MEDIA LITERACY

MEDIA LITERACY

Keys to Interpreting Media Messages

THIRD EDITION

Art Silverblatt

PRAEGER

Westport, Connecticut
London

Library of Congress Cataloging-in-Publication Data

Silverblatt, Art.
Media literacy : keys to interpreting media messages / Art Silverblatt. — 3rd ed.
p. cm.
Includes bibliographical references and index.
ISBN 978-0-275-99222-4 (alk. paper) — ISBN 978-0-275-99258-3 (pbk : alk. paper)
1. Media literacy. I. Title.
P96.M4S594 2008
302.23—dc22 2007028755

British Library Cataloguing in Publication Data is available.

Library of Congress Catalog Card Number: 2007028755
ISBN: 978-0-275-99222-4
978-0-275-99258-3 (pbk.)

First published in 2008

Praeger Publishers, 88 Post Road West, Westport, CT 06881
An imprint of Greenwood Publishing Group, Inc.
www.praeger.com

Printed in the United States of America

The paper used in this book complies with the Permanent Paper Standard issued by the National Information Standards Organization (Z39.48–1984).

10 9 8 7 6 5 4 3 2 1

To my "second generation" of Michigan friends:
Michael Sprout, Joe Heagany, Jim & Margaret Jajich,
Debbie Route, and Mort

CONTENTS

PREFACE

Media Literacy: Keys to Interpreting Media Messages offers a critical approach that enables students to better understand the information conveyed through the channels of mass communication—print, photography, film, radio, television, and digital media. One of the principal goals of *Media Literacy* is to provide students with the tools to develop a healthy independence from the pervasive influence of the media.

Although the organization of the third edition remains essentially the same as the previous editions, the material has been divided into smaller chapters, so that students should find the material easier to digest:

- Part 1 (Chapter 1) presents an introduction to the discipline of media literacy.
- Part 2 (Sections 1–4) presents a theoretical framework for the critical analysis of media text—the Keys to Interpreting Media Messages.
- Part 3 (Chapters 12–15) gives students the opportunity to apply this methodological framework to a variety of media formats: journalism, advertising, American political communications, and digital media.
- Part 4 (Chapters 16 and 17) consists of a brief consideration of mass media issues (violence in the media, media and children, media and social change, and global communications), and a discussion of potential outcomes once people have become media literate.

Since the first edition of this text was published in 1995, much has happened in the world of media. The third edition contains the following new features:

- ***Conceptual Changes.*** Since the book was published, I have refined some concepts designed to strengthen the text. Chapter 17, Outcomes, highlights applications of media literacy in various *sectors*. In addition, Chapter 5, Historical Context, includes a section that offers a way to examine the history of various media, using a *systems approach* that identifies patterns of development.
- ***New Developments.*** Although the Keys to Interpreting Media Messages continues to be the basic theoretical construct, the text has been reworked to keep up with developments in journalism, American political communications, and digital media (Part 3, Media Formats).
- ***Updated References and Examples.*** Many of the examples that illustrate, support, and extend concepts in the text have been updated, with current examples.

I am indebted to my media literacy students at Webster University who raised penetrating questions and, in many cases, prompted me to make some useful refinements in my thinking. I would also like to thank Research Assistants Don Miller and Angela Sherman for their diligence and hard work, as well as the assistance of my colleague, Ellen Elicieri, Head of Reference and Public Services, Webster University Library.

PART 1

INTRODUCTION

CHAPTER 1

INTRODUCTION TO MEDIA LITERACY

When children 4–6 were asked in a survey, "Which do you like better, TV or your daddy," 54 percent said "TV."[1]

The media have assumed a large role in the lives of the average American family. For instance:

- Only 59 percent of adults talk with other family members during the course of an evening.[2]
- Only 34 percent of parents spend time with their children during the evening.[3]
- The average American married couple spends only 4 minutes a day in "serious" conversation.[4]
- Parents spend an average of 5.5 minutes per day in "meaningful conversation" with their children.[5]

At the same time:

- Watching TV is the dominant leisure activity of Americans, consuming more than double the amount of time we spend socializing.[6]
- Average Americans watch 4 hours and 39 minutes of TV each day (more than 70 days of nonstop viewing per year).[7]
- In the United States, the average one-year-old child watches television for 6 hours per week.[8]
- 40 percent of Americans always or often watch television while eating dinner.[9]
- 25 percent of Americans fall asleep with the TV on at least three nights a week.[10]

And remember that television represents only *one* media system.

The traditional definition of literacy applies only to print: "having a knowledge of letters; instructed; learned." However, in light of the emergence of the channels of mass communications (i.e., print, photography, film, radio, television, and digital media), this definition of literacy must be expanded. The National Telemedia Council defines media literacy as "the ability to choose, to understand—within the context of content, form/style, impact, industry and production—to question, to evaluate, to create and/or produce and to respond thoughtfully to the media we consume. It is mindful viewing, reflective judgment."[11]

At the National Conference on Media Literacy, sponsored by the Aspen Institute in December 1992, the groups' representatives settled on a basic definition of media literacy: "It is the ability of a citizen to access, analyze, and produce information for specific outcomes."[12]

This author's definition of media literacy builds on the preceding ideas but emphasizes the following elements:

1. *Media literacy promotes the critical thinking skills that enable people to make independent choices with regard to: 1) which media programming to select; and 2) how to interpret the information that they receive through the channels of mass communication.* Media literacy is, first and foremost, a critical thinking skill that is applied to the source of most of the information we receive: the channels of mass communication. However, for a variety of reasons that will be discussed later in the chapter, we often blindly accept the information that we receive through the media—with disastrous results. We develop brand loyalties that have little to do with the quality of the product. We take the word (or pictures) of journalists to provide us with a clear understanding of our world. And we vote for candidates on the basis of "gut reactions" to political spots devised by clever political media consultants.

Rather than tuning to a specific program, all too often the audience simply tunes into the *medium* ("I'm gonna watch TV"). Indeed, 40 percent of TV viewers don't bother to check the TV listings before turning on the set; instead, they simply flip through the channels to determine what they want to see (or what is least objectionable).[13]

One of the criteria of becoming an educated person is developing the critical faculties to understand one's environment—an environment that, increasingly, is being shaped by the media. As Bill Moyers observes, "At stake is our sense of meaning and language, our sense of history, democracy, citizenship and our very notions of beauty and truth."[14]

2. *Understanding the process of mass communication.* Media literacy requires an understanding of the elements involved in the process of media communications: 1) the function (or purpose) of a media presentation; 2) the media communicator; 3) comparative media—the distinguishing characteristics of each medium; and 4) the audience (see Chapters 2 to 5).

3. *An awareness of the impact of the media on the individual and society.* The media have transformed the way we think about the world, each other, and ourselves. Media presentations convey cumulative messages that *shape*, *reflect*, and *reinforce* attitudes, values, behaviors, preoccupations, and myths that define a culture. Indeed, media literacy education has had an impact on young students' behaviors and attitudes with regard to alcohol,[15] tobacco usage,[16] and eating disorders.[17] In addition, media literacy "interventions" have helped curb aggressive and anti-social behaviors among third and fourth grade children.[18]

However, it should be noted that, by itself, a medium is simply a channel of communication and, consequently, is neither good nor evil. A number of factors determines the impact of a media presentation, including: 1) who is producing the presentation; 2) what is the function (or purpose) behind the production of the presentation; and 3) who is the intended audience.

4. *The development of strategies with which to analyze and discuss media messages.* Media literacy furnishes strategies that enable individuals to decipher the information they receive through the channels of mass communications. These keys also provide a framework that can facilitate the *discussion* of media content with others—including children, peers, and the people responsible for producing media programming.

5. *An awareness of media content as a "text" that provides insight into our contemporary culture and ourselves.* As we will see in Chapter 6, media presentations often reveal the attitudes, values, behaviors, preoccupations, patterns of thought, and myths that define a culture. And conversely, an understanding of a culture can furnish perspective into media presentations produced in that culture.

6. *The cultivation of an enhanced enjoyment, understanding, and appreciation of media content.* Media literacy should not be considered as merely an opportunity to bash the media. It is important to note that media is simply a channel of communications. As such, it is neither good nor evil. What determines the value and effectiveness of a media message is a number of elements, including: who is producing the message, what the function is, and the target audience. Within this context, critical analysis can heighten your awareness of media at its best: insightful articles, informative news programs, and uplifting films.

Moreover, an understanding of media literacy principles should not detract from your enjoyment of programs but, rather, enhance your appreciation of media content.

7. *In the case of media communicators: the ability to produce effective and responsible media messages.* In order to be successful, professionals in the field of media must demonstrate an awareness of the mass communication process, as well as a mastery of production techniques and strategies. But in order to truly improve the media industry, media communicators

must also be aware of the challenges and responsibilities involved in producing thoughtful programming that serves the best interests of the public.

OBSTACLES TO MEDIA LITERACY

One would think that the development of mass communication would eliminate the traditional barriers to literacy. After all, one must be educated in order to read. On the other hand, all that is required to watch television is a strong thumb to operate the remote control.

However, universal *access* to the media should not be confused with media literacy. Despite the pervasiveness of the channels of mass communication, media illiteracy remains a problem, for several reasons.

Elitism

In a study asking "To what degree does the media have an effect on society?," 80 percent of respondents "Strongly Agreed" that media had an impact on society as a whole. At the same time, however, only 12 percent of these respondents "Strongly Agreed" that media had a personal influence on them.[19]

The implications of this survey are both intriguing and disturbing. Participants in the study apparently had no difficulty seeing the influence of the media on *other* people. However, these same people were unable to recognize the impact of the media on their *own* lives. And the more that people deny personal influence of mass media, the more susceptible they are to media messages.

Significantly, follow-up survey found that education was not a meaningful variable in this wide disparity between perceptions of effects of media on others and on themselves.[20] In other words, people with college degrees were as likely as high school graduates to recognize the impact of the media on others while, at the same time, discounting its effects on their own lives. One possible explanation for this finding is that educated people are embarrassed to admit that they watch "Judge Judy" and scan the *National Enquirer* while standing at the check-out counter, like everyone else. As a result, well-educated people (in the traditional sense) are as susceptible to the influence of media messages as the general population.

Consequently, a first step in becoming media literate requires an admission that you are indeed exposed to numerous messages daily through the media and that these messages can influence your attitudes, values, and behavior.

Affective Nature of Photography, Film, Television, Radio, and Digital Media

Imagine glancing up from this text and gazing out the window. Suddenly, you spot a small, unattended toddler wandering into the street. Your immediate reaction might include:

- Experiencing a sudden jolt as your nervous system carries this information to your brain.
- Feeling a tightening sensation in your stomach.
- Breaking out in an immediate sweat.
- Struggling to translate these feelings into words and actions to help the child.

In contrast with print, visual and aural stimuli initially touch us on an *affective*, or emotional, level. In his discussion of the impact of the visual image, art historian E. H. Gombrich observes,

> The power of visual impressions to arouse our emotions has been observed since ancient times.... Preachers and teachers preceded modern advertisers in the knowledge of the ways in which the visual image can affect us, whether we want it to or not. The succulent fruit, the seductive nude, the repellent caricature, the hair-raising horror can all play on our emotions and engage our attention.[21]

Because of the affective nature of visual and aural media, it may seem more natural (and considerably easier) to simply "experience" a song or film rather than undertake the arduous task of conceptualizing, articulating, and analyzing your emotional responses. Consequently, the level of discourse about media programming is often reduced to emotional responses; in the words of Beavis and Butt-head, programs are either "cool" or they "suck."

But while affective responses may initially discourage discussion, your emotional reactions can serve as a springboard for in-depth analysis and discussion. As a result, one effective strategy for the interpretation of media messages is to ask *why* you reacted as you did while watching a program. (For further discussion, see Chapter 8, Affective Response.)

Audience Behavior Patterns

During the communication process, audience members select the most pertinent bits of information to store and assimilate into meaning. However, audiences are often engaged in competing activities while receiving media messages. Because your primary attention may be focused on other activities (driving while listening to the radio, for instance), you may be susceptible to subtle messages which can affect your attitudes and behaviors. Further, if you answer the phone or leave the room for a portion of a telecast, the text of information from which to select has been altered. As a result, you may be receiving an altogether *different* message than was originally intended by the media communicator. (For further discussion, see Chapter 4, Audience.)

Audience Expectations

In many instances, the function, or purpose behind your decision to engage in a media activity has nothing to do with the critical analysis of media content. For instance, after a long, stress-filled day at school, you may turn on your television to wind down and put the day's events in perspective. This form of "electronic meditation" signals to others that you are not in the mood for conversation. But at the same time, on these occasions, you do not feel particularly inclined to analyze media content. And the only way to *discover* media messages is to *look* for media messages.

Nature of Programming

The American media system is a market-driven industry predicated on turning a profit. Feature films, popular music, and newspapers must attract and maintain a sizeable audience to remain in business. As a result, journalists are now pressured to present the news in an entertaining fashion. This trend toward "infotainment" has severely compromised the content of many news programs.

Nevertheless, programs that were never intended to instruct the public *do* convey messages about how the world operates, provide models of acceptable and unacceptable behavior, and reinforce cultural definitions of success and failure.

Credibility of Media

Audiences are predisposed to believe what appears in the media. One particularly dangerous media message is that information presented on television or in the newspaper must be *true*, simply because it appears in the media. To illustrate, a Times-Mirror poll found that 50 percent of those who watch crime re-creation TV shows interpret the footage as news, even though disclaimers appear at the bottom of the TV screen, declaring that the programs are dramatic reenactments of a crime.[22]

In its ability to preserve a moment of time in space, photography creates the illusion of *verisimilitude*, or lifelike quality. We must remember, however, that photographs only present a distorted picture of reality. A photograph captures only a brief instant, without the context that gives it meaning. In addition, the viewer's attention is confined to the space within the frame. We only see what the photographer or filmmaker *wants* us to see; we cannot see what is happening outside of the boundary of the camera lens. Further, digital technology now enables a photographer to alter images seamlessly. As a result, a photograph may not represent what originally was captured by the camera.

Indeed, the very presence of the media alters the event intended to be captured. Consider the typical wedding. The photographer does not hesitate to interrupt the proceedings and whisk the newlyweds away from the celebration. Like trained seals, the bride and groom strike the conventional poses:

holding the rose, cutting the cake, and standing in formation with assorted relatives. The entire occasion has been transformed into a photo session, to be enjoyed later, when the couple leafs through the photo album.

Thus, one of the principal media literacy concepts identified by the Canadian Association for Media Literacy is that "All media are constructions of reality":

> This is arguably the most important concept. The media do not simply reflect external reality. Rather, they present carefully crafted constructions that reflect many decisions and are the result of many determining factors. Media Literacy works towards deconstructing these constructions (i.e., to taking them apart to show how they are made).[23]

Audience members must learn to look at the information presented through the media with a healthy skepticism and determine for themselves whether the content is accurate.

Complexity of the Language of Media

As mentioned earlier, for a person to be considered literate in the traditional sense, a certain amount of education is mandatory. In like fashion, media literacy requires an understanding of the sign and symbol system of media. For instance, in movies, the story is generally presented in chronological order; however, the filmmaker often manipulates its time sequence to establish relationships between people, locations, and events. Thus, a flashback is a production technique in which a past event is inserted in the narrative to show the influence of the past on the present.

According to Mark Crispin Miller, audiences often underestimate the "language" of media production. "Most Americans still perceive the media image as transparent, a sign that simply says what it means and means what it says. They therefore tend to dismiss any intensive explication as a case study of reading too much into it."[24]

For instance, young audience members often have initial difficulty understanding the spatial and temporal inferences depicted on screen. Daniel Anderson found that four-year-olds found it particularly difficult to draw temporal inferences, and that inferences of space were "of intermediate difficulty": "[Children's] failure to comprehend cinematic transitions cumulatively gives them a fragmented comprehension of lengthy televised narratives. With age and viewing experience, however, the child more rapidly and automatically makes the bridging inferences necessary to achieve connected comprehension."[25]

Thus, a familiarity with various production elements (i.e., editing, color, lighting, shot selection) can enhance your understanding and appreciation of media content. (For additional discussion of *production elements* see Chapter 13.)

LEVELS OF MEANING: MANIFEST AND LATENT MESSAGES

Manifest messages are direct and clear to the audience. We generally have little trouble recognizing these messages when we are paying full attention to a media presentation. For instance, have you ever noticed how many commercials *tell* you to do something?

- "Insist on Blue Coal" (Radio broadcast, 1947)
- "American Express: Don't leave home without it"
- "Just Do It" (Nike)

But in addition, media presentations may also contain *latent messages*. Latent messages are indirect and beneath the surface, and, consequently, escape our immediate attention. Latent messages may reinforce manifest messages or they may suggest entirely different meanings. For example, "G.I. Joe" commercials are designed to promote their line of war toys. But at the same time, the G.I. Joe ad campaign conveys latent messages glorifying war and equating violence with masculinity.

Cumulative Messages

Cumulative messages occur with such frequency over time that they form new meanings, independent of any individual production. Consistent messages recur throughout many media presentations with regard to gender roles, definitions of success, and racial and cultural stereotypes. As an example, taken by itself, *The Chronicles of Riddick* (2004) is simply an action-entertainment film. However, this macho image, repeated in countless other media presentations, sends an aggregate message about the ideal of masculinity.

Point of View

Point of view refers to the perspective on events. In any media presentation, there can be a range of points of view:

- The media communicator
- The characters in the presentation
- The prevailing point of view of the period in which it was produced
- Your own point of view

Point of view has an impact on: 1) how a story is told; 2) what information is conveyed; and 3) how the audience responds to the information being presented.

Identifying the prevailing point of view in a media presentation is an important step in developing a critical distance from what you are reading or watching. Identifying the point of view of the media presentation enables you to filter the information. As an example, the Fox television news channel maintains a conservative point of view that supports the agenda of George W. Bush's administration. But there is nothing wrong with using an ideological station such as Fox News as a news source, so long as you know what it *is* and what it *isn't*. The danger lies in thinking that Fox (or, for that matter, a liberal media presentation like "Democracy Now!") is presenting objective news. (For further discussion, see Chapter 12, Journalism.) The Keys to Interpreting Media Messages provide you with tools to identify the point of view of the media communicator or primary character in the presentation.

Affective Strategies

As mentioned earlier, media communicators can influence the attitudes and behavior of audiences by appealing to their emotions. For instance, some advertisers sell products by appealing to guilt or the primal need for acceptance.

Visual and aural media (photography, film, television, radio, and digital media) are particularly well suited to emotional appeals. Production elements such as color, shape, lighting, and size convey meaning by evoking emotional responses in the audience.

Embedded Values

Media content may reflect the value system of the media communicator, as well as widely held cultural values and attitudes that, in turn, reinforce and shape attitudes and values among members of the audience.

Media communicators convey meaning by manipulating production elements such as editing decisions, point of view, and connotative words and images. Thus, a consideration of these elements can reveal the values of the media communicators. To illustrate, consider the following headlines for two newspaper stories reporting on a car bombing incident in Baghdad on October 28, 2003:

"Five Consecutive Martyrdom Operations Rock Baghdad"[26]
"Bloodied Baghdad; Four Coordinated Suicide Car Bombings Kill 34, Wound 224"[27]

In the first headline, which appeared in an Egyptian government-owned newspaper, the word "martyrdom" is an indication that the media communicator regarded this action as morally justifiable. In contrast, the term "suicide bombings" in *Newsday*, a mainstream American publication, reveals that the reporter considered this attack to be brutal and senseless.

NOTES

1. Berkeley Pop Culture Project, *The Whole Pop Catalog* (Berkeley, CA: Avon Books, 1991), 547.
2. Joe Schwartz, "Is There Life Before Bed?" *American Demographics* (March 1990), 12.
3. Ibid.
4. NBC, 1991.
5. Media Reform Info Center, "TV Facts," www.enviroweb.org.
6. "No Excuse: We All Have More Free Time Than We Think, Experts Say," *St. Louis Post-Dispatch*, June 6, 1997, 2A.
7. Shelly Freierman, "Drilling Down; We're Spending More Time Watching TV," *New York Times*, January 9, 2006.
8. Frank Baker, "Media Use Statistics Resources on Media Habits of Children, Youth and Adults ... the Benefits and Minimize the Harm of Mass Media on Children through ..." (www.frankwbaker.com/mediause.htm).
9. Ibid.
10. Harper's Index, January 1996 (www.harpers.org).
11. "The National Telemedia Council," *Telemedium* vol. 38, Third-Fourth Quarter 1992, 12
12. Presented at the Aspen Institute, "National Leadership Conference on Media Literacy," Queenstown, Maryland, 7–9 December 1992.
13. Frank Absher, "Media on Media," *St. Louis Journalism Review,* October 1999, 3.
14. Bill Moyers, *The Public Mind: Consuming Images,* Public Broadcasting Service, November 8, 1989.
15. Erica Austin and Kristine Johnson, "Effects of General and Alcohol-Specific Media Literacy Training on Children's Decision Making about Alcohol," *Journal of Health Communication* 2(1997), 17–42.
16. Richard Beltramini and Patrick Bridge, "Relationship between Tobacco Advertising and Youth Smoking: Assessing the Effectiveness of a School-based, Antismoking Intervention Program," *Journal of Consumer Affairs* 35(Winter 2001), 2:263–227.
17. Dianne Neumark-Sztainer et al., "Primary Prevention of Disordered Eating among Preadolescent Girls: Feasibility and Short-term Effect of a Community-based Intervention," *Journal of the American Dietetic Association* (December 2000) (www.findarticles.com/cf_0/m0822/12_100/68739951/p1/article.jhtml?term=neumark-sztainer+%22primary+prevention+of+disordered+eating+among+preadolescent+girls%22; accessed 31 July 2003).
18. Thomas Robinson et al., "Effects of Reducing Children's Television and Video Game Use on Aggressive Behavior," *Archives of Pediatric Adolescent Medicine* 155(2001), 1:17–23.
19. James Tiedge, "Public Opinion on Mass Media Effects: Perceived Societal Effects and Perceived Personal Effects," Paper presented at Speech Communication Association Convention, Minneapolis, 1980.
20. James Tiedge, Arthur Silverblatt, Michael J. Havice, and Richard Rosenfeld, "The Third-Person Effects Hypothesis: Scope, Magnitude, and Contributing Factors," *Journalism Quarterly* 68(Spring-Summer 1991), 141–154.
21. E. H. Gombrich, "The Visual Image," in *Media and Symbols: The Forms of Expression, Communication, and Education.* Publication of the National Society

for the Study of Education, Vol. 73, Pt.1, ed. David R. Olson (Chicago: University of Chicago Press, 1974), 244.

22. Thomas B. Rosensteil, "Viewers Found to Confuse TV Entertainment With News," *Los Angeles Times,* August 17, 1989, I17.

23. "Key Concepts of Media Literacy, the Association for Media Literacy," Ontario Ministry of Education, 1987.

24. David Considine and Gail Haley, *Visual Messages: Integrating Imagery into Instruction* (Englewood, CO: Teacher Ideas Press, 1992), 3.

25. Daniel R. Anderson, "Online Cognitive Processing of Television," in *Psychological Processes and Advertising Effects,* eds. Linda F. Alwitt and Andrew A. Mitchell (Hillsdale, NJ: Lawrence Erlbaum Associates, 1985), 191.

26. "Five Consecutive Martyrdom Operations Rock Baghdad," *Al Gumhuria,* October 23, 2003.

27. Mohamad Bazzi, "Bloodied Baghdad; Four Coordinated Suicide Car Bombings Kill 34, Wound 224," *Newsday,* October 23, 2003.

PART

2

KEYS TO INTERPRETING MEDIA MESSAGES

The Keys to Interpreting Media Messages provide a theoretical framework for the systematic analysis of *media messages* (that is, the underlying themes or ideas contained in a media presentation).

Think of these keys as a series of lenses. Each lens will provide you with fresh insights into media-carried content. Depending on the specific focus of study, one key may be more useful than others. Obviously, the production of film elements would not be relevant to an analysis of newspapers. Use only those keys that will be most applicable to the particular media format.

But in all cases, what determines the validity of the interpretation is the following: 1) the analysis must be systematically applied and 2) the analysis must be supported with concrete examples from *media presentations* (i.e., films, television episodes, newspaper articles, video games, or advertisements).

SECTION

1

PROCESS

CHAPTER

2

OVERVIEW: ELEMENTS OF COMMUNICATION

In order to become media literate, you must first develop an understanding of the communications process.

Communication is an active, dynamic experience that demands your fullest attention and energy. The moment that someone approaches you and initiates a conversation, you become engaged in a rapid sequence of activities:

- Receiving a message
- Selecting relevant information
- Forming appropriate responses
- Responding to the message

Immediately after you have formed an appropriate response, the roles are reversed: you shift from audience to communicator, and vice versa.

In order for people to communicate effectively, a relationship of mutual trust and respect must be established. The communicator and audience formulate a communication contract that governs their conduct. Both parties agree to abide by the rules. For instance, the participants implicitly agree to maintain a comfortable distance from one another during conversations (neither too close nor too distant). There is also an unwritten understanding that one person should not dominate the conversation. Any violation of these agreements results in an instant breakdown of the social contract. For instance, if you feel that the person to whom you are conversing isn't really listening to you or doesn't respect what you have to say, then the conversation is doomed.

People typically engage in three types of communication. *Intrapersonal communication* takes place internally within yourself. It is the basis of all forms of communication, because until we know what it is that we want to say, we will not be able to communicate effectively with other people. *Interpersonal communication* is based upon face-to-face interaction with another person. In *mass communication*, messages are communicated through a mass medium (e.g., radio or television) to a large group of people who may not be in direct contact with the communicator.

THE COMMUNICATIONS MODEL

The basic *communications model* consists of the following elements:

- The *communicator* is the person who delivers the message.
- The *message* is the information being communicated.
- The *channel* refers to the passage through which the information is being conveyed. For example, you use your voice, eyes, and facial expressions as channels for interpersonal communication.

  In mass communication, the media—newspapers, photographs, film, radio, television, and the Internet—serve as channels for the communication of information to large groups of people who are separated in time and/or space from the media communicator.
- The *audience* consists of the person or people who receive the message.

Two elements are critical to the communications process: *feedback* and *interference.*

Feedback

Feedback occurs when audience members ask questions or comment, in order to better understand what the communicator is trying to say. Feedback can also be used to reassure the communicator. When listeners nod their heads, smile, or repeat key phrases, they are letting the communicator know they are alert, interested, and involved in the conversation.

Interference

Interference refers to those factors that can hinder the communications process. Interference can occur at all points of the communications model.

Communicator interference arises when the communicator obstructs the message. Sometimes people have difficulty expressing themselves clearly. Or communicators may not know exactly what they want to say. In this instance, the communicator might ramble on, until the listener eventually loses interest. Communicator interference also takes place if the communicator is not *self-aware*. For instance, you may be angry at a friend but are unwilling to admit it—even to yourself. As a result, you may be sending mixed messages—denying that you are angry at the same time that your behavior is contentious and abrupt.

Channel interference occurs when a glitch in the channel distorts the message. For example, if you have laryngitis, your audience may be unable to understand you. In mass communications, channel interference arises when the television picture suddenly goes blank or your computer freezes while you are on the Internet.

Channel interference may also result from using an *inappropriate* channel to send a particular type of message. As we will discuss in Chapter 4, a particular medium may not be the most effective channel to convey specific types of information. As a result, corporations may spend enormous amounts of money on promotional videos, when the detailed information they are trying to convey would be more suitable in print.

Environmental interference refers to distractions within the setting in which the information is received. For example, we have all attended movies in which people behind us have talked throughout the picture, or have had our view blocked by tall people seated in front of us.

Audience interference occurs when the audience obstructs the communication process. The following psychological principles explain how individuals misinterpret information:

- *Selective exposure* refers to the audience's program choices, based on personal values and interests. People often seek out information with which they agree, while avoiding communication that offers a different perspective. This principle also extends to mass communication. Sports fans may tune into ESPN, while people disinterested in sports will watch something else. Audiences are also selective with regard to the people who appear in the media. If you are a Tom Cruise fan, you will make an effort to see his movies. If not, you will make an effort to avoid films starring Cruise.
- *Selective perception* is the phenomenon in which people's interpretation of content is colored by their predispositions and preconceptions. To illustrate, in a series of interviews, reporter Richard Berke found that respondents' observations of President George W. Bush simply reinforced their initial impressions—negative or positive:

  > Supporters are impressed that President Bush is secure enough to surround himself with capable advisers. His detractors say he is so unprepared that he has no choice but to lean heavily on others. His admirers say Mr. Bush's unadorned speaking style strikes them as refreshingly honest. His detractors say they are embarrassed by Mr. Bush's sometimes jumbled syntax.[1]

  In this case, groups felt that *whatever* Bush did or said supported the point of view that each had maintained before watching the program.
- *Selective retention* occurs when a person selectively remembers (or forgets) information. People tend to tune out conversations when they are exposed to subject

matter in which their interest level is low. For instance, if you decide to talk about a subject I know nothing about (e.g., nuclear physics), I will focus my attention elsewhere, where I am more comfortable. An individual's recall of information may be influenced by a number of other factors as well: whether the person was distracted at the time, a sense of nostalgia (reconstructing past events so that they appear more positive), or the impulse to minimize unpleasant thoughts or experiences.

- *Attention span* may also be a factor in audience interference. As mentioned previously, communication is an active process that demands concentration and energy. Occasionally we'll just take a break and tune out the speaker. This option is particularly tempting when we are presented with information outside of our personal frames of reference.
- Finally, audience members often filter messages through their *egos*. That is, they only hear those aspects of a conversation that pertain to them, ignoring the rest of the message. Audience members are not always paying strict attention while the other person is speaking. Instead, they are busily formulating their responses or are anxiously awaiting their chance to talk.

Differences between Interpersonal and Mass Communication

While the principles discussed above apply to all forms of communication, some significant differences exist between interpersonal and mass communication.

Mass Communications Model. When Marshall McLuhan declared, "The medium is the message," he was suggesting that the media have reconfigured the traditional communications model. The channels of mass communications have now assumed a primary role in determining choice of communicator content, and the audience.

To illustrate, in broadcast news programming, the medium of television dictates the choice of *communicator:* anchorpersons must be likable, convincing, and attractive. To that end, the Fox News Network keeps stylists on staff whose task is to make their anchors and reporters more appealing to a young audience.[2] In the process, journalistic ability has become subordinate to performance skills.

The characteristics of a medium also affect the *content* of a news presentation. Print journalism lends itself to the detailed presentation of complex issues. Consequently, newspaper coverage of a story tends to be issues-oriented, providing detailed context and background.

To be sure, television is less successful in its ability to present the context, interpretation, and implications of these incidents than its print counterpart. However, because of the visual properties of television, television news is an ideal medium for showing events in the process of unfolding. In order to take advantage of the visual capabilities of the medium, television news often emphasizes *events* rather than *issues*.

In addition, TV news is influenced by the entertainment sensibility of television. News producers tend to select stories that are dramatic, sensational,

Table 2.1
Audience Preferences, Based on Media Attributes

	Provides Greatest Experience	Is the Most Informative	Gives Me Greatest Control	Is the First I Turn On	Is the Easiest to Use
TV	46%	20%	22%	40%	42%
Magazines	3%	5%	3%	1%	3%
Newspapers	3%	23%	9%	12%	7%
Internet	27%	37%	49%	34%	24%
Radio	3%	4%	2%	9%	7%
All Are Equal	18%	11%	15%	5%	17%

Source: InsightExpress. Base = 500 people surveyed online on September 17, 2004.

have an identifiable cast of characters, and a clear narrative structure (with a beginning, middle, and conclusion).

Finally, the choice of medium has a significant impact on the *audience*. To illustrate, television is the most credible source of news, including word of mouth.[3]

Feedback in Mass Communications. Without immediate contact with the audience, the media communicator has only one opportunity to convey a message. As a result, media presentations must be carefully planned in order to anticipate any ambiguities or questions raised by the audience.

However, the media communicator has no immediate way of knowing whether the audience is truly involved in the communication process. Much of the feedback in the mass communication process is delayed. Because of the time/space differential between the media communicator and audience, a significant amount of time often elapses before the audience member can register a response with the media communicator. Examples of delayed audience response include letters to the editor, petitions, or phone calls.

Certain types of media programming, such as advertising, political spots, and certain kinds of religious programming call for very specific *cognitive, attitudinal,* or *behavioral responses* from the audience (e.g., buy this, or vote for this proposition). In addition, the mass communication process does provide several indirect feedback opportunities for the audience as well.

- *Participatory responses* refer to occasions in which individuals respond directly to programs through laughter, anger, or personal boycotts of programs and products. Individuals may also become participants in talk radio programs, as part of a studio audience, or by commenting on bulletin boards on the Internet.
- Since immediate responses frequently are not observable, mass communications feedback is often *cumulative* (reflecting a collective opinion) and *quantifiable* (presenting some numerical information data about the success of the programming). For example, television ratings disclose how many people watch a

particular program. Significantly, however, these ratings do not measure whether the audience actually *enjoyed* the program.

- Revenue is another cumulative, quantifiable mass communication feedback mechanism. The success of a film, CD, or newspaper is measured by the amount of money (and profit) it generates.
- *Critical responses* comprise another category of mass communication feedback. For example, critical reviews offer feedback for filmmakers and provide an opportunity for the public to learn about the merit of a production. Awards like the Oscars and the New York Film Critics Circle Awards also acknowledge artistic accomplishments. And each year, festivals at Cannes, Sundance, and other venues recognize outstanding achievements in film.

Saturation of the Mass Media. In interpersonal communications, the speaker enjoys direct, personal access to the audience; however, the size of this audience is limited. On the other hand, a media communicator can reach a vast audience simultaneously with the same, undistorted message. For example, it took nearly two months for news of the signing of the Treaty of Ghent (officially ending the war of 1812) to reach America. In contrast, the death of Princess Diana in 1997 generated what *Newsweek* magazine referred to as an immediate "global outburst of online mourning."[4] Clearly, the mass communicator is in a unique position to influence a wide range of people at one time.

But although mass communications is unrivaled at providing a *breadth* of information, there are limits to the *depth* of information it can furnish. Clearly, some media are more confining than others. But whether it is a five-minute news report or a two-hour documentary, media presentations operate within distinct time limits that may or may not meet the informational needs of the audience.

Ability to Preserve a Message. In interpersonal communication, information is exchanged on an informal basis. Consequently, we may forget precisely what we said. Or we may choose to reinterpret the conversation on the basis of what we *meant* to say—particularly if we said something silly or embarrassing.

In contrast, media presentations (e.g., newspapers, DVDs, CDs) are distinguished by a degree of permanence, which means that they can be scrutinized and re-examined by the audience. As a result, mass communicators are highly accountable for the material that they produce and must be prepared to accept responsibility for their work.

Media as Collaborative Process. Unlike interpersonal communications, the production of a newspaper, news broadcast, or ad campaign is a collaborative process requiring the input of numerous people. For example, a Hollywood film crew includes the following positions:

- The *producer* is responsible for the business arrangements (e.g., financing, business planning, insurance, contracts, and personnel).

- The *scriptwriter* develops the screenplay. The scriptwriter may be solely responsible for the original treatment, or be part of a team. Also, additional writers may be brought in to revise a script that has been obtained by a producer or studio.
- The *director* is the film's principal creative authority, responsible for the presentation of the script on screen.
- *First and second assistant directors* assist with cast and crew management, crowd control, and coordination of the schedule.
- The *continuity* department is charged with making sure that the props, clothing, and makeup remain consistent. This can be a difficult task, given that scenes are often filmed out of sequence.
- The *cast* includes the stars, supporting players, bit players, and uncredited extras. Additional cast members consist of stunt doubles, who perform dangerous shots, and stand-ins, who work with the crew to set up the proper camera positions and lighting for the performers.
- The *cinematographer* is responsible for the artistic and technical quality of the film, including: lighting, framing, and color values.
- The *production designer*, or art director, is responsible for set design.
- The *editor* assembles, arranges, and selects the footage, often in concert with the director.

Other crew members include a gaffer (chief electrician), best boy (gaffer's assistant), grips (who haul heavy lights), costume designer, music director, sound editors, and publicity teams.

Because members of the crew may hold different opinions about content and approach, compromise is a large part of the decision-making process. As a result, the final presentation is sometimes disjointed and confusing.

It should be noted, however, that one of the distinguishing features of interactive media is that one person can, in fact, assume most (if not all) of the production responsibilities. One person can shoot and edit video, produce animation, and integrate graphics into the production.

Media as Industry. Media programming is extremely expensive to produce. For instance, in 2005, the average cost to make and market a movie was $96.2 million.[5] Indeed, the cost of making the blockbuster film *Titanic* (1997) exceeded $200 million—more than the cost of building the original ship. As a result, producers are often reluctant to take artistic risks, relying instead on "bankable" stars and genres. Consequently, rather than challenging the audience artistically, studios bankroll films that rely on violence, sex, and flashy music.

The first key to interpreting media messages—*process*—consists of the following four elements:

- *Function*
- *Comparative Media*
- *Media Communicator*
- *Audience*

NOTES

1. Richard L. Berke, "Little Change in Views of Bush 3 Months Into His Presidency," *New York Times,* April 21, 2001.

2. Frank Absher, "Hair Brain," *St. Louis Journalism Review* (November 1998), 3.

3. Joe Saltzman, "Who Do You Trust and Why," *USA Today* (Society for the Advancement of Education), January 1, 2000 (http://findarticles.com/p/articles/mi_m1272/is_2656_128/ai_58576589).

4. "Dawn of e-life," *Newsweek*, September 20, 1999, 39.

5. Laura M. Holson, "Hollywood Puts the Squeeze on Talent," *New York Times*, November 6, 2006, C1.

CHAPTER 3

PROCESS

- Media Communicator
- Function

MEDIA COMMUNICATOR

In interpersonal communications, the communicator and audience are in direct and immediate contact. In contrast, in mass communications, the media communicator is separated both in time and space from the audience and, therefore, is largely unknown to the audience. An old movie that you watch on television may have been produced 40 years ago, by someone you never met, who lived in another part of the world.

As a result, it can be very difficult for the audience to determine the identity of the media communicator. Although we generally assume that the person in front of the camera or microphone is the person who is responsible for what is being said, this performer or model may have been instructed in what to say by someone who is unseen by the audience. Indeed, it can be argued that the "on-camera talent" are rather like ventriloquist dummies, who are simply mouthing the words penned by a team of scriptwriters.

Thus, identifying the hidden person or organization responsible for a media presentation can furnish perspective into the content and outlook of the media production. Consider the following example, detailed by reporter Joe Rhodes:

The MySpace page appeared in early November (2006).... It was a fan page with a hot pink background, a tribute to a one-hit Canadian teenage pop star from the early 1990s.

"As Robin Sparkle's #1 Fan, it was my duty to create this page," read the copy in the About Me section. "She's just so cute and her music is so great. She must be the greatest pop singer from Canada ever!".... It was just gushing enough to be real. But it wasn't. The Robin Sparkles MySpace page was a plant, concocted by the producers of the CBS sitcom "How I Met Your Mother" to play off a storyline in the show's Nov. 20 episode.

By the next morning, the number of "friends" on the Robin Sparkles fan page had jumped from fewer than 100 to more than 5,000, and the video was one of the most viewed on both MySpace and YouTube. More important, the ratings for "How I Met Your Mother" jumped the next week, increasing by more than a million viewers in the age 18-to-34 demographic group. That gave the show, a critical favorite but a middling ratings success, its highest overall ratings of the season.[1]

The following polls and studies that appeared in newspapers and magazines were sponsored by groups that have a vested interest in the outcomes:

- Americans believe the best learning and information source today is the Internet. (Sponsored by Internet provider Prodigy.)
- The majority of Americans polled plan to travel during the holidays. (Sponsored by online travel service Expedia.com.)
- More Americans are afraid of getting sick from germs in a public restroom than in any other place. (Sponsored by Kimberly-Clark, which makes tissues, towels, and soaps used in public restrooms.)
- More than half of all Americans say their legs ache several days a week. (Sponsored by Futuro, makers of support hose.)
- More than 75 percent of American women want more choices in birth control. (Sponsored by Ortho-McNeil, which makes prescriptive birth-control.)
- Two out of three doctors who offer nutritional advice to their patients recommend that said patients eat more yogurt. (Sponsored by the Dannon yogurt company.)[2]

Although these survey results may indeed be accurate, the identities of these media communicators calls their findings into question.

Because the actual media communicators are not visible, they are able to deflect responsibility for the content of the programming. As an example, in 2007, radio "shock jock" Don Imus referred to the members of the Rutgers University women's basketball team as "nappy-headed hos." In a statement, MSNBC said that "while simulcast by MSNBC, 'Imus in the Morning' is not a production of the cable network and is produced by WFAN Radio.... As Imus makes clear every day, his views are not those of MSNBC.... We regret that his remarks were aired on MSNBC and apologize for these offensive comments." CBS Radio issued this statement: "We are disappointed by Imus' actions earlier this week which we find completely inappropriate. We fully agree that a sincere apology was called for and will continue to monitor the program's content going forward."[3] But significantly, after the public outcry over Imus's remarks prompted advertisers like Procter & Gamble and Sprint—the *actual* media communicators—to withdraw their sponsorship, NBC and CBS radio fired Imus.

Ownership Patterns

Who are the most powerful and influential people in Hollywood?

Entertainment Weekly's list of the top 10 Hollywood elite in 2006 included some recognizable names, to be sure: director Steven Spielberg, Steve Jobs, CEO of Apple Computers, and producer Jerry Bruckheimer (of the "CSI" television franchise and *Pirates of the Caribbean* among others). However, the majority of names on this list may be unfamiliar:

- Barry Meyer, chairman-CEO, and Alan Horn, president-COO, of Warner Bros. Entertainment (#2)
- Jim Gianopulos and Tom Rothman, chairmen and CEOs of Fox Filmed Entertainment (#3)
- Richard Cook, chairman of Disney Studios, and Nina Jacobson, president of Buena Vista Motion Pictures Group (#5)
- Tom Freston (president and CEO of Viacom) and Brad Grey (chairman-CEO of Paramount Motion Pictures Group) (#6)
- Richard Lovett (president of Creative Artists Agency) (#7)
- Michael Lynton (chairman and CEO of Sony Pictures) and Amy Pascal (vice-chairman of Sony Pictures) (#8)
- Ron Meyer (president/COO of Universal Studios), Marc Shmuger (chairman of Universal Studios), and David Linde (co-chairman of Universal Studios) (#9)[4]

While these behind-the-scenes executives may not be household names, they exercise enormous influence over content we receive through the media. These important media figures determine not only *what* appears but *who* appears as well.

Identifying the media communicator often extends beyond individuals to those companies that are responsible for the production and distribution of media presentations. As an example, in 2003, Mordecai Wiczyk, Ariel Emanuel, Patrick Whitesell, and Asif Satchu, established Media Rights Capital, a powerful Hollywood talent agency that put together deals for high-profile movie projects—like Alejandro González Iñárritu's *Babel* and the comedic actor Sacha Baron Cohen's planned

Bruno—in which the agency was given part ownership in return for helping to find film projects and make deals. Without an agency like Media Rights Capital, many writers, actors, and musicians would labor in complete anonymity. (For more discussion of ownership patterns, see Chapter 7, Structure.)

The Architects

The second line of media communicators (behind the owners) consists of those individuals who conceptualize, write, produce, direct, and edit a media presentation. On a more immediate level, the content of a specific program is a product of these media architects.

Identifying the background and worldview of these architects can furnish perspective into the content of media presentations. To illustrate, the writers of TV situation comedies are predominantly young white males. According to reporter Christopher Nixon, sitcom writers are "often undersocialized, smart-alecky guys for whom *Portnoy's Complaint* and *American Pie* are sacred texts—who are cooped up together in small spaces late into the night."[5]

During the writing sessions, the humor can become infantile—to say the least. In 1999, Amaani Lyle a former writers' assistant who was fired from the NBC sitcom *Friends*, filed a sexual harassment suit against Warner Brothers Television; Bright/Kauffman/Crane Productions; and three writers. Amaani Lyle contended that while doing her job, she was subjected to crude language, naughty doodles, and sexual fantasies involving cast members. The locker-room sensibility of the writers also found its way onto the show, with countless sexual references—including, ironically, comments from male characters who expressed insecurities about their anatomies and attractiveness to women.

One of the major challenges facing these architects is producing programming for an audience that has a different background and mindset. For instance, the hit television series *Zoey 101* (Nickelodeon) targets a "tween" audience, between the ages of nine and 12. But although Dan Schneider, the creator of the series, is an adult, his background as a former child actor helped prepare him to produce the series. (Schneider played the character Dennis Blunden on the ABC sitcom *Head of the Class* from 1986 to 1991.) Moreover, Schneider says that he spends considerable time doing research to help him connect with his young audience. For instance, to gauge the response of his viewers, he reads Internet message boards: "I think that they want to see kids that reflect what their friends are like. But they also want to see kids that are like the friends they wish they had. I can't tell you how much work we put into casting this show."[6]

Figure 3.1
The real voice behind the person appearing in the media presentation may (be from) a different background. Their efforts to appear "young" and "hip" can lead to confusion. To illustrate, the comic strip *Boondocks* plays on a McDonald's ad campaign, in which the term "hit it" is a slang expression for a sexual encounter. Credit: The Boondocks © Aaron McGruder. Dist. by Universal Press Syndicate. Reprinted by permission.

MEDIA LITERACY TIPS

MEDIA COMMUNICATOR

The following questions are useful in considering the role of the media communicator:

✓ Who is responsible for creating the media production?

✓ What are the demographic characteristics of the media communicator(s)?
- Age
- Income
- Race/Ethnicity
- Gender

✓ How do these characteristics affect the content and outlook of the media production?

FUNCTION

A simple communication activity may be motivated by many purposes, or *functions.*

Expression. In these situations, speakers inform the listener of their frame of mind—what they are thinking at that moment, how they are feeling, or their attitudes toward people and issues. As E. H. Gombrich observes, "A speaker can inform his partner of a state of affairs past, present or future, observable or distant, actual or conditional."[7]

Description can provide elaboration on general statements, providing concrete examples and details.

Instruction refers to occasions in which the purpose is either 1) to inform the audience about a subject with which it is unfamiliar, or 2) to furnish *additional* information about a subject with which the audience is already acquainted. Examples include giving directions to the airport or watching the evening news on television.

Information exchange refers to an occasion in which all parties benefit by sharing knowledge.

Persuasion is a function in which the communicator's objective is to promote a particular idea or motivate the audience to specific behaviors or attitude change. The ultimate purpose of persuasion is *control.* For example, advertising attempts to persuade you to think positively about a product and, ultimately, to purchase a particular brand.

Entertainment is a deceptively strategic communication function. Humor is a social mechanism that brings people together. Jokes, stories, and gossip divert people from the more serious and pressing matters of the day. Sharing laughter is also a time-honored way to break down traditional barriers. To illustrate, accomplished public speakers often begin with an amusing anecdote that makes the audience feel comfortable. And in political communications, humor is used to attack a person or undermine an opponent's position.

Creative Expression. Novelists, painters, and experimental videographers express themselves through their art and share their artistic vision with the audience. Thanks to digital technology, independent artists and nonprofessionals have the means to produce, edit, and distribute works of art.

Exploration. Sometimes communicators are not clear what they want to say but are merely involved in exploration. Stalling techniques (like interspersing "uh" and "you know" between words) gives the speaker a bit of space to figure out where to go next. However, we still say things that we wish we could take back.

Mass communicators typically present polished information that has been prepared in advance. However, with many hours to fill and a limited amount of programming, media communicators are frequently forced to ad lib. For instance, during the Michael Jackson trial in 2005, cable talk shows rehashed the day's events, even if nothing significant had transpired. Reporters remained talking on-air even when there was nothing new to report. Max Frankel observes that this "oral media" has changed the level of discourse in the media:

> Listen to the frothy chatter of hosts and guests on the "all news" stations of CNN, Fox, or NBC and compare them with the deft essays of Ted Koppel on ABC or Bill Moyers on PBS. The blatherers are handicapped not only by the speed of their discourse but also by their inability to stop and think, to reread their notes, look up a word, dig into a relevant book and expurge the angry epithet. Nor can they retreat from an unwarranted opinion or stupid prediction.
>
> In the oral media, thoughts fly from the top of the head, causing even smart people to sound ignorant. The camera permits no pauses, even for feigned reflection. To escape the gaps in their knowledge, television ad-libbers seek safety in mere opinion, speculation, and prophecy, which can be contradicted but not easily proved false.[8]

Ritual. As it pertains to communication, a ritual is a verbal or written exchange that has an underlying social significance. As an example, a number of international students have expressed bewilderment over Americans' habit of greeting people with, "How are you?" and then moving on without waiting for a reply. However, what the students have mistaken for superficiality is actually a cultural ritual, in which people are making a formal connection with one another. "Small talk" is another ritual intended to make social situations more comfortable.

Performance. A surprising proportion of our communication is devoted to performance. Think of the dynamics that occur in singles bars. A fellow may be talking about his job, his astrological sign, or telling an amusing story, but the latent purpose of the conversation is to create a favorable impression. This function also carries over into the world of mass media. Production elements reinforce the themes, mood, or messages of the media presentation. All too often, however, media communicators include dazzling special effects and elaborate camera movements in order to impress the audience with their expertise (see further discussion in Chapters 13 and 14).

Emotional Catharsis. Emotional catharsis includes spontaneous expressions of love, passion, anger, pain, happiness, or the release of tension. These expressions may not be coherent or planned—what did you say the last time someone dented the fender of your car?—but your speech can be startlingly clear and graphic.

Media figures—whether they are interviewers or interviewees—are trained to control these revealing outbursts. However, when people are under constant media scrutiny, restraint is not always possible. These moments provide brief but candid glimpses behind the images that are so carefully cultivated for public view.

Disengagement. At times, the objective is to *discourage* extended conversation. Perhaps you are in a hurry but find yourself in an awkward or tedious conversation. In this instance, you might adopt strategies designed to terminate discussion—by responding in monosyllabic answers or furnishing verbal cues intended to accelerate the conversation (e.g., "And then ...?").

Profit. In the American media industry, profit is most likely an underlying function. Of course, advertising and commercial media entertainment are geared to generate revenue. However, journalists are also torn between serving the public's Right to Know and the profit imperative. As Allen Neuharth, chairman of the Gannett newspaper chain has noted, "Wall Street didn't give a damn if we put out a good paper in Niagara Falls. They just wanted to know if our profits would be in the 15–20 percent range."[9]

Latent Function

Latent function refers to instances in which the media communicator's intentions are not immediately obvious to the audience. For instance, we have all been involved in an exchange of information in which it eventually becomes clear that the other person is not really interested in your opinions but instead is intent on converting you to a particular point of view. In this case, the latent function is *persuasion*.

Often, the manifest function is designed to *divert* the audience's attention away from the principal latent purpose behind a message. As an example, *America's Army*, a popular online video game produced by the Army, recorded over 7.5 million registered users in 2006. Players interact with the "Real Heroes" characters during the training stages of the game and watch videos about those soldiers' experiences in the real Army. But beyond its entertainment value, the game doubles as a recruiting tool for the United States Army. According to Chris Chambers, the deputy director of the Army Game Project,

> We are out there meeting young people on the Internet and introducing them to the Army. (The Web site pages, action figures, and virtual characters) put a real face on what has been a generic story about the Army.[10]

Indeed, it is astounding to discover how frequently the manifest function is irrelevant—or at least, subordinate—to other, latent purposes, like impressing the audience or making a profit. According to author Stuart Ewan, these latent commercial functions ultimately undermine the meaning initially ascribed to "sacred" images such as elected officials and the American flag: "All people make images sacred as a way of commenting on their world and ascribing meaning to culture. Now this has been transformed into merchandise—the general meaning is lost."[11]

Although the principal function of children's programming on commercial stations is to entertain, children may be unaware that its underlying purpose is to generate product sales. Media lawyer Chris Kelleher points out that children's programs on public television also have a latent profit function:

> Once a show gets some traction to it, then they negotiate with toy manufacturers to make and distribute the characters. One of the biggest offenders in the "tie in" department is PBS, with Barney, Teletubbies and Arthur. Although PBS's roots are in "educational TV," these characters have generated millions in sales for the toy companies through never ending exposure on "non commercial" TV. PBS then gets a cut of the profits.[12]

At times, the latent function can be very subtle, escaping the attention of the young audience. For instance, a latent function of the after-school programming on the WB network is to induce its young viewers to switch channels to the Cartoon Network when the WB cartoon programming is over. Because both networks are properties of the parent company, AOL/Time Warner, this cross-promotion is designed to cultivate a large audience share, which drives up the company's advertising rates.

Multiple Function

Multiple function refers to a communications exchange which serves more than one function at a time. To illustrate, you may have participated in conversations during which the function of the person talking to you shifts from information exchange to persuasion.

Although multiple functions are often harmonious, at other times they may work at cross-purposes. For instance, in order to remain competitive, broadcast journalists are pressured to present information in an entertaining fashion. Consequently, the information and entertainment functions frequently conflict with one another. Some information is complex and difficult (if not tedious) to understand. However, journalists often feel compelled to dress up these reports, which alters the content.

To illustrate, in 2004, the ABC newsmagazine *20/20* featured a story about adoption, entitled, "Be My Baby," that followed a 16-year-old mother from Ohio as she selected among five couples vying to raise her baby. Leading up to the segment, co-anchors John Stossel and Barbara Walters promoted the story as if it was a reality show. Stossel declared, "Barbara will bring you what might be called the ultimate reality show. As you watch, a pregnant teenager will decide which of five couples gets her baby." Walters added, "It's like *The Bachelor* or *The Bachelorette*; you are in or out tonight." However, this effort to capitalize on the popularity of reality shows undermined the legitimate news value of the story.[13]

But at the same time, a program with multiple functions can become successful by attracting a diverse audience. For instance, Rush Limbaugh's radio program is intended to be informational and persuasive. At the same time, the show is designed to be entertaining; Limbaugh's tongue-in-cheek manner verges on self-parody. As a result, the program offers something for everyone. The Limbaugh shows are "camp," or satire for liberals, but serious politic polemic for conservatives.

Undefined function occurs when the media communicator does not have a clear intention in mind. The absence of a clearly defined function can result in a muddled, directionless presentation. For instance, we have all attended movies in which it seems the director could not decide whether the film should be a comedy or tragedy. And, as a result, it is neither.

NOTES

1. Joe Rhodes, "A Fictional Video on MySpace Puts a TV Show's Promotion Into Hyperspace," *New York Times*, April 9, 2007, C8.
2. "Survey Readers Beware: Ridiculous Claims Ahead," *St. Louis Post-Dispatch* Everyday Magazine on Monday, December 17, 2001, Knight Ridder.
3. Lisa de Moraes, "Sorry Excuses: MSNBC's Form Apology," *Washington Post,* April 7, 2007, C01.
4. "Hollywood Power List," *Entertainment Weekly* (June 2006), 22–37.
5. Christopher Nixon, "Television Without Pity," *New York Times,* October 17, 2004.
6. Kate Authur, "The Awesome Tales of the Tweens," *New York Times*, August 7, 2005.
7. E. H. Gombrich, "The Visual Image," in *Media and Symbols: The Forms of Expression, Communication, and Education,* Publication of the National Society for the Study of Education, Vol. 73, Pt.1, ed. David R Olson (Chicago: University of Chicago Press, 1974), 242.

8. Max Frankel, "What's Happened to The Media?," *New York Times Magazine*, March 21, 1999, 38–40.

9. Ben Bagdikian, *The Media Monopoly*, 3rd ed. (Boston: Beacon Press, 1990), xxi.

10. Maria Aspan, "A Game With Real Soldiers," *New York Times*, September 18, 2006, C6.

11. Bill Moyers, *The Public Mind: Consuming Images*, Public Broadcasting Service, November 8, 1989.

12. Chris Kelleher, interview by author, September 23, 1999.

13. Bill Carter, "'The Ultimate Reality Show' On Adoption," *New York Times*, April 28, 2004, E1.

CHAPTER 4

PROCESS

- Comparative Media
- Audience

COMPARATIVE MEDIA

Each medium is defined by a set of distinctive characteristics that influence how it presents information. For instance, radio obviously cannot employ visuals in transmitting information. However, the radio producer can appeal to the listeners' imaginations through creative use of words and sound effects.

Consequently, one of the principles of media literacy involves the value of a balanced media diet. That is, consumers of media must learn to use media in *combination* to take advantage of the distinctive attributes of each medium. As discussed earlier, the stories selected for broadcast news are unparalleled at showing events as they unfold. In contrast, print stories contain essential detail and context. Consequently, using *both* media provides the audience with a more comprehensive understanding of the news event.

The following considerations can be helpful in assessing the characteristics of a medium:

- The *senses* involved in receiving information affect people's ability to assimilate certain kinds of information, as well as the ways in which they respond to the content.

- The *pace* of the presentation refers to the rhythm or rate at which information should be assimilated.
- The *environment* in which the medium is presented is a characteristic. The physical surroundings affect how an individual comprehends and responds to a media presentation.
- *Dissemination patterns* refer to 1) the amount of time it takes for information to be conveyed through a particular medium, and 2) the route that it takes to get to the public.

Print. Print is a tangible medium. Books are bound, collected, and passed from generation to generation. Although the primary sense used in reading is sight, readers also employ the sense of touch; you can hold printed material in your hands, smell the paper, and, in the case of newspapers, feel newsprint rubbing off on your hands. Printed material can be re-read and examined in depth. In addition, authors' names generally appear in their published work, so that they are accountable for the accuracy of their statements.

Print is a portable medium. You can take your book with you anywhere—the library, the park, or the subway. The major factor in location is adequate lighting.

To all outward appearances, you may be simply lounging about with a book in your hands at this moment. However, reading is a physical activity that demands an intense level of concentration and energy.

Reading is generally a primary experience. Unless you are reading a story to a small child, you tend to read silently, by yourself. Reading requires relative solitude. Try reading this textbook while engaged in other activities (driving or talking on the phone, for instance). Then see if you can clearly summarize the major points in the chapter. One activity or the other will surely suffer. Increasingly, however, publications like *USA Today* are designed with simplified information and colorful graphs, which enables readers to participate in other activities simultaneously.

Print lends itself to the detailed presentation of information and discussion of complex issues. Print also enables the author to describe internal states of consciousness: not merely what people are *doing* but what they are *thinking* as well. For instance, Henry James's novel *Portrait of a Lady* examines the interior life of the heroine, Isabelle Archer, and the principal inhabitants of her world. The following passage, detailing a chance meeting between Isabelle's husband, Osmond, and the nefarious Madame Merle, offers James the opportunity to discuss the subtext behind this simple, everyday encounter:

> In the manner and tone of these two persons, on first meeting at any juncture, and especially when they met in the presence of others, was something indirect and circumspect, as if they had approached each other obliquely and addressed each other

> by implication. The effect of each appeared to be to intensify to an appreciable degree the self-consciousness of the other. Madame Merle of course carried off any embarrassment better than her friend; but even Madame Merle had not on this occasion the form she would have liked to have—the perfect self-possession she would have wished to wear for her host. The point to be made is, however, that at a certain moment the element between them, whatever it was, always leveled itself and left them more closely face to face than either ever was with anyone else. This was what had happened now. They stood there knowing each other well and each on the whole willing to accept the satisfaction of knowing as a compensation for the inconvenience—whatever it might be—of being known.[1]

In print, the author clearly establishes the pace in which the material is received. The density of information and sentence structure requires a particular reading rate. As you doubtless noticed, Henry James's novels demand careful attention. James's style is characterized by long, complex narrative prose with frequent interpolations. On the other hand, the spare writing style and colorful graphics of *USA Today* enables readers to skim the paper, so that they can incorporate this task into their busy routines.

However, the reader does exercise an element of control over the pace. If you decide to put this text down now, there is very little that this author can do about it. If you decide to read more rapidly or skip entire paragraphs, that is ultimately your choice.

The dissemination schedule for print is comparatively deliberate. Newspapers are published on a daily basis. Consequently, if you do not get the opportunity to read your morning paper at breakfast, it may well be "old news" by the time you pick it up in the evening. Magazines may come out once a week or even bimonthly. Moreover, it normally takes a year or more for a book to be written, edited, published, and distributed. However, publishers now scramble to release a book on a popular subject before interest in the subject subsides. For example, three days after the death of Pope John Paul II on April 2, 2005, a biography of the pope was released, published by Cliff Street Books.

Photography. We live in a visual environment. We see billboards in crowds, wear images on our clothes, and leaf through magazines in a variety of public places, as well as at home. Photography has become a primary means of documenting our lives. The family photo album furnishes an important record of who we are and where we came from. Photos keep a record of significant rites of passage in the family, such as birthdays, holidays, graduations, and weddings. Indeed, a household with children is more likely to have at least one camera than a household in which there are no children.[2] Pictures have become particularly precious in contemporary culture, when, in so many cases, the extended family is no longer in close proximity. A photograph possesses an almost mystical quality; a person achieves a measure of immortality through photographs. Examine a picture from your childhood. Although you have changed, your image remains forever young. And looking at your photo book can stir memories, bringing the past into the present.

Although photographs have a distinct feel and smell, the primary way in which we appreciate photographs is through the sense of sight. As mentioned earlier, we tend to respond to visually oriented media in an *affective*, or emotional way. Consequently, photographers can convey media messages by evoking particular emotional responses in the audience.

In photography, the pace is primarily determined by the audience. The viewer determines how much time to devote to examining a photograph. However, the skilled photographer is able to direct the attention of the viewer to certain aspects of the photograph through the selection and arrangement of the subject matter. Further, the image-maker can use the visual tools at hand to create a mood that subtly conveys media messages. (For additional discussion, see Chapters 10 and 11, Production Elements.)

The dissemination schedule for photographs varies, from a delay of days in traditional chemical photographic processing to the immediate "grabbing" and downloading of a digital image.

Film. Like photography, film is an affective medium that generates an immediate emotional response. Adding the element of sound to the visuals makes film a particularly effective communication vehicle. Finally, the illusion of motion in film seemingly brings the film images to life, adding another layer of *verisimilitude* (or lifelike quality) to the medium.

Because film is more movement-oriented than print, plots that emphasize action—people doing things—play particularly well on screen. In contrast, the film version of Henry James's *Portrait of a Lady* (1996) did not translate easily from novel to film. As discussed earlier, in James's novel, the plot is subordinate to the exploration of character and theme. Thus, in its attempt to play up the action of the storyline, the film version lost much of the beauty and charm of the original work.

Unfortunately, many feature films are merely celebrations of movement, filled with car chases and wanton violence, which also fails to take full advantage of the medium. At its best, a film uses plot to furnish insight into character and theme; that is, the events in the story cause the main characters to undergo significant changes or come to important realizations about themselves, the world depicted in the film, or its inhabitants.

Watching a film in a movie theater is a primary experience. In contrast with other media, you must travel to a designated area. One of the attractions of going to the movies is simply getting away from the pressures and routines of home. The theater is dark and comfortable. The sound and images on the large screen can be overwhelming, moving you into a new realm of experience.

In addition, attending a movie is a social occasion. Who can forget their first date at the movies—the tension about whether to hold hands, sharing popcorn, and what to talk about after the show. Members of the audience are involved in a communal experience—responding to the program at the same moment. On the other hand, the audience can serve as a major distraction, when cell phones ring or the people behind you are chattering as though they're at home in their living rooms watching TV.

The pace of film is primarily determined by the filmmaker. We cannot stop the film if we decide to buy popcorn or visit the restroom. Movies are intended to be viewed in their entirety, in one sitting. The audience may be bored or overwhelmed by the pace of a film, but they have very little choice in the matter, other than leaving the theater.

The dissemination schedule for film is the most deliberate of all media. A Hollywood film project can take over three years from conception to exhibition in theaters. This process consists of four distinct stages:

- *Preproduction* includes all the preliminary creative, developmental, and planning stages, including the writing of the script, the negotiation for film rights, casting the film, contract negotiations with the performers' agents, building of studio sets, and deciding on locations. This stage generally requires between three months and two years.
- *Production* involves shooting the primary film footage, with accompanying recorded dialogue. This phase normally lasts between 30 and 80 days. Each day of shooting covers approximately three pages of the script and generates two or three minutes of final used footage.
- The *postproduction* stage includes editing, dubbing voices, sound mixing, creating and adding the musical score, addition of special effects, studio previewing, and reshooting of specific scenes. This stage can require three months to one year.
- The *promotion* stage consists of distribution, exhibition, and publicity. Many films never make it to this stage and are never released.

The script is likely to undergo many transformations during this protracted process, so that it may not even resemble the original screenplay. This prolonged process makes it difficult for a filmmaker to gauge whether a film will be topical by the time it is released.

In recent years, the domestic film industry in the United States has suffered. In 2005, the box office ticket sales dropped by 5 percent from the previous year.[3] This decline is the result of several factors: the competition of CD sales, improvements in home viewing, such as big screen televisions and high definition quality, and the reduced time between its theatrical run and its availability for home viewing.

However, the international film industry continues to flourish. The most prolific center of filmmaking in the world is Bombay, India. Over 800 films per year come out of "Bollywood." Another center of film production is "Nollywood," Nigeria, which produces 416 films per year (an industry regulation limits itself to releasing eight titles per week).[4]

Radio. Radio is an integral part of our everyday experience. In 2006, 93 percent of all American consumers over 12 years of age listen to the radio during the course of a week. The average radio consumer spends more than 10 hours per week listening to the radio.[5] Almost all Americans own at least one radio, and the average per household is 5.6 radios.[6]

Radio is continuous and accessible 24 hours per day. The clock radio puts people to sleep at night and wakes them up in the morning. Consequently, radio has assumed a remarkable personal significance in our lives. Hearing an old song on the radio may awaken memories of a summer long ago, perhaps, or of old friends, or a first romance. In that sense, it often is not the song that we are reacting to (in fact, we may dislike the particular tune). However, the media program has become internalized as a part of our personal experience, and we feel nostalgic about a program because it has put us in touch with ourselves and our pasts.

The invention of the car radio and the transistor radio transformed radio into a very portable medium. Radios accompany us everywhere. In 2006, most workday radio listening occured away from the home. From 7 A.M. to 7 P.M., the majority of radio listening occurs in the car, at work or in some location other than the listeners' homes.[7] Through refinements in this technology, radio can be incorporated into a person's active lifestyle, as we walk or jog. In addition, Internet radio usage was up 50 percent between 2005–2006.[8] E-radio, which is radio delivered through the Internet, gives the audience access to a wide range of stations from around the world. In addition, satellite radio is a special radio that receives signals broadcast by communications satellite. Subscribers are able to receive a wide range of commercial-free programming, free of signal breakup; audio interference characteristic of traditional radio relies on the transmission of radio signals, which usually can only travel about 30 or 40 miles from their source.

Radio relies entirely upon the listener's sense of hearing. Consequently, we must use our imaginations to envision what is being described over the air. On one level, this can be liberating—enabling us to project our own mental pictures onto the events. Old-time baseball announcers like Ronald "Dutch" Reagan (who later became the 40th president of the United States), relayed Western Union accounts of the action over the radio, learning to take advantage of the imaginative possibilities of the medium. Rather than simply announce the progress of the game, they embellished the report with fictitious details, sweeping emphasis, and artificial crowd noise to dramatize the action.

In radio, the pace of the presentation is controlled entirely by the communicator. As a result, the radio announcer is trained to speak slowly and distinctly, with a pleasing modulation of tone. Increasingly however, the pace of radio is controlled by a third agent—the station managers. A computer software program enables studio engineers to compress a speaker's presentation. Thus, by speeding up the delivery of the speaker, eliminating pauses, and removing what is known as "redundant" data from within words—for example, shortening a long syllable—engineers have been able to free an additional four minutes per hour for additional commercials. However, by accelerating the pace of the presentation, the station managers have potentially altered its meaning. Alex Kuczynski notes, "The new device has angered radio denizens like (Rush) Limbaugh, who says he uses pauses for emphasis much like an actor raises an eyebrow on stage."[9] Moreover, condensing the presentation is sometimes difficult to follow, which affects how the audience receives and interprets the messages.

Although radio remains separated in space from its audience, it operates live, in "real time." Morning radio is geared to helping you wake up and getting you to work on time. Most stations strive to insure that their weather information, news, and traffic reports are current and timely. The disc jockey takes dedications from fans and makes references to local celebrities, events, and landmarks. As a result, radio audiences develop intense loyalties to particular stations and radio personalities. Radio listeners may listen to two or three stations but are loyal to one in particular.[10]

The dissemination schedule for radio is immediate; as soon as radio broadcasters become aware of a story, they can put it on the air. This, combined with the easy accessibility of radio, makes this medium a primary source of information in times of crisis.

Listening to the radio is primarily a secondary activity. That is, the radio may serve as background, as a mood enhancer, or as a companion while we are engaged in other activities at home, school, or work. While the car radio is on, for example, our principal attention is (or should be) to keep the vehicle on the road. Consequently, because the radio audience is focusing its primary attention elsewhere, they may be susceptible to media messages conveyed through radio broadcasts.

Television. TV has emerged as the dominant leisure activity in the United States. It is easily accessible; more than 99 percent of homes in the United States have TV sets.[11] Broadcast television is free; anyone with a television can tune in. In addition, television is continuous. Generally speaking, broadcast television is on the air for 24 hours per day.

Like film, television combines sight, sound, motion, and color. TV hits us on an affective level, presenting images that move us emotionally.

Television is primarily an in-home experience, shared by a single individual or small group. Because complete darkness is not essential for viewing, people are often engaged in competing activities while they are watching television. According to one survey, over 70 percent of the television audience participates in at least one other activity while watching or listening to TV.[12] This may account for the formulaic nature of media; the predictability and simplicity of television programming enables the

Figure 4.1
Average time (in minutes) spent listening to the radio weekly, from 1997 to 2007.

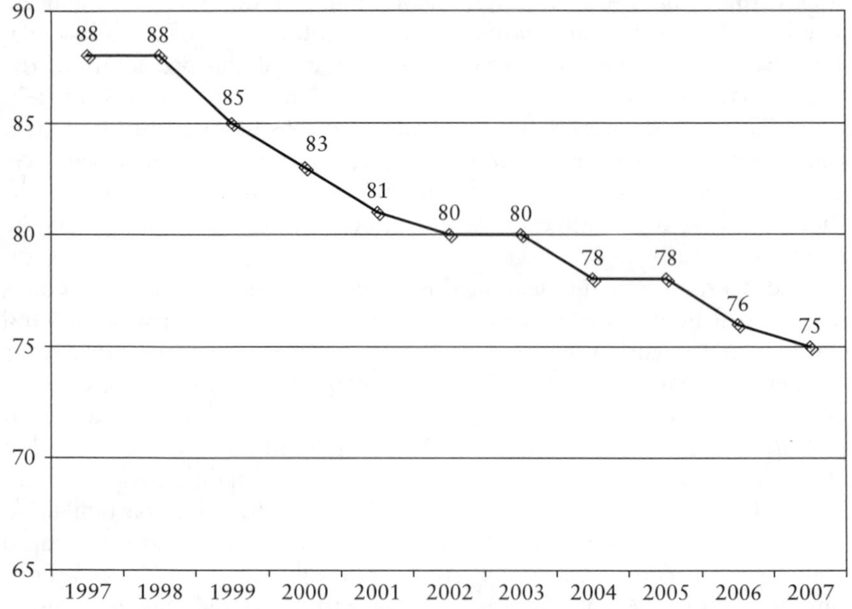

audience to follow the narrative while talking on the phone, reading, or cleaning the house.

The television set has been incorporated into the interior design of the home, much as the medium has become integrated into our daily activities. Think about the primary television viewing area in your home. The furniture is arranged around the television set; indeed, it is often difficult for people to face one another without craning their necks. Television has emerged as a prominent member of the family.

Television is an ideal medium for showing events in the process of unfolding. The standard format for TV programming is the series, which is brought into your home on a regular basis, over an extended time span (ranging from four weeks to, in the case of the soap opera *As the World Turns*, over 50 years. In contrast to film, which is one complete production, TV episodes are installments in a much longer, more complex story.

The ongoing nature of television also contributes to a unique personal dynamic between the performers and the audience. As an example Oprah Winfrey's television show is simply known as *Oprah*, reflecting the public's personal relationship with the star—they are on a first-name basis with the star.

Media technologies enable audiences to assume a major responsibility for the pace of television programming. DVD players, which have become a common component in American homes, allow viewers to pause or repeat a sequence, as well as record programs. In 2006, nearly 80 percent of American households owned at least one DVD player.[13]

Thanks to video technology and communications satellites, the dissemination schedule for television is now almost instantaneous. In 2006, the Hurricane Katrina tragedy was updated regularly, so that the public could participate in these news stories "in progress." However, television is less suitable for presenting the context, interpretation, and implications of this incident.

Despite the advent of large screen televisions, the style of television programming still harkens back to a time when the image on most television sets was a fraction of the size of the screen in the movie theater. Thus, instead of showing vast exteriors, television presents interior sets. As Herbert Zettl notes, television is an expressive medium which is well-suited to focus on relationships: "Film derives its energy from landscapes as well as people; in television, it is primarily people with all their complexity who power a scene, while the landscape aspects take a back seat."[14]

In addition, television programs currently employ more closeups than are commonly found in film. For example, in the soap opera genre, the significance is not so much on the action but on the *reaction* of the characters. Soaps devote much of their attention on the effects of various events on relationships between characters and on the larger soap opera community. This emphasis on facial expression means that people appearing in front of the camera must maintain their composure. An inappropriate smirk, twitch, or tear by a broadcaster or politician can speak volumes to an audience.

However, widescreen television sets have reduced this distinction between film image and television picture. This technology has yet to affect the intimate production style of television, but as the screens become more prevalent, the style may change as well.

To this point, the production quality of most video shot for television has been noticeably different from film, which affects how the information is presented. However, the arrival of digital video and high resolution HDTV has already reduced these aesthetic differences between video and film. Recent breakthroughs in technology have made it possible to capture movies using high-definition digital videocameras with fidelity comparable to 35-millimeter film and to project them digitally in theaters with no loss of image quality. According to Rob Sabin, this new video technology will revolutionize filmmaking:

> For filmmakers, exhibitors and moviegoers alike, digital cinema promises, over time, the single most significant enhancement of the movie experience since "The Jazz Singer" introduced sound in 1927. A shift to digital cameras will allow dramatic reductions in costs and new possibilities in special effects. On the

distribution end, digital projection could open avenues for the exhibition of less commercial films, creating more choices for consumers. And it will allow movie lovers to see, for the first time in history, exactly what the director sees in his final cut, without the degradation of image that is inevitable with film prints.[15]

Released in 2002, George Lucas's *Star Wars: Episode II* was the first major feature to be shot entirely in video, using high-definition digital video cameras, instead of the usual 35-millimeter film camera. Further, technology has made it possible to project video productions digitally in theaters with negligible loss of image quality.

Digital media. *Digital media* is not a new medium, per se, but a combination of existing media (print, photography, graphics, video, and audio). As such, this medium combines many of the distinctive characteristics of established media, including printed text, photographic images, sound, and motion.

Unlike other mass media, interactive communications is non-linear, replicating the impulses and thought patterns that characterize human interpersonal communications. As a result, the individual exercises extraordinary control over the pace of the presentation. To illustrate, if you log on to a web page on Franklin Roosevelt, you may suddenly develop a curiosity about the Depression. At this point, you may click on a link that moves you into a more thorough discussion of this ancillary topic. From there, you may select a link that focuses on films of the Depression. And so on ...

In the 1950s, the UNIVAC computer took up an entire room. Today, with the advent of the computer chip, computers have become increasingly portable, so that the BlackBerry you hold in your hand is more powerful than that original UNIVAC.

One of the remarkable characteristics of interactive technology is the accelerated dissemination schedule of the medium. Information is nearly instantaneous; indeed, it is ironic how impatiently we now wait for the few seconds required to "grab" graphics or find reference information on the Internet.

Of all media, the digital domain offers the most depth of information on a particular topic. Web pages generally include links to additional sources and related articles. Entire libraries filled with information are literally at our fingertips. Consequently, it is no coincidence that the audience for online news is particularly interested in information that newspapers and television do not cover in-depth: science, health, finance, and technology.[16]

The distinctive features of this new medium affect the structure, style, and content of media presentations. To illustrate, as the media industry began producing popular programming specifically for mobile phones, called *mobisodes*, it became clear that creating a program for a pocket-size screen is far different from making a program for a 27-inch television set. Producer Eric Young, hired to create a series of mobile episodes for a spin-off of the hit drama "24," declared, "We are all experimenting to see what works. Every new medium finds its own way and rules. It will be true for this one, too."[17]

In addition, the structure of these mobisodes has to be short—one minute in length—to accommodate the busy schedules of the average cellphone user. Consequently, producers developed a "serial" format, consisting of one-minute-long stories. All of these episodes adhere to the following formulaic structure: 1) begin with a conflict; 2) continue with dialogue; and 3) conclude with a cliffhanger to entice viewers to watch the next episode.

The style of the dramatic genre also had to be modified for this new channel. Because panoramic shots appeared blurry, approximately 70 percent of the images were close-ups of actors. In addition, small images such as bullet holes were difficult for the audience to see. As a result, Young was forced to make the bullet holes extra large for gunshot wounds and to double the amount of blood so they could be easily identified on the small screen.

Even the narrative itself is influenced by this new digital TV platform. Adventure dramas such as "24: Conspiracy" feature a lot of action to make best use of the small screen. In addition, because of the preponderance of young cellphone users, youth-oriented genres appearing on cellphones include reality shows, comedies, and animated shorts.

However, many interactive media communicators have yet to take full advantage of the potential of this medium. Many digital media communicators lack a clear objective for using interactive media. Companies often operate according to the *double negative* syndrome with respect to interactive media. That is, although they can see no good reason to put up a web site, they are afraid *not* to, for fear of falling behind their competition. As a result, web sites are often simply repetitions of print ads and so fail to take full advantage of the unique properties of this medium.

In addition, digital media communicators must learn to take advantage of each medium's ability to present particular types of information. As mentioned earlier, detailed information can best be conveyed through use of print. Graphics can help illustrate or clarify complex statistical information. And photographs and video can provide a record of events.

But digital communicators have yet to use the different media in combination to accommodate the different learning styles of individuals. For instance, people who retain visual information may rely on this mode of communication, with support from print and audio.

Occasionally, digital media communicators try to dazzle the audience with their technical wizardry. However, the inclusion of glitzy effects simply to impress the audience can actually *interfere* with the communication process.

AUDIENCE

Audience Identification

Because media communicators have no direct contact with their audience, a great deal of time and attention is devoted to *audience identification.* Media communicators often engage marketing specialists to develop a clear sense of audience. For example, John Merrill provides this marketing profile of the radio news-talk audience:

> Listeners of radio's format-leading news/talk demo (are) typically in the 35-plus age range, strongly skewed toward males (59%), overwhelmingly white (88%), usually married (64%), homeowners (76%) and with no offspring currently living in the household (61%). Different sectors of the population have distinct, identifiable interests and backgrounds and look for specific objectives or gratifications in media programming.[18]

Some media programming may be targeted simultaneously at both a *manifest* and *latent* audience. For instance, Saturday morning commercials are directed at children. However, a secondary target audience consists of *parents*, who are pressured to purchase the products featured in the commercial for their children.

Over time, media communicators have changed their audience identification strategy from a *broadcasting* philosophy to *narrowcasting.* Over time, the media market has become so large that it became profitable to direct messages at specialized interests, tastes, and groups. For example, if you turn your radio dial, you will find AM stations geared to African Americans, young people, and country music lovers. Because of the huge mass audience, it is no longer necessary to appeal to every viewer. ESPN can realize a profit if they can reach all of the sports fans in the audience. (For more discussion of narrowcasting, see Chapter 5, Historical Context.) Narrowcasting enables media communicators to tailor their presentations to the background and interests of particular subgroups.

This narrowcasting strategy enables the media communicator to develop *communication strategies* that are tailored to its audience. As an example, Procter & Gamble, maker of household items, has long promoted a conservative, wholesome image that has resonated with its traditional market—housewives. However, because the P & G online audience is younger and more freethinking, its ad strategy must be unconventional as well. For instance a 2006 online ad campaign for ThermaCare menstrual pain reliever asserts that the product can alleviate *male* menstrual cramps. Reporter Stuart Elliott explains,

> A marketer once known as much for its moral rectitude as its soaps and detergents is pushing further into the brave world of new media with a provocative effort asserting that men can suffer from menstrual cramps.

> Not long ago, the company, Procter & Gamble, wou[illegible]e shied away from a public discussion of women's menstrual cramps, muc[illegible] sponsoring a playful campaign pretending that they afflict men, too. But ti[illegible]e changed, and even Procter, the nation's largest advertiser, is looking to p[illegible]e envelope with viral campaigns online.
>
> Major marketers believe they can take greater risks online because Internet users tend to be younger and more accustomed to irreverent humor … The ThermaCare products intended to treat women with menstrual pain are behind the elaborate new campaign, known as "Men With Cramps." The effort, with a budget estimated at $1 million, includes two special Web sites, a fake documentary and video clips, all purportedly the work of an imaginary institute that is studying the imaginary problem of "cyclical nonuterine dysmenorrhea"—i.e., men with cramps. (There are traditional ads for the other types of ThermaCare products, with spending last year of about $35 million.)[19]

Second, creating an audience profile enables media communicators to modify the *style* of the presentation to the audience. For instance, in 2005, two major book publishers began publishing their books in a larger size to accommodate the needs of their aging market. Penguin Group and Simon & Schuster began publishing their paperbacks in larger type, with more space between lines for baby boomers, who are finding it more difficult to read the small print in paperbacks. Jack Romanos, the chief executive of Simon & Schuster explains, "We've been losing the foundation of our customer base because their eyesight is getting worse, and the books are getting harder and harder to read."[20]

Narrowcasting further enables media communicators to customize the *content* of their media presentations on the basis of the background and interests of its audience. Unfortunately, narrowcasting can also lead to *cultural segregation*, in which individuals remain insulated within their particular spheres of interest and belief systems. For example, if you are only interested in country music, you are never in a position to be exposed to hip-hop. Narrowcasting enables the media to respond to the background and interests of particular subgroups; however, at the same time, this trend can also have the effect of further insulating individuals. As a result, audiences can become locked into this demographic straitjacket and, consequently, are not exposed to perspectives of other groups. An essential aspect of media literacy involves looking beyond the materials that have been directed at your particular demographic group, in order to get a broader perspective. For instance, magazines like *Ebony*, *Essence*, and *Jet* provide insight into the interests and concerns of the African-American community. Other subgroups like Asian Americans and Hispanics have developed their own specialized media. Similarly, it is also important to become exposed to media presentations that offer different ideological perspectives. For instance, *The Nation* and *The Progressive* are magazines with a liberal orientation, while the *National Review* and

U.S. News and World Report provide a conservative perspective on events.

Post-Modern Mass Communications Model

In this rapidly evolving media landscape, the mass communications model discussed earlier must be reconfigured yet again. Because the American media is a market-driven system, producers must take their audience into consideration at an earlier stage of the communication process (see Table 4.1).

Each medium (or particular application of the medium) is directed at a particular audience. As an example, most people who attend movies in the United States are between the ages of 18 to 24. Producers then devote their attention to finding actors and actresses who resonate with this audience, as well as stories that appeal to this group.

In many instances, the audience now determines the choice of *media communicator.* For instance, producers of news programs now recruit youthful hosts who can "relate" to the young audiences they wish to attract. Amanda Congdon, news presenter for ABCNews.com, is the embodiment of her audience. Congdon, who was recruited from the popular webcast news show Rocketboom, is young, informal, and has "attitude." Virginia Heffernan explains,

> On [Ms. Congdon's] first minishow, Ms. Congdon shows up in a taut Steely Dan T-shirt and opens with her trademark girly casualness: "O.K., this is weird." ... Like a teenager, she seems exaggeratedly puzzled by whatever's at hand; she's too cool for almost everything, and good for her ... Slim, swan-necked, with the upright bearing of a dancer or cadet, she doesn't exactly lean in for intimacy with the viewer. She's not relatable. She seems a touch abstemious. The news, it seems, kind of grosses her out ... If it's not good and evil that preoccupy her, it's at least

Table 4.1
Communications Models

Interpersonal Communications Model	Mass Communications Model	Post-Modern Communications Model
Communicator	Channel	Channel
•	•	•
Message	Communicator	Audience
•	•	•
Channel	Message	Communicator
•	•	•
Audience	Audience	Message

"cool" and "weird." And that's not entirely trivial. On Rocketboom she used expressions and interjections (Cool! Weird!) to interpret and inflect primary sources, and often that was enough. Last year her report on Hurricane Katrina simply played various television interviews in New Orleans. Then the camera returned to her. She gave a loose, flinging shrug that tersely conveyed disbelief, fury and sadness. It was an editorial in itself ... This works well in the ultrashort news clips she'll be doing on ABCNews.com.

Though Ms. Congdon quickly offsets that show of exuberance with a dash of sarcasm, it's still unmistakably there. She's plainly an enthusiast: for new media, for old media, for Amanda Congdon, for the possibility of being smart and pretty at the same time and furthermore doing something cool and kind of like weird.[21]

In the evolution of media, the channel and the audience have assumed a primary (first) role in the mass communications process.

The audience now plays a role in defining the media communicator. Consequently, Ms. Congdon can be seen as a reflection of the informal appearance and attitude found in her youthful audience.

Figure 4.2

The audience now plays a role in defining the media communicator. For example, Amanda Congdon, who was hired as news presenter for ABCnews.com, reflects the informal appearance and attitude found in her youthful audience. Courtesy of Amanda Congdon.

In this post-modern communications model, the audience can even determine the *content* of media presentations. A 2006 study of newspapers around the United States found that the audience largely determines the ideology of newspapers. Economist Jesse M. Shapiro explains, "The data suggests that newspapers are targeting their political slant to their customers' demand and choosing the amount of slant that will maximize their sales."[22]

One of the distinguishing features of the post-modern communications model is that the audience is able to bypass the traditional media gatekeepers and act as their own content providers. With the appearance of Internet sites featuring music, blogs, and film reviews, the audience selects media content for each other, providing an alternative to corporate media communicators as sources of information and entertainment. Courtney Holt, executive vice president for digital music at MTV, explains, "The tools for programming are in the hands of consumers ... Right now it almost feels like a fanzine culture, but it's going to turn into mainstream culture. The consumer is looking for it."[23]

As an example, Pandora.com is a streaming Internet radio service that customizes the playlist for you by compiling a database of your musical tastes. Reporter Jeff Leeds explains,

> Services like Pandora have become the latest example of how technology is shaking up the hierarchy of tastemakers across popular culture ... All told, music consumers are increasingly turning away from the traditional gatekeepers and looking instead to one another—to fellow fans, even those they've never met—to guide their choices.[24]

As a result, you no longer have to rely on commercial radio stations that are owned by mega-corporations and play a standard playlist determined by the corporate headquarters. Instead, Pandora.com enables you to compile and refine your own playlist (with the assistance, at times, of other members of the audience).

Established industries have begun to work off of this post-modern communications model as well. For instance, advertisers are now producing and distributing their own television commercials over the Internet without going through traditional ad agencies. Some companies simply provide websites for the audience, who contribute the content. For instance, Plastics.com promotes itself as "a live collaboration of the Web's readers and the smartest editors—a place to suggest discuss the most worthwhile news, opinions, rumors, humor and anecdotes online." As Joey Anuff, editor in chief of Plastics.com explains, "It's kind of a news exchange. It's run by editors, but it's fueled by an audience."[25]

Ironically, in the post-modern mass communication model, the message often is the *final* consideration. All too often, the audience dictates choices in programming. For instance, because the typical moviegoer is between the ages of 18–24, studios and distributors look for films with subject matter dealing with teenage angst and young adulthood, steering away from subjects that would be of interest to mature audiences. Indeed, film studios frequently rely on the input of focus groups, made up of their target audience, before deciding on the finished product—much to the chagrin of the filmmakers. Agent Bob Broder explains, "Too many times a writer is asked to add or change an element or character of a show, even if it makes no creative sense, merely in an attempt to reach a specific demographic."[26]

Audience considerations also play a role in the content of news programming. Newspapers such as the *Miami Herald* conduct reader-preference surveys to identify what the audience wants to know—a far cry from the traditional news imperative of providing what the audience "needs" to know. In television news, surveys reveal that a large segment of the population wants "entertaining and enjoyable news presented by personalities who deliver it in a caring way."[27] Consequently, in their drive to make the news entertaining to the audience, entertainment has become news.

Audience Behavior Patterns

What are audience members doing while they are receiving media messages? Audience behavior patterns refer to an individual's aggregate experience while exposed to a media presentation.

Competing Activities. Audience members are frequently engaged in competing activities while receiving media messages (driving while listening to the radio, for instance). A study conducted in 2005 found that the subjects (representing a broad range of age) were *multitasking* about a third of the time they were using media. Colleen Fahey Rush, executive vice president for research at MTV Networks, notes, "Our research showed that people somehow managed to shoehorn 31 hours of activity into a 24-hour day. That's from being able to do two things at once."[28]

Unfortunately, the brain appears to have a finite amount of space for all of the tasks that require concentrated attention. A study using magnetic resonance images of brain activity reveals that engaging in competing activities impairs an individual's ability to perform *either* task effectively. Reporter Sandra Blakeslee explains,

> When people try to drive in heavy traffic and talk, brain activity does not double. The amount of brain activity devoted to each task actually decreases. As a result, people performing two demanding tasks simultaneously do neither one as well as they do each one alone.[29]

Thus, although your brain can become more proficient at carrying out multiple tasks, your performance levels are never as high as when the tasks are carried out independently. Because of this divided attention, you may not be giving critical attention to *either* activity. Consequently, you may be susceptible to subtle messages that can affect your attitudes and behaviors. Despite their years of training, young people are overwhelmed by this barrage of images, sounds, and messages. Andrew Blau declares,

> There is more media produced than can ever be seen … Even young people who can multitask in ways that make older heads spin will not be able to keep up with the growing amount of media available on the growing number of surfaces, devices, and screens of all kinds.[30]

Further, studies indicate that half of the audience leaves the room at least once during the course of a TV show—while the media communicator is "talking" to the audience. And approximately one-third of the audience deserts the typical hour-long program before it is over, switching to another channel or turning off the television. Significantly, if you answer the phone or leave the room for a portion of a telecast, the text has been altered; if you miss the ending of a police drama, before the criminals are caught, you may be left with the message that crime *does* pay.

Significantly, this multitasking often involves *multiple-media* activities:

- About 80 percent of teens regularly use more than one media type at a given time,
- More than 60 percent of teens say they regularly go online while watching TV.
- Nearly 60 percent use instant messaging and about 35 percent listen to the radio while watching TV.[31]

As a result of this merging of images, printed text, dialogue, and music, you may be receiving an altogether *different* message than was originally intended by the media communicator.

Table 4.2
Percent of Individuals Who Utilize Other Media When:

Watching Television	67.9%
Listening to the Radio	56.4%
Reading the Newspaper	68.9%
Surfing the Internet	70.7%

Source: BIGresearch

MEDIA MULTITASKING

AUDIENCE BEHAVIOR PATTERNS

The media are so pervasive that sometimes we don't realize how these channels have been incorporated into our everyday lives. If you kept a daily record of your exposure to media, you might well find that the following variables play a role in your media behavior:

- Media Formats
  We are accustomed to thinking of media appearing in conventional formats: on the television screen, newspaper page, or movie theater. However, these media now appear in a variety of formats, including billboards and T-shirts. In addition, media messages appear in unusual settings, such as grocery stores and elevators. Be sensitive to the various media surrounding you.
  In the course of a single day, how much time did you spend with:
  - Print
  - Photography
  - Radio
  - Film
  - Television
  - Computer
  - Other

  In addition to the established media systems cited above (e.g., photography, film, television), what other media did you encounter?
  - Billboards
  - T-shirts
  - Video Games
  - Other
- Multiple Media
  People are frequently involved in more than one media activity at a time (e.g., listening to the radio while you are reading this book). This barrage of media affects the amount of attention you can devote to any one message. Multiple media may even combine to form a separate, independent meaning.
  - How much of your time was devoted to multiple media?
  - Which media were used in combination?

  As a result you may be susceptible to subtle messages which can affect our attitudes and behaviors.
  - How much of your media time involved competing activities?
  - What activities competed with your media time?
- Voluntary vs. Involuntary Media
  Voluntary media consists of times when *you* choose a particular medium or program. Involuntary media refers to the times when someone *else* has made a media selection, and you are exposed to messages beyond your control (e.g., someone blasting the radio in the next room while you are trying to sleep).

MEDIA MULTITASKING (*continued*)

Involuntary media activity is also *embedded within* a voluntary media activity. For instance, for every "half hour" news broadcast, up to eight minutes are devoted to advertisements.

- How much of your media activity was voluntary?
- How much media activity was involuntary?
- How much involuntary media activity was *embedded* in voluntary media?

- Weekend vs. Weekday Activity
  Media activities are often closely associated with our daily routines. Consequently, because our routines often change during the weekends, so does our media usage:
  Do you devote more or less time to media-related activities during the weekend?
  Are your choices of specific types of media (television, radio, etc.) different?
  How many of your weekend social activities revolve around the use of media?

Audience Interpretation of Media Content

What role does the audience play in the interpretation of media content?

Two schools of thought provide explanations with respect to the responsibility of the audience in the interpretation of content: 1) the hegemonic model and 2) the reception theory.

In the hegemonic model, the audience assumes a passive role in the communications process. The media communicator establishes a *preferred reading*, in which the text dictates the responses of the audience. The preferred reading asks the audience to assume the role, perspective, and orientation of the heroes and heroines. The plot establishes the accepted point of view of the narrative. In addition, production elements such as lighting and angle distinguish the heroes from the villains and, consequently, directs how the audience is to respond to these characters.

The reception theory posits that the audience assumes an active role in *negotiating*, or interpreting the information they receive through mass media, filtered through their particular experiences and backgrounds. According to this construct, audience members may negotiate a meaning that is entirely different from the preferred reading dictated by the media communicator. Within this construct, particular subcultures may react differently to a media presentation, based on the common experiences of the group. Thus, women may be more sensitive to messages about violence against females in film than men.

But in addition, an individual's own expectations or frames of reference can influence how they respond to a media presentation. Art historian E. H. Gombrich points out,

The information extracted from an image can be quite independent of the intention of its maker. A holiday snapshot of a group on a beach may be scrutinized by an intelligence officer preparing for a landing, and the Pompeiian mosaic might provide new information to a historian of dog breeding.[32]

AUDIENCE-RECEPTION THEORY

What is the role of the audience with regard to the interpretation of media content? According to the *reception theory,* the audience assumes an active role in interpreting, or "negotiating," the information they receive through mass media, based on their particular experiences and backgrounds.

The following variables affect how an individual interprets media content:

- *Background*
  How much does the audience already know about the subject?
- *Interest Level*
  How interested is the audience in the subject? How attentive is the audience?
- *Predisposition*
  What is the attitude of the audience toward the subject (positive or negative) going into the conversation?
- *Priorities*
  What issues are of particular concern to the audience? Why?
- *Demographic Profile*
  - National origin
  - Gender
  - Race
  - Ethnic origin
  - Age
  - Education
  - Income
- *Psychological Profile*
  - Self-concept
  - Primary relationships
  - Significant life experiences
  - Ways of relating to others
  - Ways of dealing with emotions
  - Personal aspirations
- *Communications Environment*
  - What is the size of the audience?
  - What are they *doing* while they are receiving the information?
- *Stage of Development*
  Have you ever re-read a novel and reacted differently than you did the first time? The content did not change, but *you* did. As people grow older, their experiences influence their perception of what they see. In addition, the maturation process alters how people interpret their world—including media content.

Thus, according to the reception theory, when considering the ways in which the audience comprehends media content, it is important to consider the following questions:

- What values, experiences, and perspectives are shared by the audience?
- Do these shared values, experiences, or perspectives influence their understanding or interpretation of the presentation?
- How do the experiences and perspectives of the *individual* audience member affect the interpretation of the presentation?

In addition, the reception theory addresses the issue of *taste*—why certain people derive pleasure from particular media presentations.

Which perspective on audience interpretation is correct—the hegemonic model or the reception theory? *Probably both.* Although audience members are encouraged to assume the point of view of the preferred reading, they also negotiate their own meaning, based on their individual backgrounds, orientations, and experiences.

SUMMARY

Keys to Interpreting Media Messages: Process

Communication is a very complex activity. This process is even more challenging in mass communications, when the communicator is removed in time and space from the audience. However, in both cases, the successful communicator:

- Understands the communication process
- Recognizes the purpose of the communication
- Is self-aware
- Understands the message (knows what he or she wants to say)
- Understands the characteristics of the channel being used
- Can identify the audience
- Uses feedback to insure that the audience comprehends the message

Applying the following questions related to process can provide insight into media messages:

A. Media Communicator

1. Who is responsible for creating the media production?
2. What are the demographic characteristics of the media communicator(s)?
3. How do these characteristics affect the content and outlook of the media production?

B. Function

1. What is the purpose behind the production?
2. Does the media communicator want you to think or behave in a particular way as a result of receiving the information?
3. Does the production contain any of the following:
    a. Latent functions
    b. Multiple functions
    c. Undefined functions

C. Comparative Media

1. What are the medium's distinctive characteristics?
2. In what ways does the choice of medium affect:
    a. The communication strategy
    b. The communication style
    c. The content

D. Audience

1. Audience Identification
    a. For whom is the media presentation produced?
    b. Is there more than one intended audience?
    c. What values, experiences, and perspectives are shared by the audience?
    d. What does the *communication strategy, content,* and *style* of a media presentation reveal about the intended audience?
2. Audience Behavior Patterns
    a. What is the audience doing while they are receiving media messages?
    b. What is the environment in which the audience is receiving media messages?
    c. In what ways does the behavior of the audience affect how the messages are received?
3. Audience Interpretation of Media Content
    a. Do these shared values, experiences, or perspectives influence their understanding or interpretation of the presentation?
    b. How do the experiences and perspectives of the *individual* audience member affect his or her interpretation of the presentation?
    c. How does the choice of audience influence the *strategy, style*, and *content* of the media presentation?
    d. Do the strategy, style, and content of the media presentation provide insight into the intended audience(s)?

NOTES

1. Henry James, *Portrait of a Lady* (New York: The Modern Library, 1966), 239.

2. E. H. Gombrich, "The Visual Image," *Media and Symbols: The Forms of Expression, Communication, and Education,* Publication of the National Society for the Study of Education, Vol. 73, Pt.1, ed. David R Olson (Chicago: University of Chicago Press, 1974), 249.

3. "Plummeting 2005 Box Office Sparks Hollywood Crisis," Breitbart.com, December 13, 2005 (www.breitbart.com/news/2005/12/13/051213173239.bo5ciosh.html).

4. Norimitsu Orishi, "Step Aside, L.A. and Bombay, Hooray for Nollywood," *New York Times,* September 16, 2002, A1.

5. Radio Today 2006 Edition, Arbitron (www.arbitron.com/radio_stations/home.htm).

6. Rebecca Pirrto, "Why Radio Thrives," *American Demographics* 16:5(May 1994), 40 (7).

7. Radio Today 2006 Edition, Arbitron.

8. Listener Survey, American Media Services, April 19, 2006 (www.americanmediaservices.com/news/press_releases/archives/000036.shtml).

9. Alex Kuczyanski, "Radio Squeezes Empty Air Space for Profit," *New York Times*, January 6, 2000 (www.nytimes.com).

10. Pirrto, "Why Radio Thrives."

11. Media Reform Info Center, "TV Facts" (www.enviroweb.org)

12. Ellen Gray, "Some TV Viewers Might Just Be Listening," *St. Louis Post-Dispatch*, October 18–24, 1998, Television Guide, 46.

13. Gigi Sohn, president and co-founder, Public Knowledge, Testimony to Committee on the Judiciary, June 21, 2006 (http://judiciary.senate.gov/testimony.cfm?id=1956&wit_id=5459).

14. Herbert Zettl, *Sight Sound Motion: Applied Media Aesthetics* (Belmont, CA: Wadsworth, l990), 95.

15. Rob Sabin, "The Movies' Digital Future Is in Sight and It Works," *New York Times,* November 26, 2000.

16. Pew Research Center Biennial News Consumption Survey, "Event-Driven News Audiences."

17. Laura M. Holson, "Now Playing on a Tiny Screen," *New York Times,* October 17, 2005.

18. John Meril, "Listening Down in 98," in 1998 Radio Format Study Interep.

19. Stuart Elliott, "Online, P. & G. Gets a Little Crazy," *New York Times,* December 14, 2006, C3.

20. Edward Wyatt, "Books, Not Tales, Get Taller Before Baby Boomers' Eyes," *New York Times,* August 12, 2005.

21. Virginia Heffernan, "An Online Newscaster's Appealing Bafflement," *New York Times,* December 13, 2006, B2.

22. Austan Goolsbee, "Lean Left? Lean Right? News Media May Take Their Cues From Customers," *New York Times*, December 7, 2006.

23. Jeff Leeds, "The New Tastemakers," *New York Times,* September 3, 2006.

24. Ibid.

25. Susan Stellin, "Media Talk: Putting Readers in the Assignment Desk," *New York Times,* January 22, 2001.

26. Bill Carter, "Shrinking Network TV Audiences Set Off Alarm and Reassessment," *New York Times*, November 22, 1998 (www.nytimes.com).

27. Pew Research Center Biennial News Consumption Survey, "Event-Driven News Audiences."

28. Sharon Waxman, "At an Industry Media Lab, Close Views of Multitasking," *New York Times*, May 15, 2006.

29. Sandra Blakeslee, "Car Calls May Leave Brain Short-Handed," *New York Times*, July 31, 2001, F1.

30. Andrew Blau, "Deep Focus," National Alliance for Media Arts and Culture, (January 2005), 15.

31. Kevin Downey, "Huge Challenge for Advertisers to Get Noticed," *Media Life*, September 25, 2003.

32. Gombrich, "The Visual Image," 249.

SECTION

2

CONTEXT

Context refers to those surrounding elements that subtly shape meaning and convey messages.

CHAPTER

5

HISTORICAL CONTEXT

Media presentations derive their significance from the events of the day. Clearly, the primary goal of the journalist is to record events that have political or social significance. But entertainment programming and advertising are also influenced by current events. A historical approach to media analysis offers a way to put prominent events and figures of the day into meaningful perspective.

Historical context can follow several lines of inquiry:

A media presentation can add to our understanding of historical events. Individuals look to news programming such as newspapers and television news programming to keep abreast of the day's events. But in addition, individuals are looking to entertainment programming like Comedy Central's *The Daily Show* as a principal source of political news. Reports indicate 46 percent of high school students get news and information at least once a week from entertainment shows such as *The Daily Show*, *The Colbert Report*, and *South Park*.[1] Media communicators often draw from current events as fodder for programming. To illustrate, Don Wolf, creator and executive producer of the *Law & Order* television crime drama franchise, often scans the newspaper for items that can be used in episodes of the series:

> When Mr. Wolf, 59, maneuvered his 6-foot-4 frame behind a table at the Four Seasons Hotel in Manhattan for breakfast recently, his mood was ebullient, his enthusiasm for his surviving shows seemingly undiminished. The main reason, at least at that moment, was a front-page headline in that morning's *New York Post*, which blared: "King of Bling Busted—Jacob the jeweler in Coke-Cash Rap."

Paraphrasing the story for a visitor, Mr. Wolf described how Jacob Arabo, an immigrant from Uzbekistan whose creations had draped Madonna, Diddy and other performers, was being accused of laundering money for a drug network in Detroit. "That," he said with assurance, "will be a 'Law & Order' next year."[2]

Thus, fans of popular programs are immersed in current events. Alessandra Stanley explains,

Sometimes the Iraq conflict takes over an entire plotline: an episode of "Criminal Minds," a CBS series about serial killers and psychopaths, turned its focus to a Muslim terrorist suspect being held at Guantánamo—without due process. (He is thrown on the floor of an interrogation room in his underpants, hands and feet bound by chains and his face bruised from beatings.)[3]

Because many popular media presentations derive their meaning from the historical events of the day, older media presentations can furnish perspective into the historical period in which it was produced. For instance, *Invasion of the Body Snatchers* (1956) is a science-fiction thriller that was made during the Cold War. Understanding the geopolitics of this historical period can furnish considerable perspective into the film. The story, about an invasion of pods from outer space, is a parable about a takeover of the United States by the Soviet Union. The pods descend on a rural American community and assume the identity of citizens once they fall asleep. These inhuman creatures have no souls and feel no emotion. Like ants, they operate within a collective mentality. Significantly, once the pods were discovered, they were easily destroyed. Thus, as with the Communist threat, the primary defense against these creatures was eternal vigilance.

Conversely, an understanding of historical events can furnish perspective into a media presentation. To illustrate, columnist Stuart Elliott's critique of the 2007 Super Bowl ads discussed ways in which overtones of the Iraq war could be found throughout the commercial spots:

No commercial that appeared last night during Super Bowl XLI directly addressed Iraq, unlike a patriotic spot for Budweiser beer that ran during the game two years ago. But the ongoing war seemed to linger just below the surface of many of this year's commercials.

More than a dozen spots celebrated violence in an exaggerated, cartoonlike vein that was intended to be humorous, but often came across as cruel or callous. For instance, in a commercial for Bud Light beer ... one man beat the other at a game of rock, paper, scissors by throwing a rock at his opponent's head....

Those who wish the last four years of history had never happened could find solace in several commercials that used the device of ending an awful tale by revealing it was only a dream. The best of the batch was a commercial for General Motors by Deutsch, part of the Interpublic Group of Companies, in which a factory robot "obsessed about quality" imagined the dire outcome of making a mistake. The same gag, turned inside out, accounted for one of the funniest spots, a Nationwide Financial commercial by TM Advertising, also owned by Interpublic. The spot began with the singer Kevin Federline as the prosperous star of an elaborate rap video clip. But viewers learned at the end it was only the dream of a forlorn fry cook at a fast-food joint.

Then, too, there was the unfortunate homonym at the heart of a commercial from Prudential Financial, titled "What Can a Rock Do?" The problem with the spot, created internally at Prudential, was that whenever the announcer said, "a rock"—invoking the Prudential logo, the rock of Gibraltar—it sounded as if he were saying, yes, "Iraq."[4]

A media presentation can serve as a barometer of current attitudes toward historical events. Traditionally, media programming has been a source of commentary on historical events. John Leland explains,

In the 18th century, songwriters responded to current events by writing new lyrics to existing melodies. "Benjamin Franklin used to write broadside ballads every time a disaster struck," said Elijah Wald, a music historian, and sell the printed lyrics in the street that afternoon. This tradition of responding culturally to terrible events had almost been forgotten, Mr. Wald said, but in the wake of Hurricane Katrina, it may be making a comeback, with the obvious difference that, where Franklin would have sold a few song sheets to his fellow Philadelphians, the Internet allows artists today to reach the whole world.[5]

In 2006, Bruce Springsteen released an album consisting of songs composed by longtime activist folksinger Pete Seeger. Springsteen launched his promotional tour at the 37th annual Jazz and Heritage Festival in New Orleans, Louisiana, which was still struggling to rebuild after being ravaged by Hurricane Katrina in 2005. By resurrecting Seeger's protest songs like "Eyes on the Prize" and "Mary Don't You Weep," Springsteen voiced the frustration and pain of the many displaced residents of the city. Springsteen made this commentary even more topical by adding his own lyrics to the 1929 song, "How Can a Poor Man Stand Such Times and Live?": "[Bush] gave a little pep talk, said I'm with you, then he took a walk."

Recognizing historical references can furnish clues into themes and messages contained in media presentations. Popular films, music, and television programs frequently contain historical references. For instance, in a 2007 episode of *Without a Trace* (CBS), an F.B.I. agent described a potentially disastrous pipe leak in the ocean as "the ecological equivalent of Iraq."[6]

Critic Frank Rich points out that Steven Spielberg's 2005 film version of *War of the Worlds* contains numerous references to 9/11:

The alien attack on America is the work of sleeper cells; the garments of the dead rain down on those fleeing urban apocalypse; poignant fliers are posted for The Missing. There is also a sterling American military that rides to the rescue. Deep in the credits for "War of the Worlds" is a thank-you to the Department of Defense and some half-dozen actual units that participated in the movie, from the Virginia Army National Guard to a Marine battalion from Camp Pendleton, Calif. Indeed, Mr. Spielberg seems to have had markedly more success in recruiting extras for his film than the Pentagon has had of late in drumming up troops for Iraq.

In not terribly coded dialogue, the film makes clear that its Americans know very well how to distinguish a war of choice like that in Iraq from a war of necessity, like that prompted by Al Qaeda's attack on America. Tim Robbins—who else?—pops up to declare that when aliens occupy a country, the "occupations always fail." Even Tom Cruise's doltish teenage screen son is writing a school report on "the French occupation of Algeria."[7]

In countries with restricted civil liberties, media communicators are able to comment on public affairs issues in an indirect fashion. For instance, *Barareh Nights* is a popular Iranian soap opera, which takes place about 70 years ago in the little village of Barareh. This distant setting enables the producers to comment indirectly about contemporary conditions in Iran. *Barareh Nights*, which is watched by 90 percent of people with access to a television (now most of Iran's 69 million people) deals with issues of corruption, rigged elections, tensions between the social classes, and women's rights that plague Iran today. Indeed, in one subplot, Barareh "enriches" its staple food, peas, in a clear parallel with Iran's disputed uranium enrichment program. Viewer Ahmad Eslami comments, "This show is just beautiful. The whole Islamic Republic is right here."[8]

At times, media presentations even forecast historical events. Because the American media industry relies so heavily on current events and trends as the source of media programming, entertainment programming frequently anticipates historical events. Television critic Alessandra Stanley provides the following example:

> The first season of the Showtime series "Sleeper Cell," about an undercover agent who infiltrates a cell of Muslim conspirators in Los Angeles, eerily presaged the London plot (of July 7, 2005)—including Western terrorists who converted to Islam.[9]

Media communicators often conduct extensive research that they incorporate into the plot. To illustrate, the film *The Day After Tomorrow* (2004) presents a futuristic scenario in which the world has been ravaged by climate changes, as super storms destroy Western Europe, and Manhattan has been covered in a sheet of ice. In preparation, Director Roland Emmerich consulted a report entitled "An Abrupt Climate Change Scenario and Its Implications for United States National Security," commissioned by Andrew W. Marshall, head of the Pentagon's office of long-term threat assessment. Although Emmerich exaggerated the immediacy of the threat for dramatic effect, the film does point to risks of future climate shocks. Emmerich notes, "It's a popcorn movie that's actually a little subversive."[10]

Examining a media program from a different era can furnish perspective into the cultural attitudes, values, and behaviors of the period in which it was produced. For instance, the majority of old films feature women in subservient roles. One striking exception was *City for Conquest* (1940), starring Jimmy Cagney and Ann Sheridan. In this movie, Peggy Nash (Sheridan) is a dancer who is forced to choose between a career and her boyfriend, Danny Kenny (Cagney). However, mesmerized by ambition, Peggy deserts Danny and, within the context of the film, betrays herself. It is only when she gives up her career and devotes herself to Danny that she again becomes a "whole" woman. However disturbing to a modern audience, this film provides a useful glimpse into the gender politics of the times.

The phenomenon of the "remake" also furnishes perspective on the interests, preoccupations, and values that characterize different eras. To illustrate, *Invasion of the Body Snatchers*, discussed above, has been remade three times: 1978, 1993, and 2006. These different versions can be understood within the context of the historical events that define the

Figure 5.1
In *City for Conquest* (1940), Murray Burns (Anthony Quinn) is an unscrupulous dancer who appeals to the ambitions of Peggy Nash (Ann Sheridan) in order to come between her and Danny Kenny (James Cagney). Photograph © 1940 Turner Entertainment Co. All Rights Reserved.

periods. The original version was a product of the Cold War era. But as research assistant Don Miller notes, the 1978 adaptation offers commentary on the historical events that shaped that period:

> The 1978 re-make took place after the Viet Nam War and Watergate, when the public's mistrust of the American government was deep-seated. In one scene, the protagonist, Matthew Bennell (Donald Sutherland) contacts Washington, D.C., for help, only to discover that his call has been intercepted; the person on the other end of the line knows Bennell's name before he announces it. In the worldview of *Invasion of the Body Snatchers*, the pod people have taken over the government and are monitoring Bennell's activities.[11]

Media presentations can also distort historical events. In entertainment programming, historical events are often altered for dramatic emphasis. To illustrate, in 2006, ABC produced a dramatic miniseries "The Path to 9/11," which was criticized for including historically inaccurate scenes, including the depiction of members of the Clinton Administration being negligent in their efforts to stop Osama bin Laden in the years leading up to the attacks. Marc E. Platt, an executive producer of the miniseries declared, "We never tried to take a political point of view. And we tried to be fair within the context of a dramatization."[12] However, two retired F.B.I. agents resigned from advisory roles during the production of the miniseries because of concerns about the program's accuracy. According to Thomas E. Nicoletti, one of the agents, the miniseries included scenes that put people at places they weren't or plotted the narrative action out of chronological order: "There were some of the scenes that were total fiction ... I'm well aware of what's dramatic license and what's historical inaccuracy. And this had a lot of historical inaccuracy."[13]

The network subsequently edited out some of the disputed scenes and added a disclaimer, saying that "for dramatic and narrative purposes, the movie contains fictionalized scenes, composite and representative characters and dialogue, as well as time compression." However, former representative Lee H. Hamilton of Indiana, the vice chairman of the Sept. 11 commission, declared, "It suggests to me that news and entertainment are getting dangerously intertwined, and I do not think that is good for the country, because an event of this consequence is very hard to understand. To distort it, or not to present it factually in this kind of presentation does not serve the country well."[14]

Docudramas frequently romanticize a historical period for entertainment purposes, while glossing over the social and economic conditions that precipitated the event. These dramatizations generally focus on the impact of historical events on the personal lives of the characters. But Michael Parenti observes that although these entertainment media programs are not intended to serve as an historical record, the audience often believes that a docudrama presents an accurate account of events—with dangerous consequences:

In the minds of many Americans, movie and television dramas are the final chapter of history, the most lasting impression they have of what the past was like, what little of it they may have been exposed to. For the most part, make-believe history is an insipid costume epic, a personalized affair, the plotting, strutting, and yearnings of court figures and state leaders. Tyrants become humanly likable as the social realities of their tyranny are ignored. The revolutionary populace is represented as tyrannical and irrational, while the sources of their anger and misery remain unexplained. Conflicts and wars just seem to happen, arising out of personal motives and ambitions. In these ways make-believe history reinforces the historical illiteracy fostered in the schools and in political life in general.[15]

Further, news programming may not necessarily be a complete and accurate record of historical events. Ian I. Mitroff and Warren Bennis contend that TV news presents information in isolation, without the historical context that provides meaning:

With very few exceptions, most issues on network television news are presented in a completely historical context or no context whatsoever. Most news issues, especially local items, merely appear; they drop in from out of the blue ... The overall effect is one of dazzling confusion. Little or no attempt is made to present a larger view in which the issues could be located in a coherent framework....[16]

As discussed earlier, print journalism lends itself to a more detailed analysis of historical events than television news; however, newspapers also face space limitations that impose restrictions on their ability to present the full historical context necessary for a comprehensive understanding of the events of the day. As a result, it may be necessary to read a variety of articles or books on the topic. (For more discussion, see Chapter 12, Journalism.)

Examining the historical events depicted in both news and entertainment media presentations can serve as a useful springboard for additional research, focusing on the following questions:

- Does the media presentation present an accurate portrait of events?
- Are the causes leading to the events in the presentation clear?
- Does the information provided in the narrative provide a complete picture of the historical period? What (if anything) was left out?
- What were the consequences of the dramatized events?

Media History: A Systems Approach

In any historical analysis, isolated facts derive their meaning only when understood within a broader perspective. We all recall, with horror, high school history classes that required the memorization of assorted names and dates for a multiple choice or true-false exam. Although cramming for an exam may have some character-building value, it served no particular educational purpose; immediately after the examination, we would mentally delete those names and dates that we had struggled so valiantly to master. But more importantly, by focusing our attention on the details, we lost sight of how these events fit into a broader historical framework.

A *systems* approach to the history of media is designed to place events within a broader historical context. Details such as names and dates acquire meaning in terms of how they fit into (and influence) these historical patterns. And by recognizing patterns that have emerged, we are better able to understand present conditions and, indeed, anticipate future developments.

Biological Systems. One very useful analogy for the analysis of media history can be found in the study of biological systems. Biologists regard living creatures as systems composed of smaller *interrelated* and *interdependent* systems. For example, the cells of the human body have a life of their own, but they also interact to make up larger units, such as the digestive, reproductive, and respiratory systems. Each of these systems depends upon the others for selected, specialized functions; the respiratory system, for example, cannot serve the functions of the digestive system. These systems, in turn, are parts of a still larger system—the human body.

In like fashion, the mass media is a complex "system." Each medium is made up of interrelated and interdependent subsystems. For example, a newspaper is made up of a number of departments, such as the publisher, editorial department, news desk, features, and the advertising division. Each "subsystem" of the newspaper plays a distinct role in the publication of the paper. Thus, the advertising department determines how many news stories can be carried in a particular edition. But at the same time, these departments are interdependent. As an example, it is not uncommon for articles to be "cut" to accommodate the insertion of a last-minute advertisement. Moreover, an ongoing ethical dilemma facing newspaper editors involves how they should treat stories involving prominent clients, on whom the paper depends for advertising revenue.

At the same time, each medium (e.g., film, radio, or the Internet) is part of a larger system, commonly referred to as "the media." As is the case in biological systems, these media are also interrelated and interdependent. Conglomerates frequently own different media (e.g., newspapers and television stations), so that they share ownership philosophies and resources. For instance, Rupert Murdoch's News Corporation is a conglomerate that owns television stations, newspapers, book publishing companies, and Internet sites. Through cross-promotion, programs serve to publicize the programming of another holding.

In addition, media systems frequently rely on one another as sources of information and programming. To illustrate, nearly three-quarters of all radio stations rely on local newspapers as a primary source of news.[17]

Media subsystems may also have an overlapping influence on *style*. For instance, print journalism had a profound influence on the literary style of twentieth century authors such as Ernest Hemingway. More recently, the medium of film has had an impact on modern literature; current novels are written in a very visual, plot-oriented style, which can easily be adapted into film and television scripts.

Finally, "the media" is part of a network of interrelated social institutions that include church, schools, government, and family. Significantly, when Mikhail Gorbachev initiated social reforms in the Soviet Union in 1987, he began by opening up the media system (Glasnost). This change led to restructuring the political and economic systems as well.

Principles of Evolution. Evolution refers to patterns by which all species develop from earlier forms of life. According to scientists, life forms began as simple organisms. Over time, these organisms became more complex in order to adapt to new circumstances and environments. Those life forms unable to adapt, like the dinosaur, became extinct.

Natural selection is a related biological principle. During the process of evolution, the best features of an organism are retained and the unnecessary elements are eliminated. To illustrate, the appendix is an organ that has no current physiological function in humans. Scientists believe that at one time, this organ probably aided in cellulose digestion. In other animals, the appendix is much larger and provides a pouch off the main intestinal tract, in which cellulose can be trapped and be subjected to prolonged digestion. Dr. Mabel Rodrigues speculates that the appendix will gradually disappear in human beings, as our diet no longer includes cellulose.[18]

The major media systems follow a readily identifiable pattern of evolution:

I. The Inception Stage. This initial stage of development refers to the period surrounding the invention of the medium. This stage is generally *decentralized*. Individual inventors conducted their research in relative isolation. In some cases, individuals were working on the same invention simultaneously. For instance, radio was developed by a number of inventors from different countries:

- In 1887, Heinrich Hertz set up the first spark transmitter and receiver.
- In 1892, a French inventor, Edouard Branly, created a tube containing loose zinc and silver filings, with contact plugs on each end. The shavings would stick together after the first spark was received; a method of separating them for the next signal was necessary.
- In 1893, a Serbian, Nikola Tesla carried out the first demonstration of wireless communication.
- In 1895, an Italian, Guglielmo Marconi experimented with Hertzian waves and was able to send and receive messages over a mile and a quarter.
- In 1906, American William De Forest developed the audion, a device that made it easier to receive voice and music transmissions.

Similarly, three men were working on the invention of the television at the same time. In 1923, Russian Vladimir Zworkin invented the inconoscope (camera tube) and the kinescope receiving unit in 1926. In 1925, John Logie Baird, a Scottish inventor, achieved the world's first real television picture in his laboratory, which used spinning disks to scan pictures. In 1927, Philo Farnsworth, an American, produced the first all-electronic television picture and on Sept. 7, 1927, transmitted the first electronic television image.

Moreover, "packet switching," the technological foundation of the Internet, was developed independently by two scientists: Donald Davies in England and Paul Baran in the United States between 1966 and 1969.

At this stage, the inventors of these media systems are consumed with the scientific possibilities of their projects, never imagining the commercial implications of their work. Reporter Jeff Kisseloff recounts,

> The earliest pioneers (of television) vividly recall the thrill of exploration, of building something from nothing, to please not some corporate sponsor but themselves. Nobody knew what television was or would be, so there were no molds to fit into. Mostly, they proceeded on curiosity and raw intelligence and a willingness to experiment in an atmosphere that not only tolerated resourceful thinking but depended on it.[19]

Historical events play a role in the development of media systems as well. For instance, World War I greatly accelerated the growth of the radio industry, as the armed forces began to rely on the communications capability of this medium. By the war's end, over 100,000 people had been trained in the use of radio.

However, the emergence of television as a popular medium was *slowed* by the Great Depression and World War II, when resources were committed to the war effort. Between 1948–1952, the American Federal Communications Commission (FCC) imposed a freeze on all new applications for TV stations and the number of station licenses awarded, in order to devote time to develop technical standards and procedures for the use of the airwaves.

The invention of the Internet was a product of the Cold War. After the Soviet Union's 1957 launch of Sputnik, the first manmade satellite to orbit the Earth, the U.S. Defense Department's Advance Research Projects Agency (ARPA) was formed. This agency provided money and computers so that U.S. scientists could compete with their Cold War adversaries. By the mid-1960s, the U.S. Defense Department became concerned about the vulnerability of its defense system. If a targeted area was decimated by a nuclear warhead, all of the defense information at that site would cease. Thus, the Arpanet project (from which the Internet eventually evolved) was created to allow rapid, electronic distribution of defense information.

In the inception stage, the programming is generally a demonstration of the capabilities of the medium. For instance, in the early twentieth century, pioneer filmmakers Auguste and Louis Lumiere invented a machine that served as projector, camera, and film printer. Their early films were simply celebrations of movement. One was called, *Train Coming into Station*; another showed workers leaving the Lumiere Factory.

In like manner, one of the first television broadcasts, U.S. President Franklin Roosevelt's address during the 1939 World's Fair, was designed to demonstrate the immediate transmission of picture and sound.

II. The Embryonic Stage. As the commercial potential of a young medium becomes apparent, corporations agree to sponsor the research of these individual inventors and hobbyists. For instance, in 1920, Frank Conrad, an amateur radio operator and engineer for Westinghouse Electric began broadcasting programs from his garage on amateur station 8XK in Wilkinsburg, Pennsylvania. The broadcasts generated such interest that Westinghouse built KDKA, the first broadcasting station.

Attempts to develop a media system into a profitable industry often become a race between corporations, and the object of dramatic patent wars and monopoly litigation. For instance, in 1919, Radio Corporation of America (RCA) was formed to head off the dominance of the British-dominated Marconi Company.

As television reached the embryonic stage, RCA wanted to extend the monopoly RCA enjoyed in radio to the new technology. Consequently, the corporation connived to wrest control from inventor Philo Farnsworth. Evan I. Schwartz explains,

> In a bid to copy Farnsworth's idea, (RCA President David) Sarnoff sent his top engineer, Vladimir Zworykin, to Farnsworth's lab. Then Sarnoff himself paid a visit. Still unable to match Farnsworth's work in RCA's labs and unwilling to pay him royalties, Sarnoff tied Farnsworth up in a court battle that hamstrung the inventor for many years.
>
> Even though the US Patent Office eventually determined that Farnsworth was the true inventor of electronic television, the massive RCA publicity machine ensured that Sarnoff would receive credit for bringing television to the world. That PR campaign peaked with a much-ballyhooed demonstration of a TV at the 1939 World's Fair. 'This started at the World's Fair, when Sarnoff announced that RCA was now introducing television—a series of untruths that were accepted by everybody and are still accepted, and are in the history books,' says Russell Farnsworth (Philo's son).[20]

By 1932, NBC installed a television station in the newly built Empire State Building, and Zworykin was employed as director of RCA's electronic research laboratory.

During the embryonic stage, the media hardware (radio receivers, television sets, computers) is extremely expensive to produce and, as a result, is nearly prohibitive in cost for the average consumer. For instance, in the early 1950s, television sets sold for over $1,000 that, factoring in inflation, is the equivalent of approximately $8,400 today. In like fashion, in 1985, the first color LCD home computers cost approximately $3,000, which would amount to $5,657 today.[21]

As a result, the programming is directed toward an elite, affluent audience. To illustrate, after Johann Gutenberg invented moveable type (the basis of the printing press) in 1454, the first printed documents were religious texts and government papers. Both audiences were literate, so that they could read the materials, and affluent enough to afford these documents, which were expensive to produce. To cite another example, the first commercial radio programs consisted of opera and public information shows.

At the same time, the embryonic phase is characterized by experimentation in the style, structure, and content of programming, as the media communicators learn about the possibilities of the medium. Before the formulaic conventions of genres have been established, early work is characterized by innovations that are only seen again after the medium has been well established and the conventions have been thoroughly explored by media communicators. For instance, early filmmaker Georges Méliès experimented with special effects in his work, including stop action animation. In television, Ernie Kovaks was a comic genius who began experimenting with the medium in the 1940s, before the conventions of television had been established. Kovaks concocted elaborate gags involving camera angles, lenses, music, live audiences, and immediate transmission.

In many instances, media communicators were forced to find creative ways to work within the economic and technological limitations of the medium. Kisseloff explains,

> Because no spare parts were available, Arch Brolly used a pickle jar to complete his transmitter and keep WBKB, Chicago's most important station, on the air during World War II. When Brolly's boss, the redoubtable Captain Bill Eddy, needed a camera base that could be raised and lowered, he created one from a barber chair....
>
> When the producers of "Captain Video" needed a ray gun, Charles Polachek, the director, grabbed a spark plug, muffler, rearview mirror and ashtray from the automotive department, glued them together himself and called it the 'opticom scillometer'.[22]

III. The Popular Stage. At this stage of development, the size of the audience has expanded to the degree that a profitable mass audience base exists:

- Photography was invented with the development of the daguerreotype in 1839. With the development of the "dry plate" (purchased and ready to use), photography emerged as a popular medium at the beginning of the twentieth century, with people taking personal "snapshots."
- Radio's "golden age" was the decade of the 1930s. In 1930, almost 50 percent of American households had radios. But by 1940, 90 percent of American homes

had radios. During this decade, radio advertising revenues rose from $25 million to more than $70 million.[23]

- The 1940s was a period of unprecedented popularity for the film industry. Between 1942–1945, the American public spent approximately 23 percent of its total recreation dollar going to the movies. By the late 1940s, the weekly attendance at the cinema totaled 90 million people.[24]
- Television experienced a surge of popularity during the decade of the 1950s. For instance, in 1950, television sets were in 9 percent of American homes. By 1956, two-thirds of American households had at least one TV set. And by 1960, 90 percent of the country (45 million homes) owned at least one TV set.[25]
- The Internet remained the territory of academics and government until the early 1990s, when the evolution of technology made computers smaller and more affordable for personal use. The development of the Web during the 1990s was astonishing. In July 1988, there were approximately 33,000 Internet hosts. Ten years later, that number had increased to 739,000. And in December 1994, there were approximately 1,579,000 subscribers to America Online. By December 1998, the number of subscribers to AOL had increased to 15,000,000.[26]

During the popular stage, the media "hardware" (i.e., television sets, radio receivers, or computers) becomes less expensive, making the purchase of the hardware more affordable for the average consumer. One reason for this cost reduction can be attributed to mass production. Making more units at one time cuts down on the cost of each individual unit. But in addition, industry executives discovered that the most fruitful revenue source was not the *hardware* (the media equipment), but rather in the *software*. To illustrate:

- During the 1930s, radio companies discovered that the greatest source of profit was not the radio receiver, but, rather, in the revenue generated by the advertising. Consequently, it behooved the radio companies to lower the cost of the radio set in order to put a set in every consumer's hands. Indeed, in many radio contests during the Depression, the prizes were radio receivers—a shrewd strategy to put more radios in the hands of consumers.
- The original cost of a consumer video recorder was $800. The price of a VCR eventually dropped to under $100, as media companies generated their profits through the sale and rental of videotapes. This devaluation has also been enhanced by the introduction of a new technology (DVDs) that supplanted videotapes.
- The cost of a home computer has steadily dropped, from approximately $2,000 in the 1990s. In 2006, the nonprofit project One Laptop Per Child announced plans to produce laptops for worldwide distribution at a cost of $150.[27] This type of drastic cost reduction creates a large and profitable market for computer software, as well as goods advertised over the Internet.

At this stage, the market is far from saturated. Consequently, the various industries pursue a broadcasting strategy, in which they strive to

Figure 5.2
Media history—a systems approach: information evolution.

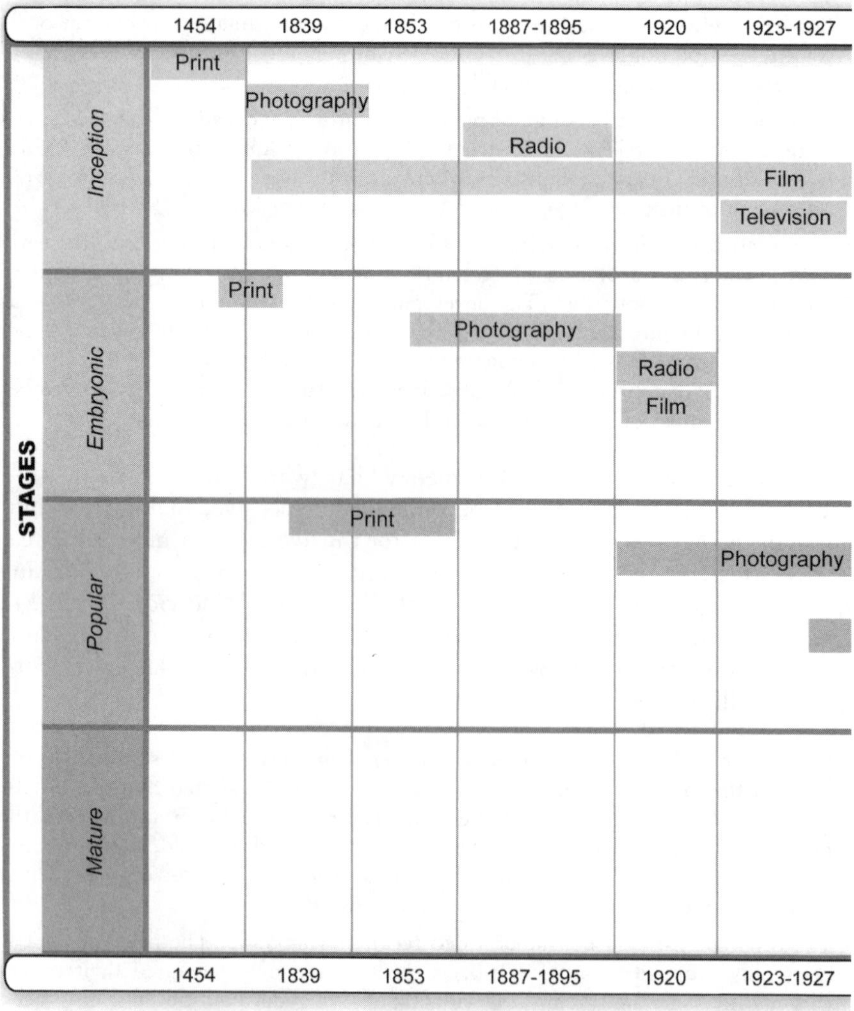

appeal to a mass audience. For instance, in the early 1950s, not everyone had a TV set yet, and those who did generally had one set for the entire family, which was stationed in the "TV room."

In order to insure a profit, it is necessary to attract as much of the mass audience as possible. Consequently, programming is developed that is designed to appeal to the interests and tastes of the majority of the public. In television, for example, the 1950s was an era in which, due to the

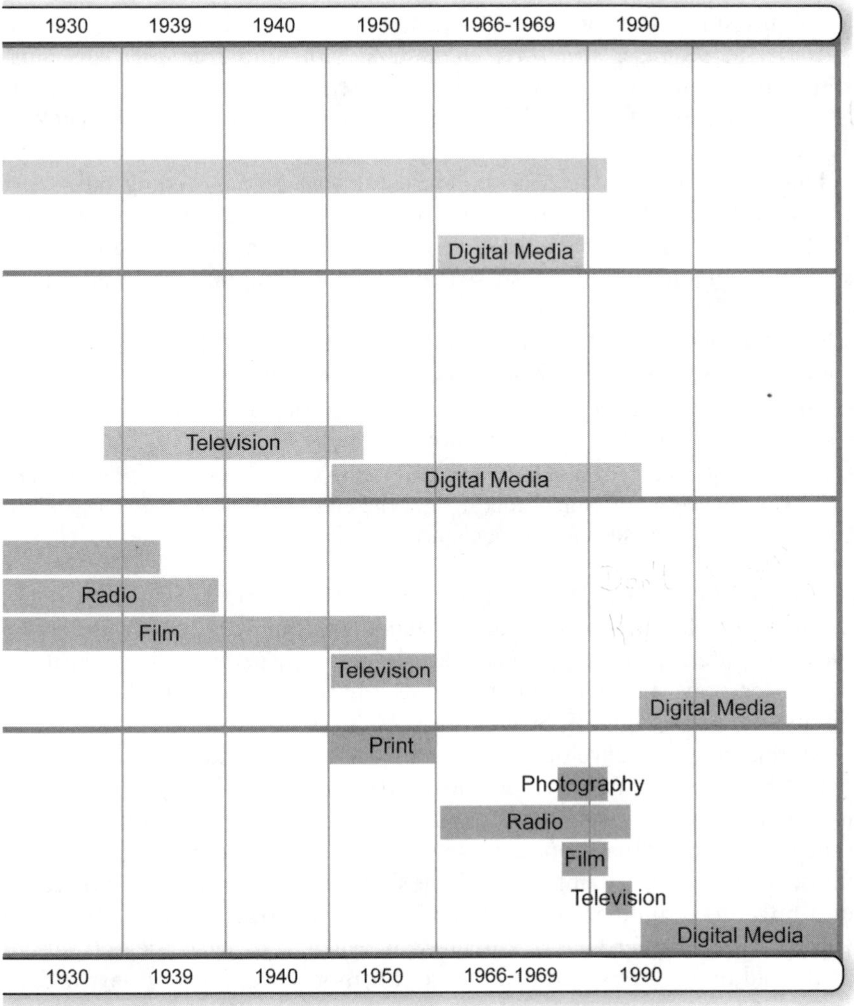

economic necessity of attracting a large mass audience, family viewing was encouraged by the industry. Thus, variety programs like the *Ed Sullivan Show* flourished during the 1950s. In the course of one hour, the *Ed Sullivan Show* routinely featured puppet shows, comedians, opera singers, and rock stars.

During this popularization stage, genres are established within the medium. The word *genre* simply means "order." As applied to artistic works, a genre is a type, class, or category of presentation, which shares distinctive and easily identifiable features. Examples of genres include romances, science fiction, situation comedies, and news programming.

At this stage, the formula of a genre is established. Formula refers to patterns in *premise*, *structure*, *characters*, *plot*, and *trappings*. To illustrate, the evening talk show genre hit its stride with *The Tonight Show, Starring Johnny Carson*, which dominated the genre for 30 years (1962 to 1992).

During Carson's tenure, the standard formula of the evening talk show was established. The program time was reduced from 90 to 60 minutes. Each show featured a blend of comedians, musicians, and movie or television stars. In addition, the basic structure of each program was established:

- First, Carson presented a monologue. This session included joshing with sidemen, such as Ed McMahon and bandleader Doc Severinsen.
- Carson then moved over to the primary set, consisting of a desk, which the host sat behind, and a sofa for the announcer and guests.
- The pecking order of the guests was also established in order of celebrity. The most renowned guest would appear first; the end of the show was relegated to relative unknowns, such as young comics or authors.

IV. Mature Stage. During the mature stage, media companies are absorbed by large conglomerates. Media presentations are regarded by these corporations as a product, like shoes, rugs, or any other consumer item. Decisions are made on the basis of its profit potential (for more discussion, see Chapter 7, Structure).

At this stage of development, the media market has become so large that it becomes profitable to pursue a *narrowcasting* strategy, appealing to minority interests and tastes. To illustrate, cable television features a wide range of channels that appeal to specialized interests, including news, old films, religious programming, cooking shows, and country music. Because of a huge mass audience base, it is no longer necessary to appeal to every viewer. Thus, Turner Classic Movies can realize a profit if they attract all of the old movie buffs in the audience (for more discussion of narrowcasting, see Chapter 4).

At the same time, considerable competition emerges within each subcategory of programming. For instance, the competition for the *Tonight Show* on broadcast television alone now includes *Late Show with David Letterman* (CBS), *Conan O'Brien* (NBC), *Late, Late Show/Craig Ferguson* (CBS), and *Jimmy Kimmel Live* (ABC). In addition, talk shows began appearing in the morning and afternoon slots as well.

At this stage of development, programs experiment with the established formula of genres in order to keep it fresh. For instance, during the 1970s, Hollywood released a number of films that played off of the conventional formula of genres, including: Westerns (*Little Big Man*, 1973; *McCabe and Mrs. Miller*, 1971), Police Dramas (*Serpico*, 1973), and Detective Stories (*The Long Goodbye*, 1973).

International Media History. These same stages of development also appear in the media systems of other countries, at the time in which their media systems begin to evolve. To illustrate, 2000–2005 was India's "golden age" of television. During this period, the number of homes with televisions grew from 88 million to 105 million—the same as in the United States. Advertising spending on Indian television increased by 21 percent a year, on average, from 1995 to 2005, when it reached $1.6 billion.

Often, in the case of countries in which the development of the media appears later than in the United States, this schedule of development is accelerated. As an example, the pace of change in India is supercharged because the country is catching up to, and in some cases leapfrogging, developments that took decades to play out elsewhere. As Vikram Kaushik, the chief executive of Tata Sky, a satellite-TV provider, declares, "Everything that happened in the rest of the world in 10 years, is happening here in two years."[28]

Principles of Ecology. The principles of *ecology* offer a useful construct for understanding the complex relationship between media systems, particularly in the wake of the emergence of digital media. Ecology refers to the biological principle of co-existence. In some cases, organisms are antagonistic to one another. Thus, in Africa, lions are predators who feast on a variety of animals, including buffalo, zebra, antelope, giraffe, and warthog. In other instances, organisms operate in a state of *symbiosis*, in that both organisms prosper through their relationship with one another.

Phase I: New Medium as Threat. The introduction of a new medium is generally regarded as a threat to the established media systems. For instance, threatened by a loss of cultural control, members of elite culture dismissed new media as detrimental to the culture. In the eighteenth century, women were advised not to read novels for fear that it would make their brains soft. In 1859, poet Charles Baudelaire warned, "By invading the territories of art, this industry [photography] has become art's most mortal enemy."[29] More recently, educator Allan Bloom has decried the influence of popular music: "It ruins the imagination of young people and makes it very difficult for them to have a passionate relationship to the art and the thought that are the substance of liberal education."[30]

The emergence of a new medium poses a threat to existing media on several levels:

- An emerging medium "borrows" its programming from the established media, creating an enormous vacuum in those media systems. To illustrate, in the 1930s, radio took its programming from magazines, comic strips, novels, short stories, and vaudeville. For instance, the genre of soap operas originated in nineteenth-century domestic fiction and, then, romance magazines. And specific

Figure 5.3
Principles of ecology.

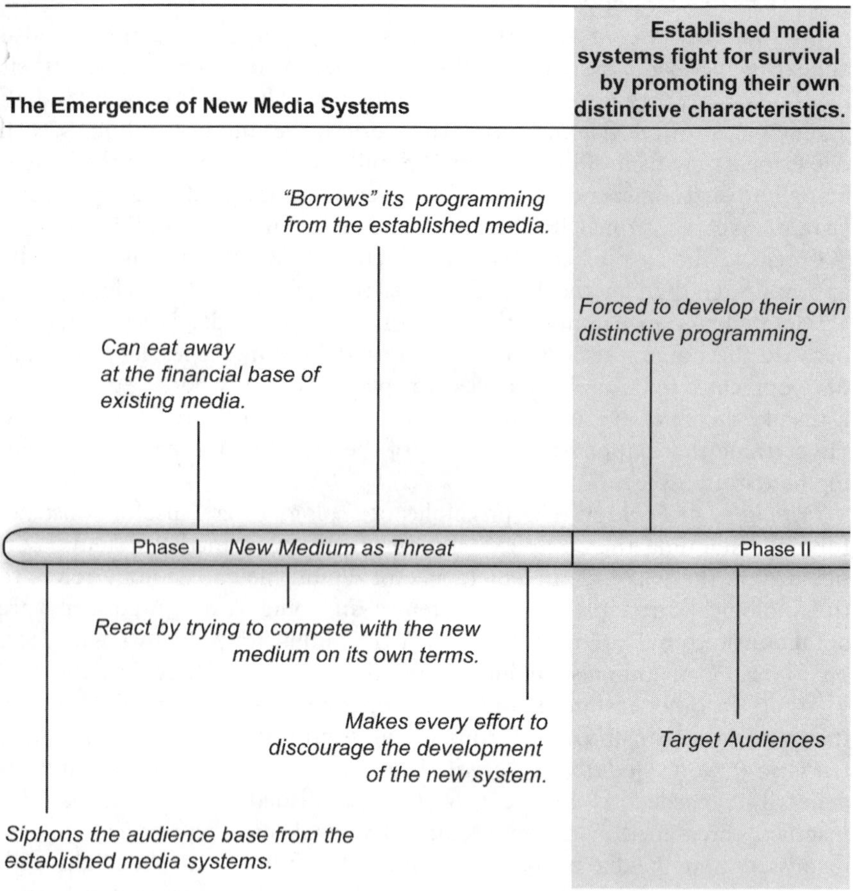
The Emergence of New Media Systems
Established media systems fight for survival by promoting their own distinctive characteristics.
"Borrows" its programming from the established media.
Forced to develop their own distinctive programming.
Can eat away at the financial base of existing media.
Phase I
New Medium as Threat
Phase II
React by trying to compete with the new medium on its own terms.
Makes every effort to discourage the development of the new system.
Target Audiences
Siphons the audience base from the established media systems.

programs, like "Superman" first appeared in comic books before being converted into a radio serial in 1940.

But then, in the early 1950s, radio began to lose its programming to the newest medium—television. Situation comedies such as *I Love Lucy* and *The Jack Benny Show* moved over to television, causing considerable panic within the radio industry. Other popular genres that moved from radio to television included soap operas and quiz shows.

- The emergence of a new medium siphons the *audience base* from the established media systems. To illustrate, in 1946, the weekly film attendance in the United States had swelled to 90 million per week—equivalent to half of the population of the country. However, this was also the same year that television began daily

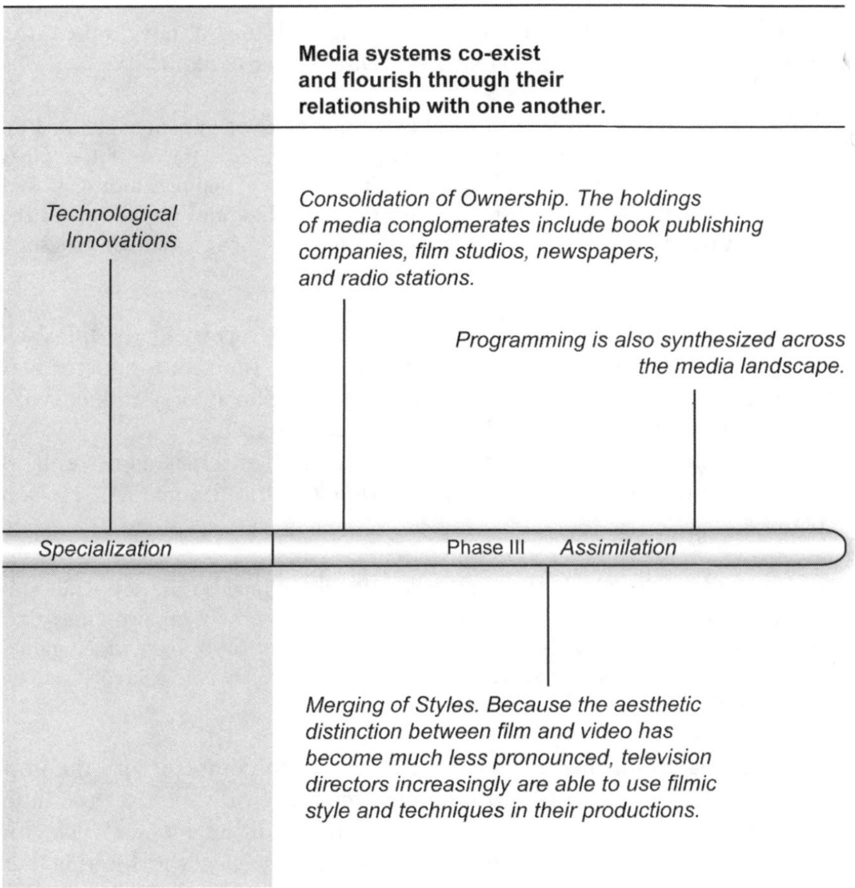
Media systems co-exist and flourish through their relationship with one another.
Technological Innovations
Consolidation of Ownership. The holdings of media conglomerates include book publishing companies, film studios, newspapers, and radio stations.
Programming is also synthesized across the media landscape.
Specialization
Phase III Assimilation
Merging of Styles. Because the aesthetic distinction between film and video has become much less pronounced, television directors increasingly are able to use filmic style and techniques in their productions.

broadcasts in New York. By the following year, as the commercial television industry began to operate in earnest and the number of television sets in the United States increased to 1 million, movie attendance dropped to 70 million per week.

To cite a more recent example, video games are eating away at television viewership. A 2005 article in *USA Today* explains,

If video killed the radio star in the 1980s, then it seems video games are trying to do the same thing to TV in this decade ... 24% of gamers reduced their TV watching over the past year and 18% expect to cut small-screen viewership next year.

Video gamers watched 11.1% less TV than last year, dropping their weekly TV viewership to 16 hours, compared with 18 hours in 2004.[31]

Significantly, the technical advances in digital media have taken the audience from a range of media systems. David Carr explains,

Newspapers felt the pain of technological disruption first, when people had dial-up modems capable of transmitting modest, largely text-based data. As fatter pipes developed, music performed a jailbreak, leaving behind a maimed industry. And now, with the number of ever-faster connections spreading and the advent of the Flash player, television seems positioned as roadkill, with great big movie files soon to fall after that.[32]

The emergence of new media systems can also eat away at the *financial base* of existing media. For instance, in the 1950s, the radio industry was faced with a financial crisis, as the sponsors of soap operas moved with the programs to finance their television counterparts.

Likewise, in 2006, the film industry found itself in crisis as a result of the competition from "new media." Media critic Laura M. Holson explained,

The growth of new media threatens to undermine traditional businesses, while studios are flummoxed about how to take advantage of the new opportunities they represent. And movies and TV also face tough new competition from video games and online social networking sites. Even cellphones have become a favorite diversion among the young.[33]

Initially, the established media react by trying to compete with the new medium on its own terms; unfortunately, this tactic only exposes the limitations of the older media. For instance, the traditional news cycle for print newspapers is approximately 12 hours. However, the Internet has virtually eliminated production and distribution time. Because of this "virtual deadline," the pressure to bring information to the public has played a major role in changing the standards and practices of traditional journalism. Instead of the traditional guidelines of requiring two sources to confirm the facts of a story, editors have reduced this procedure to one source—sometimes with disastrous results. For instance, in their haste to announce the winner of the 2000 U.S. presidential race, CBS announced that the winner of the U.S. presidential election was Al Gore.

Another tactic of the established media industries is to make every effort to discourage the development of the new system. For instance, in the 1950s, American film studios exerted pressure to prevent their film stars from appearing on television, forcing the new medium to recruit minor movie actors for their shows or develop its own stable of stars. In addition, the studios refused to release their features for presentation on television. The film industry also launched an intensive publicity campaign, with the slogan "Movies Are Better Than Ever!" to counter the growing popularity of television.

Another response to the diminishing profits is to demand that actors and directors lower their fees or risk having their projects dropped. In 2006, 20th Century Fox and Universal Pictures walked away from *Halo*, a movie based on the popular video game, after the executive producer, Peter Jackson, and others refused to reduce their fees. Russell Crowe dropped out of negotiations to star in a new movie being directed by Baz Luhrmann and produced by 20th Century Fox. Crowe explained, "I do charity work, but I don't do charity work for major studios."[34]

Brian Grazer, an Academy Award winner who produced the blockbuster *The Da Vinci Code*, explained, "You are faced with a new reality. Do you want to stick to your price and be forced to stand in the parking lot instead of playing on the field? That is cause for conflict between talent and studios."

Phase II: Specialization. Eventually, the established media systems fight for their survival by promoting their own distinctive characteristics. This specialization occurs in three ways:

Technological Innovations. In the 1950s, the film industry introduced a series of technical advances to compete with television, which was in its popular stage of evolution. Because television screens were only 13 inches, film studios produced movies in widescreen formats such as Cinemascope and Cinerama. Further, during this era, television programming was primarily delivered in black and white—color was introduced in 1954 but was expensive and exclusive until the 1960s. Consequently, the film studios produced movies in Technicolor—a rich, super-saturated color that, again, provided a contrast with black and white TV sets. In addition, because the tiny speakers in TV sets could not deliver quality sound, the film industry enhanced their audio delivery systems, including "Surround Sound." The film industry even resorted to technological gimmicks to attract audiences, producing movies in 3-D, "Smellorama," and "Psychorama."

During this period, radio responded to the threat of television with two technical innovations: the transistor and the car radio. The early television sets were large, bulky, and required being near an electrical outlet. However, the transistor radio could accompany listeners anywhere—to the beach, or on a picnic. The car radio was another innovation that fit into the American lifestyle. Because Americans were spending an increasing amount of time driving, the car radio was a welcome companion that (unlike television) would not be a distraction for the motorist. The audience for radio boomed.

Programming. Over time, the evolution of a new medium actually *liberates* the established media, so that they are forced to develop their own distinctive programming. For instance, the development of photography in the nineteenth century ultimately freed painters to explore other realms of visual expression. Rather than striving for verisimilitude in landscapes and portraits, nineteenth-century impressionists like Monet and Manet were free to capture how the world appeared to the subjective, human eye. Thus, in the twentieth century, Expressionism emerged as a school of art, in which the intention was to reveal the inner state of the artist. Expressionistic painters like Wassily Kandinsky, Franz Marc, George Grosz, and Amadeo Modigliani expressed on canvas how they felt about what they saw and experienced.

During the 1950s, the film industry took advantage of the medium's capacity for size by displaying grand landscapes. And by extension, film could present grand *themes* as well. Film studios released a series of epic films such as *The Ten Commandments* (1956) and *Ben-Hur* (1959), befitting the size of the screen.

At the same time, radio was faced with a programming vacuum when soap operas, quiz shows, and Westerns moved to television. In response, radio turned to a programming format for which the poor audio quality of television was unequipped—music. Thus, the Top 40 format became popular in the 1950s.

Narrowcasting. Because established media are further advanced on the evolutionary cycle, they are in a position to direct their programming at target audiences, while the new media system is still establishing its mass audience base. Thus, while television was pursuing a *broadcasting* strategy in the 1950s, the film industry took advantage of the burgeoning teen market to produce films about adolescence, including *The Wild One* (1953) and *Rebel Without a Cause* (1955). At the same time, films with "mature" themes like *Written on the Wind* (1956) and *Peyton Place* (1957) were designed to attract an adult audience.

Radio also targeted an adolescent audience through its new Top 40 format. Radio played a pivotal role in the popularity of rock-'n'-roll and its teen heartthrobs such as Elvis. As a result, despite the gloomy forecasts about the future of the radio industry, the number of radios in use in the United States increased, from 105,300,000 in 1952 to 183,800,000 in 1962.[35]

Phase III Assimilation. Eventually, media systems not only co-exist, but flourish through their relationship with one another.

Consolidation of Ownership. The holdings of media conglomerates include book publishing companies, film studios, newspapers, and radio stations. Thus, Twentieth Century Fox is part of a media empire, News Corp, which includes Fox television and the London *Times*. The distribution of media presentations has also become assimilated. As an example, the theatrical release of a film now is closely followed by its presentation on cable television and, then, DVD sales and rentals.

Technical Convergence. Computers and digital technologies have transformed all media systems. For instance, digital photography captures images through an electronic process, replacing the traditional chemical process. In like fashion, digital video and high resolution television (HDTV) greatly reduce the aesthetic differences between video and film. Recent breakthroughs in digital technology have made it possible to capture movies using high-definition digital videocameras with fidelity comparable to 35-millimeter film and to project them digitally in theaters with no loss of image quality.

Programming is also synthesized across the media landscape. For instance, in 2006:

- Approximately 7 million U.S. subscribers watched television programs on their cellphones.[36]
- *CBS Evening News With Katie Couric* became the first evening newscast to be entirely simulcasted live on the Internet.
- Consumers are now able to download episodes of network television programs like *Desperate Housewives* and *Lost* on iPods through iTunes.
- Major film studios, including the Walt Disney Company, Twentieth Century Fox, Warner Brothers, and Universal Studios, have also added feature movies to the iTunes music store.

Merging of Styles. Because the aesthetic distinction between film and video has become much less pronounced, television directors increasingly are able to use filmic style and techniques in their productions.

Cycle

A medium may re-experience the same ecological pattern as it adapts to the inception of a new medium. Just as the radio industry had to scramble in the face of the arrival of television in the 1950s, radio is currently struggling, competing with the Internet, which has appropriated the environment, format, and structure of radio. Richard Siklos explains,

> Although more than 9 out of 10 Americans still listen to traditional radio each week, they are listening *less*. And the industry is having to confront many challenges like those that have enticed Mr. Costa, including streaming audio, podcasting, iPods and Howard Stern on satellite radio.
>
> As a result, the prospects of radio companies have dimmed significantly since the late 1990s, when broadcast barons were tripping over themselves to buy more stations. Radio revenue growth has stagnated and the number of listeners is dropping. The amount of time people tune into radio over the course of a week has fallen by 14 percent over the last decade, according to Arbitron ratings.[37]

Once again, the radio industry is moving into Stage II: Specialization, as it battles for survival.

- *Programming*. Radio was left with an enormous programming hole, as digital media devices have appropriated the music format, with significant improvements in quality of sound and accessibility of content—you can program your own selections. One way in which the radio industry is responding is through the format of talk radio, which offers a type of programming that is unique to this medium. In addition, the satellite radio provides uninterrupted music, in a format of your choice. This "format" selects songs, providing a "surprise" element that the audience enjoys, and offers an exhaustive playlist that introduces the audiences to new songs. And finally, the radio industry is relying more on syndicated programs—not just to save money but as a way to attract a large audience. For instance, superstar Rush Limbaugh reaches 20 million listeners weekly through 500 radio stations.

- *Technology.* The radio industry is using digital technology to increase the appeal of the medium. Satellite radio brings the programming discussed above to the subscriber.

Indeed, the radio industry is already entering Stage III: Assimilation. Radio is providing content for many of the venues created by digital media. For instance, individuals can download radio programming for play on their iPods.

NOTES

1. Future of the First Amendment (source: www.firstamendmentfuture.org)
2. Jacques Steinberg, "'Law & Order' Meets the Law of Supply and Demand," *New York Times*, July 16, 2006.
3. Alessandra Stanley, "All Terrorism All the Time: Fear Becomes Reality Show," *New York Times*, August 12, 2006.
4. Stuart Elliott, "Super Bowl Ads of Cartoonish Violence, Perhaps Reflecting Toll of War," *New York Times*, February 5, 2007.
5. John Leland, "Art Born of Outrage in the Internet Age," *New York Times*, September 25, 2005.
6. Alessandra Stanley, "The Drama of Iraq, While It Still Rages," *New York Times,* July 27, 2005.
7. Frank Rich, "The Two Wars of the Worlds," *New York Times*, July 3, 2005.
8. Reuters, "As Iran Turns: Corruption in a Soap Opera Town," *New York Times*, December 27, 2005.
9. Alessandra Stanley, "All Terrorism All the Time: Fear Becomes Reality Show," *New York Times*, August 12, 2006.
10. Andrew C. Revkin, "The Sky is Falling! Say Hollywood and, Yes, the Pentagon," *New York Times*, February 29, 2004 (www.nytimes.com).
11. Don Miller, Unpublished Paper, Webster University, August 11, 2006.
12. Edward Wyatt, "More Questions of Accuracy Raised About ABC Mini-Series on 9/11 Prelude," *New York Times*, September 12, 2006.
13. Ibid.
14. Ibid.
15. Michael Parenti, *Make Believe Media* (New York: St. Martin's Press, 1992), 68.
16. Ian I. Mitroff and Warren Bennis, *The Unreality Industry* (New York: Oxford University Press, 1989), 13.

17. Needham, Harper & Steers Advertising, Washington D.C., conducted on the Associated Press Broadcasting Services. Yahoo! Internet Life.

18. Dr. Mabel Rodrigues, "Ask a Scientist©," Zoology Archive. June 29, 2005 (www.newton.dep.anl.gov/askasci/zoo00/zoo00015.htm).

19. Jeff Kisseloff, "In the Television's Beginning, There Was Risk-Taking," *New York Times*, November 29, 1998.

20. Don Aucoin, "Televisionary Decades After the Fact, the World is Just Tuning in to the Work of TV Inventor Philo T. Farnsworth," *Boston Globe*, September 7, 2002.

21. U.S. Department of Labor, Bureau of Labor Statistics (www.bis.gov)

22. Kisseloff, "In the Television's Beginning, There Was Risk-Taking."

23. Michael W. Gamble and Teri Kwai Gamble, *Introducing Mass Communication* (New York: McGraw-Hill Book Company, 1986), 1166.

24. Kristin Thompson and David Bordwell, *Film History: An Introduction* (New York: McGraw Hill, 2002), 125.

25. Brad J. Bushman and Craig A. Anderson, "Media Violence and the American Public," *American Psychologist* (June/July 2001), 477.

26. "Ticker," *Brill's Content* (December 1998/January1999), 140.

27. John Markoff, "For $150, Third-World Laptop Stirs a Big Debate," *New York Times*, November 30, 2006.

28. Vikas Bajai, "In India, the Golden Age of Television Is Now," *New York Times,* February 11, 2007.

29. Helmut Gernsheim and Alison Gernsheim, *The History of Photography* (New York: McGraw-Hill Book Company, 1969), 243.

30. David Considine and Gail Haley, *Visual Messages: Integrating Imagery into Instruction* (Englewood, CO: Teacher Idea Press, 1992), 3.

31. "Gamers' TV Time Going Down the Tube," *USA Today*, August 8, 2005.

32. David Carr, "Idiosyncratic and Personal, PC Edges TV," *New York Times*, October 16, 2006.

33. Laura M. Holson, "Hollywood Puts the Squeeze on Talent," *New York Times*, November 6, 2006.

34. Ibid.

35. Shirley Biagi, *Media Impact* (CA: Wadsworth Publishing, 1988), 105.

36. Edward C. Baig, "The Era of Living Wirelessly; Ready to Get Unplugged?," *USA Today*, June 26, 2001.

37. Richard Siklos, "Changing Its Tune," *New York Times*. September 15, 2006.

CHAPTER 6

CULTURAL CONTEXT

What can we learn by studying a media presentation as a cultural "text"?

Anthropologists study ancient civilizations by unearthing artifacts, as a way to reconstruct a portrait of the society. In the same manner, the study of popular culture has a *hermeneutic*, or interpretive function, furnishing a means of understanding culture.

Russel B. Nye offers a comprehensive definition of *popular culture*:

> Popular culture describes those productions, both artistic and commercial, designed for mass consumption, which appeal to and express the tastes and understanding of the majority of the public, free of control by minority standards. They reflect the values, convictions, and patterns of thought and feeling generally dispersed through and approved by American society.[1]

Nye traces the origin of popular culture in the Western world to the industrial-democratic revolution of the eighteenth century. Democratization, urbanization, education, increased income and leisure time, and industrialization contributed to the emergence of a middle class (predominately white and male), that created a new market for popular art. Nye observes, "This mass society had leisure time, money, and cultural unity; it needed a new art—neither folk nor elite—to instruct and entertain it."[2]

Popular artists discovered that they could make a living by attracting a mass audience that would patronize their art. In this sense, popular art became a consumer product, not unlike a pair of shoes or a new rug. These new market considerations also altered the traditional relationship between the artist and the audience. To illustrate, imagine novelist James Joyce jogging around a track with a group of his admirers. If the audience is unable to keep up with Joyce, they are out of luck. Indeed, in novels such as *Ulysses* and *Finnegans Wake*, Joyce is contemptuous of his audience, regarding them as incapable of appreciating the complexities of his work.

Now imagine filmmaker Steven Spielberg running the track with his fans. If he pulls ahead of the pack, he ... *slows down*. In popular art, the burden of understanding shifts to the artist. Successful mass communicators must learn to anticipate the interests and concerns of the audience—to offer content that is interesting and challenging, without being so far afield that they lose their audience entirely.

This relationship between the popular artist and audience might best be characterized as *reciprocal*. Clearly, media presentations are beyond the immediate control of the audience; in that sense, the media is prescriptive. However, because the Western media is a market-driven industry rooted in popular culture, media communicators must be responsive to the needs and interests of their audience. Gifted media communicators intuitively sense what people are interested in and are able to anticipate potential questions and concerns.

According to Nye, *elite* art is defined by the following characteristics:

- *Exclusivity.* Elite art is intended to be enjoyed by a select few.
- *Aesthetic Complexity.* Technical and thematic complexity is regarded as a virtue.
- *Historical Context.* Elite art is part of a larger artistic tradition.
- *Innovation.* Elite art is unconventional and exploratory.

Though useful, Nye's distinction between elite and popular art is far from absolute. For instance, popular artists William Shakespeare, Charles Dickens, and Mark Twain were elevated to elite status after their deaths, when it became evident that their popularity was in many respects due to the elite characteristics of their work. To further confuse the issue, some programming within a popular genre become "classics," which have endured over time because the artists were able to work so skillfully within the accepted format. Examples would include the classic western film *Shane*, the detective novel/film *The Maltese Falcon*, and the radio/television situation comedy *I Love Lucy*.

Clearly, the media are channels of mass communication that sometimes carry elite art (e.g., operas, independent films, and PBS specials). However, it can be said that the majority of the content carried by the channels of mass communication meet Nye's definition of popular art.

Media and Popular Culture

The term "popular" connotes acceptance, approval, and shared values among large numbers of people. We admire the popular set because of who they *are* (attitudes and values) and for what they *do* (behaviors). This notion of popularity also applies to media presentations. People only watch programs that meet their approval. If we are truly offended by violent programs, we won't watch them. And in the market-driven media industry, programs with low ratings are soon cancelled. Consequently, media programming can be regarded as a text, reflecting the attitudes, values, and behaviors that define a culture.

As an example, journalist David M. Halbfinger points out that the following recurring themes appeared in the lineup of the 2007 Sundance Film Festival: sexual oddities and sexual abuse, the ravages of war, the challenges of immigration, human disabilities, and the writer's life. Geoffrey Gilmore, the festival's director observes, "It's a completely different horizon. It feels as if we're at the cusp of a new era.... You start to watch films gradually thinking about not only that sense that the world's about to change, but how to change it."[3]

Media-carried text can also reflect *cultural preoccupations*; that is, the relative importance that a culture places on particular issues. For instance, a survey of topics on *The Jerry Springer Show* (which generally appears twice a day in the St. Louis market) during the summer of 2006 reveals an ongoing preoccupation in American society—sexual infidelity.

July 12, 2006
9 AM A woman suspects her boyfriend is cheating with a prostitute who is also his cousin; a woman falls for an older man but her ex-boyfriend won't let go.
10 AM An 18-year-old woman sleeps with her boyfriend's stepfather; a man cheats on his girlfriend.

July 18, 2006
9 AM Men cheat with their girlfriends' cousins.
10 AM A man must choose between his wife and his sister; a woman hates her gay cousin.

July 27, 2006
10 AM A woman confronts her boyfriend and the mother of his child; a love triangle involves strippers.

August 2, 2006
10 AM A woman wants a divorce so she can marry her husband's brother; a woman finds out her boyfriend is cheating with her cousin.

August 9, 2006
9 AM A man suspects his girlfriend is sleeping with his uncle; a woman's boyfriend cheats with her friend.
10 AM A man admits he has been cheating with the babysitter; a woman is not sure she can trust her fiancé anymore.

August 10, 2006
9 AM A man cheats on his wife with their roommate; a man says he cheated on his girlfriend because she does not dress sexily enough.
10 AM A prostitute introduces her pimp to her family.

August 21, 2006
9 AM A man tells his wife he is a bigamist and his other wife is pregnant; a man sleeps with his girlfriend's roommate.
10 AM A man has an affair with his girlfriend's friend; a stripper fears that her boyfriend is sleeping with another stripper; Dominique reveals the truth about his gender.

August 24, 2006
9 AM A woman cheats on her boyfriend with their co-worker.
10 AM A woman confronts her friend about having an affair with her lover; a man reveals his infidelity to his boyfriend; a woman tells her husband what she has been doing to make ends meet.

August 26, 2006
9 AM Two brides fight over one man; a man's mother lures his girlfriend away; a woman becomes fed up with her man's secret fetish and gives him an ultimatum.
10 AM A man cancels his wedding; a woman steals her sister's man.

August 28, 2006
9 AM Two sisters are involved with one man; a woman wants to tell her boyfriend of ten years that she is leaving him for a co-worker.
10 AM A man cheats on his girlfriend with her sister; a man cheats on his wife with his stepsister.[4]

Media content may also reflect *cultural myths*. Cultural myths are sets of beliefs which may not be true, but nevertheless tell us about ourselves and our culture. As Foster Hirsch observes, "A culture does not buy fantasies that have no connection to it."[5] For instance, popular song titles often pay homage to a cultural myth which might be entitled "The All-Sufficiency of Love," in which a person's identity is totally dependent upon a partner (as opposed to self):

- "One Heart One Love"
- "All You Need Is Love"
- "How Do I Live (Without You)?"
- "You Are My Everything"
- "I Believe I Can Fly"
- "All I Wanna Do (Is Keep On Loving You)"
- "One Love"
- "Lost Without You"
- "Made to Love"

According to this cultural myth, romantic love is a mysterious, mystical force that leads to loss of control ("I Can't Help Myself"). Thus, while romantic love is dangerous ("Devil with the Blue Dress On," "Cupid's Chokehold"), it is essential for survival.

Within this context, it's easy to understand the sense of urgency involved in finding romance ("It's Now or Never"). The end of a relationship has ramifications beyond the loss of your partner; you lose your identity, your self-esteem, and your reason for living.

Over time, cultural myths (such as the all-sufficiency of love) can assume a *mythic reality* as people buy into it. The danger presented by mythic realities is that people sometimes make decisions on the basis of these myths. For instance, an individual might react to the all-sufficiency myth by marrying someone out of fear of being alone.

Media presentations also reflect *changes* in the culture. For example, the topic of divorce is a social phenomenon in American culture that has long been considered taboo in advertising. However, Allen P. Adamson, managing director of the marketing company Landor Associates declares, "Divorce is so common that I don't think people view it as sad and depressing anymore. It's on every movie, every TV show. There aren't any more 'Leave It to Beaver' families around."[6] To illustrate, a 2006 television commercial for the Ford Freestyle acknowledges the ever-growing number of family members affected by divorce:

> The Ford commercial shows two parents, two children and a dog spending a weekend shopping, driving and hanging out at the beach—but at the end of the day, the father is dropped off at his apartment. "Thanks for inviting me this weekend," he says while hugging his children. "Sure," responds his apparent ex-wife, perched behind the wheel of the Ford Freestyle. The commercial ends with the father waving as the car drives away.[7]

Finally, media presentations reflect *cultural attitudes toward particular groups*, such as women, Muslims, or businesspeople. To illustrate, numerous films released in 2006, including *Scoop*, *Brothers of the Head*, *Thank You for Smoking*, and *Superman Returns,* depict reporters as drunks, crooks, or prostitutes. This portrait of reporters reflects the American public's lack of confidence in the competence, integrity, and ethics in reporters' coverage of a range of important issues facing the country. Joseph Saltzman, director of the Image of the Journalist in Popular Culture project, explains,

> The anger and lack of confidence most Americans have in the news media today is partly based on real-life examples they have seen and heard. But much of the image of the journalist as a money-grubbing, selfish, arrogant scoundrel is based on images from movies and television.[8]

In addition, popular culture not only *reflects* but also *reinforces* cultural attitudes, values, behaviors, preoccupations, and myths. What does it mean to be a success in this culture? How should men and women relate to each other? These cumulative messages are reinforced through the countless hours of media programming that repeats, directly or indirectly, the cultural script.

As an example, in an effort to boost the sagging ratings of its reality series *Survivor*, CBS announced in 2006 that it would divide its teams along racial lines—blacks, Asian Americans, Hispanics, and whites. In previous seasons, the composition of the teams was more diverse. According to producer Mark Burnett, this new format plays on the racial and ethnic polarization that already exists in the United States: "In New York you will find areas like Little Afghanistan," he said. "Maybe in the year 3010, when we're all coffee-colored, it really will make no difference. But right now, it is what it is."[9]

However, pitting racial and ethnic groups against one another only further reinforces the racial tensions that already exist within the culture. The audience is supposed to be rooting for their own racial team to win—and the other groups to lose. Moreover, because the premise of the show features the "survival of the fittest," the contest has the effect of determining the racial superiority of the winners.

Significantly, a number of major advertisers withdrew their sponsorship for the series, including Campbell Soup, Coca-Cola, General Motors, Home Depot, and Procter & Gamble.

Finally, the media does not merely reflect or reinforce culture but in fact *shapes* thinking. We all had to receive messages for the first time. In this sense, the media also plays a role in inculcating, or educating, us in regard to cultural values, attitudes, behaviors, and preoccupations.

Worldview

When you watch television, play a video game, or read the newspaper, what kind of world is depicted?

Popular artists construct a complete world out of their imaginations. The premise, plot, and characters of fictional narratives are based on certain fundamental assumptions about how this world operates. Even when we watch nonfiction programming like the news, we receive overall impressions about worldview. Consequently, worldview can be a valuable key to discover manifest and latent messages contained in media programming.

Cultural Ideologies. What kind of culture or cultures populate the world of a media presentation? *Ideology* refers to the system of beliefs characteristic of an individual, group, or culture. An ideology contains assumptions about how the world should operate, who should oversee this world, and the proper and appropriate relationships among its inhabitants.

Cultural Studies is a critical approach that focuses attention on the role of the media as a principal means by which ideology is introduced and reinforced within contemporary culture. One of the central tenets of cultural studies is that the media promote the dominant ideology of a culture. The media industry is owned by those people, groups, and interests that maintain economic and social control of the culture.

This imposition of an ideology within a culture is referred to as *hegemony.* As discussed earlier, media presentations contain their own *preferred readings*, based on the social position/orientation of the media communicator. In this way, the sympathies of the audience are aligned with the values and beliefs of this dominant culture (for further discussion of the hegemonic model, see Chapter 16). Alan O'Connor declares that the media serve as "... processes of persuasion in which we are invited to understand the world in certain ways but not in others."[10] Thus, the media create (or re-create) representations of reality that support the dominant ideology as a means of maintaining cultural control.

Generally speaking, the worldview of television continues to reflect the dominant ideology. Studies of the representation of various subcultures during the 2002 television season revealed that prime-time television continues to present a male-dominated world. According to the 2001 U.S. census, females outnumbered males, 145 million to 140 million. However, nearly 63 percent of all white and African American characters on prime-time television were men. For Latinos, the figure was 56 percent.[11] The representation of other minorities during the 2002 prime-time television season was as follows:

- White characters accounted for 81 percent of screen time.[12]
- African American characters accounted for about 15 percent of screen time.[13] (African Americans made up 13 percent of the population.)[14]
- Latino characters accounted for 3 percent of screen time.[15] (Latinos made up 13 percent of the nation's population.)[16]
- Asian Americans accounted for 1 percent of screen time while accounting for about 4 percent of the population.[17]
- Although Americans 60 and older constitute 18 percent of the population, these individuals comprised only 4 percent of major characters in prime-time television during the 2002–2003 season.[18]
- Native Americans were again invisible, although they made up nearly 1 percent of the population.[19]

The preeminence of dominant ideology in the media is further supported by a study by Gerbner and Signorielli, which identified the groups most frequently victimized by violence on prime-time television (in order):

- Women of all ages (particularly young adult and elderly women)
- Young boys
- Non-whites
- "Foreigners"
- Members of the lower and upper class[20]

The group conspicuously absent from this list consists of white, middle-class/upper-middle-class males—the people primarily responsible for producing media programming. One can almost imagine these men sitting around a Hollywood pool vicariously killing off these other subgroups.

In reality, the groups most victimized by crime are (in order):

- Young black males. In 1988, approximately 40 percent of black males who died were victims of homicide. At greatest risk among this group were lower-class black males.
- White males/black females (18–24 year olds). These groups fell roughly into the same levels, depending on the type of crime.
- White females statistically were victimized far less frequently.[21]

Another example of cultural re-creation can be found in media messages about women. In her book *The Beauty Myth*, Naomi Wolf observes that the cumulative media messages about female sexuality cause young girls "to absorb the dominant culture's fantasies as [their] own."

> The books and films [young girls] see [are] from the young boy's point of view—his first touch of a girl's thighs, his first glimpse of her breasts. The girls sit listening, absorbing ... learning how to leave their bodies and watch them from the outside. Since their bodies are seen from the point of view of strangeness and desire, it is no wonder that what should be familiar, felt to be whole, becomes estranged and divided into parts. What little girls learn is not the desire for the other, but the desire to be desired.[22]

According to Wolf, the cumulative messages about women contained in media presentations are clear: "The woman learns from these images that no matter how assertive she may be in the world, her private submission to control is what makes her desirable."[23]

Susan G. Cole warns that these messages can have disturbing repercussions:

> In spite of hopes to the contrary, pornography and mass culture are working to collapse sexuality with rape, reinforcing the patterns of male dominance and female submission so that many young people believe this is simply the way sex is. This means that many of the rapists of the future will believe they are behaving within socially accepted norms.[24]

Media Stereotyping. A stereotype is an oversimplified depiction of a person, group, or event. This term is derived from the Greek word *steros,* (hard or solid), which underscores the inflexible, absolute nature of stereotypes.

Stereotyping is an *associative* process; that is, ideas about groups are based upon a shared understanding about a group. According to philosopher Friedrich Nietzsche, people often base their opinions about a person on one distinctive characteristic, which becomes the basis of the stereotype:

> In the eyes of people who are seeing us for the first time ... usually we are nothing more than a single individual trait which leaps to the eye and determines the whole impression we make. Thus the gentlest and most reasonable of men can, if he wears a large moustache ... usually be seen as no more than the appurtenance of a large moustache, that is to say a military type, easily angered and occasionally violent—and as such he will be treated.[25]

For example, take a moment to picture a "typical" scientist....

Now, compare your profile to the following version of the stereotypical scientist, compiled through a *New York Times* survey: "A scientist is a short, unattractive, old man who is bald, has few friends, is clumsy, silly, and is hard to understand. In some cases, he is dangerous."[26]

If there is a general consensus of opinion, then we have a working stereotype.

Stereotyping is a natural coping mechanism. We make decisions based upon generalizations in order to function on an everyday basis. As an example, if you look outside and see dark clouds forming, you automatically take an umbrella with you. But although *prejudging* can be a useful device (it can prevent you from getting wet, for example), *prejudice* is a reductive principle that interferes with people's ability to appreciate the unique characteristics of individuals. According to William B. Helmerich, this grouping principle is often inaccurate, negative, and dangerous: "Approximately one-third of stereotypes can be said to have a good deal of truth to them, and that the accurate stereotypes are predominately positive, whereas those that seem highly inaccurate tend by and large to be negative."[27]

Racial stereotyping continues to play a powerful role in an individual's chances for success in America. According to a 2007 study, light-skinned immigrants in the United States make more money on average than those with darker complexions, and the chief reason appears to be discrimination. Professor Joni Hersch declared, "On average, being one shade lighter has about the same effect as having an additional year of education."[28]

The media industry is particularly well suited for stereotyping. Media communicators do not have the luxury of time to develop a unique set of characters; indeed, over the past ten years, the amount of time in which a network television program could run before facing cancellation has been reduced from thirteen to four weeks—hardly a time frame during which the audience can become familiar with a full cast of complex, unique characters. Consequently, media communicators tap into the cumulative experience of the audience; audience members recognize a character who appears on screen because they have seen him (or a character like him) dozens of times before. In addition, the stereotypes appear very *natural* in media presentations. No one in the presentation (and certainly not the protagonists) questions the veracity of the characterizations.

Media communicators also rely on stereotypes to compensate for their limited ability to collect information firsthand. To illustrate, it has become increasingly dangerous for correspondents covering the Iraq war to venture out of the protected "Green Zone." Consequently, they rely on official military briefings for their information or hire untrained Iraqis to go out into the field and bring back stories. As a result, coverage of the conflict has reflected only a general, stereotyped understanding of the Iraqi communities.

Stereotyping Techniques. Media stereotyping techniques can be quite subtle. For instance, the *Boston Globe* carried the following review of Susan Monsky's novel, *Midnight Suppers:*

> Monsky tells the story in a soft-spoken Southern accent which doesn't quite seem to go with her Semitic features and intellectual-looking wire-rimmed glasses.[29]

On close inspection, this passage invites questions about several stereotypes:

- What are "Semitic" features?
- Why would Monsky's Semitic appearance contrast with her "soft spoken" accent?
- And doesn't this review suggest that Southern women are not intellectual?

Editing decisions—what to omit or include in a media presentation—also reinforce stereotypes. The issue is not necessarily that a particular stereotypical behavior is depicted by the media, but, rather, that this characteristic consistently is the *only* dimension presented. On the surface, it may appear harmless to depict a black man as silly and confused; after all, these qualities are central to comedy—and certainly, it is easy to find corresponding examples of buffoonery among white male performers. For instance, in *You, Me and Dupree* (2006), Owen Wilson plays a man/boy who, having been fired from his job and evicted from his apartment, moves in with his best friend and his new wife. This "slacker" is an annoying, crude, and clueless houseguest, disrupting the marriage of his friend. However, if this character trait was the *only* way that white males are presented in media presentations, then this characterization would perpetuate a cultural stereotype.

Media programming continues to reinforce cultural stereotypes. To illustrate, women on television are depicted in ways that support the traditional female stereotypes:

- As they age, women characters in entertainment programs are increasingly portrayed as evil.[30]
- In news and public affairs programs, about 87 percent of the sound bites used from those referred to as experts are from men.[31]
- Only 10 percent of educational television programming features female protagonists.[32]

To be sure, shows like *Grace Under Fire*, *ER*, and *CSI* have broken through many of the female stereotypes over the last decade. However, contemporary programs often present only the *appearance* of transcending stereotypes. Many of the strong, independent female characters depicted in contemporary media presentations appear as supernatural creatures, such as vampires (*Underworld*), witches (*Bewitched*, *Charmed*), or psychics (*Medium*). Giving these characters superpowers removes these strong females from the context of everyday experience, making them more acceptable to the general public.

For example, the comedy *My Super Ex-Girlfriend* (2006) tells the story of Matt Saunders (Luke Wilson) who meets the perfect girl, who is a super heroine named G-Girl. Matt discovers that G-Girl is too needy, controlling, and jealous and decides to break up with her. Jenny doesn't take it well and decides to get back at him by using her superpowers.

This film, which was written by a male (Don Payne), reflects what reporter Manohla Dargis refers to as the "fear of a female planet." Despite her superpowers, what holds this superheroine back are the stereotypical female traits: jealousy, vanity, superficiality, and erratic temperament:

> Why G-Girl and not G-Woman? For the same reason that this particular superhero can access her powers only after she slips on something tighter and a whole lot less comfortable-looking: she's a joke.... Alas, as if by clockwork or the professional lout's handbook, she turns out to be wildly insecure, possessive, needy, the whole crazy-woman nine yards, which means that, at least as far as the filmmakers are concerned, she's both a drag and a threat.[33]

Moreover, independent female characters are often cast as villains, or as characters whose "femininity" has been compromised by their assertiveness. To illustrate, *The Devil Wears Prada* is a 2006 film adaptation of Lauren Weisberger's novel about the fashion industry. Meryl Streep plays Miranda Priestly, the ruthless editor of a top fashion magazine. Her staff fears her—in part because she has adopted many of the assertive traits that characterize male CEOs. The film tells the story of Andy Sachs (Anne Hathaway), a young woman who finds a job in New York

City as an assistant to Miranda Priestly, editor of an influential fashion magazine. Priestly (played by Meryl Streep) is a satanic figure who abuses everyone around her. Indeed, the publicity poster of the film depicts fashionable high heels (belonging to Ms. Priestly); the heel is the devil's scepter.

David Carr points out that the characteristics that make Miranda a villainess reflect the double standard that exists in American culture with regard to women in the workplace:

> One of the movie's running jokes occurs when Miranda Priestly, Ms. Wintour's cinematic doppelganger, arrives at work and flings all manner of jillion-dollar handbags and coats on the desk of her hapless assistant.... Male media stars can ingest illegal drugs, make obscene phone calls or hire prostitutes without apparent consequence, but the failure of a female media figure to say please when ordering coffee can lead to wholesale indictment.[34]

As the story progresses, Andy discovers that her professional success is attained at the expense of her personal life—just like her mentor, Miranda. Carr observes, "However, the movie's ... chief preoccupation—is Miranda Priestly ... really happy?—seems entirely beside the point. It is a question that seems to come up only when the successful executive happens to wear a dress.[35]

However, it is encouraging that actors such as Sidney Poitier, Denzel Washington, and Tony Shalhoub play roles that are not tied to their race or ethnicity and, consequently, broaden the dimensions of minority groups as they appear in the media.

MEDIA LITERACY TIPS

CONTENT ANALYSIS

One way to identify media stereotypes is by conducting a content analysis, which employs quantitative techniques to look for patterns, messages, symbols, language, art forms, and potential biases in print and electronic media.

Conducting a content analysis consists of the following steps:

- Defining the categories to be studied
- Tabulating and summarizing the data
- Making inferences—that is, drawing conclusions from the patterns identified

Content analysis can be conducted on many levels, ranging from simply tabulating types of occurrences (as outlined here) to sophisticated computer-assisted analyses of media content.

As you conduct the content analysis, keep in mind the following:

1. Obviously, some of these categories are subjective. It is important, however, to strive for clarity and consistency in categorization.

MEDIA LITERACY TIPS (*continued*)

2. Categories should be identified through behavior (e.g., patting a person on the head as evidence of nurturing behavior).
3. You must fill out one tally sheet for *each* character.
4. To complete the analysis, tabulate the results, and then draw your inferences, or conclusions.
5. It should be noted that the size of this sample is too limited to yield conclusive results. However, this type of limited study can provide a useful indication of stereotypes, as well as making you more sensitive to the portrayal of groups in the media.

Content Analysis Tally Sheet

1. Name of program
2. Medium (e.g., film, television)
3. Genre of program (e.g., adventure, romance, news)
4. Name of character viewed
5. Male or female
6. Was this character *the main character* in the program? (Judge by number of minutes on air)
7. Occupation
   a. Student
   b. Unemployed
   c. Unskilled labor
   d. Skilled or trained labor
   e. Job requiring at least a college degree
   f. "Prominent" or highly visible position
   g. Other
8. Level of education
   a. Grade school or under
   b. High school
   c. College
   d. Other
9. Race
   a. African American
   b. White
   c. Asian
   d. Latino
   e. Native American
   f. Bi-racial
   g. Other

MEDIA LITERACY TIPS (*continued*)

10. Marital status
    a. Single
    b. Married
    c. Divorced
    d. Widowed
    e. Living with "significant other"
    f. Other
11. Age (approximate)
    a. 0–5 years old
    b. 6–12 years old
    c. 13–18 years old
    d. 19–25 years old
    e. 26–35 years old
    f. 36–50 years old
    g. 51–65 years old
    h. Over 65 years old
12. Number of children
    a. 0
    b. 1
    c. 2
    d. 3
    e. 4
    f. Over 4
13. Appearance
    a. Attractive by traditional standards
    b. Glamorous
    c. Unattractive by traditional standards
    d. Average by traditional standards
    e. Other (please indicate)
14. Body Type
    a. Slender or thin
    b. Average
    c. Voluptuous
    d. Above average weight
    e. Athletic
    f. Heavy
    g. Other (please indicate)

MEDIA LITERACY TIPS (*continued*)

15. Personal characteristics (check as many as apply) displayed by the character in the episode:
    a. Nurturing
    b. Abrupt
    c. Devious
    d. Straightforward
    e. Flirtatious
    f. Sarcastic
    g. Self-reliant
    h. Dependent
    i. Emotional
        1) Cries
        2) Laughs
        3) Yells
        4) Whines
        5) Becomes physically violent
        6) Other (please indicate)
    j. Physically affectionate
    k. Sexual
    l. Intelligent
    m. Slow-witted
    n. Humorous
    o. Object of humor/ridicule
    p. In control of situation
    q. Passive
    r. Other (please indicate)
16. Role of the Character in Narrative
    a. Hero or heroine
    b. Villain
    c. Supporting character
    d. Romantic figure
    e. Comedic character
17. Impact of Character in Narrative
    a. Positively affects outcome of the narrative
    b. Negatively affects outcome of the narrative
    c. Has no impact on the outcome of the narrative

Romantic Ideal. The worldview reflected in many popular media presentations reflects a *Romantic Ideal.* As Richard Harter Fogle observes, this ideal presumes an ordered universe: "The center of romanticism ... lies in a new and different vision, in which everything is alive, related, and meaningful."[36]

In this ordered universe, nature is a microcosm of heaven, defined by an absolute value system:

- Truth
- Love
- Beauty
- Faith
- Justice

These values are unified and interchangeable; one virtue cannot exist in isolation from the others. Beauty is merely the external manifestation of the other, less tangible virtues. Justice ultimately prevails. Love triumphs, the truth is revealed, and faith is rewarded. Even in action/adventure films, violence is a necessary means of restoring and preserving this ideal order.

Within this context, the individualism that characterizes romanticism is a celebration of the divinity in human beings. In *Song of Myself*, Walt Whitman declares,

I celebrate myself and sing myself,
And what I assume you shall assume,
For every atom belonging to me as good belongs to you.[37]

An important issue in the romantic worldview is *control.* A formulaic plotline in many popular genres involves the protagonist taking charge of a chaotic situation, despite overwhelming odds. Control is a central issue in advertising as well. Beyond selling a particular product, a latent message in many ads is the promise that the product will enable consumers to assume control of their lives. For instance, a television commercial for Chevrolet begins with a rock singer in the foreground. The song lyrics announce:

I get what I want
I go where I please....

The latent message of control even extends to the worldview of broadcast news. No matter how catastrophic the news, the broadcast anchor is trained to present the information in a measured—and controlled—fashion.

But significantly, women in media presentations often inhabit a world in which they are powerless. They live in fear of the elements, of men, and of their own natures. Their only chance for happiness is through male benevolence and protection.

To be sure, we are exposed to entertainment and informational programming that departs from this romantic ideal. The horror genre presents a world of evil and chaos, in which human beings are powerless and vulnerable. This genre explores concerns that are fundamentally terrifying to humans: fear of death, of demons, of worlds beyond our understanding, and of our own Promethean delusions that are manifested in the creation of nuclear-inspired monsters (giant ants, for instance). However, order is generally restored at the conclusion, which re-establishes this romantic ideal—at least until the sequel is released.

Values Hierarchy. How can you identify the value system operating within the worldview of a media presentation?

Milton Rokeach defines the notion of values as "An enduring belief that a specific mode of conduct or end-state of existence is personally or socially preferable to alternate modes of conduct or end-state of existence."[38]

The values system operating in a media presentation generally represents the culmination of layers of belief systems. The personal values of the media communicator are interwoven with membership in a number of subcultures based upon gender (male-female), ethnic/racial identity (e.g., African American, Jewish), stage of life (college student), and class—which operate according to separate value systems. To add to the confusion, media communicators are also products of the larger value system of the dominant culture, which then provide order and meaning for that culture. Thus, in order to identify a value system operating in a media production, it is of paramount importance to define its culture (or subculture).

Some strategies for identifying the values system operating in a media presentation include the following:

Analyzing the Characters. In media presentations, characters can be considered personifications of values. Heroes and heroines embody those qualities that society considers admirable. Heroes generally prevail in media entertainment programming because they embody the values that are esteemed within the culture. For instance, Superman is committed to "Truth, Justice, and the American Way." Indeed, these values are often the source of the hero's courage and strength. Western heroes must adhere to a strict moral code: never draw first or shoot a man in the back. Although this code sometimes puts the hero at a momentary disadvantage, any violation of these principles would mean his downfall.

In contrast, villains generally epitomize those negative values that pose a threat to the worldview of the presentation. Villains are not bound by the moral constraints to which heroes must adhere; they are free to draw first, lie, and cheat. However, these momentary advantages are not powerful enough to contest the moral order of the universe. Villains are inevitably brought to justice for their crimes—and, in a larger sense, for their transgressions against the moral order of the universe (as defined by the media presentation).

Even nonfiction heroes who are presented in the media, such as Albert Einstein, Princess Diana, and Michael Jordan, are celebrated because they embody these cultural values. In reality, however, few people can fulfill these expectations. Public figures fall from grace once their flaws have been exposed by the media—almost as though the public cannot forgive them for being human.

Examining the Conclusion. As the protagonists and villains engage in conflict, the values that they personify are also in opposition:

- Good versus evil
- Justice versus injustice
- Truth versus falsehood
- Love versus hate
- Internal satisfaction versus material acquisitions
- Immediate satisfaction versus delayed gratification

The outcome of the production establishes a hierarchy of values. For instance, with the culminating battle scene in the action film *The League of Extraordinary Gentlemen* (2003), the conflict between good and evil is resolved. As the good guys win and justice prevails, a system of values has been firmly established.

Measuring Success. Media programming can provide insight into definitions of success, as defined by the culture in which the presentation was produced. Success can be identified through the *kinds* of behavior that are rewarded in media presentations and *how* they are rewarded.

By examining cumulative media messages, it is possible to construct a composite picture of success in American culture:

As Validation. The roots of the American myth of success can be traced to our Puritan tradition. According to the Puritan doctrine of predestination, God foreordained all things, especially the salvation of individuals' souls. This doctrine also provided an elaborate rationale and justification for personal achievement. Material success on earth was regarded as a sign that a person was predestined to go to heaven.

A secular version of Puritanism has translated easily into the American capitalistic definitions of success. A very subtle system of morality justifies the system of capitalism. Those who succeed are somehow deserving; those who fail are unworthy.

As Immortality. The notion of "upward mobility" suggests a heaven on Earth, beyond worldly cares and concerns. Successful people attract public attention and adulation. Fame makes them appear bigger than life; truly successful people leave a legacy that lives on after their deaths.

As Conquest. Striving for success is often portrayed as a test of personal resolve, requiring discipline, sacrifice, and commitment. In an 1888 instructional book on success, entitled *Road to Success; a Book for Boys and Young Men*, the Reverend Aaron Wanner declares that success is not for the frail: "A weak, sickly body is a great impediment in the way to one's success. It is like a broken, leaky roof, which subjects everything in the house to injury."[39]

As Self-Determination. Successful media figures are in control, free to determine their own fates. They are also in a position to assert their individuality. For instance, in the *Lethal Weapon* films, Officer Martin Riggs (Mel Gibson) is part of the system. Yet, he dresses in street clothes, wears his hair long, drives his own car, and breaks the rules when it suits him. Riggs possesses a clear sense of identity. He is confident, possesses self-knowledge, and knows what direction in life he wants to pursue.

As Physical Ideal. Movie stars like Brad Pitt and Angelina Jolie are objects of admiration because of their appearance. Moreover, athletes are revered for their athletic prowess.

As a Contest. Success is a sport, in which people compete against one another. Champions like Donald Trump and Bill Gates have been able to devise strategies to come out on top. Popular books suggest techniques that promise to give individuals the advantage they need to prevail:

- *Winning through Intimidation*, Robert Ringer
- *Nonverbal Communication for Business Success*, Ken Cooper
- *The Psychology of Effective Living*, Roger C. Bailey

As American Dream. According to the Horatio Alger myth, anyone can succeed through hard work. If you believe enough in your dream, it will come true. However, this myth also serves as an elaborate defense of the status quo. Those members of minority groups who manage to succeed are offered as proof that the system works for everyone. In the process, the Horatio Alger myth minimizes the effort required for minorities to overcome cultural hurdles. And by extension, those who do not succeed must be slackers.

As Acquisition. For some, the accumulation of possessions is the ultimate measure of success. Within this orientation, notions of an afterlife are not even considered; existence has been confined to this world. Consequently, life's meaning is reduced to a contest: in the words of the popular bumper sticker, "The one who dies with the most toys wins." Through some sort of consumer transmutation, we become what we purchase. If we *look* successful, we *are* successful.

NOTES

1. Russel B. Nye, "Notes on a Rationale for Popular Culture," *A Popular Culture Reader*, ed. Jack Nachbar, Deborah Weiser, and John L. Wright (Bowling Green, OH: Bowling Green University Popular Press, 1978), 22.

2. Ibid., 20

3. David M. Halbfinger, "Coming to Sundance: New Crop of Engaged Indie Films," *New York Times*, November 30, 2006.

4. "Today's Talk Shows," *St. Louis Post-Dispatch* (www.stltoday.com).

5. Foster Hirsch, *The Dark Side of the Screen* (New York: Da Capo Press, 2001).

6. Julie Bosman, "Hey, Just Because He's Divorced Doesn't Mean He Can't Sell Things," *New York Times*, August 17, 2006, C6.

7. Ibid.

8. David Carr, "Reporters on Film: Drunks and Tarts," *New York Times*, August 14, 2006, C1.

9. Bill Carter, "'Survivor' to Divide Teams Along Racial Lines," *New York Times*, August 24, 2006, C6.

10. Alan O'Connor, "Culture and Communication," *Questioning the Media: A Critical Introduction*, ed. John Downing, Ali Mohammadi, and Annabelle Sreberny-Mohammadi (Newbury Park, CA: Sage Publications, 1990), 37.

11. U.S. Census Bureau, www.census.gov.

12. "White Characters Dominate Prime-Time Television While Latinos Are Significantly Underrepresented, UCLA Study Finds," 2003 UCLA News (http://newsroom.ucla.edu/page.asp?id=4325).

13. Ibid.

14. U.S. Census.

15. "White Characters Dominate Prime-Time."

16. U.S. Census.

17. "White Characters Dominate Prime-Time."

18. Martha M. Lauzen and David M. Dozier, "Recognition and Respect Revisited: Portrayals of Age and Gender in Prime-Time Television," *Mass Communication & Society* 8:3(2005), 241–256.

19. "White Characters Dominate Prime-Time."

20. George Gerbner and Nancy Signorielli, "Violence Profile 1967 Through 1988–89; Enduring Patterns," January 1990.

21. Richard Rosenfeld, interview by author, April 22, 2007.

22. Naomi Wolf, *The Beauty Myth* (New York: William Morrow and Company, 1991), 156–157.

23. Ibid., 133.

24. Ibid., 167.

25. Freidrich Neitzsche, *The Consolations of Philosophy*, Alain de Botton (New York: Pantheon Books, 2000), 206.

26. Malcolm W. Browne, "Television Blocks the View," *New York Times*, January 27, 1981, C2.

27. William B. Helmreich, *The Things They Say Behind Your Back: Stereotypes & the Myths Behind Them* (New Brunswick, NJ: Transaction Pubs., 1983), 44.

28. Associated Press, "Study of Immigrants Links Lighter Skin and Higher Income," *New York Times*, January 28, 2007, A19.

29. Carol Stocker, "Published on the First Try," *Boston Globe,* February 11, 1983.

30. Eric Effron, "Just Between Us," *Brill's Content* (April 1999), 47.

31. Neda Raouf, "NOW Targets Portrayal of Women," *Los Angeles Times*, July 4, 1999, 6B.

32. Ibid.

33. Manohla Dargis, "In 'My Super Ex-Girlfriend,' Luke Wilson Is Just Not That Into Uma Thurman," *New York Times*, July 21, 2006.

34. David Carr, "The Devil Wears Teflon," *New York Times*, July 10, 2006, C1.

35. Ibid.

36. Richard Harter Fogle, ed., *The Romantic Movement in American Fiction* (New York: The Odyssey Press, 1966), 3.

37. Walt Whitman, *Leaves of Grass* (New York: The Viking Press, 1959), 26.

38. Milton Rokeach, *Beliefs, Attitudes, and Values: A Theory of Organization and Change* (San Francisco: Jossey-Bass, 1968), 113.

39. Rev. Aaron Wanner, *Road to Success; a Book for Boys and Young Men* (Reading, PA: Daniel Miller, 1888), 12.

CHAPTER 7

STRUCTURE

In the United States, the *concentration of ownership* in the media industry has become an extremely troubling trend. In 1981, Ben Bagdikian found that 46 corporations owned or controlled the majority of media outlets in the United States. However, as of 2006, that number had shrunk to eight corporations: Time/Warner, Disney, Vivendi Universal, Viacom, Sony, the News Corporation, General Electric, and Bertelsmann. This ownership model fits F. M. Sherer and D. Ross's definition of an *oligopoly*:

> Oligopoly refers to an industry characterized by a few mutually interdependent firms, with relatively similar shares, producing either a homogeneous product (a perfect oligopoly) or heterogeneous products (an imperfect oligopoly). Under such a market structure, the industry leader often sets the price.[1]

Impact of Consolidation of Media Ownership on Content

The ownership of media production companies in the United States has a significant impact on media content, in several respects.

Homogeneity of Content. Because of the concentration of ownership, the content that we receive through the media is controlled by a very few corporations. Media outlets owned by a mega-corporation have a uniform style, content, and operating philosophy. As an example, radio is a medium that was primarily made up of small, independent, locally owned stations. Increasingly, however, small radio stations have been purchased by large conglomerates. As a result, roughly one in every 10 radio stations in the country is owned by Clear Channel, Inc. Further, a conglomerate can dominate a particular region. To illustrate, Clear Channel, Inc., owns all six commercial stations in Minot, North Dakota, the state's fourth-largest city, with a population nearing 37,000.

Radio stations owned by the same conglomerate have identical formats, playlists, promotions, and jokes, dictated by the corporation. Thus, despite its local flavor, the playlist of a radio station in one city is identical to its corporate counterpart in another area.

These media conglomerates subcontract with national news services eliminating the cost of producing their own programming. Metro Networks, a Houston-based company, provides news, sports, weather, and other information to more than 2,200 radio and television stations in over 80 markets in the United States, reaching an audience of nearly 100 million listeners. Metro Networks may serve several stations in one market; in New York, for example, nearly 100 stations subcontract with Metro. Although the news staff at each station rewrites the copy to make it appear distinctive, this practice reduces the diversity of news sources.

Media organizations also save expenses by purchasing *syndicated* programs. A syndicated program is produced in one location and then sold to stations throughout the country. Thus, if a radio station carries Rush Limbaugh instead of producing a local talk program, they are spared the cost of hiring a host, producer, and engineer. Unfortunately, the radio listeners are also denied the opportunity to hear and discuss issues from a local perspective.

Support of Status Quo. The conglomerates that own media companies are beneficiaries of the existing political and economic systems. As a result, while media companies may call for some refinements within the existing system, they cannot be counted upon to press for significant changes in the current system. Ben Bagdikian declares, "The lords of the global village have their own political agenda. All resist economic changes that do not support their own financial interests."[2] For example, one avenue for political campaign reform calls for television, as a guardian of the public airwaves, making free airtime available for political ads. Needless to say, the media conglomerates do not support this idea.

Programming as "Product." As part of a corporate empire, media presentations are thought of simply as products, like shoes or showerheads, to be manufactured and sold. In this market-driven media system, the primary goal is to maximize profit. To illustrate, in the 1950s, television news was considered a public service. Television executives counted on entertainment programming underwriting the cost of producing the news. However, by the 1970s, the news operation was expected to pay for itself by breaking even. Today, the news operation has emerged as the primary source of profit for local television stations. This economic imperative has had a dramatic impact on news content. As Max Frankel explains, news stations now select sensational, sentimental, or dramatic stories. In a desperate attempt to attract viewers:

> (News operations) are pressured to find a mass audience with maudlin tales of individual struggle, worshipful portraits of pop celebrities and photogenic scandals that are easily grasped. Anything long or complicated would shrink the audience.[3]

To illustrate, during the quarterly ratings period known as the "sweeps," local television stations commonly feature week-long "news" stories on provocative topics like wrestling, prostitution, and breast implants in hopes of attracting the largest possible audience.

Derivative Programming. One of the prime reasons that mega-corporations acquire media companies is for their cash flow potential—which is considerable. For instance, in 2005, *Star Wars Episode III: Revenge of the Sith* grossed $158.5 million during its first weekend of release in North America. Indeed, CBS radio accounts for 14 percent of the parent company's revenue.[4]

Because the economic bottom line is paramount, the media industry is increasingly reluctant to take programming risks: Bill Carter observes,

> Though there is near uniform agreement that only shows with truly original concepts seem to be connecting with viewers, an unwillingness to take risks often derails ideas before they are even tried, several executives said.
>
> One head of a television production studio, who spoke on condition of anonymity, outlined how the fear of risk undermined the networks' acknowledged need for truly new ideas. We go into development meetings after they see how all their shows are failing, and they tell us we have to give them our wildest, most creative ideas, the executive said.
>
> So we tell our writers to come up with most original ideas they can. Then we come back, and we've got about eight ideas to pitch, four that are truly out there and four that are more like original spins on familiar formats.
>
> The first thing that happens is they throw out the four wilder ideas because they're just too risky. Then they start to tinker with the others. And every change they suggest makes the show more conventional. Then they give you a list for actors and say don't cast anyone not on this list. Then there's a list for directors. And by the time they get the shows, they wonder why they have no original ideas.[5]

To illustrate, one of the reasons that television executives first introduced the Reality genre is because the programs are so inexpensive to produce. Producing programming without having to hire professional actors and writers generates extraordinary profits for the stations and their owners. The fact that the genre became popular has only added to the glut of profit.

In addition, film studios only produce movies with formulaic plots, sequels and "bankable" stars. As Rick Lyman and Laura M. Holson point

Figure 7.1
Market value of the Big Eight companies in 2007, in billions of dollars.

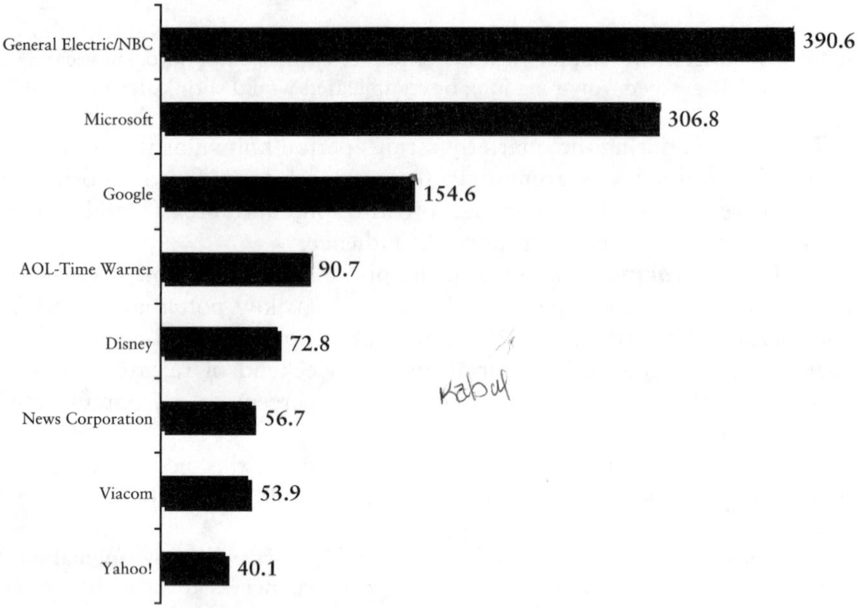

out, this profit imperative has an impact on the choices of films that are released over the Christmas holidays:

> Gradually over several years, and particularly this year, the prestige studio movies—like *Schindler's List*—have all but disappeared from the holiday schedule. In their place, with a few notable exceptions, come more and more sequels, remakes, spin-offs and other risk-averse, mass-market fare driven by the need for fast dollars.[6]

Cross-promotion. Media programs sometimes are presented for the sole purpose of promoting other holdings within the corporate empire. As an example, in 2004, St. Louis television critic Gail Pennington examined the local news stories on NBC affiliate KSDK and found the following instances in which local news stories were actually thinly disguised promotions for network programming:

- One story profiled Donald Trump, star of "one of the most successful reality shows on television, '*The Apprentice*,' airing 'right here on News Channel 5.'"
- Another story took viewers behind the scenes on *Law & Order: Special Victims Unit*, another NBC series.
- *Cover Story* visited *Saturday Night Live*, marking "30 years of SNL on Newschannel 5."

- A recurring segment called "Monday's Movers and Shakers" featured NBC personalities, such as retiring news anchor Tom Brokaw and *Hardball* host Chris Matthews of MSNBC.[7]

Because of the breadth and depth of available programming, conglomerates also can direct audiences from one program to another carried under one corporate banner. For instance, after-school cartoons on the WB network carry advertisements designed to induce its young audience to change to the Cartoon Network when the WB show is over.

Unfortunately, this promotional strategy may be difficult to detect, unless you are familiar with all of the vast holdings of a media conglomerate. Jeff MacGregor observes,

> To the casual consumer of entertainment, it's almost impossible to discern the linkages between product and promoter. Until recently, for example, TV Guide was owned by the News Corporation, Rupert Murdoch's umbrella for his global communications company. News Corp. also owns 20th Century Fox. And the Fox network. Does that account then for the substantial number of decorative cover stories over the last few seasons devoted to "The Simpsons" and "The X-Files"? What about a show like "The Practice," which was the subject of a cover story last season slugged "the best show you're not watching"? But that's on the ABC network, you say. Yes, it is. But it's produced by the Fox studio, 20th Century Fox Television.[8]

Conflicts of Interest. Conflicts arise when a media conglomerate covers stories in which the parent company has an interest. To illustrate, General Electric's reliance on the defense technology as a principal source of revenue raises questions of conflict of interest with respect to how NBC might cover military-related stories. In 2002, General Electric, one of the world's leading manufacturers of jet engines for military aircraft was awarded $1.7 billion in contracts from the U.S. Defense Department. General Electric also has a very lucrative business exporting defense equipment internationally. During the second quarter of 2000, G.E. received more than $600 million in military contracts, including the Air Force of the Republic of Korea. To be clear, it is by no means certain that NBC is influenced by the business dealings of its parent company. However, the vast holdings of these conglomerates puts their media subsidiaries in the uncomfortable position of covering events in which the conglomerate is directly involved.

In addition, the executives of these wealthy and influential media conglomerates may have ties to the political establishment, creating conflicts of interest that can affect their presentation of information. As an example, Tom Hicks, vice-chairman of Clear Channel, Inc., has had longtime financial ties to President George W. Bush. Consequently, after Natalie Maines, lead singer of the Dixie Chicks, publicly criticized Bush in 2003, Clear Channel banned playing the group's music on their stations and, further, organized an outdoor event in Louisiana, in which Dixie Chicks'

CDs were trampled by a tractor. The company subsequently banned over 160 songs that they considered to be "dangerous," including:

- "New York, New York," Frank Sinatra
- "What a Wonderful World," Louis Armstrong
- "Mack the Knife," Bobby Darin
- "He Ain't Heavy, He's My Brother," The Hollies
- "Walk Like an Egyptian," The Bangles
- "Imagine," John Lennon

Ignoring Public Service Responsibilities. The drive to maximize profit can even jeopardize public health and security. As an example, in 2002, a train derailed in Minot, North Dakota, leaking thousands of gallons of toxic chemicals into the air. One person died and hundreds were treated for immediate health problems. After the town's Emergency Alert System failed, local officials and panic-stricken residents tried to call one of their stations, KCJB (910 AM), which was the town's designated local emergency broadcaster, but no one answered. Instead of providing emergency information to the city's residents, the stations continued to play music piped in from out of state. None of the city's six commercial radio stations—all owned by Clear Channel Communications—aired warnings for local residents.

Professor Eric Klinenberg declares that media consolidation has compromised our capacity to broadcast emergency information:

> (Clear Channel has) replaced live local talent, deejays, talk show hosts, programmers, with automated programming, oftentimes faked to sound like it's local, even though it's programmed in a remote studio thousands of miles away. That night in Minot, North Dakota, there was no one in any of those six stations.... The result is that when the Emergency Alert System failed, there was no way to get the word out.
>
> I think this is a story that Americans need to know, because when we make policy decisions to allow more consolidated media ownership, to allow one company to own six stations, it's my belief, my experience, that we compromise our local security, our national security.[9]

Internal Structure

The *internal structure* of a media organization consists of the following elements: the *resources* of the production company, the *organizational framework* (i.e., different departments, lines of responsibility), and the *process of decision-making*. These organizational factors have an impact on day-to-day decisions, as well as long-range planning.

Case Study: *Television News Operation.* To illustrate, consider the organizational structure of a television news operation, and its impact on news content.

The resources of the station. The resources of a news operation can have a dramatic affect on a station's ability to gather the news. Local television stations range from skeletal one-person news departments to sophisticated operations with $30 million budgets.

As Max Frankel explains, the size of the staff (writers, reporters, videographers, and editors) drastically affects the depth and quality of news coverage:

> Television news staffs could not possibly show a profit if they rigorously tried to investigate a crime wave or social trend or school performance. A camera-wielding crew of experienced reporters would have to spend days, even weeks, on assignment to do such stories. Most local stations, seeking profit margins of 35 to 50 percent, could never pay for such talent. So they chase squad cars and ambulances and stand "live" before brick walls and try to validate glib judgments about the performance of a mayor, warden, or fire chief. And their anchors merely smile and opine their way through the day's headlines about murder, disease, weather, and sports.[10]

Other big-budget items include subscriptions to several news services, satellite transmission, and sophisticated mini-cams—all of which can be cut to save expenses. Unfortunately, large media conglomerates often cut back on its personnel in the newsroom in order to maximize profits. For example, in 2007, Telemundo announced plans to cut 700 jobs throughout its television operations. The local news organization was replaced by regional bureaus based in southern California and Texas.

Because of the lack of resources, local television news operations are sometimes forced to rely on video news packages (VNR), which are mailed to broadcast stations by public relations companies. But although VNRs look like news, they actually promote the company represented by the public relations firm. Jeff Pooley explains, "VNRs—which *USA Today* once described as 'Hamburger Helper for newscasters'—are a boon to cash-strapped newsrooms, which rarely identify the source of the footage."[11]

To illustrate, the public relations firm representing General Mills sent out a video "news" release announcing a university study citing the health benefits of whole oat grains. As the voice-over discussed the study, the visuals depicted a well-dressed woman pouring Cheerios into her crystal bowl—clearly not news footage but a staged shot. This public relations video was carried as part of news broadcasts around the country and, consequently, was interpreted by audiences as news.

In January 2004 it was discovered that the Bush administration had violated federal law by producing and distributing VNRs to local news outlets throughout the United States promoting its Medicare program, disguised as television news segments. The video stories contained all of the formulaic elements of broadcast news stories, including a voice-over by a person who signed off, "In Washington, I'm Karen Ryan reporting." Investigation

Figure 7.2
The typical organization of a TV news operation.

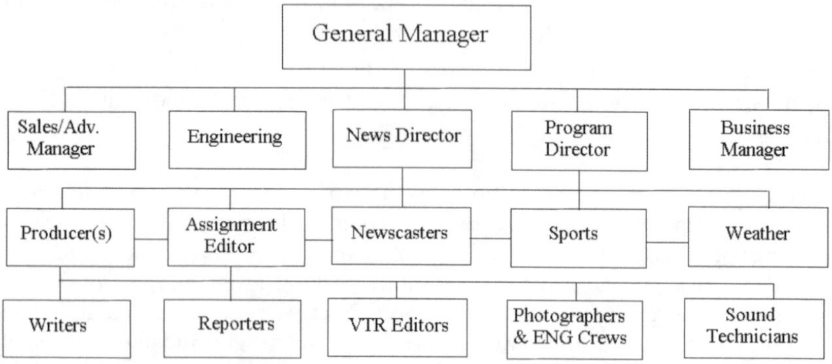

revealed that Karen Ryan was not a journalist but, instead, an employee of the public relations firm that the government hired to produce the VNRs. The Government Accountability Office, an investigative arm of Congress, has determined that videos such as these "constitute covert propaganda" because the government was not identified as the source of the materials and violated the prohibition on using taxpayer money for propaganda.[12] Thus, although the audience was expecting to receive an informative report about the Medicare program, they were instead presented with the Bush administration's "spin" about the program.

The organization of the newsroom. As the chief operating officer of the television station, the *general manager* is primarily responsible for the overall operation of the station, including long-term planning, community service, programming, and budgetary considerations. Ordinarily, the general manager is not involved in the day-to-day activities in the newsroom; however, if he or she becomes enamored of a pet project for the news, it usually finds its way on the air.

The *business manager* is responsible for all financial aspects of the news station. As such, he or she monitors the entire operation from a fiscal point of view, including costs associated with the news broadcast. The recommendations of the business manager on the purchase of newsgathering equipment, salaries for writers, reporters, and anchors can have a significant impact on the quality of the newscast.

The *news director* is directly responsible for the station's daily newscasts. However, according to Jim Willis and Diane B. Willis, the news director's mission to produce the news often is compromised by the pressure to maintain strong ratings:

Often the quality that the news director would like to have in the newscasts is deemed too expensive to produce by owners and upper management. One key reason this is true is that too many upper-level managers tend to look at newsroom expenses as costs rather than investments that will pay dividends later in a quality news product.... Often, too, the kind of patience a news director would like to exhibit to give his or her staff a chance to shine is cut short by the demands of upper management and owners to produce first-place newscasts sooner rather than later.

These tensions often cause news directors to leave their position and move on to other markets. The average length of employment of many news directors at any single station is often less than two years.[13]

The decision-making process in the broadcast newsroom can also influence the selection and presentation of information. The decision-making process in broadcast journalism involves the following considerations:

- Who is the initial gatekeeper for news stories?

While the assignment editor is generally the person responsible for assigning stories to reporters, in larger stations the initial gatekeeper may be a person in an entry-level position. This person, who opens the mail and answers the phones only passes along the information he or she considers newsworthy. Thus, questions to ask regarding the Assignment Editor include:

- What are the criteria for the selection of stories?
- Is the process of news selection arbitrary (one person) or consultative?
- Is there an appeals process?
- How is it determined which crews (reporters and camera people) are assigned to a story?
- How are deadlines for stories determined?

Time constraints can have a direct bearing on the quality of news coverage. For example, journalists often rely on particular sources for information based on the "rule of the Rolodex"—that is, once they have found a source who is not only a good interview but is also readily available, they often go back to this person again and again.

The decision-making process in the entertainment media industry has become so bureaucratic that it often affects the creative process. According to Larry Doyle, an idea first must clear a panel of executives—nearly an impossible task:

There are any number of logical theories to explain the bureaucratic swarming—Chinese-box conglomeration, network ownership by parts manufacturers; panic ... but still, it's an amazing thing to see. It is not unusual these days for a television series creator to have to answer to 10 or more executives.... "Can we start the story sooner?" "Can we raise the stakes?" "Can we make the lead more rootable?" they ask interchangeably, not moron so much as joylessly correct automaton.[14]

Media and Government Regulation

The relationship between a country's media system and its government's regulatory policy shapes the quality and diversity of media messages. Each country maintains its own policy with regard to the content and dissemination of information through the channels of mass communication.

In the United States, the First Amendment to the Constitution declares that "Congress shall make no laws abridging the freedom of speech, or of the press." Over the years, the term has been expanded to include any governmental body, local or federal. The First Amendment was established on the premise that the United States is a marketplace of ideas. All forms of ideas should be expressed, and each individual must be able to decide what is right and appropriate.

The Supreme Court has ruled that five categories of speech are not protected by the First Amendment: *obscenity, false advertising, "fighting words," inciting to riot*, and *defamation*. The challenge, then, is to determine the scope and the limits of these categories.

Legislating restrictions on speech is a complex and delicate matter. For instance, what people consider to be obscene changes over time. The original conception of obscenity referred to material which aroused "impure thoughts." This definition of obscenity is subjective; what is obscene to one person may not be to another.

Obscene material must be judged on the basis of the following criteria:

- "The material (taken as a whole) depicts or describes in a patently offensive manner sexual conduct specified by state or local law." However, the minimum standard of what is "patently offensive" is obscure.
- "An average person, applying contemporary community standards, looking at the work taken as a whole, determines that it appeals to the prurient interest." In this case, a court would apply a local, not a national community standard, which means that a work of art could be considered obscene in Little Rock but protected by the First Amendment in Chicago, Illinois. Thus, a community may pass its own laws declaring material obscene, but they must clearly define what constitutes obscenity.
- "The material taken as a whole lacks serious scientific, political, literary, or artistic value."

A legal precedent has been established (*Pope v. Illinois*, 1987), that a jury must use what a reasonable person under the circumstances would consider has scientific, literary, or artistic value as its guideline.

For material to be declared obscene, it must meet all three criteria. For example, in 1989, the City of Cincinnati charged the Cincinnati Museum of Art with six separate obscenity law violations for displaying a collection of photographs by photographer Robert Mapplethorpe. While the jury found that the photos met the first and second criteria, they ruled that the material did have artistic value, and, accordingly, the case was dismissed.

Unlike print media, broadcasting over the airwaves is regulated by the Federal Communications Commission (FCC). The rationale often given for allowing the government to regulate (and license) this form of speech is as follows:

- *Scarcity of the airwaves.*
  Because only a limited number of broadcast frequencies are available, a formal procedure for licensing and use of the airwaves is necessary.
- *Public ownership.*
  The airwaves are owned by the people. Broadcasters therefore are entrusted with using the airwaves, so long as they serve the public interest.
- *Characteristics of broadcast media.*
  The broadcasting media (radio and television) are pervasive. Because broadcast programming comes directly into the home, the public needs protection from misuse.

As a result, broadcast stations have an obligation to serve the public interest. In their study of the historical foundations of the First Amendment, Dwight L. Teeter, Jr. and Don A. Le Duc observe,

> In essence, the [Supreme Court] held that by accepting the privilege of using the limited and valuable public resource of spectrum space, each broadcast licensee also assumed an obligation to exercise this privilege for the benefit of the public; an obligation the FCC had the authority to enforce on behalf of the public.[15]

However, this imperative to serve the public interest is often in conflict with the pressure on stations to generate profits.

In order for stations to operate, they must be awarded a license from the FCC (the duration of a TV license is for five years; a radio license is good for seven years). The criteria for acceptance are as follows:

- *Threshold.* All applicants must meet minimum criteria for citizenship, character, financial and technical ability.
- *Comparative licensing.* Consideration is given to applicants who can provide the best service, as well as to groups which reflect cultural diversity. When a frequency becomes available, the FCC must hold public hearings to consider applications. However, there is generally an expectancy of renewal, giving the current license holder the advantage. Although the FCC is prohibited from censoring content, they are charged with maintaining the following programming standards:
- *Obscene or indecent programming.* Under current regulations, this type of programming is absolutely prohibited.
- *Personal attack & editorial.* The FCC establishes parameters for public debate on controversial issues and makes a distinction between personal attacks and political debate.

The development of new media technologies is redefining the philosophical basis for the regulation of broadcasting content. Unlike broadcast technology, cable television (as well as cable radio) can carry considerably more channels. In addition, cable television is a service that the audience purchases; we invite cable into our home, as opposed to the more pervasive nature of traditional broadcast technology.

Attorney Michael Kahn contends that these technological changes are having an impact on the content of the broadcast media:

> The whole intellectual framework for regulating radio and traditional television is based on radio and television technologies that are more than fifty years old. While the public may own the air, the cable companies own their cables. These days, it's cheaper to operate a local cable station than a local newspaper. As a result, reasons given for limiting the reach of the First Amendment in the regulation of radio and traditional TV don't easily transfer to cable TV. This is all good news for both consumers of news and producers of media, in that the basic First Amendment freedoms should be given more breathing space through cable technology than under the old regulation scheme of the FCC.[16]

Copyright

Copyright refers to the legal right of artists or their publishers to control the use and reproduction of their original works. However, enforcing national copyright laws—especially in an international arena—has been nearly impossible to enforce. International piracy of American films and music results in the loss of tens of thousands of jobs both inside and outside the industry and costs billions of dollars in lost wages, lost tax revenue, and diminished overall economic output. A study commissioned by the Motion Picture Association of America found that in 2005, movie companies lost $6.1 billion in revenues due to piracy.[17]

Efforts by the United States to pressure other countries to establish copyright laws have been a delicate matter. However, in 2007, the United States announced that it would impose strict tariffs on Chinese manufactured goods in retaliation for its violation of trade agreements. Chinese citizens are among the most blatant culprits of copyright infringements.

SUMMARY

Context refers to those surrounding elements that shape meanings and convey messages. Historical context, cultural context, and structure affect the content and style of a media presentation and thus provide keys to interpreting media messages.

Keys to Interpreting Media Messages: Context

Applying the following questions related to *Context* can provide insight into media messages:

SUMMARY

A. Historical Context

1. What does the media production tell us about the period in which it was produced?
    a. When was this media production first presented?
    b. What events were occurring when the presentation was produced?
    c. How has the media presentation been influenced by the events of the day?
    d. Does the media presentation comment on the events of the day?
    e. How does an understanding of these events furnish perspective into the presentation?
2. Does an understanding of historical events provide insight into the media presentation?
    a. Media presentations made during a particular historical period
        1) What events were occurring when the presentation was produced?
        2) What prior events led to the climate in which this media presentation was produced?
        3) How did people react to the production when it was first presented? Why?
            a) How do people react to the production today?
            b) How do you account for any differences in reaction?
        4) How does an understanding of these events furnish perspective into the presentation?
    b. Historical references
        1) Are there historical references in the media production?
        2) How does an understanding of these historical references affect your understanding of the media presentation?
3. Does a media presentation furnish perspective into current attitudes toward historical events?
4. Did the media presentation anticipate or foreshadow any political or historical events? Explain.
5. Did the presentation play any role in shaping the events of the day? Explain.
6. In the case of *entertainment* programming, is the dramatization an accurate portrait of events? Compare the presentation with historically accurate accounts of the event or period.
    a. Are the causes leading to the events in the presentation clear?
    b. What were the consequences of the dramatized events?
7. In the case of a *news* story, how much historical context has been provided? Where would you find the answers to these unanswered questions?

8. In countries with restricted civil liberties, does media programming comment on political and cultural issues in an indirect fashion? Explain.
9. Can a media program from a different era furnish perspective into the cultural attitudes, values, and behaviors of the period in which it was produced? Explain.
10. Systems Approach to Media History: Evolution of Media Systems
    a. In what ways does the history of a medium fit into the following Stages of Evolution:
        1) Inception stage
            a) Decentralization
            b) Innovation
            c) Impact of historical events on the development of the medium
        2) Embryonic stage
            a) Corporate sponsorship
            b) Expensive technology
            c) Affluent, elite audience
            d) Programming
                1) Innovative
                2) Elite
        3) Popular stage
            a) Rapid growth of audience
            b) Technology becomes more affordable
            c) Formulas and conventions of genres are established
            d) Broadcasting approach to programming
        4) Mature stage
            a) Bought by mega-corporations; profit incentive affects programming
            b) Narrowcasting/microcasting approach to programming
            c) Innovations in programming—to "break through the clutter"
    b. In what ways (if any) does the history of this medium *depart* from the patterns discussed in the chapter? What are the implications of these departures?
11. Systems Approach to Media History: Phases of Media Ecology
    a. In what ways does the history of a medium fit into the following phases?
        1) Phase I: New medium as threat
            a) Appropriating programming
            b) Siphoning audience base

2) Phase II: Specialization
   a) Technology
   b) Programming
   c) Target audience
3) Phase III: Assimilation
   a) Technical convergence
   b) Programming
   c) Consolidation of ownership

b. In what ways (if any) does the history of these media *depart* from the patterns discussed in the chapter? What are the implications of these departures?

B. Cultural Context

1. Media & Popular Culture
   a. In what ways does the media presentation *reflect*:
      1) Cultural attitudes
      2) Values
      3) Behaviors
      4) Preoccupations
      5) Myths
      6) Cultural changes
      7) Attitudes toward groups
   b. In what ways does the media presentation *reinforce*:
      1) Cultural attitudes
      2) Values
      3) Behaviors
      4) Preoccupations
      5) Myths
   c. In what ways does the media presentation *shape*:
      1) Cultural attitudes
      2) Values
      3) Behaviors
      4) Preoccupations
      5) Myths
2. *Worldview:* What kind of world is depicted in the media presentation?
   a. What culture or cultures populate this world?
      1) What kinds of people populate this world?
      2) What is the ideology of this culture?

b. What do we know about the people who populate this world?
    1) Are characters presented in a stereotypical manner?
    2) What does this tell us about the cultural stereotype of this group?
c. Does this world present an optimistic or pessimistic view of life?
    1) Are the characters in the presentation happy?
    2) Do the characters have a *chance* to be happy?
d. Are people in control of their own destinies?
    1) Is there a supernatural presence in this world?
    2) Are the characters under the influence of other people?
e. What hierarchy of values is in operation in this worldview?
    1) What embedded values can be found in the production?
    2) What values are embodied in the characters?
    3) What values prevail through the resolution?
    4) What does it mean to be a success in this world?
        a) How does a person succeed in this world?
        b) What kinds of behavior are rewarded in this world?

C. Structure

1. What are the ownership patterns within the media industry?
    a. What are the ownership patterns within the particular media system you are examining? (e.g., television, film, radio)
    b. Who owns the production company that has produced the presentation you are examining? (e.g., television station, newspaper, film company)
2. Does the ownership of the media presentation have an impact on its content?
    a. Support of status quo
    b. Homogeneity of content
    c. Programming for profit
    d. Cross-promotion
3. Does government regulation affect the media presentation?
4. What is the internal structure of the media organization responsible for producing the media presentation? How does this internal structure influence content?
    a. What are the resources of the production company?
    b. What is the organizational framework of the production company?
    c. What is the process of decision-making in the production company?

NOTES

1. Frederic M. Sherer and David Ross, *Industrial Market Structure and Economic Performance*, 3rd ed. (Boston: Houghton Mifflin, 1990).

2. Ben Bagdikian, *The Media Monopoly*, 5th ed. (Boston: Beacon Press, 1997), 36.

3. Max Frankel, "What's Happened to The Media?," *New York Times Magazine* (March 21, 1999), 38–40.

4. Jeff Leeds, "Amid Turbulence at CBS Radio, an Old Hand Is Back," *New York Times*, April 16, 2007, C4.

5. Bill Carter, "Shrinking Network TV Audiences Set Off Alarm and Reassessment," *New York Times*, November 22, 1998 (http://nytimes.com).

6. Rick Lyman and Laura M. Holson, "Holidays Turn Into Hollywood's Hot Season," *New York Times*, November 24, 2002.

7. Gail Pennington, "Newschannel 5: Where the Fluff Comes First," *St. Louis Post-Dispatch*, November 18, 2004, F01.

8. Jeff MacGregor, "Why It Takes 400 Pages to Tell You What's On," *New York Times*, October 11, 1998.

9. Eric Klinenberg, interview on Democracy Now!, January 26, 2007 (www.democracynow.com).

10. Frankel, "What's Happened to The Media?"

11. Jeff Pooley, "Hamburger Helper for Newscasters," *Brill's Content* (December 1998/January 1999), 46.

12. John Files, "Bush's Drug Videos Broke Law, Accountability Office Decides," *New York Times*, January 7, 2005, A16.

13. Jim Willis and Diane B. Willis, *New Directions in Media Management* (Boston: Allyn and Bacon, 1993), 198–199.

14. Larry Doyle, "Executive Privilege," *New York Times Magazine*, February 28, 1999, 31.

15. Michael Kahn (attorney, Stinson, Mag & Fizzell), interview by author, June 6, 1999.

16. Ibid.

17. Steven McElroy, ed., "Financial Impact of Film Piracy," *New York Times*, September 30, 2006, B8.

SECTION

3

FRAMEWORK

CHAPTER

8

FRAMEWORK

- Introduction
- Plot

INTRODUCTION

The introduction often foreshadows what to expect in the course of a media presentation. The opening of a film, television, or radio program acquaints the audience with the primary characters, plot outline, and the worldview of the programming. For example, the initial scene in *Rocky* (1976) begins in the midst of a boxing match between two club fighters. The fight is being held in a church recreation hall. A picture of Christ is suspended over the ring, underscoring that that this is not merely a physical conflict but a spiritual struggle as well, requiring faith, courage, and conviction.

Rocky is an awkward boxer whose fate appears certain; he will lose. As the fight progresses, however, Rocky's determination, heart, and spirit enable him to transcend his physical limitations. This introductory bout, like the film itself, ends in triumph. The remainder of the film is essentially an elaboration of its first five minutes. Even though he loses that fight, he wins a rematch and prevails.

Title

The *title* of a media presentation often encapsulates the essential meaning of the media presentation. Due to the competitive nature of the media industry, newspaper headlines, advertising slogans, political mottos, song and movie titles also must generate interest in the presentation. Some titles suggest thematic concerns; others titillate with promises of sex and violence. Even titles for film sequels, such as *Mission Impossible: III* or *Clerks II* announce that the audience should expect more of the same formulaic characters, action, and plot.

Indeed, the title is so critical that before Hollywood film producer Roger Corman would launch a film project, he would first conduct market research to find a film title that would catch the interest and imagination of the audience, such as *Naked Paradise* and *Attack of the Crab Monsters* (1957). He then created an entire film around these titles.[1]

Illogical Premise

A premise refers to the initial circumstances, situation, or assumption which serves as the point of origin in the narrative. A description of premise usually answers the question, "What is this program about?"

According to Samuel Taylor Coleridge, our response to fiction is determined by a "willing suspension of disbelief," in which the audience accepts the premise of the program, no matter how outlandish. This suspension of disbelief enables us to participate in the fantasy world of *Star Wars*, which existed "long ago and far away," or thrill as dinosaurs come to life in *Jurassic Park*.

Once the initial premise has been accepted, the remainder of the narrative progresses in a logical fashion. To illustrate, examine the following premise carefully:

> A scientist in a galaxy far from Earth discovers that his planet faces imminent destruction. He does not have the time to save himself or his wife; however, he is able to construct a small rocket for his infant son. The rocket, carrying the boy, lifts off just before the planet explodes.
>
> The rocket finds its way to Earth. Significantly, because of the Earth's atmosphere, the boy has super powers; he can fly, has super strength and hearing, and never needs a haircut.

Once the audience has accepted this extraordinary premise for *Superman*, the remainder of the narrative proceeds naturally: the boy assumes a human identity, moves to the city, finds a job, and fights crime.

In some cases, the audience accepts, without question, a premise with ideological overtones. For example, the premise of police shows like *Homicide* assumes the following: 1) that we live in a dangerous world; 2) that members of lower classes and African Americans are predators who pose a threat to the dominant culture; 3) that the heroes know (without a trial) who is innocent and who is guilty; and 4) what is needed is a strong, undeterred authoritarian presence to remedy these problems. The reactionary political ideology behind this premise, in which civil liberties are sacrificed in the name of law and order, is made to look like an appealing option in this turbulent world.

Advertising frequently relies on an illogical premise to sell products. Once its premise has been accepted, an ad can be very persuasive. For instance, one television commercial begins with a shot of a door, with the title, "The Ponds Institute" etched on the glass. The door swings open, and the audience is thrust into the midst of a group of people in lab coats walking purposefully as they conduct their business. A voice-over announces that "Here at the Ponds Institute, we are concerned with combating the effects of aging on the skin." This scenario instills us with confidence in Ponds products. Upon reflection, however, several questions arise regarding the premise:

- Exactly where is the Ponds Institute?
- Can you get a degree from the Ponds Institute?
- Is it located near the Sassoon Academy?
- What kind of research is conducted at the Ponds Institute?
- What kind of methodology is employed in its research?
- Can we obtain a copy of the results of the research?

Thus, as you begin to watch a film, see an ad, or read the newspaper, examine the underlying assumptions behind the premise of the presentation. At that point, you can make a conscious decision whether or not to suspend your disbelief.

PLOT

"Let me tell you about the movie I just saw."

A plot is a series of actions planned by the artist to build upon one another, with an introduction, body, and conclusion. The foundation of plot is *conflict*. Characters are initially confronted with a dilemma, which is resolved by the end of the story.

Explicit Content

One way to approach the study of plot is through an analysis of *explicit* and *implicit* content.

Explicit content refers to events and activities in the plot that are displayed through visible action. The audience constructs meaning by selecting the essential pieces of explicit information in the story, which answers the following question: "What was the program about?" To illustrate, consider the following scenario:

A man bops another fellow over the head with a bat, takes his money, and flees. Later in the program he is caught and carted off to jail.

The audience constructs meaning by selecting the essential pieces of explicit information in the story. In this example, five distinct actions are described: 1) clubbing; 2) theft; 3) flight; 4) apprehension; and 5) incarceration.

In his study of children's comprehension of television content, W. Andrew Collins found that young children typically have difficulty remembering explicit details and identifying important scenes:

- Eighth graders recalled 92 percent of the scenes that adults had judged as essential to the plot.
- Fifth graders recalled 84 percent of the scenes that adults had judged as essential to the plot.
- Second graders recalled an average of only 66 percent of the scenes that adults had judged as essential to the plot.[2]

According to Collins, young children's limited grasp of explicit story material impairs their ability to interpret media content:

> Young children fail to comprehend observed actions and events in an adult-like way because they arrive at different interpretations of the various actors' plans or intentions.... Thus, it is possible that second and third graders take away not only a less complete understanding of the program than fifth and eighth graders do, they may also be perceiving the content of the program somewhat *differently* because they retain (and work off of) a different set of cues.[3]

Significantly, the standard against which the children's performance is measured consists of a sample of *adults*. However, there is no guarantee that these adults have successfully identified all of the essential scenes. Although adults are generally more knowledgeable than children, they are not necessarily informed or interested in all topics. In addition, because adults are frequently distracted by competing activities, they are often unable to devote their full attention to a media presentation and may miss essential scenes.

Moreover, reaching the age of 21 does not necessarily *guarantee* intellectual or emotional maturity. Some adults have an impaired ability to identify essential content. For instance, cult figure Charles Manson claimed that popular media instructed him to lead his "family" on a series of mass murders. Manson selected certain portions of the Bible and the Beatles as "essential content," devising a warped but quite intricate rationale to justify his monstrous crimes.

As mentioned in the discussion on Audience Reception Theory (see Chapter 4), a number of factors influence how an individual processes media content:

- *Background*
  How much does an individual already know about the subject?

- *Interest level*
  How interested in the subject is the member of the audience? How attentive is he/she?
- *Predisposition*
  What is the attitude of the audience member toward the subject (positive or negative) going into the conversation?
- *Priorities*
  What issues are of particular concern to the audience member? Why?
- *Demographic Profile*
  National origin
  Gender
  Race
  Ethnic origin
  Age
  Education
  Income
- *Psychological Profile*
  Self-concept
  Primary relationships
  Significant life experiences
  Ways of relating to others
  Ways of dealing with emotions
  Personal aspirations
- *Communications Environment*
  What is the size of the audience?
  What are they *doing* while they are receiving the information?
- *Stage of Development*
  At what stage of development is the individual?
- Chronological
- Cognitive
- Emotional

Implicit Content

Let's re-examine the scintillating scene that was presented earlier in our discussion on explicit content:

A man bops another fellow over the head with a bat, takes his money, and flees. Later in the program he is caught and carted off to jail.

In addition to the essential events (i.e., explicit content), a number of questions remain:

Why did the first man hit the second fellow? Was there a prior relationship between the two men? Why does the first man run? Why is he punished at the end of the story?

Implicit content refers to those elements of plot that remain under the surface:

- What are the *motives* behind characters' decisions and actions? Motive answers the question *why* the characters behaved as they did.
- What are the *connections between events* that occur in the plot?
- What are the *connections between the characters* that occur in the plot?
- Are the *consequences* for characters' actions made clear?

W. Andrew Collins's study revealed that children had even greater difficulty identifying *implicit* content than they had deciphering the *explicit* content:

- Eighth graders recalled 77 percent of the items that adults had agreed upon.
- Fifth graders recalled 67 percent of the items that adults had agreed upon.
- Second graders had an overall score of fewer than half (47 percent) of the items that adults had agreed upon.[4]

These results suggest that young children are developmentally incapable of recognizing the relationships between events. Interestingly, the second grade girls outperformed the boys, "... who appear to be performing at about chance level (between 30 percent and 40 percent) on this level of inference."

Thus, despite the best intentions of some media communicators to attach a moral to programs, children may be receiving a message about a world without consequence. And once again, the standard of measurement in the study is the highly subjective comprehension level of adults. Some adults may also be unclear about the cause-effect relationship of events depicted in the media.

To further complicate the issue, many media programs present a world seemingly free of consequence. Heroes in action films routinely violate laws in the name of a higher moral good. High-speed car chases, destruction of property, and assault without just cause would not go unpunished in real life but are somehow justifiable in media-carried content.

Subplots

Narratives often contain secondary stories, called *subplots*. Subplots may initially appear to be unrelated to one another. However, because the characters operate within the same worldview, the subplots may comment on different aspects of the same thematic concerns. Consequently, identifying connections between the subplots can furnish perspective into the themes and messages in the presentation.

To illustrate, *As Good as It Gets* (1997) is a film that features three seemingly unrelated subplots, revolving around each of the major characters: Melvin Udall (Jack Nicholson) is a misanthropic, obsessive-compulsive writer, whose only pleasurable contact with another human being is Carol

MEDIA LITERACY TIPS

TAKING NOTES ON FILM/TELEVISION PROGRAMMING

Explicit and Implicit Content

Identifying *explicit content* is an essential first step in the thorough and systematic analysis of media messages. The most effective way to identify the explicit content is to take notes during the presentation. Record relevant scenes and significant bits of dialogue. Making vague generalizations will not suffice. You must refer to specific detail from the narrative to support your position.

Unlike print, which provides a text on which to reflect, this note-taking process is particularly tricky when viewing film or television. You are writing in darkness, recording what just occurred while new events are unfolding. However, as you become more comfortable with this process, you will become more comfortable with it and will be prepared to present a clear, defensible analysis of media programming.

Screening a film or television program for analytical purposes requires active involvement on your part. It is important that you take notes, so that you can make sense of the film after the screening.

As you screen a film or TV program, take notes on *Explicit Content*:

I. Background Information
   A. Title
   B. Year
   C. Director
   D. Actors
   E. Names of significant characters
   F. Other significant information (e.g., Studio, Producer)
II. Note significant scenes
   A. Essential events in these scenes
   B. Significant bits of dialogue

After the screening, review your notes to identify *Implicit Content:*

Implicit content consists of those elements of plot that remain under the surface.

I. What were the motives behind the behaviors of the characters? (Why did the characters behave in the manner that they did?)
II. What were the connections between the significant events in the narrative?
III. Was there any foreshadowing of events?
   Significant events that reoccur later in the narrative?
   Significant dialogue that recurs later in the narrative?
IV. What was the relationship between:
   A. The significant events in the narrative?
   B. The characters in the narrative?

Does this examination of explicit and implicit content provide any perspective into themes or messages in the media presentation? Explain.

Connelly (Helen Hunt), the waitress who serves him breakfast every morning. Melvin also derives some pleasure from tormenting his neighbor Simon Bishop (Greg Kinnear), a gay artist. For instance, annoyed by the yapping of Simon's dog Verdell (Jill the Dog), Melvin stuffs the pooch down the laundry chute.

But while these three characters differ markedly from one another, their situations are similar: each one exists in a state of isolation.

Melvin's isolation is largely self-imposed; he is a misanthrope who has only contempt for other human beings. In addition, Melvin has a compulsive disorder that makes him phobic about order. This makes it difficult for him to interact with people, who are, by nature, complicated and messy—both physically and emotionally.

Carol is a character whose life has been shaped by circumstances. Her primary focus is caring for her sickly son. She is lonely, poor, and must concentrate on survival.

Simon is a successful artist. But after he is brutally beaten, Simon finds himself in need of financial and emotional support. Simon discovers that he is terribly alone—he has been ostracized by his parents because of his sexual orientation and even loses the affection of Verdell to Melvin.

In the early stages of the film, the stories of these three disparate characters are unconnected. However, after Simon is beaten and hospitalized, Melvin is left to care for Simon's dog Verdell and eventually, with Carol's help, to help Simon as well.

The interweaving of these subplots enables writer/director James L. Brooks to comment about the value of community. Each of these characters was leading a life of quiet desperation, needing help and support. But in the process of providing support for others, they each find joy and peace in their own lives.

Affective Response

We often experience a range of emotions while reading a novel or watching a film. According to Walt Disney, the true Disney experience—and a key to its success—is that the films put children in touch with their emotions:

> What is the difference between our product and the other? ... Giving it "heart." Others haven't understood the public. We developed a psychological approach to everything we do here. We seem to know when to "tap the heart." Others have hit the intellect. We can hit them in an emotional way. Those who appeal to the intellect only appeal to a very limited group.[5]

To illustrate, *101 Dalmatians* (1961 and 1996) touches a range of very intense feelings in the young audience. First, children watch the formation of a family, as two Dalmatians (Pongo and Perdita) meet, fall in love, and raise 15 puppies. The next few scenes are filled with warmth and affection, featuring the antics of the puppies. At this point, a villainess (Cruella De Vil) appears. The young audience reacts with sadness, grief, and anger, as the puppies are kidnapped and imprisoned in an old mansion. There they wait to be slaughtered, so that their fur can be converted to a coat for Cruella. But by the conclusion of the film, as the puppies are rescued and order is restored, the children experience an emotional catharsis. These feelings of relief and happiness complete the emotional cycle.

Within this context, a media presentation can have a therapeutic function, making us feel alive. Joseph Campbell explains,

> People say that what we're all seeking is a meaning for life. I don't think that's what we're really seeking. I think that what we're seeking is an experience of being alive, so that our life experiences on the purely physical plane will have resonances within our own innermost being and reality, so that we actually feel the rapture of being alive.[6]

Psychologist Barbara Thompson declares, "The scariness (of horror movies) makes us feel like kids again. What kid isn't scared of the monster beneath the bed? I remember racing up the basement stairs because I was frightened to be down there alone."[7]

In addition, media presentations can provide a healthy emotional release for audiences. When we watch scary movies, the theater becomes a safe place to confront our wildest fears. Wes Craven, director of the Scream horror films, observes,

> It's like boot camp for the psyche. In real life human beings are packaged in the flimsiest of packages, threatened by real and sometimes horrifying dangers, events like the Columbine (school massacre). But the narrative form puts those fears into a manageable series of events. It gives us a way of thinking rationally about our fears.[8]

Media communicators often strive to elicit an emotional reaction from the audience for dramatic purposes. "Show, don't tell" is an adage that can be applied to media presentations. That is, rather than simply talking about a subject, it is always more effective to arrange for the audience to experience emotions that enrich their understanding of the content.

Indeed, one particularly effective dramatic device is for the media communicator to generate the same emotional reactions in the audience members that are being experienced by the characters on-screen. For instance, in the 1956 version of *Invasion of the Body Snatchers* (see discussion, Chapter 5), director Don Siegel begins with the town doctor (a prototypical 1950s authority figure) paying a house call on a family. A boy runs to the car, screaming, "My mother's not really my mother." The camera cuts to an emotionless zombie, who calls to her "son" to come to the house. This revelation is particularly chilling to children who (according to proponents of psychoanalytic attachment theory) often suffer from fear of separation from their parents.[9] Young audience members project these primal feelings back onto the screen, making the film that much more terrifying.

The effective media communicator has learned to anticipate how the audience should react at each point of the presentation and then strives to elicit that particular response. As an example, Hollywood director George Cukor, whose work included *The Women*, *Holiday*, and *Dinner at Eight*, was not known for his technical expertise. Instead, he surrounded himself with the best available cast and crew and, stationing himself by the camera, acted as his *own* audience while the action unfolded. If he was moved by the scene, he was satisfied. If not, he would gather his experts around him to discuss strategies that would produce the intended response.

Because the story is geared toward the climax, the feelings that we experience in the process often fade from memory. However, one useful way to approach the analysis of media presentations is to think along with the media communicator. How does the media communicator want you to be feeling at particular points in the plot? Sad? Happy? Scared? Insecure? Envious?

The next step involves investigating *why* the media communicator is attempting to elicit that intended emotional response from the audience. Advertisers and politicians frequently use affective appeals to influence the attitudes and behaviors of the audience. Advertisements which display animals or babies are intended to evoke a warm response, which the media communicator hopes will be transferred to the product. Political figures routinely arrange for "photo opportunities" with children, elderly people, and their own family members in hopes that we will feel positively toward them and, as a result, support them and their policies.

Moreover, paying attention to your affective responses during a media program can furnish valuable perspective into your personal belief system. A good illustration can be found in Charlotte Brontë's novel *Jane Eyre*. Jane is a governess who goes to work in the household of a gentleman named Rochester. The two fall in love and plan to marry. However, as the wedding day approaches, Jane becomes aware of strange and disturbing noises in the attic. It is clear that whatever is in the attic is some dreaded secret which, if uncovered, might jeopardize their future together.

Should Jane clear up this mystery before she weds Rochester, or should she marry Rochester and *then* make a trip to the attic? Is marriage an institution of refuge, where people blindly seek comfort regardless of consequence? Should people marry for security or love (or both)? What is the role of trust in relationships? Your emotional response can serve as the basis for critical self-analysis.

NOTES

1. Philip di Franco, ed., *The Movie World of Roger Corman* (New York: Chelsea House Publishers, 1979).

2. W. Andrew Collins, "Children's Comprehension of Television Content," in *Children Communicating*, ed. Ellen Wartella (Beverly Hills, CA: Sage Publications, 1979), 27.

3. Ibid., 28.

4. Ibid., 29.

5. Bob Thomas, *Walt Disney: An American Original* (New York: Simon and Schuster, 1976), 278.

6. Joseph Campbell, with Bill Moyers, *The Power of Myth* (New York: Doubleday, 1988), 5.

7. Holly Selby, "Eeek! Why People Love to Be Scared (But Not Too Scared) by Films," *Baltimore Sun,* September 15, 2000, E3.

8. David Blum, "Embracing Fear as Fun to Practice for Reality," *New York Times*, October 30, 1999.

9. R. W. Zaslow, "Bonding and Attachment," *Encyclopedia of Psychology*, ed. Raymond J. Corsini (New York: Wiley and Sons, 1984), 160–162.

8, 9, 12, 13

CHAPTER

9

FRAMEWORK

- Genre
- Conclusion

GENRE

We have all watched dozens of situation comedies on television. But what exactly *is* a situation comedy? What elements are common to all of these programs? These shared characteristics make up the *genre* of situation comedies.

The word genre itself simply means "order." A genre is a standardized format which is distinctive and easily identifiable. Examples include horror films, romances, sci-fi, situation comedies, westerns, and the evening news. A genre is not confined to one medium. For instance, at one time or another, westerns have appeared in print, on radio, television, and film.

Formula

Genres are characterized by *formula;* that is, patterns in *premise, structure*, and *plot, characters, setting,* and *trappings*. Individual programs generally conform to the formula of the genre. As John Cawelti observes, "Individual works are ephemeral, but the formula lingers on, evolving and changing with time, yet still basically recognizable."[1]

Formulas provide cues about how the audience should respond to media content. Film critic Neal Gabler explains,

> You show an audience an attractive young man and woman who playfully bicker at the beginning of a movie and it roots for them to wind up together at the end. Or show a bully pushing around a decent fellow and viewers root for the latter to defeat the former. The audience reacts not because it knows the formula—it reacts because the formula knows the audience.[2]

In discussing the formulaic aspects of genre, it might be useful to focus on the genre of the TV situation comedy (or sitcom).

Formulaic Premise. How would you describe a typical sitcom?

A *formulaic premise* refers to an identifiable situation which characterizes a genre. A formulaic premise answers the question, "What is this genre about?" For example, Lawrence E. Mintz describes the sitcom premise in the following manner: "a half-hour series focused on episodes involving recurring characters within the same premise. (That is, each week we encounter the same people in essentially the same setting)."[3]

As its name suggests, the comedy is generated through everyday situations rather than stand-up monologues. The stories feature the characters coping with everyday life (e.g., Homer Simpson gets a promotion). Contending with these everyday situations enables the characters (and, by extension, the audience) to put life's minor irritations and problems into perspective. The cumulative message behind the sitcom premise is that life is a maze, filled with traps. However, these situations are always relatively minor and can be resolved within a 30-minute episode.

Formulaic Structure. A genre generally fits within an identifiable, unvarying *structure*, or organizational pattern. In many genres (including the sitcom), the standard formula is order/chaos/order. The initial order of the story is disrupted almost immediately. The chaotic stage takes up the majority of the program and is the source of much of its humor. The status quo is finally restored in the conclusion. The cumulative message behind this structure is that problems are all solvable, and justice always prevails.

Formulaic Plot. Only a finite number of general *plots*, or stories, appear within a given genre. As an example, the sitcom operates according to a finite number of plot possibilities. For instance, episodes of the popular NBC sitcom *Scrubs* generally fall into the following plot categories:

- An outsider intrudes on the community of *Scrubs*
- Events create internal problems within the community of *Scrubs*
- A member of the *Scrubs* community lies or deceives others and suffers the consequences
- A misunderstanding disrupts the *Scrubs* community
- Events affect a character, who finds comfort and support from the *Scrubs* community
- Romance affects a character and, consequently, the entire *Scrubs* community

Although these general plots are predictable, the embellishments, detail, and small nuances *within* these plots keep each episode fresh and interesting.

Many of the plots revolve around misunderstandings between the characters. Communication is clearly valued as a means of both preventing and resolving problems.

Plot complications also occur due to acts of deception. A cumulative message of formulaic plots in sitcoms involves the value of truthfulness. Sitcom characters do not murder each other. Instead, they tell "white lies" or are guilty of some minor transgression. However, deception never pays in the world of the sitcom; the characters always get caught.

Another common locus of conflict is excess *hubris*, or pride. Characters who possess too much pride and ambition disrupt their world and become isolated from the members of their community. These characters are not evil, for evil does not exist in the world of the sitcom; they are simply misguided. Due to an inflated sense of self, they make errors in judgment. At the conclusion of the episode, the character's *hubris* is exposed to the other characters (and to the audience as well).

Another cumulative message found in formulaic sitcom plots is related to *identity*. Know yourself and be satisfied with who you are. Characters who have violated the moral code of sitcoms by trying to be someone they're not suffer the consequences. Ultimately, self-knowledge and personal happiness are more important than achievement and material gain.

A *conventional storyline* is a recurring incident that is characteristic of a particular genre. Examples include the gun duel in a western, the wedding scene in a romance, or the car chase in the action genre. Because conventional storylines appear so frequently in a particular genre, these incidents assume a meaning that is commonly associated with the genre. Consequently, a conventional storyline in a program can be used to convey messages.

For instance, the *perp walk*, in which a suspect is shown walking into the police station in the custody of the police, is a conventional storyline in television news. Ray Suarez observes that the perp walk sends the message that the suspect is guilty:

> More than merely a visual cliche, the perp walk has helped to collapse the distinctions between suspect and criminal. My voice in countless narrations said all the right words—"accused" and "alleged" and "according to police"—but the pictures said "guilty," "guilty" and "guilty." The visuals became part of our nightly melodrama, our dispatches from the war zone, flashed to an increasingly suburban audience. The suspects, shorn of their presumption of innocence by the exigencies of television and the public relations aims of the police, could not refuse to participate in the ritual.[4]

Stock Characters. Stock characters appear so frequently in a particular genre that they have become instantly recognizable when they appear in a program. For instance, when we watch a western, we are already acquainted with the hero's sidekick; we have met the old coot a thousand times before. As a result, the audience immediately is drawn into the story. These stock characters frequently mirror cultural stereotypes. The familiarity of these characters indicates the degree to which this stereotype is accepted in our culture. Indeed, much of the humor of these characters is derived from the exaggerated mannerisms and appearance of these stereotypes. Other examples of stock characters include: the honest friend, the talkative old woman, the suave gambler, the simple country boy, the blundering drunkard, the super sleuth, the eccentric scientist, and the folksy TV weatherman.

Sitcom characters must be generally friendly and likable. Carl Reiner observes, "Warm is an important word. You laugh easier when funny things are happening to nice people."[5] It is permissible for characters to be eccentric and annoying, however, so long as they are not malicious. In this world, people are basically good. The principal characters recognize the essential goodness beneath a character's imperfect exterior and accept them because they are a part of their community—at home or at work.

Formulaic Setting. A formulaic setting refers to a standard background against which the action takes place. A limited number of sets are employed in any sitcom. Most of the activity centers around the interior, with only brief exterior shots used to establish the setting. Shifts in the formulaic setting often reflect corresponding changes in the culture:

- In the 1950s, sitcoms like *Leave It to Beaver* took place in the home, reflecting (and reinforcing) the American cultural myth of the conventional family structure.
- In the 1970s, sitcoms like *The Mary Tyler Moore Show* moved to the workplace, reflecting the breakup of the nuclear family.
- In the 1990s, the conventional setting shifted to a public hangout, such as the coffee shop in *Friends*.

The setting connects the characters, who come from very diverse backgrounds. For instance, the title of the sitcom *The Office* derives from the workplace, which is where nearly all of the action occurs. In the series, the locations within the set correspond to particular behaviors. For instance, the water cooler is the place in which gossip is exchanged; the lunchroom a place in which interactions between characters occurs, and the boss's office is a locale in which differences in status between manager Michael Scott (Steve Carell) and his employees become very obvious.

Conventional Trappings. Conventional trappings are props and costumes that appear so often that they become identifiable with a genre. These trappings furnish the audience with cues about people, events, and situations in the presentation. For instance, the white coats and surgical masks worn by the cast of *ER* signals that these characters are doctors.

The appearance of tents and jeeps in a film like *Letters from Iwo Jima* (2006) signals that a presentation is part of the war genre. And westerns like the HBO series *Deadwood* are recognizable by the appearance of horses, six-guns, boots, ten-gallon hats, and saloons, complete with swinging doors, a long bar, gambling tables, and saloon girls.

The trappings of a genre may change over time. For instance, the western appears to have disappeared as a popular TV genre. However, it can be argued that the police show has emerged as an updated version of the western. Although the urban landscape has replaced the frontier, and the car has supplanted the horse, the function, characters, and essential premise remain the same. The lawman still fights crime, even though the outlaws are rustling drugs instead of cattle.

Variations in the Formula. In order to appear distinctive and fresh, *generic programming* (i.e., programming belonging to a particular genre) often features slight variations in elements of the formula. Areas of variation within the formula include:

- *Characters.* In some generic programs, the main variation is a change in the gender, age, or sexual orientation of the characters. For instance, discussing the addition of two new "youth dramas" to its 2004–2005 television season, Jordan Levin, chief executive of the WB network observed, "It's a reinvention of the family-dynasty soap like 'Dallas,' 'Dynasty,' 'Falcon Crest,' by aging it down."[6]
- *Setting.* In 2004, with *Las Vegas*, NBC loaded its fall schedule with shows that were derivative in setting, including *LAX* (set in an airport, not a casino) and *Hawaii.*

But even those works that challenge the parameters of the genre are highly conscious of the formula. For instance, *Arrested Development* departed from the usual sitcom formulas. The series bounces off of the sitcom formula, playing with the audience's expectations for comedic purposes. As an example, the end of an episode often includes a "teaser" that previews the next week's episode. However, the teaser often turns out to be a stand-alone joke, made funnier because of the audience's anticipation of a new plot development.

Function

Genres share common manifest objectives. For instance, the primary function of the situation comedy is to entertain or amuse the audience. But in addition, a genre may contain shared latent functions. The sitcom is a morality play that offers instruction to the audience. Garry Marshall (producer of *Happy Days*, *Laverne and Shirley*, and *Mork & Mindy*) observes, "We tried to be useful. We did shows about mental health, about diabetes, about death, blindness, and epilepsy. Tolerance. That's what we tried to teach. Be nice to each other."[7]

In addition, genres touch a range of primal feelings within the individual. The horror genre arouses feelings of fear. Comedies permit the audience to laugh. Action films tap into feelings of anger. Tragedies make us cry. In this era in which people (particularly males) are not encouraged to confront their emotions, media presentations put people in touch with their feelings. Consequently, genres serve a therapeutic function, providing a very healthy release for audiences.

Evolution of a Genre

Tracing the evolution of a genre can provide considerable perspective into corresponding changes in the culture. To illustrate, 1950s soap operas sometimes alluded to "the other woman" (accompanied by the single, sinister note of an organ). Today, entire programs are dedicated to "the other woman," signaling the culture's more permissive sexual mores, as well as society's preoccupation with sex.

The situation comedy of the 1950s reflected the cultural life of the period. After the disruption of World War II, the United States was preoccupied with a return to normalcy. Consequently, the biggest challenge facing the 1950s sitcom characters was change. For example, in *Leave It to Beaver,* disruptive elements like puberty and girlfriends threatened the sanctity of the Cleaver household. However, each episode concluded with the comforting return to normalcy. Within this context, the 1950s sitcoms featured a zany character who was surrounded by a rational supporting cast. For instance, much of the humor in *I Love Lucy* stemmed from Lucy's efforts to fit into a normal world.

The setting for *I Love Lucy* was the home. Lucy's world consisted of her husband and child and her neighbors, Fred and Ethel Mertz. One of the formulaic plots consisted of Lucy's efforts to break into show business. Ricky Ricardo refused to allow his wife to realize her ambition and, within the context of the show, with good reason. Lucy was deluded; she had no talent and was incapable of functioning on her own. (In actuality, Lucy was an enormously talented comedienne and the star of the show.) But in order to realize her dream, Lucy willfully disobeyed her husband. Ricky would inevitably get wind of this deceit and "teach her a lesson." The message was clear: Lucy's place was in the home.

By the 1970s, the formula of the sitcom had shifted, reflecting corresponding changes in the culture. In an era characterized by cultural change, the role of the central figure was to provide stability in what had become an absurd and chaotic world. Thus, the central figures such as Mary Richards (*The Mary Tyler Moore Show*), Alex Rieger (*Taxi*) and Barney Miller were rational characters surrounded by a zany cast. Change was now accepted as inevitable. The supporting characters became the source of the humor in these series. The chief concern became how to maintain a sense of balance in the face of change.

Sitcoms such as *All in the Family* began to deal with topics of cultural concern, such as racism and homosexuality. Female characters like Mary Tyler Moore were depicted succeeding on their own, without the support of a male. Moreover, the family at home had been supplanted by the "family" at work, reflecting the breakup of the family and emergence of the workplace as the center of activity. The crew at *WKRP in Cincinnati* may have bickered among themselves, but they rallied when a member of their community needed support.

By the 1980s, the genre of the situation comedy evolved into a number of different subgenres due, in part, to the narrowcasting of the audience into distinct categories. Rick Mitz identified seven subgenres within the situation comedy format: l) Domestic sitcoms; 2) Kidcoms; 3) Couplecoms; 4) SciFicoms; 5) Corncoms; 6) Ethnicoms; 7) Careercoms; and 8) Historycoms.[8]

Each subgenre has a slightly different setting, cast of characters, and specific plotlines. For instance, a couplecom like *Mad About You* took place in a domestic setting, revolved around a young married couple, and their friends and relatives. The plots revolved around the intricacies of adapting to married life. These subgenres reflected the cultural concerns, preoccupations, and myths surrounding subcultures in America. At the same time, however, these subgenres continued to adhere to the general formula (premise, structure, and thematic concerns) that define the genre.

In general, the sitcoms of the 1990s focused on the characters' attempts to adapt to the complexities of modern culture. Programs featured an array of people in transition. For instance, in *Frasier*, the main character was adjusting to a new stage of life. Although he was successful professionally, Frasier was locked into a state of perennial adolescence. He was divorced and has moved to a new city. Frasier lived at home with his father and was still working out his personal issues with his dad and brother. Many of the plots revolved around Frasier's attempts to validate himself to his father and brother.

As with previous sitcoms, 1990s sitcoms operated according to the order/chaos/order structure. At the beginning of an episode, things were calm. Then something occurred to throw them off balance. But although the circumstance, by itself, may be harmless (e.g., Frasier getting his dad a birthday gift), the incidents took place within a larger context that revealed why the character was in a state of eternal dissatisfaction (Frasier was never been able to please his father).

Unlike the 1950s sitcoms, the return to order is not so much a resolution of issues but is, instead, a momentary truce in the long-term effort to contend with the complexities of modern life. In the 1990s sitcom, the community of characters plays an important role in providing support for one another. But in this complex world of diminished expectations, all they can provide is comfort, rather than solutions.

In the world of the 1990s sitcom, gratification often comes from small pleasures. Indeed, the most popular sitcom of the nineties, *Seinfeld*, was "a show about nothing." In one scene from *Everybody Loves Raymond*, Raymond's dad eats a delicious piece of chocolate cake made by his wife and comments, "This cake almost makes it all worthwhile." In a larger sense, the sitcoms of the 1990s served this function for the audience, providing a momentary diversion from the stresses of contemporary culture.

Post-millennium sitcoms reflect much of the uncertainty that typified the United States in the wake of the tragedy of 9/11. In this post-9/11 environment, audiences preferred the comforting worldview of sitcoms. Jeff Zucker, president of NBC entertainment, explained, "After Sept. 11 there was a rush to familiar faces and familiar friends, programs where you knew the characters and cared about them. That's why shows like 'Frasier' and 'Raymond' and 'Friends' have prospered."[9]

After the country had begun to heal from the effects of 9/11, sitcoms again began to look into the foibles of the culture and its inhabitants. According to Alessandra Stanley, *Curb Your Enthusiasm* is an extension—and a magnification of—the self-indulgence and self-absorption of Larry David's previous sitcom hit, *Seinfeld*:

> As on "Seinfeld," the NBC show Mr. David created with Jerry Seinfeld in 1990, Larry and his sidekicks are mostly idle, self-absorbed and argumentative. But this show is even more uncensored, veined with the pessimism, loony narcissism and political incorrectness that are at the core of Mr. David's comedy.
>
> His comedy is stripped of all sentimentality, which is part of its subversive appeal. When Larry's mother is dying, his father does not inform him, saying his mother didn't want to "bother" him while he was shooting a film in New York with (Martin) Scorsese. Larry is shocked, but quickly realizes he can use his mother's death as an excuse to avoid bores, cancel a dinner party, and persuade his wife to have sex.
>
> "Curb" is impious about religion, race, gender, politics, charity, sex, money, death, immigrants, celebrity, politics, terrorism and the underclass, and its creator has unerring aim for even the best-cloaked Hollywood hypocrisies—one reason the show is so popular with the show-business crowd.... On the show, Larry is a truth seeker who gets in trouble for saying out loud what most people think privately.[10]

CONCLUSION

Because the conclusion of a media presentation is the last segment that an audience is exposed to, it influences how we respond to the narrative as a whole. Consequently, examining the conclusion can be a valuable key to interpreting media messages.

Illogical Conclusion

In *The French Lieutenant's Woman*, novelist John Fowles argues the conclusion of a narrative must be a logical extension of the initial premise, characters, and worldview, free of further intrusion by the artist:

> You may think novelists always have fixed plans to which they work, so that the future predicted by Chapter One is always inexorably the actuality of Chapter Thirteen ... [But] *we wish to create worlds as real as, but other than the world that is.* Or was. This is why we cannot plan. We know a world is an organism, not a machine. We also know that a genuinely created world must be independent of its creator ... It is not only that [the character] has begun to gain an autonomy; I must respect it, and disrespect all my quasi-divine plans for him, if I wish him to be real.[11]

Fowles compares the process of writing a novel to giving birth. After creating the characters, setting, and worldview of the novel, the artist must then let go, allowing the characters to fulfill their destinies. Although this process can be agonizing for the parent/author, Fowles declares, "I let the fight proceed and take no more than a recording part in it."[12]

In light of Fowles's observations, it is striking that conclusions to popular media presentations are so often false, confused, or simply illogical when considered within the flow of the program.

One explanation can be found in the study of popular culture. In order to attract and maintain an audience, media presentations focus on complex issues, reflecting cultural interests, concerns, and preoccupations. Unfortunately, these complicated issues must be resolved within strict time constraints (e.g., 30 minutes for a sitcom). These conditions often result in conclusions that offer simplistic answers to complex problems. Tide detergent will make you a better mother. Wearing Tommy Hilfiger clothes will make you popular. And Ultra Brite toothpaste will make you irresistible.

Illogical conclusions also respond to the audience's desire for a happy ending. In his study of fairy tales, Bruno Bettelheim observes,

> The dominant culture wishes to pretend ... that the dark side of man does not exist, and professes a belief in an optimistic meliorism ... The message that fairy tales get across ... [is] that a struggle against severe difficulties in life is unavoidable, is an intrinsic part of human existence—but that if one does not shy away, but steadfastly meets unexpected and often unjust hardships, one masters all obstacles and at the end emerges victorious.[13]

Mindful of this demand for a satisfying resolution, media communicators feel compelled to insert an artificial ending that makes the audience leave the theater with smiles on their faces. Indeed, film studios compete to release the "feel good movie of the year."

A third explanation stems from industry considerations. Film studios, Broadway producers, and authors now routinely protect their investments by conducting focus groups before releasing their final product. If the survey results are negative, the media communicators are not hesitant to alter the ending. For instance, the conclusion of *A Stranger Among Us* (1992) was reshot after an unsuccessful preview at Cannes. Producer Howard Rosenman explained, "After our second preview, we knew we had to reshoot. We were losing our target audience (women under 30) because (the heroine Emily, played by Melanie Griffith) ended up with the wrong guy … We retested in Pasadena, and the scores went up considerably."[14] However, director Michael Apted (Thunderheart) cautions, "Suddenly, you're pandering to the public and treating movies like soap suds, instead of somebody's vision."[15]

The history of Hollywood films is replete with instances in which the endings of films have been altered:

- After completing *The Magnificent Ambersons* (1942), director Orson Welles discovered that the film studio, which owned the film, had reshot the tragic ending, giving the film a hopeful, sentimental turn.
- *Dying Young* (1991), a tragedy about a victim of AIDS, was re-worked, so that in an ending that negated the title, the patient survived.
- *Daylight* (1999), an adventure film starring Sylvester Stallone, originally concluded with the hero sacrificing himself in the waters off of Manhattan. In the version that was released, however, Stallone survived.

However, the artificial conclusion often undermines the manifest message of the media presentation. To illustrate, in *Fatal Attraction* (1987), happily married New York lawyer Dan Gallagher (Michael Douglas) has an affair with Alex Forrest (Glenn Close). But after Alex informs Dan that she is pregnant, her behavior becomes more erratic. Dan then decides to end the affair.

According to scriptwriter James Dearden, *Fatal Attraction* initially was written as a morality tale: "It was a commentary on human responsibility, on the moral consequences of one's actions."[16] Thus, in the original ending, Alex commits suicide, Dan's fingerprints are discovered on the weapon (he had held the knife in a previous scene), and it is insinuated that Dan will be punished for his moral transgression.

However, test audiences responded negatively to this ending. Director Adrian Lyne said, "They would have thrown rocks…. (The audience) had grown to hate this woman … to the degree that they wanted retribution."[17] As a result, the studio spent $1.3 million to reshoot the ending. In the revised version, Alex is a psychopath who terrorizes Gallagher and his family. This substitute ending reframes the meaning of the film. Dan is no longer responsible for his infidelity but, instead, is a victim of an obsessed stalker. Ultimately it is Dan's wife Beth (Anne Archer) who saves herself, her family, and her marriage by stabbing the deranged Alex. According to Richard Corliss, by killing Alex, Beth not only saves her family, but in essence, forgives Dan's cheating.[18] In the final shot sequence, Dan and Beth stand with their arms around one another (a sign of protection). The camera then pans to a close-up of a family photograph: order has been restored.

Significantly, although the test audience was not comfortable with good-guy Gallagher being responsible for the betrayal of his family, they were willing to accept the vilification of a sexually aggressive, independent woman. Professor Jane Ferry declares, "The film's message is clear. Single professional women are psychotic and ... must be silenced, especially if they seek more than the limited role of wife and mother."[19]

Audiences accustomed to the swift and immediate resolution of entertainment programming are often unprepared to contend with media coverage of news events. For example, when the Iraq war began in 2003, television coverage was continuous. However, as the situation became prolonged, without apparent end in sight, the public (and, consequently, the networks) began to lose interest in the crisis.

Media Literacy Strategies. Envisioning a conclusion consistent with the logical flow of a narrative can be an effective strategy for identifying latent messages. A good example can be found in the highly successful 1950s TV sitcom *The Honeymooners*. The lead character, Ralph Kramden (Jackie Gleason) is a big, blustery bus-driver who, each week, becomes embroiled in a harebrained scheme, so that he can get what "he deserves." However, once the comedic elements have been stripped away, Ralph is a terribly unhappy and selfish person, plagued with *hubris* and a deluded sense of self. When he doesn't get his way, Ralph "playfully" threatens his wife Alice and pal Ed Norton. ("Pow—to the moon!") In order to launch his get-rich-quick scheme, Ralph continually deceives Alice, lying to her or pilfering the household money.

At the end of each episode, the folly of Ralph's excessive ego has been exposed. Ralph parades in front of Alice, looking repentant and trying to find the words to ask for forgiveness. After some hesitation, Alice always relents. The program inevitably concludes with an embrace of reconciliation, with Ralph declaring, "Baby, you're the greatest."

This illogical conclusion conveys clear manifest messages about the importance of forgiveness and support in marriage. However, what would be the *logical conclusion* of an episode of *The Honeymooners?* Possible scenarios include the following:

- Ralph goes into therapy
- Ralph and Alice see a marriage counselor
- Alice leaves Ralph

Suggesting an ending consistent with the logical flow of *The Honeymooners* provides insight into the cultural attitudes of the period about marriage and relationships. A key to identifying media messages is, then: given the initial premise, characters, and worldview, how *should* the presentation logically end?

A related line of inquiry is *preferred conclusion:* how do you *want* the story to end? Your response reveals a great deal about your personal belief system. In the case of *The Honeymooners*, should one minimize problems to keep a marriage going? Is this Ralph's problem solely, or does

Figure 9.1
In *The Honeymooners*, Ralph Kramden (Jackie Gleason) bullies his buddy Ed Norton (Art Carney), much to the displeasure of wife Alice (Audrey Meadows). The happy ending at the conclusion of each episode offers a simplistic conclusion that is not consistent with the logical flow of the program. Photograph courtesy of Globe Photos, Inc.

Alice share in the responsibility? What is Ralph's attitude toward women? Why is Ralph so driven to make "the big score"? Any preferred conclusion to *The Honeymooners* reveals your personal attitudes toward marriage, sex roles, and relationships.

Another useful line of inquiry involves identifying the function, or purpose, behind the insertion of an artificial ending in a media presentation. As an example, in the 1955 animated version of George Orwell's *Animal Farm*, the conclusion was markedly different from the original novel. Written in 1945, the book is an allegory about the struggle between the capitalist farmers, and the proletariat farm animals. At the conclusion of the novel, the farm animals look back and forth at the exploitative human farmers and the tyrannical pigs (who represented the totalitarian Soviet communist regime) and find it "impossible to say which was which."

"However, in the animated film, the farm animals direct their criticism only at the Communist pigs. Journalist Frances Stonor Saunders uncovered evidence that the conclusion of this media presentation was secretly altered, as the latent function was switched from *entertainment* to *propaganda*. After Orwell's death in 1950, the U.S. Central Intelligence Agency (CIA) purchased the film rights to *Animal Farm*, altering the ending to make its messages more overtly anti-Communist.[20]

Character Development

Character development gives an artist the opportunity to make thematic statements. During the course of a narrative, characters often engage in a process of self-discovery, developing a new outlook that enables them to succeed at the conclusion.

A useful method for detecting media messages is to examine the ways in which characters have been affected by the events in the story:

- Have the major characters changed as a result of the events in the story? How? Why?
- What have the characters learned as a result of their experience?

SUMMARY

Framework refers to various structural elements of a production: Introduction, Plot, Genre, and Conclusion.

Keys to Interpreting Media Messages: Framework

Applying the following questions related to Framework can provide insight into media messages:

A. Introduction

1. *Title*: What does the title of the presentation signify?

2. *Introduction as Foreshadowing Device*:
    a. What events constitute the introduction of the media presentation?
    b. What does the introduction tell us about the presentation?
    c. Does the introduction foreshadow events and themes in the body of the production?
3. *Illogical Premise*
    a. Is the premise of the presentation logical?
    b. What are the underlying assumptions behind the premise of the presentation?
    c. What is the impact of this premise on the messages conveyed in the presentation?
    d. Do you accept the underlying premise in the presentation?
    e. If not, are you willing to suspend your disbelief?

B. Plot

1. *Explicit Content:* What are the significant events in the story?
2. *Implicit Content*
    a. What is the relationship between the significant events in the narrative?
    b. What is the relationship between the characters in the narrative?
    c. What are the characters' motives for their actions?
    d. Are the consequences to specific behaviors defined?
3. Subplots
    a. Can you identify any subplots in the narrative?
    b. Are there any connections between the subplots that provide insight into the worldview, characters, and themes in the production?
4. Affective Response
    a. How does the media communicator want you to be *feeling* at particular points in the plot?
        1) Why does the media communicator want you to be feeling this way?
        2) Is the media communicator successful in eliciting this intended emotional response?
    b. Do your affective responses provide insight into media messages? Explain.
    c. Do your affective responses provide insight into *your* personal belief system? Explain.

C. Genre

1. Does the presentation belong to any recognizable genre?
2. Is there a predictable formula for the genre? What insights does this formula provide into the genre? Into the specific program?

        a. Formulaic Function
        b. Formulaic Premise
        c. Formulaic Structure
        d. Formulaic Plot
        e. Conventional Storyline
        f. Stock Characters
        g. Setting
        h. Conventional Trappings
    3. What does this genre suggest about:
        a. Cultural attitudes and values?
        b. Cultural preoccupations?
        c. Cultural myths?
        d. Worldview?
    4. Can you trace the evolution of this genre?
        a. Have there been shifts in the genre over time?
        b. What do these shifts in genre reveal about changes in the culture?

D. Conclusion
    1. *Function*
        a. What is the purpose behind the conclusion of the narrative?
        b. Is there a latent function behind the conclusion? Explain.
    2. *Character Development*
        a. Have the major characters changed as a result of the events in the story? How? Why?
        b. What have the characters learned as a result of their experience?
    3. *Illogical Conclusion*
        a. Does the conclusion of the presentation follow logically from the established premise, characters, and worldview?
        b. If not, how should the presentation have ended, given the established premise, characters, and worldview?
        c. How would you have *preferred* for the story to end? Why?

NOTES

1. John Cawelti, "Myth, Symbol, and Formula," *Journal of Popular Culture* 8 (Summer 1974), 15.
2. Neal Gabler, "The Nation: The Illusion of Entertainment; Just Like a Movie, But It's Not," *New York Times*, August 4, 2002.

3. Lawrence E. Mintz, "Situation Comedy," in *TV Genres,* ed. Brian G. Rose (Westport, CT: Greenwood Press, 1985), 119.

4. Ray Suarez, "But What If the 'Perp' Walks?," *New York Times*, March 13, 1999, A27.

5. Mintz, 114.

6. Bill Carter and Stuart Elliott, "ABC and WB Announce Lineups They Hope Will Bring a Turnaround from Disappointing Seasons," *New York Times,* May 18, 2004, C9.

7. Ibid., 115.

8. Rick Mitz, *The Great TV Sitcom Book* (Westport, CT: Richard Marek, 1980).

9. Bernard Weintraub, "TV's Comforting Laugh Track," *New York Times*, October 31, 2001.

10. Alessandra Stanley, "Rough-Edged Cultural Touchstone," *New York Times*, November 16, 2002, B7.

11. John Fowles, *A French Lieutenant's Woman* (Boston: Little, Brown and Company, 1969), 105–106.

12. Ibid., 417.

13. Bruno Bettelheim, *The Uses of Enchantment: The Meaning and Importance of Fairy Tales* (New York: Vintage Books, 1976), 7.

14. Glenn Fowles, "It Ain't Over Until It's Happy," Knight-Ridder Newspapers. Reprinted in the *St. Louis Post-Dispatch*, July 7, 1992, 4D.

15. Ibid.

16. Susan Faludi, *Backlash: The Undeclared War against American Women* (New York: Doubleday, 1991), 120.

17. Adrian Lyne, interview, "'Fatal Attraction' Director Analyzes the Success of His Movie, and Rejoices," *New York Times*, by Ajean Harmetz, October 5, 1987, C17.

18. Richard Corliss, "Killer," *Time*, November 16, 1987, 72.

19. Jane Ferry, "Babylonian Babe: Boffo at the Box Office," unpublished paper, October 1997.

20. Laurence Zuckerman, "How the C.I.A. Played Dirty Tricks With Culture," *New York Times*, March 18, 2000.

SECTION

4

PRODUCTION ELEMENTS

Production elements have an impact on the *style* and *quality* of a media presentation. Production values are roughly analogous to grammar in print, in that these elements influence:

- *The ways in which the audience receives the information*
- *The emphasis, or interpretation, placed on the information by the media communicator*
- *The reactions of the audience to the information*

The clever mass communicator uses production values to engage the audience in the media experience. To illustrate, in *Paradise Lost* John Milton uses a literary technique that allows the reader to vicariously participate in Satan's descent into hell. *Read the following passage aloud:*

> Him the Almighty Power
> Hurl'd headlong flaming from th' Ethereal Sky
> With hideous ruin and combustion down
> To bottomless perdition, there to dwell
> In Adamantine Chains and penal Fire,
> Who durst defy th' Omnipotent to Arms,

Nine times the Space that measures Day and Night
To mortal men, he with his horrid crew
Lay vanquisht, rowling in the fiery Gulf
Confounded though immortal.[1]

By the time that you have finished reading this exhaustive run-on sentence, you are out of breath and have, on some level, experienced Satan's fall from grace.

These stylistic elements operate on an affective, or emotional, level that frequently escapes our conscious attention. Referring to visual language, Rudolf Arnheim observes, "In fact, these purely visual qualities of appearance are the most powerful of all. It is they that reach us most directly and deeply."[2] Consequently, production elements can create a mood that reinforces manifest messages or themes in a media presentation. For example, in horror films, manipulation of lighting, music, and screen space arouse intense feelings of terror in the audience. Further, these stylistic elements may convey independent messages (e.g., the glamour associated with screen violence).

NOTES

1. John Milton, *Paradise Lost, Paradise Regained, and Samson Agonistes* (Garden City, NY: Doubleday & Company, 1969), 20.
2. Rudolf Arnheim, *Art and Visual Perception* (Berkeley: University of California Press, 1974), 97.

CHAPTER

10

PRODUCTION ELEMENTS

- Editing
- Color
- Lighting
- Shape
- Scale
- Relative Position
- Movement

EDITING

Editing refers to the selection and arrangement of information. Editing decisions send messages regarding the significance of content. For instance, radio and television journalist Walter Cronkite closed his broadcasts with his signature, "And that's the way it is," which implies that the only events of the day worth considering had been covered on that evening's program.

However, all media presentations are faced with the challenge of fitting the information within the existing time and space constraints of the medium. For instance, the front page of a newspaper typically includes approximately six stories. In any given day, it is safe to say that a hundred items are important enough to be included on the front page. Editors are faced with the task of whittling down the number of stories, as well as the amount of time or space allotted to each. In addition, editing decisions are often made for pragmatic reasons. For instance, it is not uncommon for newspaper articles to be condensed to make room for additional advertising.

Consequently, a fundamental rule for media practitioners is: "Don't fall in love with your work." The filmmaker who becomes too attached to a project may find it painful to cut the movie to a length that audiences will willingly sit through and the studio will release.

Editing decisions often fall into the following categories.

Inclusion and Omission. Given the time and space limitations, critical decisions involve both what to *include* and what to *omit* from a media presentation. Because these decisions have been reached before the presentation reaches the public, the audience is often unaware of the selection process.

For instance, only a limited number of people in a newsroom actually make the editorial decisions, which then affect our understanding of our world. Newspaper staffs generally designate one person to keep the "daybook" of events that will be covered by the paper that day. As an example, Chris Hedges provides the following portrait of Tom McElroy, who decides what stories are carried by the Associated Press:

> Tom McElroy, 39, an editor at the Associated Press with a silver stud in his left ear and a black bicycle helmet tossed casually on his desk, would not make anyone's list of media heavyweights. But from his small, cluttered cubicle in Rockefeller Center, covered with pages of faxes and news releases, he puts together the Associated daybook. This Press daybook, a schedule of daily events in the city, often determines what gets covered in New York and what does not.
>
> Groggy editors and reporters at newspapers and at radio and television stations check the daybook daily as they start work. And public relations people, knowing that it is the holy grail of city journalism, sit dog-faced in their offices if their clients' events are not posted on it.
>
> "If an event is not listed on the A.P. daybook it is not worth doing," said Edward Skyler, who works in the public relations department at Bloomberg.
>
> The daybook is compiled to give members of the media an agenda for major events taking place each day in the city. These events can be news conferences by the mayor or wacky promotional events that are used to leaven the nightly news. All those who subscribe to the A.P. metro or broadcast wires, including this newspaper, receive the service.
>
> "This will be good," he said, setting the notice down next to his computer. He routinely tosses out a lot of the blatant promotional events, he said. "Even on a busy day I try to put some little nonprofit on that cannot afford a big public relations firm and wants coverage," he said. "When I go home and see it on the news it makes me feel good."[1]

One way to gain insight into this *preproduction selection process* is to compare coverage of different media presentations. As an example, in 2003, a story appeared in various news publications about three elderly Iraqi women who were detained by the American military in the Iraqi town of Chaldea. This arrest was part of an American military strategy that National Public Radio reporter Deborah Amos described was "aimed at quelling attacks on US forces by jailing the mothers so their sons will give themselves up."[2] This incident was the cause of widespread anti-American demonstrations in the area.

But aside from this NPR report, the episode received very little attention from the Western press. However, Arabic-language television stations provided extensive coverage of the incident. The nephew of the women, Nihad Fuazph, declared, "They cover also our demonstrations and convey our opinion to the whole world. To the Arabian tribes, it's a very important and big thing."[3]

A particularly useful line of inquiry is to examine a variety of newspapers or to compare the nightly news with unedited C-SPAN coverage of events. What has been included? What has been omitted?

Arrangement of Information. Cronkite's signature statement not only promised to present all of the news; he also pledged to give us the news in *order of importance*. The arrangement of information makes a statement about the relative merit and value of content. What appears first is, obviously, most essential. What appears last is of lesser importance.

Temporal and Spatial Inferences. Media communicators manipulate time and space as a means of establishing relationships between people, locations, and events. Although narratives generally move in chronological order, media communicators are able to manipulate the order to draw connections between these time periods. For instance, a flashback is a stylistic technique in which a past event is inserted in the narrative to show the influence of the past on the present.

Filmmakers also use *parallel action* to create the illusion that events on screen are occurring simultaneously. This can be accomplished by the editing technique of *cross-cutting,* in which footage from different locations is juxtaposed to give the impression of events occurring at the same moment. For instance, the classic Russian film *Potemkin* (1925) tells the story of a riot at the battleship *Potemkin*. Soviet filmmaker Sergei M. Eisenstein selected a succession of images (called a montage), consisting of soldiers, a woman crying, and a baby carriage bouncing down the steps out of control. This juxtaposition of shots underscores the relationship between the authoritarian power of the Cossacks, the suffering of the people, and the devastation of the town.

In like fashion, spacial inferences draw connections between occurrences at particular sites. For instance, a formulaic establishment shot in television consists of a wide shot of a building. The camera zooms in, dissolving into an interior scene. The inference is that the interior scene is taking place in the building that was shown in the exterior shot.

Editing can also suggest *causality*. The juxtaposition of scenes can show the consequences of actions (e.g., the villain admitting guilt, followed by a shot of the villain going to jail). Sequencing one shot after another can also dramatize the impact of events on people. In soap operas, a revelation

Figure 10.1
Media communicators are able to manipulate time and space as a means of establishing relationships between people, locations, and events. The classic Russian film *Potemkin* (1925) tells the story of a riot at the battleship *Potemkin*. Soviet filmmaker Sergei M. Eisenstein selected a succession of images (called a montage) to comment on the relationship between the authoritarian power of the Cossacks, the suffering of the people, and the devastation of the town.

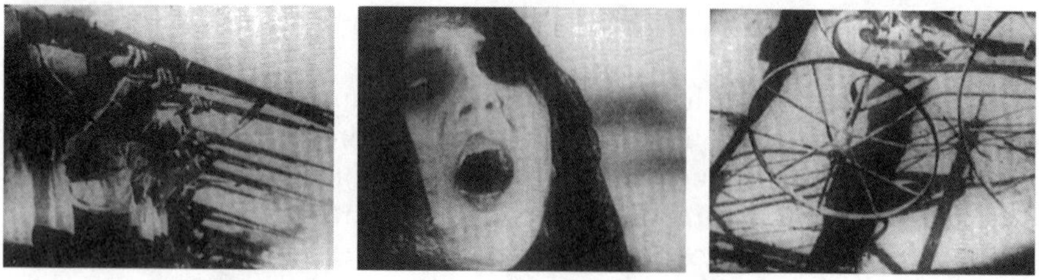

in the story is frequently followed by reaction shots, which reveal how all of the principal characters are affected by the goings-on.

COLOR

Color is a visual element that has a powerful effect on audiences. Wallace S. Baldinger declares, "[Color] affects our waking moments, consciously or unconsciously, and also, when we are dreaming, our sleeping moments. It influences—sometimes to a frightening extent—our moods and states of mind, soothing or amusing us, stimulating or revolting us, driving us even to madness."[4]

"I am feeling blue," "He is green with envy," and "This news is red hot" are examples of how colors are associated with, and inspire, particular emotions.

According to Baldinger, the affective nature of colors is tied to universal human experience:

> Owing to association with certain experiences and objects, we feel that certain hues are "warm" and others "cool." By association with late-afternoon sunshine, fire, or heated iron, on the one hand, and with nightfall, water, ice, snow, on the other, we group yellow, orange, and red together as warm hues and green, blue, and violet together as cool. The artist draws on the ideas which we thus connect with color when he selects and organizes hues, sometimes even making us feel hot or cold by reaction to them.[5]

In general, the affective properties of colors are as follows:

- *Warm colors, like red, orange, and yellow, tend to make us feel happy, secure, positive, and intensely involved.*

- *Cool colors, like blue or violet, make us feel calm.*
- *Dead colors, like gray or black, make us feel sad, alone, or uncomfortable.*

To illustrate, a group of preschool children from Reggio Emilia, Italy, were asked to describe four pictures of a tiger. These pictures were identical, with one exception: each version was reproduced in a different color. The children described these pictures in very different terms, revealing the influence of color on perception:

- *Yellow tone*
  "It's an enchanted and hot forest, full of sun like an enormous fire."
  "The tiger is also on fire and ferocious."
- *Blue tone*
  "It seems to be a dream. The tiger seems to be a fantasy."
  "It's like a forest at the bottom of the sea. Or else a land far away in the clouds."
- *Green tone*
  "It's like being immersed in a sea of tall grass. It's the most normal because it's green."
  "It's a quiet forest. It makes me feel (sleepy)."
  "You can almost smell the scent of mint."
- *Gray tone*
  "It's frightening, scary, because it's dark like the night. There isn't even a ray of sun."
  "It's a magical forest with strange noises. It's like being in a place that doesn't exist, like a ghost town."[6]

Color contrast may also evoke particular moods. Warm colors and pleasing color contrasts generate a positive response in the audience. However, contrasting color combinations, such as red and purple, produce a visual tension which is sensed by the audience.

Interior designers take these affective properties of color into consideration when they decorate public spaces, such as business offices, hospitals, and schools. To illustrate, restaurants make generous use of the color orange, which has been found to stimulate the appetite.[7] Faber Birren describes the ideal color scheme for schools:

> Carefully planned experiments by psychologists have well proven that modern principles of color applied to schools will improve in a striking way the scholastic performance of school students.... A well designed environment not only facilitates learning new subject matter, but reduces behavioral problems....
>
> It is good standard practice to use white for all ceilings, both for consistent appearance and to reflect an abundance of shadow-free illumination.... Libraries, rest rooms for teachers, school offices ... could well be in the subdued tones of Pale Gold, Fern Green, Colonial Green, Smoky Blue.
>
> Cafeterias should be in Peach, Coral, Rose, Pumpkin, Flamingo. All of which are cheerful and appetizing.

> The gymnasiums, shops, manual training, and domestic arts rooms probably are best in luminous tones of Soft Yellow, Peach, Beige. Locker rooms and dressing rooms in Coral will reflect a flattering light.[8]

However, the precise meaning associated with a particular color can depend on several factors. Primary colors contain degrees of saturation, or shades, which often evoke a range of emotions. Thus, while blue is generally thought of as a cool color, a light blue feels warm and enveloping.

Further, the *context* in which a color appears can determine its meaning. For instance, green is often associated with nature and health. However, in *The Wizard of Oz* (1939) the green complexion of the Wicked Witch of the West looks unnatural and evil.

Finally, *cultural context* can play a role in the meaning of color. That is, colors sometimes assume a special significance within a particular culture. To illustrate, while the color black is associated with mourning in most Western cultures, other colors assume the same connotative meaning in many Asian cultures. Robert L. Stevenson explains,

> Imagine receiving a Christmas present wrapped in black paper or a sympathy card in neon pink. You could make a comparable mistake by offering red roses to a German or Polish acquaintance, yellow or white chrysanthemums to most Europeans, any purple flowers to a Brazilian, or white lilies to a Canadian. All of these are associated with funerals or death in the respective cultures.[9]

Color schemes can serve as a dramatic device that reinforces themes and messages in a media presentation. An example of thematic use of color occurs in *The Wizard of Oz*. The beginning of the film is shot in black and white, reflecting Dorothy's rather mundane existence in Kansas. After her home has been uprooted by a tornado, she opens the door to discover that she has landed in Oz. And what a world! At this point, the film is transformed into color. Oz is portrayed as a warm, enchanting place, thanks in large measure to the pastel color scheme. The set is dominated by delicate shades of gold, blue, and green.

This dramatic effect is in marked contrast to a subsequent scene in which Dorothy and her friends enter the forest on their way to meet the Wizard of Oz. The scene is dominated by dark colors, including the sky and costume of the Wicked Witch of the West. This color scheme reinforces the notion of the forest as a dark, foreboding place.

LIGHTING

Lighting can subtly affect the mood of a media presentation. A brightly lit photograph evokes feelings of security and happiness. In contrast, a dark picture filled with shadows creates a mysterious atmosphere that evokes fear and apprehension in the audience. Dim lighting can also trigger a sense of powerlessness and loss of control, as the viewer must struggle to grasp a clear visual understanding of the environment.

Lighting also can be used for dramatic emphasis. Those aspects of a page or screen that are in the light attract attention and are therefore considered to be of prime importance, while objects that remain in the dark are of little consequence. Flat lighting exposes everything equally and, as a result, makes the world of the photo appear dull and monotonous. However, different gradations of light are more lively and create an interesting and exciting world.

The *source* of light is another device for dramatic effect and thematic expression. Rudolf Arnheim describes a painting by Rembrandt, entitled *Descent from the Cross*:

> ... the (hidden) light ... brightens the body of Christ, which is being taken down from the cross. The ceremony is performed in a dark world. But as the light falls from below, it heightens the limp body and imparts the majesty of life to the image of death. Thus the light source within the picture tells the story of the New Testament—that is, the story of the divine light transferred to the earth and ennobling it by its presence.[10]

In a two-dimensional form such as photography, film, or television, lighting casts shadows that are as substantial as any of the "real" objects being depicted. Consequently, shadows can be employed as a narrative device, dramatizing relationships by literally connecting people or objects. For instance, in Alfred Hitchcock's suspense classic *Dial M for Murder* (1954), Tony (Ray Milland) devises an elaborate scheme to murder his wife Margot (Grace Kelly). However, Margo resists this attempt on her life and kills the intruder in self-defense. Tony then frames Margo, so that it appears that Margo had killed the man in an act of premeditated murder. However, with the arrival of Inspector Hubbard (John Williams), Tony's plan begins to unravel. As Tony shows the inspector around the apartment, he opens the door to the kitchen, which has bars across the windows (out of sight of the camera). The light through the window casts a shadow of bars across the doorway, foreshadowing Tony's eventual incarceration.

According to David Goen, lighting has its own distinct code of meaning:

Bright Lighting	Dim Lighting
Innocence	Death
Purity	Evil
Religious faith	Lack of communication
Delicacy	Pollution
Delight	A problem of religious faith
Joy and good will	Foreshadowing trouble
Life	Something hidden[11]
Discovery	Force and strength

Figure 10.2
Standard lighting techniques. A, *Key light*: principal light source—directional spot. B, *Back light*: rims top and separates object from background—directional spot. C, *Fill light*: slows shadow falloff—flood or soft (spread) spot. D, *Side light*: spotlight coming from the side (usually opposite key) directional. E, *Kicker light*: directional spot from back, off to one side, usually from below. Photographs by Timothy Merritt; model, Loren Munder.

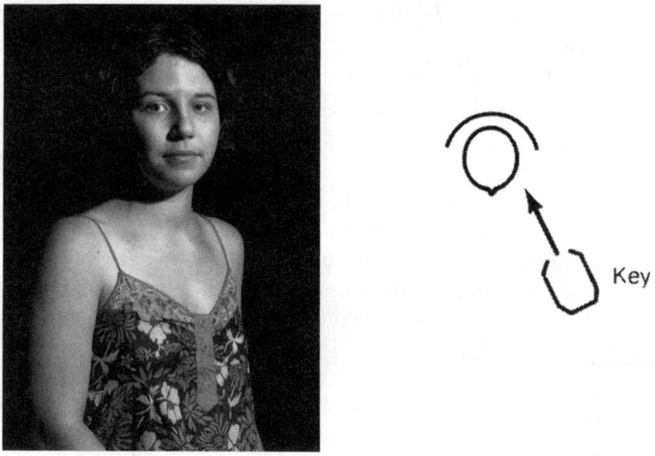

(a)

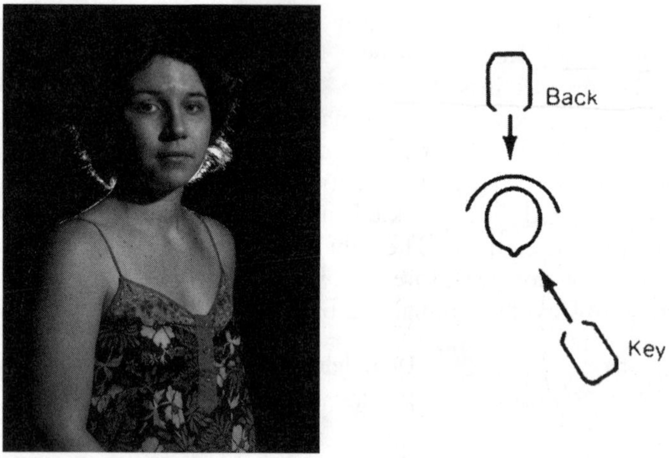

(b)

Figure 10.2. (*Continued*)

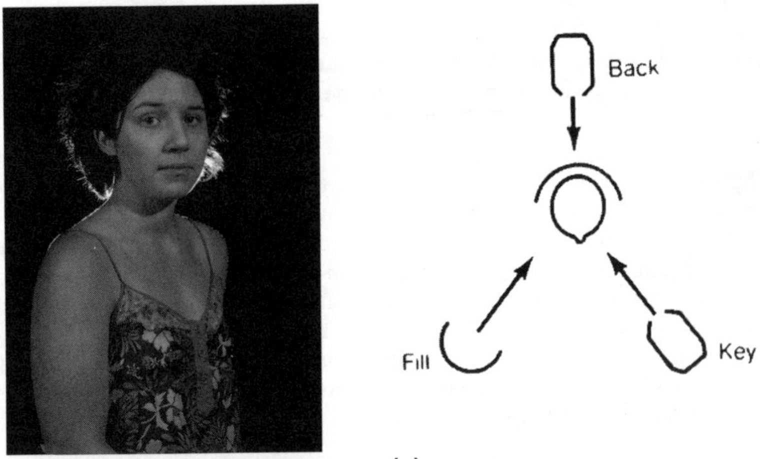

(c)

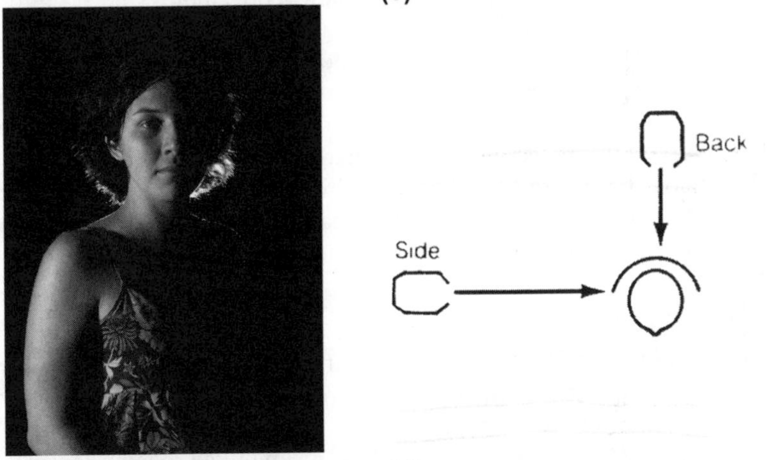

(d)

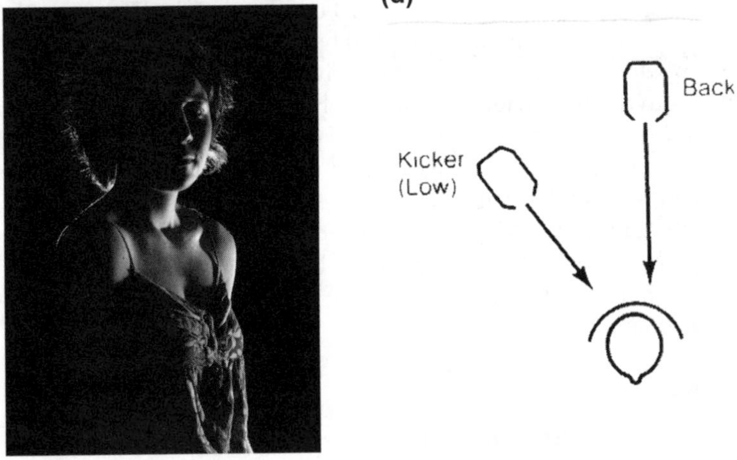

(e)

The *quality* of light—hard or soft—comments on the objects depicted in the picture. Lighting can either flatter characters or produce a glare which accentuates their flaws, depending on the intention of the communicator. Goen explains:

> Soft light creates minimal contrast: It seems to wrap around an object, enveloping and bathing it, obscuring defects and minimizing surface detail. It is light that doesn't seem to come from any particular direction. Soft light can reveal the subtleties of gradation of tone, that is, the transition of light to dark tones.
>
> Hard light creates high contrast: Light that produces sharply defined outlines brings out any texture in the subject and can seem harsh and brutal.... High contrast lighting shows a much more limited range of tones. Your shadow under a direct light, such as a bare light bulb or the midday sun, is much more consistent in tone and is a fairly uniform darkness.[12]

In *Blade Runner* (1982), director Ridley Scott employs hard lighting to create a pessimistic world of the future. Due to humanity's abuses of the environment, the climate is dark and gloomy, and it is continually raining. From an aerial view, flames leap up at the camera, from some unknown fuel source, conjuring up biblical images of hell. There is no natural source of light in the film, reflecting man's unnatural condition. Instead, the street is illuminated by hideous neon signs, which only accentuate the imperfections in the faces of the people who inhabit this world. A sense of hopelessness permeates the film, much of it due to the use of lighting.

SHAPE

The primary unit of visual communication is the *dot*. The dot is a reference point which attracts the eye of the viewer and delineates space on the page by defining the space around the dot. The dot is also the beginning of a more complex visual plan; a series of dots, when linked together, form a *line*.

A line suggests a sense of direction. For instance, in Western culture, a diagonal line running from the left-hand bottom corner to the right-hand top has an *ascending* quality, suggesting positive feelings of progress and enlightenment. Conversely, a diagonal from left-hand top to right hand bottom has a *descending* quality, producing a sense of pessimism, danger, and failure.

Lines may also convey messages based upon the amount of pressure that the artist applies to the paper. A delicate line can suggest caution, refinement, or hesitancy. A bold line connotes conviction or passion.

A *shape* is created when a line comes back to itself and is distinct from any other shape or space. Each of the three basic shapes has its own distinctive character.

The Circle

The *circle* possesses a mystical quality. This shape has direction and is complete; as a result, it is associated with endlessness, wholeness, and the cyclical conception of time (e.g., the zodiac and clock faces). In Mayan culture, the circle was viewed as a "symbol of perfection" or the "balancing of forces." In many cultures, the circle is a symbol of the sun and, as a result, signifies warmth and life.

In ancient civilizations, the circle was a symbol of protection. For example, in antediluvian Babylonian culture, laying a circle of flour around a person's sickbed was a ritual designed to keep demons away. Within this context, the circle *separates*, setting objects apart (e.g., a "social circle"). However, a circle can also serve as a symbol that *joins* people and things together within its parameters. In medieval Europe, magicians used the circle to delineate sacred space:

> ... the circle is not only intended to keep something out but also to keep something in—the magical energy which the magicians will summon up from within themselves in the course of the ceremony.... If it were not for the circle the energy would flow off in all directions and be dissipated. The circle keeps it inside a small area and so concentrates it. The same motive lies behind the circle of people who link their hands at a séance.[13]

Stonehenge and Avebury are examples of ancient uses of the circle to mark the boundary of a sacred area. According to Eva C. Hangen, the circle image has a universal significance that can be traced through a variety of cultural artifacts:

- Circle of fire: monastic chastity, magic, inviolability
- Wedding ring: continuing devotion and love
- Four circles linked to a fifth, larger one: the words of wisdom
- In Mexico, two serpents entwined into a ring: time without end
- In China, a circle separating two serpents: the two Principles claiming the universe[14]

Because the circle is smooth, round, and has no edges, it has a friendly, non-threatening quality. Media presentations reflect this sensibility. The roundness of cartoon characters like the Teletubbies, Mickey Mouse, or the Pillsbury Doughboy gives them a lovable quality, while villains like the Big Bad Wolf are angular.

Shape has an impact on the popularity of consumer products. Thus, according to reporter Natalie Angier, making products into a round shape—known as the "cute factor"—bolsters its commercial appeal:

> Sales of petite, willfully cute cars like the Toyota Prius and the Mini Cooper (have) soared, while those of noncute sport utility vehicles tanked.... As though the original Volkswagen Beetle wasn't considered cute enough, the updated edition was made rounder and shinier still. "The new Beetle looks like a smiley face," said Miles Orvell, professor of American studies at Temple University in Philadelphia.[15]

The Square

In contrast to the circle, the *square* is very much of this world. A square is precise, consisting of horizontal and vertical direction. College students asked to describe the square came up with the following properties:

Fair	Honest
Precise	Dull
Dependable	Ordinary
Solid	Boring
Stable	Lacking imagination
Straight	

The Triangle

A *triangle* consists of radical angles. Paul Martin Lester explains, "Triangles are the most dynamic and active of shapes. As energetic objects, they convey direction, but they can burden a design with the tension they can create."[16] Triangles are associated with motion, conflict, tension, abandonment, and power. The tension between the angles endows this shape with a mysterious power. The ancient Egyptians claimed that the triangular structure of the pyramids preserved the bodies and spirits of the kings buried within their walls. Richard Cavendish explains, "The true pyramid was merely a representation in stone of the sun's rays shining to earth through a gap in the clouds, and by its possession the king could transport himself at will to the celestial kingdom of the sun god."[17]

Similarly, a modern legend claims that the Bermuda Triangle, formed by the southern tip of Florida, Puerto Rico, and Bermuda, is the locus of some "sinister force field." Since 1854, approximately fifty ships have been lost without a trace in this area of water.

Hangen has identified the following meanings ascribed to triangles:

- In general symbolism: equality, democratic thinking, perfection
- In Christian symbolism: the Trinity
- When pictured with divergent rays: eternity, the rays indicative of glory and brightness
- In art and architecture, in designs with apex pointing upward: heaven
- In flower arrangement:—triangular form lying on long side: repose—standing on the acute angle: stateliness and power—standing in an inclined position: dynamic force

SCALE

Scale refers to the relative size between objects. Scale is a very basic means of conveying messages; the larger an object appears, the more important it is.

Scale can also serve as a thematic device. For example, in *King Kong* (1933), the relative size of objects on screen is a metaphor for the complex relationship between man and nature. The scene that introduces King Kong juxtaposes the giant ape with the diminutive heroine, Ann Darrow (Fay Wray). Where Kong (or nature) is powerful, human beings are frail, weak, and ineffectual. Ann is particularly vulnerable, a victim of her own feminine nature (as defined by 1930s American culture).

After King Kong has been captured, Ann relaxes in her Manhattan apartment with her boyfriend, Robert Armstrong (Carl Denham). Within the sanctity of these walls, which are scaled to the dimensions of its human occupants, Armstrong reassures Ann: "You're safe now, dear." But alas, Kong has escaped. At this moment, the huge ape's face appears at her window, reducing the "normal" bedroom to dollhouse proportions. The ape's huge arm sweeps into the room, brushing off Armstrong's feeble defense and snatching the heroine. Civilization is again exposed as a rather thin facade. Nature (including human impulses and needs) looms large in all of us, despite our pretenses of civilization and control.

Figure 10.3
In *King Kong* (1933), relative size served as a metaphor for the complex relationship between mankind and nature. In this scene, King Kong overwhelms the powerless Ann (Fay Wray). Photograph © 1933 RKO Pictures, Inc. All Rights Reserved.

Figure 10.4
King Kong pays a house call on Ann (Fay Wray). Civilization is exposed as a feeble refuge against the forces of nature. Photograph © 1933 RKO Pictures, Inc. All Rights Reserved.

At the climax of the film, King Kong seeks refuge atop the Empire State Building. Significantly, in this shot, a *tiny* Kong clings to the mammoth structure. Once again, scale reflects relative *power*; Kong (and by extension, nature), has ultimately become a victim of civilization. For the moment, humans have succeeded in denying their own natures, including instinct, passion, and devotion, as symbolized by King Kong. The ape gently lays Ann on a ledge before plunging to his death. Fay is left only with her cultivated, uninspiring boyfriend and some vague, ambiguous emotions.

RELATIVE POSITION

Where a character or object appears on the screen (or page) sends a distinct message to the audience. Objects appearing toward the front attract immediate attention, whereas objects placed in the background are generally considered to be of secondary importance. Moreover, in Western cultures, people tend to pay more attention to objects situated on the *right* side of the screen. Herbert Zettl explains:

Figure 10.5
King Kong climbs the Empire State Building. Tiny Kong ultimately has become a victim of civilization. Photograph © 1933 RKO Pictures, Inc. All Rights Reserved.

In practice, this means that if you have a choice, you should place the more important event on the right side of the screen. In an interview show, for example, if you consider the guest more important than the host, place the guest on screen-right rather than the host. Most prominent hosts, however, do not want to be upstaged, and so they occupy the more conspicuous screen-right position.[18]

Human beings tend to look for balance; that is, an equal distribution around the center. Because of this natural predisposition to order, or *gestalt*, the audience tends to feel unsettled if all the activity is placed on one corner of the screen. Consequently, media communicators can convey a message by taking advantage of the audience's natural predisposition for order.

Table 10.1
Relative Position: Where the Character or Object Appears on the Screen (or Page) Sends Distinct Messages to the Audience

3	6	1
	7	
4	5	2

For instance, in the classic romantic film *Camille* (1936), starring Greta Garbo and Robert Taylor, the two lovers are positioned so that their faces are equidistant from the center of the screen. This use of space establishes a sense of romantic harmony and anticipates the climax of the love scene, when the lovers' lips meet in the exact center of the screen.

In addition, media communicators create a tension through *imbalance* in order to convey themes and messages. As art educator Albert Henry Munsell has observed, "Any long duration of unbalance, either mental, physical or spiritual is an aggravated form of disease.... Yet short periods of unbalance are very stimulating in the effort which they produce to regain balance."[19]

In addition, the space *outside* of the screen is frequently employed in suspense and horror genres for dramatic effect. The space outside the visual control of the viewer represents the unknown and can be employed to surprise or shock the audience. In *The Blair Witch Project* (1999), the camera remains fixed on the film's protagonists, so that the audience never

Figure 10.6
In *Camille* (1936), Marguerite (Greta Garbo) and Armand (Robert Taylor) are deep in reverie. The two lovers are positioned so that their faces are equal distance from the center of the screen. This use of space establishes a sense of anticipation, when the lovers' lips meet in the exact center of the screen at the climax of the love scene. Photograph © 1936 Turner Entertainment Co. All Rights Reserved.

knows who (or what) is stalking the characters. *Aliens* (1986), directed by James Cameron, takes this principle a step further. In this film, the source of terror is hidden *within* the characters, waiting to emerge at the opportune moment.

The media communicator can employ relative position to draw connections between people, objects, or events. To illustrate, in Alfred Hitchcock's classic suspense film *Psycho* (1960), there is a scene in which the relative position provides insight into the character of Norman Bates (Anthony Perkins). Norman and Marion (Janet Leigh) are in the parlor of the Bates Hotel. Norman has fixed a sandwich for Marion, who is staying overnight at the Bates Motel. She is fleeing after having stolen money from her boss. The shots of Norman talking include stuffed birds in the background. Marion comments on the stuffed birds, which leads to a moment in which Hitchcock reveals something about the tortured soul that is just beneath Norman's charming demeanor. Norman says, "I think we're all in our private traps ... and none of us can ever get out. We scratch and claw, but only at the air and only at each other and never break out of it." The stuffed birds in the background suggest that Norman is both predator and victim of his past.

MOVEMENT

Because movement makes the world on-screen appear so lifelike, people often assume that the events depicted are real and believe the messages that are conveyed in the programming.

To illustrate, in 1895, during the infancy of film, the Lumiere brothers produced a film entitled, *Arrival of a Train.* As the title suggests, this celebration of movement consisted of a train pulling into a station at an angle 45 degrees from a stationary camera. Reportedly, audience members fled from the theater, terrified.

The direction of movement conveys distinct messages:

- Movement directed *toward* the audience can either be friendly (e.g., an invitation or sign of intimacy), aggressive, or menacing.
- Movement directed *away* from the audience can signal either abandonment, retreat, avoidance, or resolution.
- Movement directed *upward* often is a positive sign (something going to heaven or, perhaps, outer space).
- Movement directed *downward* often is a negative sign (e.g., crashes or fights), or signals defeat.

The exact meaning of the movement is, to some degree, determined by the context in which the motion takes place. For instance, in David Puttnam's film *The Mission* (1987), an early scene shows a young missionary

Figure 10.7
Arrival of a Train **(1895), a documentary, was shot during the infancy of film at the turn of the century by the Lumiere brothers. Audiences found the movement of the train in the film to be disturbingly lifelike.**

(Jeremy Irons) struggling to scale a steep mountain in order to reach a South American Indian tribe. His climb up the mountain is contrasted with the falling action of a majestic waterfall. Water cascades from the cliffs above, showering the young missionary as he ascends the mountain. This juxtaposition of movement reinforces thematic concerns that are examined throughout the film: while it is difficult for man to control his nature and ascend to heaven, it is all too easy to fall from grace.

Motion involves not only direction but also *rhythm*: that is, the rate or pace at which movement occurs. A slow camera movement or the use of slow motion, can be very restful and reassuring. Commonly employed in sporting events and newscasts, slow motion also furnishes the viewer with the opportunity to study detail in a shot, in order to understand both *what* happened and *how* it occurred.

Many media communicators are sensitive to the psychological principles of movement. In Western culture, left-to-right movements are considered more restful and natural than right-to-left movements, due in part to the way that those people are trained to read. Western filmmakers often employ left-to-right movements to establish a positive and harmonious atmosphere and right-to-left movements to intensify feelings of tension and disharmony.[20]

The media communicator must also respect the natural *logic* of movement. A car moving from left to right across the screen must continue this directional flow, or *vector*, unless the director deliberately shows the car changing directions. Otherwise, the audience feels disoriented and may dissociate from the action.

NOTES

1. Chris Hedges, "Journalists Really Do Have an Agenda," *New York Times*, January 6, 2001.
2. Deborah Amos, "Demonstrations in Iraq Over the Arrest of the Mothers of Suspected Militants," *All Things Considered*, National Public Radio, October 24, 2003.
3. Ibid.
4. Wallace S. Baldinger, *The Visual Arts* (New York: Holt, Rinehart, and Winston, 1960), 16.
5. Ibid., 15.
6. George Forman, "Viewer's Guide to 'The Hundred Languages of Children'" (University of Massachusetts/Amherst, 1991) (Mimeographed).
7. NBC Radio, June 19, 1992.
8. Faber Birren, *Light, Color, and Environment* (New York: Van Nostrand Reinhold Company, 1982), 81–82.
9. Robert L. Stevenson, *Global Communication in the 21st Century* (New York: Longman Publications, 1994), 63–64.
10. Rudolf Arnheim, *Art and Visual Perception: A Psychology of the Creative Eye* (Berkeley: University of California Press, 1974).
11. David Goen, "Attaining Visual Literacy: How Pictures Function as Signs and Symbols" (M.A. thesis, Webster University, 1991), 54–55.
12. Ibid.
13. Richard Cavendish, ed., *Man, Myth, and Magic* (Wichita, KS: McCormick-Armstrong, 1962), s.v. "Circle."
14. Eva C. Hangen, *Symbols: Our Universal Language* (Wichita, KS: McCormick-Armstrong, 1962), 72.
15. Natalie Angier, "The Cute Factor," *New York Times*, January 3, 2006.
16. Paul Martin Lester, *Visual Communication: Images with Messages* (Belmont, CA: Wadsworth, 1995), 44.
17. Cavendish, *Man, Myth, and Magic*, s.v. "Pyramid."
18. Herbert Zettl, *Sight, Sound, Motion: Applied Media Aesthetics* (Belmont, CA; Wadsworth, 1990), 112.
19. Albert Henry Munsell, *A Grammar of Color* (New York: Van Nostrand Reinhold Company, 1969), 14.
20. Richard L. Stromgren and Martin F. Norden, *Movies: A Language in Light* (Englewood Cliffs, NJ: Prentice Hall, 1984), 49.

CHAPTER

11

PRODUCTION ELEMENTS

- Point of View
- Angle
- Word Choice
- Connotative Images
- Performance
- Sound Elements

POINT OF VIEW

Writers can present information from a range of perspectives:

- The *first person* point of view presents the action as interpreted by one character. For instance, Herman Melville's classic American novel *Moby Dick* begins, "Call me Ishmael." The reader's understanding of the story is colored by the predispositions and values of Ishmael, an obscure member of the crew.
- The *second person* point of view makes the reader the primary participant in the story. This perspective makes use of the pronoun "you."
- The *third person* point of view describes the activities and internal processes of one character. The third person point of view commonly employs the pronouns "he" or "she." The author is privy to the thoughts and activities of this character but retains some critical distance and is therefore not accountable for the behavior for the character.
- The *omniscient,* or all-knowing point of view enables the author to enter the heads of any and all of the characters, so that the reader has a comprehensive

exposure to the people and events depicted in the work. This point of view is used frequently in journalism, which creates the appearance of objectivity in news coverage.

While writers generally try to maintain a consistent perspective, they may occasionally adopt a *panoramic* point of view, in which the perspective is constantly shifting. For instance, during the climactic whale-hunting scene, *Moby Dick* shifts from a first-person perspective to an omniscient narrator. The audience somehow overhears Captain Ahab's dialogue, even though Ishmael is stationed in a different boat. Journalists may also adopt this panoramic point of view, by incorporating their own (first person) perspective into an "objective," third person account through production techniques such as connotative words and images, space, and editing decisions.

Camera Proximity in Film & Television

In video and film, the point of view of the camera determines what the audience sees on screen. A shift in camera proximity (i.e., close-ups or wide-angle shots) not only gives the audience a different view, but also provides them with a new way to think about the subject.

Filmmakers can create a literal first person point of view by employing a *subjective camera technique*. For instance, in *The Lady in the Lake* (1947), the camera assumes the perspective of the protagonist, Philip Marlowe (Robert Montgomery), so that the audience sees the world through the eyes of the main character. The only time that Marlow actually is in *front* of the camera occurs when his reflection briefly appears in a mirror. This first-person perspective was effective—for a brief period. However, without a focal character to watch, the film proved disorienting. For example, the fight scene degenerated into a burlesque in which the camera spun around (as "Marlow" was hit). The effect was to make the audience dizzy.

Film and television can also *approximate* the first person perspective through use of the *Extreme Close-up* camera shot (XCU). Through subtle facial reactions such as a lifted eyebrow or wry smile, gifted actors like Robert De Niro or Johnny Depp reveal their innermost thoughts and emotions to the audience.

Obviously, the second person ("you") perspective is nearly impossible to achieve in television and film, unless you actually appear on screen. However, TV and filmmakers will simulate the second person perspective by selecting performers who are intended to represent you. The "man in the street" approach in advertising casts normal, everyday people who are supposed to represent your concerns and interests. Other examples include audience participation programs such as game shows and talk shows such as *Oprah* and *Larry King Live* that encourage "average" people to call in to express their concerns.

Figure 11.1
In *The Lady in the Lake* (1947), a battered Philip Marlow (Robert Montgomery) checks his wounds in the mirror with Audrey Totter (Adrienna Fronsett). In this experiment in subjective camera techniques, the camera assumes the perspective of Marlow. This fleeting image in the mirror provides the only opportunity in the film for the audience to see Marlow. Photograph © 1946 Turner Entertainment Co. All Rights Reserved.

The *Medium Shot (MS)* is analogous to the third person perspective in print, in that it simply records the actions and interactions of the characters. This shot frequently takes in several actors in the frame. A third person perspective can also be attained by shooting over the shoulder of one participant and then the other. Herbert Zettl explains,

> Are we now using the camera subjectively, with the viewer alternately associating with the person not seen on the screen? Not really. Even if the person on the screen (A) speaks directly to the camera, we know from the context that person A's target is not us, the viewers, but person B ... We are not in any way involved in the exchange ... and are, therefore, not enticed to participate in the event or to assume person B's role.[1]

Film and television employ several different production techniques to simulate the omniscient perspective employed in print. The *Extreme Long Shot (XLS)* takes in a wide expanse of visual information and often establishes the setting at the beginning of a scene. This shot provides broad context for the subsequent action. The viewer can see a great deal within the frame and thus has a measure of control in terms of what to watch. The *omniscient* camera moves freely in time and space, enabling the director to focus on characters in different settings (unbeknownst to the other characters).

Moreover, "ultra-tram" technology now provides viewers with an omniscient perspective that enables the audience to see the world in entirely new ways. For instance, in televised golf matches, lipstick cameras placed near the ball give the audience an unfettered look at a Tiger Woods tee shot. Moreover, super slow motion provides intimate examination of shots. And "under the hoop" floor cams now enable the fans of TV poker to peek at the cards of all of the players in a poker game.

In film and television, point of view can be employed as a narrative device. TV series such as *Law & Order: Criminal Intent* employ a narrative technique, in which, through an initial scene, the omniscient camera (and by extension, the audience) knows "who done it" only the members of the cast remain unaware of the guilty party. The narrative then becomes a matter of watching Detectives Goren (Vincent D'Onofrio) and Eames (Kathryn Erbe) discover what the audience already knows.

The simplest way to determine the point of view in a film or television program is to ask: *whose story is this?* Another tip-off is: in screen romances, who is facing the camera when the couple embraces? The main character is the one receiving the attention from the other character, and the audience vicariously assumes the position of the subordinate character.

Television news typically establishes an omniscient point of view. Technical innovations such as satellite transmission and videotape enable the television news industry to transmit reports instantaneously from around the globe. This omniscient perspective also contributes to the impression that the information contained in the broadcasts is unimpeachable and that the broadcast journalist is all-knowing.

ANGLE

Angle refers to the level at which the camera is shooting in relation to the subject. The choice of angle can affect the audience's attitude toward the subject. For instance, in the Nickelodeon program *Rugrats* (2001–2004), the camera height was stationed at the eye-level of the children (rather than looking down at them from an "adult" perspective). This camera angle sends the message that the audience should take these children seriously and treat them (and their concerns) with consideration.

A person filmed from a high angle looks small, weak, frightened, or vulnerable. Conversely, a person filmed from a low angle appears larger, more important, and powerful. Joseph V. Mascelli observes, "In the right

Figure 11.2
This dramatic image of Adolf Hitler is taken from *Triumph of the Will* (1935), Leni Riefenstahl's documentary about Hitler's first party convention at Nuremberg. Riefenstahl's use of camera angles made Hitler look powerful and imposing on screen.

dramatic context the angle can create a feeling of subjective fear in the audience especially if used in conjunction with a wide angle lens."[2]

A classic example of the dramatic use of angle is Leni Riefenstahl's *Triumph of the Will* (1935), a Nazi propaganda film documenting Adolf Hitler's first party convention at Nuremberg. The camera was continually tilted upward at Hitler to create a sense of divine presence and to inspire awe in the audience. The documentary was so successful in its effort to deify Hitler that the Allies banned the film for several years after the end of the war.

WORD CHOICE

Language is not simply a vehicle for conveying information but actually shapes the audience's understanding. According to linguist Kenneth Burke, language *precedes* thought. That is, ideas, concepts, and things do not really exist until there are words to recall, categorize, and talk about them. To illustrate, because Russian meals consist of *breakfast*, *dinner* (early afternoon) and *supper*, the concept of a "business lunch" was difficult to understand and explain. However, as Russian businesspeople were introduced to the "business lunch" in their travels, they brought the concept back with them. Now, business lunches are part of the Russian culture.

Words can derive new meanings from the cultural developments. For example, according to UrbanDictionary.com, "jump the couch" has now become slang for "a defining moment when you know someone has gone off the deep end." This term was inspired by Tom Cruise's behavior on "Oprah," in which he bounced off of the couch to profess his love for Katie Holmes. Indeed, new words are continually being invented as societies evolve. As an example, William Safire notes the introduction of the following terms related to Internet blogs:

> A ping is not just the word for a sound anymore. It is also an acronym for "packet Internet gopher," a program that tests whether a destination is online and can also be the gently noisy notification sent when a blog needs updating or has been updated. Link love is "an unsolicited, posted link that aims only to amuse or interest." Other blogophiles call it linky love and stress a more intimate sense of reciprocity: "to link to another blogger because that person has linked to you." One who carries this yearning for online linkage to extremes is called a link slut or worse. Bloggers do not treat this as prurient, nor is "the discovery that some other blogger has posted an identical thought at the same time," which they call simultaneous blogasm.
>
> Delicious, though an adjective in standard usage, is both a noun and a verb in blargon: Adlam defines it as "a social bookmarking service that allows users to share their bookmarked sites with others. To del.icio.us someone is to add them to your delicious bookmarks. Many bloggers strive to make it onto the del.icio.us front page (otherwise known as being popular)." This has led to the verbal noun or gerund deliciousing.[3]

The selection of particular words in a media presentation can provide insight into the media communicator's attitude toward the subject. The following language configurations can affect the essential meaning of a concept.

Connotative Words

Connotation refers to the meaning associated with a word beyond its *denotative* (dictionary) definition. The meaning of a connotative word is universally understood and agreed upon. For instance, the word "house" simply describes a structure. However, "home" suggests a much richer meaning—a family gathered around the hearth, children playing video games, and the smells of dinner wafting in from the kitchen.

Sometimes the connotative meaning of a word has a cultural context. For example, in the United States, the sun has a positive connotation; to have a "sunny disposition" is a compliment. But in Egypt, which is largely desert, the sun is perceived as cruel. As a result, to be described as "a ray of sunshine" would be an unfavorable comment. Instead, being compared to moonlight would be considered a compliment.[4]

Advertising often relies on connotative words to sell products. Brand names like Country Time lemonade conjures up positive associations from America's mythic past to sell the product. (For further discussion, see Chapter 13, Advertising.)

Euphemisms

Euphemisms are terms that are intended to minimize the reaction of the audience to media messages. For instance, at some hospitals, instead of dying, some people simply experience *negative patient-care outcome*.[5]

Advertisers employ euphemisms to change public perceptions of products. For instance, the California fruit industry has changed the name prunes (with its medicinal connotation) to *dried plums*.

Public relations firms also rely upon euphemisms as a strategy to sell unpopular policies and programs. As an example, as the gambling industry devised its campaign to legalize casinos throughout the United States, polls revealed that some people considered *gambling* to be immoral. Consequently, efforts to legalize casinos met with less resistance when the name of the industry was changed from gambling to *gaming*.

Politicians rely on euphemisms to present information that might be unfavorably received by the public. Thus, rather than using the word "hunger" to describe the 12 percent of Americans (35 million) who could not put food on their table at least part of the year, the Agriculture Department now describes these people as experiencing *very low food security*. (For further discussion, see Chapter 14, American Political Communications.)

Public figures who are caught in scandals use the following euphemisms to explain their resignations: "To spend more time with my family" or "To pursue other interests."

CONNOTATIVE IMAGES

Some images possess universal associative properties. Photographs of animals generate a positive response among audiences, regardless of variables like culture, gender, income, or race. Other images are sure to generate other affective responses such as fear, laughter, or repulsion. For instance, images of babies evoke warm feelings associated with innocence, life, and love. An image of a rose is a symbol of romantic love.

However, other images derive their meaning through *context*. For instance, fire can symbolize either protection or destruction—the precise connotative meaning becomes clear through the context of the presentation. Other connotative images derive their meaning through their cultural context. As an example, long before the swastika became the emblem of

Figure 11.3
Some images engender universal responses. For instance, the photo of young Elijah Operhall evokes a universally warm emotional reaction from the audience. Photograph by Harriet Worobey.

the Nazi party in the 1920s, it was regarded as a positive symbol throughout the world. The word "swastika" is actually derived from the Sanskrit word "svastika," which means well being and good fortune. The earliest known swastikas date from 2500 or 3000 BC in India and Central Asia. Synagogues in North Africa, Palestine, and Hartford were built with swastika mosaics. Indeed, Buddha's footprints were said to be swastikas.

In the early twentieth century, the swastika was a common icon in the United States as well. Coca-Cola issued a swastika pendant as an advertising promotion. And during World War I, the American 45th Infantry division wore a shoulder patch adorned with an orange swastika. Only after the Nazis adopted this symbol was the swastika associated with evil.

Astute media communicators are able to use connotative images to their advantage. For example, in 2003, George W. Bush landed a plane on the USS *Abraham Lincoln* to announce that the mission in Iraq was successfully concluded. As he emerged from the plane in his pilot gear, he projected an image of a warrior who had successfully protected the United States from an impending threat.

Photographs can be altered through the manipulation of digital images to construct a new reality. In August 2006, it was discovered that freelance Lebanese photographer Adnan Hajj had doctored an image of the aftermath of an Israeli air strike on Beirut. The photo, which was taken for Reuters the global news and information agency, showed thick black

Figure 11.4
Photographs may also convey unintended messages. To illustrate, in 2007, BBC News captured a photo of Defense Minister Amir Peretz watching military maneuvers of Israeli troops in the Golan Heights through binoculars that still had the lens caps on, as Israeli army's new chief of staff, Gen. Gabi Ashkenazi explained what was in view. This image reinforced the popular conception of Peretz (and the Israeli administration) as inept in the handling of the invasion of Lebanon in 2006. [AP Images]

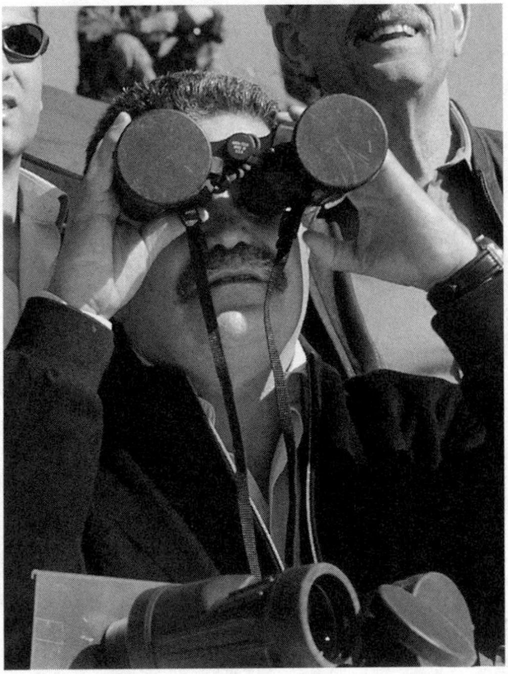

smoke rising above buildings in the Lebanese capital after an Israeli air raid. By adding the smoke, the photographer was commenting on the devastation of the attack and the culpability of the Israelis.

PERFORMANCE

A strong performance can transform a mediocre film, TV, or radio script into an electrifying experience. The keys to a good performance are nonverbal and verbal performance skills.

Nonverbal Performance Skills

Mahima Ranjan Kundu defines nonverbal communication skills as "all the gestures, expressions, postures, etc. that are used in the process of communication."[6] Communications scholars estimate that nonverbal communication comprises 65 percent of all communication between people.[7]

Figure 11.5
The clear and persuasive nature of nonverbal communication is epitomized in the performance of silent film stars like Charlie Chaplin. His walk, gestures, and facial expressions were a central part of his familiar endearing persona—the Little Tramp.

According to media relations consultant Tripp Frohlichstein, nonverbal elements such as appearance, costume, facial expression, body type, gestures, and movement play a role in hiring selections, work appraisals, and promotions.

- *Eye contact.* Good eye contact is important in convincing the viewer of your credibility. Wandering eyes may represent deceit, confusion, or lack of sincerity. When on television, maintain eye contact with the reporter asking the questions. If you are on a talk show, talk primarily to the host and do not look at the camera. If someone else is talking, look at them to show your interest. Even with a print reporter or a radio host, maintain solid eye contact. Some reporters assume that shifty eyes signal shifty thoughts.
- *Gestures.* Use gestures when appropriate and natural. Since we think in pictures, gestures can help augment points being addressed.... Do not use broad sweeping gestures for TV because the camera sees only a limited area. (When standing, keep your hands at your side except when gesturing.)
- *Open face.* Keep your eyebrows up and smile when appropriate. This helps you better convey your pride, as well as intensity. When the eyebrows are flat, so are your voice and feelings. When your eyebrows are down, so is the interview and you may be perceived as angry or negative.
- *Nodding.* Don't nod in agreement if the interviewer is reciting a litany of your company's negatives. You may simply be saying, "I'm listening" but this could be perceived by the audience as agreeing with those negatives.
- *Glasses.* Avoid shiny metal or chrome frames which will catch and reflect the light. Thin tortoise shell frames are best. Neutral shades that blend with your hair and skin tone are recommended. Make sure they fit correctly so you are not always pushing them up on your nose.
- *Mannerisms*

DO	*DON'T*
Sit up straight	Fold your arms
Lean forward	Make fists
Keep your hands folded in your lap or on chair	Dig fingers into arms of the arm of your chair when not talking
Keep your head perpendicular to your shoulders to add to your authority	Pick cuticles
Pay attention to the person who is talking (mentally and physically)	Fiddle with pencils
Keep an open face and smile when appropriate	Slouch
Sit with legs together or crossed at the knee	Swivel back and forth on a swivel chair
	Smoke
	Tap fingers
	Jiggle legs

In addition to the above rules, women have several additional guidelines to observe:

DO	*DON'T*
May sit with legs crossed at the ankles	Cross your legs at all if your skirt is short
	Coyly tilt your head
	Have purse visible
	Play with earrings or hair

- *Costume* and *makeup* are other important ingredients in performance.

Frohlichstein includes the following tips for men:

- Blue, tan, and gray apparel
- Blue or pastel shirts
- Outfit that explains your profession (doctors, construction, businessmen, etc.)
- Polished shoes
- No black, brown, yellow-red, red-orange, or loud, clashing colors (causes bleeding and blurring on home screen)
- No sunglasses outside or photogray glasses inside (makes you look like a criminal)
- Makeup (if offered)

In addition to the rules cited above, women should observe the following guidelines:

- Wear closed-toe shoes
- Avoid sexy or frilly outfits
- Avoid clunky or glittering jewelry (distracting)
- Red, gray, and blue are acceptable colors for women
- Women shouldn't wear too much lipstick. The same color as one's tongue looks natural. Women should get a pancake makeup as close to skin tone as possible, cheating toward a slightly darker shade if you can't get an exact match. Test it on the back of your hand.... Put on exposed areas, including back of hands.[8]

Nonverbal performance elements play a particularly significant role in television news presentations. A shrug, lifted eyebrow, or frown provides commentary on the script. Indeed, Brian Mullen identified a link between a newscaster's facial expressions and the voting behaviors of the audience. Mullen monitored the nonverbal performances of the network anchormen (with the sound off) during the week prior to the 1984 U.S. presidential election, rating the anchors' facial expressions when they mentioned presidential candidates Ronald Reagan and Walter Mondale.

Mullen next surveyed a cross-section of Americans to determine: 1) their choice of presidential candidate; and 2) the television newscaster they watched most often. Mullen discovered the following:

- Peter Jennings of ABC consistently appeared more positive when referring to Ronald Reagan.
- The voters who regularly watched Jennings were more likely than others to vote for Reagan.

Mullen concluded that the results "are consistent with a link between newscasters' facial expressions and viewers' voting behaviors."[9] Mullen hastened to qualify the results of his study. The methodology was admittedly subjective (after all, what *is* a positive expression?). Moreover, it remains unclear whether Jennings actually influenced his audience or merely attracted those viewers *already* predisposed to support Reagan.

However, this study demonstrates that performance does influence the public, even in the "objective" world of broadcast journalism. Undoubtedly, Jennings was unaware that he exhibited positive behaviors when he spoke of Reagan; nevertheless, this nonverbal message was clear to the public. Audiences look to media figures for approval and disapproval on a wide variety of topics. Consequently, media communicators should be aware that even subtle nonverbal expressions can have a powerful influence on the public.

Verbal Performance Skills

When used effectively, a performer's voice quality and delivery reinforce media messages. Frohlichstein offers the following advice on various aspects of verbal performance.

- *Volume*. Do not use loudness to make a point—you'll lose warmth. Too soft a voice makes you hard to hear and the listener loses the message.... Also, low volume lacks emotional commitment.
- *Tone*. Tone refers to the quality or character of sound. A deep tone suggests authority, power, and confidence. Frohlichstein observes, "Exercise your voice before doing interviews. Use varying pitch and modulation."
- *Clarity*. People must understand the words you are saying. "Nuance" can become "new ants."
- *Speed*. Too fast and listeners can't follow you. Too slow and you become ponderous and boring.
- *Pacing*. Vary it to keep listeners' interest.
- *Feelings*. It is vital that your voice reflects your interest and concern with the topic.[10]

Beyond all of the technical reasons for an actor's success, there is also an intangible quality to performance. As an example, Marilyn Monroe enjoyed a special relationship with the camera. The camera seemed almost to look inside Ms. Monroe, revealing her vulnerable self. Marilyn Monroe did indeed look larger than life on the silver screen, which is one reason why Monroe has retained her following long after her death.

SOUND ELEMENTS

The element of sound can send very subtle messages, by either enhancing or altering moods. Sound occurs in three different forms in media productions: *dialogue, music*, and *background sound*.

Dialogue is written material intended to *sound* like conversation. However, if you transcribed a conversation between a small group of people, you would probably discover that it is confusing to read. The conversation would be filled with interruptions and times when several people are speaking at once. Further, this transcript would be characterized by interpolations, such as "you know" and "like," which are intended to give the speaker extra time to think and decide what to say.

In contrast, scripted dialogue is clear and free of interruptions. An excellent example of effective dialogue can be found in Ted Tally's screenplay of Thomas Harris's novel, *The Silence of the Lambs* (1991). Consider the first encounter between FBI candidate Clarice Starling and the sophisticated, nefarious Dr. Hannibal "The Cannibal" Lecter:

DR. LECTER: You're so ambitious, aren't you ... ? You know what you look like to me, with your good bag and your cheap shoes? You look like a rube. A well-scrubbed, hustling rube with a little taste ... Good nutrition has given you some length of bone, but you're not more than one generation from poor white trash, are you—Agent Starling ... ? That accent you've tried so desperately to shed—pure West Virginia. What is your father, dear? Is he a coal miner? Does he stink of the lamp?

His every word strikes her like a small, precise dart.

DR. LECTER (cont.): And oh, how quickly the boys found you! All those tedious, sticky fumblings, in the back seats of cars, while you could only dream of getting out. Getting anywhere, yes? Getting all the way to the F ... B ... I.

CLARICE (shaken): You see a lot, Dr. Lecter. But are you strong enough to point that high-powered perception at yourself? How about it ... ? Look at yourself and write down the truth. (She slams the tray back at him) Or maybe you're afraid to.

DR. LECTER: You're a tough one, aren't you?

CLARICE: Reasonably so. Yes.

DR. LECTER: And you'd hate to think you were common. My, wouldn't that sting! Well you're far from common, Clarice Starling. All you have is the fear of it. (pause) Now please excuse me. Good day.

A great deal has occurred in this very brief bit of dialogue. Although Clarice is conducting the interview, it is clear that Dr. Lecter is very much in control. Clarice (and the audience) discover that Dr. Lecter is far from a common criminal. He is extraordinarily charming, intelligent, and perceptive—dangerous qualities when combined with Lecter's vicious nature.

We also learn about Clarice in this sequence. Dr. Lecter has zeroed in her background and motivation for pursuing a career in the FBI. She feels violated—with good reason, as Lecter coldheartedly exposes her deepest fears and insecurities. However, Clarice fights back, showing Lecter (and us as well) that she is indeed tough enough to withstand the trials awaiting her in the remainder of the film.

Moreover, a strange, complex relationship forms between Starling and Dr. Lecter during this scene. Clarice is fascinated by Lecter's certainty about the world, his powers of perception, and even the evil that drives him. Lecter has been testing the novice FBI agent. However, Clarice has successfully withstood his attempt to intimidate her and destroy her resolve. By the end of the conversation, Lecter acknowledges that Clarice is "far from common." This admission, however, does not prevent him from continuing to play games with Agent Starling, a challenge which she recognizes and accepts.

Thus, a script may contain a great deal of information and complex layers of meaning. As a result, it is not always easy to follow dialogue in radio, film, and television. There are limits to the amount of information that a person can absorb strictly through their sense of hearing. And because dialogue is presented very rapidly, like speech, the audience member can easily confuse the message being delivered.

Music can have a subtle, yet powerful influence, enhancing our moods or distracting us from our immediate concerns. Indeed, music therapy is an effective form of treatment for a variety of physical conditions. As an example, soothing music can help premature babies use oxygen more effectively, gain weight faster, and leave the hospital more quickly.[11] Stroke patients have also learned to develop their cadence, stride, and foot placement by moving to synchronized music.[12]

Music is frequently used to manipulate attitudes and behaviors in public settings. Some companies have installed pre-programmed Muzak in the workplace, in an effort to improve office productivity.

Music may also be selected carefully to accelerate the turnover rate of customers. Some 7-Eleven convenience stores play classical music to dissuade teens from congregating. According to Stephanie Coulter, some restaurants play fast-paced songs at a high volume "to get people agitated so they eat faster, talk more, drink more."[13] One study found that people chew an average of 4.4 bites a minute to fast music, but only 3.88 bites a minute to slow music.[14]

Music is also used as a narrative device in film and television presentations. Music can function as a *convention* that conveys subtle cues to the audience about the narrative. For instance, theme music for the evening news often simulates the rhythm of teletypes. In this case, the musical score helps to establish the seriousness and legitimacy of the news operation. Music is particularly effective in foreign films, in which the audience is largely unfamiliar with the language in the film. (For further discussion of conventions, see Chapter 10.)

A film score is often used in conjunction with the visuals, to "punctuate," or emphasize themes and messages. In the documentary *Fahrenheit 9/11* (2004), filmmaker Michael Moore included a very moving scene showing the aftermath of the tragic attack on the World Trade Center. The falling motion of the debris from the explosion falling to earth (which was shown in slow motion) served as a metaphor for the fallen hopes and dreams of the country in the wake of the tragedy. The score of this scene consisted mainly of a piano, playing scales, from high to low, accentuating the feel of the falling debris.

Musical scores can also articulate themes in a media presentation. As an example, at the conclusion of *Garden State* (2004), Andrew (Zach Braff) has announced his decision to return to Los Angeles to "work some things out," leaving Sam (Natalie Portman) behind. The song "Let Go" plays over shots of Sam sitting in the airport crying. At the end of the song, Andrew reappears: he is "letting go" of his emotional baggage and returns to work things out with Sam.

Finally, a tune, rhythm, or chord can also signal a narrative shift, preparing the audience for a transition between scenes, and foreshadowing upcoming events. For instance, the infamous theme from *Jaws* (1975) always signaled the approach of the killer shark before he attacked his next victim.

Background Sound: Natural Sound and Sound Effects

Natural sound refers to the sounds that normally occur within a setting, such as crowd noise at a baseball game or waves lapping up on the beach. To add a feeling of realism, natural sound is frequently added to "sweeten" the audio track of a film and television programming. Indeed, a beach scene would be noticeably artificial if we did *not* hear the waves hitting the shore or the squeal of seagulls. Without this background noise, the message would be one of *omission*; that what we are watching, in fact, is a movie and not real life.

Sound effects are pre-recorded sounds such as doors closing, horses galloping, and spurs jingling that are added to broadcast presentations for dramatic emphasis. For instance, radio serials from the 1930s made generous use of sound effects to advance the plot. Sound effects are also used in film and television. Much of the dramatic thrust of martial arts movies is created during the post-production process, when the action is "sweetened" by thumping rugs, tearing sheets, and dropping bags of flour. In addition, the synthesizer has emerged as an important technological innovation that produces a range of sound effects—from the most mundane to the eerie and supernatural.

The relationship between these three areas of sound—music, dialogue, and natural sound—can also convey messages. To illustrate, in *The Adventures of Robin Hood* (1938), starring Errol Flynn, the climax of the film is a scene in which Robin's men storm the castle to dethrone Prince John and restore King Richard to the throne of England. In the midst of the fray, Robin meets the villainous Sir Guy of Gisbourne in combat and emerges victorious. Erich Wolfgang Korngold's stirring film score dominates the soundtrack, heightening the romance and drama of the duel.

However, *Robin Hood: Prince of Thieves* (1991) used natural sound as the dominant element of the soundtrack in the climactic scene (i.e., the clanging of the swords and the grunting of the two warriors). Consequently, this version of the scene emphasized the violence and danger of the battle, as opposed to the romantic feel of the 1939 original.

SUMMARY

Mindful of the principle of economy, the skillful media communicator uses style not merely as ornamentation but as a means of reinforcing messages. Production values subtly affect how the audience responds to media content.

Media communicators often make conscious decisions with regard to production values such as color, lighting, and angle. However, at other times they may make an intuitive choice—because it "feels right." In this case, media communicators instinctively select the color scheme or camera angle that best fits the intended mood of the presentation. Consequently, even if communicators do not articulate the reasons behind their selections, they nevertheless are making decisions based on the affective properties of production values.

A sensitivity to production elements is therefore a useful way to approach the interpretation of media messages.

NOTES

1. Herbert Zettl, *Sight, Sound, Motion: Applied Media Aesthetics* (Belmont, CA: Wadsworth, 1990), 225.
2. Joseph V. Mascelli, *The Five C's of Cinematography* (Hollywood, CA: Cine/Graphic, 1965), 115.
3. William Safire, "Blargon," *New York Times Magazine*, February 19, 2006.

4. Marieke K. de Mooij, *Global Marketing and Advertising: Understanding Cultural Paradoxes* (Thousand Oaks, CA: Sage, 1998), 52.
5. Charles Downey, "Word Processing," *St. Louis Post-Dispatch*, October 22, 1994, D1.
6. Mahima Ranjan Kundu, "Visual Literacy: Teaching Non-Verbal Communication Through Television," *Educational Technology* l6:8 (August 1976), 31.
7. Ibid.
8. Tripp Frohlichstein, *Media Training Handbook* (St. Louis, MO: MediaMasters, 1991), 31–37.
9. Ruth Moss, "Candidate Camera," *Psychology Today,* December 1986, 20.
10. Frohlichstein, *Media Training Handbook,* 31.
11. Bob Condor, "Used to Improve Health, Mind, and Mood, Music Therapy Is Sounding Better All the Time," *Chicago Tribune,* December 28, 1998.
12. Ibid.
13. *St. Louis Post-Dispatch*, January 5, 1998, B15.
14. Ibid.

KEYS TO INTERPRETING MEDIA MESSAGES

These pages may be used as a reference for media literacy analysis:

I. Process

A. Media Communicator

1. Who is responsible for creating the media production?
2. What are the demographic characteristics of the media communicator(s)?
3. How do these characteristics affect the content and outlook of the media production?

B. Function

1. What is the purpose behind the production?
2. Does the media communicator want you to think or behave in a particular way as a result of receiving the information?
3. Does the production contain any of the following?
    a. Latent functions
    b. Multiple functions
    c. Undefined functions
    d. False functions
    e. Competing functions

C. Comparative Media

1. What are the medium's distinctive characteristics?
2. In what ways does the choice of medium affect:
    a. The communication strategy?
    b. The communication style?
    c. The content?

D. Audience

1. For whom is the media presentation produced?
2. Is there more than one intended audience?
3. What values, experiences, and perspectives are shared by the audience? Do these shared values, experiences, or perspectives influence their understanding or interpretation of the presentation?
4. How do the experiences and perspectives of the individual audience member affect his or her interpretation of the presentation?
5. How does the choice of audience influence the strategy, style, and content of the media presentation?
6. Do the strategy, style, and content of the media presentation provide insight into the intended audience(s)?

II. Context

A. Historical Context

1. What does the media production tell us about the period in which it was produced?

   a. When was this media production first presented?

   b. What events were occurring when the presentation was produced?

   c. How has the media presentation been influenced by the events of the day?

   d. Does the media presentation comment on the events of the day?

   e. How does an understanding of these events furnish perspective into the presentation?

2. Does an understanding of historical events provide insight into the media presentation?

   a. Media presentations made during a particular historical period:

      1) What events were occurring when the presentation was produced?

      2) What prior events led to the climate in which this media presentation was produced?

      3) How did people react to the production when it was first presented? Why?

         a) How do people react to the production today?

         b) How do you account for any differences in reaction?

      4) How does an understanding of these events furnish perspective into the presentation?

   b. Historical References

      1) Are there historical references in the media production?

      2) How does an understanding of these historical references affect your understanding of the media presentation?

3. Does a media presentation furnish perspective into current attitudes toward historical events?

4. Did the media presentation anticipate or foreshadow any political or historical events? Explain.

5. Did the presentation play any role in shaping the events of the day? Explain.

6. In the case of *entertainment* programming, is the dramatization an accurate portrait of events? Compare the presentation with historically accurate accounts of the event or period.

   a. Are the causes leading to the events in the presentation clear?

   b. What were the consequences of the dramatized events?

7. In the case of a *news* story, how much historical context has been provided? Where would you find the answers to these unanswered questions?

8. In countries with restricted civil liberties, does media programming comment on political and cultural issues in an indirect fashion? Explain.
9. Can a media program from a different era furnish perspective into the cultural attitudes, values, and behaviors of the period in which it was produced? Explain.
10. Systems Approach to Media History: Evolution of Media Systems
    a. In what ways does the history of a medium fit into the following Stages of Evolution:
        1) Inception Stage
            a) Decentralization
            b) Innovation
            c) Impact of historical events on the development of the medium
        2) Embryonic Stage
            a) Corporate sponsorship
            b) Expensive technology
            c) Affluent, elite audience
            d) Programming
                1) Innovative
                2) Elite
        3) Popular Stage
            a) Rapid growth of audience
            b) Technology becomes more affordable
            c) Formulas and conventions of genres are established
            d) Broadcasting approach to programming
        4) Mature Stage
            a) Bought by mega-corporations; profit incentive affects programming
            b) Narrowcasting/microcasting approach to programming
            c) Innovations in programming—to "break through the clutter"
    b. In what ways (if any) does the history of this medium *depart* from the patterns discussed in the chapter? What are the implications of these departures?
11. Systems Approach to Media History: Phases of Media Ecology
    a. In what ways does the history of a medium fit into the following phases?
        1) Phase I: New Medium as Threat
            a) Appropriating programming
            b) Siphoning audience base

2) Phase II: Specialization
    a) Technology
    b) Programming
    c) Target audience
3) Phase III: Assimilation
    a) Technical convergence
    b) Programming
    c) Consolidation of ownership

b. In what ways (if any) does the history of these media *depart* from the patterns discussed in the chapter? What are the implications of these departures?

B. Cultural Context

1. Media & Popular Culture

a. In what ways does the media presentation *reflect*:
    1) Cultural attitudes
    2) Values
    3) Behaviors
    4) Preoccupations
    5) Myths
    6) Cultural changes
    7) Attitudes toward groups

b. In what ways does the media presentation *reinforce*:
    1) Cultural attitudes
    2) Values
    3) Behaviors
    4) Preoccupations
    5) Myths

c. In what ways does the media presentation *shape*:
    1) Cultural attitudes
    2) Values
    3) Behaviors
    4) Preoccupations
    5) Myths

2. *Worldview:* What kind of world is depicted in the media presentation?

a. What culture or cultures populate this world?
    1) What kinds of people populate this world?
    2) What is the ideology of this culture?

b. What do we know about the people who populate this world?
   1) Are characters presented in a stereotypical manner?
   2) What does this tell us about the cultural stereotype of this group?

c. Does this world present an optimistic or pessimistic view of life?
   1) Are the characters in the presentation happy?
   2) Do the characters have a *chance* to be happy?

d. Are people in control of their own destinies?
   1) Is there a supernatural presence in this world?
   2) Are the characters under the influence of other people?

e. What hierarchy of values is in operation in this worldview?
   1) What embedded values can be found in the production?
   2) What values are embodied in the characters?
   3) What values prevail through the resolution?
   4) What does it mean to be a success in this world?
      a) How does a person succeed in this world?
      b) What kinds of behavior are rewarded in this world?

C. Structure

1. What are the ownership patterns within the media industry?
   a. What are the ownership patterns within the particular media system you are examining? (e.g., television, film, radio)
   b. Who owns the production company which has produced the presentation you are examining? (e.g., television station, newspaper, film company)
2. Does the ownership of the media presentation have an impact on its content?
   a. Support of status quo
   b. Homogeneity of content
   c. Programming for profit
   d. Cross-promotion
3. Does government regulation affect the media presentation?
4. What is the internal structure of the media organization responsible for producing the media presentation? How does this internal structure influence content?
   a. What are the resources of the production company?
   b. What is the organizational framework of the production company?
   c. What is the process of decision-making in the production company?

III. Framework

A. Introduction

1. Title: What does the title of the presentation signify?
2. Introduction as Foreshadowing Device:
    a. What events constitute the introduction of the media presentation?
    b. What does the introduction tell us about the presentation?
    c. Does the introduction foreshadow events and themes in the body of the production?
3. Illogical Premise
    a. Is the premise of the presentation logical?
    b. What are the underlying assumptions behind the premise of the presentation?
    c. What is the impact of this premise on the messages conveyed in the presentation?
    d. Do you accept the underlying premise in the presentation?
    e. If not, are you willing to suspend your disbelief?

B. Plot

1. Explicit Content: What are the significant events in the story?
2. Affective Response
    a. How does the media communicator want you to be feeling at particular points in the plot?
        1) Why does the media communicator want you to be feeling this way?
        2) Is the media communicator successful in eliciting this intended emotional response?
    b. Do your affective responses provide insight into media messages? Explain.
    c. Do your affective responses provide insight into your personal belief system? Explain.
3. Implicit Content
    a. What is the relationship between the significant events in the narrative?
    b. What is the relationship between the characters in the narrative?
    c. What are the characters' motives for their actions?
    d. Are the consequences to specific behaviors defined?
4. Subplots
    a. Can you identify any subplots in the narrative?
    b. Are there any connections between the subplots that provide insight into the worldview, characters, and themes in the production?

C. Genre
   1. Does the presentation belong to any recognizable genre?
   2. Is there a predictable formula for the genre? What insights do these formula provide into the genre? Into the specific program?
      a. Formulaic Function
      b. Formulaic Premise
      c. Formulaic Structure
      d. Formulaic Plot
      e. Conventions
         1) Conventional Storyline
         2) Setting
         3) Stock characters
         4) Trappings
   3. What does this genre suggest about:
      a. Cultural attitudes and values?
      b. Cultural preoccupations?
      c. Cultural myths?
      d. Worldview?
   4. Can you trace the evolution of this genre?
      a. Have there been shifts in the genre over time?
      b. What do these shifts in genre reveal about changes in the culture?
D. Conclusion
   1. Character Development
      a. Have the major characters changed as a result of the events in the story? How? Why?
      b. What have the characters learned as a result of their experience?
   2. Illogical Conclusion
      a. Does the conclusion of the presentation follow logically from the established premise, characters, and worldview?
      b. If not, how should the presentation have ended, given the established premise, characters, and worldview?
      c. How would you have preferred for the story to end? Why?

IV. Production Elements
   A. Editing
   B. Color
   C. Lighting
   D. Shape
   E. Scale

F. Relative Position
G. Movement
H. Point of View
I. Angle
J. Connotation
   1. Words
   2. Image
K. Performance
L. Sound
   1. Music
   2. Dialogue
   3. Background Sound

*What *manifest messages* are in the presentation?

*What *latent messages* were you able to identify?

PART

3

MEDIA FORMATS

CHAPTER 12

JOURNALISM

PROCESS: FUNCTION

American news channels, such as newspapers, magazines, radio, television, and the Internet, serve a variety of manifest functions.

Information. In the United States, news outlets are essential to the public's ability to make informed decisions. The Society of Professional Journalists' Code of Ethics declares:

> The public's right to know of events of public importance and interest is the overriding mission of the mass media. The purpose of distributing news and enlightened opinion is to serve the general welfare.
>
> Journalists who use their professional status as representatives of the public for selfish or other unworthy motives violate a high trust.[1]

One of the principal functions of news outlets is to provide *hard news* coverage. Hard news stories focus on topical events and issues that furnish readers with a vital connection to the nation and the world.

News programs also present vital information about the reader's community. Newspapers, radio reports, and local television programming provide weather forecasts, television listings, and calendars of events that help individuals function on an everyday basis. Moreover, birth announcements, weddings, and obituaries keep the reader informed about significant rites of passage.

Persuasion. The press serves as a forum for debate and offers a point of view on events for the consideration of its readers. Journalists take this charge seriously. To illustrate, the *St. Louis Post-Dispatch* carries an editorial platform authored by Joseph Pulitzer in 1907 which clearly defines this function:

> I know that my retirement will make no difference in its cardinal principles, that it will always fight for progress and reform, never tolerate injustice or corruption, always fight demagogues of all parties, never belong to any party, always oppose privileged classes and public plunderers, never lack sympathy with the poor, always remain devoted to the public welfare, never be satisfied with merely printing news, always be drastically independent, never be afraid to attack wrong, whether by predatory plutocracy or predatory poverty.

Ideally, the persuasive function is confined to the editorial section of the paper or is accompanied by an identifying graphic on the TV screen. However, journalists can also subtly influence public opinion through such production elements as word choice, editing decisions, and story placement.

Disclosure. The American press plays a critical role in detecting injustices and abuses within the system. Watergate is a prime example; in the 1970s, investigative reporters Bob Woodward and Carl Bernstein of the *Washington Post* uncovered a story leading to criminal convictions, a presidential resignation, and legislative reforms. A more recent example occurred in 2007, when the *Washington Post* published a series of articles revealing that Walter Reed Hospital was providing substandard care for military veterans—not just veterans of Iraq but of the Vietnam war as well. In response, President Bush formed a commission to investigate the matter, as well as the broader issue of veterans' benefits.

Entertainment. Because of market considerations, newspapers are now pressured to present *entertainment as news*. Features, sports, and celebrity gossip frequently appear in the news section of the newspaper. Further, television programs like *Entertainment Tonight* and *NFL Today* employ the conventions of news programs, such as desks, anchorpeople, and video backdrops, further blurring the distinction between news and entertainment.

Agenda Setting. Even if a newspaper or TV news program doesn't tell us what to think, they do tell us what to think *about*. Newspapers are not always successful in persuading their audience to adopt their position on issues like national health care or legalized abortion; however, there is little doubt that media coverage brings these issues to the attention of the public as matters of consequence.

Profit. As a market-driven industry, American news operations are geared to produce a profit. Consequently, news programming increasingly presents *news as entertainment*. TV news programming is influenced by the entertainment sensibility of television. News producers tend to select stories that are dramatic, sensational, have an identifiable cast of characters, and a clear narrative structure (with a beginning, middle, and conclusion). Former presidential press secretary Mike McCurry laments,

> (The Press) has lost any sense of nobility about their profession. Just go channel surfing and you see pro wrestling, and you see roller derby, and you see *Hardball* with Chris Matthews and you see *Crossfire*; it's kind of all the same genre. It's false conflict presented as serious discussion.[2]

The entertainment sensibility also affects the selection of stories in news broadcasts. In 2006, 60 percent of local TV newscasts—once traffic, weather and sports are excluded—consisted of crime and accident stories.[3]

But significantly, a survey reveals that 62 percent of the American public thinks that the news is too sensationalized, and 76 percent said the press spent too much time reporting on the private lives of public officials.[4] This would suggest that newspapers might be more successful if they were less driven by profit and instead concentrated on their role as a public service.

Propaganda. In countries that feature a state-owned media system such as China and North Korea, the media is clearly an instrument of the government. But even in countries in which the media is privately owned, governments have used the media as a vehicle for propaganda. As an example, in 2005, *USA Today* disclosed that conservative commentator and columnist Armstrong Williams was paid $240,000 by the Education Department to promote the No Child Left Behind Act on his syndicated television program, without revealing that the government paid him to make these comments on the air. Consequently, while the manifest function of his remarks was to *inform* the public, his latent purpose was to *persuade* his audience to support the education initiative.

Comparative Media

Thanks to innovations in media technology, individuals have much more choice with regard to the channel through which the news is delivered. Print newspapers, radio, television, and the Internet are the primary channels, but individuals are able to get news updates on their BlackBerries and cellphones as well. Although television remains the most popular source of news (with nearly half of the population spending at least 30 minutes a day getting their news from TV), the number of people who regularly watch nightly network news is down to 28 percent, half the total from 1993. And early-evening news ratings for local TV were down 13 percent.[5]

Although the choice of media may have shifted, Americans spend about the same time keeping up on the news (just over an hour a day) as they did a decade ago.[6] Approximately one-third of U.S. residents get their news online, while only one in 50 did a decade ago.[7] Seven percent of those polled looked for news on "new media" such as cellphones, personal digital assistants, and podcasts. (Among those 18–29 years of age, the number is 13 percent.)[8] And although newspaper circulation fell 2.6 percent during the first six months of 2006, newspaper-run web sites reported an 8 percent increase in viewers over the same time period.

It must be emphasized that, depending on the medium selected, the audience is getting a different *kind* of news. Watching the news on television provides insight into the events as they unfold, while print journalism furnishes valuable perspective into these events. Consequently, the best course of action is a *balanced media diet*, consulting different media to get a broader understanding of events. Indeed, after President Bush announced his support for limited stem cell research in 2001, CBS anchorperson Dan Rather advised his television audience that they should also read the newspaper to grasp this complex issue:

> Obviously, this is a very complicated subject. It's the kind of subject that, frankly, radio and television have some difficulty with, because it requires such depth into the complexities of it. We can with, I think, impunity, recommend that if you're really interested in this, you'll want to read in detail one of the better newspapers tomorrow.[9]

Print. The most radical decline with regard to the consumption of news is print media. In 2006, just over four in 10 adults said they had read a newspaper, in print or online, the previous day, compared with 58 percent in 1994.[10] American daily newspaper consumption is in decline. The average daily circulation of newspapers decreased by 2.8 percent during the six-month period ending September 30, 2006, compared with the same period of the previous year, the steepest in any comparable six-month period in at least 15 years.[11] Papers in major metropolitan areas, where more homes are wired for broadband Internet, fared worse than those in smaller markets. To illustrate, the *Los Angeles Times* lost 8 percent of its daily circulation and 6 percent on Sunday. The *Boston Globe*, owned by The New York Times Company, lost 6.7 percent of its daily circulation and almost 10 percent on Sunday.[12]

However, local and community news remain big attractions for traditional newspapers. Because of the concentration of media ownership, local news and information are often overlooked. But small, locally owned community newspapers remain a vital source of information. One study indicates that 61 percent of consumers look to their newspapers as an essential source for local news, events, and sports, followed by television (58 percent) and radio (35 percent).[13]

Radio. In the United States, commercial radio news is on the decline. For instance, in Philadelphia, over the past quarter century, the number of AM radio stations that feature news coverage has shrunk from five to two.[14]

To be sure, talk radio is a format that promotes discussion on current events. Talk-radio hosts are broadcast by more than 1,200 radio stations, plus the Internet, satellite radio, and television. They reach more than 100 million Americans weekly—about a third of the nation. However, the function of this format is not *information* but *persuasion*.

In radio, the audience can only process information aurally. As a result, it can be difficult to assimilate complex information and intricate sentence structure. Consequently, news broadcast on radio must be clear and concise. The content should be kept general, because people tend to get confused when they hear only a litany of facts and figures.

Television. Although TV remains the most popular source of news, viewership has declined. The number of people who regularly watch nightly network news was down to 28 percent in 2006, half the total from 1993.[15] Network evening news ratings dropped 6 percent and morning show ratings 4 percent. Early-evening news ratings for local TV were down 13 percent.[16]

Television remains a primary source of information about national and international issues. Seventy-one percent of respondents say they rely on network, cable, and satellite TV for national news.[17]

Digital Media. News programming is exploding on the Internet, in a variety of formats.

- Most newspapers have added an Internet component to their news operation, so that readers can access their information online.
- Online papers (that have no print companion) have emerged.
- Blogs

The Internet offers a choice of media within one newscast. The audience can use print, video, graphics, and audio, giving them different dimensions of a story within one medium.

Another significant feature of digital media is that the audience has unprecedented control. You can decide what features (e.g., video or photos) you want to see, or hit a "hot link" to learn more about particular aspects of a story. Howard Kurtz observes," The good news is that the average consumer can ... choose from sources he trusts and enjoys rather than being spoon-fed by a handful of big corporations."[18]

Young people primarily turn to the Internet for news. A 2006 Knight Foundation Study reveals that of high school students:

- 66 percent get their news and information from the news pages of Internet portals such as Google and Yahoo!
- 45 percent from national TV news web sites
- 34 percent from local TV or newspaper web sites
- 32 percent from blogs and
- 21 percent from national newspaper sites[19]

In addition, 7 percent of Americans got their news from new technologies such as cellphones, personal digital assistants, and podcasts. Among those aged 18–29, the number was 13 percent.[20]

But surprisingly, 31 percent of adults regularly logged in for news as well. Indeed, people in their forties were even more likely to go online for news than younger adults. People who go online for news cite the convenience and speed as factors in their preference for web sites like Yahoo, CNN, and MSNBC to get news. Google and AOL were also among the more popular sites.[21]

Media Communicator

Media Ownership and News Content. The ownership of a news organization has a dramatic impact on the content of news programming. For instance, according to an FCC study, local ownership of television stations adds almost five and a half minutes of total news to broadcasts and more than three minutes of "on-location" news.[22]

Because the media are a major industry in the United States, the corporate worldview has become predominant in media-carried content. Ben Bagdikian observes,

> No sacred cow has been so protected and has left more generous residues in the news than the American corporation.... (At the same time), large classes of people are ignored in the news, are reported as exotic fads, or appear only at their worst—minorities, blue-collar workers, the lower middle class, the poor. They become publicized mainly when they are in spectacular accidents, go on strike, or are arrested.... But since World War I hardly a mainstream American news medium has failed to grant its most favored treatment to corporate life.[23]

As part of the corporate community, newspaper owners may be susceptible to conflicts of interests that compromise their coverage. As an example, the *St. Louis Post-Dispatch* is an investor in the St. Louis Cardinals baseball team, which puts the newspaper in a compromising position with respect to its sports coverage.

Moreover, the owners of these wealthy and influential media companies frequently have ties to the political establishment, which affects their point of view. To illustrate, at the outset of the Iraq war in 2002, Clear Channel Inc., the largest radio conglomerate in the United States, organized and paid for a series of pro-war rallies in numerous U.S. cities, including Cleveland, Atlanta, and Philadelphia. Clear Channel Inc., is a corporation whose vice-chairman, Tom Hicks, has had longstanding and extensive financial ties to President George W. Bush.

On occasion, owners have directly intervened in editorial decisions when the issues affected their political interests. To illustrate, Rupert Murdoch, chairman of News Corporation (which owns Fox News), is a staunch supporter of the policies of the Bush administration. According to former Fox reporter John Du Pree, Murdoch informed his news staff that there was too much coverage of racial issues and HIV related stories and instructed them to include stories that discredited and embarrassed the Reverend Jesse Jackson.[24]

Reporting Personnel. The more familiar you are with the individuals who report and produce news programming, the better prepared you are to interpret their stories. In print journalism, the people who write the stories are relatively anonymous. Articles typically are accompanied only by the name of the reporter. In contrast, because of the visual nature of television news, broadcast anchors and reporters are recognizable; indeed, these journalists are often regarded as celebrities. However, it should be noted that essential personnel who influence the content of broadcast news programs, such as the owners, news directors, producers, writers, and editors, remain anonymous, behind the camera.

Becoming familiar with the media communicator remains the most challenging aspect of analyzing news presented on the Internet. Currently, there is no system of accountability for web pages and blogs; the writer may be using a pseudonym, may have no expertise in the field, or may have a distinct point of view that they bring to the coverage of an issue. (For more discussion, see Chapter 15, Digital Media.)

Editorials that appear in the newspaper may be unsigned, so you have no way to identify the writer. In the case of a guest editorial, a brief blurb generally accompanies the article that identifies the contributor. However, an alarming trend in print journalism is *selective disclosure*, in which only part of a contributor's background and affiliations are presented. For example, in 1998, Brent Scowcroft and Arnold Kanter wrote an op-ed piece for the *Washington Times*, entitled, "What technology went where and why," in which the authors declared that charges about Chinese technological espionage were "melodramatic." The article identified the authors as follows:

> Scowcroft, President of the Forum for International Policy, was national security advisor under Presidents Ford and Bush. Kanter, a senior fellow at the Forum for International Policy, served as undersecretary of state for Political Affairs from 1991 to 1993.

However, what went unmentioned was that Scowcroft was president and Kanter was a principal of The Scowcroft Group, a consulting firm that helps its corporate clients, including China, attract international business.[25] Clearly, this background information furnishes significant perspective into the point of view of this source.

Identifying the background of journalists has become even more problematic, due to newspapers' increasing reliance on news services, such as the Associated Press. In this cost-saving measure, a local copywriter takes a report sent over the "wire" by the news service and edits it to fit the available space in their papers. In the process, the reader has no way to know who wrote the original story.

Sources. Reporters often rely on a network of sources as they research stories, for several reasons. These sources may have access to information that would otherwise be unavailable. In addition, since industry pressures demand that reporters cover a wide range of topics within a limited time span, journalists must depend on experts, who can assimilate and interpret this complex information.

Identifying the sources that appear in the paper can help to put their contributions into perspective. The media often rely on a few sources that appear repeatedly in the media. A White House correspondent is quoted by Stephen Hess as explaining, "We're in small quarters with access to only a small number of official people, getting the same information. So we write similar stories and move on the same issues."[26]

To illustrate, the lineup for the Sunday morning television news on April 5, 2003, featured some familiar names that rotated from show to show:

- "Meet the Press" 8 A.M., Channel 5
  Deputy Defense Secretary Paul Wolfowitz and Gen. Peter Pace, vice chairman, Joint Chiefs of Staff.
- "Fox News Sunday" 9 A.M., Channel 2
  Deputy Defense Secretary Paul Wolfowitz and Kanan Makiya, Iraqi National Congress.
- "Face the Nation" 9:30 A.M., Channel 4
  Deputy Defense Secretary Paul Wolfowitz
- "This Week" 10 A.M., Channel 30
  Gen. Peter Pace, vice chairman, Joint Chiefs of Staff; and Sens. John Warner, R-Va., and Joseph Biden, D-Del.
- "Late Edition" 11 A.M., CNN
  Gen. Peter Pace, vice chairman, Joint Chiefs of Staff; and Sens. John Warner, R-Va., and Carl Levin, D-Mich.[27]

Assembling a *demographic profile* of these journalistic sources can furnish perspective into an expert's opinions. Factors that should be considered in identifying sources include *gender, age, economic bracket, educational background,* and *professional background.* For instance, the sources above are well-educated, white males over 50 years of age who are members of the Bush administration. Other important factors to consider include the following.

Ideology. The political orientation of a source influences how that person interprets the events of the day. For instance, an article may refer to a source as a member of the Heritage Foundation, "a conservative think tank." But what does this mean? Who funds this organization? And what is its mission?

In 2006, Media Matters, a progressive web-based research and information center, found that during the first quarter of 2006, the guests on TV political talk shows were predominantly conservative in their ideology:

On each show, Republicans and conservatives outnumbered Democrats and progressives in total guest appearances. *Face the Nation* featured nearly *twice* as many Republicans and conservatives as Democrats and progressives during the second quarter. That disparity was in line with the findings from the first quarter, which showed that 47 percent of the show's guests were Republicans and conservatives, while only 32 percent were Democrats and progressives. Compared with the first quarter, *Meet the Press* showed improvement in the second quarter; however, the program still hosted more Republicans and conservatives than Democrats and progressives.[28]

Motive. Why has a source agreed to appear in the newspaper? Understanding motive is critical to putting a source's contributions into perspective. When a news presentation relies heavily on contributions from a source, the audience would be well-served by asking the following questions:

- Why is the source volunteering this information?
- What is the anticipated outcome of this contribution?
- Does this information reflect a personal or professional bias on the part of the source?

It is also important to consider the *reporter's* motive for using a source. *Los Angeles Times* staffer David Shaw charges that reporters sometimes speak through sources, by selecting experts who will corroborate their own points of view: "Reporters often call a source because they want a quotation to illustrate a particular point, and they are sure to get exactly what they want if they call a source whose attitudes they already know."[29]

At other times, reporters select sources simply because the reporters are lazy and the sources are *available*. Daniel Okrent, the public editor of the *New York Times*, explains,

Bad reporters find experts by calling up university press relations officials or brokerage research departments and saying, in effect, "Gimme an expert"; some academic publicity machines send out rosters, complete with phone numbers, e-mail addresses and areas of expertise, so that the lazy journalist doesn't even have to make that first call.[30]

Areas of Expertise. It is also valuable to consider the source's level of expertise. Sources are expected to provide analysis, clarification, or background on a subject in which they have a particular expertise. Instead, sources sometimes give opinions on a wide range of topics outside their area of specialty.

Moreover, according to *New York Times* columnist Tom Wicker, a reporter's over-reliance on sources can actually *undermine* the integrity of its news coverage. A source can punish reporters in a number of ways, including "lost access, complaints to editors and publishers, social penalties, leaks to competitors, (and) a variety of responses no one wants."[31] Wendell Rawls, Jr., assistant managing editor of the *Atlanta Journal and Constitution* admits, "Yes, there are times when I feel uncomfortable reporting facts that I imagine will cause a source some pain. I deal with it by calling up the source and telling him what I'm going to do. I don't let the source get ambushed."[32]

Anonymous Sources. Identifying sources is often complicated by the issue of anonymity. Using unnamed sources gives reporters wider access to inside information, by enabling informed individuals to talk without fear of recrimination. To illustrate, during the Watergate investigation, *Washington Post* reporters Woodward and Bernstein depended on a confidential source within the Nixon administration (codenamed "Deep Throat") to obtain vital inside information which otherwise would not have been available. (Thirty years later, it was revealed that "Deep Throat" was Mark Felt, the number two man at the FBI at the time.)

Anonymous sources can go "off the record" in several ways:

- The most common use of anonymous sources occurs when the source remains confidential, but the reporter is free to publish the information.
- Sources may provide *deep background*—that is, providing the context that puts a story into a broader perspective and points the reporter in a particular direction. As a result, the source is not directly acknowledged in the story.
- Both the source and the information remain confidential. However, the reporter is free to seek corroboration elsewhere.

The use of anonymous sources makes it impossible for the reader to ascertain the credibility, affiliation, and motive of the person providing essential information. Martin Lee and Norman Soloman explain,

> If the unnamed source is a whistleblower speaking accurately and truthfully about his or her boss or agency, the information can be considered a "leak," and in all likelihood the reporter will be serving the public interest. If, on the other hand, the unnamed source is the voice of a government agency and there's no legitimate reason for the source to be unnamed, the information can be considered a "plant," and in all likelihood the reporter will be serving the interest of the agency, not the public.[33]

But even if the motive is unclear, what is certain, according to Robert Booth, is that "all unauthorized disclosures are committed by people who ultimately wish to influence outcomes, events and opinions."[34]

An example of the damage of unspecified motives occurred during the run-up to the war in Iraq. The *New York Times* made extensive use of anonymous sources who declared that Iraq had weapons of mass destruction. However, after the invasion, no one was able to locate these weapons of mass destruction. Further, it was disclosed that these anonymous sources were Iraqis who stood to personally benefit from a U.S. invasion. Consequently in 2004, the *New York Times* published a public apology for failing to shed light on the motives of their sources:

> Accounts of Iraqi defectors were not always weighed against their strong desire to have Saddam Hussein ousted.... The most prominent of the anti-Saddam campaigners, Ahmad Chalabi, has been named as an occasional source in Times articles since at least 1991, and has introduced reporters to other exiles. He became a favorite of hard-liners within the Bush administration and a paid broker of information from Iraqi exiles.[35]

In a positive development, some news organizations have taken steps to cite the motive for a source choosing to remain anonymous. As an example, an article appearing in the *New York Times* in 2006 discussed the interrogation tactics employed by Americans on Al-Qaeda official Abu Zubaydah at secret detention centers. The story included contributions by former and current law enforcement and intelligence officials, who spoke on the condition of anonymity. The article included the following explanation:

> The officials spoke on the condition that they not be identified because many aspects of the handling of Mr. Zubaydah remain classified and because some of the officials may be witnesses in future prosecutions involving Mr. Zubaydah.[36]

Every country has its own regulations with regard to protection of sources. In the United States, 49 states and the District of Columbia have passed some version of a shield law, which permits reporters to maintain the confidentiality of sources. Thirteen of these states and the District of Columbia have passed shield laws with absolute authority, meaning that under no circumstances can the state override the journalist's right to withhold privileged information. In 36 other states, the journalist-source privilege is qualified, meaning that the government can require a journalist to reveal confidential information if the government can prove that it has exhausted alternative ways of obtaining the information and that the information is necessary to serve a compelling state interest. Indeed, reporters can be jailed for defying court orders to reveal the names of sources. The Bush administration has made a concerted effort to clamp down on leaks. Citing the espionage act of 1918, officials maintain that the federal government has the authority to prosecute and jail journalists who disclose classified information.

Journalist Judith Miller, then of the *New York Times*, was imprisoned for 85 days for refusing to divulge the name of her source with regard to the leak of CIA operative Valerie Plame. In addition, Josh Woolf spent over six months in jail for refusing to reveal the names of his sources in his coverage of an anti-G8 demonstration in San Francisco protests. Media lawyer Theodore J. Boutrous Jr. declares, "Every tenet and every pact that existed between the government and the press has been broken."[37]

Many journalists and civil libertarians are advocates for the establishment of a federal shield law. Law Professor Geoffrey R. Stone declares,

> Congress should expeditiously enact a federal journalist-source privilege law, which would protect journalists from compelled disclosure of their sources' confidential communications in the same way psychiatrists and lawyers are protected. Importantly, neither Congress nor the press should be unwilling to compromise when the alternative is to forgo such a privilege altogether. A strong and effective journalist-source privilege is essential to a robust and independent press and to a well-functioning democratic society. It is in society's interest to encourage those who possess information of significant public value to convey it to the public, but without a journalist-source privilege, such communication will often be chilled because sources fear retribution, embarrassment or just plain getting involved. As we have seen over the past several years, particularly with the federal investigation of the leak of the identity of former C.I.A. operative Valerie Plame, the absence of a journalist-source privilege leads to confusion, uncertainty and injustice. At the hands of unrestrained federal prosecutors, journalists have taken a serious battering.[38]

Point of View: The Illusion of Objectivity in the Press. The American press adheres to the principles of accuracy and objectivity. The Society of Professional Journalists' Code of Ethics declares,

> Good faith with the public is the foundation of all worthy journalism.
>
> 1. Truth is our ultimate goal.
> 2. Objectivity in reporting the news is another goal which serves as the mark of an experienced professional. It is a standard of performance toward which we strive. We honor those who achieve it.

This code assumes that an absolute Truth exists and that journalists are in a position to present this ideal Truth, without distortion or personal bias. However, we live in a complex, subjective world in which the truth may be difficult to identify.

As Walter Lippmann has observed, news can only be expected to approach Truth in cases of quantifiable information, such as the temperature, sports scores, and election results. But even in these cases, information can be far from absolute. For instance, weather reports can only accurately measure the specific place where the temperature is being calibrated. Variables such as the proportion of green space versus highly constructed areas, wind patterns, and amount of sunshine can cause a fluctuation of several degrees in temperature within a 30-mile radius.

Readers often confuse the statement of fact with truth. To illustrate, in August 2006, the following headline appeared in the *New York Times*: "Rumsfeld Says War Critics Haven't Learned Lessons of History."[39] But although it is a *fact* that Rumsfeld made the comment, his statement is not necessarily *true*.

Since there is no universal agreement on Truth, faithfulness to the ideal of objectivity becomes an impossibility. The press is frequently the target of criticism for biased reporting from both the left and the right, depending upon the commentators' *own* versions of the truth. Ted J. Smith observes,

> Critics on the left ... attack journalists for being insufficiently critical of mainstream policies, leaders, and institutions, for excluding minority views, and for unreflective repetition of the assumptions and values of capitalist economics and bourgeois democracy. Supported by numerous academic studies, there can be little doubt about the basic validity of this claim.
>
> Among conservatives, belief in the liberal bias of the media is almost an article of faith.... Conservatives base their case on the claims that journalists, especially in the prestigious national media, are liberal in their political views, and that those views are reflected in coverage.[40]

However, some scholars find this notion of objectivity in the press to be not only *unrealistic* but *undesirable*. Ben Bagdikian maintains that the basis of solid journalism is values: "Objectivity contradicts the essentially subjective nature of journalism. Every basic step in the journalistic process involves a value-laden decision."[41]

Author Mark Hertsgaard argues that American journalists have become trapped by the modern ethic of objectivity, forcing the press to forego its responsibility as an opinion leader: "How could the public be expected to develop an opinion on a given issue unless that issue was posed for their consideration. In the American system, that was the responsibility of the press. Yet the modern ethic of objectivity precluded such journalism."[42]

Moreover, this ideal of objectivity limits journalists to reporting only in cases in which an event has occurred or if an outside agent has brought up an issue. As a result, journalists are limited to reporting the official positions of those in authority as news. Hertsgaard asserts that the U.S. press generally reflects the official State Department policy: "In accordance with their avoidance of partisanship, many journalists seemed to regard strenuous challenging of the government as an improper violation of the rules of objectivity. Honest adversarial journalism they equated with, and often dismissed as, 'advocacy' journalism."[43]

Consequently, a key to the interpretation of news programming is to dispel this myth of objectivity. In a discussion about Fox News, an executive from another network observed, "There is a place for [what Fox does]. But call it what it is. There's no need to work under the cloak of darkness."[44] Identifying the point of view of Fox News (or *The Nation*, a progressive magazine) enables you to put the news report into perspective.

Objectivity and Intention. An important consideration in a discussion of objectivity concerns the issue of *intention:* Are reporters surreptitiously trying to sway readers to their point of view? Certainly, there are times in which a careful analysis of content reveals the embedded values of the journalist. However, at times, the journalistic process itself calls for choices that inevitably suggest a particular point of view. For instance, in reporting a story, one side must always be mentioned first; this placement conveys the message that this is the legitimate position.

Ultimately, however, the question of intention is irrelevant. Journalists must recognize that decisions they make in writing and editing the news convey messages that influence the reader. As a result, journalists must be more conscious of the ramifications of the choices they make.

For its part, the audience must understand that objectivity is in many cases an unobtainable ideal. In that way, the audience will be able to take the point of view of the article into consideration as they read newspapers, watch television, or check a web site. Rather than *objectivity*, a more realistic and constructive set of journalistic principles are *judgment*, *fairness*, *transparency*, and *perspective*.

- *Judgment.* Journalism is as much an art as it is a craft; that is, in the many individual cases that come across an editor's desk, the situations are complex. Editors and reporters must rely upon *news judgment*, based upon journalistic principles and collective experience. However, at times, there may be disagreement, even among veteran journalists, about how to treat a story.
- *Fairness.* Understanding that it is difficult to uncover an Absolute Truth, journalists have a responsibility to represent all sides of an issue. Byron Calame, public editor of the *New York Times*, explains,

> Getting both sides of a story and sorting them out for readers is the basic job of newspaper reporters and editors. This is a key to creating a newspaper that is fair—both to readers and to the people and institutions that are the subjects of stories. Seeking comment from those written about, especially when they are put in an unfavorable light, is a particularly important aspect of fair coverage. It helps ensure that readers get the most complete and accurate view possible of a newsworthy development.[45]

- *Transparency.* Being clear about the point of view of the publication, the reporter's perspective, and the background and motive of sources enables the audience members to filter the information and make up their own minds about the topic.
- *Perspective.* In a world in which events often appear unconnected and consequences only appear over time, journalists have a responsibility to put these events into meaningful perspective. At the same time, however, the audience has the responsibility to challenge these assertions to make sure that journalists handle this charge responsibly.

Moreover, we live in a complex world, in which events occurring in one part of the world reverberate in other regions—sometimes years after its original occurrence. One such example is global warming; the greenhouse gasses released in the air have contributed to a gradual climate change that affects all nations—regardless of their direct culpability in the matter. Consequently, a *post-modern approach* to journalistic principles borrows from the concepts of explicit and implicit content outlined by W. Andrew Collins in Chapter 8. The five journalistic questions that defined the parameters of journalism during the second half of the twentieth century—who, when, where, why, and how—fit roughly into Collins' notion of *explicit content*: identifying the significant events that need to be covered. However, the press's failure to cover events after 9/11 demands that reporting focus on the *implicit information* as well:

- Motive
- Connection between events
- Connections between people
- Consequences

Disclosure versus Privacy. At times the point of view of the press is disturbingly intimate—particularly with regard to coverage of public figures. In the United States, people can be subjected to media scrutiny as "public figures" if they have met the following criteria:

- Voluntarily stepped into the spotlight
- Assumed an important role in the resolution of important public issues
- Had an impact on a public issue
- Become a public figure through means other than simply media attention.[46]

Unfortunately, however, unscrupulous journalists abuse this journalistic license, intruding into the personal affairs of celebrities. For instance, in April 1992, *USA Today* learned that former tennis star Arthur Ashe had been infected with the HIV virus during heart surgery in 1988. A reporter then called Ashe to ask for confirmation before running the story. Ashe, who had kept the matter private out of concern for his family, was then forced to go public with the information. After the story was published, former tennis pro and friend Billie Jean King declared angrily, "Can't (the press) just leave him alone? Can't they leave people alone, just once?"[47]

The intrusion of the press was even more dramatic in the case of Princess Diana. In 1997, Diana, Princess of Wales, was killed in a high-speed automobile crash, as a result of being pursued by paparazzi.

Citizen Journalism. A general dissatisfaction with the mainstream press has led to the establishment of the *citizen journalism* movement. Citizen journalism refers to the use of blogs and video to develop an audience-driven source of news production and distribution that circumvents the traditional gatekeepers of news and information such as newspapers, radio, and television news programming. Blogs have emerged as an influential source of news and information. Senator Harry Reid (D-Nevada), the majority leader of the Senate observes, "I do believe that each day, (bloggers) have more impact.... One of the reasons I so admire them is they have the ability to spread the truth like no entities I've dealt with in recent years. We could never have won the battle to stop privatization of Social Security without them."[48]

The term "blog" is derived from the phrase "web-logging." Like most logs, they list regular entries, with the most recent first. Web logs may also include hotlinks to related and referenced sites and ways for readers to post responses. The idea of blogs harkens back to the American Revolutionary War period, when pamphleteers like Thomas Paine wrote, printed, and distributed information that made the case for American independence from Britain. Blogs are maintained by a variety of contributors: professional journalists who are discouraged by what they see as the corruption of the American journalism system, activists, and amateurs with an interest in the field of journalism or a specific interest in an issue. By the end of 2004, about eight million people had created a blog.[49] These publications are relatively inexpensive to produce, since web journalists are spared the costs of printing and distribution.

Citizen journalism fulfills an essential role of societal watchdog, calling attention to important information that is under-reported by the mainstream media, as well as putting this information into meaningful perspective. Due to the pervasive nature of media technology, journalistic "correspondents" capture events that cannot be covered by the mainstream press. In December 2006, a video shot on a cellphone captured the hanging of former Iraq president Saddam Hussein. Despite efforts to keep the graphic depiction of this event secret, the videos, evidently taken by one of the guards or witnesses at the execution, were released over the Internet.

Because of the pervasiveness of the media, political figures no longer have the luxury of "back stage activities"—areas of privacy previously hidden from public view. Before the age of modern media, politicians could retain some semblance of privacy. But now, newsmakers must assume that all public functions are being recorded, regardless of locale. To illustrate, in November 2006, comedian Michael Richards unleashed a barrage of vicious racist remarks at patrons at a comedy club where he was performing. While in the past, the incident would be minimized, a video of the event, captured by cellphone, was posted on YouTube.

Moreover, blogs and videos give people "glimpses" into a particular realm of experience, relatively unedited. In an editorial at the end of 2006, the *New York Times* declared,

Reading the bloggers has helped to fill one of the big gaps in Americans' view of the war in Iraq. Danger in the streets and security fears for anyone seen speaking with Western reporters has made it increasingly hard to get real glimpses of what it's like for the people who have to live there.[50]

Wired magazine and NewAssignment.Net are spearheading a collaborative approach called "crowdsourcing," in which members of the public, serving as citizen correspondents, contribute their knowledge and research to coverage of one story.

However, at this inception stage time, Citizen Journalism currently faces some limitations as a serious form of journalism. Because few bloggers find full-time job opportunities, little original reporting is produced. A 2006 study found that only 1 percent of the posts that day involved a blogger interviewing someone else and only 5 percent contained some other original work, such as examining documents.[51]

In addition, quality standards and practices haven't yet been established. While some blogs are well-researched and fair in their coverage of issues, others are merely personal reflections. Citations and references are frequently not cited. And finally, there is no way to verify information on authors, including their background, credentials, and possible motives for contributing. In a "Letter to the Editor" of the *Boston Globe* in 2006, Tim Harrigan observed,

Bloggers can cloak themselves as they choose and reincarnate as often as a character in a video game. There is no accountability and there are no standards. The Web may be digital, but communication is organic. When and if a blog has a real person behind it and when it fact-checks like a newspaper, I may find the time to read it. Until then, there are plenty of real news outlets and real people reporting real news.[52]

In addition, because of the intense competition, some bloggers may feel pressured to sensationalize their entries to attract an audience. David Carr admits,

The desire to connect is a pure impulse, but it can lead to bad behavior on the part of writers. Sometimes, I feel a little lonely on my Oscar blog. The solution: I take a rhetorical baseball bat to a fan favorite, *Borat,* and hundreds of rabid commentators appear. Hey, I've got readers.

... At some point, ratings (which print journalists, unlike their television counterparts, have never had to contend with) will start to impinge on news judgment. "You can bemoan the crass decision-making driving by ratings, but you can't really avoid the fact that page views are increasingly the coin of the realm," said Jim Warren, co-managing editor of the *Chicago Tribune*.

"The best thing about the Web—you have so much information about how people use it—is also the worst thing," said Jim Brady, executive editor of Washingtonpost.com. "You can drive yourself crazy with that stuff. News judgment has to rule the day, and the home page cannot become a popularity contest."[53]

However, the establishment of standards of accuracy, thoroughness, fairness, reliability, ethics, and transparency in Citizen Journalism is currently in process. Edelman, CEO of the public relations giant of the same name, observes, "Bloggers do not need to disclose their sources, but they should attribute specific content to a company or another blogger if used verbatim."[54] At the 2006 YearlyKos Convention of bloggers, Jennifer Palmieri, former deputy White House press secretary under President Bill Clinton, held a "pundit project training," where she told bloggers how to present themselves in television interviews—what to wear, how to sit, and what to say.[55]

In addition, new resources are being developed to help formalize this field, such as the Technorati web site, which tracks what is being discussed in the blogosphere, including French, German, Italian, Korean, and Chinese, Japanese, and English sites.

It should be noted, however, that even though Citizen Journalism was developed as a response to what is perceived as the corrupt, bottom-line sensibility of the mainstream press, blogs and video sites are already becoming prey to the market forces that have compromised established journalism venues. Carr states,

> One of the overlords of the blogosphere with 15 sites and enough buzz to arm every doorbell in the nation, Nick Denton, the founder of Gawker Media, has watched page views at his sites double in the last year; Gawker Media and Nielsen/NetRatings put monthly unique visitors at 4.2 million. So it comes as a bit of a surprise that Mr. Denton celebrated a very upbeat stretch in the blogging industry by putting two of his sites on the block, reorganizing others and laying off several people.
>
> Laying off journalists? How very old media.
>
> "We are becoming a lot more like a traditional media company," Mr. Denton said. "You launch a site, you have great hopes for it and it does not grow as much as you wanted. You have to have the discipline to recognize what isn't working and put your money and efforts into those sites that are."[56]

Audience

Print. The newspaper audience is physically removed from the writer. However, research provides a clear portrait of the regular newspaper reader. Although newspapers are readily available, the audience is selective; as was mentioned earlier, reading presupposes a certain level of education. Clearly, the newspaper has emerged as an elite medium. The typical audience member is older, well-educated, and of relatively high income.[57] This demographic pattern cuts across racial and gender lines. Older, well-educated, and affluent African Americans read newspapers even more faithfully than their white counterparts. And working women are more likely to read newspapers than women who do not work outside of the home.[58]

People tend to read the newspaper for the following reasons:

- Immediacy and thoroughness
- Local awareness and utility
- Habit
- Entertainment
- Social extension or gossip[59]

Although almost all readers (92 percent) leaf through the entire newspaper, people generally read only about one-fifth of the paper. At the same time, over 50 percent turn to a newspaper two or more times in a given 24-hour period. This would suggest that the newspaper serves as a reference at various times of the day (i.e., consulting the paper for sales or movie schedules).[60]

Habit plays a large role in newspaper consumption. One advantage still held by the newspaper over fast-paced outlets such as radio, TV, and the Internet is that a majority of people find it relaxing to read the newspaper.[61]

Content preferences among readers remain remarkably stable over time. People read the paper according to an established order (e.g., the sports section first, then the front page …). Thus, although some sections of the newspaper may be of interest to a relatively small number of people, those readers maintain a fierce loyalty to that section.

Young people are largely indifferent to the print medium. Newspaper reading among people 30 and under has dropped over the past decade. Young people often regard newspapers as:

- An "old people's habit … something you see old people do while waiting for a bus"
- Speaking for the status quo and against societal change
- Cold and impersonal
- A middle-aged medium (produced by older adults for an older audience)[62]

However, role-modeling can be a factor in determining newspaper consumption patterns among young people. College students are far more likely to read the paper if their parents routinely read newspapers. In fact, students are likely to read the paper at the same time of day and in the same location as their parents.[63] This would suggest that one way for parents to encourage their offspring to read the newspaper is simply to read the paper themselves.

Significantly, the availability of newspapers online has helped keep young adults interested in papers. A Newspaper Association of America Foundation (NAAF) survey found that during the third quarter of 2006,

57 million people visited a newspaper web site, an increase of 24 percent over the same period a year before.[64]

STRUCTURE

Economic Factors—Impact on Content

Economic factors have a significant impact on the content of news programming. For instance, about 60 percent of newspaper space is devoted to advertisements (see Figure 12.1). Another 16 percent of space is devoted to public relations–oriented content, including public relations releases, story memos, or suggestions that come from corporations. Martin A. Lee and Norman Soloman explain,

> PR copy from real estate agents, developers and industrial firms typically masquerades as authentic news stories. It's not unusual for articles about fashion, for example, to be lifted straight from press releases by designers and fashion shows. Food editors rely heavily on food company blurbs for recipes and stories. Sections on home improvement, travel, and entertainment are likewise filled with PR-related fluff. [65]

Moreover, news organizations routinely cover *staged events*. These speeches and ribbon cutting ceremonies have little news value, primarily serving the interests of the sponsoring organizations. Obviously, this leaves little room for actual news content in the newspaper.

Economic developments have contributed to the *homogenization of news content*, in several respects:

- *One-newspaper cities.* Between 1940 and 2001, the percentage of one-newspaper cities has increased from 43 percent to 87 percent to 98 percent.[66] This movement toward one-newspaper cities reduces the range of perspectives available to readers.

Figure 12.1
Distribution of newspaper space.

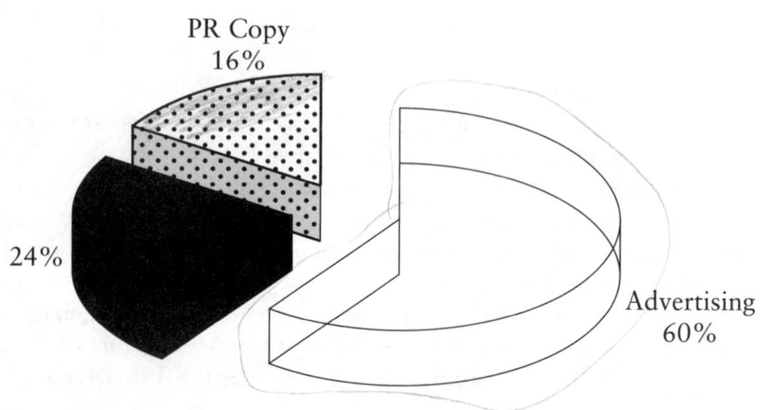

In multi-newspaper cities, the newspapers often present opposing editorial positions—one is liberal, the other conservative. As a result, the readers are exposed to a range of political perspectives. In response, some one-city papers offer both liberal and conservative perspectives on their op-ed page. But unfortunately, this approach often means that *neither* side has much of a forum for opinion.

- *Newspaper chains.* A newspaper chain refers to a large company that owns a series of newspapers in different locations throughout the country. In the United States, newspaper chains dominate the journalistic landscape. In 2002, the 22 largest newspaper chains owned 39 percent of all the newspapers in the country (562 papers). Yet those papers represent 70 percent of daily circulation and 73 percent of Sunday. Further, the top 10 chains account for more than half of all circulation in the United States (51 percent daily and 56 percent Sunday).[67]

  According to Ben Bagdikian, newspapers that have made the transition from an independent company to part of a conglomerate have seen an increase in advertising, accompanied by a decrease in news content. In addition, editorial policies either reflect the ideology of corporate ownership or "become bland to avoid controversy." Bagdikian also cites studies that found that chains tend to hire less-qualified journalists to curb expenses.[68] → local politis

- *Conglomeratization of Alternative Newspapers.* Alternative papers generally began as "underground" publications that covered local politics, avant garde arts activities, and alternative lifestyles in the community. However, these alternative newspapers are being absorbed by national chains. As an example, New Times Inc., based in Phoenix, Arizona, has purchased alternative newspapers in Miami, Dallas, Houston, St. Louis, Phoenix, Denver, Los Angeles, and San Francisco. Moreover, a striking shift in content has occurred in alternative papers that have been bought by chains, with far more entertainment coverage than social commentary or political coverage. Papers owned by The New Times Inc. are not allowed to endorse political candidates, since this might alienate potential readers. In addition, the staff cuts that characterize daily newspapers (see above) are also occurring at the alternative press. In 2005, New Times acquired the *Village Voice*, long considered a voice of liberal ideology throughout the nation. In 2006, the New Times Inc. eliminated 20 staff positions, including five senior editors, some of whom had been at the paper since 1969. Tom Robbins, a longtime reporter and union steward at the *Village Voice* said: "All of a sudden we get hit with these very deep cuts and firings … who helped put *The Voice* on the map. It cuts the heart right out of the paper."[69]

- *Reliance on Syndicated Stories.* In this arrangement, individual papers throughout the country purchase the rights to carry a columnist. Although this arrangement eliminates the salary of a local reporter, the audience loses a valuable local perspective on issues and events. In addition, syndicated stories are generally picked up long after they have originally appeared, losing their timeliness. As an example, *New York Times* columnist Maureen Dowd's editorial commentary regularly appears in that publication on Saturdays. However, the same column is run in the *St. Louis Post-Dispatch* on the following Wednesday. Dowd's column, which comments on the events of the day, often loses its edge, original meaning, and value when it appears four days later.

Thus, while there are more news outlets in 2006 than ever before, there are actually *fewer* voices. The Project for Excellence in Journalism examined how a

✗ no them. imp.

variety of news outlets in the United States, including newspapers, television, radio, and the Internet, covered a single day's worth of news and found that there was enormous repetition and amplification of just two dozen stories. Largely because of economic constraints, there was virtually no original investigative reporting. As a result, although "Google News" offered access to 14,000 stories within two clicks, they were actually accounts of just 24 news events.[70]

Influence of Advertising on News Content. Advertisers, who account for 75 percent of newspapers' revenue, can have an enormous impact on news content, in a number of respects:

- *Favorable treatment in the press.* News programming are often preferential in their coverage of influential corporations. Russell Baker provides the following example:

> During Robert Sam Anson's brief tenure as editor of Los Angeles magazine, the business side committed to a fifteen-page supplement, to be written by the editorial side and called "The Mercedes Golf Special." Mercedes didn't promise to take any ads, but it was hoped that the car maker would think kindly of the magazine for future issues.[71]

- *Self-censorship.* A subtle form of self-censorship exists in the press, in which editors either suppress or rewrite a story without being asked, for fear of offending advertisers. Newspapers and magazines are leery of writing about the health hazards of cigarettes, for fear of losing the advertising dollars from the tobacco industry. Baker provides the following example:

> The tobacco companies' hefty advertising in many a magazine seems in inverse proportion to the publication's willingness to criticize it. Over at the American Cancer Society, media director Susan Islam says that women's magazines tend to cover some concerns adequately, but not lung cancer: "Many more women die of lung cancer, yet there have hardly been any articles on it."[72]

- *Merging of editorial content and advertising.* The merging of editorial content and advertising raises concerns about independent control of coverage and potential conflicts of interest. In 2007, the *Philadelphia Inquirer* announced plans to carry a new "sponsored column" called PhillyInc., written by Inquirer reporters and editors, on the first page of its business section. However, this column was to be sponsored by a local advertiser, Citizens Bank. Plans called for the column to carry the bank's logo and be outlined in the bank's distinctive green ink. The bank will also run ads across the bottom of the page and in an upper corner. According to *New York Times* reporter Katharine Q. Seelye, "This rankles many in the newsroom because it looks as if the newspaper's editorial content has been co-opted."[73]

  In addition, ads sometimes appear in the form of editorial content, as *advertorials.* Advertorials blur the distinction between ads and editorial content. Very little effort is made to distinguish these advertorials from other stories featured in the newspaper. The disclaimer "advertisement" is often buried in the ad, placed away from the visual field. At other times, the ad simply includes the name of the product in small print.

For example, in the October 2006 edition of *Cosmogirl!*, a number of articles promote specific brands. "Runway to hallway: totally '80s," "Private Eyes," and "Look Polished" mention the brand names, the prices of the products, and—in many cases—the location of where they can be purchased. Research Assistant Don Miller points out, "The verb 'try' is used in some of these articles ('*Try* the darkest shade in the ... line; *try* ... eye shadow; *try* ... nail lacquer.') The use of the verb 'try' is a subtle call to action, so many of these articles could easily be interpreted as advertisements rather than actual magazine text or content."[74]

- *Advertisers Prescribing Content.* At times, advertisers assume a direct role in the editing of *editorial content* (editorial content refers to news content: everything in the newspaper that is not paid space). To illustrate, in 2006, the *L.A. Times* published a review of the Pontiac G6, by columnist Dan Neil, in which he called for the dismissal of two senior G.M. executives, holding them accountable for the company's recent drop in sales. In response, General Motors announced that it would stop running its advertising in the newspaper "until further notice." G.M. was the newspaper's second biggest advertiser, spending more than $10 million a year in advertising. Michael Drexler, chief executive at Optimedia International U.S. observes, "No advertiser wants to appear in a poor light, so the first reaction is to hit 'em in the pocketbook."[75]

Internal Organization

News organizations are acquired for the purpose of generating cash flow for their parent corporations. In 2004, the profit margins of some of these news organizations were very healthy:

- Tribune Company publishing division: 25.9 percent
- Gannett: 32 percent
- E.W. Scripps: 31.3 percent
- Lee: 27.4 percent
- Journal Register: 27.3 percent

However, at the same time, these conglomerates are devoting *fewer* resources to the coverage of the news. Between 2000–2006, news organizations eliminated more than 3,500 staff positions, a drop of 7 percent.[76] In 2006–2007, the following newspapers cut their staffs as a cost-cutting measure:

- The *Philadelphia Inquirer* announced that it planned to lay off 68 to 71 employees, or about 17 percent of the newsroom staff, just seven months after a group of local businessmen took over the newspaper.
- The *Washington Post* cut 80 newsroom jobs through voluntary buyouts, the second such offer in just over two years, and attrition.
- The *Dallas Morning News* announced that more than 100 of its 580 newsroom staff members accepted severance packages, reducing the size of the newsroom by roughly 20 percent.

- The *Cleveland Plain Dealer* announced plans to cut 17 percent of its staff.
- 101 jobs were eliminated at the *San Jose Mercury News*.
- The *St. Paul Pioneer Press* cut 40 full-time positions at the paper.
- The owners of *Los Angeles Daily News* laid off the paper's publisher and 20 other employees.

At the *Los Angeles Times,* the nation's fourth largest newspaper, publisher Jeffrey Johnson and editor Dean Baquet were fired by executives of the Tribune Company after they defied orders to eliminate more newsroom positions.[77]

Radio has been similarly affected by staff cuts. A study of radio stations in three U.S. cities found that only 14 percent of stories involved sending reporters out in the field—and most of those were pieces picked up from syndicates or National Public Radio.[78]

And finally, television news operations have experienced staff cutbacks as well. In 2006, NBC News officials announced that they had begun laying off employees connected to its flagship programs—including *Today, NBC Nightly News With Brian Williams*, and *Dateline NBC*—as part of companywide budget cuts dictated by the division's corporate parent, NBC Universal. In total, the cuts at *Dateline* will represent about 10 percent of the program's staff. In addition, NBC eliminated locally originated news programming in six cities: San Jose (Ca.), Phoenix, Dallas, San Antonio, Houston, and Denver.

Often, this step involves offering buy-outs to senior reporters and producers, retaining the less-experienced staff members, who command lower salaries but lack the contacts and know-how of their older counterparts. Working with limited resources affects the types of stories that those reporters who remain on staff are able to cover. *St. Louis Journalism Review* publisher Charles Klotzer explains,

> "If a story needs a real investment of time and money, we don't do it anymore." The speaker is a forty-something reporter on a mid-sized Illinois daily. "In assignment meetings, we dream up 'talker' stories, stuff that will attract attention and get us talked about, tidbits for busy folks who clip items from the paper and stick them on the fridge."

He adds ruefully: "Who the hell cares about corruption in city government, anyway, much less dying Bosnians?"[79]

Moreover, many news organizations have closed foreign bureaus, reducing their coverage of international events, and instead focus mainly on local and regional news. Former managing editor Stuart Wilk explains,

> Best case, I think it will look like a paper with really strong local coverage and a lot of good wire stories. The national and international coverage will be the same coverage that you see in the Sioux Falls paper and the Elkhart, Ind., paper and in

the Fort Worth paper. And to those of us who see newspapers as something other than local, covering City Hall and covering the Rangers, that's really sad.[80]

Moreover, the allocation of staff and equipment in the newsroom is often tied to the popularity—and profitability—of a news segment. In local television news, ratings are now delivered in 15 minute increments, so that news directors can measure whether the audience share goes up or down as a news program moves from one segment to another. The *Los Angeles Times* has adopted a "market-oriented approach to news," in which each section of the paper, such as editorial or sports, runs as an independent business unit. Each unit is expected to pay its way through advertising revenue or increased readership.[81] Thus, if the consumer reporting segment records an audience decline, the reporter—and the segment itself—may be in jeopardy.

Homogeneity in the Newsroom. The typical newsroom is predominantly young, male, and white. This lack of diversity can influence the selection of stories that appear in the newspaper, overlooking stories of interest to members of subcultures. Tim McGuire, managing editor of the *Minneapolis Star Tribune*, observes, "It's time we stop and listen to minority voices that have an understanding and perspective white editors and reporters don't have."[82]

The composition of the newsroom staff also has an effect on the *treatment* of stories. To illustrate, on a CNN Headline News Program broadcast on November 14, 2006 (after the mid-term congressional elections), CNN host Glenn Beck interviewed Keith Ellison, who had just become the first Muslim ever elected to Congress. Ellison is a U.S. citizen, born and raised in Detroit, Michigan, before winning the Congressional seat in Minnesota. In this interview, Beck made clear his bias against people who hold Muslim religious beliefs:

GLENN BECK: I, I will tell you. May I? May we have five minutes here where we're just politically incorrect and I play the cards face up on the table?

KEITH ELLISON: Go there.

GLENN BECK: Ok. No offense, and I know Muslims, I like Muslims, I've been to mosques. I really don't believe that Islam is a religion of evil. I think it's been hijacked, quite frankly. With that being said, you are a Democrat. You are saying let's cut and run and I have to tell you, I have been nervous about this interview with you, because what I feel like saying is sir, prove to me that you are not working with our enemies and I don't—I know you're not. I'm not accusing you of being an enemy, but that's the way I feel and I think a lot of Americans are feeling that way.

KEITH ELLISON: Well, let me tell you the people of the 5th Congressional District know that I have a deep love and affection for my country. There's no one who is more patriotic than I am. And so, I don't need to prove, to prove my patriotic stripes.[83]

This is not to suggest that this reporter necessarily is a vicious bigot. However, because people are limited by their own experience, he is certainly guilty of a *benign racism*; in which he is oblivious to information or wording that would be offensive to Muslims. Although Beck can easily dismiss this media stereotype of Arabs as harmless, he would surely take the matter more seriously if the characterization disparaged his own racial/ethnic group. More diversity among decision-makers would avert this type of problem.

At a Poynter Institute conference entitled, "Redefining the News: Reaching New Audiences Through Diversity," professionals and scholars made four recommendations designed to infuse a diversity of viewpoints in the newspaper:

- *Develop story ideas within the community*
- *Cultivate sources from a variety of backgrounds and perspectives*
- *Redesign news beats*
- *Reshape newsroom culture*

Efforts to diversify newsrooms in America have been uneven. In 2005, minorities comprised 22.2 percent of local television news staffs, compared with 21.2 percent in 2004. At non-Hispanic stations, the minority workforce was 20.4 percent, also an increase over the previous year. However, in local radio, the minority workforce fell to 6.4 percent, down from 7.9 percent in 2004. (The highest level ever recorded was in 2001, when minorities held 24.6 percent of TV news jobs.)

The percentage of women in the television news workforce was 40 percent in 2005, up from 39.3 percent the previous year. The percentage of women news directors was 25.2 percent, up from 21.3 percent in 2004. But at the same time, the percentage of women in radio news fell to 24.8 percent from 27.5 percent in 2004, while the percentage of women radio news directors dropped from 24.7 percent to 20.4 percent.[84] Seymour Topping, director of editorial development for New York Times Co. Regional Newspapers declares, "We must forge ahead even more strongly to reach the ... goals of accurately representing the diversity in American society."[85]

Introduction

The introduction of a news story furnishes perspective into the point of view and underlying messages of a story. For example, an article by Simon Romero published in the *New York Times* on February 23, 2007, contains journalistic techniques that convey negative messages about Venezuela, supporting U.S. State Department policy.

Premise. The *premise* can furnish perspective into the unwritten assumptions behind an article. For instance, in February 2007, an article by Simon Romero appeared in the *New York Times*: "Venezuela Rivals

U.S. in Aid to Bolivia," that focused on an aid package that Venezuelan President Hugo Chavez gave to Bolivia. The premise of the story supports the official position of the U.S. government with regard to Venezuela as foe. An analysis of the article reveals the following assumptions:

- *That Venezuela's aid to Bolivia is a strike against the United States.*
  The wording of the headline, "Venezuela *Rivals* U.S. in Aid to Bolivia" establishes the subtext: the rivalry between Venezuela and the United States. Romero inserts his opinion as fact that one of Venezuela's foreign policy goals is "limiting the regional influence of the United States."[86]
- *That Venezuela is a threat to the well-being of Bolivia.*
  The article suggests that Venezuela's aid is a weapon used to dictate Bolivia's affairs. The reporter quotes a Bolivian "opposition leader" who puts the Venezuelan aid package in a negative light: "'We've become a client state of Venezuela, in what is a new form of imperialism,' said Óscar Ortiz, an opposition senator with the Podemos Party who has publicly criticized Bolivia's relationship with Venezuela."[87]
- *That U.S. aid is good, while Venezuelan aid is bad.*
  The objective of all foreign aid is to put the benefactor in a position of influence within the recipient country. But although the United States is involved in the same tactic, the article makes it appear that the Venezuelan aid is a surreptitious and underhanded activity: according to Romero," it was difficult to know the exact amount of Venezuelan aid because many of the agreements between Venezuela and Bolivia were not made public."[88]

The article acknowledges that the preponderance of the aid is in agricultural products—Venezuela purchased a large portion of Bolivia's soybean crop, purchasing 300 tons of Bolivian beef and 7,500 tons of beans and poultry, and donating 300 tractors. However, the article then suggests that Venezuela is also involved in military shipments to Latin American countries. Romero declares that "(Venezuela's) military assistance has attracted the most scrutiny," although no evidence is cited. This is followed by a vague suggestion that this aid poses a military threat:

> The International Institute for Strategic Studies, a British research group, said in a recent report that Venezuela, which is undertaking a rapid armaments buildup, *could be* (author's emphasis) providing Bolivia with weapons and financing for new military bases.[89]

But even if the reporter's allegations are true, selling arms is not illegal. Indeed, the United States is the largest arms dealer in the world.

Print Headlines. Readers receive their initial impressions about a newspaper or magazine story through headlines. However, headlines are rarely composed by the reporter who wrote the story. Instead, this task is delegated to a local copywriter who may not understand the intent, or even the main point of the story.

A primary function of a headline is to *inform* the reader about the principal thrust of the story. Consequently, the headlines that appear in newspapers may vary widely. For example, headlines announcing the results of the U.S. mid-term congressional elections of November 7, 2006, reflected global points of view and perspectives on the story:

- "Bush Crushed in US Mid-Terms": The *Sun* (UK)
- "Voters 'as mad as hell, and determined not to take it'": *The Independent*
- "Thank you, America": *The Guardian (UK)*

Another striking example can be found in a story about a speech given by Vice President Dick Cheney in April 2004. A headline, which appeared on page A3 of the *New York Times,* was "Cheney Urges China to Press North Korea on A-Bombs."[90] However, this headline was rewritten for the News Summary column, which appeared on page A2 of the *same* paper: "Cheney Warns Chinese Leaders."[91] Clearly, while the first headline is neutral, the second headline puts a more threatening spin on the story.

In addition, a headline also must *attract attention* by being provocative, if not sensational. Unfortunately, these competing functions can work at cross purposes, altering the meaning of the story—sometimes with humorous results. Consider the following headlines:

"Safety Experts Say School Bus Passengers Should Be Belted"
"Typhoon Rips Through Cemetery; Hundreds Dead"
"Iraqi head seeks arms"[92]

At times, headlines can actually *conceal* meaning. To illustrate, a 2006 story in the *New York Times* reporting on the presidential election in Venezuela carried the following headline:

"Venezuelans Give Chavez a Mandate to Tighten His Grip"[93]

This headline seems to suggest that recent events have given Venezuelan President Hugo Chavez the power to assert dictatorial control over the population. In reality, this "mandate" was an election, in which Chavez was freely chosen by an overwhelming majority of the Venezuelan people.

But at the same time, headlines may also inadvertently *disclose* latent meanings in an article. A classic example can be found in a story that appeared in the *St. Louis Post-Dispatch* in 1991 about William Kennedy Smith, who was charged with rape in Florida. Significantly, the headline, "Trial Starts in Kennedy Rape Case," was inaccurate; the name of the alleged perpetrator was not Kennedy but *Smith*. Nevertheless, the headline did furnish perspective into the real story—the ongoing saga of the Kennedys, a family that remains the object of national fascination. Moreover, the headline helps explain why a rape case in Florida would make the front page news in Missouri.[94]

Television and radio news programs often employ promotional slogans designed to attract an audience. But in the process, these slogans shape the audiences' perception of the programming. For instance, Fox News uses the slogan "Fair and Balanced," which promotes their perspective as objective. But as discussed earlier, a latent function of Fox News is to promote the agenda of the Bush administration.

Front Page/Cover. The front page of newspapers now includes stories that were formerly placed in other sections of the paper—sports, business, human interest, and entertainment news. Many newspapers now place "teasers" (headlines and photos highlighting features in the rest of the paper) above the fold. In 1996, the *Pittsburgh Post-Gazette* took this trend a step further by eliminating news stories *entirely* from the front page of its early Sunday edition and filling the page with teasers. After the paper reported a 1 percent increase in newsstand sales, the *Milwaukee Journal-Sentinel*, *Dallas Morning News*, and *The Fort Worth Star-Telegram* subsequently adopted the same format.[95]

The Introductory Paragraph. In print journalism, the most essential information is positioned in the first paragraph of the story. This *inverted pyramid style* of American journalism dates back to the nineteenth century with the invention of the telegraph. Concerned that the telegraph lines would go down at any moment, editors insisted that reporters send the most important information across the wires first. Background information and details were then included later in the story. The pyramid structure also enables editors to make room for late-breaking stories or additional advertisements at the last minute by cutting the least essential information from the end of the story. Readers should therefore expect to find the answers to the following questions in the first paragraph: *who*, *what*, *when*, *how*, and *why*.

The body of the story is designed to elaborate on the information presented in the lead paragraph. At times, however, the first paragraph is an incomplete or even inaccurate summary of the body of the story. To illustrate, a 2007 article in the *New York Times*, "Venezuela Spending on Arms Soars to World's Top Ranks," begins with the following paragraph:

> CARACAS, Venezuela, Feb. 24—Venezuela's arms spending has climbed to more than $4 billion in the past two years, transforming the nation into Latin America's largest weapons buyer and placing it ahead of other major purchasers in international arms markets like Pakistan and Iran.[96]

However, beginning at the eighteenth paragraph, the reporter adds information that puts this arms "buildup" into meaningful perspective:

> Supporters of the arms buildup contend that under Mr. Chávez, who has been in power for eight years, Venezuela has spent proportionately less on its military in relation to the size of its economy than the United States or than other South American countries like Chile and Colombia.

In 2004, the last year for which comparative data were immediately available and before Venezuela's arms buildup intensified, overall defense spending by Venezuela, including arms contracts, was about $1.3 billion and accounted for about 1.4 percent of gross domestic product, compared with 4 percent in the United States and 3.8 percent in Colombia, according to the Stockholm International Peace Research Institute, which tracks military spending.

Doubts persist as to how powerful Venezuela's armed forces have become in a regional context, even as they acquire new weapons. Military experts here say pilots in the air force still need training to start flying their new Russian fighters. And in terms of troop strength, Venezuela's 34,000-soldier active-duty army still lags behind the armies of Argentina and Brazil, with about 41,400 and 200,000 members respectively, according to GlobalSecurity.org, a Web site that compiles data on military topics.[97]

Consequently, when reading newspaper articles, it is important to verify whether the lead paragraph indeed encapsulates the major thrust of the article.

Plot

Explicit Content. *Reportorial persuasion techniques.* The following journalistic persuasion techniques can, intentionally or unintentionally, affect the point of view of a story.

Presentation of opinion as fact refers to the technique in which reporters inject opinion into a story disguised as fact. For example, in a news article reporting on Cuba on the eve of Fidel Castro's 80th birthday celebration, reporter Marc Lacey makes a series of statements that are founded in opinion rather than fact:

> Mr. Castro's Cuba is very much a work in progress. Its education and health care systems are universal, but socialism has not wiped out classism or racism, freedom to speak out is clearly restricted and life for most people is humble, at best.[98]

Vague authority refers to instances in which reporters cite undocumented or generalized groups to support a particular point of view. For instance, in a story about Iraqi cleric Muqtada al-Sadyr on National Public Radio, reporter Anne Garrels commented, "The minister of the Interior has no power, a view that is privately shared *by many U.S. officials*."[99]

One person cross-section is a persuasion technique in which one person is used as a metaphor for a larger group—which may not be the case. For example, in a March 2006 Associated Press article reporting on American troop morale in Iraq, journalist Antonio Castaneda cites the comments of Sergeant Jon Beck to make the case that troop morale among American soldiers remains positive: "I was volunteering to come back. It's our generation's war. And it's the place where the money is as an infantryman."[100]

However, statistical information suggests quite the opposite. According to a poll of forces in Iraq conducted when the article appeared, 72 percent of 944 military members polled there said all the troops should be sent home within 12 months. And more than a quarter said American forces should leave immediately.[101]

The designated spokesperson. Sometimes the press arbitrarily appoints a spokesperson who assumes a position of authority and leadership in relation to a particular issue or event. They may indeed be leaders of an organization or an "expert" (e.g., university professor). But whether these people actually enjoy the support of a broad constituency is open to question.

The slanted sample. Sampling the public for their response to issues and events is a very common journalistic approach. However, this sample may be chosen in an arbitrary fashion and therefore is not representative of the public at large. For instance, an article that appeared in the *St. Louis Post-Dispatch* in 2001, entitled "Waking up a Sleepy City," furnishes a good example. The article began as follows:

> The *Post-Dispatch* recently gathered together six young adults who are native to St. Louis. They have faced and are facing choices about where to live and work. They exemplify the kind of talented, young adults that American cities are trying to attract.[102]

In the article, these young people discussed St. Louis and its future. The story was accompanied by a photograph of the six young men and women—all white.

The *Post-Dispatch* received numerous letters to the editor commenting on the slanted sample of the article, and the messages that it conveys, including the following comment from journalist Alvin A. Reid:

> Once again, "Imagine St. Louis" has decided to discuss the future of St. Louis without the input of any African Americans. Six young people interviewed, six photos on cover, two on the inside and no black people.... insulting. It's disgusting. Since the subject is "The Brain Drain" I guess I am to assume:
>
> A) Black people don't leave St. Louis for greener pastures, or visit other metropolitan areas, thus they could not have an opinion.
>
> B) Black people have no brains.
>
> C) You couldn't find any African Americans to interview.
>
> D) You didn't try to find any African Americans to interview. (This is the answer that I believe to be true.)
>
> I ask the editors of this page, "If a black person were visiting St. Louis from San Francisco, Washington, or another metropolitan area, what would they think after seeing "Imagine St. Louis"?[103]

The "not available" ploy. Investigative pieces that include the statement that "the subject was unavailable for comment" implies that the subject was uncooperative, ducking the reporter, and had something to hide. This statement often neglects to clarify the circumstances:

- Whether the person was in town
- When the person was contacted (i.e., day or evening)
- Where a person was contacted (i.e., at home or at work)
- How often the reporter attempted to reach the person
- The time frame in which the reporter attempted to contact the subject (i.e., over a three day period)

Some newspapers now provide the context behind this information (e.g., "repeated attempts to reach x over a three-day period were unsuccessful").

The passive catch-phrase. Sentences can be written in either the *active* or *passive* voice. In the active voice, the subject is explicitly responsible for the action (e.g., Bob threw the ball). But in the passive voice, the subject is the *receiver* of the action (e.g., The ball was thrown to Bob). The passive voice is particularly useful in describing an action in which the actor is unknown. To illustrate, in the sentence, "The door had been closed before we arrived," it is unclear who closed the door.

In addition, the passive voice can also be used to deflect responsibility for the action, since it is unstated *who* initiated the action. For example, when confronted with evidence of White House interference into the dismissals of eight federal prosecutors in 2005, Attorney General Alberto R. Gonzales acknowledged that "mistakes were made."[104] This statement deflects responsibility for the action, since it is unstated *who* made the mistake. Use of the passive voice also creates the impression that an opinion is common knowledge or generally accepted.

Selective quotes. Reporters can influence the meaning of a story by deciding *when* to use quotes, *whose* quotes to include, and *which parts* of the person's interview to extract into a quote. Quotes can be manipulated in the following ways:

- Including only those statements that support a particular point of view
- Taking quotes out of context to magnify or distort its meaning
- Juxtaposing separate statements together to form an entirely new meaning
- Including grammatical or syntactical errors to make a person appear unprepared, uneducated, or foolish
- Cleaning up a quote to make a subject appear more knowledgeable and authoritative

Inaccurate paraphrase. Instead of directly quoting a subject, reporters sometimes opt to paraphrase what their subject said. However, a reporter's summary may not always be an accurate interpretation. For instance, in her review of Al Gore's book *Earth in the Balance*, Michiko Kakutani observes,

Mr. Gore writes of undergoing a midlife crisis around the same time. He says that in 1989, having just turned 40, lost a presidential campaign and seen his son, Albert, nearly die in an automobile accident, he became "impatient with my own tendency to put a finger to the political winds and proceed cautiously."

However, an editorial in the Internet newspaper the *Daily Howler* pointed out that Gore never used the term "midlife crisis":

The diagnosis is that of the thoroughly unlicensed professional therapist, Dr. Kakutani.... And since we can assume that Gore is aware of the term, the truth about this is really quite simple: in this book, Gore deliberately chose not to write of "undergoing a midlife crisis." In fact, he seems to describe a different sort of experience—he talks in this same section about "an outer manifestation of an inner crisis that is, for want of a better term, spiritual."

Well, Kakutani had a "better term" in mind, and she put it in Gore's mouth—"midlife crisis." It played well with her theme that Gore is a bit strange, and consumed with "New Age psychobabble." What do you do if you want to say that, and your subject won't cooperate by using such terms?

Simple—you paraphrase! You put the desired words in his mouth—and tell readers that that's what he "said."

Welcome to the world of paraphrase, where inventive journalists find clever ways to get hopefuls to "say" things they like. The power of paraphrase is the power to spin, and the press corps tends to use power freely.[105]

Extraneous inclusion is a reportorial technique in which information is added to a story that, on the surface, appears to be immaterial to the story. However, this extraneous information can influence readers' attitudes about the story. To illustrate, in 2006, 72 professors, administrators and graduate students at Georgetown University protested the administrative appointment of former Under Secretary of Defense Douglas J. Feith to a faculty position in its School of Foreign Service. Some even accused him of war crimes in connection to his role in the Iraq conflict.

An article discussing the negative reaction of the faculty appeared in the *International Herald Tribune*. The article, written by Jason DeParle, included the following passage:

Professors in the school were widely opposed.... One is Susan Terrio, who has appointments in anthropology and French *and whose resume lists several writings about French chocolate makers. ("From Master Chocolatiers Today: Bayonne and the Basque Coast.")* She complained that Mr. Feith's appointment was "*presented as a fait accompli.*" (Emphasis Mine)[106]

The inclusion of the extraneous information about Terrio conveys the message that the professor (and, by extension, many of the professors) protesting Feith's appointment are silly, effete academics who are unqualified to make a judgment about Feith's qualifications for the teaching appointment.

Biased interviewing strategies. A reporter can slant a story through the type of questions posed to subjects:

- *Compliance as Assertion*

  Reporters may come to an interview prepared with a point of view (and a quote) to include in an article and is only asking for the *consent* of the subject. In this case, reporters may phrase a question, "Would you agree that…?", "Would you say that …?" or "So what you are saying is…."

- *Leading or Loaded Questions*

  Reporters ask questions that contain a false premise or are loaded with negative allegations or a false premise. An example would be, "Are you concerned that higher rates as proposed by the electric company might force many people to give up their service?" Any response to a question phrased like this (even a denial) legitimizes the position of the reporter.

- *"Gotcha" Questions*

  In this practice, reporters' questions take the form of a pop quiz, the ostensible goal being to test the veracity of a subject's claims. For instance, before the 2000 U.S. presidential election, a Boston television reporter asked George W. Bush to name the leaders of a series of foreign countries. He could not.

  But whether or not Bush could provide the names of foreign leaders is not a true indication of whether he has a comprehensive understanding of foreign policy. Instead, it is a technique that attracts public attention to the reporter and the particular news programming.

- *Hypothetical Question*

  Questions beginning with phrases such as "What would happen if …?" puts the subject in a speculative position that is then presented as fact. In addition, hypothetical questions frequently catch the interviewee off-guard, so that he/she may offer an opinion that is not thoroughly considered.

- *Either/Or Choices*

  In this persuasive technique, reporters offer a limited range of responses to their interviewees. Like students taking a multiple choice exam, subjects may then feel compelled to select the best answer among the choices offered, even though it may not actually be the "best" answer. However, Tripp Frohlichstein reminds the public that "There are five different responses to an 'either/or' question. If the choices are 'a' or 'b', you can respond with:

  1) 'a'
  2) 'b'
  3) both 'a' and 'b'
  4) Neither 'a' or 'b'
  5) 'c' (an alternative not given by the reporter)[107]

Television offers an additional set of visual techniques that enable TV journalists to sway the opinion of the audience. In the documentary *Outfoxed*, filmmaker Robert Greenwald identifies the following techniques employed in Fox News programs:

- *Nonverbals.* Former Fox reporter Jon Du Pre describes the practice of giving "a wink and a nod" to signal approval of a story.
- *Ad-libs.* Making a comment after a story enables the reporters to cross the line from a news report to a commentary. Du Pre maintains that during the 2004 presidential campaign, ad-libs that castigated Democrats such as "North Korea loves John Kerry" got an "attaboy" and pat on the back.[108]

Implicit content. As mentioned earlier in the chapter, television is a medium better equipped to focus on news' *explicit* content (i.e., events) than print. However, newspaper accounts are better suited to examine the *implicit* content (i.e., causes, connections, and consequences) *behind* events or issues. However, even in a newspaper article, the complex factors contributing to an event (e.g., the situation in the Middle East) may be difficult to include in the limited space allotted for the article. Moreover, a news story may only represent an installment in a far larger story, which is still in the process of unfolding. As writer Ben Hecht once observed, trying to determine what is going on in the world by reading newspapers is like trying to tell time by watching the second hand of a clock.[109] Thus, while newspapers provide information on the day's events—the *who*, *what*, *when*, *where*, and *how* questions that are the hallmarks of journalism—they may not have the space to consider the broader *why* question. Moreover, the consequences of an event may not be readily apparent. For instance, it will be many years before the ramifications of global warming become fully evident.

MEDIA LITERACY TIPS

IMPLICIT CONTACT

In light of the complexity of events, it is particularly critical to give some thought to *implicit content* when reading articles. When you are reading a story, ask:

- *Why did this event occur?*
- *What are the possible connections between events?*
- *What are the possible consequences of these events?*
- *Which questions does the story answer?*
  1) *Who?*
  2) *When?*
  3) *Where?*
  4) *How?*
  5) *Why?*
- *Have any of the above questions been omitted? How does this omission affect your understanding of the story?*
- Where would you find the answers to these unanswered questions?

PRODUCTION ELEMENTS

Journalists find themselves in something of a dilemma with regard to the use of production elements. For instance, repeating one word throughout a story (e.g., "he said, she said") is considered bland and uninteresting writing. On the other hand, synonyms (e.g., "he argued, she declared") possess connotative meanings that can make an article appear biased. In like fashion, on any given day, there may be 15 stories that arguably belong on the front page. However, because of space limitations, the editors must select six stories, which signals the relative importance of news stories. At other times, however, journalists use production elements such as placement of stories, word choice, and connotative images to convey messages to the reader. But regardless of the intention of the media communicator, examining production elements is a valuable way to identify media messages.

Editing

When preparing a story, a reporter assembles an abundance of information that must be condensed into a clear, coherent, and concise presentation, free of grammatical errors, stylistically consistent, and accurate with respect to facts and citations. In addition, journalists make a number of other editing decisions that convey subtle messages.

What stories to include and omit. Certain stories are given attention in the press, while other stories are ignored. These editing decisions are often very subjective, reflecting the priorities and values of the newspaper staff. As Frohlichstein observes, "News is whatever the editor says it is."[110]

To illustrate, in the wake of a terrorism alert issued by the White House in August 2004, it was found that the further a publication was situated from the New York and Washington areas, where the risk was said to be greatest, the less coverage the threats received.[111] For three days following the alert, the *Washington Post* and the *New York Times* each carried at least two front-page articles—and nearly two full pages or more inside the paper. In contrast, the *Austin American-Statesman* (Texas) carried only one front-page article about the warnings from the New York Times News Service or the Associated Press. According to managing editor Fred Zipp, the immediate impact of a story on the community is a major factor in the amount of coverage a story receives: "If the warning had been that Al Qaeda is going to attack the tower on the University of Texas campus or a University of Texas football game, then we would have been ... aggressive." Philip Taubman, the Washington bureau chief of the *New York Times*, adds, "For *The New York Times* and *Washington Post,* this is personal. Our readers live in these communities. Many of our staff members live in these communities."[112]

Each year *Project Censored* publishes its list of the Top 10 Under-reported News Stories of the year. A panel of distinguished media professionals and scholars collaborate to "seek, identify, and publicize stories on important issues that have been overlooked or under-reported by the news media." The most under-reported stories of 2006 included the following:

1. Future of Internet Debate Ignored by Media
2. Halliburton Charged with Selling Nuclear Technologies to Iran
3. Oceans of the World in Extreme Danger
4. Hunger and Homelessness Increasing in the United States
5. High-Tech Genocide in Congo
6. Federal Whistleblower Protection in Jeopardy
7. U.S. Operatives Torture Detainees to Death in Afghanistan and Iraq
8. Pentagon Exempt from Freedom of Information Act
9. The World Bank Funds Israel-Palestine Wall
10. Expanded Air War in Iraq Kills More Civilians[113]

At the same time, Katherine Albergate, Lesley Amberger, Lindsay San Martin, and Kate Sims identified the top ten "Junk Food News" stories—the most over-reported news stories of 2006. The following stories received much more coverage than they deserved:

1. Angelina Jolie and Brad Pitt get together
2. Nick Lachey and Jessica Simpson
3. American Idol hits an all-time high
4. The Runaway Bride that didn't
5. Martha Stewart is back in town
6. Brokeback Mountain breaks through
7. Britney Spears (it just wouldn't be a list without her)
8. Myspace infiltrates our space
9. Steroids in Baseball get pumped up
10. The DaVinci Code ad nauseum[114]

What information to include (and omit) in a story. Decisions about what to include and what to omit in a particular story shape an audience's understanding of a news event. Again, these editing decisions can be subjective, reflecting the collective judgment of reporters and editors. As an example, a study of 200 American and international journalists covering the Iraq war, found that 17 percent of them worked for organizations that would not publish pictures of the dead to accompany the stories, and 42 percent had rules discouraging the practice.[115]

Decisions about what information to include in a story can serve as an indication of prevailing attitudes and policies, reinforced by the mainstream media. As an example, on June 24, 2006, two alleged Hamas members were captured by Israeli soldiers who had crossed the border into Gaza. This event was covered by a number of American mainstream media outlets, including the Associated Press and Fox News. The Fox report began as follows:

> Saturday June 24, 2006
>
> "Israeli Forces Capture Two Hamas Members in First Gaza Arrest Raid Since Withdrawal"
>
> GAZA CITY, Gaza Strip—Israeli forces swept into southern Gaza under the cover of darkness early Saturday, rounding up two Palestinian militants in the first arrest raid in the coastal strip since Israel withdrew from the area last year.
>
> The Israeli army said the two Hamas members were planning a large attack against Israel in the near future. No shots were fired, and the troops withdrew from the area immediately after the pinpoint operation, the army said.[116]

The following day, on June 25, Hamas retaliated by kidnapping two Israeli soldiers. This act touched off a three-week, full-scale invasion of Lebanon by Israel.

From that point on, however, there was no mention in the mainstream press of the Israeli kidnapping that had occurred on June 24. By consistently omitting this information about the initial incident, it appeared that Hamas' action against U.S. ally Israel was unprovoked and justified.

The composition of a story also may be determined by time and space constraints. In television news, stories are rarely longer than two minutes in length. Newspaper editors also face a daily challenge of fitting the information into the allotted time or space. *New York Times* managing editor John Geddes explains,

> The four (basic news) sections—on, say, a Wednesday—run about 200 columns. The day, in terms of space, begins about 11 o'clock when one of our senior editors goes to each of the individual desks and asks, what do you have? Do you need any space? Is there anything of note? That is brought to me or whoever's doing space that day at about 11:30. And we try to pass judgment. Is this meritorious? How do we stand with our budget? Do I have five long stories for which space is being requested for tomorrow? Is that too much for the reader? Is there an option to hold for another day, or is there news that's forcing this to run right now? We balance all those things. And then we give that request for space to our colleagues in production. They take the news requirements and the advertising requirements, combine them to make up the whole paper.[117]

When examining a news story, it is appropriate to ask:

- What essential information is included in the story?
- What is the reporter's justification for including the information contained in the story?
- What essential information is missing? What additional information would be valuable for understanding the story?

The order in which information is presented. The order in which information is presented is a sign of its importance. Geddes explains,

Remember, journalism is about telling me what's important and telling me what's important in the order of its importance. It's always a compared-to-what. Something happened on Day One, when nothing's going on in the world, it may merit one column of coverage. The same thing happening on a very busy day may merit an inch of coverage.[118]

For instance, on August 17, 2006, all three networks began their evening newscasts with a story about a man who confessed to the 1986 murder of child beauty queen JonBenet Ramsey. This was followed by a story about a ruling by Federal court Judge Anna Diggs Taylor that the U.S. government's wiretapping surveillance program was unconstitutional. Clearly, the sequence of stories conveys the message that the Ramsey story was more significant than the wiretapping report.

Depth of coverage. Decisions about how much attention is given to a story signals how important it is. Brief mention of a subject suggests that the issue is of minimal importance, whereas in-depth stories send the message that the public should treat the subject seriously. Geddes explains, "We're trying to capture what's important today in a given space. And we're trying to relay that to readers using the relative size of the story and the coverage as an indicator of importance."[119]

To illustrate, cable and radio talk shows spent far more time discussing Anna Nicole Smith than the Iraq war on the two days following her death (February 8–9, 2007). According to the Project for Excellence in Journalism, cable and radio talk shows dedicated 37 percent of their programming to her death; 14 percent of the programming focused on the debate over Iraq; and less than 10 percent focused on the race for the White House.[120]

But even more surprising, a study conducted by ThinkProgress.org, found that on March 2, three weeks after Anna Nicole Smith's death, Fox News still devoted *12 times* more coverage to Ms. Smith than the breaking news about the treatment of veterans at Walter Reed Hospital.[121]

A related editing decision involves the amount of emphasis to devote to particular *aspects* of a story. Reporters will provide more detailed explanation of those elements of a story that they deem to be important. For instance, stories about candidates vying for their party's nomination for president of the United States often dwell on the amount of money that they have raised, as opposed to their positions on issues.

Sustained coverage. The frequency with which a story appears keeps certain issues in the public's consciousness and signals that the editors consider the story to be of importance. In contrast, sporadic coverage of an issue sends the message that it is relatively unimportant. To illustrate, ABC News devoted a total of only 18 minutes to the genocide taking place in Darfur, Sudan, throughout all of its 2005 newscasts. NBC had only five minutes of coverage during all of its evening newscasts, and CBS only three minutes—about a minute of coverage for every 100,000 deaths in that country. In contrast, Martha Stewart was the subject of 130 minutes of coverage by the three networks during its 2005 nightly newscasts.[122]

Whose perspectives are presented, and in what order? In order to maintain a balance, reporters should include all sides to a story—although this isn't always the case. Even when all sides are presented, the viewpoint presented first is often considered to be the more legitimate, established point of view.

Post-Production Editing Decisions

After a story has been completed by a reporter, a copy editor revises the material, correcting grammatical errors and syntactical mistakes. The story also may be rearranged to improve the flow of information. Finally, portions of a story can be eliminated to prevent redundancies.

Although the copy editor tries not to tamper with the content of a story, he or she may not comprehend the reporter's rationale for including a particular phrase or specific quote in an article. Further, the copy editor may be pressed to condense an article when a timely story is added at the last moment, or if advertisers want more space—even if the content is affected.

In television news, the post-production process is a major part of creating a news story. Editors are charged with assembling the story, which involves: 1) compressing the story to fit the prescribed time limit; 2) selecting the visuals that will accompany the reporter's narrative; 3) intercutting interviews with other elements of the story; 4) adding a voice-over in the editing suite (if necessary).

Scale

Print. The size of a headline sends a signal about the importance of the story. Consider the following headlines:

The heavy, bold headline in the *Post-Dispatch* ("JonBenet case collapses") calls attention to the hoopla surrounding this unsolved murder case. The 72 headline alone takes up 1/4 of the page and is placed in a prominent position above the fold to draw the reader's attention. The size of the headline makes it seem as if all other news is of little importance compared to this 10-year-old murder investigation. In contrast, the headline for the story in that day's *New York Times* carries only a 20-point headline, signaling that this is a story of relatively minor significance.

By way of comparison, approximately 50 years ago the *New York Times*' headline for the Japanese surrender, which ended WWII, was only slightly larger (80 points) and used a much thinner font than the JonBenet Ramsey story. Clearly, the size differential is not indicative of the relative importance of these two events. Instead, the scale of the *Post-Dispatch* story conveys a latent message about the sensationalization of news in the current era, as part of a larger effort to attract readers and maximize profits.

Relative Position

The relative position of stories has an influence on the significance we attach to a story. On a practical level, most of us start to read a section of a paper at the beginning. As a result, an article placed on page five is not as likely to be read as a story appearing on page two. *Chicago Tribune* managing editor Dick Siccone points out that many factors enter into decisions about story placement, including available space, the local interest of the story, and other local priorities. However, Siccone acknowledges that story placement does send messages regarding the relative importance of news items:

> One of the most important things a paper does is give readers guidance about what is the most meaningful. The stories which are most desirable for readers appear in consecutive order ... page one, page two, page three. (Placement) signals to readers exactly what they most need to read.[123]

Story placement often varies widely from newspaper to newspaper. For instance, the September 16, 2006, edition of the *New York Times* carried a front page story detailing an outbreak of E. coli linked to fresh prepackaged spinach, which had reached 94 cases in 20 states.[124] But on the same day, the story was carried on page 8 of the *St. Louis Post-Dispatch*.[125]

In 2004, the editors of the *New York Times* conducted a self-study on its coverage of events leading to the Iraq war and concluded that its placement of stories supported the Bush administration's case for going to war in Iraq. The report notes, "Articles (making) dire claims about Iraq tended to get prominent display, while follow-up articles that called the original ones into question were sometimes buried in the back pages. In some cases, there was no follow-up at all."[126]

However, the *New York Times* continued this practice long after this self-study was released. On January 28, 2007, a story about an anti-war protest in Washington, D.C. that attracted hundreds of thousands of people from around the country was buried on page 20 of the paper, whereas an article about tennis player Serena Williams occupied page 1.

Word Choice

Examining word choice can be a valuable way to identify the point of view of the media communicator. In an article on Al Jazeera English, an English-language counterpart to Al Jazeera Arabic TV, columnist Judea Pearl points out how the use of language reveals the political ideology of the station:

> For example, the phrase "war on terror" is invariably preceded by the contemptuous prefix "so-called." The words "terror" and "insurgency" are rarely uttered with a straight face, usually replaced with "resistance" or "struggle." The phrase "war in Iraq" is often replaced by "war on Iraq" or "war against Iraq." A suicide bombing is called a "commando attack" or, occasionally, a "paradise operation."[127]

One useful line of inquiry for the analysis of word choice involves breaking down a sentence according to parts of speech. Journalists are presented with a range of choices in the selection of *nouns.* (A noun is a word used to describe a person, place, or thing.) Columnist John Leo explains, "'Actress-model' and 'onetime beauty queen' really mean 'bimbo,' whereas 'womanizer' means 'lecher.'"[128]

To illustrate, the *Dictionary of Cautionary Words and Phrases*, compiled by a group of professional journalists, includes the following connotative nouns:

- "Community" implies a monolithic culture in which people act, think, and vote in the same way. Do not use, as in Asian, Hispanic, black, or gay community. Be more specific as to what the group is: e.g., Black residents in a north side neighborhood.
- Avoid gender enders. For instance: actress, comedienne, heroine, poetess, and starlet. Instead, use gender-neutral terms such as actor, comedian, executor, hero, poet, and star.
- Use "leader" with caution. Be more specific: Black politician, black activist. Implies person has approval of an entire group of people.
- "Man" may be used when both men and women are involved and a more clearly defined term is not available. Frequently the best choice is a substitute, such as "humanity," "a person," or "an individual."[129]

Adjectives are complements to nouns, providing additional information about a person, place, or thing (e.g, a *tall* person). To illustrate, when Senator Joseph Biden (D-Delaware) announced his candidacy for the presidency in February 2007, he characterized his opponent, Senator Barack Obama as "the first mainstream African American who is articulate and bright and clean and a nice-looking guy."[130] While the use of the word "articulate" is, on the surface, a compliment, the adjective is considered offensive when used to describe an African American. Professor Michael Eric Dyson explains that the implication is that most African Americans do not fit into that category: "Historically, it was meant to signal the exceptional Negro. The implication is that most black people do not have

Figure 12.2
The word choice used in the two photos to describe the survivors of Hurricane Katrina reveals racist attitudes. While the white couple are described as "finding food," the black people who are engaged in the same activity are described as "looters." One way to discover the impact of a connotative word is to substitute synonyms and see how the meaning changes. In this case, the white couple would be "looters" and the black man as simply "finding food" furnishes perspective into the assumptions about subcultures that lie behind this use of language. Top photograph courtesy of Agence France; bottom photograph courtesy of AP.

the capacity to engage in articulate speech, when white people are automatically assumed to be articulate."[131]

The selection of *verbs* and *adverbs* can also influence readers' attitudes. Verbs describe action (e.g., walking, strolling, or rushing someplace). Adverbs describe *how* something is done (e.g., quickly, carelessly). To illustrate, the adverbs in the following articles (see italics) furnish commentary about the attitudes behind the actions of the newsmakers.

- Just before the congressional elections of 2004, ABC World News reported, "Just two years ago, Mr. Bush won over 75% of the vote (in Nebraska). Now, he is *desperately* trying to keep this reddest of districts from turning blue, something it hasn't been in nearly half a century."[132]
- *Washington Post* columnist George F. Will castigates the neoconservatives "who *arrogantly* push the administration toward more misadventures abroad."[133]

One way to discover the meaning of a connotative word is to substitute synonyms and see how the meaning changes. Consulting with a thesaurus provides you with a list of words that have roughly the same denotative meaning but contain other connotative, or associative meanings as well.

Connotative Image

Photographs can add a particular emphasis to a story or, in some cases, convey entirely separate messages. But although we tend to believe what we see in the newspaper or on the television screen, photographs present only a *version* of reality. Many photographs are posed; indeed, newspapers often rely on *file photos* that may have been taken long before the event being covered. The public relations department of a company may also provide photographs if a story involves one of their employees.

The framing of a picture establishes arbitrary boundaries which can affect our perceptions of reality. For instance, a photographer can establish relationships that do not exist by isolating two figures in a crowd. Tabloids take this principle a step further by creating composite pictures; that is, positioning two images next to one another to create a new meaning. Photojournalist Howard Chapnick explains,

> Over the years, I have seen many examples of journalistic distortion by pictures taken out of context, by the use of prejudicial rhetoric in captioning of photographs, and by editors making composites of two separate news photographs and publishing it as one image. There are dozens of ways to alter reality if journalistic integrity is absent.[134]

Now, thanks to digital technology, objects in photographs can be manipulated or eliminated altogether (for more discussion, see Chapter 4).

MEDIA LITERACY TIPS

PHOTOGRAPHS

The following questions are useful in considering the role of *photographs* within the context of print journalism articles:

- *What is the function of the photo?*
- *How do I feel as a result of looking at the photograph? (What is your affective response?)*
- *Is this a posed or spontaneous shot? What does this reveal?*
- *What is the relationship between the print article and the photograph?*
- *What messages are conveyed by the photo?*

Graphics

Both broadcast and print journalism rely on graphics in order to cater to the skimming habits of its readership and attract readers. However, this format is frequently more flashy than informative. For instance, the graphics for Fox News Alert originally conveyed the message that what was to follow was important. But now, the graphic is used indiscriminately—simply to call for the attention of the audience. For instance, the News Alert was used to announce the breakup of Jennifer Lopez and Ben Affleck.

CASE STUDY: GESTALT ANALYSIS

The arrangement of stories *within* a single page also affects the audience's perception of news content. Stories on the top half of the page are accorded greater importance by the reader than stories appearing near the bottom.

Readers often regard the composition of a newspaper page as a collection of separate stories. However, editors often consider the relationship between the stories when laying out the stories. As Dick Siccone observes, "Some days you make statements, some days you don't."[135] By activating our gestalt and seeing the page as a whole, we can draw connections between events and identify cultural preoccupations and concerns. To illustrate, Nick Johnson, a graduate student in Media Communications at Webster University, conducted the following media analysis of a front page of the *New York Times*, using selected keys to interpreting media messages:

An analysis of the front page of the November 8, 2006 edition of the *New York Times* furnishes considerable insight into the point of view of the paper on the day following the midterm elections, when the Democrats took the majority of seats in both houses of Congress.

Figure 12.3
The arrangement of stories within a single page affects the audience's perception of news content. By activating our gestalt and seeing the stories appearing on a single page as a whole, we can draw connections between events and identify cultural preoccupations and concerns. Nick Johnson, a graduate student in Media Communications at Webster University, conducted a media analysis of this front page of the *New York Times*, using selected keys to interpreting media messages (see below). Copyright © 2006 by The New York Times Co. Reprinted with permission.

"All the News That's Fit to Print"

The New York Times

Late Edition
New York: Today, rainy, windy, high 59. Tonight, rain ends, some clearing, low 54. Tomorrow, partly cloudy and very mild, high 68. Yesterday, high 59, low 47. Weather map is on Page A18.

VOL. CLVI . . No. 53,757 + NEW YORK, WEDNESDAY, NOVEMBER 8, 2006 ONE DOLLAR

DEMOCRATS TAKE HOUSE

WHITE HOUSE CONCEDES DEFEAT; SENATE IS TIGHT; SPITZER IN ROUT; MENENDEZ AND LIEBERMAN WIN

THE '06 ELECTION

THE REGION
Menendez Wins Handily; Comeback for Lieberman

THE HOUSE
New Faces in Congress

COMPTROLLER
Hevesi Hangs On

GOVERNORS
A First in Massachusetts

BALLOT QUESTIONS
No to an Abortion Ban

Voters in South Dakota rejected the most sweeping abortion ban proposed in the nation in more than a decade, an effort to challenge Roe v. Wade. Michigan voters approved a measure barring affirmative action by public institutions in education, employment or contracting. PAGE P9

ONLINE

For the latest results of House, Senate and regional races.
News and analysis from the New York Times political staff.
Interactive graphics to highlight who will control the next Congress.
The Caucus and Empire Zone blogs on national and local races.
The Midterm Madness blog of politics with a partisan eye.
nytimes.com

Democrats, including Representative Nancy Pelosi, celebrated victories from coast to coast.

Senator Joseph I. Lieberman thanked supporters.

Eliot Spitzer enjoying his victory in Manhattan.

12-Year Run Over, Balance May Rest on Virginia Race

By ADAM NAGOURNEY

Democrats seized control of the House of Representatives and defeated at least three Republican senators yesterday, riding a wave of voter discontent with President Bush and the war in Iraq.

Continued on Page P3

NEWS ANALYSIS

A Loud Message for Bush

By ROBIN TONER

Everything is different now for President Bush.

President Bush arriving at the White House yesterday.

Continued on Page P2

For Democrats, Time to Savor Victory at Last

By JEFF ZELENY and KATE ZERNIKE

Democrats, at least in this millennium, have not been accustomed to much celebration.

Continued on Page P3

Clinton and Democrats Sweep Top Contests in New York State

By PATRICK HEALY

Continued on Page P15

INSIDE

Nicaraguans' Votes Are In, and Ortega Is Back

Daniel Ortega's main competitor for the presidency conceded defeat, fulfilling the 16-year struggle of Mr. Ortega, right, to return to power. Mr. Ortega, once a fiery Marxist, promises a new pragmatism in governing. PAGE A14

Terror Sentence in Britain

A British Muslim received at least 40 years for planning attacks in the United States and Britain. The police called the defendant "a very important Al Qaeda figure." PAGE A13

Drilling Into the Depths

Companies are using new technology to venture farther and deeper into the Gulf of Mexico in the quest for oil. BUSINESS DAY, PAGE C1

Rebuilding Ties in Darfur

Some refugees in Darfur have returned home, and are learning to live alongside former enemies. PAGE A14

Newspaper Editor Forced Out

Dean Baquet, the editor of The Los Angeles Times who defied his parent company's orders to cut jobs, was forced out. BUSINESS DAY, PAGE C1

Updated news: nytimes.com
Tomorrow in The Times: Page C20

The main headline on the page, "Democrats Take House," is written from the point of view of the Democrats. Written from the opponents' point of view, the headline would read, "Republicans lose." Coupled with the dominant photograph of Capitol Hill Democrats, cheering, linked hand in hand, this story offers a resounding "hooray" in unison for the readers.

The headline of an accompanying story is "For Democrats, Time to Savor the Victory *at Last*" [emphasis added]. The main subheading on the story, "White House Concedes Defeat," implies that George W. Bush was running for re-election and adds the perspective that Bush will be a lame duck in the remainder of his term. Below this heading is a third tier: "12-Year Run Ends—Chafee and Santorum Are Out," another pointed choice of words. While many incumbents were defeated that day, for many liberals, Santorum has been Public Enemy Number Two, just behind Bush. His strong anti–gay rights stance has even caused famed sex columnist Dan Savage (not affiliated with the *New York Times)* to coin the word "santorum" to stand for an unmentionable byproduct of sex.

A portion of the body copy reads, "The *parade* of departing Republican Senators includes Rick Santorum of Pennsylvania ...," again highlighting this polarizing figure. This statement, however, does much more. By referring to this as a parade, it almost likens Santorum and others to members of a sideshow, ones who voters are cheering and applauding as they leave Washington.

Finally, at the bottom right hand column, another story proclaims that the election is "A Loud Message for Bush," again implying that the election was a referendum against Bush. The story is accompanied by a small photograph of President Bush waving at the camera. According to journalistic convention, the subjects of pictures should face toward the inside of the page. If necessary, a photo can be moved to the other side of the page, or the negative can be reversed. So within this context, the page designers have clearly made it look like he is waving goodbye and walking off the page.

NOTES

1. *The Quill* (November/December 1991).
2. Samer Farha, "TVSpy," in *Shoptalk*, September 24, 1998, shoptalk@listserv.syr.edu.
3. Will Lester, "Growth of Online News Readers Levels Off," Associated Press Online, July 30, 2006.
4. Roper Center (http://newseum.org).
5. Paul J. Gough, "Study: TV Still Tops for Those Seeking News," August 2, 2006 (http://news.yahoo.com/s/nm/20060802/tv_nm/news_dc_1).
6. Lester, "Growth of Online News."
7. Gough, "Study."
8. Lester, "Growth of Online News."
9. Gail Pennington, "Rather Tells Viewers to Read the Paper for Details on Stem Cells," *St. Louis Post-Dispatch*, August 12, 2001.
10. Lester, "Growth of Online News."
11. Seth Sutel, "U.S. Newspaper Circulation Declines 2.6 Percent," Associated Press Worldstream, May 8, 2006, Business News.

12. Katharine Q. Seelye, "Newspaper Circulation Falls Sharply," *New York Times*, October 31, 2006, C1.
13. Lester, "Growth of Online News Readers Levels Off."
14. Howard Kurtz, "The Big News: Shrinking Reportage," *Washington Post*, March 13, 2006, C01.
15. Lester, "Growth of Online News."
16. Kurtz, "The Big News."
17. Lester, "Growth of Online News."
18. Kurtz, "The Big News."
19. Future of the First Amendment (www.firstamendmentfuture.org).
20. Lester, "Growth of Online News."
21. Ibid.
22. John Dunbar, "FCC Study Opposing Rule Was Destroyed," *St. Louis Post-Dispatch*, September 15, 2006, A11.
23. Ben Bagdikian, *The Media Monopoly*, 3rd ed. (Boston: Beacon Press, 1990), 18.
24. *Outfoxed,* Robert Greenwald, Director. Carolina Productions, 2004.
25. Jeff Pooley, "Sins of Omission," *Brill's Content* (December 1998–January 1999), 40–42.
26. Howard Kurtz, "Dallas Paper's Story traveled Far Before Being Shot Down," *Washington Post*, January 28, 1998, D1.
27. TV Updates, *St. Louis Post-Dispatch*, April 5, 2003.
28. "Third Time's Not a Charm: Sunday Morning Talk Shows Still Imbalanced," Media Matters (http://mediamatters.org/items/200607200006).
29. Martin A. Lee and Norman Soloman, *Unreliable Sources: A Guide to Detecting Bias in the News Media* (Secaucus, NJ: Carol Publishing Group, 1990), 17.
30. Daniel Okrent, "Analysts Say Experts Are Hazardous to Your Newspaper," *New York Times*, October 31, 2004.
31. Lee and Soloman, *Unreliable Sources,* 17.
32. Martin Gottlieb, "Dangerous Liaisons," *Columbia Journalism Review* (July/August 1989), 26.
33. Lee and Soloman, *Unreliable Sources,* 17.
34. Robert Booth, "Full Disclosure on Leaks," *New York Times*, October 22, 2003.
35. From the Editors, "The Times and Iraq," *New York Times*, May 26, 2004.
36. David Johnston, "At a Secret Interrogation, Dispute Flared Over Tactics," *New York Times*, September 10, 2006, 1A.
37. Adam Liptak, "After Libby Trial, New Era for Government and Press," *New York Times*, March 8, 2007, A18.
38. Geoffrey R. Stone, "Half a Shield Is Better Than None," *New York Times*, February 21, 2007.
39. David S. Cloud, "Rumsfeld Says War Critics Haven't Learned Lessons of History," *New York Times*, August 30, 2006, A4.
40. Ted J. Smith, III, "The Watchdog's Bite," *The American Enterprise* (January/February 1990), 63–64.
41. Bagdikian, *Media Monopoly*, 63.
42. Mark Hertsgaard, *On Bended Knee* (New York: Farrar Straus Giroux, 1988), 334.

43. Hertsgaard, *On Bended Knee,* 65.

44. Rifka Rosenwein, "Meet the Cast of Characters on Fox News," *Brill's Content* (October 1999).

45. Byron Calame, "Listening to Both Sides, in the Pursuit of Fairness," *New York Times,* The Public Editor, November 5, 2006.

46. William E. Francois, *Mass Media Law and Regulation*, 2nd ed. (Ohio: Drake University School of Journalism, 1978), 137–138.

47. Joan Ryan, "The Greatest Tragedy Is That Ashe Didn't Have A Choice," *The Sporting News*, April 20, 1992, 4.

48. Adam Nagourney, "Gathering Highlights Power of the Blog," *New York Times,* June 10, 2006, A10.

49. "Pew Internet and American Life Project" (www.pewinternet.org).

50. "Life During Wartime," Editorial, *New York Times,* June 13, 2006, A22.

51. Katharine Q. Seelye, "Study Finds More News Media Outlets, Covering Less News," *New York Times*, March 13, 2006.

52. Tim Harrigan, "Lessons from the Blogosphere in the Case of Jill Carroll," Letter to the Editor," *Boston Globe,* April 10, 2006.

53. David Carr, "24-Hour Newspaper People," *New York Times*, January 15, 2007, C1.

54. Kurtz, "The Big News."

55. Nagourney, "Gathering Highlights Power of the Blog."

56. David Carr, "A Blog Mogul Turns Bearish on Blogs," *New York Times,* July 3, 2006.

57. Lee and Soloman, *Unreliable Sources*, 110.

58. "Why Newspapers?" (www.naa.org/info/whynewspapers/1.html).

59. Ibid.

60. Leo Jeffres, *Mass Media Processes and Effects* (Prospect Heights, IL: Waveland Press, 1986), 123–124.

61. Lester, "Growth of Online News."

62. Lee and Solomon, *Unreliable Sources*, 122.

63. Gerald C. Stone, *Examining Newspapers* (Newbury Park, CA: Sage Publications, 1987), 109.

64. Katharine Q. Seelye, "Newspaper Circulation Falls Sharply," *New York Times,* October 31, 2006, C1.

65. Lee and Soloman, *Unreliable Sources*, 66.

66. Eli M. Naom, "Media Concentration in the United States: Testimony Before the US Senate Committee on Commerce Science and Transportation," Washington, DC, July 17, 2001 (www.vii.org/papers/medconc.htm-42k).

67. Editor and Publisher Yearbook; PEJ research in "The State of the News Media 2004," *American Journalism Review* (www.stateofthenewsmedia.org/narrative_newspapers_ownership.asp?cat=5&media=2).

68. Ben Bagdikian, *The Media Monopoly*, 3rd ed. (Boston: Beacon Press, 1990), 66.

69. Moto Rich, "Village Voice Dismisses 8, Including Senior Arts Editors," *New York Times,* September 1, 2006.

70. Seelye, "Study Finds More News."

71. Russell Baker, "The Great Media Meltdown," *New York Times*, September 19, 1999 (www.nytimes.com).

72. Ibid.

73. Katharine Q. Seelye, "Philadelphia Journalism's New Order," *New York Times*, April 23, 2007, C1.

74. Don Miller, "Media and Youth Culture: Buy it Now!" unpublished paper, MEDC 5981, Webster University, December 2006.

75. Stuart Elliott, "G.M.'s Snub of The Los Angeles Times Is Just the Latest Battle between Marketers and Media Outlets," *New York Times*, April 11, 2005, C6.

76. Kurtz, "The Big News."

77. "Headlines," Democracy Now!, November 16, 2006 (www.democracynow.org).

78. Kurtz, "The Big News."

79. Charles L. Klotzer, "There," *St. Louis Journalism Review* (November 1997), 4.

80. Julie Bosman, "Newsroom Buyouts May Cut Dallas Paper's Staff by 20%," *New York Times*, September 11, 2006, C4.

81. Neil Hickey, "Money Lust: How Pressure for Profit Is Perverting Journalism," *Columbia Journalism Review* (July/August 1998) (www.cjr.org).

82. Klotzer, "There."

83. *Democracy*, November 13, 2006.

84. "Minorities Gain on Local Television News Staffs," Radio and Television News Directors Association, July 6, 2006 (www.rtnda.org/news/2006/070606.shtml).

85. Pat Widder, "Minority's Newsroom Presence Edges Higher," *Chicago Tribune*, Bus. Sec., 3.

86. Simon Romero, "Venezuela Rivals U.S. in Aid to Bolivia," *New York Times*, February 23, 2007, A3.

87. Ibid.

88. Ibid.

89. Ibid.

90. "Cheney Urges China to Press North Korea on A-Bombs," *New York Times*, April 15, 2004, A3.

91. "Cheney Warns Chinese Leaders," *New York Times*, News Summary, April 15, 2004, 2A.

92. Michael Hartley, "Silly Newspaper Headlines" (www.mvhs.net/~salvo/texts/sillyhead.html).

93. Simon Romero, "Venezuelans Give Chávez a Mandate to Tighten His Grip," *New York Times,* December 5, 2006.

94. "Trial Starts in Kennedy Rape Case," *St. Louis Post-Dispatch*. Compiled from News Services, December 3, 1991, 1A.

95. Dylan Loeb McClain, "Some Newspapers Try a No-News Front Page," *New York Times*, June 1, 1998 (www.nytimes.com).

96. Simon Romero, "Venezuela Spending on Arms Soars to World's Top Ranks," *New York Times*, February 25, 2007.

97. Ibid.

98. Marc Lacey, "A Rare Silence Reverberates in Castro's Long Goodbye," *New York Times*, December 3, 2006, A3.

99. Ann Garrells, *All Things Considered*, National Public Radio, September 22, 2006.

100. Antonio Castaneda, "Troop Morale Holds Steady in Iraq," *St. Louis Post-Dispatch*, March 19, 2006, A8.

101. Drew Brown, "Most U.S. Troops in Iraq Support Withdrawal, Poll Finds," Knight Ridder Washington Bureau, March 18, 2006.
102. Greg Jonsson, "Waking Up a Sleepy City," *St. Louis Post-Dispatch*, March 11, 2001.
103. Alvin A. Reid, Letters to the Editor, *St. Louis Post-Dispatch,* March 11, 2001.
104. John M. Broder, "Familiar Fallback for Officials: 'Mistakes Were Made,'" *New York Times*, March 14, 2007.
105. Daily Howler, December 8, 1999 (www.dailyhowler.com).
106. Jason DeParle, "Out of the Frying Pan, into the Freezing Cold," *International Herald Tribune*, May 26, 2006, 5.
107. Tripp Frohlichstein, *Media Training Handbook* (St. Louis, MO: MediaMasters, 1991), 54–56.
108. *Outfoxed.*
109. Ben Schott, "The Year in Questions," *New York Times*, December 31, 2006, Section 4, Pg. 9.
110. Tripp Frohlichstein, interview by author, July 21, 1992.
111. Jacques Steinberg, "After the Peaks of Journalism, Budget Realities," *New York Times*, June 14, 2004, C1.
112. Ibid.
113. Peter Phillips & Project Censored, *Censored 2007* (New York: Seven Stories Press).
114. Ibid., 214.
115. David Carr, "Show Me the Bodies," *New York Times*, June 5, 2006, C1.
116. Foxnews.com (www.foxnews.com).
117. Byron Calame, "All the News That Fits the Allocated Space," The Public Editor, *New York Times,* January 29, 2006.
118. Ibid.
119. Ibid.
120. "All Anna Nicole Smith, All The Time," *Democracy Now!*, February 19, 2007 (www.democracynow.org/article.pl?sid=07/02/19/1545210).
121. "Anna Nicole Smith Gets 12x As Much Coverage as Walter Reed," *Democracy Now!*, March 6, 2007 (www.democracynow.org).
122. Nicholas D. Kristof, "All Ears for Tom Cruise, All Eyes on Brad Pitt," *New York Times*, July 26, 2005.
123. Dick Siccone, managing editor, *Chicago Tribune*, interview by author, April 28, 1992.
124. Monica Davey and Julia Preston, "Likely Source of Bad Spinach Is Named as Outbreak Widens," *New York Times,* A1.
125. Alsha Sultan, "Stores Remove Bagged Spinach amid 20-State E. coli Outbreak," *St. Louis Post-Dispatch,* September 16, 2006, A8.
126. From the editors, "The Times and Iraq," *New York Times*, May 26, 2004.
127. Judea Pearl, "Another Perspective, or Jihad TV?" *New York Times,* January 17, 2007, op-ed contributor.
128. John Leo, "Reading Between the Hyphens," *U.S. News & World Report*, May 21, 1990, 23.
129. *1989 Multicultural Management Program Fellows Dictionary of Cautionary Words and Phrases: An Excerpt From the Newspaper Content Analysis Compiled*

by 1989 Multicultural Management Program Fellows (Columbia, MO: University of Missouri School of Journalism, 1989).

130. Lynette Clementon, "The Racial Politics of Speaking Well," *New York Times*, February 4, 2007.

131. Ibid.

132. "Bush Rallies GOP Voters In Red States," *The Frontrunner,* November 6, 2006, Section: Washington News.

133. Cathy Young, "A Chasm in Conservatism," *The Boston Globe,* July 24, 2006, A9.

134. Howard Chapnick, "Markets & Careers," *Popular Photography* (August 1982), 42.

135. Nick Johnson, "Journalism Analysis—Post-November Election," (December 2006) unpublished paper, Webster University.

CHAPTER 13

ADVERTISING

OVERVIEW

The average American is immersed in advertising:

- U.S. ad spending in 2006 reached a record $285 billion—the equivalent of $950.00 for every person in the United States.[1]
- An hour of prime-time network programming contains 18 minutes of advertising, down from 16 minutes in 2003 and 12 minutes in the 1980s.[2]
- By the age of 65, the average American has seen two million TV commercials.[3]
- American children are exposed to 40,000 ads per year.[4]
- When *Dateline NBC* recently asked children to choose between a banana and a rock with a Scooby-Doo sticker on it for breakfast, nearly all chose the rock.[5]

It is safe to say that the United States has arrived at the stage of *ubiquitous advertising*, in which all conceivable public space is dedicated to advertising, including checkout lines, gas pumps, ATM machines, and urinals. In addition, *place-based video screens* show advertisements in public spaces. As an example, AccentHealth, a marketing company, has placed TV screens in 10,800 doctor's offices across the country.[6] Advertisers also reach consumers in nontraditional ways, including podcasts, blogs, video games, e-mail messages, cellphones, and video-on-demand.

Some disagreement exists about the effectiveness of advertising messages. Studies show that nine out of 10 people can't remember the product or company featured in the last commercial they watched, even if it was less than five minutes ago.[7] However, Tony Schwartz makes an important distinction between *memory* and *recall* in advertising:

> Researchers narrowly focus their questions on a subject's recollection of commercial content, which they consider the essence of what makes a message effective.... [However,] if we make a deep attachment to the product in the commercial, there is no need to depend on their remembering the name of the product.
>
> Seeing the product in the store should evoke the association attached to the product in the commercial.[8]

Thus, although you may not remember specific information about an advertisement, the ad may make the product appear familiar to you when you are wandering down the grocery store aisle. By the age of two, children have developed a loyalty to specific brands.[9]

And further, beyond promoting particular brands, advertisements send cumulative messages about what kind of world we live in, media stereotypes, sexual roles, and measures of success.

Function

Advertising performs a variety of manifest functions:

- Informing the public about a product
- Attracting the attention of the consumer to the product
- Motivating the consumer to action
- Stimulating markets
- Supporting the business community
- Establishing and maintaining a lasting relationship between the consumer and a company

American consumers rely on advertising for services and goods. We scan the papers for bargains, entertainment information, holiday gift ideas, and trends in fashion. Public service spots warn us about dangers in society (e.g., "Say no to drugs") and encourage us to be better citizens by giving to various charities.

At the same time, advertising serves a number of *latent* functions:

Persuasion. Advertising cannot convince consumers to purchase something that they truly don't want: if you don't like coconut, no ad will convince you that you do. However, impulse displays located by the checkout counters in stores stimulate a desire for items that you do fancy but may not be thinking about at the moment. And in cases in which the customer is already shopping for a product, ads are designed to steer the consumer to their particular brand.

Nevertheless, advertisers try to convince us that we don't merely want a product but, in fact, *need* it. Indeed, advertising copy is often phrased in the form of an imperative, or command (e.g., "Buy it today!").

Shaping Attitudes. Before advertisers can influence specific consumer behaviors, they are often faced with the more fundamental problem of shaping *attitudes*. The agency of Campbell-Mithun-Esty sees its primary task as creating "desired attitudes" among consumers: "What attitudes must we establish or change? What habits do we want formed? Do we want that person to know something new has happened, or become aware of additional product uses, or sample our product, or change a negative attitude or misconception?"[10]

Some ad campaigns are designed to create a positive *image* for the company rather than sell a product. For example, in 2006, major oil companies such as ExxonMobil and the British Petroleum Company (BP) ran television ads, conveying messages about how the company cleans up the environment and searches for new solutions to energy problems.

When encountering a public relations advertisement, it is also appropriate to ask *why* the company has chosen to solicit the good will of the public. In this case, the ad campaign was designed to enhance the credibility of the oil industry, which has reported record profits while at the same time hiking up the price of gasoline.

Fostering Consumer Culture. One of the cumulative messages found in advertising involves the value of consumerism in American culture. Advertisers encourage the audience to think of themselves in terms of their consumer behavior. Advertising promotes membership in a group (e.g., "The Pepsi Generation"), united by common consumer habits. Indeed, by wearing designer labels or sweatshirts with commercial logos, consumers have been transformed into walking billboards, advertising these products.

This conditioning begins early. The premise of a popular board game called "Mall Madness" is a trip to the mall, complete with no-limit credit cards. An ad for the game uses a jingle containing the lyrics, "It's our world, girls, so let's SHOP!" But according to a sixth grade media literacy student at Rossman School in St. Louis, Missouri, the toy manufacturer "wants us to think the most important thing to girls is shopping—but it ISN'T!"[11]

In contemporary culture, education has been reduced to knowledgeable *consumerism*. In the past, an educated person was regarded as someone who was exposed to the world of ideas and had developed the critical skills that enabled him or her to ask questions, analyze options, reach logical conclusions, and make decisions. Today, however, an educated consumer is measured by whether he or she has the background and ability to be a "smart shopper." Thus, the slogan on the web site for Syms Department Stores is, "An educated consumer is our best customer."[12] Indeed, the chain refers to their salespeople as "educators"; they have taken over the teacher's role of instructing their "pupils" on matters of importance—that is, how to consume wisely.

Establishing Standards of Behavior and Lifestyle. Advertising is in the business of establishing standards of behavior—how to look, where to go, and what to do with our time. In addition, ads have become a part of our lifestyles. Ad slogans have been incorporated into peoples' common vernacular (e.g., "Drop the Chalupa").

Advertising also has assumed a principal role in the delineation of taste. A marketing executive for Pepsi-Cola once offered the opinion that his competitor, Diet Coke, had made a conscious decision to keep the taste of its product indistinct: although nobody initially *liked* Diet Coke, no one *disliked* the product either. Then, through clever promotion ("Just for the taste of it"), consumers learned that it was stylish to drink Diet Coke and eventually developed a taste for the soft drink.

Entertainment. Advertising was one of the first public communications formats to realize that any message, if presented in an entertaining fashion, will attract the interest of the public. For instance, one of the prime attractions of the Super Bowl is the ceremonial unveiling of new commercials. Indeed, the Super Bowl commercials have become such an entertainment spectacle that in 2007 a separate program was aired on CBS to host "Super Bowl's Greatest Commercials 2007," hosted by Jim Nantz and Daisy Fuentes.

However, advertising must not be so entertaining that it distracts the audience from its primary function of promoting a product. Robert K. Passikoff, president at Brand Keys, observes, "Entertainment is not the same as engagement. People looked at the Ellen DeGeneres commercials and said, 'This is the funniest thing, so clever.' And then they pulled out [the product]—their Visa card."[13]

As Principal Message. Instead of simply supporting programming, in some cases, the programs themselves are advertisements. The Home Shopping Network attracts large numbers of viewers who enjoy the merchandising of products. Only slightly less subtle is MTV. In addition to the sponsors of MTV programming, the entertainment content *itself* is advertising—the music videos provide exposure for recording artists, promoting artists' concerts and CDs.

Media Communicator

In advertisements, the media communicator plays a major role in influencing the intended audience. Advertisers strive to establish a *parasocial* relationship with the audience, making the consumer feel known, appreciated, and special. The Campbell-Mithun-Esty Ad Agency observes, "We must come into our customers' homes and lives as understanding friends and remain as welcome guests because of the honesty and good grace with which we present ourselves."[14]

Although ads are presented through channels of mass media, they often assume an interpersonal tone. It should not come as a surprise that the personal pronoun "you" is the most frequent word used in advertising. For instance, a radio spot for Hampton Inn includes the following claim:

At Hampton Inn, we know how you feel.... Hampton Inn—We're with you all the way.

Because Hampton Inn "knows you" so well, they are in a unique position to provide for all of your lodging needs.

These ads emphasize the longstanding relationship between a company and its customers, so that advertisers can ask for (and expect) consumer loyalty. The word "trust" is another frequently used word in advertising (e.g., "Wal-Mart stands for 'trust.'").

Identifying the hidden media communicator in an ad is an important step in the analysis of media messages. To illustrate, advertisers increasingly invent online profiles who appear on sites like MySpace and Facebook to reach young people who avoid television commercials. Saul Hansell provides the following example:

(In 2007), a Facebook member using the name Brody Ruckus, who said he was a Virginia Tech student, created a group on Facebook and said that if 100,000 people joined it, his girlfriend would agree to have sex with him and another woman at the same time. The group soon attracted 430,000 members.

Some members became suspicious, however, and discovered that there was no Brody Ruckus registered at Virginia Tech. They traced the group to Ruckus Network, a college-oriented music service. Facebook shut down the group, citing its policy against commercial activities by members (unless, of course, they are paying advertisers).[15]

In this case, teenagers in the audience had accepted these messages from their "peers," little realizing that the jargon was written by adults, whose interests, values, and motives differ markedly from the kids in the audience.

Ads directed at children often feature actors and models who are a bit older than the target audience members and, as a result, serve as role models. The thought process of young audience members works according to the following syllogism: 1) The kids in the ad are cool and popular; 2) These kids use the product; 3) I want to be like them; 4) I want to purchase the product.

Adults make the same mistake of thinking that the performers in ads are the actual media communicators. Thus, an ad in which Tiger Woods endorses a deodorant operates according to the same syllogism: 1) Tiger is cool and popular; 2) Tiger uses the product; 3) I want to be like Tiger; 4) I want to purchase the product.

Performers in advertisements fall into the following categories:

Actors. Casting directors screen candidates carefully to find actors who will be most convincing in the role. Hooper White advises advertising executives,

> You should furnish the casting director with a complete written description of the actor you have in mind. Is he or she hard nosed or easygoing, aggressive or passive, funny or serious, quiet or loud? Don't limit the written description to physical details. Be sure to discuss, in writing, the *entire characterization.* You will find that this forces you to clearly identify the character, thereby helping the casting director to find the right actor.[16]

Personas. Some characters have become a staple of a company's advertising strategy. Because the audience has known characters like the Marlboro Man, Mr. Whipple, Madge the manicurist, and Juan Valdez for decades, they are regarded as real people who can be trusted to tell the truth about the benefits of the product. As a result, the actor who portrays "Juan Valdez" has become a worldwide celebrity:

> When Juan Valdez walks the streets of Manhattan or Paris, a poncho over his shoulder, delighted passers-by point, yell greetings and ask for autographs. He is thronged. "It's astonishing the power of publicity," said the man who has portrayed Juan Valdez since 1969, Carlos Sanchez. "My Colombian friends see how the American people receive me, taking photos, and they say it is crazy."[17]

More recently, Volkswagen created a profile page for "Helga," the virtual German character in some of its commercials, on MySpace. Participants could add Helga to their list of friends. In addition, they could see and comment on the commercials and download Helga ringtones, buddy icons, and life-size images.

Celebrities like Jessica Simpson frequently are hired to serve as spokespeople for products. The rationale is that consumers who admire Ms. Simpson will accept her recommendation to use a particular product. Indeed, taking this strategy a bit further, some celebrities have their own line of products, such as Jessica Simpson's line of cosmetics, called Dessert. We should remember, however, that these performers are paid hefty fees, whether or not they actually use the products they endorse. Moreover, celebrity ads often elevate these spokespeople to positions of undue authority, such as former weatherman Willard Scott endorsing Riopan Plus II cold medicine or Hollywood actors promoting political candidates.

Models. Advertisements frequently use models who display the desired "look" that the target audience admires. These models also embody a cultural ideal, which in many cases is not only unrealistic, but unhealthy. The female models in fashion and cosmetics ads are, on average, between 13 and 19 pounds underweight which, according to the American

Psychiatric Association, falls within the range of anorexia.[18] Women are constantly asked to compare themselves to the models and actresses who appear in advertising. In order to sell their products, ads continually tell their female audience members that they are inadequate—overweight, need cosmetic "support" to look better, or simply are too old. This barrage of messages can have a harmful effect on the self-image of young girls and women.

Icons. Cartoon characters like Charlie Tuna, Tony the Tiger, and the Keebler Elves are icons that have been created to personalize the company. They must be likable, memorable, and project qualities that can be associated with the product. However, these fictitious characters have no connection whatsoever with product quality or company policy. To illustrate, in 2001, a sex discrimination lawsuit was filed against Metlife, a life insurance corporation, which has licensed the Peanuts character Snoopy to represent its corporate image. There is no small irony in this loveable symbol representing a company that has been anything but endearing to its workers.

A related strategy involves creating fictitious people like Betty Crocker and Aunt Jemima who become associated with a product. In some cases, a succession of models have been selected, projecting an image of the ideal homemaker that is more in line with the times.

Real People. Testimonials from "average people" lend authenticity and credibility to an ad. The more amateur their performance, the more the audience identifies with them and believes their testimony. This "real people" approach should not be confused with a strategy in which actors *portray* average consumers.

A variation on this strategy involves using actual company personnel to sell the product. CEOs like August Busch III, head of Anheuser Busch Brewery, are not polished pitchmen; however, the consumer enjoys seeing the corporate heads of companies as "regular guys" who believe in their product.

Attention Getters. Every local television station carries commercials by outrageous pitchmen who attract attention by screaming, roller-skating, dressing up in ape suits, or by offering "crazy, crazy low prices." Of course, it is not unreasonable to ask: why would anyone want to buy a product from a person who is either that crazy or that annoying?

Product as Character. In addition, agencies strive to establish an identity for their product in the mind of the public. John Ferrill, executive vice president and creative director of Young & Rubicam, explains,

> Every product has a personality. Whether the clients have consciously thought about it or not, people perceive a brand in a certain way. Jell-O is a member of the family; it's friendly, it's fun. Anacin is very businesslike; it gets the job done, but it does it in a very straight, unglamorous, matter-of-fact kind of way. I could name almost any product and you'd have some impressions on … really what it is. The

brand personality is the description of a product stated as though that product were a person.

If you're trying to write a statement for Oil of Olay, you might characterize the brand as "feminine". You might say she is mysterious, possibly foreign in origin. She understands beauty secrets and the needs of women. She is an authoritative friend.[19]

Comparative Media

One of the most formidable challenges facing advertisers involves finding the most efficient way to reach their target audience. The most direct means of convincing a consumer is through face-to-face communication, so that customers can actually feel, smell, see, and taste the product for themselves. However, in order to reach a mass audience, advertisers must rely on *indirect* experience to promote the merits of their product. For instance, beer ads must rely on visuals to suggest the taste and texture of the beverage. To illustrate, in a classic Miller Draft Beer ad, opening the bottle instantly transforms a hot climate into a frosty winter world. In this case, the visuals call to mind the cold, crisp taste of Miller Beer.

Every medium has its own distinctive characteristics that determine its ability to promote particular types of products to specific audiences. Jay Schulberg of the Ogilvy and Mather Advertising Agency explains,

> ... the media can do different things. TV can create awareness more quickly with a larger percentage of the population at a lower cost. To do that in print becomes prohibitively expensive; it's almost impossible. However, print can inform better.
>
> If one has a complicated message, or where the consumer is spending a lot of money for a product, such as a VCR or a television set, people want information, and you can get a lot more into print than you can get into a 30-second spot. So where TV may create the awareness, say, for a car, people want to read about what the car has, in my view.[20]

Advertisers consider the following factors when deciding on which medium to use:

- Which medium is best suited to convey the advertising message?
- Which medium is the target audience most likely to use?
- Which medium can display the product most attractively and effectively?
- Given the costs and benefits associated with each medium, how can clients make the most efficient use of their advertising budgets?

Print. The medium of print is unmatched in its ability to convey detailed information about a product. In addition, the tangible nature of print allows consumers to refer back to ads when they want specific information. Consequently, people rely on newspapers more than any other medium when they are ready to make a purchase.[21]

Table 13.1
Media Comparisons

Advantages	Disadvantages
Newspapers	
Geographic Market Selectivity Flexibility — Ease of Ad Insertion Editorial Support Broad Coverage Considerable Reader Interest	Lack of Permanence Poor Printing Quality Limited Demographic Orientation Wasted Circulation High Cost for National Advertisers Ad Can Be Buried
Magazines	
Demographic Market Selectivity Long-Life Ad Capability Good Quality Print Production Editorial Support Reader Interest Upscale Audience/Prestige	Lack of Flexibility in Last-Minute Changes Limited Availability High Cost—Especially for Color Limited Local Ad Opportunities Ad Can Be Buried
Radio	
Geographic and Demographic Market Selectivity Universal Accessibility Relatively Inexpensive Personal Nature of Radio Pace Determined by Advertiser Local Appeal Portability Costs for Ads Have Remained Stable Growth of the Radio Audience Flexible Format Time can be bought on short notice Changes can be made on short notice	Lack of Permanence Perishability Clutter Lack of Visual Support Limited Impact—Background Medium
Television	
Visualization of Product Geographic Market Selectivity Significant Market Penetration Can Deliver Huge Audiences Legitimacy of Medium	Perishable Ad Message Unless Repeated Relatively Expensive Clutter-Messages Lost in Group of Ads Not Terribly Selective Medium Limited Time for Presentation Relatively Inflexible Format Ad slots often bought up well in advance of presentation
Internet	
Flexibility—Ability to Update Ads Can Blend in with Editorial Text Can Use Multiple Media to Convey Information Ad More Effective Outreach to Potential Costumers Ability to Track Consumer's Other Purchases Ability to Track Effectiveness of Ads Ability to Target Audience-Microcasting	Ad Can Be Immediately Deleted Can Get Lost in Clutter Expensive to Maintain Site Difficult for Consumer to Locate the Ad—Lack of Comprehensive Web Index

Print ads also have the advantage of blending in with editorial content. For instance, in fashion magazines it is often difficult to distinguish between fashion articles and ads promoting a line of apparel. Moreover, readers tend to associate print ads with the publication in which it is published; consequently, ads placed in prestigious periodicals are accorded commensurate respect.

Print ads generally are very carefully crafted. In contrast with a 30-second television spot, an advertising team concentrates on the equivalent of one frame for a print ad. All elements have been carefully selected in this one moment to fulfill the objective of the ad.

Radio. The lack of visual support in radio obviously makes it impossible for an ad to actually show the features of a product. However, radio advertisers can take advantage of the imaginative possibilities of the medium to sell their product. For instance, a radio spot for the Volkswagen Jetta asks, "How do I help you visualize the Volkswagen Jetta?" The narrator then plays a variety of classical selections to suggest gracefulness, performance, and being "at one" with the car. He concludes by inviting us to "imagine the difference between mere transportation and pure driving pleasure."

Like print ads, radio commercials can blend in with the regular programming. To illustrate, in 2007, KZPS FM in Dallas, Texas, announced plans to promote its products conversationally in what the company calls "integration." A prototype provided by the station offers the following scenario for advertising Southwest Airlines:

> The D.J. later discusses the South by Southwest music festival, a popular annual event held in Austin, and concludes, "You know, the best way to get down to Austin for South by Southwest is Southwest Airlines. They have tons of flights. It's the way I travel."[22]

Radio ads feature catchy jingles, as well as sophisticated recording techniques and performance. In fact, former ad composer Barry Manilow was able to parlay his understanding of jingles (simple melodies and snappy lyrics) into a successful career as a popular artist.

The radio advertiser must condense information into the abbreviated time allotted, at the same time making sure that the information is presented clearly enough to be easily followed. The message must be simplified and the presentation concise. The radio advertiser is limited to one minute, or approximately 200–300 words; in contrast, the print advertiser can use as many as 1,000 words to promote the product.[23] The pace is determined by the advertiser, so that if the audience is inattentive, the message is irretrievably lost. But, as mentioned earlier, radio listeners are often engaged in competing activities, so they may be particularly susceptible to advertising messages.

Television. Television is certainly the most prestigious advertising medium. Merely by appearing on the airwaves, products (and companies) assume a measure of legitimacy. No mater how goofy the local pitchmen may act, they enjoy a minor celebrity status in their community, simply by appearing in front of the camera.

According to Arthur Bellaire, an effective television spot must combine visuals, sound, and narrative information to convey its message:

The video and the corresponding audio should relate. Don't be demonstrating one sales feature while talking about another.... While the audio should be relevant to the video, don't waste words by describing what is obvious in the picture. Rather, see that the words interpret the picture and thereby advance the thought. Rely on the video to carry more than half the weight. Being a visual medium, television is more effective at showing than telling. Avoid static scenes. Provide for camera movement and changes of scenes.[24]

Television offers the following advantages in the promotion of products:

- *Demonstration.* Television is supreme in its ability to show how a product is used.
- *Dramatization.* Advertisers find that ads are effective when they "activate" the product by showing it being used by people. Beyond simply demonstrating how a product is used, television ads present a scenario in which the product makes a significant impact on the lives of the characters.
- *Performance.* More than other media, television is particularly adept at presenting people who are consuming and enjoying the product. A convincing performance can make a difference in persuading its audience to purchase the product.
- *Affective Appeal.* The combination of music and pictures can touch the emotions of the viewer. pics + sounds

Innovations in media technology have added to the challenges facing TV advertisers. Although advertisers spend about $70 billion a year on television commercials, digital video recorders now enable viewers to skip the ads altogether.[25] Indeed, 88 percent of the TV commercials went unwatched in homes that had the black box.[26]

In response, advertisers have developed the following strategies to keep people tuned to the ads:

- Airing one-second ad spots called "blinks." Presenting brief commercial spots doesn't give listeners time to change the station before the message is delivered.[27]
- Producing commercials in which the product being advertised is unclear. This "mystery" keeps people in suspense (and watching).
- Personalizing ad messages to appeal to the specific interests and needs of the audience.
- Emphasizing the quality of production, so that the entertainment value of the spots is, in some cases, superior to the programming.

Digital Media. The Internet has certainly revolutionized the advertising industry. In the early days of mass media, advertisers used a *broadcasting* strategy, in which they used direct mail, radio, print, and television, hoping to interest some of the mass audience within this broad sweep. As print, radio, and television became more sophisticated, marketers were able to *narrowcast* their messages, developing a demographic profile of their target audience and then devising an ad strategy to reach their intended audience.

Interactive technology enables advertisers to move to a *microcast strategy,* in which advertising messages are personalized to meet an individual's specific interests, buying habits, and financial capacity.

Web sites commonly install *cookies*, a piece of software which plants small, traceable files on the computers of the people who visit their site. This *meta information* (i.e., information about the information) enables advertisers to track activity on the Internet, so that they can gather precise information about the individual consumer. In 2006, Internet companies Yahoo and AOL developed the capacity to instantaneously analyze what their users searched for on the Web and then construct an advertisement that takes their personal interests into consideration. Josh Bernoff observes,

> An audience of 200,000 people you know intimately might be as valuable as an amorphous mass of 20 million. After all, a person with a deep interest in a subject is more likely to watch an ad about that subject. "You and I may not care to watch a commercial for Preparation H. But for someone with hemorrhoids, it might be the thing he is most eager to hear about. And he's the one the makers of Preparation H want to talk to."[28]

To illustrate, if you visit the Sears web page to purchase camping equipment, Sears will upload not merely any purchases but also other areas that you have browsed through, such as cowboy boots. The next time that you visit Sears on the Web, the homepage will be personalized, notifying you about any bargains in boots. In addition, if the web site has personal information on you (either by buying the information from another web site or by giving you a "prize" to fill out a form), the homepage will be able to give you advance notice of a relative's birthday and then make suggestions for an appropriate gift.

After browsing through the virtual selection of boots at the Sears site, you may begin to receive unsolicited e-mails from other companies about sales for boots. It is now commonplace for this "preference" information about an individual to be sold throughout cyberspace—so now every boot company on the planet knows of your interest.

A related marketing technique is called *performance-based advertising,* in which a company establishes a network of web sites with links to its site and then pays these "affiliates" for referrals. To illustrate, C-net has signed up thousands of individuals and companies to post a link to C-net on their web sites. C-net then pays the affiliate for every referral. This system is potentially a very lucrative source of income for Internet search directories and content providers, giving these sites an impetus to attract as many visitors as possible. Consequently, it is important to consider *why* particular links appear on a web site.

The fluid nature of interactive media also makes it easy to camouflage the advertising function, so that advertising is often difficult to detect. Advertising links may be inserted into editorial copy, without being labeled accordingly, so that individuals seeking additional information on a topic instead find themselves in an advertiser's web site. These links may also be included because the web owner is being paid an advertising fee. Eric Effron explains,

> For example, nytimes.com offers a link to barnesandnoble.com next to its online book reviews, and *The New York Times* gets a piece of the action if anyone buys a book via that route. Because it's the *Times*, we can be fairly sure that reviews aren't skewed to help sales. But it has to be noted that the *Times* now has a financial interest in that book being reviewed that it didn't have before. And it's not coincidental that ... while most of the newspaper's past articles are available online for just one year and can only be retrieved by paying a fee, the *Times* has made 19 years of book reviews available for free (with the Barnes & Noble "buy option," of course).[29]

The banner, or pop-up ad automatically appears on the desktop as the user hits a particular site. In 2006, 30 percent of consumers sometimes clicked on banner advertisements on the Web. And 61 percent report later visiting the web sites advertised.[30]

Finally, television and web technology are converging, so that the old television set is being transformed into an "entertainment monitor." The large screen will be divided, with the left-hand side reserved for continuous advertising. The world on-screen will then become a virtual display window; if you fancy a pair of shoes that an actor or actress is wearing on a situation comedy, you will be able to click on the image and order the item.

AUDIENCE

The American Marketing Association offers a rather curious definition of advertising: "A paid form of a *non-personal* presentation and promotion of ideas, goods, or service by an identified sponsor aimed at a particular target market and audience [emphasis mine]."[31]

However, it can be argued that in many respects, advertising is an extraordinarily *personal* form of mass communications. After all, the success of an ad depends upon advertisers' ability to identify and then persuade one person. Indeed, John O'Toole, chairman of Foote, Cone & Belding Advertising, regards advertising as a form of interpersonal communication. He observes, "When the chord is struck in one, the vibrations reverberate in millions."[32]

Advertisers devote considerable attention to research to become familiar with their audience. *Demographic* research refers to the study of human populations. Demographic categories include: *age, gender, income, education, occupation, race, religion,* and *family size*. Demographic considerations such as geographical location can play a large role in consumer buying patterns. For example, black is the predominant automobile color on the East Coast, while white and lighter shades of cars are preferred on the West Coast.

Psychographic research identifies the attitudes, values, and lifestyles shared by groups falling within these demographic categories. Psychographic research enables advertisers to identify the consumption patterns of particular subgroups. To illustrate, Otto Kleppner predicts that after completing college, you will go through the following stages of consumerism:

- *Young single.* You have moved to your own apartment and begun to make your own buying decisions. A high proportion of this income is spent on clothes, personal care, recreation, and entertainment.
- *Young marrieds, no children.* In general, you become more home-oriented. For all but a small proportion of these households, the wife works, providing a higher standard of living for the household. Most consumer buying decisions begin to be made by the female.
- *Young marrieds, children under six.* At this stage, the couple becomes tied down. If the wife quits her job, the family income goes down—although in most cases, the wife continues to work. A move to a larger apartment or house is required.
- *Young marrieds, children over six.* Your children have entered school. At this point, the wife has more freedom for activities outside of the home. The children begin to influence purchasing decisions.
- *Older marrieds with children.* Your expenses increase for education, weddings, etc. You begin to engage in more activities away from home. For instance, you begin to travel more frequently.
- *Older marrieds, no children.* Your children have left home. Smaller living quarters are now required. Your consumption patterns no longer need to consider the children.
- *Older singles.* At this stage you have become widows, widowers, divorcees, and unmarried men or women. You experience a dramatic change in lifestyle as your income is reduced.[33]

Advertisers have discovered that lifestyle has a direct bearing on consumer patterns. For instance, automobile purchases are most numerous among young married couples with no children, as well as young married couples with children over six. And because young marrieds with small children are generally less mobile than other groups, they are the most promising prospects for television purchases.

Advertisers can even predict consumer buying patterns on the basis of a consumer's previous purchases. The BBDO Advertising Agency uses a system of *Lifestyle Indicators (LSI)* to predict cross-product consumer buying patterns: "[We can] relate the usage of your product to the usage of other products. Through this method we can determine whether your prime prospects drink wine or beer, if they travel outside the U.S., what kinds of cars they drive, what books they read, etc."[34] Thus, after you have made a purchase, you may be flooded with e-mails promoting other products that, according to Lifestyle Indicators, will be of interest to you.

Through psychographic research, advertisers have become particularly adept at identifying the fears, anxieties, and areas of insecurity of their target audience, and then flooding them with personalized messages that, first, trigger their insecurities, and then present their product as the solution to their "problem." Reporter Lisa W. Foderaro provides the following illustration:

> Pam Fitzgerald, managing partner of a marketing company in Virginia who struggles with her weight, bristles at the diet-plan spam, wondering "who knows how much I weigh." And her heart aches for one of her young employees, the only one in the small firm not to have finished college, who seems to be a magnet for spam pushing Johnny-come-lately bachelor's degree programs. "It's rubbing him raw day in and day out," she said. Worsening the psychic toll is the increasingly focused tailoring of spam of all stripes.[35]

Multiple Audiences. Media programming may be directed simultaneously at both a manifest and latent audience. To illustrate, ads that appear in women's magazines such as *Cosmopolitan* or *Vogue* are often surprisingly alluring and seductive, given that the target audience consists primarily of heterosexual women. One way to account for this sexually titillating advertising is that the latent audience actually consists of *males*. Women readers project themselves into the role of the model and then respond to the ads from a male perspective. ("How would he like me in this outfit?") This explanation has some rather disturbing implications. For although progressive magazines like *Cosmopolitan* purport to be fashionably liberated, this advertising strategy suggests that women still depend upon male approval in American culture.

CONTEXT

Historical Context

In order to reach people in the most immediate manner possible, advertising is extraordinarily sensitive to historical events. These events provide a context of meaning for the commercial message. For instance, after the terrorist attack of 9/11, Calvin Klein altered its campaign from a sexy appeal to a more "poignant" approach—snippets of film, in home-video style, of family moments, shot in retro black and white, set to the 1960s Burt Bacharach song, "What the World Needs Now Is Love."

Cultural Context

Advertising and Popular Culture. Advertising may furnish perspective into cultural attitudes and values. As an example, in 2004 the Staples office supply chain launched an advertising campaign in which customers pushed an "Easy Button," that demonstrates how convenient it is to shop at their stores. The Easy Button says "Easy" on top and "Staples" along the side. Pushing the button activates a recording of Staples' slogan: "That was easy!" The popularity of this prop was so overwhelming that Staples began merchandising the Easy Button for $4.99. As of 2006, the chain sold nearly 1.5 million "Easy Buttons."[36]

One way to account for the unexpected popularity of the promotion is that it taps into the concerns of individuals who are struggling to contend with a world in which they feel overwhelmed and powerless. One ad executive speculated in *Brandweek* that the Easy Button is an "elegant metaphor, speaking to a yearning for solutions to the complexities of the modern world."[37] Thus, the commercials present scenarios in which pushing the Easy Button instantaneously solves difficult problems. In one ad, an Easy Button builds the Great Wall of China, just in time to thwart an invading army. According to reporter Rob Walker, people turn to the Easy Button to solve their problems.

> According to Shira Goodman, Staples' top marketing executive, the company has received letters and tracked reports of a dizzying array of Easy Button uses, from people pressing it to cheer on the kids during kitchen homework sessions to, somewhat incredibly, a woman who took one to her mother's chemotherapy sessions. The Canadian prime minister was famously filmed with an Easy Button in his office. "This one is a little scary," Goodman says, "but I've personally been on airplanes and seen them in the cockpit."[38]

Reflection of Cultural Preoccupations. Advertising can also disclose areas of cultural interest and concern. In that respect, ads can furnish perspective into the following *cultural preoccupations*.

Sex. American advertisements reflect our culture's ambivalent, adolescent preoccupation with sex. What are some of the cumulative messages about sex which can be found in American advertising?

- *Sex is a cultural obsession.* The sheer quantity of sexually oriented ads suggests that sex is a national fixation. All products (from perfume to automobiles) have sexual implications. Sex is always on our minds.
- *Sex is dirty.* American ads encourage a voyeuristic approach to sex. The audience peeks at models on the printed page or screen, which provides much of the sexual tension in the ads. Female models are posed in a posture of innocence, seemingly unaware that they are objects of desire. If they look at us boldly, they fall into the category of "bad girls."

American ads convey the message that sex is dirty and must be repressed. In contrast, European advertisements generally are much more explicit than their American counterparts. Nudity is not uncommon, either in print or television ads.

- *Appearance is everything.* You are only as sexy as you look. We do not accept imperfections, either in our sex objects or, by extension, in ourselves. Consumer items, then, assume a magical quality, transforming people into desirable, sexy creatures.
- *Sex is confined to a narrow stage of life.* Sex is a youth-oriented activity. In advertising, sex ends with marriage. Advertising rarely depicts older adults in sexually suggestive situations.
- *Sex is objectified.* In many ads, women are reduced to sexual objects. Ads often show only part of females' bodies, reinforcing the notion that sex appeal is associated with certain parts of the anatomy. Sex is not presented as an aspect of a larger relationship but an end in itself.
- *Sex is a contact sport.* Sex is a contest, in which people compete for the attention of others. That's why we need all the commodities we can muster. Sex has very little to do with one's partner but instead is an ego-centered performance, undertaken for the approval and admiration of others.
- *Sex is a consumer item.* The sexual style of ads has become its substance: products are sexy. In the ultimate depersonalization of sex, we are asked to believe that the products advertised in a seductive fashion, like cars, have sexual properties.

Aging. Americans' preoccupation with youth is reflected in advertising. Ads for a range of products reinforce the ideal of youth by featuring models who are young, healthy, and fit. Julia Smillie observes, "Constant exposure to images of youth create an impression that youthfulness is the norm and that in order to be accepted, (the consumer) must strive to stay young."[39] In a television ad for Just for Men Hair Coloring, a group of young people, male and female, are gathered together. One of the people has grey hair. His entire figure is washed out and devoid of color. Thus, gray is equated with being dull and boring, dreary and unattractive. The ad then instructs the man to "Get back in the game" by getting rid of grey hair. Once he has committed to using the product, color is restored to his image, and he is no longer ostracized from the group.

An ad for New Age hair color promises that the product will "restore your hair to its natural color," inferring that aging is an unnatural process. An ad for Shiseido skin cream establishes age as an enemy: "The fragile skin around your eyes. This is where time strikes first." Advertising for cosmetics, plastic surgery, exercise equipment, and hair replacement plans make the very ambitious promise of restoring youth. The headline for an Oil of Olay ad declares, "I don't plan to grow old gracefully, I intend to fight it every step of the way."

Cleanliness. American advertising often plays on our cultural insecurities about cleanliness. Asked where this antibacterial fetishism comes from, Dr. Jeffrey S. Duchin replies, "A lot of it is not based on science. It is based on our national psyche and what we value – purity and cleanliness."[40]

Over the years, ad campaigns for Listerine mouthwash have been directed at a range of anxieties related to halitosis:

- *"Could I be happy with him in spite of THAT?"* (1923)
- *"It brought him untold misery; yet only he himself was to blame."* (1924)
- *"Often a bridesmaid but never a bride."* (1924)
- *"Why had he changed so in his attentions?"* (1924)
- *"Their first conversation betrayed the fact that she was not fastidious."* (1925)[41]

Cultural Myths. American ads frequently tap into cultural myths, including the following.

Progress. According to this cultural myth, new is better. Change is good for its own sake. Advertisers persuade customers that this year's models are superior to last year's. Advertisers create new markets by denigrating the old model, breaking last year's promise of quality and durability.

Appeal to Mythic Past. At the same time, a nostalgic appeal to our mythic past establishes confidence in the product. For example, the highly successful Motel 6 ad campaign positions the hotel chain as a throwback to simpler times. Spokesperson Tom Bodett is a latter day Will Rogers who offers country wisdom and hospitality in a depersonalized corporate world. With country fiddle music playing in the background, Bodett assures us, "We'll leave the light on for ya."

Individualism. Americans like to see themselves as rugged individualists, in the mold of John Wayne and Clint Eastwood. However, a delicate balance exists between *individualism* and *conformity.* People who are *too* different become cultural rejects (nerds, geeks, etc.). The trick to rugged individualism, then, is to stand out by being the epitome of style. The Marlboro man simply leads the pack of conformists.

Advertising sends the message that the way to assert one's individuality in contemporary society is through consumer behavior. Ironically, then, our range of individual expression has been reduced to the creative selection of products.

Cultural Change. Ads may also function as a barometer of cultural change. To illustrate, in a TV spot for Toyota Tercel, a young man has been commandeered to drive his friends to some unknown destination in his new automobile. He is clearly uncomfortable in this role and lays down a series of rules to protect his new Toyota. ("No eating in the car.... No fooling around.... You have to help me wash it afterward.") The voice-over declares, "Because your values may change, but your friends don't." The message here is clear. As part of his upward mobility, this baby boomer now treasures material goods (i.e., his Toyota), even more than his friendship with his old buddies. The commercial makes this statement without apology; according to the ad, this is as it *should* be—part of the maturation of the American consumer. These old friends have become a source of aggravation and embarrassment. The implication is that if they don't grow up (as responsible consumers), they will be left behind.

Worldview. What kind of world is portrayed through advertising?

In many ads, what is really being sold is the *worldview* of the commercial. When you buy a designer shirt or sunglasses, you are purchasing far more than the product; you are entering the upscale and trendy world depicted in the ad campaigns. Jennifer Steinhauer observes,

> To promote a lifestyle, a company must obsessively market its products through ad campaigns in which the product is not nearly as central as the people using it.... In most Nine West ads, it is hard to make out the shoes or bag for sale. But the women are young and sexy and never far from a great-looking guy and a romantic setting. A shopper is meant to believe that if she buys the whole package—clothes, tables, sheets and bras—she will join the elite club of those living out the brand's lifestyle in its ads.[42]

The inference is that purchasing the product somehow admits you into the world of the ad.

Thus, mentally airbrushing the product out of an advertisement can identify the worldview surrounding the product. Imagine a beer commercial, in which young people are cavorting on the beach. Now, mentally delete the product from the scene. What remains is a delightful social occasion, replete with plenty of music, flirting, and celebrating. But when the product is placed in the center of the activity, the ad conveys the message that beer is central to this good time—indeed, you can't really have a party without someone bringing a keg.

Beyond the promotion of specific products, ads convey cumulative messages about the world of advertising. Some of these elements include the following.

- *A Material World.* The worldview of ads is reduced to what we can see, feel, touch—and buy. In the here-and-now world of advertising, style has become substance. People discover meaning through the acquisition of consumer goods. To illustrate, in November 2000, a billboard was posted in the Westfarms mall in Hartford, Connecticut, which said, "This holiday season let's all take a moment to wish for peace on Earth." However, as part of the advertisement, the words "for peace on Earth" were intentionally crossed out, replaced with the wish "that you'll be one of the lucky winners to get all your Visa purchases for free."[43]

  In the world of advertising, identity has become a disposable commodity. We can (to all appearances) become anyone we want on the basis of how we look and what lifestyle we adopt. As Andre Agassi, former tennis star and pitchman for Canon cameras observed, "Image is everything." Appearance becomes ascendant; the emphasis is now on youth, looks, and health.

- *An Uncomplicated World.* This world offers simple solutions to complex problems: all issues can be resolved by purchasing the right product. The advertising world is populated by uncomplicated people who find fulfillment through laundry detergents and car wax.
- *World of Immediate Gratification.* According to cultural historian David Shi, Americans suffer from "acceleration syndrome," in which they are increasingly impatient:

> Waiting has become an intolerable circumstance. We get on an elevator and immediately rush to close the door button for fear of waiting 10 seconds ... Technology has helped create products designed to save time: fax machines, express checkout lines, speed dialing, remote controls, overnight mail delivery, e-mail. But in saving time, these products are making us even more impatient.[44]

This sense of urgency permeates the world of advertising. In commercials, people cannot postpone their gratification for more than 30 seconds. In a McDonald's ad campaign, the merits of the product are sung to the tune "Temptation," enticing us to rush to McDonald's. To rewrite an old adage, "Nothing worth having is worth waiting for."

- *A Self-Absorbed World.* In this narcissistic world, satisfaction does not stem from helping others. Instead, pleasure comes from helping yourself to as many products as you can afford. Why buy L'Oreal hair coloring? "Because I'm worth it." Why spend your money at McDonald's? Because "You deserve a break today." A pre-Christmas radio spot for The Cheese Place asks, "Don't we owe ourselves a little self indulgence? So why not be a little selfish before the gift giving begins?"[45]
- *A Competitive World.* Advertising creates a competitive environment, in which consumers are continually asked to compare themselves to others. For instance, women are told that they are overweight, need cosmetic "support" to look better, or simply are too old. This barrage of messages can have a dramatic impact on the self-image of young girls and women.

  However, advertising fosters an unattainable ideal of female beauty. Through digital imaging (a computer manipulation technique), fashion photographers eliminate models' wrinkles and imperfections. For example, a photograph of actress Michelle Pfieffer for the cover of *Esquire* magazine required extensive retouching—costing over $1,300—before the image was suitable. A work order for the job included the following directions: "Soften eye-lines, soften smile line, trim chin, remove neck lines, add blush to cheek, add hair on top of head."[46] Ironically, then, even those models who have become our standards of female beauty fail to measure up to this ideal.
- *An Optimistic World.* Ultimately, the worldview of advertising is optimistic, in that even the most troublesome problems can be resolved through the acquisition of consumer goods. Ads show happy people celebrating their good fortune. And we too can "discover the possibilities" of life and assume control of our own destinies through prudent consumerism. However, Stephanie Coontz warns,

> The flip side of the urge to have it all is the fear of settling for too little ... Some individuals turn even leisure into a form of relentless work as they strive to avoid "missing out" on opportunities. Others are terrified by the possibility of "premature" commitment: The sense that all choice is good and more choice is better is a profoundly destabilizing one for interpersonal relationships.[47]

- *A Class Segmented World.* The world of advertising is divided into two groups: the haves and the have-nots. Advertisers for Nike and Reebok have built a market for $300 basketball shoes by convincing teenagers that these items are the keys to status. Many young consumers feel pressured to keep up with this fashion trend, despite the inflated cost of the shoe.

Images of Success. In an attempt to present products in their most positive light, ads associate their products with success. As an example, a classic ad campaign, "Where you're going it's Michelob," presents the product as a metaphor for success in American culture.

Michelob is a premium beer which is targeted at an upscale audience. In the television version of this ad, a variety of people are headed toward a state of being called "Michelob." The first sequence follows two characters ascending a mountain (accompanied to a jingle which begins, "You're on your way to the top."). These upwardly mobile characters overcome odds and are in complete control of their environment. The commercial is choreographed in such a way that all of the characters (mountain climbers, businesspeople, a truck driver, a young couple hustling to meet one another, and people at a barbecue) appear active and purposeful. These fast-paced commercials are characterized by a series of quick cuts. The latent message is that the Michelob lifestyle is exciting and glamorous.

Michelob is equated with self-knowledge, certainty, confidence, and a sense of direction. The music reminds us:

> Where you're going it's Michelob.
> And along the way you know just where you are and where you're going.
> You've always known it.

These characters are all young, beautiful, and physically fit—there is not a beer belly in the crowd. The main figures are always in the middle of the frame, the center of attention. Everyone is watching (and admiring) them. And because the use of the personal pronoun "you" projects the audience into the advertisement, we are by extension watching people adoring us.

The culmination of the characters' quest ("Where they're going") is the earthly equivalent of heaven—success, or at least, a frosty Michelob. Michelob is a just reward for hard work and an acknowledgement of achievement. As a metaphor for success, Michelob offers an easy solution to complex problems. Thus, even if you are a total failure, you can maintain the *illusion* of success by drinking a Michelob.

Figure 13.1
This Michelob ad offers a composite picture of success in American culture. The ad appeals to the audience by associating the product with these images of success. Courtesy of Anheuser-Busch Companies, Inc. and Fleishman-Hillard, Inc.

MEDIA LITERACY TIPS

WORLDVIEW

Questions to ask with regard to *worldview* in advertising include:

- *What kind of world is being depicted in the ad?*
- *What kind of lifestyle is promoted in the ad?*
  Consumers may actually be attracted to the lifestyle depicted in the ad, of which the product is only a small part.
- *What is the role of the product within the worldview of the ad?*
  Imagine the ad without the product to see whether that consumer item is indeed an essential part of that world.
- *If you did not know what product was being promoted, what would you think was being advertised?*
  Consumers who are interested in the primary product may also be compelled to purchase the other consumer items depicted in the ad.

Ideology. The world of advertising is dominated by mainstream culture. Increasingly, however, advertisers recognize that subcultures represent a substantial market. As an example, the buying power of African Americans grew by 127 percent in 14 years (from $318 billion in 1990 to $723 billion in 2003).[48] As a result, many ads now target the African American community. However, as John Leo points out, some of these marketing strategies continue to exploit poor segments of the African American community to sell their products: "The malt liquors, marketed primarily to poor members of minority groups, use cobra, bull, dragon, tiger, stallion, and pit bull. The idea is to sell wildness and power to the powerless (high alcohol content is part of the same strategy)."[49]

The G. Heilman Brewing Company took this approach one step further, introducing a strong malt liquor with the brand name of *PowerMaster.* However, this overt promise of empowerment-through-alcohol generated protests by minority groups, and the Bureau of Alcohol, Tobacco and Firearms withdrew its approval for the brand name. But as Leo points out, "So long as this theme is covert, nobody seems to object, but the G. Heilman Brewing Co. found out what happens when the fig leaf is dropped."[50]

Media Stereotyping. Because advertisers have a limited amount of time to reach their audience, they rely heavily on stereotypes. To illustrate, a 2006 television spot for Gillette Razors takes place at the Gillette "lab," where two "scientists" test the quality of the latest innovations in their shaving gear. The first is an older gentleman—he is short, with unruly hair, and speaks with a thick German accent. The other scientist is a younger Asian man. Both are wearing white lab coats.

Advertising promotes membership in a group (e.g., "The Pepsi Generation"), based upon common buying patterns. Indeed, by wearing designer labels or sweatshirts with commercials logos, consumers have been transformed into living advertisements for products.

However, groups portrayed in ads are depicted mainly in consumer-oriented terms. The heritage and political ideology of groups are stripped away, leaving only their appearance and lifestyle as their only distinguishing features.

Moreover, subcultures that are not part of the mainstream are often presented as stereotypical buffoons. A Wendy's ad campaign depicted various "fringe" groups like hippies, who foolishly wanted such unsavory food as alfalfa sprouts. This caricature had the trappings of the 1960s hippie—the long hair, mannerisms, and language—but was devoid of the political and social ideology of the counterculture.

MEDIA LITERACY TIPS

IDEOLOGY & STEREOTYPES

As you analyze ads, ask the following questions with regard to *ideology* and *stereotype:*

- *To what groups (or subgroups) do the characters belong?*
- *In what settings are they presented?*
- *Are they the primary or secondary characters?*
- *Are they at home or at work?*
- *What kinds of products do they promote?*
- *What do the stereotypes reveal about cultural attitudes toward these groups?*

Hierarchy of Values. Advertising often associates products with traditional values such as family and Christmas spirit. For instance, some ads equate consumerism with American democracy. An ad campaign for Chevrolet announces that its new line of trucks is "An American Revolution." Freedom has been reduced to the freedom to *buy.*

MEDIA LITERACY TIPS

HIERARCHY OF VALUES

Questions to ask in regard to *values hierarchy* include:

- *What manifest values are being used in the promotion?*
- *What connection does the product have with these values?*
- *What latent values seem to be most prized in the advertisement?*

Figure 13.2
Many ads associate the purchase of products with traditional values such as family, Christmas spirit, and patriotism. This ad campaign for Chevrolet cites its trucks as part of "An American Revolution." However, this appeal to sell products only cheapens the actual values it pretends to espouse. Courtesy General Motors Media Archive.

Social Marketing. Media literacy can be a useful tool in shaping messages that influence the attitudes and behaviors of individuals. The rationale behind social marketing is that the tools of media literacy can be used to promote pro-social behaviors. To illustrate, one study found that young Massachusetts adolescents were significantly less likely to smoke if they were exposed to an anti-smoking media campaign. Smoking rates declined by 50 percent among 12- to 14-year-olds who were exposed to the messages, compared with those who didn't recall the ads.[51] In Florida, an anti-smoking campaign featuring a series of television commercials produced a 54 percent decline in middle school tobacco use over the past two years, and a 24 percent drop among high school students.[52] By examining media presentations as a cultural text, social marketers can identify the attitudes and concerns of the audience and, then, construct media messages that influence its intended audience. To illustrate, an examination of popular media programming would suggest that messages dealing with *appearance* would be far more effective with this audience than *health* messages. Twelve year olds don't internalize messages about the likelihood of cancer 60 years from now; however, they do respond to ads in which a member of the opposite sex is turned off because the smoker's breath smells.

Structure

Ownership Patterns. In the market-driven American media system, programming is often subordinate to advertising. As an ABC network executive explains, "The network is paying affiliates to carry commercials, not programs. What we are is a distribution system for Procter & Gamble."[53] As an indication of the importance of advertising revenue, during radio's golden era of the 1930s, the stars took second billing in many shows to the sponsors. Examples included "The Kraft Music Hall (starring Bing Crosby)" and "The Pepsodent Program (starring Bob Hope)." This practice changed only after advertisers realized the power of a celebrity to attract an audience.

Recently, sponsors have begun to produce original programming for cable television, obtaining final control over all aspects of programming. In 2006, Unilever put together two specials built around its Axe Shower body wash: "Gamekillers" on MTV and "Exposing the Order of the Serpentine on SpikeTV." And in the same vein, toy manufacturers Mattel and Hasbro developed movie versions of Hot Wheels, G.I. Joe, Bionicle toys, Super Soaker squirt guns, and My Little Pony to promote their products. The companies have veto power over the script and the writers. Jim Wagner, senior vice president for entertainment marketing at Mattel, explained, "We need the entertainment to create a brand for us that's long term."[54]

According to Edward S. Herman and Noam Chomsky, advertisers insist on bland content that supports the status quo:

> Advertisers … choose selectively among programs on the basis of their own principles. With rare exceptions these are culturally and politically conservative.… Advertisers will want, more generally, to avoid programs with serious complexities and disturbing controversies that interfere with the "buying mood." They seek programs that will lightly entertain and thus fit in with the spirit of the primary purpose of program purchases—the dissemination of a selling message.[55]

Ronald K. L. Collins cites instances in which reporters have been called off of stories involving advertisers: "In a confidential survey of 42 real-estate editors by the *Washington Journalism Review*, nearly half said publishers and senior editors had prohibited critical coverage of the industry for fear of offending advertisers."[56]

Advertising and Government Regulation. The Federal Trade Commission (FTC) was created by Congress in 1914. It is headed by five commissioners appointed by the president. In 1938, the FTC was given the authority to protect consumers from unfair and deceptive advertising. If there is an illegal activity, both the company and the advertising agency may be held responsible.

According to Lee Peeler, associate director of the FTC, advertisements must comply with three basic rules: 1) An ad cannot be deceptive—that is, mislead consumers to their detriment; 2) Objective claims must be supported with competent studies; and 3) Advertisers are responsible for the reasonable implications of their ads to consumers. Peeler explains, "If an advertiser says 'I didn't really mean to convey that,' well, that doesn't get them off the hook. All of advertising law is based on what consumers take from the ad."[57]

Although Congress has not provided a comprehensive definition of the term "deceptive," the FTC considers the following criteria in determining whether an advertisement is deceptive:

- The nature of the misstatements (i.e., Is it likely to deceive someone?)
- The nature of the audience targeted by the ad (e.g., children, senior citizens)
- The significance of the ad to the consumer's decision to purchase the product (i.e., Is it likely to play a material role in the decision to buy?)

Once a company is found guilty of using deceptive advertising, it may choose to comply voluntarily with the recommendations of the FTC; in this case, a consent order may be filed with the court, in which the company agrees to halt the ad without technically admitting guilt. Another option is to seek a thorough litigation. The FTC also may simply notify the public that an offense has occurred. Finally, in some cases the FTC may require corrective advertising, whereby the advertiser must for a reasonable amount of time include corrective statements in their advertisements.

The question remains, however—if regulatory policies and enforcement procedures have been in force for more than half a century with regard to deceptive advertising, why do misleading ads continue to appear in the media?

In 2005, the FTC filed 77 actions in federal district court to protect consumers against unfair and deceptive trade practices and obtained 103 judgments ordering more than $824 million in consumer redress, and 15 judgments ordering payment of more than $6.6 million in civil penalties. But according to attorney Michael Kahn, most of the cases of misleading advertising are never brought to the attention of the FTC:

> Nothing is officially "deceptive" until declared so by an appropriate tribunal. More than 90 percent (of allegedly misleading ads) are never brought to anybody's attention. The FTC is a woefully understaffed organization, not set up to handle a large volume of complaints. They are reduced to looking for the worst examples, the ones they can win. For every one they target, there are probably a hundred others out there.[58]

Moreover, advertisements may not be misleading in a legal sense but induce the public to buy a product by appealing to the emotions or making subtle promises about the benefits of the product. According to Joseph R. Baca, director of the office of compliance at the FDA's Center for Food Safety and Applied Nutrition, "The thing is, a lot of claims we see out there are puffery. But they don't get to the point where we can call them fake or misleading."[59]

FRAMEWORK

Introduction

In advertising, the introduction is intended to attract the consumer's attention, lead the consumer into the rest of the ad, and to encompass the essence of the product.

Beyond mere identification, a *brand name* creates an immediate impression and establishes the character of a product. For example, "Hamburger Helper" creates a positive, distinctive image, whereas "Cheap Cereal Filler Meat Supplement" puts a less rosy spin on this type of product. Some brand names are intentionally exotic or mysterious, conveying the message that the product is unexpected, new, and fresh.

Selecting brand names has become more complicated in a global market. Some words may be difficult to recall in a foreign language or suffer from an unflattering translation. For instance, the literal Spanish translation for the Chevrolet Nova is "No go." Worse yet, the name "Coca-Cola" in Chinese was first rendered as "Ke-kou-ke-la," which means "Bite the wax tadpole," or "female horse stuffed with wax," depending on the dialect. Coke then found a close phonetic equivalent in Chinese, "ko-kou-ko-le," which is loosely translated as "happiness in the mouth."

As a result, the strongest trademarks are often *neologisms*—words which have been invented for products. The look and sound of these neologisms are designed to suggest connotative meanings about the essence of the product. For instance, when Amtrak unveiled its new high speed train, the Acela Express, to serve the Northeast, Amtrak president George D. Warrington explained that this neologism was selected to represent a new conceptual orientation for the railroad:

> Acela is more than just a name for Amtrak's new high speed trains, Acela is a brand representing a whole new way of doing business. A combination of acceleration and excellence, Acela means high speed and high quality—we are changing the journey for every customer on every train with faster trip times, comfortable amenities and highly personalized service.[60]

At times, a brand name can give the consumer a false impression about the product. For instance, Hostess came out with "Hostess Cupcakes Lite," which claimed to be one-third fewer calories than the regular cupcakes.

However, a close examination of the label reveals that the Lite cupcakes are actually one-third *smaller* than the original version. One can easily imagine a "superlite" concept, with 50 percent fewer calories, with a package containing one cupcake.

A catchy *slogan* is also integral to the success of an ad. Five times as many people read the headline than the copy in the body of the ad. Memorable slogans are clever, rhythmical, alliterative, and manage to capture the intended character, or spirit of the product.

For instance, "Just do it" is a very sophisticated and effective motto, even though the name of the product (Nike) is never mentioned. The slogan lauds athletic effort and tells us that we can succeed despite the odds (or excuses). Buoyed by this pep talk, we are prepared to achieve our goals. The latent message is that Nike athletic footwear will provide essential support in this quest.

Ultimately, the slogan is a not-so-subtle imperative to buy the product: "Just do it."

As with brand names, advertising slogans may assume a different meaning with an international audience. For instance, when Kentucky Fried Chicken advertised in China, it did not realize that its slogan, "Finger-lickin' good" was translated into "Eat your fingers off"—not a very appetizing prospect.

The *package* can create a positive first impression and make a product appear unique. Consumers are drawn to distinctive *packaging*, as though the *product* was different.

To illustrate, Classico pasta sauces are packaged in a mason jar, which suggests a homemade quality for the product. Thomas Hine explains,

> (The ornate Classico jar) encourages people to taste the sauce not as the common commodity it has become but rather as an expression of a place, with its own culture and distinctive ingredients. It makes people feel they are not simply opening a jar of sauce but doing something just a little more special.[61]

Hine points out that a package like Classico provides a sense of membership and identity for the consumer:

> It's flattering to the buyer: "We know you've traveled, and we know you don't buy industrial tomato sauce, that you're a more discriminating buyer and are willing to pay a price of about 40 to 50 percent more than Ragu."[62]

In 2007, R.J. Reynolds introduced a new line of Camel cigarettes for women, in which the only differences were the name of the brand and the package. Stuart Elliott explains,

> Camel No. 9, has a name that evokes women's fragrances like Chanel No. 19, as well as a song about romance, "Love Potion No. 9." Camel No. 9 signals its

with subtler cues like its colors, a hot-pink fuchsia and a minty-
slogan, "Light and luscious"; and the flowers that surround the
ine ads.[63]

because companies repackage products to meet the emerging customers, packaging concepts can also provide insight into cultural changes. For instance, Campbell's "Soup for One" was developed in response to the increasing number of people who live alone, as well as those whose hectic schedules prevent them from sitting down for the traditional family meal.

Illogical Premise. Ads that appear perfectly reasonable on the surface may be based on an illogical premise. To illustrate, a television ad for Coors Light beer promotes its product as a health drink. As young men and women cavort around the beach in swimwear, the voice-over reminds us that you do not want a beer that will "slow you down." However, upon reflection, it is obvious that a steady diet of beer—regular or light—will hardly keep you trim and fit.

The ad campaign "Newport Lights—Alive with pleasure" provides another excellent example. Given the medical evidence about the health hazards of smoking (which by law must be cited in the ads), this claim could hardly be more absurd.

Plot

Explicit Content. When a product is unique, clearly superior to its competition, or of public benefit, the advertiser's task is easy. However, if a product is indistinguishable from other brands on the market, the advertiser must devise strategies that make the product appear alluring and distinctive. This task is even more of a challenge when a product is harmful to the public, such as alcohol or cigarettes.

Consumers should remain skeptical of false and misleading ads. Some ads present an *incomplete* or *distorted* message, telling only a half-truth in order to present the product in the best possible light. To illustrate, the FDA issued a statement that advertisements for COX-2 drugs Celebrex and Bextra are misleading by failing to disclose the side effects of the drugs. The FDA cited five print and television ads for making "unsubstantiated effectiveness claims."

Examining explicit content can disclose the following inconsistencies, fallacies, and incongruities in advertisements.

The Big Promise is a claim that is far beyond the capacity of the product. As an example, Axe deodorant has emerged as the top brand in less than four years by promising to help men attract more women. An ad on the Axe web site depicts a scene in which a mob of bikini clad women charge madly toward the beach; they come upon a man who is spraying himself with Axe deodorant. The ad slogan suggests a cause/effect relationship between the deodorant and attracting women: "Spray More. Get More. The Axe Effect."

MEDIA LITERACY TIPS
THE BIG PROMISE
When examining ads, consider the following questions with regard to the *big promise*: 1. *What promises does the ad make with regard to the product?* 2. *Which promises can the product reasonably keep?* 3. *Which promises are beyond the capabilities of the product?*

Although the Big Promise in an ad may well be more subtle than the above example, its message is conveyed quite clearly to members of the audience. In 1997, a Michigan man sued Anheuser-Busch for false advertising, claiming that he did not have success with women after drinking the product. He said the implicit promises in the beer advertisements did not come true for him, causing physical and mental injury and emotional distress, so he sued the beer manufacturer for $10,000.[64]

Hyperbole is a part of the American storytelling tradition, which relies upon exaggeration or absurd overstatement to make a point. Examples can be found in such tales as George Washington's coin toss across the Delaware River and the legendary Paul Bunyan. In a country of seemingly limitless resources, Americans magnify events and locations for emphasis and dramatic effect. This literary device also capitalizes on the American competitive spirit. Everything we do (or own) must be the best. However, advertising sometimes makes claims (e.g., "Milwaukee's finest beer") which are, in fact, merely a statement of opinion.

A *simile* is a literary device which refers to a direct comparison between two things; such comparisons are introduced by *like* or *as.* According to William Lutz, similes are employed "whenever advertisers want you to stop thinking about the product and start thinking about something bigger, better, or more attractive than the product."[65] For instance, a wine that claims "It's like taking a trip to France" is designed to induce the consumer into romantic reverie about Paris instead of thinking about the taste of the wine.

Parity statements refer to ads which are worded in a way that suggests that a product is unique, when what the ad is *actually* stating is that the product is indistinguishable from its competition. For example, Rick Berkoff points out that the Personna Double II slogan ("There is no finer razor made. Period.") could be rephrased as follows: "Personna Double II: It's no better than its competition. Period."[66]

In 1996, Eveready Battery Company registered a complaint with the National Advertising Division of the Better Business Bureau about the excessive claims of the Duracell Battery Company, as encapsulated in their slogan, "The World's Most Advanced Battery." In response, Duracell changed the slogan to a parity statement which only *implied* product superiority: "No Battery is More Advanced."

Extraneous Inclusion occurs when superfluous information appears in the ad that suggests a relationship to the claims of the product. For instance, the FTC filed a claim against Winston Cigarettes for an ad campaign in which they claimed that their product had "no additives." Lee Peeler explained, "The ads left the implication that no additives made Winston safer than other cigarettes, and that's not true."[67] The terms of the settlement required that the ads include the disclaimer, "No additives in our tobacco does NOT mean a safer cigarette."

A syllogism is a subtle line of reasoning that seems true but is actually false or deceptive. For example, a magazine ad for California Almonds has the slogan, "California Almonds: A Tasty Snack & Nutritional Feast." The copy of the ad presents the following logic:

- Roasted almonds are tasty
- Roasted almonds are healthy
- So, "whenever the urge to snack comes out, make sure California almonds are in."

The ad suddenly shifts from promoting the *product* (almonds) to a particular *brand* (California Almonds). The question to be asked, then, is: even if you believe the first part of this syllogism, couldn't you then buy another brand of almonds?

Unfinished statements make implied claims that advertisers are unable to stand behind. Instead, they leave it to the consumer to complete the statement. Lutz provides the following examples:

- Batteries that "last *up to* twice as long." Twice as long as what?
- "You can be sure if it's Westinghouse." Just exactly what we can be sure of is never explained.
- "Magnavox gives you more." This slogan never details what you get more of. [68]

Qualifier words should also send a white flag to the consumer. However, phrases such as "some restrictions apply" are either quickly flashed on the TV screen or uttered with inhuman rapidity by the announcer, insinuating that this information is inconsequential. Some qualifier words try to create the illusion of quality, but in fact negate this claim. For instance, the term "chocolate flavored" candy suggests that you are eating chocolate, when in reality you are ingesting artificial ingredients that simulate the taste of chocolate.

Lutz has identified other qualifier words commonly used in advertising:

- *Help.* The next time you see an ad for a cold medicine that promises that it "helps relieve cold symptoms fast," don't rush out to buy it. Ask yourself what this claim is really saying.... "Help" only means to aid or assist, nothing more. It does not mean to conquer, stop, eliminate, end, solve, heal, cure, or anything else. But once the ad says "help," it can say just about anything after that because "help" qualifies everything coming after it. The trick is that ... you forget the word "help" and concentrate only on the dramatic claim. You read into the ad a message that the ad does not contain. More importantly, the advertiser is not responsible for the claim that you read into the ad, even though the advertiser wrote the ad so you would read that claim into it.[69]
- *Virtually.* Lutz warns that claims like "virtually spotless" are deceptive. "After all, what does 'virtually' mean? It means 'in essence or effect, although not in fact.' Look at that definition again. 'Virtually' means *not in fact.* It does *not* mean 'almost' or 'just about the same as,' or anything else."[70]
- *New and Improved.* An advertiser can present a product as "new" if there has been a "material functional change" in the item. In the same way, a product advertised as "improved" suggests that it has been "made better." However, ads frequently make such claims for products that feature only slight modifications (e.g., changing the shape of a stick deodorant).

MEDIA LITERACY TIPS

EXPLICIT CONTENT

A Consumer Guide to Advertising invites the public to consider the following questions in regard to the *explicit content* of ads:

- *Can the advertiser support its claims?*
- Be wary of any claims, and search for independent confirmation, particularly for large purchases like automobiles and appliances.
- *After watching the ad, do you really know what the product is or does?*
- As amusing as some ads can be, do they provide us with anything more than a brand name? What about price, value, size, shape, and nutritional content? A wise consumer ... focuses on all of the information needed to make an informed choice.
- *What's not in the ad?*
- Sometimes the most important information is not even mentioned in the ad. It could be that the 15- or 30-second spot is just too tight to fit everything in, but it could also be a deliberate evasion or half-truth on the part of the advertiser.... Know what you're getting before (making a purchase).[71]

Affective Response. Advertisements often present scenarios that trigger emotions and then manipulate these feelings to sell their product. Despite working within a very limited format (e.g., a 30-second TV spot), ads are able to evoke intense emotional reactions among members of the audience. Advertisers recognize that products are purchased for psychological as well as product satisfaction. Consequently, ads often strive to accentuate the *emotional benefits* of a product. Thus, the phone company is not merely selling a communications system but furnishes the means by which you can "reach out and touch someone" you love. This approach may be used even when the product does not have a clear emotional benefit. As an example, a Christmas radio spot for Kretchmeyer Hams presents the product as a vital part of a family holiday celebration. After dinner, a young man offers a moving toast: "There is no place I'd rather be right now than with my family." This may indeed be true; however, the ham can claim no more responsibility for the emotional richness of the moment than the silverware or canned peas.

Ads featuring puppies and babies are guaranteed to produce a warm reaction. The advertiser hopes that the consumer will transfer these positive feelings to the product. Humorous ads work on a similar principle. Laughter is a positive emotional response; we are grateful to people who make us laugh. Arthur Bijur, president of the Freeman Advertising Agency explains,

> If you can share a smile with someone, you've made a friend. Humor works because it warms people up and relaxes them. Humor creates connection, opens a window to get a message in and makes people feel good about your brand.[72]

Emotional appeals are tailored to generate a response from the target audience. For example, a Michelin Tire advertising campaign featured the slogan, "Because so much is riding on your tires," accompanied by a picture of a cute infant sitting on one of their products. In this case, the ad was directed at young parents, capitalizing on their protective instincts.

Ads may be directed at one of the following intrinsic *psychological motivations*.

Quest for Identity. From the moment we are born, we are engaged in a quest to discover who we are. One effective ad strategy involves promoting the product as the culmination of this search for identity: products assume a significance because they tell you (and others) exactly who you are. To illustrate, consider the text in a print ad for the Mercury Cougar:

In the Beginning
You look like everybody else.
Then something happens
Maybe it starts with the way you wear your hair.
Or the colors you put together.
But pretty soon, you don't look like everybody else.
You look like you.
And then something really funny happens.
Everybody else wants to look like you.

Love. An untold number of products have been promoted in the name of love. Consumer products are positioned as tangible symbols of affection, affirming the depth, sincerity, and permanence of your love.

Some ads position their product as an essential ingredient in the courtship ritual. Using the right product will make you more attractive and desirable ("Making close comfortable"—Norelco Shavers). Giving the proper present can win a person's heart. And some products even promise improved performance in lovemaking ("Make it last a little longer"—Big Red Gum).

These ads call attention to the pleasure that you'll bring your loved one through a thoughtful purchase. But at the same time, this approach is a subtle appeal to the ego of the purchaser; imagine how grateful your partner will be upon receiving the gift, and how wonderful you are for giving it.

Love between family members is another very powerful psychological motivation. A McDonald's television commercial begins with a young man walking wistfully through a children's playground. He stops at a McDonald's and orders a breakfast to go: "I'm having breakfast with my daughter," he explains to the young woman at the counter. The next scene shows the young man at the hospital, gazing fondly at his newborn child. The ad suggests that daddy's Egg McMuffin has played a significant role in this deeply personal moment. However illogical, this very powerful latent message about the connection between father and daughter reinforces the manifest pitch for McDonald's.

Need for Approval. From infancy, all human beings share a longing for approval. A persistent latent message in advertising is that people can satisfy their need for acceptance through their consumer behavior. One particularly effective version of this appeal centers around the complex relationship between children and their parents. For instance, a television spot for the U.S. Marines begins with a young, tough looking young man returning home from boot camp. He is met at the train by his younger brother. The Marine immediately asks whether his dad is still angry with him for having enlisted in the Marines. Behind this rugged facade, the soldier is still a little boy seeking his father's approval.

The scene shifts to the Marine entering his old house. He is dressed in full military regalia. His father looks at him from across the room. Silence. Suddenly, Dad moves toward his son and embraces him. This reconciliation scene touches young males in the audience who may be sorting out their own complex feelings toward their fathers. The underlying message is that by joining the Marines, a young man can find the resolution to this fundamental need for acceptance.

Guilt. American culture can be characterized as exceedingly guilt-ridden. We feel remorse for any number of real and imagined transgressions. Advertisers capitalize on these irrational feelings to promote their product. For instance, the ad campaign for Michelin tires discussed earlier ("Because so much is riding on your tires") depicts an infant surrounded (and protected) by the product. The latent message is that parents who care about their children must buy Michelin tires. However, this affective appeal does not hold up under rational scrutiny: Is the choice of brands critical to being a good parent? (Why not buy new Goodyear tires, for instance?) Does buying Michelin tires automatically make you a good parent? And if you're a responsible parent, shouldn't you worry about the other features of the car as well (e.g., the fuel line or transmission), as well as other drivers and *their* tires? The list could go on and on.

> MEDIA LITERACY TIPS
>
> GUILT-PROVOKING ADS
>
> When confronted by *guilt provoking ads,* ask the following questions:
>
> - *Why am I feeling guilty?*
> - *How will purchasing the product assuage my guilt?*
> - *Is the choice of brand important?*
> - *Could an advertiser exploit these feelings of guilt to sell me other products?*

Nostalgia for Significant Moments. These ads attempt to associate products with those significant moments that touch people's lives. For instance, ads about first experiences cleverly tie the product into individuals' sense of nostalgia. An online ad for the virtual dating service match.com shows formally dressed boys and girls at a dance. The slogan declares, "Love is Complicated. Match.com is simple." The black-and-white photo signals that this is an old photo and that the pre-teens are reminiscent of the baby boomers who are considering enrolling in the service. The photo recalls a simple, innocent time, when finding romance was easy.

This "snapshot" evokes memories of similar events in their lives that subtly encourages consumers to think positively about the service.

Another line of ads exploits the audience's sentimental attachment to *holidays*, such as Christmas, Fourth of July, and Thanksgiving. Advertisers link their products with holidays ("Kretchmeyer: Your Christmas Ham"), in hopes that these good feelings will be transferred to the product. The business community seizes upon holidays like Mother's Day or Valentine's Day as excuses for special promotions (i.e., "Halloween Madness sales"). Taking this promotional tack to the extreme, the business community has even *invented* holidays such as Grandparent's Day as advertising gimmicks to stimulate sales.

Fixation with Death. Sigmund Freud theorized that from birth, people experience a primal attraction to death. H. J. Eysenck explains,

> Freud postulates that the organism has an innate tendency to revert to its initial state. This instinct, which would lead to self-destruction, has to be diverted

outward by the developing organism.... The death instinct represents one of the two major classes or drives and motives, which—for psychoanalysts—comprise all motivational processes.[73]

Freud's theory of the death instinct might help to account for why people race cars, skydive, and find other ways to live "close to the edge" of death.

Several different ad strategies are manifestations of our love/hate relationship with death:

- *Denial of Death.* This ad strategy promotes products as a safeguard against death. Castleguard Security system reminds us that, in an impermanent world, "Give the most valuable gift of all ... the gift of security." Advertisements for diamonds are even more blatant, selling immortality in the form of their product. A diamond insures that love will be permanent, and that the fortunate couple will live happily ever after.
- *Loss of Control.* Death represents the ultimate loss of control. BBDO advertising offers the following insight into how the Gillette Deodorant campaign, "Never Let Them See You Sweat," capitalized on our primal need to maintain control in our lives:

> The "Product" stance is that it "goes on dry, stays dry". But this did not differentiate this superior performing product until the "You" attitude was added: Control, Aspiration. The resulting theme line, "Never Let Them See You Sweat," and the campaign featuring rising young entertainers, has helped revitalize the brand.[74]

- *Abandonment.* A classic TV commercial promoting the Prudential Insurance Agency focuses on the testimony of a grieving widow. She has been abandoned by her husband and now must contend with the emptiness of her life. "We thought it would never happen to us," she laments, realizing that she is not only alone but impoverished as well. In this case, the insurance represents both financial and emotional comfort and security.
- *Longing for the Past.* An ad for Tyson chicken reminds us, "So for over 50 years, we've made sure that Tyson's chicken is the leanest and meatiest that they can be." This ad establishes a tradition which makes us feel rooted and safe. At the same time, this return to the past provides us with a sense of confidence in the future.
- *Fear of Failure.* In American culture, failure is regarded as a form of death-in-life. To illustrate, Thornton C. Lockwood analyzed a series of "Slice of Death" AT&T ads, featuring testimonials by businesspeople who have been let down by their current phone system:

> The problem the agency chose to dramatize ... was phone failure and the problems that creates for business people; loss of credibility with clients, lost sales, demoralized workers, management confusion, and ultimately, even business failure.[75]

Significantly, the first test storyboard scenario was even more overt: a malfunctioning (and malevolent) telephone swallows a young woman who is taking phone orders at a restaurant.

- *Fear of the Unknown.* An ad for "The Travelers" contains a photo with religious overtones: a skyscape, with streaks of light shining through the clouds. The headline reads,

  Financial Serenity
  The Strength to Leap
  Beyond the World of Worry

  Armed with the protection afforded by The Travelers (with its slogan, "You're better off under the Umbrella"), the audience is prepared to meet whatever challenges lie ahead.

However, affective appeals like those cited above offer only superficial, antiseptic emotional experiences that ultimately trivialize genuine emotional experiences. We are spared the complications and consequences that are a part of any genuine emotional commitment. Our involvement need only last for 30 seconds; then we can move on.

Implicit Content. Nowhere is consequence portrayed as more direct and immediate than in the world of advertising. The relationship between the significant events in the narrative is clear. Ads dramatize how products fulfill needs and solve personal problems. Ads show smiling, satisfied consumers who have benefited from the purchase of the product.

However, the long-term consequences generally go unmentioned in these ads. For instance, the calories and cholesterol contained in fast food, over time, make American children the most obese in the world. Or the debt accrued by credit card holders, who do not consider that they eventually have to pay for their purchases (with hefty interest charges).

Genre

In order to be instantly recognizable, advertisements often borrow from established genres, such as the drama, music video, and sitcom. For instance, TV infomercials for health products and self-motivation materials mirror the format of the talk show, complete with host, desk, audience, and a "guest" who hawks the product.

At the same time, advertising can be considered a distinct genre of its own, with a distinct structure, plot, and characters.

Formulaic Structure. Advertisements generally operate within the format of order/chaos/order.

- *A problem is quickly introduced which throws the character's world into chaos.*
- *The product is presented as a means of solving the problem.*
- *Order is restored through use of the product.*

The conclusion is geared to inspire the consumer to action.

Indeed, some ad campaigns first *create* a problem and then offer a solution—in the form of their product. For instance, "ring around the collar" was not an area of tremendous concern until the makers of Wisk brought this situation to the attention of the public.

Print ads offer a variation of this formula, with the visual emphasis on the restoration of order. The problem is either indirectly alluded to (e.g., AT&T's ad, "Six Cities. Two Days. Easy"), or left entirely to our imaginations (e.g., pictures of beautiful women wearing Maybelline eyeliner). In this case, audience members are asked to believe that the purchase of the product will transform an ordinary looking woman into one of the exotic looking models in the ad.

Formulaic Plot. In a television commercial, the plot dramatizes the effectiveness of the product, as well as its benefits for the consumer. In the process, however, ads frequently exaggerate the value of the product and its impact on the individual. The product is generally central to the narrative, the latent message being that the product plays an integral role in our lives as well.

One type of ad campaign features a repetition of the plot; only the specific nuances differ. For instance, the Charmin toilet paper ad campaign, featuring Mr. Whipple, always replays the same basic plot:

> Several women pause while grocery shopping to squeeze the Charmin, commenting that they cannot resist the temptation because Charmin is so "squeezably soft." Mr. Whipple appears and, warning the ladies not to squeeze the Charmin, confiscates the goods. However, to Mr. Whipple's embarrassment, the ladies point out that he, too, is fondling the toilet paper—a testament to the irresistible softness of Charmin.

Between 1964 and 1985, Charmin's agency, D'Arcy Masius Benton & Bowles Communications, produced over 500 Mr. Whipple spots—all with the same formulaic plot. This approach was so successful that Mr. Whipple was brought out of retirement in 1999.

Conventions. In order to compensate for the limited time and space in which to present their message, ads commonly use costumes, props, and sets to send subtle cues about the product. For instance, an ad promoting a headache remedy may feature an actor who is wearing a white lab coat. The unstated message is that this spokesperson is a medical expert whose advice should be heeded.

Advertising relies on a stable of stock characters (e.g., The Harried Housewife, Out-of-it Husband, Sex Siren). These stereotypes evoke instant recognition by the audience by drawing upon a common cultural understanding and consensus.

MEDIA LITERACY TIPS

ADVERTISING CONVENTIONS

The following questions are useful in considering the role of *advertising conventions*:

- *What conventions are used in the ad?*
- *How are these conventions used in the ad?*
- *What messages are these conventions designed to convey?*
- *How are these conventions used to promote the product?*

Illogical Conclusion

Advertisements do not always follow logically from their initial premise. As mentioned earlier, ads frequently conclude with a Big Promise: the product will bring you happiness or success. An example would be the Head and Shoulders ad, in which a young man finds romantic fulfillment after washing his hair. At the very least, advertising exaggerates the importance of a product. For instance, the ads in which a couple jump in the air to celebrate their purchase of a Toyota would appear to be something of an overreaction.

PRODUCTION ELEMENTS

In advertising, as with all media formats, style reinforces messages. The originality of a presentation is an indication that the product is unique as well and encourages the audience to see (and think about) the product in a new way. Production elements can also create a mood that affects how we react to the product. And in some cases, style may make a product look better than it is.

Editing

Copywriters for print advertising strive to keep their messages brief, concise, and simple. John Caples advises ad copywriters to write to the level of a sixth-grade student.[76] At the same time, an effective copywriter elaborates and clarifies, "creating a word picture that makes crystal-clear the specific advantage of every feature."[77] Variety in sentence structure avoids monotony and creates a fresh, energetic mood which will carry over to the product. Caples observes that short sentences "put speed and excitement into your ad" and move the audience to action, while long sentences can furnish useful explanations about the product.[78]

In television, a director can condense a vast amount of information into a limited time frame through editing. Television commercials contain a myriad of images and information. Directors are faced with the challenge of cutting up to 16,000 feet of raw footage to 45 feet for a 30-second ad. Because each second becomes critical, an enormous amount of attention is devoted to the selection and arrangement of images.

For instance, in a 30-second ad selling Kodak camera equipment, a series of photographs encompass the lifetime of a woman.

In addition, the television soundtrack and picture are commonly speeded up by as much as 25 percent without being noticed by the audience. Dr. James MacLachlan claims that this method increases the unaided recall of the content by 40 percent.[79]

The editing technique of quick cuts is also geared to attract and maintain the attention of the audience. This "MTV" style generates a sense of excitement, sending the latent message that the product is exciting as well. In addition, this style is considered avant-garde, which indirectly comments on the "hipness" of the product.

Color

The selection of bright colors and dramatic color contrasts attracts the attention of the consumer—which is the principal goal of an advertisement. But in addition, the choice of colors sends other subtle messages about the product. Otto Kleppner observes,

> Color talks its own psychological language: To make a drink look cool, there will be plenty of blue in the background; to make a room look warm (for heating advertisements), there will be plenty of red in the background; springtime suggests light colors, and autumn the dark tones. Thus a clue to the choice of the dominating color may often be found in the mood in which the product is being shown.[80]

The choice of colors may also be tied to the psychographic profile of the target audience. John Lyons points out that commercials targeting young girls are often shot through pink and green filters to create a warm, romantic, and traditionally "feminine" tone which subtly influences young girls' response to the product.[81]

Scale

The magnification of images can be a very deceptive ad technique. For example, extreme close-ups make small products look big. As a result, toys that look impressive and durable on screen may in fact be small and flimsy.

Relative Position

The layout of an advertisement can dictate the response of the audience. In Western culture, a person glancing at an ad is most likely to focus initially on the upper right-hand portion of the page.

Advertising directors often employ the technique of *structured motion*, in which the layout is designed to lead the audience through an ad in a predetermined way. Otto Kleppner explains,

> The art is to attract attention at the head of the page, and by having optical stepping-stones leading from there to the end, hold the ad together and lead the reader through the copy. Flow may also be helped by the line of direction of the artwork, sweeping across the page. It may be helped by *gaze motion*, that is, having the people in the picture look toward or, perhaps with other elements of the ad, lead the eye to the center of attention.[82]

To illustrate, every summer, TV ads for Lipton's Ice Tea appear, in which beautiful young people frolic around a swimming pool. Just as our eyes are drawn to these alluring male and female bodies, these images dissolve and are replaced by shots of the product and the brand label.

Ads frequently position their product as the center of the world of the commercial, suggesting that it is an essential part of the situation presented in the advertisement. As mentioned earlier, in beer ads, the product is placed in the middle of the activity. Consequently, these ads convey the message that beer not only accompanies a good time, but it is impossible to have fun without a provision of beer.

Figure 13.3
A variety of structured motion patterns—ways in which people look at ads.

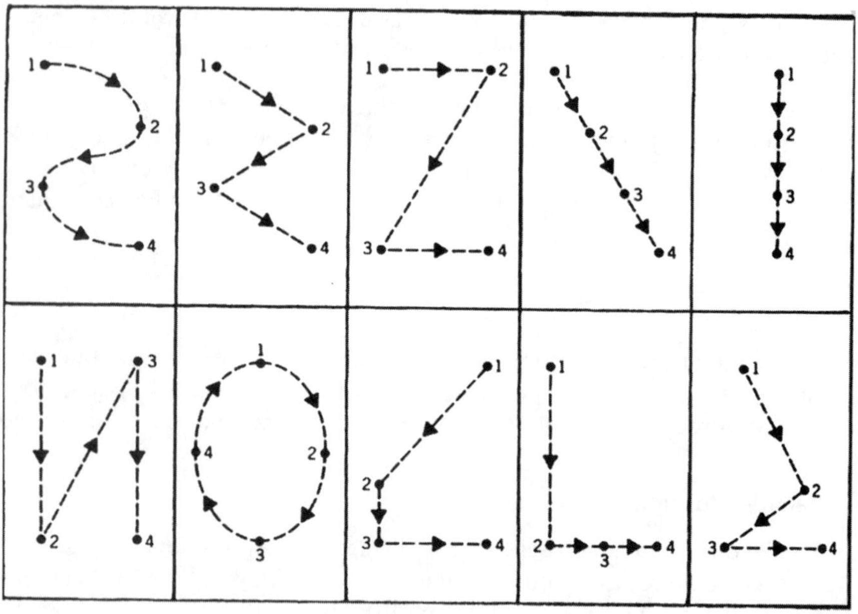

Ads often depict situations in which the person modeling the product is the center of attention—presumably due to the consumer item being advertised. The advertiser encourages the audience to identify with this principal figure, so that the audience vicariously receives approval by using the product.

Advertising Space and Gender Role. In the 1970s, Erving Goffman conducted a study of the use of ad space as a reflection of cultural attitudes toward women (see Figure 13.4). More recent photographs show women in a greater diversity of poses, reflecting the changing role of women in contemporary culture. For instance, the March 2007 issue of *Vogue* included ads in which the models were looking straight into the camera. In several of the ads, the model's pelvis is thrust forward, so that it is the closest body part to the camera. The models appear comfortable with their sexuality as a vital part of their total identity; this nonverbal behavior, then, reflects a growing acceptance of the total integration of a woman. However, it can be argued that this contemporary body language signals only the *appearance* of change. Samantha L. Harms observes that this trend also can be regarded as a further exploitation of a "bad girl" image: "In these ads, the company logos are placed prominently near the models' open legs, in an effort to attract the attention of the readers. Thus, the ads definitely associate their products with sex."[83]

Camouflaged Warnings. Product warnings are designed to be as inconspicuous as possible. For example, the disclaimers in cigarette advertisements appear in very small print and are separated from the main visual field. Sometimes the disclaimer is camouflaged by the color and graphics of the ad. In 1999, Mazda Motors of America was fined $5.25 million for failing to make adequate consumer leasing disclosures in its television ad campaign. The FTC ruled that the disclosures that appeared in the commercials were in small and unreadable print, offset by distracting images and sounds.[84]

MEDIA LITERACY TIPS

EFFECTIVE AD LAYOUTS

Otto Kleppner outlines the following criteria for effective ad layouts:

- *Is it arresting?*
- *Is it clear?*
- *Is it orderly?*
- *Is the most important idea given the most important attention?*
- *Does it invite reading?*
- *If the trademark is needed to identify the product, is it sufficiently visible?*
- *Does the layout leave the desired impression about the product?*[85]

Product Placement

Product placement refers to an advertising strategy in which the products are incorporated into media presentations. Product placements in media presentations have become commonplace in the world of advertising, generating $4 billion annually.[86]

Figure 13.4
A, *Upper/lower space*: Men are frequently situated in a higher physical space in ads, in contrast to females who are lying down or sitting on the floor. Goffman contends that being relegated to a lower space symbolizes women's social status in a male-dominated world. B, *Cant*: Female models often pose in a "cant" position, in which the head or body is bowed. The latent messge of this body language is deference, submission, and subordination. C, *Attentional vectors*: Women frequently direct their attention toward the male, who is clearly the center of attention. The male has been empowered to the degree that he is free to focus his attention elsewhere. This visual cue instructs the audience to place more importance on the male. D, *Shielding*: Female models are often screened from direct contact with the world of the ad, suggesting that women are dependent and require protection. Women are often stationed behind a barrier or peek out behind another person (generally a male). Women may also be positioned in the background or at the edge of the frame, which suggests a subservient position. Photographs by Carolyn Slonim.

Figure 13.4. (*Continued*)

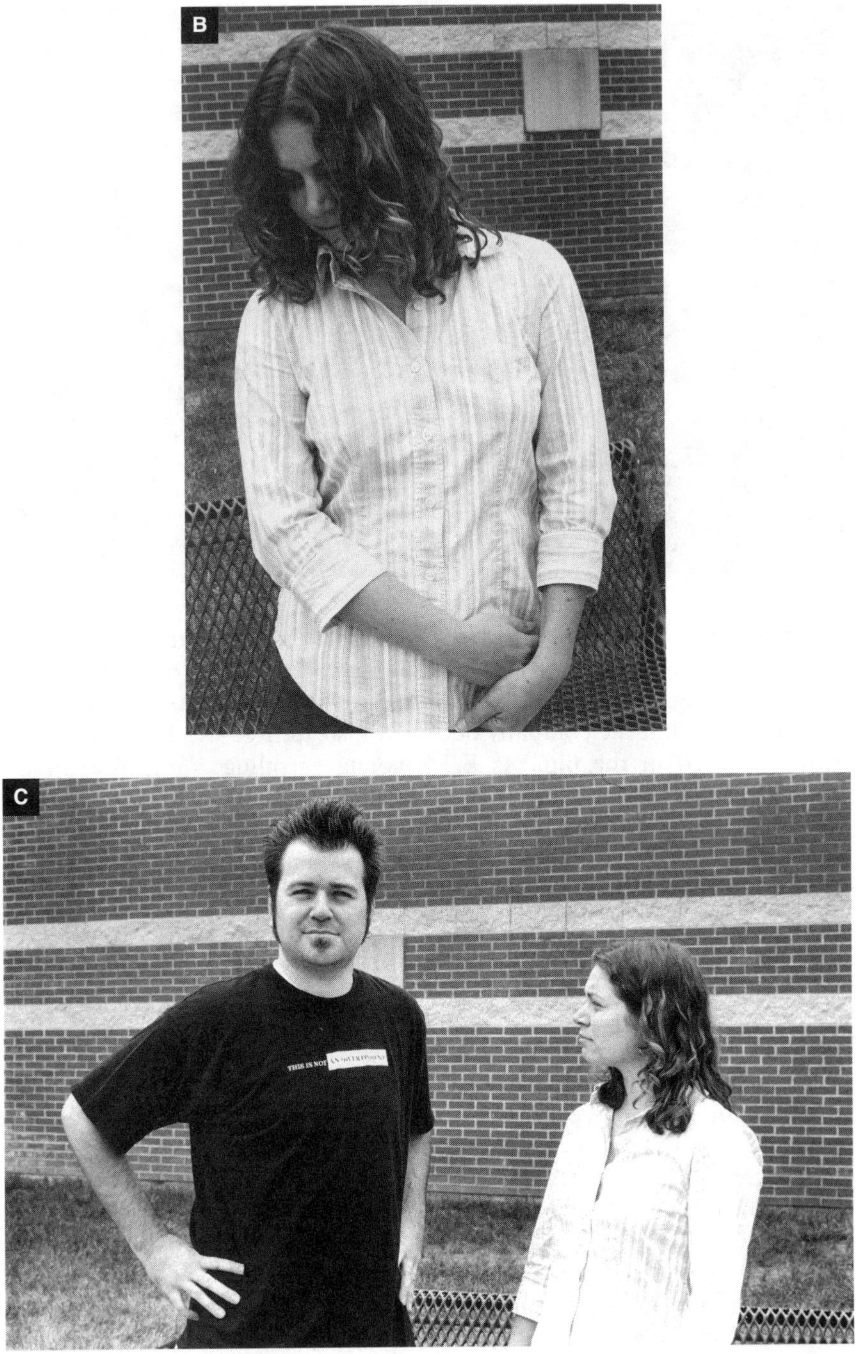

Figure 13.4. (*Continued*)

Is product placement an effective promotional vehicle? In 1982, the producers of the film *E.T.* approached Mars, Inc., the makers of M&M's candies, proposing a deal in which in return for a fee, the candy would appear in the film; the company declined. Instead, Reeses's Pieces were visually displayed in the film, as E.T.'s young earthling companion Elliott used the candy to mark a trail for the alien to follow. Within a month of the premiere of the film, sales for the candy jumped by 65 percent.[87]

In 2004, the product placement market jumped by 30.5 percent to $3.46 billion, $1.87 billion of it in TV. Overall, the number of placements on TV rose to 107,839 in 2005, from 81,739 in 2004.[88] The media research firm PQ Media predicts that by 2009, the overall number will reach $6.94 billion.[89] In 2005, Volkswagen signed a long-term product placement deal with NBC Universal that cost the automaker an estimated $200 million. Under the terms of this agreement, Volkswagens will appear in movies released by Universal Studios, as well as television programs appearing on NBC and other networks owned by General Electric, such as Bravo, SciFi, and USA.

On a per-episode basis, the number of product placements is staggering. In 2006, the telecasts of the reality show "Contender" averaged 500.9 individual occurrences of products placed in its shows—almost 30 times that of traditional commercial messaging.[90]

In a typical product placement arrangement, an agency signs a client for a retainer and places the product as many times as is appropriate and possible. Increasingly, advertisers have become reliant on this strategy. Ray Warren, managing director at OMD USA declares, "If there's going to be a can of soda on a table, it might as well be our client's can of soda."[91] Thus, it is no surprise that in an episode of the television series "Five Days to Midnight," Mountain Dew (a product of PepsiCo) made three appearances along with a Pepsi-Cola vending machine and a clock decorated with vintage Pepsi-Cola logos.

Advertisers have now begun directing product placement at their target audiences. For instance, in 2006, Dodge paid several million dollars and committed more than $10 million more in marketing to place its vehicle in the teen action film *Fantastic Four: Rise of the Silver Surfer.* In addition, U.S. advertisers have now begun directing product placement at children. For instance, in one scene of *Curious George* (2006) an animated movie for very young children, George is seen relaxing amid broken crates of Dole produce, with the product spilling out. His guardian, the Man in the Yellow Hat, drives a Volkswagen.

Product placement is now becoming commonplace in all media. As an example, in 2005, HarperCollins Publishers released a children's book, entitled "Cashmere if You Can." The plot of the book follows the adventures of Wawa Hohhot and her family of Mongolian cashmere goats who live on the roof of Saks's Midtown Manhattan store. Although there is no clear disclosure of Saks's involvement, the setting of the story is hardly an accident; a Saks Fifth Avenue marketing executive came up with the idea, and the department store chain owns the text copyright.

Product placement can also be found in popular music as well. In the top 20 songs of 2005, Mercedes-Benz was mentioned 100 times, Nike 63, Cadillac 62, Bentley 51, and Rolls-Royce 46.[92]

Some genres are particularly well-suited for product placements. For instance, the Reality genre lends itself to product placements, in part because the sets must include branded products as part of its "real" look. As a result, in 2005, Reality programs contained an average of 11:05 minutes per hour of brand appearances, as compared to 3:07 per hour for scripted entertainment programming.

Product placements are beginning to appear in newscasts as well. A 2006 survey asked 266 marketing executives if they had ever paid for product placement in newscasts. Nearly half said yes. And nearly 46 percent of those who had not paid for placement replied that they would consider doing so in the future.[93]

Product placement strategy is designed to create an identity for the product by matching it with the characters that project its desired image. For instance, General Motors vehicles Pontiac, Cadillac, and Buick were featured throughout the first season of the sexy TV drama "Falcon Beach." Each vehicle was matched with the character most closely mirroring the consumer profile of the brand. Thus, Paige (Jennifer Kydd), the lead female character, was depicted driving a sleek Pontiac Solstice, while her mother (Allison Hossack) drove a reliable, sturdy (but stylish) Cadillac SRX.

Using products as props or part of the set legitimizes the product and is therefore a very subtle form of persuasion. For instance, in a 2006 episode of the NBC drama series *Friday Night Lights*, two characters met for dinner at an Applebee's restaurant.

A more subtle form of product placement is *product integration*, in which products are cleverly embedded into the narrative. Products become central to the story, conveying the message that these items are essential to the characters (and the audience as well). For instance, in a 2006 episode of *Seventh Heaven*, sponsored by the makers of Oreo cookies, a young suitor proposed to his girlfriend, by giving her a diamond ring embedded in an Oreo cookie. Product placement is also becoming central to character development in a narrative. Marc Graser provides the following example from *The New Adventures of Old Christine*, a situation comedy on CBS starring Julia Louis-Dreyfus:

> Toyota's plucky hybrid has become synonymous with Julia Louis-Dreyfus' environmentally conscious character on the CBS sitcom. It helps that the car has been central to many of the show's plots, including one where it has a run-in with a gas-guzzling Hummer.[94]

Indeed, product placement has become such an effective advertising vehicle that in some cases, the entire storyline is conceived with product placement in mind. In 2006, Lifetime, a cable network, consummated a deal with Perfectmatch.com that extended through the entire 13-episode run of its sitcom *Lovespring International*. Perfectmatch.com, an actual online dating service, is incorporated into the series as an archrival of the fictitious company in the series. In the first episode, the owner of the agency screams at her staff about their poor performance: "Do you know how many people have signed up for Perfectmatch.com in the last five minutes? 1,623." In another episode, a dissatisfied client declares, "I would have had better luck on Perfectmatch.com."[95]

However, some writers and producers complain that the imperative to slip product promotion into a script can undermine the integrity of the story. Scott Miller, a story producer on the reality show *American Dream Derby*, a horse-racing contest that appeared on GSN earlier this year, said he was required to get Diet Dr. Pepper into every episode, regardless of what was happening on-screen:

> These were moments when people were crying, or two cast members were screaming at each other, or two allies were sneaking off to strategize, and there were several times when it was: Let me stop and make sure everyone has a can of Diet Dr. Pepper. I'd literally be below the frame line, handing a can of Diet Dr. Pepper

to someone who didn't have one. First and foremost, I want to tell a good story. I'm not necessarily there to help make a commercial.[96]

In 2005, a collective of show business unions, including The Writers Guild of America, West, and the Writers Guild of America, East, and the Screen Actors Guild, denounced the practice of "stealth advertising" and called for a code of conduct to govern this practice. The group issued a position paper saying,

We are being told to write the lines that sell this merchandise, and to deftly disguise the sale as story. Our writers are being told to perform the function of ad copywriter, but to disguise this as storytelling.[97]

Movement

Movement can play a significant role in television advertising. Movement can also draw the attention of the consumer to specific features of the ad. In addition, the technique of slow motion enables the audience to scrutinize the product demonstration, adding to the dramatic emphasis of the ad.

The motion can also set the tone for the promotion. Motion can lend a dynamic feel to the media presentation, giving the impression that the product is exciting and glamorous.

The *direction* of the movement also conveys messages. For instance, in a television spot for *Sports Illustrated*, a sports nut leans toward the camera to tell us about "a great deal" if we subscribe to the magazine. This movement suggests a familiarity and confidentiality with the audience which inspires trust.

Many advertisers now favor the "shaky camera technique," in which the camera jumps around, much like an amateur home video. In contrast with the slick style found in conventional TV spots, this style produces a genuine, "just folks" impression. In addition, Thornton C. Lockwood found that the shaky camera technique employed in an AT&T "business reality" ad campaign "underscored the stress and discomfort the characters experienced" by not using AT&T.[98]

Word Choice

Connotative Words. Words are very carefully chosen in advertising. However, upon close inspection, these words can convey a false impression. For instance, processed foods with healthy sounding names such as Lean Cuisine and Healthy Choice frozen dinners call attention to the health benefits of the product. However, according to a system called

Guiding Stars that rated the nutritional value of food on a scale of zero to three stars, these brands received *no* stars.[99]

Many of the most common and persuasive words used in advertising fall into the following categories:

- *Commencement* words suggest immediacy, importance, and a sense of urgency:

  Introducing
  Announcing
  Now
  Suddenly

- *Convenience* words appeal to the consumers' interest in products that will make their lives easier:

  Easy
  Quick

- *Transformational* words promise new levels of experience:

  Sensational
  Startling
  Amazing
  Remarkable
  Miracle
  Magic
  Revolutionary
  Improvement

- *Directives* tell the consumer what to do:

  Hurry
  Compare

- *Customer Advantage* words offer the consumer a feeling of control, vision, wisdom, and superiority:

  Bargain
  Offer
  Free
  Sale

Codewords. Codewords refer to terms that have a particular significance for the target audience. For instance, Audi, an import luxury sedan has been a longtime sponsor of NBC radio's *Wall Street Report*. "Audiwatch" spokesperson Amy O'Connor urged her audience to "put Audi on our *shortlist*." This corporate codeword (meaning a select group that has survived an elimination process) is both familiar and appealing to the upscale audience Audi is trying to attract. Indeed, identifying these codewords can be a useful method of discovering the intended audience for advertisements.

MEDIA LITERACY TIPS

CONNOTATIVE WORDS

A Consumer Guide to Advertising cautions the public about *connotative words* commonly found in the food industry:

Natural. If you think this product is automatically as good for you as fresh broccoli, think again. Read the label: on one box of cake mix "natural" included modified food starches, mono and diglycerides, gum arabic, etc. (The one exception is meat and poultry labels where natural means "minimally processed.")

Dietetic. This usually means low in sodium and does not necessarily mean reduced calories.

Light or Lite. Could mean anything, and may mean nothing. Don't assume that it's lower in calories unless it's on a meat label.

No sugar. Yes, but it could have sugar substitutes such as corn sweeteners. Watch for the words containing "glucose, sucrose, fructose, and dextrose."

No artificial ingredients. What's artificial to you may not be artificial to a food manufacturer! There are no laws that prevent ingredients such as "hydrolyzed vegetable protein" (which involves chemicals) from being included in products listed as containing "no artificial ingredients."[100]

Connotative Image

What kinds of images are most prevalent in advertising?

The public is fascinated by pictures of *people*—particularly young, attractive women. Pictures of *babies and animals* tap into a wellspring of emotional experience which are sure to generate a positive reaction in the audience. Images that emphasize the *rewards* of a product are also common. For instance, real estate ads generally show customers either learning about the sale of their home or walking into their new house. *A Consumer Guide to Advertising* suggests that the public consider whether the visual images in an ad correspond with the words:

> By playing with ... visuals, the text can be absolutely accurate, but the image in the mind's eye may suggest something very different ... Be suspicious. Don't rely on visual images alone to provide you with accurate information. Listen carefully to the words, read the labels and then decide if this product or service is for you.[101]

Some advertisers have overlooked the *cultural context* of a connotative image—with disastrous results. To illustrate, the logo of Nike AirJordon basketball shoes included the word "Air" in stylized script, which was nearly identical to the configuration of the Arabic script for "Allah." Offended by what they considered a sign of disrespect to the Muslim

Figure 13.5
Advertisers who target international audiences must be sensitive to the cultural context of words and images. This Nike logo, which bares a striking resemblance to the Arabic script for "Allah," deeply offended the Muslim community. Photograph courtesy of Cary Wolinsky/Trillium Studios.

religion, the Council on American-Islamic Relations threatened to organize a boycott among the world's one billion Muslims. Nike subsequently apologized for this unintended slight and pulled the shoes from distribution.

Sound

Music. Music serves a variety of functions in advertising. Music can generate feelings of excitement, joy, and pleasure, which advertisers hope will be transferred to the product. Music also can provide dramatic emphasis, underscoring the advertising message presented by the words and images. Music often establishes a tone (e.g., solemn, whimsical, elegant) that instructs the audience on the appropriate response to the advertising message. And finally, the rhythm and repetition of melodies can trigger the consumer's recall of a product at a later point.

The music in TV ads can make an ad not merely palatable but enjoyable. The jingles are often well-produced; in fact, in the 1970s, "I'd like to buy the world a Coke" went on to become a popular hit single. The entertainment value of the music makes it more likely that the audience will stay tuned to the commercial.

Ads customize the soundtrack to its target audience. For instance, Ford Motor Company's marketing research indicates that pickup truck buyers are likely to be country music fans.[102] As a result, Ford truck ads often feature country music to attract its intended market.

Advertisers can also purchase the rights to popular commercial songs. The cost can be prohibitive—up to $250,000 for a one year license[103]—however, using popular songs enables advertisers to transfer the popularity of a hit tune to their product.

A related approach involves using a popular tune, but inserting new lyrics with a commercial message. For instance, a classic Toyota commercial substituted the following lyrics for the Monkees' signature hit "(We're the) Monkees":

Hey hey, we're Toyota
Toyotathon time of the year
Savings are better than ever,
Come on down today.

In some cases, advertisers hire "sound alike" artists to add to the original flavor of the spot. In fact, in 1989 Bette Midler was awarded $400,000 in a suit against the New York advertising agency of Young & Rubicam for using one of her former backup singers to imitate Midler's rendition of "Do You Want to Dance" in a Ford Mercury commercial.[104]

Using *original* music and lyrics can also be an expensive undertaking, but a song that has been especially commissioned for the ad is sure to complement the messages presented through dialogue, voice-over, and visuals. In addition, an original jingle sends a message about the uniqueness of the product.

Older songs in the public domain can serve as an inexpensive way to set the tone for local ads. Because the copyright law has lapsed, this music is free. These "generic" songs can be found in most local libraries. However, because this music appears so frequently in commercials, there is no hope of any product identification with the music.

Background Sound. Sound effects dramatize the commercial message by simulating the sounds commonly associated with the product. The sound of a can opening, a carbonated beverage being poured into a glass, and people talking and laughing can contribute to the verisimilitude of a beer ad. When ads are produced in a studio, the media communicator uses sound effects to re-create the noises that the audience would expect as part of the environment of the ad. However, finding sound effects that capture the more elusive qualities of the product can present a challenge for the audio engineer. For instance, discussing the production of an ad for G.E. Halogen Headlights, Hooper White explains,

> When the G.E. Halogen Headlight was first turned on in the graphic picture, we highlighted it with a burst of white sound (an effect quite peculiar to a synthesizer). This burst was followed with a synthetic French horn statement, which became the musical logo for the headlight. This horn statement was reiterated three times as the G.E. headlight was mentioned in the voice track.[105]

CASE STUDY

Janis Valdes, a faculty member in the department of communications and journalism at Webster University, conducted the following media analysis of a print advertisement for Viagra, using selected keys to interpreting media messages:

> In early 1999, Pfizer Pharmaceuticals launched a major national ad campaign for Viagra, a drug designed to counteract erectile dysfunction. A media literacy analysis of a Viagra print ad using the keys of context, framework, and production values provides insight into American popular culture's preoccupation with youth and fulfillment of the romantic ideal. Within this context, the Viagra ad is a modern fairy tale—Cinderella or perhaps Sleeping Beauty is more to the point: a mature couple restored to youthful vigor and living happily ever after, thanks to the magical powers of Viagra.
>
> Although demographics reveal that seniors are a growing majority in the U.S., media messages bombard us with youth-worship. Americans' obsession with aging has created an enormous market for the fountain of youth in all its guises: face lifts, tummy tucks, wrinkle creams, flashy sports cars, and all manner of remedies to increase energy, memory, and sexual function. This cultural context sets the stage for Pfizer Pharmaceuticals to introduce Viagra in December 1997.

Figure 13.6
This Viagra print ad campaign reflects American popular culture's preoccupation with youth and fulfillment of the romantic ideal. Photograph courtesy of Pfizer Inc.

A full-page ad in the March 1999 issue of *Condé Nast Traveller* features a handsome, gray-templed man in a well-cut dark suit dancing with a slender, silver-haired woman who is dressed in a gold dress and jacket ensemble. The couple is dancing in what, on close inspection, appears to be the foyer of a European castle. The couple's elegant appearance, combined with the setting, create an ambiance of affluence and privilege. The background is in soft focus, bathed in a golden light that suggests sunset and romance. The dancers themselves represent a very traditional notion of a romantic couple. The man is considerably taller than the woman, so that he occupies the upper, or dominant space in the photo. His strength is evident as he easily dips his partner with just one arm, his other hand free. The woman's foot and head are slightly blurred with motion, capturing the spontaneity of the moment. Her husband is literally "sweeping her off her feet" in this romantic place. A woman discreetly descending the stairs in the center left of the background provides an audience for this rendezvous, shifting it to a public setting, which hearkens back to the notion of a ball.

Here the romantic ideal has been extended to include those over the age of 25. Nowhere do we find a trace of the unpleasant realities that aging often brings. In fact, the only hint of the couple's maturity is their hair color. In this world, age brings wealth and prestige, the freedom to do as one pleases, and power—the power to buy back one's potency, in pill form if need be. The phrase "Let the dance begin" may spark memories for a generation raised on romantic tunes like "Dancing in the Dark," "I Could Have Danced All Night," and "Shall We Dance?" "The dance" can be interpreted as a metaphor for sex, couched in delicate terms to avoid offending the intended older audience. But the big promise of the ad is that Viagra will restore not just the sex but the romance to the relationship.

The image of the spontaneous and glamorous couple in the ad trades on the romantic ideals the audience was raised on and the fairy tale ending we'd all like to believe in. In keeping with the romantic illusion of the ad, no patient information is included in the text. The inclusion of hard facts about sexual dysfunction and possible side effects would spoil the romantic mood. Ultimately, the ad is not selling a pharmaceutical product, but the most sought-after commodity of all—a return to the romance of youth.[106]

NOTES

1. B. Johnson, "It's Been a Good 5 Years Unless You're in Media," *Advertising Age* 77(50), 16.
2. Gary Levin, "Ad Glut Turns Off Viewers," *USA Today,* October 12, 2005, D1; "The Children's Ad Onslaught," *Marketing Magazine* 111(38), 13.
3. Frank Baker, "Media Use Statistics," Media Literacy Clearinghouse (www.frankwbaker.com).
4. "Ad Nauseum," *Mother Jones* (Jan/Feb 2007), 32(1).
5. Ibid.
6. Louise Story, "A Question of Eyeballs," *New York Times*, October 18, 2008, C1.
7. Ed Papazian, ed., *TV Dimensions '93* (New York: Media Dynamics, 1993), 343.
8. Tony Schwartz, *The Responsive Chord* (Garden City, NY: Anchor Books, 1973), 69–71.
9. Baker, "Media Use Statistics."
10. Charles H. Patti and Sandra E. Moriarty, *The Making of Effective Advertising* (Englewood Cliffs, NJ: Prentice-Hall), 63.
11. Interview, Rossman School, St. Louis, Missouri, September 1998.
12. Syms.com, "An Educated Consumer Is Our Best Customer" (www.syms.com).
13. Stuart Elliott, "American Express Gets Specific And Asks, 'Are You a Cardmember?'" *New York Times*, April 6, 2007, C3.
14. Patti and Moriarty, *Effective Advertising*, 62.
15. Saul Hansell, "Joining the Party, Eager to Make Friends," *New York Times,* October 16, 2006, C1.
16. Hooper White, *How to Produce an Effective TV Commercial* (Chicago: Crain Books, 1981), 139.

17. Tim Johnson, "A Man Known Everywhere Except Home: Colombian Coffee Has a Face, and It's Still Juan Valdez," *Denver Post,* August 15, 1999, M12.

18. *Adbusters Quarterly* (Summer 1993), 30.

19. Philip Burton and Scott Purvis, *Which Ad Pulled Best?* (Chicago: NTC Publishing, l988), 41.

20. Ibid., 31.

21. Newspaper Association of America Media Usage Study, 1998 (www.naa.org/info/facts/06.html).

22. Andrew Adam Newman, "In Dallas, Commercial Radio Without Commercials," *New York Times*, April 23, 2007, C2.

23. John Caples, *How to Make Your Advertising Make Money* (Englewood Cliffs, NJ: Prentice Hall, 1983), 311.

24. Otto Kleppner, *Advertising Procedure,* 6th ed. (Englewood Cliffs, NJ: Prentice-Hall, Inc., l976), 429–434.

25. Louise Story, "A Question of Eyeballs."

26. Michael Lewis, "Boom Box," *New York Times Magazine*, August 13, 2000.

27. "Ad Nauseum."

28. Lewis, "Boom Box."

29. Eric Effron, "The Big Blur," *Brill's Content* (February 1999), 44–45.

30. Alex Mindlin, "Increasingly, the Message Is in the Medium," *New York Times,* March 20, 2006, C3.

31. Dennis Everette and John Merrill, *Media Debates* (New York: Longman, 1991), 182.

32. Patti and Moriarty, *Effective Advertising,* 20.

33. Kleppner, *Advertising Procedure,* 300.

34. Patti and Moriarty, *Effective Advertising*, 53.

35. Lisa W. Foderaro, "Raining E-Blows On Egos," *New York Times*, January 28, 2007, Section 9; Pg. 1.

36. Rob Walker, "Ad Play," *New York Times*, December 17, 2006, Section 6; Pg. 40.

37. Ibid.

38. Ibid.

39. Julia Smillie, interview by author (March 16, 1992, St. Louis, MO).

40. Gina Kolata, "Extreme Hygiene; Kill All the Bacteria!," *New York Times,* January 7, 2001, Section 4; Pg. 1.

41. Edgar R. Jones, *Those Were the Good Old Days: A Happy Look at American Advertising* (New York: Simon and Schuster, 1959), 349–353.

42. Jennifer Steinhauer, "That's Not a Skim Latte. It's a Way of Life," *New York Times*, March 21, 1999 (www.postnet.com).

43. Thomas B. Goodkind, "Ultimate Offensive Advertising," The Connecticut Media Literacy Project, http://www.medialit.uconn.edu, November 2000.

44. Caroline E. Mayer, "Growing Array of Time-Saving Products Allows for Instant Everything," *Washington Post,* January 11, 2001.

45. KWMU, 90.7 FM, St. Louis, MO, December 20, 1991.

46. F. Jacobson and Laurie Anne Mazur, *Marketing Madness* (Boulder, CO: Westview Press, 1993), 198.

47. Stephanie Coontz, *The Way We Never Were* (New York: Basic Books, 1992), 176–177.

48. African American Market Profile, Magazine Publishers of America, 2002, (www.magazine.org/content/files/market_profile_black.pdf).

49. John Leo, "Hostility Among the Ice Cubes," *U.S. News & World Report*, July 15, 1991, 18.

50. Ibid.

51. Richard A. Knox, "On Teen Smoking, Ads Work Both Ways," *Boston Globe*, March 1, 2000, B1.

52. Martin Merzer and Lesley Clark, "Fewer Teens Smoking Since State Began Tough Campaign," *Miami Herald*, March 2, 2000, A1.

53. R. Collins, *Dictating Content* (Washington, D.C.: Center for the Study of Commercialism, 1992), 77.

54. Evelyn Nussenbaum, "Coming Soon to a Theater Near You: The Moviemercial," *New York Times*, September 21, 2003.

55. Edward Herman and Noam Chomsky, *Manufacturing Consent* (New York: Pantheon Books, 1988), 17–18.

56. Collins, *Dictating Content,* 25.

57. Leslie Savan, "Truth in Advertising?" *Brill's Content* (March 2000), 62.

58. Michael Kahn, attorney, Stinson, Mag & Fizzell, interview by author, June 6, 1999.

59. Andrew Martin, "The Package May Say Healthy, but This Grocer Begs to Differ," *New York Times,* November 6, 2006, 1A.

60. "Amtrak Rolls Out 'Acela' Service, High-Speed Trains for Northeast" press release March 9, 1999 (www.amtrak.com/news/pr/atk9936.html).

61. Thomas Hine, *The Total Package* (Boston: Little, Brown and Company, 1995).

62. Ibid.

63. Stuart Elliott, "A New Camel Brand Is Dressed to the Nines," *New York Times*, February 15, 2007.

64. "Examples of 'Crazy' Cases," *West News Magazine*, December 3, 1997, 7.

65. William Lutz, *Doublespeak* (New York: Harper and Row, l989), 92.

66. Rick Berkoff, "Can You Separate the Sizzle from the Steak," in *Mass Media Issues*, ed. George Rodman (Chicago: SRA, l98l), 149.

67. Savan, "Truth in Advertising?"

68. Lutz, *Doublespeak*, 95.

69. Ibid., 86.

70. Ibid.

71. Lee E. Norrgard, *A Consumer Guide to Advertising* (American Association of Retired Persons), 10–11.

72. Bernice Kanner, "Silliness Sells," Bloomberg News appeared in *St. Louis Post-Dispatch,* February 2, 1997, E1.

73. H. G. Eysenck, ed., *Encyclopedia of Psychology* (New York: Herder and Herder, 1972), 247.

74. Patti and Moriarty, *Effective Advertising,* 55.

75. Thornton K. Lockwood, "Behind the Emotion in 'Slice of Death' Advertising," *Business Marketing* (September l988), 88.

76. Caples, *Make Your Advertising Make Money,* 370.

77. Ibid., 184.

78. Ibid., 87.
79. White, *Effective TV Commercial*, 118.
80. Kleppner, *Advertising Procedure,* 374.
81. John Lyons, *Guts: Advertising from the Inside Out* (AMACOM, 1987), 292.
82. Kleppner, *Advertising Procedure,* 371–372.
83. Patti and Moriarty, *Effective Advertising,* 80.
84. Federal Trade Commission, "Mazda to Pay $5.25 Million for Violating FTC and State Orders Regarding Lease Arrangements," Federal Trade Commission, September 30, 1999.
85. "Ad Nauseum."
86. Marcelle S. Fischler, "'Grey's Anatomy' ... and Closet," *New York Times*, February 25, 2007, Section 9, p. 1.
87. "How Sweet It Is," *Time*, July 26, 1982, 39.
88. Alex Midlin, "Increasingly, the Message Is in the Medium," *New York Times,* March 20, 2006, C3.
89. Patti Summerfield with files from Lisa D'Innocenzo, "So Your Brand's a TV Star. What's It Worth?," *New York Times,* February 1, 2006, 26.
90. Mindlin, "Increasingly, the Message Is in the Medium."
91. Stuart Elliott, "There's No Place to Turn. More Embedded Pitches Will Lurk in TV Shows," *New York Times*, June 17, 2004, C4.
92. "Ad Nauseum."
93. Sara Ivry, "Marketers Say They Pay For Play in News Media," *New York Times*, June 26, 2006, C5.
94. Marc Graser, "10 Favorite Product Placement Deals," *Advertising Age* (December 18, 2006), 36.
95. Julie Bosman, "A Match Made in Product Placement Heaven," *New York Times,* May 31, 2006, C3.
96. Sharon Waxman, "Hollywood Unions Object to Product Placement on TV," *New York Times,* November 14, 2005.
97. Ibid.
98. Lockwood, "'Slice of Death' Advertising," 86.
99. Martin, "The Package May Say Healthy," 1A.
100. Norrgard, *A Consumer Guide to Advertising,* 10–11.
101. Ibid.
102. David Huron, "Music in Advertising: An Analytic Paradigm," *The Musical Quarterly* (Fall 1989), 567.
103. Steve Gordon Law, Negotiating a License for Use of Music in a National Television Campaign (http://stevegordonlaw.com/article_aslj_fall01.htm).
104. Chris Dickinson, "Sell-Outs? Maybe So; Best Sellers? Absolutely," *St. Louis Post-Dispatch*, December 8, 1996, 3D.
105. White, *Effective TV Commercial*, 182–183.
106. Janis Valdes, "Viagra: Let the Dance Begin," Webster University, unpublished paper, April 2, 2000.

CHAPTER

14

AMERICAN POLITICAL COMMUNICATIONS

The mass media have not merely altered the delivery system of information but, in fact, have transformed the American political process. Even people who say they learn nothing from political advertisements believe the claims made in them.[1]

The escalating expenses required to run a successful political media campaign necessitates that candidates have access to vast amounts of money. It is anticipated that candidates running for President of the United States in 2008 will spend a combined one billion dollars. Because current finance regulations make "only" $65 million available to each candidate for the 2008 election for president of the United States, all major candidates have rejected this option, instead relying on private donations to fund their campaigns.

Once in office, politicians must continue to raise money for reelection. As a result, elected officials are forced to devote more of their time to fund-raising than in performing their legislative duties.

The financial pressures on candidates affect political campaigns in the following ways:

Candidate Selection. The prospect of having to raise enough funds to run a campaign is a major consideration in determining the viability of a candidate. This prospect can be particularly discouraging for darkhorse candidates, who must compete with contenders who have access to ample financial resources. In February 2007, former Iowa Governor Tom Vilsack dropped out of the 2008 presidential primary, citing the pressures of fund-raising—and his inability to keep up with the campaign fund-raising of his competitors—as the chief reason for his withdrawal: "Effort and hard work are not enough. It's about the money, and with states moving (their primaries and caucuses) up on the calendar, the premium on money became higher."[2]

Campaign Viability. In the early stages of a campaign, the amount of campaign money raised by candidates has become the major criterion to measure the viability of a political candidate. Indeed, courting big donors is now regarded as the equivalent of an "invisible primary," with the winner assuming the lead position going into the actual primary election. The fund-raising totals of the candidates are tracked closely by the press, with the "winner" designated as the frontrunner. To illustrate, when Jonathan Tasini, ran for the senate in the 2006 Democratic primary against Hillary Clinton, television network Channel One refused to allow him to participate in the televised debates because he hadn't raised a set amount of funds ($500,000)—even though polls indicated that 13 percent of the voters supported Tasini.[3]

Campaign Strategy. Campaign finances affect candidates' ability to get their messages across to the voters and, by extension, their campaign strategies. For instance, John Edwards (D-N. Carolina) and Governor Tom Vilsak (D-Iowa) and Governor Mitt Romney (R-Massachusetts) formally announced their intention to run for president in January 2007—one year before the first primaries and two years before the 2008 election. Announcing one's candidacy early is a strategy that enables these candidates to solicit large contributors before the donors commit funds to an opponent. In contrast, during the 1992 election, Bill Clinton did not formally announce his candidacy until October 1991—just *three months* before the Iowa caucus.

The skyrocketing costs of mounting a political campaign—mostly associated with producing and distributing advertising over the media—has had a profound affect on the American political system. Of the nearly $30 million that Senator Hillary Clinton spent on her successful re-election bid in 2006, the vast majority was dedicated to media-related expenses.

Influence of Special Interest Groups. Special interest groups expect favorable treatment from a candidate who they have supported financially. This pressure sometimes forces politicians to take positions that they otherwise wouldn't adopt. Mark Shields cites the following example:

> According to Representative Chris Shays, a stubborn Connecticut Yankee Republican, "A majority of Republican House members today want to support a strong patients' bill of rights bill to limit the power of managed care companies." Then why is there no such GOP bill? "Soft money from HMOs and insurance companies" is the frank and courageous answer of Chris Shays. The numbers support Shays. In the most recent campaign cycle, insurance interests and HMOs gave nearly $8 million in soft money, backing Republicans over Democrats by a ratio of much more than four to one.[4]

Table 14.1
A $30 Million Campaign: A Sample of Expenses for Senator Hillary Rodham Clinton's 2006 Re-Election Campaign

Name	Fees	Service
Consultants		
RWT Production	$6,143,931	Direct Mail
O'Brien McConnell & Pearson	$3,226,336	Direct Mail
Penn Schoen & Berland	$981,105	Polling
Grunwald Communications	$932,937	Media Consulting
Mayfield Strategy Group	$404,140	Web Site and E-Mail
Donor Services Group	$330,740	Telemarketing
Merkle Response Service	$306,545	Direct Mail
Ryan Phillips Utrecht MacKinnon	$275,976	Legal Consulting
Financial Innovations	$213,659	Merchandising
Hudson Media Planners	$182,627	Media Consulting
Copernicus Analytics	$156,127	Voter Database
Miscellaneous Spending		
	$161,751	Chartered Flights
	$80,421	Audio Visual Equipment
	$51,313	Photography
	$13,169	Flowers

In some cases, these special interests play a direct role in the drafting of legislation—a right not afforded to average citizens like you and me. Internal documents released in 2002 reveal that officials from *both* political parties had repeatedly discussed policy matters—and proposals that contributors wanted to see enacted as legislation—as part of the process of soliciting political donations. As an example, in a letter to Charles A. Heimbold Jr., chief executive of the pharmaceutical company Bristol-Myers Squibb, 2002, Republican chairperson Jim Nicholson asked for a $250,000 contribution, and, in turn, welcoming his "suggestions" on health care legislation:

> We must keep the lines of communication open if we want to continue passing legislation that will benefit your industry.... Your expertise in health care and involvement in Republican politics are of great benefit to me, and I would like to get your opinion on what we have proposed. I welcome any suggestions you may have on how we can make it an even stronger plan.[5]

Lobbyists, representing special interests, make every effort to influence the decisions of legislators. Lobbyists are often former government officials who use their connections to gain access to politicians. Although these representatives of special interests are only authorized to provide information to politicians, their influence often exceeds this purely consultative role. In 2003, the House of Representatives defeated a bill designed to allow Americans to import less expensive medicines from Canada and Europe. One of the deciding factors was a letter opposing the legislation, signed by 53 senators, that was sent to all House members. But left unsaid was that lobbyists for the Pharmaceutical Research and Manufacturers Association had coordinated the signature campaign.[6]

Lobbyist Jack Abramoff, who was sentenced to six years in prison for conspiring to bribe public officials, epitomizes the abuse of influence by special interests spawned by politicians' need for money. According to a bipartisan House Government Reform Committee report, Abramoff spent almost $25,000 on meals and drinks for the White House officials and provided them with tickets to numerous sporting events and concerts. In 2001 Abramoff asked the White House to withhold an endorsement for a Republican candidate for governor of the Northern Marianas Islands, an American commonwealth in the western Pacific where Abramoff had clients; Abramoff was backing another candidate. According to the report, Abramoff received an e-mail from Susan Ralson, Abramoff's former secretary, who had joined the White House staff, which read: "You win :) KR (White House Advisor Karl Rove) said no endorsement." Abramoff also claimed credit for an administration decision to release $16.3 million to a Mississippi tribe for jail construction, despite opposition from the Justice Department.[7]

Political Action Committees (PACs) also exercise a significant influence on both national and local political campaigns. The Federal Election Campaign Act of 1971 (FECA), amended in 1974 and 1976, permits corporations, labor unions, and religious organizations to support political candidates through the formation of PACs—a "separate segregated fund" within a company or as a self-sustaining, though related organization. This legislation enables PACs to donate up to $5,000 to a candidate, circumventing the $1,000 campaign gift limit for individuals.

Despite legislation limiting campaign contributions, loopholes still exist under the rubric of "soft money." Barred from donating directly to a political candidate, individuals and corporations can contribute an unlimited amount of money to "party building activities." Thus, despite the $2,100 per election limit on contributions to individual candidates (or $4,200 for both a primary and general election), Bob J. Perry, a conservative Texas homebuilder, contributed almost $10 million to help Republican congressional candidates in 2006.[8] Consequently, in 2000, a mere 739 contributors were responsible for two-thirds of the $137 million in soft-money contributions to the Republican Party.[9]

Although soft money is supposed to pay only for party activities, like voter drives, the parties have found ways to channel the money to help candidates, usually by backing the production and distribution of political

Table 14.2
The Top 20 PAC Contributors to Federal Candidates, 2005–2006

DEMS I REPUBS I ALL PAC Name	Total Amount	Democrat %	Republican %
National Assn of Realtors	$3,756,005	49%	51%
National Beer Wholesalers Assn	$2,946,500	31%	69%
National Assn of Home Builders	$2,900,000	26%	73%
National Auto Dealers Assn	$2,821,600	30%	70%
Operating Engineers Union	$2,784,435	78%	21%
Intl Brotherhood of Electrical Workers	$2,782,875	97%	3%
American Bankers Assn	$2,747,299	36%	64%
Laborers Union	$2,680,650	85%	15%
American Assn for Justice	$2,558,000	96%	3%
Credit Union National Assn	$2,412,853	45%	54%
AT&T Inc	$2,341,683	34%	66%
Carpenters & Joiners Union	$2,293,923	74%	25%
United Parcel Service	$2,239,128	32%	67%
United Auto Workers	$2,220,350	99%	1%
American Federation of Teachers	$2,110,948	99%	1%
Teamsters Union	$2,081,100	91%	8%
American Federation of St/Cnty/ Munic Employees	$2,048,683	98%	1%
American Medical Assn	$2,011,634	31%	69%
Plumbers/Pipefitters Union	$1,950,100	91%	9%
International Assn of Fire Fighters	$1,872,105	72%	27%

commercials. In addition, spending by outside groups that are nominally unconnected to political parties is considered soft money. Tax exempt political organizations known as "527s," which are not regulated by the Federal Election Commission or a state elections commission and therefore are not subject to the same contribution limits as PACs, raised $947 million for the 2004 presidential campaign.[10]

Individual donors also exercise a disproportionate influence on politicians—to the degree that messages delivered by politicians may fulfill a latent advertising function. In 2006, when President George W. Bush announced the resignation of Defense Secretary Donald Rumsfeld, he declared, "It's tough in a time of war, when people see carnage on their *Dell* television screens." (Dell's chairperson is a major donor to the Republican Party.)[11]

These large donors, who represent a very narrow segment of American society, share a common political agenda. Bob Herbert explains,

> I doubt that many people are aware of just how elite and homogeneous the donor class is. It's a tiny group—just one-quarter of 1 percent of the population—and it

is not representative of the rest of the nation. But its money buys plenty of access. These major donors share a common political agenda. They on balance oppose national health insurance, additional anti-poverty spending and reductions in defense spending, but back gay rights and free trade. They are fairly evenly divided on environmental protection and affirmative action.[12]

Given the financial pressures of the political system, it is nearly impossible for politicians to avoid financial entanglements that compromise the performance of their duties. Political candidates are required by law to disclose the sources of their contributions. Thus, in light of the role of campaign finances in the agenda of candidates, it can be extremely worthwhile to scrutinize this information, focusing on the following information:

- How much money has each individual/organization donated to the candidate?
- What industries do they represent?
- Is there any record of policy positions in these areas?

Process: Function

The relationship between the media and politicians in America is a confusing mix of conflict and cooperation, support and opposition. For purposes of discussion, it is useful to make the following distinction:

- *The media's coverage of politics*
- *The use of the media by politicians*

These *competing functions* are reflected in the often-contradictory, confrontational nature of political communications.

The Media's Coverage of Politics. The news industry focuses on the political life of the nation. In the United States, media coverage is expected to maintain a critical distance from political figures, issues, and events. Some of the purposes of the media's coverage of politics include the following:

- *The media inform the public about the political life of the nation.* The American media educates the public about political affairs and can establish a political agenda for the nation.
- *The media provide public exposure for politicians.* Politicians depend upon the media to gain access to their constituents and get their message across. In addition, media coverage lends legitimacy to aspiring politicians. Quentin Wilson, campaign manager for former Congressman Richard Gephardt's bid for the Democratic nomination for president in 1988, relates the story of how Gephardt knocked on doors in the primary state of Iowa with little success. But it was not until the Congressman's political spots began appearing on television that these same citizens of Iowa began taking him seriously as a candidate.[13]

- *The media influence public attitudes toward politicians and issues.* Because of the influence of the channels of mass communication, politicians strive to cultivate the goodwill of the media. When James Buchanan was elected president in 1857, he went to great lengths to reconcile his differences with James Gordon Bennett, editor of the *New York Herald*. A few weeks after his inauguration, Buchanan wrote to Bennett's wife, acknowledging her congratulations:

> I am glad to learn that Mr. Bennett has promised you "to stick by my administration through thick and thin." Thus far he has given it a powerful support with occasional aberrations, for which I am always prepared and do not complain. He is an independent man and will do just what he pleases—though I know there is an undercurrent of good will towards me in his nature and he is disposed to treat me fairly. The *Herald* in his hands is a powerful instrument and it would be vain for me to deny that I desire its music should be encouraging and not hostile. Mr. Buchanan makes his mark when he strikes and his blows fall so fast and heavy it is difficult to sustain them.... It is my desire as well as my interest to be on the best of terms with him....[14]

- *The media serves as an adversary of the government.* At its best, the U.S. media serve as a societal watchdog, making the government accountable to the people. The investigative efforts of reporters (e.g., Vietnam coverage, Watergate, and Irangate) have contributed to the democratic process, leading to the deposing of leaders, policy changes, and reforms in government.
- *The media depend upon politicians as vital sources of news content and profit.* The media rely upon politicians for daily programming content. Anything that a significant political figure does is considered newsworthy. Knowing this, politicians in positions of power can withhold access if they are displeased with the way that a reporter (or their news agency) covers a story. As an example, in 2001, the mayor of Cleveland denied the city's major newspaper access to a major political event as a result of what he considered unfair coverage by the paper. Reporter Felicity Barringer explained,

> Cleveland's mayor, Michael R. White, took the step soon after a daily newspaper, *The Plain Dealer*, infuriated him with its scanty coverage of a mayoral groundbreaking ceremony for a new airport runway.
>
> Declaring that the paper had covered the three-term mayor unfairly, the mayor's press aide, Brian Rothenberg, followed his boss's orders on Wednesday and escorted *The Plain Dealer's* reporter and photographer out of the elementary school cafeteria where the mayor was announcing to the rest of the local news media that he would not seek re-election to a fourth term.
>
> The event was duly recorded by journalists from the Associated Press and local television and radio stations. But whenever a *Plain Dealer* reporter or photographer entered—and various ones did keep coming in—they were told to leave.[15]

Politicians may also exploit the competition between journalists to pressure reporters into writing favorable stories. Savvy politicians take advantage of the media's reliance on politicians for news stories. Dan Rather recalls that during his tenure as White House reporter, exclusive interviews with President Nixon were offered only to reporters who had written stories sympathetic to the administration.[16]

The Use of the Media by Politicians. Politicians also use the media to control the messages presented to the public. One example is political advertising, in which the campaign staffs for candidates produce their own ads and purchase media time to present their message. But in addition, a candidate's campaign team strives to set the news agenda for the media. Media consultant Paul Begala attributed much of the success of the Clinton campaign to "message management"; that is, he was able to focus his message and set the political agenda for the election. Within that context, Daniel Goleman suggests that citizens ask the following questions:

- *Is this what I think is important?*
- *What of importance is not being talked about?*[17]

This use of the media by politicians falls into the following categories.

Politicians use the media to protect their positions of power. Although previous administrations employed communications consultants during election campaigns, the Reagan administration was the first to adopt this approach *after* the election. The key to the Reagan communications plan is *information management*. The Reagan communications team looked at all news stories from the following perspective: does this information support (or threaten) the goals of the administration? David Gergen, director of communications under both Ronald Reagan and Bill Clinton, observes,

> For one of the first times I'm aware of, (the Reagan administration) molded a communications strategy around a legislative strategy. We very carefully thought through what were the legislative goals we were trying to achieve, and then formulated a communications strategy which supported them.[18]

This communication model has been adopted by every president since Reagan, through the administration of George W. Bush.

This approach to government/press relations consists of the following principles:

- *Plan ahead.* Each Friday, the communications team discussed upcoming events from a public relations perspective. As one participant has noted, the dominant questions were, "What are we going to do today to enhance the image of the President," and "What do we want the press to cover today, and how?"[19]
- *Stay on the offensive.* The Reagan administration made a point of controlling the agenda. The communications team would prepare its message with an eye on its potential effect on the audience. Immediately following a presidential decision, press conference, or significant news event, the Reagan communications team would circulate among the press to present the administration's interpretation, or *spin*, on the story in order to manage how information was presented, reported, and received by the public.

When faced with events that could be damaging to the administration, the communications team would focus on *damage control;* that is, the management of information during a crisis. This strategy was designed to minimize potentially harmful stories relying on the following principles:

- *Respond promptly.* The Reagan team was poised to react swiftly to news stories. The communications team then devised a strategy that downplayed negative aspects of the story.
- *Manage the flow of information.* Recognizing that the news media depends on government as a primary news source, the Reagan team made available information that they wanted conveyed and simply withheld information that they weren't prepared to discuss. As Sam Donaldson observed, "So our options are, do nothing or do it their way."[20]
- *Limit reporters' access.* Limiting access to the President reduced the chances that the administration would lose control of its agenda. It was vital, however, that Reagan maintain the *image* of accessibility. Thus, the president was often in view of the cameras, but conveniently out of earshot (e.g., photo opportunities and boarding noisy helicopters).
- *Speak in one voice.* Once an official line was decided upon, it was important that the position be presented with consistency. All administration officials presented a unified, official message. Consequently, it was imperative that the Reagan team remain discreet and loyal. This in part accounts for the Reagan administration's obsession with leaks within the administration.
- *Make it easy on the press.* The Reagan communications team provided the media with prepackaged information (which, of course, presented their perspective on events). The Reagan team manipulated media coverage by staging events such as press conferences, speeches, and conventions, which were then covered as news.

  The working assumption was that the press was inherently lazy and would accept the administration's version of news if it made their jobs easier. And as Deputy Chief of Staff Michael Deaver explained, "If you didn't have anything, they'd go *find* something."[21]
- *Take advantage of the characteristics of the medium.* The Reagan communications team took advantage of the visual nature of television to present their point of view. According to Richard Cohen, senior producer of CBS, Michael Deaver virtually functioned as Executive Producer for the television networks by setting up visually compelling backdrops and action-oriented events that the networks found irresistible. Hertsgaard explains,

  > Rather than resist the networks desire for saturation coverage of the President, the Reagan propaganda apparatus would cater to it. The networks wanted visuals of the President? Fine. But they would be visuals carefully designed to promote the Reagan agenda.[22]

- *Mislead when necessary.* The Reagan team engaged in a "disinformation" strategy, in which they deliberately released false information to achieve political goals. For instance, in 1986, the press discovered administration memos confirming that the Reagan administration had released disinformation about Moammar Gadhafi in order to destabilize the Libyan government. White House officials admitted to the disinformation campaign but minimized its significance (an example of damage control):

> We think for domestic consumption there will be no problems. It's Gadhafi. After all, whatever it takes to get rid of him is all right with us—that's the feeling, we think, in the country. On the foreign scene it will cause problems, though. We're constantly talking about the Soviet's doing disinformation. It's going to cause difficulties for us.[23]

In a classic example of disinformation, President Reagan flatly denied any government involvement in the disinformation campaign. Reagan declared, "We were not telling any lies or doing any of these disinformation things."

Latent Functions. Occasionally, American media have crossed the boundary of objective reporting and *actively* support the agenda of the government. In 1961 the *New York Times* learned of the impending Bay of Pigs invasion two days before it was scheduled to begin. President Kennedy appealed to the paper not to print the story; the *Times* complied. After the failure of the mission, Kennedy later joked that he wished that the Times had ignored his request.[24]

Another latent function involves the government using the media as a vehicle to shape public opinion. U.S. administration officials routinely "leak" information to the public through the media as a way of testing public response before policy decisions are reached. As an example, in 2006, it was disclosed that the Bush administration's Office of Cuba Broadcasting paid 10 journalists in Miami to produce programming critical of Fidel Castro; these broadcasts were disseminated to a domestic audience, as well as to Cuba through Radio and TV Martí. However, these journalists did not divulge that they were being paid by the U.S. government for their commentaries. (For more discussion of propaganda, see Chapter 3, Function.)

Dual Function. According to Kathleen Hall Jamieson, these two functions—the media's coverage of politicians versus politicians' manipulation of the media—have begun to merge, much to the detriment of the public.

> ... the differences between news and ads are blurring. News about electoral contests—"free time"—is becoming increasingly adlike. Indeed in 1988 it was no longer unusual to find segments of ads—adbites—broadcast in news stories in ways that heighten rather than diminish their power. Meanwhile, "paid TV," consisting primarily of thirty-second political spots, is becoming increasingly newslike, and in the process further fuzzing the line between news and ads. And candidate speeches, press conferences, one-on-one interviews, and debate answers are increasingly tailored with a view toward getting adlike news coverage.[25]

Process: Media Communicator

In the media age, a major criterion for selecting candidates is their ability to communicate on television. Candidates must come across as dynamic, charismatic, trustworthy, competent, and likable. In January 2007, Senator

Barack Obama's announcement of his intention to run for president was received with the excitement generally accorded a rock star. Newton Minow, a Chicago lawyer who served in the Kennedy administration, declared, "This is the sort of thing you get once in a generation. This is a connection between what the voters need and what the voters want. This is the first time I've felt it since Jack Kennedy."[26]

Consequently, media exposure has magnified the importance of the *character* of the political leaders. Former Boston Mayor Kevin White explains, "What you need in office is a man who can cope with situations as they arise, situations that no one ever thought of."[27] In that regard, political scientist James David Barber has devised a formula for predicting presidential performance, based upon distinct character types. Barber identified four character patterns, based upon his or her levels of *activity* (Activity/Passivity) and *enjoyment* (Positive/Negative affect):

- The *Active/Positive* personality is distinguished by an industrious nature, combined with the enjoyment of this level of activity. This pattern, typified by Thomas Jefferson, indicates a high level of self-esteem, success in relating to his environment, and achievement orientation.
- The *Active/Negative* character, exemplified by John Adams, combines intense effort with a relatively low emotional reward. The Active/Negative figure is compulsive, and his goal is to obtain and maintain power. As a result, an Active/Negative president such as Lyndon Johnson or Richard Nixon brought an inherently rigid approach to the presidency, resulting in escalation of policies long after the issues (e.g., Watergate, Vietnam) should have been resolved.
- A *Passive/Positive* president, such as James Madison, is a compliant figure who combines a low self-esteem with a "superficial optimism."[28] Because this personality type is primarily looking for acceptance, he or she is unlikely to take an aggressive approach to the implementation of policy.
- The *Passive/Negative* figure, personified by George Washington, "does little in politics and enjoys it less."[29] Withdrawn by nature and possessing a low sense of self-esteem, this personality type regards politics as a civic duty, often serving his term of office with reluctance.

Barber regards presidential style as an extension of internal presidential character patterns. Barber links style to performance—the way in which the president will perform his/her duties. Significantly, Roger Streitmatter has found a correlation between a president's character type and how he was treated by the media. "Robust" presidents (those who fell within Barber's Active-Positive character delineation) received at least 50 percent more newspaper coverage than presidents exhibiting less attractive character traits. Active-Positive presidents also received 87 percent more "personal news coverage" focusing on their daily activities and family.[30]

As a result, the emerging role of the media suggests a modification of Barber's theory. Style is no longer a reflection of character but instead is a carefully cultivated *image* designed to appeal to the American public and, as Streitmatter suggests, attract favorable media coverage as well. Presidential archivist Timothy Naftali declares, "Presidencies are constructed; there are whole teams of people who spend the day trying to make the president, Republican or Democrat, decisive or forward looking."[31]

Politicians strive to project an Active-Positive persona. Media staffs often stage events that make politicians appear active and dynamic, such as visiting schools, hospitals, and factories.

After the events of 9/11, President George W. Bush experienced a surge in popularity, tied to his forceful response at the site of Ground Zero. Dressed in a windbreaker, Bush grabbed a bullhorn and extemporaneously addressed the crowd, encouraging the firefighters and police.

The Bush political team subsequently sought to build on the success of this Active/Positive persona. In May 2003, Bush, outfitted in flight gear, landed in a fighter jet on the aircraft carrier USS *Abraham Lincoln* to announce "Mission Accomplished" in Iraq. This image of a vigorous leader was so popular with the public that Blue Box Toy Company merchandized a George W. Bush action figure, in which Bush was transformed into a superhero, complete with bulging biceps and "six-pack abs."

However, the successful candidate now must be able to withstand the relentless *scrutiny of the press*. After initially promoting a candidate, the media almost immediately begins to delve into the private lives of these same politicians. In December 2006, as Senator Barack Obama was considering whether to run for president, a major consideration was whether he was willing to subject himself—and his family—to the scrutiny of the press. As columnist Jeff Zeleny reported, "The next phase of his political development will inevitably draw intense and less flattering scrutiny."[32] This phase began in March 2007, when 125 newspapers throughout the country ran the story that in January, Obama had accumulated $375 in fines for outstanding parking tickets 17 years before as a student at Harvard Law School in the late 1980s. (He paid the fine in January 2007.) This media scrutiny magnifies the human flaws of these candidates and undermines public confidence in politicians.

Unfortunately, this media scrutiny limits the pool of potential candidates. It is safe to say that very few people would feel comfortable permitting the press to comb through their past. Indeed, if experience forms character, it can be argued that youthful indiscretions are an important part of growing up. To borrow a line from Groucho Marx, would you vote for anyone whose lives were so devoid of experience that he/she could survive this level of media inquiry?

Point of View. Most of the political information that we receive is filtered through media communicators. As a result, determining the point of view of the media communicator has become a vital consideration in the American political process.

Despite its lofty goals of objectivity, the press often brings a distinct point of view to its political coverage. For instance, Senator John McCain is an engaging man whose personal story, as a survivor of a North Vietnamese prisoner of war camp is truly heroic. Several reporters who have been assigned to cover McCain have admitted that, after spending time with the Senator, they have allowed their admiration for the Senator to affect their coverage. After covering McCain in the 2000 Republican presidential primary election, Jacob Weisberg, a reporter for *Slate* magazine, admitted, "When I set out to spend a few days with McCain last week, I promised my editor that I wouldn't join in this collective swoon. That proved impossible."[33] In a *Time* magazine profile of John McCain, Nancy Gibbs and John F. Dickerson admit that reporters were protective of the Arizona senator:

> A presidential candidate is not supposed to talk at length and on the record about the rules he broke or the strippers he dated, or the time he arrived so drunk that he fell through the screen door of the young lady he was wooing. The candor tells you more than the content, and reporters sometimes just decide to take him off the record because they don't want to see him flame out and burn up a great story.[34]

Comparative Media

Television has had an enormous impact on the content of political communications. Complex facts are difficult to digest on television and must therefore be simplified. Political speeches now cater to the 30-second sound bite—a brief, catchy, and memorable phrase which can be carried on television news. Who can forget "Read my lips," "He's pulling a Clinton," and Kerry the "Flip-flopper."

The number of issues in a televised presentation must be kept to a minimum. Rosser Reeves, a pioneer in political advertising, recalls working with Dwight Eisenhower on his campaign:

> I attended a speech given by General Eisenhower, and he was all over the lot. I counted twenty-seven issues ... and nobody remembered what he had said. We selected three campaign issues to feature in our campaign ads. I wanted one, but the Republican National Committee insisted on three.[35]

Media consultant Jane Squier Bruns warns that it may be a mistake to look to television for the answers to complex questions: "If you want to find [in-depth] information, you need to turn to print and other unpaid media coverage. Otherwise, you are making your choices on the wrong basis."[36]

On television, images often overwhelm verbal messages. Television reporter Leslie Stahl relates a story that illustrates this point. In 1984,

Stahl filed a news report for CBS, in which she discussed President Ronald Reagan's use of television:

> How does Ronald Reagan use television? Brilliantly.... Mr. Reagan tries to counter the memory of an unpopular issue with a carefully chosen backdrop that actually contradicts the president's policy. Look at the handicapped Olympics, or the opening ceremony of an old-age home. No hint that he tried to cut the budgets for the disabled and for federally subsidized housing for the elderly....

This script was accompanied by visuals of Reagan in action: "The president basking in a sea of flag-waving supporters, beaming beneath red-white-and-blue balloons floating skyward ... getting the Olympic torch from a runner, greeting wheelchair athletes at the handicapped Olympics, greeting senior citizens at their housing project...."

Stahl recalls that she "worried" about the response from the White House and was astonished when a Reagan official called to congratulate her. He explained,

> We're in the middle of a campaign and you gave us four and a half minutes of great pictures of Ronald Reagan. And that's all the American people see.... They won't listen to you if you're contradicting great pictures. They don't hear what you are saying if the pictures are saying something different.[37]

Ironically, Stahl fell victim to the central message of her story: it's not what you say. It's what you show. And despite what the public may experience on a day-to-day basis, they believe the images that politicians present.

Digital technology has transformed the American political landscape. In 2006, 15 percent of Americans said that they received *most* of their political information online—double the number of the previous midterm election in 2002.[38] Increasingly, candidates are turning to the Internet as a means of connecting with the voters. In January 2007, Senator Barack Obama announced his exploratory committee for president in a high-resolution video on his web site. He also used MySpace and Facebook to reach nearly 250,000 young people during the first two months of 2007.[39] Shortly after Obama's web-announcement, Senator Hillary Clinton's announcement of her intention to run for president was accompanied by a video clip posted on her web site, in which she declared that she wanted to maintain a "conversation" with the public—largely through the Internet.

Politicians also use the Internet for fundraising. Howard Dean was the first national politician to use the Internet as a fundraising vehicle, raising over $25 million in online donations during the 2004 election. Rather than relying on large contributions by a few donors, the Dean campaign relied upon small donations by a large constituency. The average amount contributed to the Dean campaign over the Internet was $77.[40]

The Internet has also emerged as a source of instant information that can affect the outcome of elections. In 2006, Senator George Allen, favored to win the race for re-election in Virginia, hurled a racial epithet at a young man of Indian descent at a campaign stop. Allen referred to S. R. Sidarth as "macaca." Macaca is a racial slur that was first used by francophone colonials in Central Africa's Belgian Congo for the native population, derived from the name of the genus comprising macaque monkeys. Allen added, "Welcome to America and the real world of Virginia." This moment was distributed on YouTube and became a gaffe that Allen could not overcome, as he went down to defeat. (For more discussion, see Chapter 12, Journalism.)

But as with any channel, the Internet can be used to mislead voters. One example is the use of "link bombs" to discredit candidates. This occurs when opponents engineer a flood of web links and cross-links to unfavorable content. As a result, negative articles about the candidate are posted at the top of the search rankings (for more information on "link-bombing," see Chapter 13, Advertising).

With the growing reliance on political web sites for information, the Democracy Online Project has developed a set of standards for online campaigning, which requires: 1) documenting positions on issues and 2) disclosing the source of materials used on web sites.[41]

Audience

Television has blurred traditional differences among political factions. Among Republicans, frequent TV viewers tended to be more liberal than occasional viewers. Among Democrats, heavy TV viewers tended to be more conservative than light viewers.[42] Further, individuals who admit to being frequent TV watchers are more likely to call themselves "moderate" and avoid the labels of "liberal" or "conservative."[43]

Generally, political messages only serve to reinforce the previously held views of voters who have strong convictions. Partisan voters do not turn to the media for answers, but rather to support their pre-existing point of view. Studies reveal that the media may influence voters on candidates and issues but *only if* allegiances are weak. For instance, in 2004, pro-Kerry viewers felt that he "won" the first presidential debate, while Republican viewers felt that Bush had emerged victorious.

Consequently, all of the energy and money of political campaigns is directed at those few voters who have not yet made up their minds. Media consultant Jane Squier Bruns explains,

> You have a spectrum across the scale of potential voters and you whittle it down ... and you finally get to the point where you know you have to reach this tiny little group in the middle. These are the undecideds who will or will not vote for your candidate—depending on what happens. And that's who the message has to go to.[44]

Post-Modern Mass Communication Model. Today the audience has assumed a predominant role in the political communication process. Politicians tailor the strategy, style, and content of their messages to their target audience (see discussion of Post-Modern Mass Communication Model, Chapter 4). Tracking polls and focus groups have become an essential means of gauging voter sentiment. As the campaign progresses, tracking polls are conducted more frequently—often on a daily basis by the end of the campaign. Squier notes,

> They're taking (the voter's) temperature all the time. Initial polls ... measure where the voters are, what they're thinking.... Their messages are very specifically targeted ... they know through the polling where they've got to reach voters.... This is not a shotgun approach. We are talking about very, very specific targeting. It's easy to do it mathematically.[45]

Political consultants conduct psychographic research to anticipate how the voters will respond to particular political appeals. Montague Kern explains, "Buttons and dials are used to test immediate nonverbal responses to televised candidate presentations."[46] "Perception analyzers" can measure how focus groups respond to a speech—line by line. William Raspberry observes,

> Imagine having your speech writers assemble a scientifically selected cross section of likely voters and try out various concepts, formulations and jokes for their effects on one group or another. You could then tailor your remarks to fit any occasion....
>
> The perception analyzer isn't the only tool in the kit by a long shot. The people who do polls and focus groups and fine-tuned surveys have gotten so good they can divide the electorate into the tiniest of issue-based pieces. Their exquisite science has given us "wedge" issues—those issues with the peculiar ability to find and exploit our political fault lines.[47]

All of this research enables political consultants to devise communication strategies that appeal to their target audience.

Cultural Context

Impact of Media on the Political Process. Today, the media not merely capture the action but have transformed the political process in the following respects.

Decline of the Party Machine. The emergence of the mass media has coincided with a decline in party affiliation among Americans. Party loyalties and organizations have declined drastically as candidates are able to get their messages directly to the voters through channels of mass communications. In 2007, 32 percent of the electorate are self-described "Independents" unaffiliated with either political party.[48]

The Rise of the Media Consultant. The primary responsibility of the media consultant is to coordinate political ads and unpaid media coverage.

However, the media consultant has branched out into all phases of a campaign, including media creation and promotion, direct mail fund-raising, and participation in the formulation of campaign strategies.

Media consultants are advertising specialists who borrow heavily from traditional advertising techniques to "sell" their candidates to the public. But media consultant Bob Goodman acknowledges that packaging a human being has distinct limitations:

> You can't put a candidate completely in a new package. You can take his polyester off and put him in a decent-looking suit. You have him blow dry his hair. You can teach him how to keep his eye on the camera. You can try to inspire certain attributes. But you don't have the complete freedom that you do when you're dealing with a bar of soap.[49]

Some critics regard political consultants as mercenaries who hire themselves out to the largest bid. Top media consulting firms can command a fee of over $1 million for a single political campaign. However, in order to continue to attract clients, consultants must maintain an impressive won-lost record. As an example, after the 2006 midterm congressional elections, attention was focused not only on the performances of the candidates but on their media consultants:

> Some of the losers to emerge from the midterm elections on Tuesday were easy to spot, particularly the Republicans who were defeated. But there were other, low-profile winners and losers along the way: the professionals who rode to victory or defeat on strategies they had created and put into place. And as the results settle in, the game of scoring their performance is under way.
>
> The most spectacular defeat was that of Senator George Allen of Virginia, who won the prize for most breathtaking downfall, not only losing his Senate seat to help hand power of the entire body to the Democrats, but also tarnishing a once-golden reputation in under three months flat. Less obvious but no less real was the damage to Mr. Allen's campaign manager, Dick Wadhams, a strategist once celebrated as the "next Karl Rove."[50]

As a result, consultants are often reluctant to take chances on "dark-horse" candidates who would benefit most from their assistance. Media consultant Sanford L. Weiner admits,

> We would all like to think we have only worked for candidates we believed in, and who represented our own individual political thinking.... Unfortunately, as with any profession, economics enter the picture. We have all from time to time, represented clients whom we didn't particularly love, but who could help us pay the overhead.[51]

However, some consultants do operate out of a core set of principles, offering their services to candidates affiliated with one political party (Republican or Democrat) or to individual candidates they respect.

Top media consultants wield an astonishing amount of power. Where candidates used to solicit the support of the party machine, they now scramble for the services of top media consultants. Candidates often defer to the judgment of the consultant—not only on campaign strategy but on policy issues as well. To illustrate, in 2006, four prominent media consultants were asked what they would do to "package" Rudolph W. Giuliani as a candidate for president of the United States in 2008. Giuliani, the former mayor of New York City is well-known throughout the country for his take-charge approach following the terrorist attack on New York City on 9/11. But although Giuliani is a Republican, he supports some "progressive" stances on social issues: he supports abortion rights, gay rights, and gun control. Significantly, two of the media consultants actually recommended that Giuliani modify his political position on abortion in order to appeal to conservatives. Mary Matalin, former counselor to Vice President Dick Cheney, declared,

> On liberal social positions: carefully evolve, but don't be a phony. Social conservatives are conviction voters. And social moderates will reject political opportunism. Indicate your respect for conservative convictions and try to "refine" your own. A late-life reversal on late-term abortion is entirely plausible and mandatory. Try to keep focus on constitutionalist judges.[52]

Paul Begala, Democratic strategist and former aide to President Bill Clinton, was even more blunt: surrender on abortion:

> You can't switch on everything. So surrender to the far right on one issue: abortion. But the only way to do it is whole hog. Use your trump card: 9/11. Tell them the death you saw that day gave you a greater appreciation for the sanctity of life. You're Saul on the road to Damascus. Praise the Lord and pass the delegates.[53]

However, Vincent Breglio complains that "Some candidates just won't listen, they won't do what they're told." He explains that "the extent to which a candidate is manageable" is a prime consideration in the selection of his clients—an alarming criterion for a national leader.[54]

The Influence of the Polls. Despite their influence, polls may not be an accurate and comprehensive barometer of public opinion. The inaccuracy of political polls occurs for several reasons. First, only the *results* of polls are generally made public, so that vital information about the polling sample is omitted. However, an important consideration in the assessment of polls is the probability that the sample of respondents will actually vote. Polls that use the *general population* as its sample are the least reliable. Other polls that use a sample of *registered voters* are considered more accurate; however, about 10 percent who say they're registered really are not.[55] The most accurate sample consists of *likely voters.*

In addition, some demographic groups are not being adequately represented in polls because of the way in which interviews are conducted. Robert Groves explains,

The data are pretty clear that you miss people who live alone, especially younger people who are more likely to be out in the evenings. You tend to over-sample people with young children because they are home. You also tend to over-interview the elderly population because they are at home and are often willing to be polled. You get the unemployed. It's an odd distribution.[56]

Further, the poll sample is skewed because polling methods are limited to people who use "land lines," as opposed to cellphones. Consequently, polls of likely voters completely miss this voter. In 2004, about 5 percent of all households relied exclusively on cellphones for telephone service. Among young adults, the number is close to 15 percent.[57]

The sample selected for the poll may also reflect a cultural bias. For instance, most national polls in the United States are conducted only in English.[58] As a result, the opinions of the Spanish-speaking population are underrepresented.

Moreover, polls only capture the mood of the moment in which they are conducted. As a result, the results may be subject to drastic swings as new events and information shape public opinion. According to Temple University Professor John Allen Paulos, polls are just snapshots: "Polls are like weather vanes. They work at the moment, but no one relies on them to say what the weather is going to be like next week."[59]

Another important consideration in evaluating poll results is the depth of conviction on the part of the voters—in other words, how strongly those polled feel about the issue or candidate they favor. Jennifer LaFleur explains,

One figure that can have an even larger outcome on the outcome of a poll is the proportion of undecided people who, come election day, actually may decide. To compensate for this factor, pollsters may force these folks into making a decision by asking them a second question such as, "If you had to decide right now, who would you pick"? The people that make a decision when forced are called "leaners."[60]

Thus, if a poll sample is made up of a number of "leaners," the level of support may be much weaker than a group with definite views.

The wording of the poll also has an impact on its results. For instance, polls designed to gauge public response to the Bush administration's eavesdropping program varied significantly depending on how the questions were worded. In a New York Times/CBS News poll, 53 percent of the respondents said they supported eavesdropping without warrants "in order to reduce the threat of terrorism." However, when the question used the phrase "terrorist surveillance system," 46 percent of those respondents approved, and 50 percent said they disapproved.[61]

A more insidious version of this tactic is the "push poll," which, under the guise of an opinion poll, is used to shape public opinion. David Broder explains:

Here's how it works: Your phone rings and someone from the "Acme Survey Center," or some other such vague name, says, "I'm taking a survey of voters. In the contest between Gwendolyn Jones and David Broder for the congressional seat in our district, would you favor Jones or Broder or are you undecided?"

If your answer is either Broder or undecided, the "interviewer" then says something like this: "If I told you that Broder's hobby is driving a high-powered sports car at dangerous speeds through residential neighborhoods and seeing how many pet cats and dogs he can run over, would that make a difference in your vote?" After another question or two, the interview closes with a repeat of the ballot question—Jones or Broder or undecided.[62]

MEDIA LITERACY TIPS

INTERPRETING PUBLIC OPINION POLLS

When faced with the results of public opinion polls, ask the following questions:

- *How old is the poll?*
  The closer to election day, the better.
- *What was the size of the sample?*
  The larger the size of the sample, the better.
- *Who was polled?*[63]
- *Who sponsored the poll?*[64]
  Polls paid for by news organizations use safeguards not used by parties in the quick polls that candidates and parties use to guide strategy.[65]
- *Is the poll state or national?*[66]
  State polls, usually a few days older, tell you if a presidential candidate is within striking distance of your state's electoral votes. But national polls can detect last-minute trends.
- *What is the margin of error in the poll?*
  Because polls ask a sample of the population, the numbers can only approximate the tabulation of the entire target population. Statisticians are able to compute a reasonable "margin of error" for each poll, based on its sample size and methodology. If a poll has a three percentage point margin of error, the totals are likely to fall within plus or minus three percentage points—a six point swing. In this case, if a poll reports that a Republican candidate is ahead by two percentage points, the Republican could be ahead as much as five percentage points, or behind by one percentage point.

Media and the Balance of Power. The media has greatly enhanced the power of the executive branch of government. As Bill Clinton and George W. Bush have so effectively demonstrated, presidents can now circumvent the Congress and appeal directly to the American people through the media. Chris Matthews, former press secretary to Senate Majority Leader Tip O'Neill and currently host of MSNBC's "Hardball," observes, "It is amazing how the monarchy translates so well into the television age and legislatures do not."[67]

Obsolete Political Processes. In this media age, a number of features of the American political system have been rendered obsolete.

The Primary System. The primary system for nominating party candidates was devised in a less sophisticated media era, when politicians could only gain access to voters by traveling around the country and declaring their positions on issues of regional interests and concern. This was also the only means by which the local citizens could hear what the candidates had to say.

But today, thanks to extensive media coverage, state primaries receive national exposure. As a result, candidates can no longer regionalize their messages but are forced to repeat the same menu of positions on national issues at each stop. As a result, candidates must resort to attack ads and peppy slogans to give their campaigns a fresh and dynamic appearance.

In addition, because of the national focus on state primaries, the initial contest in New Hampshire assumes an exaggerated importance. The winners of this primary actually receive very few delegates (Democratic—18 out of 2,145 needed for nomination; Republican—23 out of l,105 needed for nomination). However, the winners of these contests are anointed as the frontrunners by the media. Austin Ranney declares,

> The benefits of this early position are many. The frontrunners, no matter how behind they started, rise rapidly in the public opinion polls, and they find it much easier to raise money and enlist volunteers. Their opponents sink in the polls, find it harder to attract money and workers, and often drop out or "discontinue active campaigning."[68]

The 2008 election is moving toward a national primary. After the traditional opening primaries in Iowa and New Hampshire during January, 29 states, including California and New York moved their primaries up to February 5.

Electoral College. Surprisingly, in the United States, candidates are not elected by a direct vote of citizens. Instead, elections work according to an Electoral College system, in which voters choose a slate of electors, who select the president and vice president. Indeed, the electors are not obligated to vote for the slate chosen by his or her state's voters. Consequently, in the case of a closely contested nomination process during the party's convention (see below), the slate may be released from its "official" selection.

The electoral college system was devised at a time in which collecting and tabulating votes throughout the nation would have been unwieldy. Representative Ray LaHood, (R-Ill.) declares, "(The Electoral College) is merely a relic of times past, running counter to the democratic process."[69] The media age offers the opportunity for a quick and precise national tabulation of votes.

Political Conventions. Historically, political conventions were gatherings in which a political party's slate of candidates was selected. However, in the modern political arena, these decisions have been reached long before the convention. Instead, the convention has become strictly a media event, filled with scripted speeches, video sound bites, and rehearsed celebrations, and designed to generate momentum for the upcoming campaign.

Political Communication as Cultural Barometer. Political communication can be regarded as a text that reflects, reinforces, and shapes cultural attitudes, values, behaviors, preoccupations, and myths. For instance, campaign strategies furnish perspective into acceptable gender rules in American culture. Democratic strategist James Carville maintains that his party's failure to project a powerful, masculine image contributed to its losses after the attack of 9/11: "The fact that the party has come across as less—I don't want to say less masculine—but certainly less aggressive than Republicans, is true."[70] Thus, according to John Lapp, the former executive director of the Democratic Congressional Campaign Committee, the 2006 midterm election was notable, in part, for the return of the "Alpha Male Democrat."

> "So we went to C.I.A. agents, F.B.I. agents, N.F.L. quarterbacks, sheriffs, Iraq war vets. These are red-blooded Americans who are tough.... (New Congressman) Joe Sestak—that guy's muscular!" says Mr. Lapp. "He's a vice admiral. I've told him to spend a lot of time going on the national talk shows. He can really do a service changing the mold and the way the Democratic Party is viewed."[71]

In contrast, the word choice employed to describe female politicians frequently relies on appearance. For instance, just after the U.S. Congressional elections in November 2006, *The Daily Telegraph*, a conservative-leaning U.K. national paper ran a story about incoming Speaker of the U.S. House of Representatives Nancy Pelosi. The headline of the article is: "Liberal and Lip-glossed, The Most Powerful Woman in Washington." Reporter Toby Harnden speculates through vague authority that "some believe" she must have had plastic surgery to be so "well-preserved."[72]

In the United States, the *Washington Post* published a news story about Secretary of State Condoleezza Rice that contained the following passage:

> Secretary of State Condoleezza Rice arrived at the Wiesbaden Army Airfield ... dressed all in black. She was wearing a black skirt that hit just above the knee, and it was topped with a black coat that fell to mid-calf. The coat, with its seven gold buttons running down the front and its band collar, called to mind a Marine's dress uniform or the "save humanity" ensemble worn by Keanu Reeves in *The Matrix*.
>
> As Rice walked out to greet the troops, the coat blew open in a rather swashbuckling way to reveal the top of a pair of knee-high boots. The boots had a high, slender heel that is not particularly practical. But it is a popular silhouette because it tends to elongate and flatter the leg. In short, the boots are sexy.

> Rice's coat and boots speak of sex and power—such a volatile combination, and one that in political circles rarely leads to anything but scandal. When looking at the image of Rice in Wiesbaden, the mind searches for ways to put it all into context. It turns to fiction, to caricature. To shadowy daydreams. Dominatrix! It is as though sex and power can only co-exist in a fantasy. When a woman combines them in the real world, stubborn stereotypes have her power devolving into a form that is purely sexual.
>
> Rice's appearance at Wiesbaden—a military base with all of its attendant images of machismo, strength and power—was striking because she walked out draped in a banner of authority, power and toughness ... But the sexual frisson in Rice's look also comes from the tension of a woman dressed in vaguely masculine attire—that is, the long, military-inspired jacket.[73]

This article would be considered entirely inappropriate if its subject was a male. Indeed, it is considerably more difficult to find stories commenting on George W. Bush's legs or his shoes. This kind of article conveys the message that the basis for judging a female candidate is her appearance, which ultimately undermines confidence in her qualifications for public office.

Moreover, by framing Rice's position of power in sexual terms, the article suggests that aspiring to public office is somehow unsuitable for a woman. The article makes the point that assuming the "masculine attire" of public office creates a "sexual frisson," a term used to describe a feeling of excitement or terror, accompanied by a physical shudder or thrill. Indeed, describing Ms. Rice as a dominatrix conveys the latent message that powerful women continue to intimidate males in American culture.

Politics and Popular Culture. Politics has traditionally been the domain of "elitist" programming such as the newspaper, or traditional television panel programs such as *Meet the Press*, and *Face the Nation.* However, beginning in 1968, with Richard Nixon's appearance on the popular TV program *Laugh In*, presidential candidates have found popular media programming to be an effective means of reaching the electorate. In 2006, Senator Barack Obama appeared in a humorous spot at the start of *Monday Night Football* on ESPN, followed by an appearance on the *Oprah Winfrey Show.*

Popular media programming has emerged as a principal source of political news. According to a 2004 Pew Research Center study, 21 percent of people under the age of 30 say that their principal source of news about the presidential campaign came from satirical sources like *The Daily Show.*[74] Unfortunately, these entertainers are not bound by the same ethical guidelines about accuracy and fairness as journalists. Indeed, a staple of successful comedy is exaggeration and irreverence.

Political humor can be indicative of cultural attitudes toward politicians and issues. The success of a joke depends on a set of shared assumptions between the comic and audience; if the audience is confused about the context of the joke or disagrees with its premise, it will not get a laugh. Tim Harper explains,

> With George W. Bush's popular approval waning, the late-night shots at a U.S. president who has become a gold mine for jokes has turned into a more definitive barometer of his second term than the best work of pollsters Gallup or Harris.
>
> In the first three months of this year, according to a study by the non-partisan Center for Media and Public Affairs, Bush has been the butt of 102 jokes per month in the opening monologues of David Letterman, Jay Leno and Conan O'Brien, more than double the rate of Bush jokes in 2005. And more than any subject, they dwell on the perception that the U.S. commander-in-chief is ... well, not so bright.[75]

Popular media venues have promoted participation in the political process. For instance, in 2004 MTV sponsored "Rock the Ages," a voter registration drive that succeeded in registering approximately 1.4 million young voters.[76]

Political Communications and Cultural Myths. Many political ads capitalize upon our cultural self-image; not what we are, necessarily, but how we see ourselves—what we'd *like* to be.

- *Mythic past.* Ads featuring a nostalgic look backward at mythic America have an enormous appeal, particularly during times of cultural stress. This appeal is designed to project the legacy of the past onto the future. Politicians talk about the values of small town America. In addition, ads construct a worldview in which voters are empowered; we can make a difference. Our leaders ask for *our* support. We are momentarily important and in control. Ideals like freedom, hope, goodness, are central to this world of possibilities and prospects.
- *The American Dream* offers the promise of opportunity for the individual, in which success comes to the deserving through hard work and faith in the system. To illustrate, in 2004, John Kerry incorporated the American Dream into a campaign speech:

  > We believe that what matters most is not narrow appeals masquerading as values, but the shared values that show the true face of America; not narrow values that divide us, but the shared values that unite us: family, faith, hard work, opportunity and responsibility for all, so that every child, every adult, every parent, every worker in America has an equal shot at living up to their God-given potential. That is the American dream and the American value."[77]

- *The Romantic Ideal.* Political spots offer a worldview filled with the promise of a better future. Reagan's famous "Morning in America" ads maintained that America's best days were ahead. Other candidates pick up on this optimistic theme. In 2004, Kerry declared, "The hope is there. The sun is rising. Our best days are yet to come." Consequently, it is not surprising that the public has not been receptive to political messages asking us to sacrifice. Michael Dukakis's 1988 statement that he would have to make "tough" choices in budget allocations was countered by George H. W. Bush's more optimistic (and popular) message of *plenty:* we can have it all.

- *The Mythic Frontier* emerged in America in the nineteenth century, as the settlers spread west. According to Frederick Jackson Turner, the mythic frontier is characterized by "restless energy, individualism, self-reliance, the bounteousness and exuberance which comes with freedom."[78] As columnist Maureen Dowd has observed, much political rhetoric recently has drawn from this cultural myth: "After 9/11, Americans had responded to bellicosity, drawn to the image, as old as the Western frontier myth, of the strong father protecting the home from invaders."[79]

Structure

Media conglomerates are committed to preserving the status quo and only push for changes to make the current system work more effectively. As a product of the system, media industries are often beneficiaries of current political policies; for instance, in 2006, General Electric's net income from continuing operations increased 11.4 percent; yet, G.E. reported a tax rate of 17.2 percent, down from 18.7 percent in the first nine months of 2005.[80] As a result, the media are reluctant to advocate radical changes that might threaten its position.

As discussed earlier, because of the extraordinary demands of campaign finance, Special Interests exercise particular influence over the policies of politicians.

In addition, because of the imperative to maintain strong ratings, the media often treat politics as a form of entertainment. Newspaper coverage of debates emphasizes dramatic exchanges between candidates, often entirely ignoring any substantive news. Even more alarming is the tendency of journalists to translate good conduct into a vice. In 2000, Al Gore was described as "boring" because his conduct was not controversial or flashy enough to attract an audience.

FRAMEWORK

Introduction

Introduction as Foreshadowing Device. Campaign slogans are designed to generate immediate name recognition. For instance, "All the way with LBJ" was a memorable catch-phrase. Slogans encapsulate the central themes the candidate wishes to stress. Ironically, however, a slogan occasionally contains revealing latent messages. Gerald Ford pinned his 1976 election hopes on national inertia: "He's Our President—Let's Keep Him." Richard Nixon's pre-Watergate motto, "Nixon's the One!" foreshadowed his ouster. Pat Buchanan's slogan for the 1996 and 2000 presidential campaigns contained this veiled threat: "America First."

Illogical Premise. Upon close inspection, political ads frequently employ illogical conclusions. A good example can be found in a political advertisement produced for Senator Rick Santorum (R-Penn.) in his 2006 re-election bid against his opponent Bob Casey. The ad began with a visual of a smoke-filled room, with a group of cigar-smoking men playing cards. The narrator announces, "Meet Bob Casey's campaign team," and cites these unnamed developers and businessmen who have contributed to Mr. Casey and are now under investigation. The camera then pulls back, to reveal that the men are behind bars—in jail.

However, Factcheck.org noted the following inaccuracies:

- The men in the ad were actors.
- None of the "developers" and "businessmen" were identified.
- None of the men who were alluded to currently work for Mr. Casey.
- Some of the men alluded to had also contributed to Santorum in previous campaigns.[81]

Plot: *Explicit Content*

Examining the explicit content of political communications is a useful way to uncover fallacies, inconsistencies, and attempts to obfuscate issues or mislead the public. Political communications teams employ the following rhetorical techniques that manipulate information in order to influence how the public responds to issues and candidates.

Selective Facts. In political communications, facts may be used selectively, distorted, or omitted entirely. As an example, in March 2006, President Bush announced that "today nearly half the IEDs (Improvised Explosive Devices) in Iraq are found and disarmed before they can be detonated. In the past 18 months we have cut the casualty rate per IED attack in half." However, as ABC pointed out, the president failed to mention that the *number* of IED attacks had nearly doubled—from 5,607 to 10,593—so that although the casualty *rate* had declined, the total *number* of casualties had actually increased.[82] In the face of this bewildering array of information, facts become meaningless. Truth has thus been reduced to a matter of *faith*—whose facts the public chooses to believe.

Innuendo. Attacking an opponent by raising doubts without necessarily giving evidence. An example occurred during the 2004 presidential race, when Vice President Dick Cheney cast doubt on whether Senator John Kerry (who was awarded two Purple Hearts for his bravery in combat during the Vietnam War) was strong enough to fight terrorism, and asserted that the nation might one day face terrorists "in the middle of one of our cities with deadlier weapons than have ever before been used against us," including a nuclear bomb.[83]

Misrepresenting a Person's Position and Presenting It in a Form That People Will Reject. In 2004, Bush characterized Kerry's healthcare plan as a government program that would lead to rationing. Despite Kerry's denials, Bush persisted in repeating this mischaracterization.

Taking an Opponent's Words Out of Context. Campaign teams routinely comb through comments of their opponents to find comments that can be damaging when taken out of context. At one point during the 2004 campaign, Kerry declared, "I believe I can fight a more effective, more thoughtful, more strategic, more proactive, more *sensitive* war on terror." Vice President Dick Cheney then lifted the word "sensitive" out of this statement, declaring, "President Lincoln and General Grant did not wage sensitive warfare, nor did President Roosevelt, nor Generals Eisenhower and MacArthur." By taking Kerry's statement out of context, Cheney was able to depict Kerry as unmanly (in contrast with Bush's macho persona).

Bold assertions are terms that are employed when politicians make pronouncements without sufficient evidence. Eleanor MacLean cautions, "Words like 'unquestionably' and 'indisputably' should be looked at very closely, as should such expressions as 'But the truth' is or 'The fact is'.... Can such statements be proven?"[84]

Evading the Question. In formats such as debates and press conferences, a reporter has only one opportunity to ask a question. This enables politicians to evade the question or respond with a non-answer—that is, a response that does not properly address the question. For instance, during the third debate of the 2004 election, Bush was asked a question about minimum wage. Bush immediately moved the question to a discussion on education.

However, when reporters find themselves bullied by politicians, they can take advantage of this unique relationship between politicians and the media—that the politicians also depend upon the press. To illustrate, in 2002, reporters began "silent treatment" during a presidential press conference, forcing spokesperson Ari Fleischer to address an issue that he had been avoiding. Mark Halperin explains,

> The other day, something remarkable happened in the White House press room during spokesman Ari Fleischer's briefing: restraint.
>
> The issue on every reporter's mind was the same. Did the president really mean it when he said that the Democrat-controlled Senate was "not interested in the security of the American people?".... Mr. Fleischer arrived knowing he would be grilled on the president's comments. And he faced a difficult choice: repudiate his boss's words or stand by a statement that seemed at odds with the message of bipartisan cooperation the president has tried to convey.
>
> Of course, Mr. Fleischer also knew he had a way out if his carefully calibrated answer was not well received. When press secretaries get into trouble with the questions of one reporter, they turn to other reporters who, eager to get in their own questions or to secure an on-camera moment, raise their hands, shout and do whatever else is required to steal the floor. Another question is asked, the moment is forgotten and the press secretary gallops free.
>
> For many years, White House reporters have often undermined themselves and their cause by interrupting a colleague who may be closing in on the truth or, at least, on a nonanswer for the public record.... But now, just maybe, this era is coming to an end.

The reporter who took part in this landmark moment was Ron Fournier, of The Associated Press, who was invited by Mr. Fleischer to ask the first question. Mr. Fournier inquired about the president's intentions. "Did he misspeak," Mr. Fournier asked, "or does he really believe that Democrats are not interested in the security of the American people?"

Anticipating the issue, Mr. Fleischer gave an answer that some in Washington would call a nonresponsive response. I'm certain there were reporters in the room who thought they could ask the question in a clever way that would have compelled Mr. Fleischer to go beyond his talking points. But instead of interrupting Mr. Fournier and giving Mr. Fleischer a way out, they sat in silence.

Mr. Fournier continued, going back and forth with Mr. Fleischer, with four more versions of the same question. In the end, Mr. Fleischer never really answered directly whether Mr. Bush stood by those controversial words or not. But a point had been made.[85]

Shifting the argument. This rhetorical technique depends on the limited attention span of the audience. To illustrate, the Bush administration's rationale for the war in Iraq shifted several times:

- Iraq possessed Weapons of Mass Destruction
- Saddam's complicity in the attack of 9/11
- Bringing democracy to Iraq
- Saddam was an evil man
- Fighting in Iraq will prevent terrorism in the United States

Downplaying the Evidence. When faced with incriminating evidence, one approach is to minimize its importance by downplaying potentially damaging evidence. To illustrate, in October 2004, there were news reports that after the American invasion of Baghdad, a cache of explosives was missing. These explosives were powerful enough to shatter airplanes or tear apart buildings. In fact, the bomb that brought down Pan Am Flight 103 over Lockerbie, Scotland in 1988 used less than one pound of this type of material. However, Bush spokesperson Scott McClellen minimized its significance, saying that the stockpile contained "no nuclear materials."

Using Incriminating Evidence to Support Their Own Position. In October 2004, the Atomic Energy Commission released its definitive report on the status of weapons in Iraq, concluding that Iraq's weapons capabilities had actually *declined* since the first Gulf War; in other words, the sanctions had been working. However, the Bush administration claimed that the report actually vindicated their actions, citing one passage in the lengthy report that noted that Saddam entertained *intentions* about weapons of mass destruction; if he could have produced weapons, he probably would have.

Attacking the Person, Not the Argument is often used to circumvent the reasoning behind an opponent's position. Much of the focus on character attacks is an effort to discredit the political positions of the opponent. For instance, in 2003, Richard Clarke, chief of counter-terrorism on the U.S. National Security Council in the George W. Bush administration, criticized the war in Iraq. In response, presidential spokespeople questioned Clarke's motives, charging that he was promoting his new book.

Language Collectives are a form of personification, which ascribe human qualities to a large, all-encompassing organization or entity (e.g., "the Supreme Court said today," or "the White House claimed ..."). However, it is impossible for an organization to talk or express remorse. This misuse of language sends several messages to readers. First, language collectives make absolute claims, overlooking individual dissent or disagreement among people within the organization. In addition, language collectives invest the organization with an aura of authority.

Qualifiers are words or phrases that modify the meaning of the sentence. The use of qualifiers is designed to subtly introduce doubt in a statement. To illustrate, in January 2005, the U.S. military mistakenly dropped a 500-pound bomb on a house outside the northern city of Mosul, Iraq, killing 14 people, including seven children. The U.S. issued the following statement: The house was not the intended target for the air strike.... Multi-National Force Iraq deeply regrets the loss of *possibly* (italics mine) innocent lives." The use of the qualifier undermines the apology by raising doubts about the guilt of those killed in the attack.[86]

Implied Agreement. This technique uses future verb tense to suggest past agreement. To illustrate, in 2006, Representative Peter Hoekstra of Michigan, the Republican chairman of the House Intelligence Committee, sent a letter to President Bush, charging that the administration may have violated the law by failing to inform Congress of some secret intelligence programs. Administration officials subtly framed their responses in a way that refuted the charges against them:

> White House spokesman Frederick Jones: "We *will continue* to work closely with the chairman and other Congressional leaders on important national security issues." (italics mine)
>
> Carl Kropf, a spokesman for National Intelligence Chief John Negroponte: "We value this dialogue with Congress, and we will *continue* to provide the committee with the information they need to fulfill their responsibilities." (italics mine)
>
> Jennifer Millerwise Dyck, a spokeswoman for General Hayden: "The director believes in the important oversight role Congress plays, and he *will continue* regular and transparent interactions with members."(italics mine)[87]

The use of the verbs "will continue" subtly denies the charges by suggesting that the administration has complied with the law in the past, dodging any statement of disagreement.

Hasty Generalizations refer to a technique in which people make assertions based on only a few unrepresentative samplings, arguing that what may be true in one or more specific instances holds true for all cases. MacLean provides an example:

> If someone says, "Both Bill and Terry were on the first string basketball team; therefore both their younger brothers will probably also be stars," this person has jumped to a conclusion. The generalization is based on only two examples. Besides, human beings are too complex to be reduced to many generalizations: they often differ as much within a family as not.[88]

Affective Response. Many media messages delivered by politicians are designed to touch the emotions of the average citizen. Formal media rituals, such as the inauguration, press conferences, and the State of the Union Address, inspire feelings of awe and respect for the members of the government. And as mentioned earlier, the selective recitation of facts only stir feelings of confusion among the electorate.

Media consultant Tony Schwartz claims that the most effective political campaigns are directed at emotions—what he calls the "deep sell." Schwartz uses the public as his "workforce." He first conducts polls to identify their feelings about the candidates and the issues. Then he designs messages that tap into these preexisting emotions. In this sense, political ads do not educate, as much as they evoke an intended response.[89]

Affective Response in Political Advertising. Political advertising is designed to elicit an emotional response by the voters as a way of shaping their attitudes and voting decisions. Political TV spots frequently offer only the *appearance* (or image) of issues. To illustrate, although many political ads refer to issues, only relatively few outline a specific position on these issues. Most of the spots make issues out of emotionally laden themes.

Political ads may be directed at a range of *positive* emotions.

Reassurance appeals promote a sense of confidence about the present. As media consultant Roger Ailes observed, "The candidate who makes the public most secure will win."[90]

Patriotic ads reinforce our faith in our way of life and inspire a sense of pride in who we are.

Ads for candidates are often designed to inspire *hope* in the audience. Listening to a speech by George W. Bush in February 2000, Ellen Goodman commented, " I counted the word 'hope' until I ran out of fingers."[91]

However, political campaigns may also tap into a wellspring of *negative* emotions, including anger, frustrations, and dissatisfactions as a way of marshaling their support. Political ads tap into a range of *fears* and *insecurities:*

Fear of Annihilation. Both political parties use fear to sway voters. To illustrate, in 2006, the Republican National Committee sponsored a political ad in Tennessee attacking Representative Harold Ford that features pictures of fighter planes and control towers, as an ominous voice intones: "The threats are out there. The responsibility is clear. Knowing who the terrorists are and where they are is the only way to keep us safe."

At the same time, the Democratic Party produced a series of ads that played on the public's fears about the War on Terror and President Bush's claim that the Republican Party was stronger on national security issues. A video on the Democratic Senatorial Campaign Committee's web site called attention to the increase in terror attacks around the world. The ad showed footage of Osama bin Laden, highlighted illegal immigration, and pointed out the nuclear threat presented by Iran and North Korea, while making the point that Americans are less safe as a result of Republican policies. The Democrats then offered themselves as the political party that would provide protection and reassurance in this dark world. The ad concludes, "Feel safer? Vote for change."[92]

Fear of Change. Another common approach exploits the voter's anxiety about the future. David D. Kirkpatrick describes a 2006 congressional election, a campaign spot for Representative Heather A. Wilson (R) which emphasized the risks involved in making a change to her opponent, Patricia Madrid:

> In the spot, images of fire mutate momentarily into floating fragments of text before dissolving again into flames: "North Korea conducts nuclear tests. Reductions in military spending. The murder of any American anywhere on earth." As a picture of the North Korean dictator, Kim Jong Il, gives way to an unflattering photo of Ms. Madrid, a narrator asks: "Can we trust her? With so much at stake? Does she have the experience we need? In a world like this, is she the one who will keep our families safe? Patricia Madrid. Don't take the risk."[93]

The message essentially was that even if the voter wasn't satisfied with Wilson's overall performance, at least she was a known quantity.

A variation on this theme raises questions about presidential succession in cases in which a vice-presidential candidate is not highly regarded. For instance, a 1968 Democratic spot focused on Richard Nixon's running mate, simply featured the graphic, (Spiro) "Agnew for President," accompanied by uproarious laughter. At the conclusion, a voice-over commented, "This would be funny if it wasn't so serious."

Disenchantment with Status Quo. At the same time, voting for a change can be an empowering act for the electorate—particularly when they are dissatisfied with current conditions. Even if the politicians are not responsible for a situation, the voters can derive some satisfaction from "throwing the bums out." Thus, in the 2006 Senate race in Missouri, one of the campaign slogans employed by challenger Claire McCaskill against incumbent Jim Talent was: "Talent: It's Time for a Change."

Fear of Differences. Political ads may play upon our basic mistrust of differences in American culture. As author George Orwell pointed out in *1984*, an enemy is a very useful political device, providing a target for anger and a way of uniting the country.

During the 2006 Tennessee Senate campaign, race, a political ad financed by the Republican National Committee exploited racial fears to marshal support against the Democratic challenger, Harold E. Ford Jr. an African American. The spot consisted of a series of people in mock man-on-the street interviews talking sarcastically about Mr. Ford and his stands on issues including the estate tax and national security. One of these "interviews" featured an attractive white woman, bare-shouldered, who declared that she met Mr. Ford at a "Playboy party," and closed the commercial by looking into the camera, saying, with a wink, "Harold, call me." (Mr. Ford, who is single, was one of 3,000 people who had attended a Playboy party at the Super Bowl the previous year in Jacksonville, Florida.) According to Hilary Shelton, director of the NAACP's Washington bureau, the spot took aim at the sensitivities many Americans still have about interracial dating.[94]

Mistrust of Politicians. One constant political theme is based on the notion that whoever is in office is corrupt, and that only outsiders can reform the system. For instance, in 2007, former Massachusetts governor Mitt Romney, a Republican, declared that his status as a Washington outsider gave him an advantage as he sought his party's nomination for president: "I do not believe Washington can be transformed from within by a lifelong politician. There have been too many deals, too many favors, too many entanglements and too little real world experience managing, guiding, leading."[95]

MEDIA LITERACY TIPS

AFFECTIVE CAMPAIGN STRATEGIES

Anthony Pratkanis makes the following recommendations for critical analysis of *affective campaign strategies:*

- *Keep track of your emotions while viewing the ad.*
- *Ask yourself, "Why am I feeling (this way) now?"*
- *If you feel yourself getting manipulated this way, turn off the ad.*[96]

Implicit Content. The media have been criticized for a lack of sustained coverage of issues. This in part can be attributed to the "scoop" mentality of the press. Criminology professor Richard Rosenfeld characterizes the coverage of crime in the media as "anecdotal," without important context or long-term trends that put the information into perspective.[97] Lee Lescaze, reporter for the *Washington Post*, maintained that a story must be followed with some consistency in order to be considered important by the public: "When you've got a good story, you've got to run it more than once in a while. You can't just say it once ... because the White House writes its story every day."[98]

Further, the press often fails to draw connections between events or emphasize the consequences of political decisions. Mark Hertsgaard sees this as a lack of sufficient understanding of issues on the part of the media. For instance, Hertsgaard charges the press with "borderline economic illiteracy" in its coverage of Reagan's economic program. Reporters were incapable of grasping the full implications of "trickle-down economics" and could not even raise the critical questions which would lead to a thorough understanding of the issue they were covering.[99]

Genre: Political Advertising

Political advertising is a very influential form of discourse—particularly among young people. As a result, political ads can establish the agenda for both the media and the public through sheer saturation. Political advertising dominates news coverage by a ratio of five to one.[100]

Although only 19 percent of Americans say they are not influenced by campaign commercials, the public's understanding of many issues are, in fact, shaped by these ads. For instance, a 2004 survey found that the majority of voters believed inaccurate charges made in political ads during the presidential campaign: 61 percent of respondents accept as true the Kerry ads accusing Bush "of favoring sending American jobs overseas," and 56 percent believed Bush's ads that declared that Kerry "voted for higher taxes 350 times." But although both of those statements were repeated endlessly in campaign ads, neither is accurate.[101]

The functions of a political ad are:

- *To promote name recognition of the candidate*
- *To convince the uncommitted*
- *To give those who are committed the impetus to vote*
- *To present a positive, consistent image*
- *To produce and maintain the enthusiasm of the voters* [102]

Political ads share many of the defining characteristics of product advertising. Ads must be striking and dramatic in order to build name recognition for the candidate. In addition, political ads strive to appeal to the self-interest of the electorate, which can be particularly challenging in a mass market. Politicians make generous use of inclusive pronouns (e.g., wanting to see "*our* kids get ahead") to underscore that they share their constituents' values and concerns.

Political advertising can be considered as a genre, with distinct and recognizable functions, plots, characters, structure, and conventions. This genre has become so formulaic that media consultant Charles Guggenheim complained that he was "disenchanted" with what he called the "cookie-cutter" approach to producing political spots: "They take a technique that works in one state and apply it in another, changing only the name of the candidate."[103]

The structure of the political ad generally falls within the formula of order/chaos/order. From the relative serenity that the audience experiences before the appearance of the ad, a problem is introduced: inflation, despair, the inadequacies of the opposition. The candidate then is presented as a solution to the problem.

Due in part to their brevity, ads often rely on stereotypes, which are shortcuts that generally present an oversimplified and distorted depiction of a group of people. An anecdote can provide insight into the role of stereotypes in political advertising. Jane Squier Bruns relates a story in which her son Mark Squier, also a media consultant, told her about an upcoming project—a political spot for the Democratic Party designed to raise concerns about the Republicans' policy on Medicare. The commercial included visuals of a grandmother tending her infant grandson, while the voice-over declared that Republican initiatives would jeopardize the healthcare of both the young (the baby) and old (the grandmother). Squier told his mother that his newborn daughter Emma was being cast as the infant. Bruns, a vibrant, attractive woman who is also an actress, immediately volunteered to play the role of the grandmother. Squier responded that she "didn't look the part" of the grandmother. Bruns responded, "But Mark, I *am* the grandmother!" Instead, the role of the grandmother was played by an elderly, frumpy woman who wore a drab housedress. Ironically, Bruns was not cast for the part because she did not fit the stereotypical image of a grandmother—even though she is Emma's actual grandma.[104]

Significantly, ads often stereotype the target audience, reflecting the attitudes of the candidates toward their constituents. As an example, author Charles Baxter comments on the Minnesota 2004 Senate race between Amy Klobuchar (D) and Mark Kennedy (R):

> One such warm-and-fuzzy ad is instructive. In a staged conversation between a little old lady on a park bench and Mr. Kennedy, the Republican challenger is pestered with questions about why he keeps accusing Ms. Klobuchar of so many faults. "Because they're true," he says plaintively.
>
> What's interesting about the ad is not the predictable subject matter. It's that the little old lady is straight out of Fargo—not the city in North Dakota, but the film by the Coen brothers. She wears a hideous pink cardigan sweater, a mismatched blouse, bright purple slacks and drugstore reading glasses. The actress playing the little old lady gives her a broad Minnesota accent, along with a slight dental-plate lisp. The ad is funny, but what is satirized, or plainly mocked, is the intelligence of the electorate.[105]

Conventions such as business suits signify legitimacy, competence, and seriousness. Less formal attire, such as shirtsleeves, indicates a common bond with the people and a sympathy with their circumstances. But in many cases, these conventions have become, in the words of Charles Baxter, "'tiresome clichés': the black background, the outraged voice-over, the accusations, the snow-infested distorted image of the opponent."[106]

MEDIA LITERACY TIPS

STAGES OF CAMPAIGN ADVERTISING

Edwin Diamond and Stephen Bates have identified four stages of campaign advertising:

- *Phase One: ID Spots*
  The first stage of an advertising strategy is designed to instill the name of the candidate in the public consciousness. For instance, a 1978 ad for Paul Tsongas humorously featured children mispronouncing the name of the candidate as a means of insuring name recognition.
- *Phase Two: Argument Spots*
  This stage is intended to distinguish the candidate from others in the race; what a candidate stands for. However ... these "position ads" are often vague, slogan ads, in which the candidate expresses an emotional response toward an issue.
- *Phase Three: Attack*
  After the candidate has been defined and promoted, it is time to tear down the opposition.
- *Phase Four: "I see an America"*

The last stage of a political campaign typically presents the candidate as dignified, thoughtful, and reflective—beginning to act the part of the elected official.[107]

According to Jane Squier Bruns, the production of the political ad has become significantly more sophisticated since the 1952 Eisenhower-Stevenson presidential election:

> Technically speaking, it's evolved tremendously. We no longer see sixty second spots. We used to do five minute spots. You just don't see those anymore. The kind of production values you see today are very different. You're into the whole glitzy thing. [Political spots] now take a stricter advertising approach.[108]

Because of the improvements in technology, campaigns can immediately produce political ads in response to historical events and daily occurrences. For instance, a 2004 ad for George W. Bush featured a moving testimonial by a young girl whose mother had been a victim of the 9/11 attack. Indeed, political ads assume many of the characteristics of a dialogue, as candidates respond to criticisms, recent events, and the political ads of their opponents.

Subgenres. A number of formats—subgenres, if you will—have emerged in political advertising:

- *Humor* is an effective approach to making messages memorable. In addition, ridicule is a socially acceptable means of undermining the accomplishments of an opponent.
- Research reveals that "Man in the Street" *testimonial* ads generate the highest audience recall of all standard formats. Audience members respond to the sincerity and genuine quality of average citizens. The testimonial is an effective way to influence specific blocks of voters. This approach flatters its audience, inferring that their opinions (and votes) matter. As a result, a TV spot featuring the testimony of an elderly woman may have a significant impact on this subculture.
- A variation of the testimonial is the *just folks* ad, in which actors, playing average citizens, give a grassroots quality to the messages crafted by politicians and their staffs. To illustrate, in 1993–1994, the insurance industry launched a series of television ads featuring a fictitious couple, "Harry and Louise," that helped defeat Bill Clinton's universal health care proposal. In the ads, these "folks" sat around their kitchen table, commenting that Clinton's plan was too complex and bureaucratic.
- As in advertising, political spots borrow heavily from established television genres. The most striking example of these *TV parodies* is broadcast news: "Walter DeVries, for instance, is a believer in the 'news look' format, enhancing credibility by presenting political advertisements as mini-documentaries or press conferences, with nonpartisan, factual deliveries sometimes depicting the candidate in the role of an inquiring television news reporter."[109]

  Political ads which parody game shows and sporting events tap into the common understanding and experience of the audience. And in some respects, political ad campaigns unintentionally have evolved into soap operas, since they are ongoing, episodic, and deal with character issues familiar to this genre: betrayal, romance, and credibility.

Negative Ads. Although the *negative ad* has been receiving a great deal of attention in recent elections, historian Thomas V. DiBacco reports that negative campaigning has long been a part of the American political process.

> No campaign was filthier than that of 1884, when Democrat Grover Cleveland was accused of fathering an illegitimate child and the GOP's James Blaine of being on the take. Republicans rushed to make up their verse about the wayward candidate: "Ma, Ma, Where's My Pa?" But Democrats responded, "Gone to the White House, Ha! Ha! Ha!"[110]

However, in recent years, political campaigns have relied more on these negative ads. Campaign staffs routinely include a team of Opposition Research Specialists, who dig for damaging information on opponents which can be used in the campaign. In the past, candidates would resort to negative ads only if they were behind in the latter stages of the campaign. Today, negative ads can be employed from the very beginning of a race, regardless of where the candidate stands in the polls. Negative ads are designed to produce an affective response against the opponent. The objective of attack ads is not so much to convince the audience as to introduce doubt in their minds about the charges being made. Charles Baxter observes that, with negative ads, "You are not really being informed; you are, like a child witnessing a divorce, being asked to take sides."[111] Negative ads also are designed to put opponents in a defensive position, disrupting their ability to communicate their positions on issues, as they must spend their time denying allegations.

Ironically, although the public does not approve of negative ads, they tend to remember them more readily than less-controversial positive commercials.[112] However, this approach is not without risk. The "accuser" may alienate the voters by appearing petty and mean-spirited; people do not like a tattletale. Indeed, the use of negative ads often discourages voter turnout. In order to avoid voter backlash in the face of the public's disapproval of negative advertising, candidates have devised a number of indirect negative ad strategies. Darrell West explains, "The trick is to attach negative information to your opponent without being blamed for having gone negative."[113]

Using an opponent's own words or record against him (or her) absolves the candidate of direct responsibility. For instance, a 1960 ad for John F. Kennedy featured a film clip of President Eisenhower responding to a question about what policy contributions Vice President Nixon made to his administration. Eisenhower quipped, "I don't know.... If you give me a week, I might think of one." This off-hand statement by Nixon's boss was far more damaging than anything the Democrats could cook up.

Another technique involves letting surrogates play the heavy. As a former staff member for George W. Bush explained, "The advantage of speaking through a surrogate was that we could say sulfurous things about our opponent and put that on record without our candidate taking personal responsibility for it."[114] During the 2004 presidential race, a campaign by the Swift boat veterans who served with young Lieutenant Kerry was designed to discredit John Kerry's military service. Although these accusations were shown to be baseless, the media coverage of this smear campaign raised doubts among the electorate.

Another strategy exploits negative media commentary about opponents. During the 1992 presidential election, the George H. W. Bush campaign used a cover of *Time* magazine which asked the question "Why Don't Voters Trust Clinton?" Time/Warner Corporation sued the Bush campaign in an effort to stop the ad, claiming that the Bush people had not received permission to use the cover and that the spot misrepresented the contents of the related article.

A variation of this strategy occurs when candidates *first* leak information to the press and *then* simply quote what was reported in the media. Jane Squier comments,

> I wouldn't say it's a common, run-of-the-mill thing but, sure, it's done.... I've been in a situation where that very thing happened in a campaign on which I was working, and the debate was whether or not to do that. And it was finally shot down. It was decided not to do that—but it was considered. And there are certainly campaigns where that decision is the reverse.[115]

Finally, because the public has become uncomfortable with the use of negative advertising, a candidate can paint an opponent in a negative light by decrying their use of negative campaign tactics. Ramesh Ponnuru explains, "The method is simple: Call the other guy a dirty-trick artist; then shake your head sorrowfully about name-calling. The beauty of this self-serving accusation is that one can look altruistic while making it."[116]

Production Elements

In political communications, sophisticated production techniques generally can clarify ideas, issues, and positions. But according to Kathleen Hall Jamieson, production values can also be used to *undermine* the electorate's ability to evaluate political messages:

> By flooding us with words, sounds, and images, these stimuli reduce the time that we have to respond and overload our analytic capacity. With that reduction comes a lessened ability to dispute the offered material, a lessened ability to counterargue. Once these defenses are gone, a persuasive message that might otherwise have been challenged or rejected can slip by. Persuasion without benefit of analytic scrutiny of the message is the result.[117]

Editing. *Inclusion and Omission.* The amount of attention focused on politics by the news media can be indicative of its level of interest in the subject matter. At the same time, the amount of attention devoted in the media to politics reinforces and shapes the interest level of the audience. Thus, it is notable that in the month leading up to the 2004 presidential election, local television stations devoted eight times as much air time to car crashes and other accidents than to campaigns for the House of Representatives, state senate, city hall, and other local offices. Indeed, in the month before the Washington State gubernatorial election, 95 percent of the television newscasts in the Seattle market failed to carry any reports on the race.[118]

Given the time and space limitations of the news media, it is generally difficult to include all of the content of a political speech on the six o'clock news or in the newspaper. Consequently, news presentations extract a brief *soundbite* from a longer speech to bring pertinent information to the attention of the public. Throughout the years, the press has selected soundbites for the public; for instance, Franklin Roosevelt's famous line "The only thing to fear is fear itself" had been embedded in a longer address. Recently, however, the emphasis on the soundbite has become more pronounced. John Tierney explains, "The public's attention span is inexorably shrinking in the age of MTV, which forces anyone in search of an audience—television producers, newspaper reporters, politicians—to deliver shorter, punchier quotes."[119]

Indeed, speechwriters are now composing with soundbites in mind. Speeches are constructed around memorable, concise statements which present an idea or attitude in capsule form. Kathleen Hall Jamieson declares that voters should think carefully about messages contained in the soundbite: "It's quite possible to state a coherent position in a few seconds.... The problem with sound bits is that the one chosen for the news often doesn't have any substance."[120]

Editing Techniques. Editing techniques are generally employed to insure that the audience clearly receives the intended messages in political ads. At times, however, editing *conceals* significant information about a candidate. One famous example involved the 1964 re-election campaign of Senator Clair Engle:

> Despite recent brain surgery that had left him with a paralyzed arm and greatly deteriorated verbal and ambulatory skills, his consultants repeatedly filmed and, with difficulty, constructed a forty-two second commercial in which Engle, appearing perfectly healthy, announced his candidacy for a second term. The deception went off with only one hitch; Engle died before the primary.[121]

Creative editing has also been employed in negative ads to slander an opponent. In the 1996 senate race in Virginia, incumbent John W. Warner released a television ad accusing challenger Mark R. Warner of cavorting with "the nation's most liberal politicians." In the spot, Warner is shown shaking hands with the liberal former governor of Virginia, L. Douglas Wilder, as President Clinton stands between them, smiling. However, this handshake never occurred. Instead, Senator Warner's media team had digitally superimposed Mark Warner's face onto the body of Senator Charles Robb.

In television coverage of political events, the selection of visuals is a subtle yet powerful way to convey messages. Political staffers provide copies of speeches in advance, as well as seating charts, to make it easy for producers to coordinate images with the speech. For instance, during his acceptance speech at the Republican convention in 2004, George W. Bush presented plans to improve healthcare coverage and social security. TV directors choreographed Bush's comments with images of senior citizens in the crowd waving "Bush for President" placards. Robert Schmidt notes, "Behind the scenes, network producers and directors make editorial judgments about what to show while the president speaks. The goal is partly to entertain viewers, and partly to provide editorial context."[122]

Color. It should come as no surprise that the most common background colors employed in American politics are red, white, and blue. In addition

Figure 14.1
Digital photography has made visual manipulation in political ads almost undetectable. In this photo from the 1996 Virginia Senate race, candidate Mark Warner is shown shaking hands with "liberal" former governor Douglas L. Wilder. In reality, Wilder's face was electronically interchanged with someone else's. Photograph courtesy of Mark Squier.

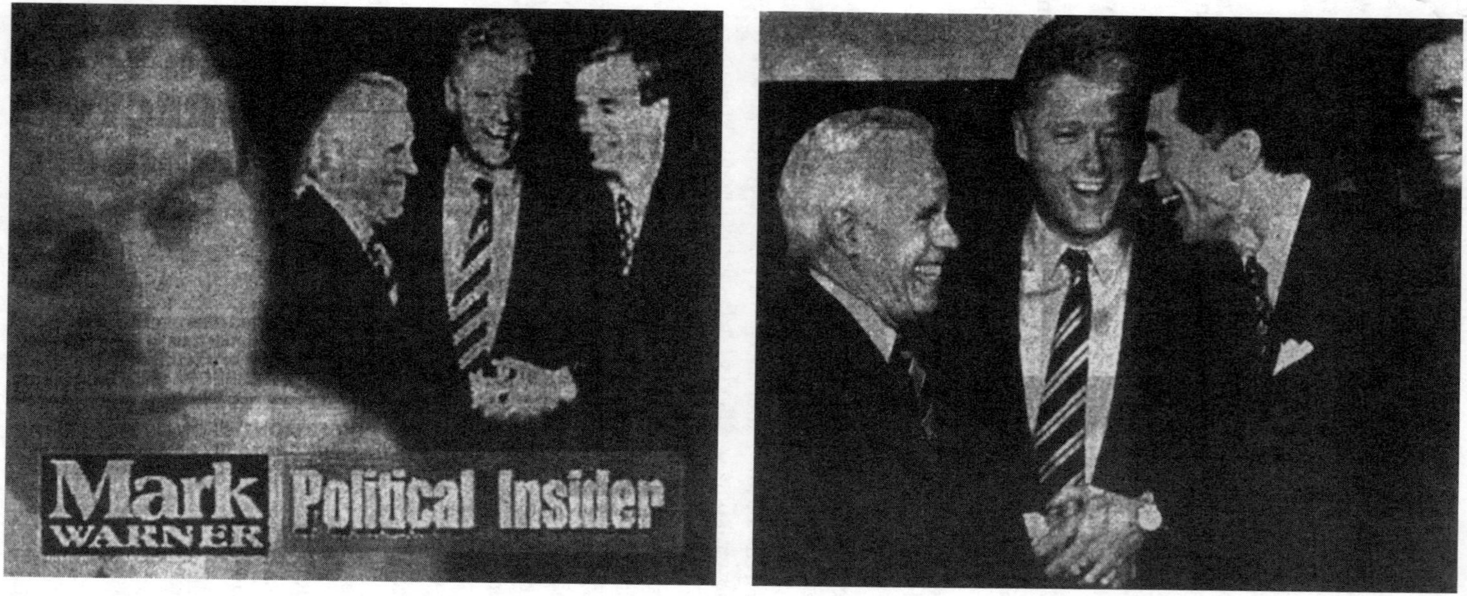

to their patriotic connotation, these warm, uplifting colors evoke positive feelings in the audience. Bright colors are also common to positive political ads.

In contrast, dark colors are frequently employed in negative advertising. One common technique consists of a "dead shot." A black-and-white photograph of the candidate's opponent, often shrouded in a black frame, is inserted into the colorful ad, providing a stark visual contrast between the two candidates.[123]

Scale. In American politics, height is often associated with power and authority. As a result, political consultants manipulate the environment to give their clients the appearance of stature. For instance, a campaign spot for diminutive John Tower of Texas was filmed in an old, reconstructed Senate Chamber, using tiny furniture to make him appear larger.[124]

Relative Position. The placement of stories sends distinct messages about political figures. For instance, on January 21, 2007, the *New York Times* carried a front-page story on Senator Hillary Clinton's announcement that she intended to run for president of the United States. At the same time, at the bottom of page 25, there was a story that Senator Sam Brownback declared *his* candidacy for the presidency. The relative placement of these two stories conveys the clear message that Senator Clinton is the more serious candidate.

Movement. Movement suggests a sense of direction, purpose, and leadership. This might explain why political ads depict politicians walking in the woods, busily engaged in legislation, and interacting with citizens.

Proximity of the Camera. In political advertisements, the proximity of the camera can promote feelings of familiarity and trust with the audience. Close-up shots of the candidates create the illusion that we know the candidate well, and inspire public confidence, suggesting that they have nothing to hide. During the 2000 presidential campaign, the ads of George W. Bush emphasized close-ups of the candidate, with the camera moving even closer as he spoke. In contrast, most of Al Gore's ads featured medium or wide-angle shots of the vice president. This production decision contributed to the impression that Bush was, indeed, a "compassionate conservative," while Gore was cold and stiff.

Angle. Political communications make use of angle in presenting media messages. The camera is often tilted up at candidates in a gesture to evoke feelings of respect and competence. For instance, a 1992 campaign ad for Bill Clinton featured the testimony of factory workers who had been laid off after years of service. These workers expressed their personal frustration with the economic policies of the Bush administration. The camera is directed up at the workers, which suggested that Clinton took them (and their problems) seriously. The camera style thus reinforced Clinton's campaign theme of "people first."

Word Choice

Because of the extraordinary power of language, politicians must be careful to select words that have the greatest impact on their audience. To illustrate, after the events of 9/11, George W. Bush addressed an international audience, proclaiming that "this crusade, this war on terrorism, is going to take a while." In 2007, Ye Xiaowen, director of China's State Bureau of Religious Affairs, denounced U.S. President George W. Bush's use of the word "crusade" to describe the War on Terrorism, contending that this term turned the war on terrorism into a religious war.[125] William Safire explains,

> (Crusade) has a religious root, meaning "taking the cross," and was coined in the 11th century to describe the first military expedition of the Crusaders, European Christians sent to recover the Holy Land from the followers of Muhammad.... In this case, a word that has traditionally been used to rally Americans was mistakenly used in the context of opposing a radical Muslim faction, and the White House spokesman promptly apologized.[126]

The implications of this choice of words are considerable. In political wars such as World War I and II, winners and losers were declared, and in both cases, the victors helped in the reconstruction of the defeated countries. But religious wars such as the Crusades last until the enemy is completely eliminated or converted.

Other lines of inquiry involving language can also provide insight into the construction of political media messages. Examining the *frequency* with which particular words in the media appear can furnish perspective into the themes that the communications team has decided to emphasize. As an example, in his speech accepting the Democratic nomination for the 2004 presidential election, John Kerry used the word "strength" 17 times, which is indicative of the Kerry campaign's decision to dispel the public sentiment that Democrats are the weaker on the issues of defense and security. Indeed, a word-frequency count of the speeches delivered during the first three days of the conventions showed that "strong" and "strength" were used 141 times. "Hope" came in a distant, but strong, second, with 98 mentions. "Values" came in third at 89.[127]

In addition, word choice can be used to define (or re-define) a position, person, or issue. To illustrate, the term *commander in chief* was only occasionally used to describe the president of the United States until the administration of George W. Bush. The reliance on this term by the Bush administration can be traced back to May 2, 2003, when President Bush, in pilot gear, landed a fighter jet on the USS *Abraham Lincoln* to announce "Mission Accomplished" in Iraq. The exterior of the plane was marked with "Navy 1" in the back and "George W. Bush Commander-in-Chief" just below the cockpit window.

The term "commander" suggests unlimited authority and power. The definition of "to command" is "To have control or authority over; to dominate; to demand obedience on the part of the person or group addressed." This characterization of the presidency as autocratic authority was reinforced by the invention of another term by Bush, when he declared, "I'm the *decider.*"[128]

The usage of this term has an ideological context which is rooted in the administration's belief in a strong executive branch of the government. In contrast, a alternative synonym, *chief executive* is derived from the word "execute," which means "to carry out, or put into effect." Thus, instead of the president simply being an executive who carries out the law of the land, he is a commander who exercises authority and control over the law. The use of "commander in chief" by the Bush administration also is designed to remind the public that the United States is at war, which gives the president wide-ranging authority.

The news media frequently adopts the vernacular of a politician's communications team, which promotes their agenda. For instance, CNN.com ran a story about the president's landing on the aircraft carrier, using the headline "Commander in Chief lands on USS Lincoln."[129]

At times, however, the word choice of politicians can backfire. As an example, in 2006, President Bush adopted the term "Stay the Course" to describe his approach to the Iraq war. At the same time, Bush used the term "Cut and Run" to define his opponents' argument for a phased withdrawal from Iraq. However, linguist George Lakoff notes that in the face of the loss of American lives and without evidence of progress in the war the president became trapped by the metaphor: "To keep staying the course, given obvious reality, is to get deeper into disaster in Iraq, while not staying the course is to abandon one's moral authority as a conservative. Either way, the president loses."[130]

Examining word choice can be an effective way to gauge the political ideology of the communicator.

Connotative words contain associated meanings that transcend the literal, dictionary definition. As applied to political communications, connotative terms fall into several categories:

- *Traditional vernacular* like "home" and "family" respond to the public's thirst for stability and meaning, given the uncertainties of contemporary culture. As such, these words are thrown around generously by politicians.
- *War rhetoric* has been applied to a variety of issues, from the "War on Drugs" to the "War on Terror." These references to war suggest a sense of mission, clear heroes and villains, and glory. At the same time, however, war rhetoric suggests a recognizable end goal, which can lead to public frustration when the situation is actually an ongoing struggle.
- *Drug rhetoric* is a very powerful metaphor to describe any social or political ill. To be "hooked" on anything conjures up images of immorality, dependency, and weakness on the part of the abuser.

- *Patriotic jargon* has always been a staple in American politics. Every politician wants to reassure their constituents that they love their country.
- Although the Constitution guarantees separation of church and state, it is always a good bet to interject *religious rhetoric* into political speeches wherever possible.
- Words that *demonize* the enemy are a time-honored way to mount public opinion against one's adversaries. As an example, in a LexisNexis search over a one-month period (December 21, 2006–January 21, 2007), over 125 North American newspapers compared Iranian President Mahmoud Ahmadinejad to Adolf Hitler.
- The *sports vernacular* in politics often reflects the male-dominated perspective of American culture. For instance, the coverage of political life often assumes the character of sporting events, with "front-runners" and "knock-out blows." Moreover, this macho vernacular suggests that political leadership ability is defined by who is the biggest and strongest.
- *Euphemisms* refer to neutral terms that are employed to minimize the impact of potentially damaging information. To illustrate, the term "extraordinary rendition" is a term used to describe a process in which the U.S. kidnaps a suspect and transports him to a country like Syria or Libya, where the individual may be tortured and kept indefinitely in total secrecy.

Indeed, political euphemisms frequently are not merely neutral but, in fact, suggest a meaning that is diametrically opposed to the actual policies. For example, *assisted feeding* describes techniques used to force nutrients into prisoners at Guantanamo Prison who had gone into hunger strikes to protest conditions. And *extraordinary rendition* describes a process in which the United States kidnaps suspects and transports them to a country like Syria or Libya, where they may be tortured and kept indefinitely in total secret.

Other euphemisms found in political communications include:

- *Degrade*: to bomb
- *Ordinance:* bomb or missile
- *Collateral damage*: civilian casualties
- *Depopulate*: to destroy towns and villages
- *Service the target*: destroy what you are aiming at

Labels are words or phrases that describe a person or group. Labels such as "oil-rich," "arch-conservative," "liberal," and "special interests" often appear with such frequency in the media that they no longer simply *describe* but, in fact, *define* the group. In the process, adjectives (e.g., "liberal") are transformed into nouns ("a liberal").

Labels send very clear signals about candidates and issues. Anthony Pratkanis explains the effectiveness of labels by citing the term *granfaloon*, which was coined by novelist Kurt Vonnegut. A granfaloon creates a we/they sensibility by promoting a false and arbitrary sense of belonging to a group. Pratkanis suggests, "Be wary of anyone who gives you a label; ask, 'Why are they dividing the world up this way?' Do not succumb to hating vague categories of people; rather, think of people as individuals."[131]

Sometimes a label can be used in a positive fashion. For instance, George W. Bush coined the label "compassionate conservative" to attract a new voter base consisting of members of both political parties. The term bridges the usual distinctions between the two political parties, combining the warmth and social concern generally attributed to Democrats with fiscal responsibility, a Republican bedrock.

Code words are terms that contain clear and distinct meaning for a subgroup within the general audience. According to historian Bruce Lincoln, George W. Bush imbeds code words into speeches directed at a general audience that convey particular messages to his conservative political base:

> As president, Bush has always been outspoken about his faith, letting evangelicals know he shares their values and vision for America. But he has also been careful. Aware that he must appeal to the center to secure reelection, he employs double-coded signals that veil much of his religious message from outsiders. Biblical references, allusions to hymns, and specialized vocabulary are keys to this communication.[132]

To illustrate, in July 2005, Bush nominated Judge John Roberts to replace Sandra Day O'Connor in the U.S. Supreme Court. In a statement, Bush emphasized Roberts's qualifications as "one of the best legal minds of his generation.... He's a man of extraordinary accomplishment and ability." But then, Bush added a surprising comment: "(Roberts) has a good heart."[133]

Then in October 2005, Bush was again called upon to fill a vacancy in the Supreme Court, with the retirement of Chief Justice William Rehnquist. His first choice was Harriet Miers, the White House counsel. Bush immediately faced opposition from liberals, as well as conservative groups. Democrats questioned Miers's experience for the position, while members of his evangelical Christian base expressed concern that she was not conservative enough—particularly with regard to her stand on the abortion issue.

Again, in citing her qualifications for the position, Bush declared, "I know her. I know her *heart*."[134] A LexisNexis search of "good heart" AND "Evangelical" disclosed that what eighteenth-century English reformer John Wesley called the "warmed heart" has become a central part of what it means to be evangelical.[135]

Thus, the use of the code word "good heart" was designed to reassure his evangelical conservative base that both Roberts and Miers are people of faith who abide by the religious and moral principles adhered to by evangelicals and who could be counted upon to support the moral principles of the Evangelical church—including the "pro-life" stance on abortion.

MEDIA LITERACY TIPS

CODE WORDS

It sometimes requires a vigilant eye to discern the meaning behind the use of code words commonly employed in political discourse. For instance, American diplomat James A. Kelly described a stormy meeting between the United States and North Korea as "frank but useful"—a term that means "no progress."

The *Glossary of Diplomatic Coverage* provides a definition for the following euphemisms:

- *A frank exchange of views*: Negotiations stopped just short of shouting and table-banging.
- *Making progress, but no breakthrough*: Still talking at cross-purposes.
- *Regret* (verb): To care, but not enough to condemn. ("We regret the loss of life in Sierra Leone. We have no intention of doing anything to stop it, mind you, but we regret that it happened.")
- *A mercurial, colorful, or controversial official*: An off-the-wall wacko.[136]

Connotative Image

In contemporary culture, visual communication has become a primary means of political discourse. Many photographs of politicians appearing in newspapers and magazines are the result of staged photo opportunities. Events such as George W. Bush jogging give photographers the opportunity to snap pictures. As Jane Squier Bruns observes, "The politician's staff asks, 'What would the message be if they took this picture?'"[137]

At times, however, a "photo-op" can backfire, undermining the intended message. In 1988, Democratic candidate Michael Dukakis posed atop a tank as a symbol of his credentials as commander in chief. Instead, observes David Wallis, Dukakis "looked more like a driving instructor than a gunnery sergeant."[138] This gaffe exemplifies former Reagan communications director Michael Deaver's dictum, "Don't use anything that's inconsistent with the candidate or what's being said, or the history and character of the person."[139]

Political connotative images fall into the following categories:

- *Primary personal experiences* show a political figure at home and play, surrounded by family members. Jane Squier Bruns observes, "The message is, 'Oh, he's a good family man and he cares about family values'.... But really, it doesn't have anything to do with the major issues in the campaign."[140]

- *Place images* associate a politician in a setting that evokes positive responses. Congressional candidates are filmed amid easily recognizable landmarks from the home state. Candidates also situate themselves in front of monuments, parks, and other sources of national recognition and pride.
- *Bonding images* consist of photographs or videos in which the politician is posing with the elderly, middle-class, or Hispanics, and so on in order to become symbolic members of the group—if only for the moment in which the photo is snapped. These images send this message: "I am with you, I share your concerns, I support you ... now, please support me."
- *Embodiment images* feature individuals who exemplify the ramifications of political policies on human beings. Many politicians now include these individuals at staged media events. For instance, in 2007, President Bush visited with military personnel and families at Fort Benning, Georgia, as well as wounded soldiers at Walter Reed Hospital.
- We expect our leaders to be courageous and resolute in times of crisis. Consequently, *strength symbols* frequently appear in political spots. George W. Bush is frequently seen clearing brush on his land, riding a mountain bike, or exercising in the gym. In addition, many political images associate American political life with a highly regarded male institution—*sports*. Bob Teeter, a Republican pollster, observes, "Sports plays a special role in our society. There are probably more people ... who would say they would rather be sports stars than actors or other things."[141] Television footage of presidents jogging, throwing out the first pitch of the major league baseball season, or congratulating winners of sports tournaments suggests that the talents and skills that are essential to success in sports are also vital to the world of politics.
- *Warm images* inspire positive responses in the viewer which then are transferred to the politician. Ever since Vice President Richard Nixon brought his dog Checkers on national television as part of his defense against charges of graft in the 1950s, dogs have served as invaluable political props for politicians. Babies are also sure bets to evoke positive feelings on the part of the audience. No president was more adept at using *warmth and sincerity symbols* than Jimmy Carter. The connotative properties associated with Carter's cardigan sweater—the informality, warmth, and comfortable appearance—convinced the electorate of his sincerity and conviction. One might even argue that Jimmy's brother Billy was a symbol of the president's down-home character.
- *Patriotic symbols* such as American flags and eagles are familiar props in political communications. Although these symbols generally remain in the background, they serve as reminders of the politician's loyalty and commitment to the country.
- Politicians frequently rely on *symbols of hope* to convey their messages. Children are a universal symbol of innocence and hope for the future. Ever since the days of Caroline and John-John Kennedy, television audiences have come to expect shots of children in political campaigns.
- Politicians also make frequent use of *competency symbols*. Politicians are often shown in professional settings, busily engaged at work (for their constituents). Shots of offices, the Senate, White House, or official ceremonies are common.

We often find candidates seated at desks, surrounded by bookcases filled with impressive-looking volumes. The implication is that the politicians have actually *read* these books and are wise and learned people.

- Negative political ads often use *negative symbols* to reinforce their messages. Montague Kern explains, "For instance, showing opponents in limousines and expensive clothes is an effective way of depicting them as rich and pampered beneficiaries of the political system who are out of touch with the concerns of the average citizen."[142]

Performance

Performance has assumed an enormous significance in contemporary American politics. According to political consultant Bill Carrick, the subtle style cues of gesture, posture, syntax, and tone of voice account for as much as 75 percent of a viewer's judgment about the electability of a candidate.[143]

Costume and hairstyle assume symbolic importance during a political campaign. Dana Wilkie explains,

> Sunglasses ... make a candidate appear less credible. Facial hair suggests insecurity. Rarely do you see a major candidate with bad teeth—which may suggest a lack of discipline. And when candidates sweep loose strands across balding patches, this leaves the impression that they try to dodge issues.[144]

Media consultants coach politicians on phrasing, intonations, facial expression, eye contact, and body language, often relying on "electronic response" mechanisms to measure viewer's reactions to politicians' nonverbal cues.[145] Media consultants also employ focus groups to gauge the public response to the most minute detail of a politician's appearance.

This emphasis on nonverbal behavior was exhibited during President Bush's State of the Union Address in January 2007. Reporter Kate Zernike observed,

> In preparation for the president's address, Nancy Pelosi of California (the new Speaker of the House of Representatives) had been coached by her staff to keep a neutral face. They warned that any raised eyebrow or pursed lip would be captured by the cameras trained on the president.
>
> Democrats had decided it was not in their interest to look churlish during the speech. Lawmakers were advised to take their cues on when to stand, sit down and applaud from Ms. Pelosi.... Her caucus said that they expected Ms. Pelosi to, in the words of Representative John B. Larson of Connecticut, show "poise, dignity, comity."

Appearances were obviously important to Ms. Pelosi, who changed from the brown suit she had worn earlier in the day to a soft green one, which offered more contrast to her dark leather speaker's chair.

However, some politicians exhibited unintentional nonverbal signals during the president's address:

> Senator Charles E. Schumer of New York cast a disapproving eye on those who stood, including Senators Joseph I. Lieberman and John Kerry. And while Secretary of State Condoleezza Rice sat forward in her seat and nodded as he described the increase in troops, Republicans who have criticized the plan, including Mr. Warner, stayed off their feet. Senator Olympia Snowe of Maine sat stone still. Across the aisle, Senator Tom Harkin of Iowa shuddered and shook his head, and Representative Charles B. Rangel of New York tipped his head back and stared at the ceiling.[146]

CONCLUSION

The mass media have transformed the American political process. Information about issues is readily available to the public; in fact, it is sometimes difficult to ignore. In addition, continuous media exposure gives constituents unprecedented access to public figures.

However, long ago, Greek philosopher Plato warned that in democratic societies, there is a danger that rhetoric (i.e., the persuasive use of language) will replace epistemology (i.e., knowledge) in the political process. That is, in today's mass-mediated environment, how something is communicated—style—can overwhelm the content. Modern politicians have learned to use the media to manipulate public attitudes and behaviors. Consequently, people tend to become more concerned with what they believe than what is true.

Media literacy can serve as an important democratic instrument that empowers individuals to make independent choices, based upon a critical awareness of the information they receive through the media. At the same time, media literacy enables individuals to recognize how the mass media are used to discourage debate, conceal information, and mislead the public.

NOTES

1. Adam Clymer, "Lie, and the Voters Will Believe," *New York Times,* May 12, 2004, A23.
2. Shir Haberman, "Vilsack Bows Out of Race; Says Finances Stretched Thin," *Portsmouth Herald,* February 24, 2007 (http://archive.seacoastonline.com/news/02242007/nhnews-ph-vilsack.html).
3. Barbara Ehrenreich, speech at the 20th anniversary event for the media watchdog group FAIR, Fairness and Accuracy in Reporting (DemocracyNow.com).
4. Mark Shields, "Hard on Soft Money," *Washington Post*, September 13, 1999 (http://washingtonpost.com).

5. Richard A. Oppel Jr., "Documents Show Parties Often Mixed Fund-Raising and Policy," *New York Times,* December 7, 2002, A15.

6. Sheryl Gay Stolberg, "Drug Lobby Pushed Letter By Senators On Medicare," *New York Times,* July 30, 2003, A15.

7. Philip Shenon, "Abramoff and Rove Had 82 Contacts, Report Says," *New York Times,* September 29, 2006, 1A.

8. Political Action, *New York Times,* January 16, 2007.

9. Frank Rich, "The Backslap Backlash," *New York Times,* June 9, 2001.

10. "Political Action: Money Focus; Industries Lose Friends on the Hill," *New York Times*, November 21, 2006, A20.

11. "Ad Nauseum," *Mother Jones* (Jan/Feb 2007).

12. Bob Herbert, "The Doner Class," *New York Times*, July 19, 1998 (www.nytimes.com).

13. Quentin Wilson, campaign manager, Rep. Richard Gephardt, interview by author, February 12, 1988.

14. John Tebbel, *The Media in America* (New York: Thomas Y. Crowell Company, 1974), 180.

15. Felicity Barringer, "Disliking Coverage, Cleveland's Mayor Retaliates," *New York Times*, May 28, 2001.

16. Dan Rather, with Mickey Herskowitz, *The Camera Never Blinks* (New York: William Morrow and Company, 1977), 222.

17. Alison Mitchell, "The Ad Campaign: A Three-Part Attack on Gore," *New York Times*, September 15, 2000, A10.

18. Mark Hertsgaard, *On Bended Knee* (New York: Farrar Straus Giroux, 1988), 108.

19. Ibid., 35.

20. Ibid., 27.

21. Ibid., 52.

22. Ibid., 53.

23. Bernard Weinraub, "'Disinformation' Risks Reagan's Credibility," *St. Louis Post-Dispatch,* October 4, 1986, 1B.

24. John Tebbel and Sarah Miles Watts, *The Press and the Presidency* (New York: Oxford University Press, 1985) 184–85.

25. Kathleen Hall Jamieson, *Packaging the Presidency*, 2nd ed. (New York: Oxford University Press, 1992), 10.

26. Jeff Zeleny, "Testing the Water, Obama Tests His Own Limits," *New York Times,* December 24, 2006.

27. Tony Schwartz, *The Responsive Chord* (Garden City, NY: Anchor Books, 1973), 103.

28. James David Barber, *The Presidential Character* (Englewood Cliffs, NJ: Prentice Hall, 1972), 13.

29. Ibid.

30. Roger Streitmatter, "The Impact of Presidential Personality on News Coverage in Major Newspapers," *Journalism Quarterly* (Spring 1985), 66–68.

31. Jim Rutenberg, "Look Ma, No Script: What That Says About Me," *New York Times,* July 23, 2006.

32. Zeleny, "Testing the Water, Obama Tests His Own Limits."

33. Howard Kurtz, "Stop Me Before I Swoon," *Washington Post*, October 18, 1999.

34. Nancy Gibbs and John F. Dickerson, "The Power and the Story," *Time Magazine*, December 13, 1999, 40–50.

35. Bill Moyers, *A Walk Through the Twentieth Century: The Thirty Second President,* Public Broadcasting Service, August 8, 1984.

36. Jane Squier Bruns, former vice president, The Communication Company, interview by author, February 24, 1992.

37. Martin Schram, *The Great American Video Game* (New York: William Morrow, 1987), 24–26.

38. Frank Davies, "Internet as Political Force Grows, Poll Finds Shift Away from TV, Papers Continues," *San Jose (Ca.) Mercury News,* January 18, 2006.

39. Adam Hochberg, "Obama, Clinton Vie for Black Support in S.C.," National Public Radio, February 19, 2007.

40. "Money and Politics," Online News Hour, November 10, 2003 (www.pbs.org/newshour/bb/politics/july-dec03/dean_11-10.html).

41. Democracy Online Project (http://democracyonline.org).

42. Leo Jeffres, *Mass Media: Processes and Effects* (Prospect Heights, IL: Waveland Press, 1986), 278.

43. George Gerbner, and others, "Political Correlates of Television Viewing," *Public Opinion Quarterly* (Spring 1984).

44. Bruns, interview by author.

45. Ibid.

46. William Raspberry, "Convictions To Fit All Occasions," *Washington Post*, August 26, 1996, A13.

47. Ibid.

48. "All Things Considered," National Public Radio, January 24, 2007.

49. Larry J. Sabato, *The Rise of Political Consultants* (New York: Basic Books, 1981), 144.

50. Anne E. Kornblut, "Another Layer of Winners and Losers," *New York Times*, November 11, 2006, A12.

51. Sabato, *Political Consultants*, 26.

52. Adam Nagourney, "For 'America's Mayor,' Tips to Take to the White House," *New York Times,* November 19, 2006.

53. Ibid.

54. Sabato, *Political Consultants*, 38.

55. Roger L. Worthington, "The Polemics of Polls," *St. Louis Post-Dispatch*, November 2, 2004, B07.

56. Don Van Natta Jr., "Polling's 'Dirty Little Secret': No Response," *New York Times,* November 21, 1999.

57. Ibid.

58. Jack Rosenthal, "Precisely False vs. Approximately Right: A Reader's Guide to Polls," *New York Times*, August 27, 2006.

59. "Experts Guide Voters on Weighing Polls," *St. Louis Post-Dispatch*, October 30, 1992, 4C.

60. Jennifer LaFleur, "Media Used Good Methods, Bad Judgment in Election Call, Experts Say," *St. Louis Post-Dispatch*, November 15, 2000.

61. Adam Nagourney and Janet Elder, "New Poll Finds Mixed Support for Wiretaps," *New York Times*, January 27, 2006.

62. David Broder, "When Push Comes to Shove, Fake Polls Become Dirty Trick," *New York Times*, October 10, 1994, 7B.

63. "Experts Guide Voters on Weighing Polls."

64. Ibid.

65. Ibid.

66. Ibid.

67. Hertsgaard, *On Bended Knee*, 51.

68. Rammey, Austin, *Channels of Power*, New York: Basic Books, Inc., 1983, 95.

69. "Lawmaker Calls Electoral College 'Relic'," *St. Louis Post-Dispatch* September 7, 1997, 5E.

70. Ryan Lizza, "The Invasion of the Alpha Male Democrat," *The New York Times* January 7, 2007, Section 4, p 1.

71. Ibid.

72. Toby Harnden, "Liberal and Lip-Glossed, the Most Powerful Woman in Washington," *Daily Telegraph*, November 9, 2006, A1.

73. Robin Givhan, "Condoleezza Rice's Commanding Clothes," *Washington Post*, February 25, 2005, C01.

74. Warren St. John, "The Week That Wasn't," *New York Times*, October 3, 2004.

75. Tim Harper, "Bush Jokes Double, Study Spots Trouble," *Toronto Star*, May 20, 2006, A03.

76. Associated Press, "Voter Group Rock the Vote $500,000 in Debt" (MSNBC.com).

77. Thinkexist.com (http://thinkexist.com/quotations/american_dream).

78. Frederick Jackson Turner, *Encyclopedia Britannica*, vol. 22 (Chicago: William Benton, 1983), 625.

79. Maureen Dowd, "Drapes of Wrath," *New York Times,* November 11, 2006, A27.

80. Kathryn Kranhold, "General Electric's Tax Boon Clouds Profit Picture," *Wall Street Journal,* December 8, 2006.

81. Robin Toner, "A Senator Bets on Party's Clout in Pennsylvania," *New York Times,* September 25, 2006, A1.

82. acmediscuss@acmecoalitition, media list, media-L@nmsu.edu, March 14, 2006.

83. Randal C. Archibold, "Cheney, Invoking the Specter of a Nuclear Attack, Questions Kerry's Strength," *New York Times*, October 20, 2004, A20.

84. George Lakoff, "Staying the Course Right Over a Cliff," *New York Times*, October 27, 2006, A19.

85. Mark Halperin, "Reporters Try the Silent Treatment," *New York Times,* September 30, 2002, A25.

86. Nick Wadhams, "Mistaken Airstrike Kills at Least 5; U.S. Acknowledges Bombing Wrong Building," *Washington Post,* January 9, 2005.

87. Eric Lichtblau and Scott Shane, "Ally Told Bush Project Secrecy Might Be Illegal," *New York Times,* July 9, 2006.

88. Eleanor MacLean, *Between the Lines* (Montreal: Black Rose Books, 1981).

89. Moyers, *Thirty-Second President.*
90. Sabato, *Political Consultants*, 7–8.
91. Ellen Goodman, "Passionate Conservatism: 1 Compassionate Conservatism: 0," *St. Louis Post-Dispatch*, February 3, 2000 (www.postnet.com).
92. Carl Hulse, "Democrats See Security as Key Issue for Fall," *New York Times,* August 15, 2006, A15.
93. David D. Kirkpatrick, "The Ad Campaign: A Firey Warning Against Taking Risks," *New York Times*, November 7, 2006, A18.
94. Robin Toner, "Ad Seen as Playing to Racial Fears," *New York Times,* October 26, 2006, A1.
95. Adam Nagourney, "Claiming Outsider Status, Romney Says He'll Seek White House," *New York Times*, February 14, 2007, Section A; Col. 1; National Desk; Pg. 22.
96. Daniel Goleman, "Voters Assailed by Unfair Persuasion," *New York Times*, October 27, 1992, C1, C8.
97. Richard Rosenfeld, professor of criminology, University of Missouri–St. Louis, interview by author, January 21, 2007.
98. Hertsgaard, *On Bended Knee*, 340.
99. Ibid., 126.
100. Jacques Steinberg, "In '04, Local TV Newscasts Were Light on Campaign Coverage, a Study Finds," *New York Times,* February 14, 2005, C4.
101. Clymer, "Lie."
102. Hertsgaard, *On Bended Knee*, 123.
103. Edwin Diamond and Stephen Bates, *The Spot: The Rise of Political Advertising on Television* (Cambridge, MA: The MIT Press, 1984), 301.
104. Bruns, interview by author.
105. Charles Baxter, "Divorce-Court Politics," *New York Times,* November 5, 2006.
106. Ibid.
107. Diamond and Bates, *The Spot.*
108. Bruns, interview by author.
109. Sabato, *Political Consultants*, 123.
110. Thomas V. DiBacco, "Dirty Campaigns—So What's New," *St. Louis Post-Dispatch*, April 22, 1992, 3C.
111. Charles Baxter, "Divorce-Court Politics."
112. Montague Kern, *30-Second Politics* (New York: Praeger, 1989), 94.
113. Howard Kurtz, "In Campaign 2000, More Mr. Nice Guy," *New York Times,* November 24, 1999.
114. J. H. Hatfield, *Fortunate Son* (Brooklyn, NY: Soft Skull Press, 2002), 112.
115. Bruns, interview by author.
116. Ramesh Ponnuru, "Accentuating the Negative," *New York Times*, December 4, 1999, A29.
117. Jamieson, *Packaging the Presidency*, 64.
118. Steinberg, "In '04."
119. Tierney, "Using Ads."
120. Jamieson, *Packaging the Presidency*, 84.
121. Sabato, *Political Consultants*, 162–163.

122. Robert Schmidt, "Who Called the Shots," *Brill's Content* (April 1999), 3.
123. Kern, *30-Second Politics*, 99.
124. Sabato, *Political Consultants*, 163.
125. Joseph Kahn, "Chinese Official Publishes Rebuke of Bush," *New York Times,* February 2, 2007, A6.
126. William Safire, "On Language; Words At War," *New York Times*, September 30, 2001.
127. "The Democrats' Week in Boston," *New York Times,* August 1, 2004.
128. Frank Bruni, "A Buzz Saw of Buzzwords," *New York Times*, December 24, 2006.
129. Mike Allen, "Bush Stresses Commander-in-Chief Role," *Washington Post,* September 13, 2004, A04.
130. George Lakoff, "Staying the Course Right Over a Cliff," *New York Times*, October 27, 2006, A19.
131. "Presidential Ecospeak," *New York Times*, October 18, 2003, A12.
132. Bruce Lincoln, "How Bush Speaks in Religious Code," *Boston Globe,* September 12, 2004, D12.
133. Peter Baker and Jim VandeHei, "Bush Chooses Roberts for Court; Appeals Judge for D.C. Has Conservative Credentials," *Washington Post*, A01.
134. Elizabeth Bumiller and David D. Kirkpatrick, "Bush Fends Off Sharp Criticism of Court Choice," *New York Times*, October 27, 2005, A1.
135. Albert L. Winseman, "U.S. Evangelicals: How Many Walk the Walk?". Gallup Poll Tuesday Briefing, 2005, The Gallup Organization (www.gallup.com).
136. Matthew Reed Baker, "Glossary of Diplomatic Coverage," *Brill's Content* (April 1999), 38.
137. Bruns, interview by author.
138. David Wallis, "Political Props and Campaigns That Take Off, or Crash," *New York Times*, April 18, 1999.
139. Ibid.
140. Bruns, interview by author.
141. James Dao and Don Van Natta, Jr., "Bradley Finally Ready to Rub Tall Shoulders," *New York Times*, October 2, 1999 (www.nytimes.com).
142. Kern, *30-Second Politics*, 100.
143. Alex Williams, "Live From Miami, a Style Showdown," *New York Times*, September 26, 2004.
144. Dana Wilkie, "Image Firms Try to Give Candidates Right Look," *San Diego Union-Tribune*, August 16, 1999, A1.
145. Kern, *30-Second Politics*, 16.
146. Kate Zernike, "A Shift in Power, Starting with 'Madame Speaker,'" *New York Times,* January 24, 2007, 1A.

CHAPTER

15

DIGITAL MEDIA COMMUNICATIONS

by Art Silverblatt and Kim William Gordon

OVERVIEW

Digital media communications has had a profound effect on the ways that we spend our time, process information, and think about our world:

- In 2005, the average American spent 154 hours on the Internet, nearly triple the amount spent four years earlier.[1]
- Digital media are drawing audiences away from the other established media. A 2006 survey found that American families that have Internet services in their homes watch 9 percent less television overall than the general population.[2]
- 53 percent of international businesspeople admitted to craving information and 54 percent claimed to get a "high" when they find what they have been seeking in an electronic search.[3]
- 46 percent of parents said their children already prefer computers to their peers.[4]
- 36 percent of parents worried that their children were overexposed to information.[5]
- Increasing numbers of people suffer ill health due to the stress of information overload.[6]

DEFINITION OF DIGITAL MEDIA COMMUNICATIONS

Digital media communications refers to a wide range of devices that we use everyday, including the Internet, cellphones, instant messaging, and digital still and video imaging devices.

A useful definition of digital media communications is as follows:

> Digital media communications refers to communication between an Initiator and Receiver, in which long-established media are combined with computer technology to emulate humans' communication patterns.

It might be helpful to break down this complex definition and expand on its major features.

"*Communication between an Initiator and Receiver* ..." Digital media is interactive; we both *retrieve* and *impart* information. As is the case with interpersonal communications, our role changes as we move from media communicator (the person initiating the dialogue) to audience (the recipient of information—both solicited and unsolicited) and back again.

"... *using a combination of long-established media* ..." Although digital media is the most current mass medium, it is actually the ultimate hybrid, combining the long-established forms of media: print, photography, graphics, audio, and video.

"... *to emulate humans' patterns of thought and expression* ..." Like no other medium, the process of digital communications approaches the dynamics of interpersonal communications. The communication style of human beings can best be described as *dynamic* and *non-linear.* We often jump from one subject to another or elect to focus our attention on a particular facet of a topic. However, print, film, radio, and television operate in a linear fashion, which means that information is presented in a predetermined, established order. This *analogue model* is exemplified by movies presented on VHS videotape. Trying to locate a particular scene on a videotape requires hitting the "rewind" or "fast forward" buttons until you reach the desired point.

In contrast, *digital technology* is uniquely capable of adapting to our non-linear patterns of thought and expression. In digital technology, information is converted through the computer to a compendium of bits—a series of 1's and 0's. When it is converted back into sound and pictures, information is no longer linear, permitting random access and retrieval. As a result, we are free to jump from subject to subject or go into one topic in depth—simulating the process of human communication.

"... *through a transparent machine* ..." It wasn't long ago that the technology of the computer was terribly intrusive. We had to attach the connection to an outside source (often through the phone line), boot up the computer, fiddle with the software, log on, and contend with technical delays and interruptions. Today, we don't really care about what "operating system" the machine uses; we are only concerned about retrieving and sending information. A significant step toward complete transparency occurred in 2007, when Xerox announced plans to build a search engine that uses a "natural language" technology, so that computers understand and process queries in plain English, rather than using keywords and URL designations.[7]

We are also moving toward the stage of *ubiquitous computers*, in which computers are fully integrated into our personal environment. Experimental models are already in place, in which Radio Frequency ID devices (RFID) are melded into personal clothing, products, animals, and people for purposes of identification, using radio waves. The next generation of interactive devices will include *Virtual Presence Systems*, in which microprocessors installed in your home will monitor your heart rate and blood pressure the moment you enter the house and automatically contact emergency services if it detects any irregularities. While dining at a restaurant, an electronic menu may help you order, taking into account any of your medical or dietary restrictions.

In addition, artificially intelligent refrigerators and pantries will monitor your home food inventory. Armed with your personal food preference profile, these computerized systems will take stock of other perishables that you may require, such as milk and cheese, arrange for payment, and coordinate delivery—all while you are playing, working, or sleeping. While driving along the highway, the in-dash system will know that you will need to purchase gas within the next few miles. The system will electronically "radio" ahead, negotiate price, review services, and prompt you with advertised options within your automobile display.

However, the application of this technology also raises some significant ethical concerns. For instance, because there is no effective way for the "carrier" to turn off the RFID, if you are wearing RFID clothing anyone with a "reader" can determine where and when you bought the clothes, and, through an immediate cross-check with prior sales records, determine your identity, financial records, where you live, and your current location.

DIGITAL MEDIA LITERACY

Selected Keys to Interpreting Media Messages can provides you with the tools to enhance your critical understanding of digital media. A media literacy approach to the study of digital media focuses on the following areas:

- The discursive style that is peculiar to each medium and that shapes its content.[8]
- The ability to decode information in a variety of forms.[9]
- The ability to make independent choices about the selection and interpretation of content.
- An understanding of the emerging structure of the Internet and its impact on content.
- An awareness of the impact of digital media on the individual and society.

- The development of strategies with which to analyze and discuss media messages conveyed through digital media.
- An awareness of digital content as a "text" that provides insight into our contemporary culture and ourselves.

PROCESS

As with all media, digital technology is simply a channel of communication that can be used in a variety of ways and for a variety of purposes. As such, digital media is neither good nor evil. Much depends on: 1) the media communicator; 2) the motives behind the communication activity; 3) how effectively the media communicator uses the medium to convey the message; and 4) how the audience receives the information.

Post-Modern Communications Model

The post-modern communications model comes into play most visibly in the world of digital communications. Digital media empowers the audience like never before, enabling individual audience members to bypass the traditional media gatekeepers. Individuals can now produce their own media presentations, edit, and distribute them over the Internet.

In this post-modern world, the audience begins to interact directly with each other. Video "gamers" are connected to a vast network, playing with people all over the world. Moreover, these same forms of simulation are being used for training and brainstorming strategies. In the world of commerce, sites like eBay are virtual flea markets, in which individuals barter and sell goods, free of corporate intervention.

Function

Understanding the *function*, or purpose, behind an interactive communications exchange is a vital consideration—both on the sending and receiving ends of the process. Initiating communication may serve a variety of functions for the *Initiator* of media messages (the individual at his/her computer):

- *Commerce.* Shopping has become a primary reason that people go online.
- *As Source of Information.* Thanks to the Internet, individuals have immediate access to an entire universe of knowledge. The Internet has become an invaluable resource for scholarship, reference information, news gathering, and product research.
- *Exchange of Ideas.* The digital domain offers numerous arenas in which individuals express their ideas. For instance, IM (instant messaging) provides opportunities to engage others in real time. Blogs have become a primary means of personal expression that run the gamut from self-published "web diaries" to Citizen Journalism accounts of the world at large (for more discussion, see Chapter 12, Journalism).
- *Persuasion.* Numerous web sites have been established with the intent of influencing the attitudes and behaviors of others. As an example, racist groups

operating within the United States now use Internet sites to spread their message: "It has become the propaganda venue of choice," declared Mark Potok.[10]

- *Artistic Expression.* The digital domain has emerged as a distribution outlet for artistic media, circumventing the powerful media conglomerates. In the past, musicians have had to attract the interest of record companies in order for their work to be distributed to a mass audience. In the process, these musicians were often forced to compromise their artistic voice to become "marketable," as defined by the recording company. Today, however, musicians whose work is not considered mainstream enough for label consideration can generate interest in their work by offering samples of their music as MP3s (an audio compression format) over the Internet. In fact, some groups are now distributing their music exclusively online through venues like Apple iTunes.
- *Entertainment.* A world of entertainment exists in virtual space. Entertainment programming is now streamed directly to your cellphones and other communication devices.
- *Exploration*, or "surfing," involves following areas of interest from link to link. Many of these explorations now begin by consulting a search engine such as Google or Yahoo!.
- *Creating and Maintaining Community.* Digital technology can cultivate a sense of community among individuals throughout the globe. To illustrate, the Master DNA Project enables individuals to submit DNA samples to a central web site to determine family lineage issues. Kim Gordon, co-author of this chapter, submitted a swab from the inside of his mouth to the web site (www.thegordondnaproject.com) for analysis and discovered family ties among the Scottish Gordon clan that had been lost for over 600 years.

Digital technology also provides an opportunity for individuals to become new members of a community centered around common interests or experiences. After he was diagnosed with a rare form of lymphoma, Lou Birenbaum joined an online discussion group, which provides essential information, support, and advice:

I logged on to the Internet with the hope of learning about the condition. I not only found a plethora of information, but also located a support group of people from around the world who shared my experience.

To my relief, I met people who had far exceeded the official life expectancy cited by doctors. I did not feel self-conscious about asking questions, since I felt that they knew what I was going through. I learned about a variety of treatments, which enabled me to discuss alternative forms of treatment with my physician. I also learned about common symptoms and the emotional reactions that accompany the disease. We even share recipes and jokes. It has been the most successful therapy I could have received.[11]

The digital culture has also become a popular venue for cultivating personal relationships. Sites like Facebook and MySpace offer virtual meeting places, where people can develop a network of friends. In addition, virtual matchmaking sites like eHarmony.com provide venues for romantic relationships, relying on database profiling systems to identify potential mates.

All too often, however, an individual may be engaged in an *undefined function*. For instance: you may have had the experience in which, rather than doing your homework, you find yourself exploring the vast digital landscape, going wherever your curiosity leads you. This "impulse browsing" can be extremely informative and entertaining. On the other hand, this can also be an enormous waste of time.

As with all media, the goal of media literacy is to address the *indiscriminate* use of the medium. Before logging on, identify the function of this communications activity, as well as the amount of time that you anticipate spending on this activity. For instance, if you decide that you would like to play a video game for the next two hours—fine. However, going online without a defined function—and time schedule—can lead to a situation in which you are up all night and suffer the consequences the next day.

Defining the function can also prevent you from turning to digital media out of boredom or habit and can help you use your time more productively.

Identifying Functions: When You Are the Receiver of Information

As discussed earlier, one of the distinguishing characteristics of digital technology is that it emulates interpersonal communications. Within this context, your role shifts from being the Initiator of messages and information to the Receiver. What, then, is the function behind the messages that are being sent *to* you?

Unsolicited Communications. Increasingly, we have become Receivers of unsolicited information from the digital landscape. These unrequested messages may fulfill a latent function that is not immediately apparent to the participant.

One latent function, unfortunately, involves sexual predators. Police Detective Bova Conti suggests that children should be told never to give out any personal information online, such as age, gender, telephone number, address, school name, or names of sports teams the child may play on. Children also should never send pictures of themselves online. Conti declares that kids themselves should be alert to red flags in conversations:

> Any time the conversation starts turning to what I call "adult things," kids should get off line. If they are asked about their body parts, or what color their panties are or whether they wear boxers or briefs. That has no place in an online conversation.[12]

Some web sites that provide information or entertainment may also contain a latent commercial function. According to Janet E. Alexander and Marsha Ann Tate, answering "yes" to any of the following questions is one way to test whether the latent function of a web site is commercial. Does the page:

- Promote a product or service?
- Provide customer support?
- Make the company's catalog available online?
- Provide product updates or new versions of a product?
- Provide documentation about a product?
- Request information about a person's lifestyle, demographics, or finances?
- Does the web site accept credit cards?[13]

Some digital sites have a latent *public relations* function that is designed to create a positive image with the public. For instance, the FBI has set up a web site for kids (www.fbi.gov/kids), with games, tips, stories, and a cartoon character named "Special Agent Bobby Bureau." The cumulative message is that the FBI is the "good guys." And further, the "FBI Adventure Game" teaches children that they can be "field agents" by monitoring and reporting suspicious behaviors to the FBI. In addition, the page encourages its young audience to consider a career in the Federal Bureau of Investigation.

Media Communicator

Identifying Anonymous Communicators. Because many messages are unsolicited and anonymous, identifying the media communicator has become an enormous challenge. At this time, it is nearly impossible to determine the identity of a person who initiates communication with you over the Internet. In many cases, the media communicators remain anonymous, using a *sock puppet*, or pseudonym to disguise his/her identity. Even if a person provides a name (or nickname), you cannot verify whether the initiator is telling the truth about his or her identity.

A letter sent to Randy Cohen's "Ethicist" column in the *New York Times* raises some intriguing ethical questions about adopting identities on the Internet:

> I persuaded a shy male friend to try Internet dating. He posted his profile and photo but never actually wrote to anyone. So I got him to let me take over. Now I am courting three women via e-mail, in the guise of a 35-year-old man. I am a woman (but, it turns out, I have a way with the ladies). This now feels a bit less innocent, but if it gets my shy friend together with a nice woman, is it wrong? Anonymous, New York

Cohen's response, in part, is as follows:

> This isn't an ethics question; it's the premise for a romantic comedy.... O.K., it is an ethics question, and one that illustrates the perils of overreaching. You did well

to help your friend look for love but erred when you engaged in impersonation.... Such misrepresentation—displaying one item when another is actually on offer—is associated more with disreputable electronics dealers than honest wooers. When the truth comes out, the women you deceived will feel hurt and embarrassed, a good guide to the impropriety of your deception....

As you know, literature offers a cautionary tale about such tactics: things didn't work out well for Cyrano or Roxanne or Christian. And so as a matter of efficacy as well as ethics, you must abandon your imposture. At a minimum, your friend must immediately replace you at the keyboard. Ideally, he'll fess up to everyone and hope, the malfeasance being well intentioned and evanescent, that his dates are more charmed than wounded by this brief and tender treachery.[14]

According to psychologist Camille Sweeney, the anonymity of the digital domain can be positive for teenagers, offering them the opportunity to experiment with new ideas, ways to relate to others, and experience different sides of self:

Herein lies the thrill of the on-line self: its malleability, its plasticity, the fact that it can be made up entirely of your own imagination. You can take your old self, or don a fresh one, and hang out in a group of jocks for a post game chat, argue the banality of Britney Spears with an international posse of pop connoisseurs, post a note to a cool-sounding guy from Detroit—all without ever having to leave your bedroom. Maybe this is the Internet's greatest asset to teendom: access, and the confidence to slip in and out of personalities, the ability to try on identities, the adolescent equivalent of playing dress-up in the attic, standing before the mirror in heels and lipstick long before you own your own.[15]

But, although meaningful relationships can certainly be developed through this channel of communication, the anonymity of the Internet can also mask the identity of people who, for various reasons, are engaged in some form of deception. As with any relationship, you should develop a relationship gradually; trust should be earned, and not assumed.

Identifying the Author of Information Posted on the Internet. Unfortunately, the name of the author of information that appears on a web site does not always appear on the site—and even if a name is included, it may be a pseudonym. But even when an authentic name does appear, there may not be any accompanying information, such as the author's background and credentials. Further, the relationship between the author and the site may be unclear. Alexander and Tate explain, "It is important to know to what extent the organization responsible for the contents of the site might influence the objectivity of the author."[16] Many web sites allow the commentary of anyone who has visited the site. Unless informed otherwise, it is best to consider the contribution as an individual's personal opinion on a topic: a virtual "letter to the editor."

But armed with the name, online research can disclose other works of the author, reviews of his/her publications, the affiliations of the author, and other places where the author has been cited as an authority.

Identifying the Ideology of the Web Site. Upon close inspection, web sites often furnish perspective about their ideology:

- *The sponsor of the web site.* A web site may be the work of an individual or an organization. If no background information is available, you can conduct research, by "Googling" the sponsor; that is, by putting the name of the organization into a search engine such as Google or Lycos.
- *A statement of the web site's agenda and mission.*
- *A listing of who provides funding for the organization.*
- *A way to contact the media communicator (e.g., an e-mail address or a direct link).*
- *References to people, issues, and events* that disclose the background and priorities of the web site.

MEDIA LITERACY TIPS

WEB SITES

Elizabeth Kirk offers the following strategies to determine the orientation of a web site if the homepage provides no clues as to its identity:

Focus on the URL, or address.

1. Can you find the web site's homepage by deleting all the information in the URL after the server name?
2. Can you tell if the page is actually part of someone's personal account, as opposed to being part of an official site? Click for help in evaluating this kind of URL.
3. If all else fails, can you find information on the server domain? Try using the Internet "Whois" server to get the name of the owner. Type the name of the server (e.g., milton.mse.jhu.edu) in the box and press "Enter."
4. You also may find the identity of a server, as well as contact names and telephone numbers, by using Network Solutions. Note that this service provides information on non-governmental and non-military sites in the U.S. only. Once you find the name of the organization owning the server, you may have enough information to judge its reputation as an information source. Remember, this is only of value for official pages from a web site.

If the page you are evaluating comes from someone's personal account, you really have no idea what their place is within the organization, or if they are in a position to represent the organization. If you are not familiar with the organization, try one of the following:

1. If it is an association of some kind, look for it at *The Scholarly Societies Project* (www.scholarly-societies.org). This web page "facilitates information about scholarly societies across the world." Is it represented?
2. For all others, search the name of the organization, enclosed in quotation marks, in AltaVista. Does anyone else have information on it?

If you cannot ascertain either the author or publisher of the page you are trying to evaluate, you are looking at information that is as anonymous as a page torn out of a book. You cannot evaluate what you cannot verify. It is unwise to use information of this nature. Look for another source.[17]

- Accredited web registries such *as Internic.net* (www.internic.net) provide information on the orientation and ownership of a web site.
- Examining the *links* on a web site can be another way to determine the character and orientation of a web site. Links are virtual passageways that lead to another part of a web site or to a different site. A link normally appears as an underlined word, phrase, or image. Clicking on the link automatically transports the user to that particular destination. Links are selected by the webmaster because they are considered to be "related" in some fashion to the original web site. Consequently, checking these links can add perspective to your understanding of the original site.

Audience (Receiver)

As discussed earlier, digital media technology enables media communicators to individualize the presentation of the message to the individual audience member:

- The Initiator can now attract the attention of the Receiver through personalized e-mail messages and banner ads.
- The Initiator is able to customize the message, factoring in the backgrounds, finances, lifestyles, and buying habits of the Receiver. For instance, a web site for a retail business that has instant access to your financial records will only show you items that you can afford. A quick credit check as you enter the site is all that is required.
- The Initiator can highlight different aspects of the message to satisfy the particular interests and expectations of the Receiver.
- The Initiator can individualize the depth of coverage, depending on the educational level of the Receiver. A fifth grader writing a report on the housefly would not need the comprehensive information required by a doctoral student on the same topic.
- The Initiator can anticipate the Receiver's questions and possible points of confusion. As an example, in 2007, Mini USA began using digital billboards that instantly customizes its message to the drivers of oncoming vehicles. Thus, one way to develop a critical understanding of the communications strategy, style, and content of a digital media presentation is through an analysis of audience. And conversely, in the case of a message that has been microcast to you personally, examining the presentation can provide perspective into what the digital media communicator knows (or thinks they know) about you.

Context: Historical Context

Because much of the discourse in digital media takes on the characteristics of dialogue, examining the topics that appear on the Internet reveal which historical events are of public interest and concern. For instance, a Google search in 2003 for "Stop the War" yielded fewer than 20,000 web page results. However, the same search in February 2007 produced 114 *million* web page results. A significant number of these results are web sites such as "antiwar.com," "stopthewarmachine.org," and "veteransforpeace.org," all of which are grassroots organizations dedicated to stopping the Iraq war. Moreover, identifying patterns within discussion venues such as blogs provides valuable insight into attitudes *toward* these historical events.

Context: Cultural Context

The evolution of the communications age has been accompanied by dramatic cultural changes. Nicholas Negroponte observes that some of these cultural trends appear, on the surface, to be contradictory:

> All things digital get bigger and smaller at the same time—most things in the middle fall out. We'll see a rise in huge corporations, airplanes, hotels, and newspaper chains in parallel with growth in mom-and-pop companies, private planes, homespun inns, and newsletters written about interests most of us did not even know humans have.[18]

Indeed, it is often the contradictory nature of these cultural trends that makes societies so complex and multifarious—perhaps mirroring the paradoxical nature of the human race.

For instance, digital technology promises to improve the quality of our lives, on many levels. For the hearing impaired, voice recognition computers installed into eyeglasses will be able to transcribe conversations into print, which will then be scrolled across the lenses. Further, Peter Schwartz predicts that by 2010, scientific breakthroughs in biotechnology and gene therapy will enable science to reverse aging. He insists that the prospect is not merely a prolonged old age but living for decades in one's biological forties.[19]

Indeed, the day is soon approaching when it is culturally acceptable for computers to be implanted *within* the human body for various purposes. Already, chips are being installed in pets that contain medical, identification, and tracking information. This technology could soon be used in supervision of Alzheimer's patients, as well as in tracking convicted felons.

Implanting a computer chip in a human being promises to endow individuals with immediate and startling capabilities. Bran Ferren, foresees the following scenario:

> An internal computer that lets you, rather than your PC, hook up to the wireless information superhighway. Why risk it? Well, imagine that you could understand any language, remember every joke, solve any equation, get the latest news, balance your checkbook, communicate with others and have near-instant access to any book every published without ever having to leave the privacy of yourself. Not bad.[20]

If the merging of humans and machines sounds too much like science fiction, it should be noted that in 1988 Kevin Warwick participated in an experiment in which a computer chip was temporarily implanted in his arm. Warwick recalls,

> A surgeon burrowed a hole between the skin and muscle on my left biceps and implanted a silicon chip enclosed in a little glass capsule.... A computer would monitor my movements and various things would happen automatically. We programmed my (department) building to say "Hello" when I came in and to tell me how many E-mails I had. Different lights would switch on as I went through various doorways. Doors opened.[21]

Of course, injecting microcomputer chips into the human body raises a series of ethical questions: Does this step turn people into machines, depriving them of their humanity? As the science and science-fiction writer John Brunner warned: "First we use machines, then we wear machines then we become machines."[22] As with all technology, the computer creates problems as it solves others.

At the same time, machines are becoming more like human beings. For instance, rather than simply gathering and processing information, some computers have the ability to draw *inferences* from information: in other words, to think.

In addition, computers now have the capacity to "reproduce." The current models of advanced computers are designing the next generation of machines. Hod Lipson, professor of mechanical and aerospace engineering at Cornell, who led the research, explains, "Self-replication is the ultimate form of self-repair."[23]

The genre of science fiction has long focused on this theme of a world in which the machines have transcended the capabilities of humankind. Films from *Forbidden Planet* (1956), *2001, A Space Odyssey* (1968), *Blade Runner* (1982), *The Terminator* (1984), and *The Matrix* (1999) have a shared premise, in which "the machines" have taken over and punish human beings for their hubris of playing God, in the creation of these omnipotent computers.

Impact on Lifestyle. Digital media culture has had an enormous influence on ways in which we relate to one another. Cellphones and BlackBerrys keep people in perpetual contact with one another, so that they never have "downtime" from work or personal relationships. Psychologists have found that this can lead to an unhealthy "wireless co-dependency" on others. Journalist Paul Brown explains, "Calling someone whenever you are in a bad mood, or have a question, may be making you less independent and less able to experience your life as fully as you should."[24] Psychologist Robert Bornstein elaborates: "The superconnected may develop a dual-dependency. They're not only counting on other people too much, they're also hooked on the devices themselves, sometimes to the point where they feel utterly disconnected, isolated and detached without them."[25]

Figure 15.1
The growth in people using the Internet, in millions.

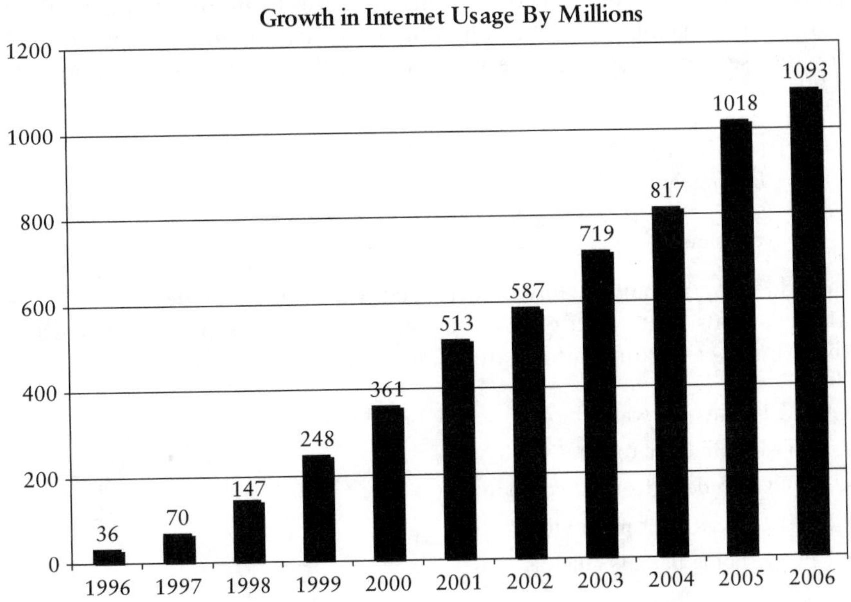

Virtual communities such as Facebook, MySpace, and Second Life have broadened and re-defined personal relationships. But according to Alex Beers, 18, although people share personal information, it is mostly superficial:

> It's a way to cultivate casual friends ... very causal. Not sharing real personal stuff but you can learn about people's lives on Facebook, but it's mostly stuff like your favorite bands. It's not like deep connection whatsoever. With Facebook, you lose a lot, like if you had physical contact with somebody, you wouldn't be able to pick up on facial cues. People miss out on that, missing subtleties, which is one of the reasons that make your friendships special.[26]

However, Leah Silverblatt, a high school senior, has signed up with the equivalent of Facebook at the college she intends to attend in the fall, which already has helped her feel connected to the community. "It's been helpful, seeing some of the people, knowing what they are interested in."[27]

Digital culture has also had a dramatic impact on language. Indeed, new words are continually being invented as societies evolve. As an example, William Safire notes the introduction of the following terms related to Internet blogs:

Digital culture has also had a dramatic impact on language. A new written form of expression has emerged in the e-mailing and text messaging conversations of young people. This modern form of hieroglyphics is based on the symbols on the computer keyboard. As an example, the following sequence of characters on the keyboard represents emotional responses:

:-) = Happy face
:-| = indifferent
: (= sad
:-<=very sad

In addition, teenagers have developed a set of *Internet Acronyms*—abbreviations that function as a code. NetLingo has published a list of these Internet Acronyms for parents, including:

- PAW: Parents are watching
- TDTM: Talk dirty to me
- NIFOC: Nude in front of computer
- LMIRL: Let's meet in real life
- KPC: Keeping parents clueless[28]

E-mail and Instant Messaging (IM) lend themselves to an informal tone and to a condensed style, which affects the way in which messages are constructed. Katie Dean explains,

> If language as communication is measured by communication and clarity, IM succeeds for being instantaneous.... But the clarity of a message can be obscured when nuances ... are lost. There will be less of a tendency to review anything you have written before you send it.... It's terse and it's understood to be terse.... (But) letters and email allow people time to reflect on what they want to say. With IM, people respond on the fly. If you're going to truncate your communications and abbreviate your emotions, then it could cause a problem.[29]

Conversion to a Global, Communications-based Economy. Digital media moved the economy from the industrial age into a global, communications-based system. This new economic model has revolutionized the way in which people conduct business.

To illustrate, let us imagine that you want to purchase a bicycle. In the system left over from the industrial age, you would drive to a nearby store, where they maintain an extensive inventory of bikes. If you were fortunate, you would find a model that met your specifications (e.g., size, color), and you would complete your transaction.

However, in a global, communications-based economy, you can shop online. First, you submit your desired bicycle specifications to an Internet auction site, where companies compete for your business. You then select the best offer, arrange for payment, and activate the order. The bicycle is then manufactured and shipped to you within 36 hours.

This economic model offers several advantages for the consumer. Shopping is convenient, accommodates your schedule, and is free of pressure by salespeople. In addition, you can purchase a bicycle manufactured to your personal specifications ("I'd like dark blue paint on the top and high visibility yellow on the bottom, and my left leg is 1/8″ longer than my right"). Further, the savings accrued by reducing inventory, labor, and marketing costs enables the manufacturer to sell this personalized bicycle for 30–60 percent cheaper than the mass-produced model sold at your neighborhood bike store. And finally, the product will be delivered straight to your door—the ultimate convenience.

This communications-based economic model offers many advantages for *businesses* as well:

- Internet commerce eliminates the expenses normally associated with setting up local stores and outlets, such as acquiring a brick and mortar storefront for displaying and selling goods.
- This new economic model eliminates the need to maintain an inventory, an expense that can double the cost of conducting business. In this new business model, however, a product is never manufactured until *after* it has been sold. Thus, the bike you have purchased online will not be assembled until you order it. At that point, the company automatically places the order over the Internet with its suppliers (e.g., bike frame manufacturers, tire and paint companies). The materials are immediately sent to a factory anywhere in the world, where the bike is assembled and shipped directly to you.
- This new economic model reduces personnel costs. Sales clerks and support and managerial staff at local retail outlets are no longer required. Further, because the bike can be primarily assembled by robots, the labor force has been reduced substantially.
- The digital domain provides new opportunities for promoting the product. Unlike the neighborhood store, all companies will have global outreach. Consequently, the new challenge for companies will involve making their product information known and accessible to an international audience, while targeting their advertising message to those individuals most likely to buy the merchandise.

This economic model is already being adopted by visionary companies. For instance, Toyota offers built-to-order automobiles via the Internet. Indeed, Dell has built its entire business model on the customization of personal computers over the Web.

However, some products still require the traditional shopping model. As an example, many customers prefer to try on clothing before making their purchase. But even in these cases, companies can adopt certain aspects of the new economic model. For instance, Levi Strauss has reduced its inventory by keeping just enough sizes and colors on hand at local outlets so that shoppers can get a general impression about the style and desirability of the item. Customers then place their orders through the Internet that are tailor-made to their exact size and style specifications. Levi Strauss then keeps a record of the customers' measurements, so that in the future, their patrons can order personalized jeans directly over the Internet.

In 2007, Intellifit began placing body scanners in malls throughout America. The exact measurements of customers are recorded on the Internet site, so that all future orders can be made to the exact specifications of the customers. Customers are then sent an e-mail message with a password for Intellifit.com, where they may select from an assortment of clothes from seven companies, including Nordstrom, Levi's, and Lands' End.

Thus, while shopping at the mall has declined (as online shopping has increased), it has not disappeared altogether. Any speculation about this new economic model must also take into consideration the customs, lifestyle preferences, and the entrepreneurial spirit of human beings. As Julie Connelly notes, shopping at the mall remains America's favorite pastime:

> The real experience that the Web cannot replicate is social. Shopping is something teenagers do with their friends, especially girls who want to show each other how cool they look in the blue sweater they just found under a load of awful green ones.
>
> "The Net kind of takes away the whole experience—the hunt, the get and the buy," said Eva Kuhn, 13, of New York who browses on line but buys in the stores. "Web shopping is just too perfect. You type in 'gray cords' and there they are. It's not fun."[30]

Cultural Trends in the Digital Age. *Globalization.* Digital media promises to obliterate traditional borders, moving the world further into Marshall McLuhan's vision of the global village. The digital domain offers social, cultural, artistic, economic, and political linkages throughout the world. Businesses have established connections and linkages throughout the world (see our earlier discussion on the Global, Communications-based Economy). As a result, a resident of Bangkok, Thailand, may have more in common with a person living in Montreal, Canada, than with her neighbor down the street.

Decentralization. At the same time, the communications age is playing a major role in the decentralization of countries. Negroponte contends that the global communications age threatens the current configuration of sovereign nations. "Nations, as we know them today, will erode because they are neither big enough to be global nor small enough to be local."[31] In fact, more than half of the world's 200 nations formed as "breakaways" after 1946. Many nations—including Brazil, Britain, Canada, China, France, Italy, and Spain—are *devolving* power to regions in various ways.[32]

This trend toward decentralization is also occurring in the United States. For instance, the federal government has been largely ineffectual in addressing major issues such as global warming. As a result, a variety of public and private concerns have taken the initiative to address this problem. In 2007, the state of California (which is the seventh largest economy in the world) instituted its own statewide initiative to cut CO_2 emissions by 25 percent by 2020. In addition, a coalition of American corporations, including General Electric, DuPont, Duke Energy, Alcoa, and Caterpillar joined with environmental groups in a meeting with Congress to issue a "call to action" for a national cap-and-trade program to limit greenhouse gas emissions.[33]

Figure 15.2

In this decentralized world, global corporations have resources comparable to many nations. This map shows the gross domestic product of selected countries and companies whose market capitalizations are about to equal them. With employees and holdings spread throughout the world, corporations are no longer beholden to these individual nations. Indeed, it can be argued that corporations are becoming such significant global entities that they have assumed much of the power and influence formally held by nation-states.

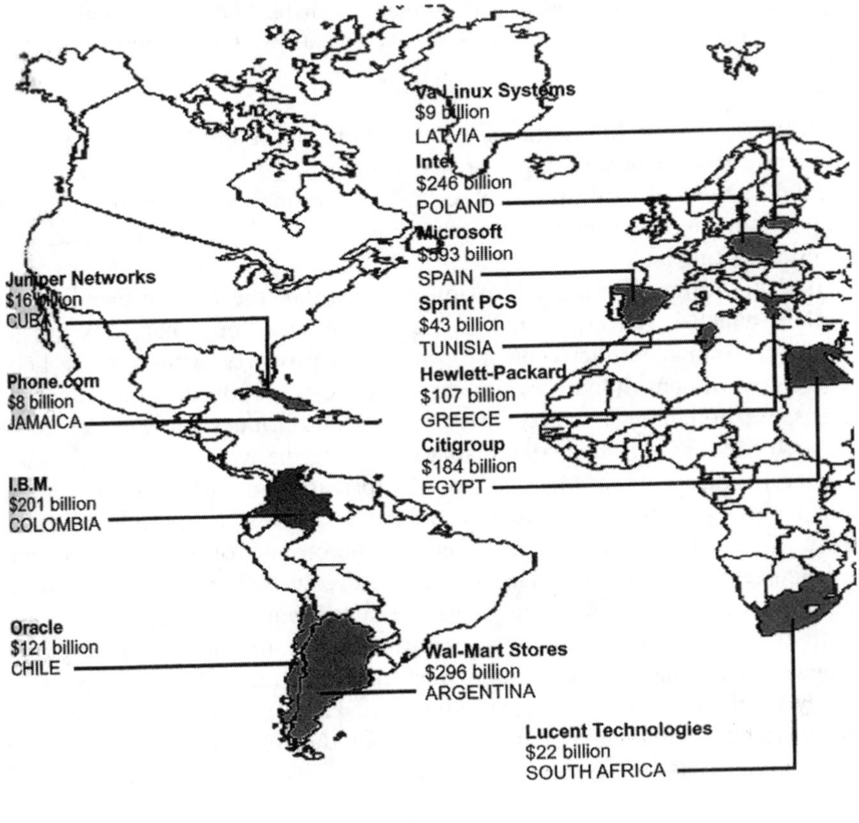

The same trend toward localization in the United States is occurring in the area of healthcare reform. Federal government programs leave 47 million people throughout the country uninsured. In response, Governor Arnold Schwarzenegger of California announced plans for a statewide healthcare program to cover all residents.

Increasingly, private companies are assuming responsibility for a range of services traditionally provided by government. Public education has been largely abandoned in the United States, in favor of private schools. Further, many municipalities are now contracting with private companies to provide sewer repair and upkeep of roads. Private security forces are being hired to maintain order in companies, public spaces such as malls, and in private gated communities. Additionally, prisons built and operated by the private sector are among the fastest growing industries. Private organizations have even begun to assume the role of governments in the conduct of foreign affairs. Increasingly, nongovernmental organizations (NGOs) are negotiating peace accords among nations. Paul Lewis explains,

> That shift (to NGOs) is a result of the growing complexity of the international agenda, of a communications revolution that has enabled NGOs to mobilize public opinion and of reduced ambitions of governments everywhere since the end of the cold war.[34]

To illustrate, the International Campaign to Ban Land Mines has played an active role in negotiating a treaty among 122 nations to ban antipersonnel mines. In addition, Amnesty International was instrumental in moving the international community into establishing the International Criminal Court.

In 2006, after the Israeli invasion of Lebanon, the Islamic group Hezbollah, which is not connected to the government, immediately began to repair the damage inflicted on the people and property. Although the Lebanese government didn't have the resources to respond immediately to the crisis, Hezbollah began to reconstruct roads and bridges and gave $12,000 to each resident who had been displaced during the war.

Decentralization has also led to the privatization of military forces. Blackwater is a private company that has become a major military presence in the Middle East. Blackwater is a mercenary force with no formal allegiance to any country. This private army, 20,000 strong, has modern equipment, including helicopters and the latest combat artillery.

In the United States, discussions are cropping up about replacing centralized government with regional territories within the United States. A study by the economists Alberto Alesina of Harvard and Enrico Spolaore of Tufts University make a strong case that the sheer size of government has hindered its ability to meet the needs of its dispersed population.[35]

According to Governor Schwarzenegger, California's ability to legislate initiatives in universal healthcare and global warming are evidence that the decentralization of power has already begun: "We are the modern equivalent of the ancient city-states of Athens and Sparta. We have the economic strength, we have the population and the technological force of a nation-state.... We are a good and global commonwealth."[36]

As an example of this trend toward regionalism in the United States, Berkshire County, a small community in Massachusetts, has begun printing its own currency, BerkShares, with the bills bearing the likeness of famous figures who made this county their home: a Mohican ($1), Robyn Van En, champion of community-supported agriculture projects ($5), W. E. B. DuBois, a founder of the civil rights movement ($10), Herman Melville ($20), and Norman Rockwell ($50). Reporter Dan Barry explains,

> The central purpose behind is to strengthen the local economy, perhaps even inoculate it against the whims of globalization, by encouraging people to support local businesses....
>
> Several dozen businesses agreed to include an alternative currency in their daily transactions and give a discount to those who used it. Now people can pay for groceries, an oil change, and even dental work with this currency.... For example, the Berkshire Co-op Market took in an astounding 160,000 BerkShares in the first three months.[37]

As Vehicle for Social Change. The Internet has emerged as a powerful tool that can be used to energize and organize grassroots political movements. A 2006 Pew survey found that 11 percent of Internet users have become online political activists (defined as users who have posted their own commentary to a newsgroup, web site, or blog, or posted or forwarded someone else's commentary, video, or audio recordings).[38] According to Lee Rainie, director of the Pew Research Center, "There's a viral, grassroots system for sharing information now that gets around the traditional gate-keeping function of the mainstream media."[39] As an example, in 2007, Brazil's government announced the establishment of the Forest People's Network, which provides free Internet access to native Indian tribes in the Amazon, including communities reachable only by riverboat. This network is designed to help protect the world's biggest rainforest by enabling tribes to report illegal logging and ranching, request help, and coordinate efforts to preserve the forest.[40]

However, the transition to a global communications age may very well be accompanied by a period of radical social upheaval. Historically, as societies have moved from one stage of economic sensibility to another (i.e., from the hunter-gatherer stage through the agrarian stage, to the industrial age), traditional lines of authority and power have been disrupted, leaving individuals to face issues of meaning and survival. To illustrate, futurist

Alvin Toffler views the American Civil War as a confrontation between the traditional agrarian society (the South) and the new industrial society (the North).

One of the truly alarming prospects of the communications age is that digital technology is widening existing divisions within societies. Jeremy Rifkin predicts that the global communications economy could result in an 80 percent unemployment rate within the next 50 years—principally in the labor, distribution, and service sectors (see above discussion, Global, Communications-based Economy).[41] According to this scenario, few people will be able to afford to purchase the goods offered over the Internet.

Thus, what Bill Clinton referred to as "the digital divide" can contribute to situations in which a considerable segment of the population feels disenfranchised, with little hope for success—conditions that are highly conducive to social upheaval. Criminologist Richard Rosenfeld observes, "Generally speaking, widening disparities will create disorder. This disorder can take the form of political process, or it can take a more individualized form such as street crime."[42]

Privacy. As discussed earlier, innovations in communications technology have made it possible to keep track of your whereabouts and activities. The Global Positioning System (GPS), a satellite-based tool, is now automatically installed in cellphones unless you manually disengage the system. Further, GPS systems like OnStar and LoJack are sold in cars as a safety feature, but in the process they function as location tracking devices.

The U.S. government has been found guilty of illegal spying on the domestic phone records and Internet activities of U.S. citizens without first obtaining a warrant. By analyzing these private communications through "data mining," the National Security Agency hoped to uncover terrorist activities. In 2006, Detroit District Court judge Anna Diggs Taylor ruled that the program is unconstitutional under the First and Fourth Amendments of the United States Constitution. However, her decision is stayed pending appeal, meaning that the domestic spying program is continuing.

Privacy has also become an issue in the workplace. By using monitoring software, employers track Internet activities of their employees and read their e-mail and computer files—in most cases, without informing the employees that they are being watched. All of this information can be placed in an employee's personnel record and used as part of a performance evaluation. In 2006, it was disclosed that Hewlett-Packard's chairwoman, Patricia Dunn, had ordered illegal spying into the phone and Internet records of her company's board of directors as part of an effort to discover who had leaked inside information to the media. In addition, RFID technology (see previous discussion) enables employers to track the physical whereabouts and daily activities of their employees.

The Organization for Economic Cooperation and Development has formulated a set of privacy guidelines, which stipulates that you have the right to expect the following:

- Any personal data that you submit over the Internet will not be used without your consent.
- You have a right to correct any errors.
- You have the right to assume the data will be protected from abuse.[43]

Ultimately, however, your best defense may be understanding that privacy is tenuous in this digital age. As CEO of Sun Microsystems Scott McNealy observes, "You have no privacy anyway. Get over it."[44] Armed with this understanding, you can take some precautions that will minimize intrusions, such as turning off the Global Positioning System on your cellphone or adding firewall software to your home computing network. Pete Slover observes,

> Experts advise a simple guideline for net activity: Assume nothing is absolutely private or safe. That includes your e-mail, browsing habits, news group postings and to be safe the contents of the hard drive of many machines hooked to the Net. Any crucial information should be backed up and, if privacy is essential, should be scrambled using encryption software widely available on the Internet.[45]

MEDIA LITERACY TIPS

PRIVACY

The Federal Trade Commission has posted the following list of steps that parents can take to protect children by safeguarding the privacy of their children online:

- Look for a privacy policy.
- Decide whether to give consent ... authorizing the web site to collect personal information from your child.
- Decide whether to approve information collection from your kids based on new uses for the information.
- Ask to see the information your child has submitted.
- Understand that you may revoke your consent at any time and have your child's information deleted.[46]

Warfare in the Digital Age. The digital culture is even affecting how countries wage war. The very concept of enemies has changed, which makes it harder to combat them. The terrorism network is not centralized in one nation. Their affiliation is no longer defined by national borders but, rather, on broader connections such as religion, history, class, and ideology.

Communications technology has emerged as a major threat to world security. John Markoff comments,

> The specter of simultaneous computer network attacks against banking, transportation, commerce and utility targets—as well as against the military—conjures up the fear of an electronic Pearl Harbor in which the nation is paralyzed without a single bullet ever being fired.[47]

It is extremely difficult for a standard military force to defend against a cyber attack. Steven Lukasik declares,

> "Preparing for cyberwar will force the nation to rethink the way it fights wars.... We've been trained to fight nuclear wars where static defenses are fatal, but in information warfare we have to rethink everything."[48]

In 2007, China successfully conducted a missile test designed to "blind" one of its older communications satellites. The implications of this test are far reaching and devastating to countries like the United States that rely on communication satellites to manage their military forces.

There are also enormous concerns about the digital domain as a terrorist target. The U.S. Pentagon has established a military center to coordinate the nation's cyberwarfare forces under the Air Force Space Command. Markoff explains,

> The new command's first mission will be to coordinate the defense of the military's computer networks against foreign threats and cyberterrorists. Soon after the mission will expand to include offense: Joint Task Force Computer Network Attack, in Pentagon jargon, designed to conduct wartime military operations against computer networks in enemy countries.[49]

Within this context, nuclear weapons assume a different role in cyber warfare. Instead of a huge arsenal used to destroy property and military forces, a small tactical nuclear weapon that releases a powerful electromagnetic pulse (EMP) can be deployed to destroy computer, telecommunications, and defense systems.

Education. Distance learning is currently trapped in the mind-set of the traditional classroom.

One of the future trends with respect to education is based on *game theory.* Video games offer sophisticated, personalized interactive learning environments in which participants learn at their own pace. In addition, these simulation learning modules apply many of the entertainment elements found in video games, including a narrative structure, characters, and storyline. As an example, a marine biology course could begin with you, the student, supplying basic information about yourself, including a photograph. From there, you would be able to see yourself in a "wetsuit," making your way to the ocean floor. The narrative flow involves learning about the environment to reach a "goal" or objective. Thus, each fish that you encounter would tell you (since, in this world, fish can talk) about themselves, which is part of the puzzle. The "winners" of the game are the students who are able to apply the principles of marine biology toward the objective.

In addition, college courses are currently being offered in Second Life, a virtual world, in which participants assume identities, called *avatars*. The instructor and students meet in virtual classrooms.

Worldview

Subcultures that are hardly visible in traditional media are a significant presence within the worldview of the digital domain. As an example, in 1999, over 2,000 web sites were dedicated to issues involving the gay community.[50] But by 2007, the same search yielded over 62 *million* web site results.

Virtual venues provide opportunities for members of subcultures to discuss areas of particular interest and concern to their communities. For instance, web pages provide information on neighborhoods, cruises, and investments.

Because the digital domain is a virtual melting pot, numerous *ideologies* are represented—from right-wing militia groups to libertarians. As an example, in 2007, there were 3.1 million sites on the Internet that referenced "anarchists."[51]

The dialogue on the Internet can also disclose ideological trends and issues. To illustrate, Populism is a political ideology that promotes the interests of ordinary people. This ideology is gaining momentum in Latin American countries such as Peru, Chile, Argentina, Bolivia, and Venezuela. "Googling" the term *Populism* yielded 2.5 million results. (Googling involves using the Google search engine to uncover how many times a concept appears throughout the virtual universe.) However, a subset of this search, "radical populism," which regards this movement as a threat, produced 644,000 results. A survey of the first page of these results furnishes perspective into the range of objections to this ideology—from populism undermining the democratic process to it being perceived as a global security threat.

In a broader sense, however, this haphazard collection of political ideologies in the digital domain is overshadowed by a more pervasive consumer ideology. Web companies are global capitalistic enterprises that regard participants solely as potential customers.

Structure

At this stage, corporations are still struggling to realize the commercial potential of the media system. During the first nine months of 2006, the combined Internet operations (which appear on its financial statement included in a category called "other") posted an operating loss of $68 million at a company that showed total operating income of $2.84 billion. Richard Siklos observes,

> We're still in the early innings, but given how much the Internet has already transformed the media and society, it's surprising how little money traditional media companies make directly from it.
>
> The optimist's view is that the spoils from this new frontier are still very much up for grabs. Only about 6 percent of all advertising spending in the United States went to the Internet in the first quarter of the year, according to Merrill Lynch.... The less-cheerful view of the traditional media companies is that all their online efforts will not translate directly into more revenue or fatter profits.... This is not to say that online will never be an important—if not central—financial contributor to media businesses of all kinds. For some companies, though, it could serve increasingly as a promotional or marketing outlet, or as a cut-rate but widely distributed version of what consumers can buy in conventional formats.... For now, though, the question of who among the media companies has this Internet thing figured out remains open.[52]

Media conglomerates are in the process of adding digital properties to their empires. In 2006, Rupert Murdoch's News Corporation bought the site MySpace.com for $580 million. MySpace.com originated as a grassroots site where teenagers could make friends with peers. However, after purchasing MySpace, News Corp has taken steps to control the content that appeared on the site, blocking information that appears without authorization of News Corp or without entering into a direct partnership with the company. According to Webster University graduate student Alex Bell, the corporate takeover will ultimately change the function of the site:

> MySpace.com flourished because teenagers and young adults found it to be a place for freedom of expression, a cultural equalizer. Anyone could get a page for self-expression or self-promotion in an increasingly high pressured music industry. Murdoch's $580 million dollar purchase of the site marks the beginning of the end of individual influence on MySpace content. This "product" will need to be highly profitable at the expense of garrulous teenagers and fledgling bands.[53]

The digital domain is a democratic medium that thus far has resisted central ownership. However, large Internet Service Providers (ISP) like AT&T, Spring, MCI, and Charter argue that they should have the right to "prioritize" the information that is distributed through their network. The criteria for this multi-tiered system would be based upon commercial considerations; the highest priority would be for those organizations conducting business with the ISP. In essence, the Internet would become a toll road. Those at the end of the line would be comprised of personal communications, academic traffic, and companies that are unable to pay the additional charges. Opponents of this measure favor a policy of *Net Neutrality*, which calls for equal access. As of 2007, this measure is being considered by the U.S. Congress. Eric Schmidt, CEO of Google, who is an advocate of Net Neutrality, declares, "Creativity, innovation, and a free and open marketplace are all at stake in this fight."[54]

Regulation of Content. The regulation of the digital domain is problematic (see earlier discussion, "Decentralization"). However, the current efforts to regulate the content and access to the digital domain originate from three sources.

International Consortiums consist of groups devoted to transnational regulatory efforts. One measure consists of designating additional *domain names*. Domain names appear at the end of the URL and identify the web site's purpose. For instance, educational institutions are ".edu," commercial enterprises are designated ".com," and government websites are ".gov." In 2004, the International Consortium for Assigned Names and Numbers opened the process of expanding the domain names. New domains under consideration include ".xxx" for sexually explicit information, and ".jobs" which identifies employment opportunities and human resource issues for businesses. However, at this point, none of the new domain names have been added.

Individual nations throughout the world are taking measures to regulate access to content on the Internet. For instance, China's extremely sophisticated filtering system prevents access to sensitive topics, including pornography, religious materials, and political dissent. In 2006, the Chinese government entered into an agreement with search engine Google; in exchange for access to 100 million Chinese consumers, Google agreed to censor material that the government found objectionable. Thus, a Google search of "Tiananmen Square," site of 1989 student protest that turned into a massacre, generates images of protesters and tanks, whereas a search through the Chinese filter produces benign images of happy tourists posing in the square.

Iran, Saudi Arabia, United Arab Emirates, Tunisia, Yeman, and Sudan also employ commercial filtering products—all developed by U.S. corporations. Nart Villeneuve warns, "In effect, U.S. corporations are in a position to determine what millions of citizens can and cannot view on the Internet."[55]

In this emerging global culture, a country's ability to enforce its laws and regulations is becoming increasingly challenging. To illustrate, the United States has its own laws restricting pornography; however, an Internet user need only tap into a web site originating in another, more permissive country, to circumvent U.S. laws. However, individual nations are attempting to make digital companies conform to their legal regulations. In 2007, a Belgian court ruled that Google's news-aggregating service, Google News, has been violating copyright laws by providing links to French-language newspapers.

Countries also encounter obstacles in the enforcement of laws regulating commerce. Governments must contend with "virtual" corporations that can change their country of residence within minutes. The *London Economist* observes, "Every day, $1.5 trillion moves around the world's foreign-exchange markets. Companies merge across national borders and even talk of changing nationality completely."[56] In this environment, the commercial regulations of one country have very limited authority.

Furthermore, it is difficult, if not impossible, for individual governments to assess taxes on global business transactions. According to the National Governor's Association, within several years states could be losing up to $12 billion in tax revenue annually.[57] To illustrate, consider the following scenario:

> I live in the United States. I open a new business. I do not manufacture a product but, instead, provide an information service. It is entirely online. The monetary transactions are credited to my account in the Netherlands. I bypass the local, national, and the international tax structure. In fact, I don't pay taxes anywhere. How can the United States government require me to pay business taxes if the machines, information, and accounting transaction systems are physically located in South Africa?

Finally, *individuals* can choose to filter out content that they find objectionable. Software is available that blocks access to certain kinds of information for themselves and their families. However, this software can be too literal, eliminating relevant sources of information. To illustrate, with some filtering systems, a student doing a report on breast cancer would find that any reference to the word "breast" blocked. Another problem is that although many adults are too intimidated by computers to install and use the software, their children know how to circumvent this software.

FRAMEWORK

Introduction

The homepage serves as the introduction to a web site. In this capacity, the homepage serves a number of functions:

- *To attract attention.* A web designer relies on glitzy media (graphics, photos, video, and audio), as well as attractive colors to draw visitors to the site.
- *To create a first impression.* The homepage affects our attitudes about the site's credibility and value. In addition, the homepage provides information about the web site's focus and mission.

- *To establish an identity, or "personality" of the web site.* One of the objectives of a web site is to develop an identity with which the intended audience feels comfortable and familiar. Within this context, examining the qualities of the web site can furnish some valuable clues about the web site's intended audience.
- *To draw the audience member deeper into the site.* The homepage is designed to convince the audience that additional information of interest can be found deeper in the site. However, at times, this homepage is a teaser designed to *redirect* your initial interest. For instance, you may hit a site looking for a vacation to Scotland, only to have a "pop-up" ad attempt to convince you that you'd rather invest in a new set of tires. It is important to remain clear about your initial purpose for visiting the site, so that you can be alert to efforts to redirect this interest. You will then be in a position to make a conscious decision about whether to pursue this new direction or find a site that provides the information you were originally seeking.
- *To serve as table of contents.* The homepage directs the audience to points of interest or importance in the site. In the process, the menu of information serves as an indicator of the priorities of the digital media communicator.

Explicit Content

How do you evaluate the information that is available in the digital universe? Because of the open nature of the network, the available information is, to be kind, uneven.

Much of what appears in traditional print is subjected to a review process to verify the validity of the content. Copy editors and editors review the text to insure clarity and accuracy. In addition, scholarly articles generally go through a rigorous peer review process. In contrast, no such guarantee exists with respect to the content that appears on the digital network. Consequently, it has become a real challenge to evaluate the information that appears on web sites. The criteria that should be used to evaluate content include:

- *Verifiability.* Is the information supported by evidence? Is it verifiable?
- *Timeliness.* One of the unique characteristics of digital media is that information can be continually revised and updated. Subjects such as technology, science, medicine, politics, media, and business are continually evolving. For these topics in particular, critical questions include: When was the information first published? And when was the site updated?

  The date of the last revision sometimes appears at the bottom of the homepage. But if you are unable to determine the currency of the information, it could be outdated and therefore should be researched further or discarded.
- *Verifiable Sources.* Does the author use sources? If so, what do you know about these sources?
- *Point of View.* What is the point of view of the text? What elements are used to reinforce that point of view?

PRODUCTION ELEMENTS

Digital media reflects a unique combination of print, photography, graphics, audio, and video. These media can complement and support each other to present information clearly and effectively. For instance, video footage can show an event unfolding, supplemented by print text that provides essential background, details, and context about the event.

On a practical level, the digital communicator can use production elements to make it easier to navigate through the digital site. As an example, web sites designed for an older audience use larger fonts, a simple graphic design, clear navigational instructions, and a voice recognition system rather than a keyboard.

In some cases, the production elements are tied to *function*. The manifest function of many web sites designed for children is to attract their attention through colorful graphics or a fun interactive approach.

As with all media, the style of a presentation should reinforce the central message.

The digital communicator should be able to individualize the style of the presentation to engage the Receiver. Production elements such as color, graphics, and music create a "look" that reflects the audience member's tastes and interests. For instance, a web site might present a conservative appearance for one visitor, and a wild look for another.

However, simply changing the style does not necessarily mean that the content is more timely and relevant. You cannot assume that a new look means that the information has been updated; the existing information may simply have been repackaged.

Style can also express an attitude about the content being presented. The production elements may suggest that the site is hip, fluid, and exciting, and that the information contained in the site is worth examining.

And, as discussed earlier, production elements like the title, graphics, photos, and slogans can provide insight into the intended target audience. For instance, colorful graphics establishes a fun interactive environment designed to attract the attention of a young audience. (For more discussion, see Chapter 4, Audience.)

At times, however, production elements can actually *interfere* with the message. The latent function of fancy graphics and animation may be to impress the audience with the designer's technical wizardry rather than to communicate a message

At the beginning of the twenty-first century, the aesthetic quality of interactive media was relatively primitive. Computers could only display 256 colors. Further, video footage consumed vast amounts of the computer's hard drive, so that clips could only be stored sparingly. However, thanks to developments such as broadband, entire movies can be downloaded onto your computer. Additional developments such as increased storage space in new model computers, video-sharing, user-generated video, and free digital storage have made video readily available.

Sophisticated media technology that in the 1990s was beyond the reach of individuals and small companies is now in the hands of anyone with a laptop computer. Technical advances now enable individuals to shoot, edit, and distribute professional level materials to a global audience, decentralizing the artistic process. As a result, independent videos have emerged as an alternative entertainment format; young people are watching (and producing) independent videos on venues like YouTube.com, instead of the predictable genres that appear on the major broadcast networks.

As of 2007, video accounts for 60 percent of the traffic on the Internet.[58] In a significant development, search engines for video such as Blinkx, TruVeo, Flurl, and ClipBlast are being developed that enable an individual to locate a video clip in the vast virtual universe, to transcribe the words uttered in a video, and to search them, using speech-recognition technology. Efforts are ongoing to develop more effective search engines that organize visual information as well as speech.

The size of the screen remains a factor in the production and presentation of content. A wide range of display monitors are now available. The average screen size on a personal laptop computer is roughly 17 inches diagonally. In addition, programs are being transmitted to cellphones and iPods, where the screen size can be considerably smaller. At the same time, there is a trend toward the large screen *entertainment monitor.* Apple TV connects the personal computer with large screen television sets (for further discussion, see Chapter 13, Advertising).

Sound has also vastly improved. The sound quality on the computer remains relatively limited, due to the small speakers; however, the systems can be wired to external high quality speakers.

Editing

Editing assumes a whole new dimension in digital media. Web developments are never "completed"—meaning that the information can be updated minute by minute if budget allows. In addition, the web page can provide considerably more information than the conventional print layout. The entire screen can be filled with headlines that contain "pull down" menus that elaborate on the topic. The additional effect of having the participant "pull down" the connected story is that the page editor now *knows what you are reading*. This is the true power of digital technology—the ability to measure each and every move the participant makes in navigating the site.

Search engines prioritize the search results that appear at the top of the list and what information is omitted entirely. It is important to remember that commercial search engines like Yahoo! are designed to generate revenue—not serve as your local library. For instance, if you are investigating the moons of Jupiter, the search engine scans the digital domain to find key words (e.g., "moons," "Jupiter"). But on commercial sites, a predetermined list of recommended sites appears, tied to financial arrangements with the search engine. In addition, in 2006, bloggers manipulated Google (called "Google bombing") so that inquiries about Republican candidates would call up a list of online sites and sources that were critical of these candidates. (For more discussion of Google bombing, see Chapter 14, Political Communications.) However, only 38 percent of searchers are aware of this distinction between paid and unpaid results among search returns.[59] Danny Sullivan, the editor of Search Engine Watch declares, "Anybody who looks for something on any search engine and thinks the results are the best or most impartial results, or that they came back completely organically is totally mistaken."[60]

It is essential to look closely at the elements of the web page to make certain that it is authentic. Unscrupulous thieves engage in "phishing" expeditions, in which they fraudulently acquire passwords and credit card details by masquerading as a legitimate business enterprise that the customer has used. These phishers construct web sites that are nearly identical to the actual business, using "screen scraping" software. Even the links send the Initiator to the identical sites. The only distinguishable difference between the phony legitimate web sites is the "web address" that appears at the top of the browser.

Because the audience assumes a major role in retrieving information, the editor must develop navigation strategies to present information in a clear, easily accessible manner. The editor works with a number of navigational elements in a web site so that the audience can move through the information easily.

The following elements are common to most commercial web sites, or *graphical user interface* (GUI):

- Site Specific Search Engines, that allow you to find information on the site
- Comprehensive Toolbars, a logical way to maneuver through the digital environment
- Advertising, either as a pop-up or embedded on the page
- Multiple Language Option
- Archive
- Video/Audio Components
- Link to the Author(s)
- Ancillary "hot links," links embedded in the copy that provide additional information
- E-mail address of "author"

- Option to forward the content/site through e-mail
- Links to graphics and maps
- Blog link
- Podcast link
- Specific links to associated sites (either through commercial contract or mutual ownership sites)
- "Opt in" notification system (so that you can request up-to-date information or sales)
- Online surveys (e.g., "What do you think of Britney Spears' new (bald) look: Hot or not?")

CONCLUSION

Applying critical analysis techniques to digital media enables individuals to make independent judgments about the information they receive and communicate through this dynamic medium. As the medium continues to evolve, an individual's ability to apply media literacy strategies will become even more acute.

NOTES

1. Evelyn Nussenbaum, "Coming Soon to a Theater Near You: The Moviemercial," *New York Times*, September 21, 2003.
2. David Carr, "Idiosyncratic and Personal, PC Edges TV," *New York Times,* October 16, 2002, C1.
3. "Some Get Internet 'Data High'. Parents Fear Kids Prefer PCs to Peers, Others Overwhelmed by Info," Reuters News Service, *St. Louis Post-Dispatch*, December 9, 1997 (www.postnet.com).
4. Ibid.
5. Ibid.
6. Glued to the Screen: An Investigation into Information Addiction Worldwide, 1996 Reuters Survey.
7. Miguel Helft, "In a Search Refinement, a Chance to Rival Google," *New York Times,* February 9, 2007, C3.
8. Kathleen Tyner, *Literacy in a Digital World* (Mahwah, NJ: Lawrence Erlbaum Associates, 1998).
9. Ibid.
10. "Group Cites Alarming Rise of Hate Sites on Internet," *St. Louis Post-Dispatch*, February 24, 1999, A4.
11. Lou Birenbaum, interview by author, September 14, 1999.
12. Deborah Peterson, "Three Recent Cases Show Cyberworld Has Dark Side Watch Young Surfers, Experts Urge," *St. Louis Post-Dispatch*, July 29, 1998, B1.
13. Janet E. Alexander and Marsha Ann Tate, *Web Wisdom: How to Evaluate and Create Information Quality on the Web* (Mahwah, NJ: Lawrence Erlbaum Associates, 1999), 63.

14. Randy Cohen, "The Way We Live Now: The Ethicist," *New York Times Magazine*, January 26, 2003, 19.

15. Camille Sweeney, "In a Chat Room You Can Be N E 1," *New York Times Magazine*, October 17, 1999, 66–70.

16. Alexander and Tate, *Web Wisdom: How to Evaluate and Create Information Quality on the Web,* 45.

17. Elizabeth Kirk, "Practical Steps in Evaluating Internet Resources," Milton's Web Page 423.99 (http://milton,mse.jhu.edu:8001/research/education/practical.html).

18. Nicholas Negroponte, "Beyond Digital," *Wired Magazine* (December 1998) (http://www.wired.com).

19. Steve Lohr, "It's Long Boom or Bust for Leading Futurist," *New York Times*, June 1, 1998.

20. Bran Ferren, "The Intercranial Internet," *New York Times Magazine*, March 15, 1998, pg. 28.

21. "Questions for Kevin Warwick," *New York Times Magazine*, October 4, 1998, 27.

22. John Brunner, *Stand on Zanizibar* (Ballantine Books, 1969), 262.

23. Kenneth Chang, "Now There Are Many: Robots that Reproduce," *New York Times*, May 17, 2005.

24. Paul B. Brown, "Wireless Codependency," *New York Times*, February 17, 2007.

25. Ibid.

26. Alex Beers, interview, "Facebook," February 27, 2007.

27. Leah Silverblatt, interview, "Facebook," February 27, 2007.

28. "Top Twenty Internet Acronyms Every Parent Needs to Know," NetLingo (www.netlingo.com/toptwentyteens.cfm).

29. Katie Dean, "The Language of IM," *Wired Magazine* (www.wired.com/news/culture).

30. Julie Connelly, "A Ripe Target for Web Retailers, Teens Keep Heading to the Mall," *New York Times*, September 22, 1999 (www.nytimes.com).

31. Nicholas Negroponte, "Beyond Digital," *Wired Magazine* (December 1998) (www.wired.com).

32. Gar Alperovitz, "California Split," *New York Times,* February 10, 2007, A27.

33. Ibid.

34. Paul Lewis, "Not Just Governments Make War or Peace," *New York Times*, November 28, 1998, A19.

35. Alperovitz, "California Split."

36. Ibid.

37. Dan Barry, "Would You Like That in Tens, Twenties or Normans?" *New York Times,* February 25, 2007, Section 1; Col. 1.

38. Frank Davies, "Internet as Political Force Grows, Poll Finds Shift Away from TV, Papers Continues," *San Jose (Ca.) Mercury News,* January 18, 2006.

39. Ibid.

40. Peter Muello, "Brazil to Offer Free Internet Access to Amazon Tribes," Associated Press Financial Wire, March 30, 2007, Business News (www.associated press.com).

41. Jeremy Rifkin, *The End of Work* (New York: Putnam Publishing Group, 1996).

42. Richard Rosenfeld, interview, September 29, 1999.

43. The Organization for Economic Cooperation and Development (www.oecd.org).

44. McNealy, Wired News.

45. Pete Slover, "Web 'cookies' are hot on the Internet," *St. Louis Post-Dispatch*, July 22, 1998 (www.postnet.com).

46. Kidz Privacy Resource Materials Federal Trade Commission (www.ftc.gov/kidzprivacy.gov).

47. John Markoff, "Blown to Bits: Cyberwarfare Breaks the Rules of Military Engagement," *New York Times*, October 17, 1999 (www.nytimes.com).

48. Ibid.

49. Ibid.

50. "Three Top Gay Online Communities Get Together," *Newsweek*, April 5, 1999 (www.newsweek.com).

51. Google (www.google.com).

52. Richard Siklos, "Waiting for the Dough on the Web," *New York Times*, June 25, 2006, 3.

53. Alex Bell, Webster University, unpublished paper, June 27, 2006 (bellawords@hotmail.com).

54. Eric Schmidt, "A Note to Google Users on Net Neutrality," Google, February 17, 2007 (www.google.com/help/netneutrality).

55. Nart Villeneuve, "The Filtering Matrix," First Monday peer-reviewed Internet journal (www.firstmonday.org).

56. Max Frankel, "A More Perfect Future," *New York Times Magazine*, January 24, 1999, 18.

57. Richard W. Stevenson, "Danger: A Tangled Web of Taxes," *New York Times*, September 27, 1998 (www.nytimes.com).

58. Jason Pontin, "Millions of Videos, and Now a Way to Search Inside Them," *New York Times*, February 25, 2007.

59. Tom Zeller Jr., "Gaming the Search Engine, in a Political Season," *New York Times,* November 6, 2006, C3.

60. Ibid.

PART

4

ISSUES AND OUTCOMES

CHAPTER 16

ISSUES IN MEDIA COMMUNICATIONS

This chapter examines the following media-related topics from a media literacy perspective:

- Media and Violence
- Media and Children
- Media and Social Change
- Global Communications

MEDIA AND VIOLENCE

In 2007 Brigadier General Patrick Finnegan, the Dean of West Point, along with experienced military and FBI interrogators asked the creative team behind the Fox television show *24* to stop using torture because American soldiers were copying the show's tactics. In five seasons of the show, there have been no less than sixty-seven torture scenes according to the Parents Television Council—that's more than one every show. Some of the torture tactics on *24* include drugging, water-boarding, electrocution, or power-drilling into a man's shoulder.[1]

Everyone has heard or read about incidents like this one, in which violent media programming has led to violence in real life. However, violence in the media is a complex issue that does not offer any simple solutions.

There is a high degree of violence throughout almost all television programming:

- The average American child sees 200,000 violent acts on TV by age 18.[2]
- By the age of 18, Americans witness 16,000 "murders" on television.
- Nearly two out of three TV programs contained violence; averaging six violent acts per hour.[3]
- There are more than twice as many violent incidents in children's programming than in other types of programming. The average child who watches two hours of cartoons a day may see more than 10,000 violent acts a year.[4]
- In nearly 75 percent of violent scenes on television, the characters showed no remorse, criticism, or penalty for the violence in the scene.[5]

Possible Explanations for Violence in the Media

Why does so much violent programming appear in the media? Possible explanations include the following:

Human Nature. Undeniably, there is a side to human nature that is attracted to violence. You may recall that as a child, while it was enjoyable to build something with blocks, it was often even *more* fun to knock them over. Audiences, of course, have the choice of watching nonviolent programming but enjoy watching programs that contain violence.

Media as Reflection of Culture. Violence is deeply ingrained in American culture. Richard Rosenfeld, co-author of *Crime and the American Dream*, declares, "The U.S. is in a category by itself in terms of homicide and serious interpersonal violence. American culture is saturated with violent images and examples that reflect the violent nature of U.S. culture."[6]

However, the media still present an exaggerated picture of violence in America. Although 1 in l0 television characters is involved in violence in any given week, the chances of an individual being a victim of a violent crime is no more than one in 100 *per year.*[7]

Industry Considerations. Violent programming is a very attractive option for an industry that is predicated on profit. In order to attract the largest possible audience, media programs generally feature the unusual and exciting. Nobody wants to watch policemen involved in the uneventful routine of their jobs, like filling out forms, walking the beat, or selling tickets to the policeman's ball. As a result, successful action/adventure films are packed with shoot-outs, car chases, and mass destruction—to the point that the audience regards violence as a part of an American agent's typical day.

In addition, violent programming is highly exportable to international markets. Although dialogue-driven programming can present some translation problems, blowing something up is a universal language. As a result, violence-laden programs like *Mission Impossible* and *Casino Royale* are popular in numerous countries, including France, Italy, Germany, Brazil, and Israel.

Characteristics of Media. One of the chief characteristics of film and television is the illusion of motion. Consequently, these media often emphasize external action, or plot. And since plot generally involves some *conflict* between characters or events, the action that takes place is often violent in nature.

Cumulative Messages: Media Violence

Audiences have been inundated with programs which, when seen as a whole, present some very clear cumulative messages about violence:

- *The world is a violent place.* Violence in entertainment media programming, coupled with the news media's extensive coverage of violent events, can affect an individual's perception of the amount of violence in society. To illustrate, in 1999, the Columbine school shooting rampage in Littleton, Colorado, which was covered extensively in the media, had an enormous impact on students' perceptions of violence in schools. Although the rate of violence in U.S. high schools decreased significantly in the 1990s, only 37 percent of high school students felt safe in school. And over half of American teenagers believed that a murderous rampage could erupt at their own schools.[8]
- *Violence is an effective solution to problems.* This is an adolescent world that is defined by Absolutes: Good versus Evil. In this world, direct action is the best way to combat "Evildoers." In police dramas like *L.A. Confidential* (1997), Officer Bud White (Russell Crowe) faces *two* adversaries: the perpetrators of the crime that he is trying to crack and the bureaucracy that frustrates his efforts to get the job done. In this world, laws and regulations only get in the way.
- *Sometimes the ends justify the means.* In many media presentations, the moral issue is not whether violence is right or wrong, but rather is it *justified*. Significantly, nearly 40 percent of the violent incidents on television are initiated by the heroes of the story—those characters most likely to be perceived as role models.[9] The Retribution film is a popular sub-genre that plays off of this notion. Initially, the hero is either personally mistreated or discovers a social injustice. At this point, the protagonist becomes the primary perpetrator of violence in their effort to restore order. Within the context of these films, the violence is justifiable: the ends justifies the means.
- *Acts of violence frequently go unpunished.* Action heroes such as Vin Diesel, The Rock, and Daniel Craig are never held accountable for the damage they inflict on people and property in the course of their films. Indeed, only 16 percent of the programs show the long-term consequences of violence.[10]
- *Violence is associated with masculinity, power, and sexual energy.* Real men are distinguished by their ability to inflict violence. Women are attracted to the strength and power of protagonists engaged in violence. Consequently, in entertainment programming, acts of violence are frequently followed by lovemaking scenes.

  In addition, violence can serve as an opportunity for male bonding between the protagonists as they fight together to defeat a common enemy.
- *Violence is fun.* Entertainment programs often feature a type of comedic violence. This type of violence operates on an adolescent level in which fighting is depicted as a fun way to let off steam and impress the girls. These scenes are

accompanied by bouncy, upbeat, or silly music, which signals that there is no danger or threat of bodily harm to the protagonists.

- *The value of human life is minimized.* Within the course of a narrative, the victims of violence operate like chess pieces, removed from the board and forgotten in the flow of the story. For instance, westerns routinely include scenes in which Indians pursue a wagon filled with white settlers. One of the passengers shoots blindly out of the window; an Indian is hit, taking a spectacular fall. Immediately thereafter, the camera resumes the chase. The condition of the Indian warrior and his horse are quickly forgotten; the death of the warrior only represents one less adversary threatening the settlers.

  Taking this a step further, in George Lucas's *Star Wars: Episode I—Phantom Menace* (1999), the army of the Trade Federation is made up entirely of robots. As a result, the mass destruction of these soldiers during the battle scenes has been completely depersonalized.
- *Some people are more important than others.* As noted above, characters in supporting roles (who are often members of minority groups) are often killed without much attention or sympathy. However, if the hero or heroine (who generally is a member of the dominant culture) suffers even a minor injury, this is presented as a crisis that commands the attention of the other characters—and the audience as well.
- *Violence is safe.* Acts of violence never hurt members of the audience.
- *Violence is sanitary.* We can all recall media presentations in which the hero is "winged" by a bullet. There is little evidence of blood. Someone bandages the wound, and the hero carries on. In reality, however, gunshot wounds are extraordinarily repulsive and hideous. Film director Sam Peckinpah, whose work included *The Wild Bunch* (1969) and *The Straw Dogs* (1971), was often criticized for the explicit scenes of violence. For instance, he would include scenes in which characters who were shot were thrown back against the wall by the force of the gunshot. The camera would then show a trail of skull fragments and blood on the wall as the character slowly slid to the floor.

  However, Peckinpah's defense was the violence in his films was not gratuitous—he was simply presenting an accurate picture of violence. On the Internet Movie Database, "dexter-3" contributed the following review of *The Wild Bunch*:

  > Critics of Sam Peckinpah generally focus on the gore and violence in his films. *The Wild Bunch* will probably not assuage these critics, but the violence is not gratuitous. In fact, it is almost perfectly meshed in this story of a group of outlaws held together by some frail and some strong bonds who realize that their era—and probably their lives—are almost at an end.... Yes the violence is on a large scale (which seems to be commonplace for films portraying the Mexican Revolution), but it is completely in place with these characters and the era in which they live. This is not always a pleasant film to watch, but it is very rewarding, and may be the best film Peckinpah made.[11]
- *Violence is glamorous.* Killings and bombings are frequently shot in slow motion, from many angles. The explosions resemble a fireworks display.
- *Violence is gratifying.* In many media presentations, the primary message is a celebration of violence. Plot and character merely provide context and rationale

that lead up to a violent climax. As Mark Crispin Miller observes, violence in the media engenders a sense of pleasure and excitement in the audience:

> Screen violence is now used primarily to invite the viewer to enjoy the feel of killing, beating, mutilating. There is no point to Rambo's long climactic rage ... other than its open invitation to become him at that moment—to ape that sneer of hate, to feel the way it feels to stand there tensed up with the Uzi.[12]

The Effects of Media Violence

Six theories offer a range of perspectives on the effects of media violence on individuals:

The arousal theory. According to this school of thought, violent programming stimulates aggression in audience members that can lead to violent behavior. The classic research of Bandura, Ross, and Ross (1963), Liebert and Baron (1972), Lukesch (1988), and Bushman and Geen (1990) support this proposition.

Studies show that the likelihood of screen-triggered aggression is increased if the violence depicted on screen:

- Is realistic and exciting, like a chase or suspense sequence that sends adrenalin levels surging.[13]
- Succeeds in righting a wrong, like helping an abused or ridiculed character get even.[14]
- Includes situations or characters similar to those in the viewer's own experience.[15]

A graphic illustration of the arousal theory of media violence occurred in Los Angeles riots on April 30, 1992, in the wake of the Rodney King verdict. Significantly, the riot was initially triggered by the media. A bystander videotaped the beating of King by police officers; otherwise, the incident wouldn't have been brought to public attention. In response to the news that the jury acquitted the police officers involved in the incident, Los Angeles erupted in violence. At least 58 people were killed and 2,383 injured. Thirteen TV station traffic helicopters furnished national coverage of the destruction, which further inflamed the situation. In Miami, Atlanta, Seattle, San Francisco, protests turned violent, and hundreds of people were arrested. Two people in Las Vegas were killed.

The cathartic theory. Paradoxically, violent programming may at times provide a healthy release for our aggressions. After watching a violent program, the audience may feel drained and purified, purged of their violent impulses. Within this context, media violence can be construed as positive and constructive.

The desensitizing theory. Some researchers have found that frequent exposure to media violence can have a numbing effect on the audience. For instance, Daniel Linz, Edward Donnerstein, and Steven Penrod found that men who watched movies depicting violence against women had relatively fewer negative emotional reactions to the films, to perceive them as significantly less violent, and to consider them significantly less degrading to women.[16]

The opiate theory. After watching enough programming, people may become passive and incapable of feeling *anything*. Fred and Merrelyn Emery found that watching television is a dissociative medium that "as a simple, constant, repetitive visual stimulus gradually closes down the nervous system of man."[17] Couch potatoes who fall asleep on Sunday afternoons while watching the brutality of NFL football would support this theory.

Cumulative effects theory. Most researchers have focused on the immediate effects of media-carried violence. However, some studies suggest that cumulative media messages regarding violence may have *long-term, indirect* effects on individuals. For instance, Malamuth and Check found correlations between exposure to sexually violent media content among male college students and aggressive attitudes, as reflected in the belief that women enjoy forced sex.[18]

Studies also suggest that the cumulative media messages with regard to violence can have a long-term effect on an individual in the following ways:

- Becoming less sensitive to the pain and suffering of others.
- Being more fearful of the world around them.
- Becoming more likely to behave in aggressive or harmful ways toward others.[19]
- Thinking of aggressive behavior as normal.[20]

The no-effects theory. This theory holds that media violence has a minimal effect on audiences. The thinking here is that what we see and hear in the media is "just entertainment" and should not be taken seriously. Thus, watching a kung-fu movie is an enjoyable experience but will not dramatically change my life. Which of these theories about the effects of media violence on individuals is correct? *All of them.*

Studies conducted on the effects of media violence are not definitive. As you have seen, studies can be found that support each of these theories. In truth, many factors contribute to an individual's particular response to media violence.

Personality Profile. An individual's psychological makeup may affect how he or she will respond to violent programming. Some studies suggest that aggressive children may be attracted to media violence, which causes them to be even more aggressive.[21] Other personality variables that may influence response to media-carried violence include:

- Introverted vs. extroverted personality
- Stable vs. unstable personality
- Tender vs. tough-mindedness

- *Identification with media content.* A media presentation may strike a responsive chord in a member of the audience. A study by Frost and Stauffer supported the theory that when media content is generally congruent with the real-life experience of the audience, the result is a marked amplification of the reality of media messages. Thus, the reaction to filmed violence can depend upon a person's identification with the characters.[22] For example, you might react more strongly to the way that the character behaves if the character on-screen resembles your ex-boyfriend or ex-girlfriend.
- *Recent experiences.* What kind of a day did you have today? If you are in a foul mood, you might react differently to a program than if you were in a jolly frame of mind.
- *Immediate environment.* Sometimes what is going on around you can influence your response to a particular media presentation. Is someone sitting directly in front of you in the movie theater, blocking your view? Is someone behind you talking on their cellphone, so that you can't hear the dialogue in the film? These distracting activities can affect viewers' reactions to the characters in the film.
- *Gender.* Some studies suggest that gender may be a factor in determining how people respond to violent programming.[23] However, Frost and Stauffer caution that these results must be seen in a broader societal context: "Since the great majority of violence in the real world is committed by males, their arousal responses to dramatized violence may differ from those of females."[24]
- *Social class.* Frost and Stauffer's study found that lower-class subjects were significantly more aroused by viewing violent programming than a sample of middle-class college students. The researchers concluded that because the environment of the lower class subjects is often more violent than that of the college students, their significantly higher arousal levels to violent stimuli may be connected to their real-life surroundings.[25]
- *Content attributes.* Barry Gunter found that a number of specific program characteristics can affect how the audience responds to violent content in the media presentation:
- *The fictional setting of a portrayal.* Violent acts committed within a realistic setting are more disturbing than similar acts depicted in fictional entertainment genres, such as westerns, science fiction, or cartoons.
- *The types of characters who were involved as perpetrators and victims of violence.* Viewers reacted dramatically when the content depicted men inflicting violence on women.
- *The type of violence depicted.* Some forms of violence are more disturbing than others. Shootings and stabbings were regarded as more "serious" forms of violence than explosions or unarmed combat.
- *The amount of attention on the suffering of victims.* Visibly harmful violence was deemed to be more disturbing to viewers than violence with no observable consequences.[26]

Given all of these theories, the most accurate statement about the effects of media violence is as follows:

Under certain circumstances, some people may respond to violent programming in a particular way.

To illustrate, in 1981 John Hinkley attempted to assassinate President Ronald Reagan, shortly after seeing the film *Taxi Driver.* But although a theater filled with people watched *Taxi Driver,* Hinkley was the *only* one who was moved to attack the president. Other members of the audience may have felt purged, drowsy, or simply entertained. Jack Valenti, former president of the Motion Picture Association of America, commented,

> I'm not saying that movies don't have an impact (on violence in society). All I know is that other countries whose children watch the same movies and (TV) shows as we do here have crime rates that are much lower. There must be other factors going on that we don't know about.[27]

Regulatory Steps. In the United States, the Telecommunications Act of 1996 made built-in V-chips mandatory in all television sets built after January 2000. These computer chips enable the consumer to block out selected programs, so that parents can eliminate violent programming from their children's menu of programming choices. The V-chip is designed to work in tandem with a voluntary ratings system created by broadcast executives in accordance with the TCA mandate.

However, these regulatory steps have not resolved the issue of children being exposed to violence in the media. Although 81 percent of Americans believe that the V-chip technology will have a positive impact on children, 73 percent of the American public do not use the V-chip in their own homes.[28] Furthermore, 19 percent of parents had never heard of the ratings system, while only five of the 11 rating categories are understood by most parents.[29]

Moreover, there is evidence that the marketing strategy of film studios is designed to entice young people to actually circumvent these restrictive ratings and see R-rated films. An internal memo from one movie studio declared that the promotional goal was "to find the elusive teen target audience and make sure everyone between the ages of 12–18 was exposed to the film."[30] Another document outlined a plan to distribute fliers and posters about an R-rated movie to organizations like the Campfire Boys and Girls in Kansas City.[31] Similarly, the study found that music with explicit content labels and violent mature-rated video games targeted underage audiences.

Adding to the complexity of the regulatory issue, questions remain about how to define violence in media programming. In the current ratings system, subtle forms of violence routinely appear in children's programming, such as acts of emotional abuse and long-term violence against self (e.g., alcohol or drug abuse). Moreover, the issue of "sanctioned" violence (e.g., sports) is also not addressed in the ratings system. Thus, the ratings system would not consider a violent sport such as a football game or boxing match inappropriate for children.

Further, the *style* of a presentation can convey violent messages. Mabel L. Rice, Altha C. Huston, and John C. Wright note,

> Rapid action, loud music, and sound effects are often associated with violence in children's programs.... The forms themselves may come to signal violence or sex typing to children, even when the content cues are minimal or nonexistent.[32]

Consequently, no completely satisfactory solution exists to the issue of violence in the media. Because there is no definitive way to predict how people might react to violent programming, it is impossible to predict how an individual copes with violent content. In a democracy, it is always dangerous to censor information. Ultimately, audiences must assume responsibility by developing a sensitivity to media messages about violence and making thoughtful choices about what media programming to select. Frank Rich observes,

> To get real results in a society with free speech and a free market, we have to vote not for pious politicians but with our pocketbooks for the culture we say we want. No one is forcing American families to subscribe to the pay-cable services that program violent movies; no one requires adults to watch Jerry Springer in eye-popping numbers (and then abandon him the moment his show is stripped of violence by a circumspect TV mogul); no one has mandated that every household purchase a bloody video or computer game (90 percent of which are bought by adults).[33]

MEDIA AND CHILDREN

No discussion of media literacy would be complete without some discussion of the influence of media in the lives of children and some strategies through which youngsters can develop a critical independence from what they read and watch.

It is undeniable that the media have emerged as a major factor in the lives of children. The use of media by children under 18 is more than 38 hours a week—or about the equivalent of a full-time job.[34]

Consider the following statistics about the role of the media in the lives of American children:

- In the United States, the average one-year-old child watches television for six hours per week.[35]
- Hours per year the average American youth spends in school: 900.[36]
- The average American youth spends 900 hours per year in school. He/she spends 1,023 hours per year watching television.[37]
- 87 percent of American children between the ages of 12–17 are connected to the Internet.[38]

Much of the time that children spend with media is unsupervised. Twenty-six percent of children under two years of age and 65 percent of children age two and over have TVs in their bedrooms.[39] Nearly 17 percent have a computer, and 36 percent have a video game system—including 47 percent of boys.[40]

Children and Advertising

Children represent a tremendously lucrative market for goods and services. In 2005, American teens spent $159 billion, exceeding the gross domestic product of countries such as Finland, Norway, Portugal, and Greece.[41] In addition, children influence about $600 billion in adult spending a year. Consequently, $17 billion a year is spent directly marketing to children, even for adult goods like cars.[42]

Because children represent the future adult consumer market, it is not surprising that marketing researchers think of children as "consumers in training." As James McNeal observes, "All of the skills, knowledge, and behavior patterns that together we call consumer behavior are purposely taught to our children right along with toilet training, toddling and talking."[43]

When asked what they do when TV commercials come on, nearly 60 percent of respondents say they watch them.[44] Among the production elements most likely to capture the attention of a young audience include humor, music, animals (real or computer-generated), and animation.[45] Significantly, these elements are also in evidence in advertising for "adult" products such as cigarettes and alcohol.

Further, the distribution of promotional paraphernalia is an extremely effective form of advertising with young people. Teenagers who own a gym bag or sports clothing with a tobacco manufacturer's logo are twice as likely to become established smokers as those who do not.[46]

"*Buy Me That: A Kid's Survival Guide to TV Advertising,*" produced by Public Media, Inc. raises some essential questions about advertising for children to consider:

- *Do commercials use tricks?*
  Commercials sometimes exaggerate the capabilities of toys to make them appear more enticing. For example, some products may appear more sturdy in ads than they really are.
- *Can toys really talk (move or sing)?*
  If they move or talk on TV ... don't be so sure. This may only be a way of dramatizing the imaginative possibilities of the product.
- *How do they make food look so good?*
  Food stylists are often employed to make food in magazine ads and television commercials look appetizing. In some cases, the product itself is not even used in

the demonstration; for instance, the ice cream that appears in television ads is actually a combination of shortening, sugar, and food coloring.

- *How do they make games look so easy?*
  In television commercials, product demonstrations always appear effortless. Through skillful editing, nobody ever makes a mistake. Consequently, children may be frustrated once they attempt to use the product on their own.
- *What does "Parts sold separately" mean?*
  Young children who cannot read the fine print at the end of an ad may be disappointed when they do not receive all of the accessories displayed in the ad.
- *Are celebrity sneakers better?*
  The relationship between a product and its celebrity spokesperson can be confusing to children. Ads suggest that a celebrity's use of a product is the secret to his/her performance; for instance, Nike ads featuring Kobe Bryant suggest that his spectacular dunks are made possible by his choice of sneakers. However, it must be made clear that buying these sneakers will not turn a youngster into another Kobe Bryant.[47]

MEDIA LITERACY TIPS

CHILDREN'S ADVERTISING

John Lyons offers some additional suggestions that will help children analyze advertisements:

- *Resist cereals named after monsters or cartoon characters.*
- *Resist anything that insinuates that it's made with fruit when it isn't.*
- *Be wary of little girl doll commercials shot through pink and green filters.*
- *Beware of toy figures shot at severe angles that distort the scale and make a tiny toy appear huge.*
- *Scorn any product whose commercial ... makes one kid look "out of it" to his peers if he doesn't have the toy. Scorn ... companies who work guilt trips on parents....*[48]

Guidelines for Media Use

The following guidelines can help children develop a critical distance from media programming and become more aware of media messages.

Moderation. The Roman comic dramatist Plautus surely could have been thinking about television viewing when he declared, "In everything the middle course is best: all things in excess bring trouble to men."[49] Studies show that too much television prohibits other activity; children who are frequent TV watchers put in much less effort on schoolwork than light viewers.[50] Another study found that sixth graders who watched less than one hour of TV daily scored 7 percent higher on academic achievement tests than classmates who watched four or more hours each day.[51]

The following tactics can combat the overuse of television:

- *Make sure that the TV is not constantly on.* Adults often leave the TV set on as "background" noise, even though they are not watching. As a result, TV watching becomes accepted as a normal part of the daily routine.
- *Watch by the show, not by the clock.* In its excellent educational packet, *Parenting in a TV Age* (PTA), the Center for Media and Values recommends that parents and children make clear choices *in advance* about what program the child should watch: "If you've set limits, they'll learn to prioritize and watch what they *really* like."[52]

  This strategy also sends the message that people should be in control of the television. The individual can decide when to watch, what to watch, and how to watch.
- *Set limits.* Parents should establish clear limits on how much TV their children should watch per day. The Center for Media and Values also recommends that parents should set the conditions for watching sensitive content like violence and sex in advance: "For example, 'You can watch *24* if you spend an hour discussing it with me afterwards.'"[53]

  Moderation can also be a wise policy with respect to children's use of digital media. Police Detective Bova Conti regards anything over 1½ to 2 hours a day on the Internet as excessive. He also suggests some other good-sense guidelines, such as forbidding late-night or excessive use.[54]
- *Participate with your child.* Parents who use the TV as an electronic babysitter are absent during a time in which their children are exposed to many ideas. However, watching television together presents opportunities for discussions between parents and children. Indeed, talking back to the television transforms a passive activity into an active, two-way interaction which encourages critical viewing on the part of the child. Later, this common reference point can serve as a springboard for further discussion.

  This principle of participation also applies to the Internet. Detective Bova Conti declares, "As a parent you should talk to your children often about what they're doing online."[55]

TV Postulates. *Parenting in a Media Age* suggests that parents stress the following postulates about TV. However, it should be noted that these postulates can be applied to other media as well, including film, satellite radio, and digital media:

- *You are smarter than your TV.* While it may be marginally entertaining to watch TV programming, it is infinitely more fun to pick it apart. Point out inconsistencies in content. Ask how the program compares to their personal experience and understanding of the world. This healthy skepticism encourages children to come to independent conclusions about the information presented on television.
- *TV's world is not real.* PTA suggests that parents and children watch a cartoon together and list all the things that could not happen in real life. This exercise reinforces the notion that much of what we see on television is true only on the tube. This activity can also be applied to other genres of media programming, such as situation comedies.

Dorr, Graves, and Phelps recommend that parents raise the following issues about the reality/fantasy of television content:

- *Entertainment programs are made up.*
- *Plots are made up.*
- *Characters are actors.*
- *Incidents are fabricated.*
- *Settings are often constructed.*
- *Entertainment programs vary in how realistic they are.*
- Viewers can decide how realistic they find entertainment programs.

Television content may be evaluated by comparing it to one's own experience, asking other people, and consulting other media sources.[56]

- *TV keeps doing the same things over and over.* By encouraging children to look for patterns in programming, children learn to anticipate these occurrences in future programming. For instance, once a child becomes sensitive to the introduction of ominous music in a program, he/she is less likely to become frightened by it. Moreover, discovering patterns together can be a useful starting point for discussion: *why* does this type of music always appear during particular moments in a program?
- *TV teaches us that some people and ideas are more important than others.* PTA suggests, Let your child use the remote control to flip through channels and count the number of different kinds of people on the screen at that instant.... Or keep a tally of "bad guys" in shows ... noting the sex and race of bad guys. Are there any patterns?[57]
- *Encourage an active selection of programming.* The digital domain offers a wide range of options with regard to media programming. The selection process requires that the children become active, critical viewers before they watch. In addition, this process enables parents and children to select a program or tape that both would enjoy watching together.

Keys To Interpreting Media Messages

Selected Keys to Interpreting Media Messages provide a clear and systematic way to put the information that children receive through the media into perspective. In addition, these strategies can serve as a springboard for later reflection and discussion.

Process

Function. By the age of three, children understand the intent of television commercials.[58] Thus, asking a child *why* an entertaining ad has been produced can make him/her a more critical consumer. Nobody likes to think of themselves as being "suckered" into doing something they don't want to do. It can be far more entertaining, as well as satisfying, to resist the ad message than succumb to it.

Audience. Studies show that three-year-old children are capable of understanding the concept of audience segmentation (that advertisements are targeted to specific groups).[59] Thus, it can be particularly enlightening for children to try to identify for whom the presentation is intended. As an example, it has been estimated that only 10 percent of children's viewing time is spent watching children's television programming. The other 90 percent of children's viewing time is devoted to watching programs designed for adults.[60] And, this statistic does not include instances in which younger children are watching programs geared for *older kids.* Having identified the target audience, discussion can then focus on how the communication strategy, style, and content have been developed to reach the intended audience.

Context

Worldview. A useful way to spark discussion about a media presentation is to ask, "What kind of world is this?" Children's programming conveys the following cumulative messages about the world:

A homogeneous world. The world of children's programming offers a distorted a picture of the composition of American society. As discussed earlier, the world depicted on prime-time television is predominately comprised of white males:

- 3.7 percent African Americans (as opposed to 11 percent in the general population)
- 16 percent women (as opposed to 52 percent)
- 3.1 percent Spanish speaking (as opposed to 6 percent)[61]

A world filled with stereotypes. Professor Linda Holtzman of Webster University conducted a class that examined stereotypes in children's Saturday morning television. After monitoring children's Saturday morning television programs, the class discovered that of 75 major characters, only six were women. Only one of those six female characters exhibited qualities that were not categorized as "traditional"—and she was a villain![62]

A violent world. As mentioned earlier, children's programs have been found to be far more violent than programming directed at adults. Violence is depicted as a natural part of life and justifiable to achieve a worthwhile goal.

An absolute world. The world of children's programming is populated by good guys and bad guys. Issues are clearly divided into right and wrong. Programs offer simple solutions to complex problems.

A material world. In the world of children's programming, things are often more important than people. Heroes and heroines are fashionably dressed and own lots of material possessions. Children also see a world in which people are presented as objects. Heroes and heroines are generally more attractive than secondary characters and are the center of attention. It is no coincidence that boys and girls think that being attractive is the most important attribute for male and female characters.[63]

A youth-dominated culture. Adults are presented as ignorant, close-minded, or inept. Adult characters are incapable of either understanding or participating in the extraordinary adventures of the children. Kids are best served by bonding together in peer groups and keeping information from their parents.

Structure. A general discussion about the economic structure of the American media system can be very enlightening for children, including the following points:

- Programs are produced to make a profit.
- Media companies rely on advertisements for revenue.
- The economic structure influences media content and style (what we see and how the information is presented).

Framework

Introduction. As discussed in Chapter 8, the introduction is a microcosm of the entire media presentation. If the opportunity presents itself (for example, when watching television, during the first commercial break), you and the child can discuss what you have learned about the characters, worldview, plots, and themes, based on the information provided in the introduction.

Illogical premise. Programming directed at children may be founded on a set of assumptions that are embedded in the premise. These assumptions play an important role in shaping the messages contained in the program.

To illustrate, approximately 500 newspapers carry a weekly syndicated "Mini Page" for kids, written by Betty Debman, which covers a range of topics.[64] One installment on "South American Countries" contains a number of ideological assumptions that affect the content:

- Progress is defined largely in terms of economic (specifically capitalistic) advancement. Debman declares that South America's future looks better because "many natural resources ... are yet to be developed to the fullest ... (including) minerals, forests, and fertile farmlands." However, the economic development of this region has been an environmental disaster, including the devastation of the rainforests, ecological imbalances, and loss of habitat for animal life.
- The capsule description of each South American country is another extension of the premise of the article. The capsule summary describes each country in economic terms (i.e., its "important exports").
- Another premise of the article is that a country's success is measured in terms of its relationship with the United States. A major reason cited for the progress of

the region is "better opportunities for trade with the United States and the rest of the world."

- The article regards illegal drugs as a major problem in South America. However, the source of the problem is identified as the poor farmers who "make money by raising crops from which illegal drugs are made." This statement shifts the blame

Figure 16.1
Illogical premise: programming directed at children may be founded on a set of assumptions that shape the message contained in the program. Reprinted with permission of the St. Louis Post-Dispatch © 1995.

MINI PAGE

By BETTY DEBNAM

Problems and Progress

South American Countries

Progress

South America's future looks better today because it has:

• governments that are elected by the people. Many countries used to have dictators.

• better opportunities for trade with the United States and the rest of the world.

• many natural resources that are yet to be developed to the fullest. It has minerals, forests and fertile farmlands.

Like most parts of the world, the countries of South America have come a long way, but some still have problems.

Problems

• large families without enough food and jobs for their members. Many people move to the cities and live in slums. There are many poor people and the number is rising. There are only a few who are rich.

• illegal drugs. Many poor farmers make money by raising crops from which illegal drugs are made. The sale of drugs causes crime, especially in Bolivia, Colombia and Peru.

• not enough products. Some countries depend on only one or two products to sell. If something goes wrong, the whole country suffers.

Below is a chart of the countries listed by size. We have given you the literacy rate. This is the percentage of people over 15 who can read and write. We have also given the per capita income (the amount of money each person would have if all of the country's income were divided equally). (Source: "The World Factbook 1993," C.I.A.)

Country	Capital	Population	Literacy	Per Capita Income
Brazil	Brasilia	156,664,223	81%	$2,350
Argentina	Buenos Aires	33,533,256	95%	$3,400
Peru	Lima	23,210,352	85%	$1,100
Colombia	Bogota	34,942,767	87%	$1,500
Bolivia	La Paz	7,544,099	78%	$670
Venezuela	Caracas	20,117,687	88%	$2,800
Chile	Santiago	13,739,759	93%	$2,550

Country	Capital	Population	Literacy	Per Capita Income
Paraguay	Asuncion	5,070,856	90%	$1,500
Ecuador	Quito	10,461,072	86%	$1,100
Guyana	Georgetown	734,640	95%	$370
Uruguay	Montevideo	3,175,050	96%	$3,100
Suriname	Paramaribo	416,321	95%	$3,300
French Guiana	Cayenne	133,376	82%	$4,390
U.S. (for comparison)	Washington, D.C.	258,103,721	97.9%	$23,400

Figure 16.1. (*Continued*)

away from the capitalists and government officials who have grown rich through the manufacturing and distribution of drugs.

Given this example, it is imperative that adults encourage kids to challenge the underlying assumptions contained in the premise of media presentations.

Explicit content. As discussed in Chapter 8, W. Andrew Collins found that young children lack the capacity to identify the "essential content" of a story being conveyed through the media. The short attention span of young children affects their ability to decode content:

- six-month-old infants gaze at the set but only sporadically.
- one-year-olds watch about 12 percent of the time that the set is on.
- By the age of two, children watch about 25 percent of the time that the set is on.
- Between the ages of 2–3, children's attention span jumps to 45 percent of the time that the set is on.
- By the age of four, children are watching 55 percent of the time that the set is on, "often even in a playroom with toys, games, and other distractions."[65]

Indeed, five-year-old children have difficulty deciding what is real or fantasy on film. The children embellish stories with their own ideas, add people and objects not in the film, and have a hard time telling when a story ends. In addition, young children have difficulty deciding whether situation comedies are real or make-believe.[66] Nearly half (14 of 30) of the children thought a person on television had spoken directly to them and six had actually answered back.[67]

However, asking a child to give a plot synopsis of the story ("what happened") provides an excellent opportunity for adults to clarify any misconceptions that they may have about a media presentation and gives children an opportunity to ask questions. In addition, because young children often focus attention on those aspects of a story that interest them, having a child reconstruct what happened in the presentation is a way to learn about the child's interests and concerns.

Implicit content. In addition, young children often have difficulty understanding *implicit content:* those elements of plot that remain under the surface. Consequently, discussing elements of implicit content can serve as a useful springboard for discussion with children.

- *Ask why things occurred in the story.* Examining the *motives* of characters. ("Why do you think he behaved like that?") As mentioned in earlier discussions, young children are often unable to identify the motives behind an act of violence. As a result, they may not judge media violence on the basis of any moral standard but rather on whether or not the behavior is successful. As David Considine observes, "The media, therefore, potentially provide a model that tells children 'might is right' and 'the end justifies the means.'"[68]
- *Discuss the connections between the characters that occur in the plot.*
- *Discuss connections between events in the plot.*
- *Discuss the consequences of characters' actions.* Frequently, the heroes do not face any consequences, even if they are responsible for destruction of property and people in the narrative. A good question to ask children to consider is what consequences *they* would face if they were in the same position.
- *Affective response.* Asking children to tune into their feelings can be a very useful springboard for discussion about a media presentation:

— How did you feel during particular points of the story?
— How did you feel about certain aspects of the program? For instance, did you like (a particular character)? Why?
— Do your affective responses provide insight into *your* personal belief system? Explain.

These questions can lead to a discussion about personal feelings and values.

Another line of inquiry involves asking the children to *empathize* with the characters:

— How do you think (the character) felt at particular points in the narrative?
— How would you feel if you were in that situation?

Identifying with characters can give children perspective into the experience of the characters in the presentation. Specifically, asking children to empathize with characters they ordinarily wouldn't identify with (such as supporting characters, members of subcultures, or a character of the opposite sex) can give a child valuable insight into the experience of the members of that group.

Illogical conclusion. Media communicators often feel compelled to insert artificial endings in media presentations that make the audience leave the theater with smiles on their faces (see discussion, Chapter 9). These illogical conclusions provide an excellent way to draw children into a discussion about the presentation:

- Did you like the ending? Why or why not?
- Does the conclusion of the presentation follow logically from the established premise, characters, and worldview?
- If not, how *should* the program have ended? Why?
- How would you have *preferred* for the program to end? Why?

Using this can raise issues about the messages in the presentation (intended and unintended), as well as providing an opportunity for children to examine their own values system.

MEDIA AND SOCIAL CHANGE

The media have been criticized at various times, both for taking too active a role in promoting social change and for obstructing needed societal change. However, the media merely provide a channel through which a communicator can reach an audience. The media's role with regard to social change is determined by the following factors:

- *The intentions of the communicator*
- *The predilections of the audience*
- *The capabilities of the medium*

Pro-social Impact of Media

Popular media programming can have a *pro-social impact*, by bringing issues to public attention. For instance, Oprah Winfrey has focused on numerous issues of social importance, including body image of females, global child prostitution rings, and communication techniques for dysfunctional families. Also featured were programs about the aftermath of Hurricane Katrina and lessons of the Holocaust. She also focused on the issues in the Sudan.

Media as Agent of Social Change

It is no coincidence that the formation of the United States occurred at a time when the media began to influence public attitudes. Historian John Tebbel argues that the activity leading to the American Revolutionary War was, in many respects, a media event, led by the press as manipulators of public opinion.[69]

By 1750, newspaper publishers in the colonies had grown so numerous that the English crown had given up trying to license them. At the same time, newspapers were becoming closely allied with the business community. Circulation and advertising had made the publishers reasonably rich. As a result, newspapers were increasingly invested in the growth of the economy and of colonial society.

In 1765, England imposed a Stamp Act on the colonists. Britain had drained much of her financial reserves during the French and Indian War, which "saved" the Protestant colonies from Catholic France. Consequently, England felt that the colonies should assume some of the financial burden.

The stamp tax was levied on all segments of the population but was most damaging to businesses relying on newsprint and legal documents. Ironically, then, the two most offended segments of the population were those capable of doing the most harm to England—newspaper publishers and lawyers.

In protest, some publishers suspended operations, upsetting the business community (which had grown reliant on newspapers for advertising), as well as the general readership. However, the majority of publishers simply evaded the law. Some published without the customary newspaper masthead or title. Others published without the required tax stamp on each issue, explaining editorially that the publisher had tried to buy stamps but had found none available.

Motivated by self-interest, these young editors mounted an effective media campaign against the British. They became advocates for democracy, charging that the Stamp Act was an assault on their freedom of the press. Tebbel observes, "They argued with fervor and dedication, if not with much devotion to the truth."[70] As an example, one paper claimed that the British were planning to impose a tax on kissing.

This public relations effort on the part of the publishers was crucial to the revolutionary movement. Newspapers kindled revolt in cities, where British tax collectors, civil servants, and soldiers were visible. In addition, newspapers were delivered in wagons to the isolated settlers in the "frontier" regions of the Ohio Valley, which otherwise would not have received news for weeks or months. As a result, the English presence in the colonies began to meet with an organized resistance, leading to the American Revolution.

More recently, media technology has provided social activists with tools to promote social change. Video games are now being developed that raise awareness of social issues among young players. Stephen Friedman, general manager of mtvU, a subsidiary of MTV declares that video games are "the next generation of activism."[71] As an example, "Darfur Is Dying" is a popular game in which players assume the role of a character—a mother, father, or child—who leaves a Sudanese village to go foraging for water in the desert. Along the path, the refugee must avoid militia, who try to capture, rape, or kill them. Reporter Sylvester Brown Jr. tried the game:

> I chose a small boy to send rummaging for water. He was captured within moments. As I played, pop-up screens told of the dangers faced by refugees and gave staggering statistics of those wounded, raped or killed daily. Next, I chose a father, then a mother and finally a little girl. They were all captured. Up popped more dire statistics, followed by interactive links urging players to write politicians, join organizations and learn more about the tragedy.[72]

Other games presented at the third annual "Games for Change" conference held in New York City in 2006 include:

- "PeaceMaker," in which players, assuming the role of either the Palestinian leader or the Israeli prime minister attempt to negotiate a peace settlement in the Middle East.
- "A Force More Powerful," in which players act as peace activists who learn to organize nonviolent demonstrations and fundraising activities.
- "Homelessness: It's No Game," in which players are faced with the challenge of providing care for homeless characters.

Media as Impediment to Social Change

However, critics also point out that the media can *obstruct* social change. Edward Herman and Noam Chomsky argue that the U.S. media operate according to a propaganda model that supports the status quo: "The propaganda model traces the routes by which money and power are able to filter out the news fit to print, marginalize dissent, and allow the government and dominant private interests to get their messages across to the public."[73]

This propaganda model consists of the following elements:

- *Size, ownership, and profit orientation of the mass media.* The American mass media industry prospers within the current system. As a result, media conglomerates benefit from the status quo policies of business and government.
- *The advertising license to do business.* Because the American media system is market-driven, media communicators are dependent upon sponsorship to produce programming. Consequently, media executives are reluctant to present content that might offend powerful advertisers. Herman and Chomsky declare, "In addition to discrimination against unfriendly media institutions, advertisers also choose selectively among programs on the basis of their own principles. With rare exceptions, these are culturally and politically conservative."[74]

  In addition, because advertisers are selective about the types of presentations they choose to support, they can exert enormous influence over programming decisions.
- *Sourcing mass media news.* Stories told through the media are shaped through the use of sources, who often represent government and corporate interests. (For further discussion, see Chapter 12, Journalism.)
- *Flak.* "Flak" refers to responses to media content, which can take the form of letters, phone calls, petitions, lawsuits, and legislative initiatives. Herman and Chomsky distinguish between individual feedback and "serious flack"—organized efforts by groups with political agendas. Indeed, some groups (e.g., the American Legal Foundation, the Capital Legal Foundation, the Media Institute, the Center for Media and Public Affairs, and Accuracy in Media) have been formed with the expressed purpose of influencing media content. The authors observe, "the ability to produce flak, and especially flak that is costly and threatening, is related to power."[75]

  > These groups are often well funded and can produce "serious flak" through contacts with the White House, heads of networks or ad agencies. These groups may also generate their own media campaigns in response to programming, or back politicians who support their points of view.

- *National security as a control mechanism.* Since the 1950s, America has used the ideology of anticommunism to control the information that reaches the public. Since the terrorist attack of 9/11, this rationale has been replaced by the broader appeal of national security.

The Media and the Iraq War. A classic example of Herman and Chomsky's propaganda model can be found in the media coverage of the Iraq War. Public perceptions and attitudes toward the Iraq War were manipulated through a carefully designed communications strategy. This communications strategy was essential to the U.S. government's marshaling of support for the military action, both at home and abroad. Media strategy was also a consideration in key military decisions. Secretary of Defense Donald Rumsfeld was initially reluctant to send in a large army to engage in a land war, principally because the resulting gore and loss of American life in hand-to-hand combat would not play well on television.

The Iraq War communications strategy included the following elements:

- *Censorship Policy.* The U.S. government insisted that all reports be carefully screened, on the pretext of military security. However, much of the censorship was designed to maintain a positive image of the war, both at home and abroad. For instance, images of dead American soldiers were not allowed, although publishing these photos had little to do with the issue of security.

  In this information vacuum, the public was left with second-hand reports about the war. The government furnished the media with waves of interviews, briefings, and press conferences—all of which presented a uniform, official perspective on the war. In the absence of hard news, the media relied heavily on "experts": i.e., former government officials, who elaborated on, but basically reinforced the same party line. Reporters were often reduced to the role of facilitators or, worse, cheerleaders for the official government line.
- *The Call to Conformity.* This cloak of secrecy cultivated an atmosphere in which complicity was equated with patriotism. Paradoxically, individuals who exercised their democratic right to question policy were considered anti-American. Support of the war and the government policy was, then, clearly defined as an act of faith.
- *Patriotic Rhetoric.* Patriotic rhetoric incited intense feelings of nationalism and coerced the public to support the conflict without question.
- *Euphemisms.* Many of the terms employed to describe the campaign itself presented an antiseptic portrait of the war. Expressions like "collateral damage," "surgical strike," "carpet bombing," and "extraordinary rendition" originated with the government but were passed along without question by the media.
- *Demonization of the Enemy.* Emotionally charged terms were applied to the enemy. George W. Bush called Saddam Hussein a "thug" and insisted that he was in some way responsible for the attack on the United States of 9/11, though there was no evidence of a link. The goal was obvious; it is easier to fight someone you hate.
- It can be argued that this media strategy worked effectively during the early stages of the Iraq war—up to President Bush's "Mission Accomplished" pronouncement in 2003. However, when it became clear that the conflict was not over, public support began to wane.

The Media and the Feminist Movements. A comparison of the media coverage of the two twentieth-century women's movements provides insight into the factors that determine whether the media accelerates or inhibits social change.

There were two women's movements in America during the twentieth century: the women's suffrage movement, which began in 1908, and the feminist movement, which originated in 1968. Francesca M. Cancian and Bonnie L. Ross tabulated the number of articles devoted to women and women's issues appearing in the press during the time period surrounding these two movements in order to address the following questions:

- What is the causal relation between the movement and the media?
- Which changes first, the quantity of news coverage or the strength of the movement?
- What is the time lag between the two events?[76]

During the rise of the women's suffrage movement, the increase in media attention was almost immediate and played a direct role in the success of the movement. Several factors can account for the responsiveness of the press. First, the movement was characterized by dramatic tactics, such as open-air meetings and parades, which lent themselves to media coverage. In addition, the leaders of the suffrage movement made a devoted effort to cultivate the favor of the media. Finally, the authors note that the suffrage movement did not threaten the male-dominated society: "The suffrage movement was not revolutionary ... but focused on the single goal of getting the vote."[77]

In contrast, the 1960s feminist movement at first was largely ignored by the press; media coverage lagged behind the movement by several years. The authors offer several explanations for the initial lack of attention by the press:

- *The 1960s movement emphasized issues rather than events.* The feminist movement originated largely through the organization of conscious-raising groups and women's liberation organizations. These activities did not lend themselves to media attention (the more dramatic bra burning demonstrations occurred later in the history of the movement).
- *The feminist movement was perceived to be anti-news organizations.* Some of the leaders of the feminist movement were openly hostile toward the media, feeling that coverage was biased, demeaning, and exploitative. Consequently, these leaders were far from receptive to media attention.
- *The feminist movement posed a threat to the power elite.* The authors maintain that the media only covers those movements and issues that are acceptable to the establishment. "Once a movement is accepted by the government, big business, labor leaders, and other members of the political establishment, it will receive considerable media coverage.[78]
- *News organizations were anti-movement.* News organizations, which were dominated by males, were threatened by the radical goals of the feminist movement. M. B. Morris contends that the press attempted to subdue the movement in its early stages—first by ignoring it, then by undermining its serious intent through frivolous coverage, and finally by "publicizing its least offensive goals and de-emphasizing its revolutionary aims."[79]

By late 1969 and early 1970, media coverage of the women's movement began to increase. Cancian and Ross suggest that by that time the movement had gradually grown in popularity and notoriety, until it crossed some "threshold level" of respectability. At that point, the authors note that the media coverage contributed to the growth of the movement: "There is considerable support for believing that the media blitz caused the movement to grow much faster than it had previously."[80]

Cancian and Ross's study underscores the paradoxical role of the media with regard to social change. Under some circumstances, a social movement is covered promptly by the press, promoting public awareness. At other times, media coverage may lag behind the beginning of a movement, inhibiting social change. However, once a movement has become mainstream and non-threatening, media attention often follows, which further contributes to the popularity of the movement.

GLOBAL COMMUNICATIONS

The discipline of media literacy is particularly relevant to the study of international communications. The ability to analyze and discuss the information being conveyed over the international channels of mass communication can lead to a broader understanding of issues and events that shape our lives.

The world of American journalism is very small indeed. Only a limited amount of attention is devoted to international news. As discussed earlier, many newspapers focus on local and community issues. The international stories that are included are picked up from wire services such as AP or UPI. A few "national" newspapers with foreign bureaus such as the *New York Times* and *Washington Post* include coverage of international issues.

Television news operates on a crisis sensibility; that is, it commits its resources (crews and equipment) to events in countries involving the U.S. or its allies—often war scenarios.

Several factors account for the sparse international news coverage in U.S. news programming. Time and space constraints demand that editors select foreign news carefully. Each country has a complex story to tell on a daily basis. For instance, if a paper provided comprehensive coverage of events in Holland, we would be reading a section nearly as large as a Dutch newspaper. If you multiply this by the 248 nations, dependent areas, and other global entities in the world, it would take the American reader a week to digest one day's worth of international news. Consequently, it is impossible to provide complete international coverage without omitting news of national and local interest.

Financial considerations further restrict foreign news coverage. Many news organizations have reduced their overhead by consolidating their foreign bureaus. The remaining correspondents, who are responsible for a large region, lack the familiarity with a single country—and the contacts—that are integral to insightful reporting.

Ethnocentrism also contributes to the lack of international coverage in American newspapers. The majority of U.S. territory is not in close physical proximity with other countries and, consequently, not directly affected by events taking place on foreign shores. As a result, many Americans remain indifferent and uninformed about other countries.

However, the meager coverage of international news reinforces the latent message that the United States is the only country that matters. Some countries, like Iraq or Lebanon, have become the center of national attention because of a crisis, such as a war, political upheaval, or natural disaster. However, according to Herbert Gans, most of the international news that appears in U.S. newspapers consists of *American* activities in other cultures:

- Implementation of U.S. foreign policy
- Stopovers by U.S. officials
- American entertainers on tour
- International events that affect Americans and American policy[81]

According to Philip Gault, certain countries and regions receive sustained coverage in the American press because of their political, commercial, and ethnic linkages with the United States:

- *Political Interests:* Russia, Central America, Southeast Asia, China
- *Commercial Ties*: Taiwan, Japan
- *Ethnic Identification*: Britain, Germany, Italy, Ireland, Israel[82]

Until recently, it has been difficult to obtain information originating from other countries. Increasingly, however, global media have become accessible to international audiences. Satellite transmission enables an individual to receive radio and television programming from around the world. For example, the "BBC World News" television program is broadcast throughout the United States on BBC America, a cable/satellite network.

In addition, the Internet has emerged as a tremendous resource for international programming.

- A wide array of foreign films is available.
- A range of international radio stations can be accessed through the Internet.
- Many news sources offer a multilingual format on the Internet. For instance, Pravda, Eurasia.org.ru, and Gazeta.ru provide daily news from Central Asia in both Russian and English. The BBC web site also provides its news in many languages.
- Many web sites provide access to international newspapers in translation. For instance, newstran.com translates more than 5,000 newspapers and magazines on a daily basis.
- Search engines such as LexisNexis enable individuals to compare daily international coverage of a particular issue.

- Listservs and mailing lists distribute translated foreign information worldwide. To illustrate, the Johnson Russia List has become a primary resource for people who have an interest in Russian affairs.[83]

However, universal *access* to the media should not be confused with media literacy. It is imperative that individuals develop the ability to analyze and discuss the plethora of information being conveyed over the channels of mass communication. Media literate individuals have learned to develop a critical distance from the information they receive through the media. In that way, they are in a position to make independent judgments about what programming they choose to watch, read, or hear, as well as how to interpret the information that they receive through the channels of mass communication.

The following keys are particularly useful in the analysis of international media messages.

Process

Function. Understanding the function, or purpose behind a media presentation, is a particularly useful key to interpreting international media messages. The purposes of global communications include the following:

To foster global community. Media technology such as the communications satellite can bring different cultures together. One of the first instances of this "global village" concept occurred in 1952, when the coronation of England's Queen Elizabeth was broadcast overseas and celebrated worldwide.

To disseminate information. Enormous differences exist in the way that various countries produce and distribute the news. Comparing the coverage of a current event in a variety of international newspapers reveals dramatic differences in presentation, content, and even different cultural definitions of news. For example, in Western papers, news about the Third World and Asia tends to be sensational, while coverage of Western items shows more balance between political coverage and sensational stories.[84]

Propaganda refers to the systematic development and dissemination of information to propagate the views and interests of a particular group. Harold D. Lasswell identified four principal strategic aims of propaganda in war:

- To mobilize hatred against the enemy
- To preserve the friendship of allies
- To preserve the friendship and, if possible, to procure the cooperation of neutrals
- To demoralize the enemy[85]

But in addition, propaganda is also deployed during peacetime to promote national interests, pave the way for diplomatic initiatives, and encourage trade, tourism, and investment.

Significantly, American entertainment programming has been one of the most effective forms of propaganda. International audiences are decidedly fans of American films, television, and music. The unbridled energy and freedom of expression convey positive cumulative messages about America. International audiences have been fans of American films, television, and music.

Profit. Regardless of the manifest function of a media presentation (e.g., entertainment or information), profit has emerged as a significant latent function. The emergence of the transnational media industry as a for-profit enterprise has had an enormous impact on the production and dissemination of media messages throughout the globe. In recognition of international markets, companies are developing communications strategies to cultivate markets and influence consumer patterns abroad.

A related function involves the use of the media *to promote economic development* in a region. For instance, Ecuadorian natives are now able to sell their crafts over the Web.[86]

Context

Because the media have become such an integral part of a nation, a media system reflects the political, historical, cultural, and economic orientations of that country. Consequently, understanding a nation's media system can furnish valuable perspective about that country. And conversely, examining these aspects of a nation can provide insight into its media system.

Political Framework. Every country's media system is shaped by its political framework—particularly on its definition of freedom of the press. In a number of countries, journalists face serious repercussions for reporting the news. In 2006, 167 journalists were killed while reporting the news.[87] The deadliest countries for journalists in the last decade were Iraq, Russia, and Colombia.[88]

Lucie Morillon, Washington director of Reporters Without Borders, declares, "There has never been a more dangerous time to be a journalist. But even more deplorable was the lack of interest, and sometimes even the failure, by democratic countries in defending everywhere the values they are supposed to incarnate."[89]

Historical Sensibility. A country's media programming often reflects its particular point of view with respect to a historical event. For instance, what Americans refer to as the "Vietnam war" is thought of in Vietnam as "The Great American War." Clearly, the historical assumptions on which media content is based differ between these two countries.

The historical sensibility of a country also has an impact on its coverage of current events. Historian Nikolai Zlobin explains, "Each nation has its own historical memory and mentality."[90] To illustrate, the reaction of the Chinese media to the Iraq War was tempered by its own historical experience. Zlobin observes, "In its five thousand year history, China has seen dozens of dictators like Saddam Hasseim come and go. They were not about to panic over one more."[91]

Cultural Sensibility. Every country has its own distinct cultural sensibility that affects the content of its media programming. Cultural sensibility refers to a country's distinctive customs, informal codes of conduct, norms, and mores. Zlobin provides the following example: "I once asked an Italian journalist if he could write an article criticizing the Pope. He said, 'No way. There is no law. However, it would never occur to me to do it.' It was outside of his cultural mentality."[92]

Examining the media presentation of a country can furnish perspective into its cultural sensibility. To illustrate, in 2006, *The Yacoubian Building*, a film adaptation of the novel by Egyptian Alaa Al Aswany, focuses on the lives of residents both rich and poor of the Yacoubian, an actual apartment building in downtown Cairo. Journalist Peter Kenyon comments,

> *The Yacoubian Building* describes a country that is corrupt, unfair and thuggish.... Yacoubian takes a look at sometimes uncomfortable truths about life in contemporary Egypt. It tackles subjects considered taboo in traditional Egyptian society, such as homosexuality, and even features a corrupt imam.[93]

Wahid Hamed, who wrote the screenplay for *Yacoubian*, observes, "I think [the movie] will be like a document of the time we live in," noting that the movie says in public what many citizens are thinking in private.[94]

Mistakes in international news accounts frequently occur because reporters are unaware of the cultural nuances of a country. For instance, Zlobin recounts that in 1999, the international press reported that Russian President Boris Yeltsin had issued a warning that a military strike against Iraq by a U.S.-led coalition would lead to a "world war." This story caused understandable consternation within the global community. But according to Yeltsin spokesperson Sergei Yastrzhembsky, the Western media had overreacted because they misinterpreted Yeltsin's use of Russian slang. (*Naryvatsya* which means "run-in," was interpreted by the Western media as signifying a much more serious confrontation.)[95]

International advertisers have also been hurt by their insensitivity to the cultural nuances of its foreign market. To illustrate, Gillette mounted an expensive ad campaign in France promoting its shaving accoutrements. But to the surprise of the company, the ads were ineffective. However, as Zlobin explains, the demonstration of the product made no sense to the French audience: "The commercials showed men shaving in the morning before going to work. However, in France, it is customary to shave at night before retiring."[96]

National Stereotyping. Media programming is a principal means by which people from different cultures learn about one another. Unless you have personally visited another country, what you know about that culture is derived primarily from the media depictions of other cultures. *National stereotyping* refers to the generalized conception associated with members of a particular country. These stereotypes are generally not very flattering. For instance, an episode of the English comedy *Fawlty Towers* depicts Americans as vulgar, materialistic, and shallow. American advertising often pokes fun at other nationalities as a way to flatter the American consumer in comparison. For example, a Wendy's Hamburgers ad campaign portrays Russians as ugly, ignorant peasants; the message is that Americans are blessed with both the taste and freedom of choice to buy Wendy's Hamburgers.

Media and Cultural Identity. In some traditional cultures, the channels of mass communications have introduced new and different ideas that have disrupted the established values system. To illustrate, in his study of the effects of Western media on Indonesia, Asep Sutresna found that younger Indonesians are losing touch with traditional Indonesian culture: "Young Indonesians are not familiar with traditional cultures anymore, such as ephics which contain Indonesian ancestors' philosophy of life. They are not familiar with the figures in those ephics or traditional stories. They tend to view these cultures as being for rural people's consumption."[97]

The widespread presence of the media has led to a schism between generations. Sutresna explains, "Young Indonesians tend to view the traditional values and ethics as too strict and obsolete. Those are their parents' values and ethics."[98] Instead, the younger generation has adopted Western values, including the definition of success: "The success for young Indonesian are rich (materialistic), popular, independent, and individualistic."[99]

In 2006, Playboy Enterprises announced plans to publish a version of *Playboy* magazine in India, reflecting the rapid Westernization of the country. Thus, the Indian version of the magazine would focus on topics related to high living, pop culture, celebrity, and fashion. Reporter Anand Giridharadas explains,

> (India is) overflowing with ambition, as a small but growing class of young, urban, world-traveling men with disposable income find their way to a new upper class. The democratization of affluence is creating would-be male connoisseurs, keen for tutelage in ways of the high life.[100]

Because the mores of the country prohibit the graphic Western type of sexuality, the Indian version of the magazine contains no nudity. However, Venkatesh Abdev, a top official of the World Hindu Council, a conservative organization declared, "They are going to spoil our culture. We are not giving as much importance to sex as them. Free sex is not allowed in our culture."[101]

Further, Indian law prohibits the sale or possession of material that is "lascivious or appeals to the prurient interest" and that is without redeeming artistic, literary or religious merit. And on a more practical level, even though the younger generation welcomes this new version of sexuality, they tend to live at home with their parents, who definitely are not comfortable with the "new" sexuality. N. Radhakrishnan, editor of Man's World, explains, "In urban India, the concept of single men living alone is quite new. Here, most men, until they're married, live at home. Once you're married, your wife wonders what you're reading."[102]

Some media systems that are considered repressive by Western standards are actually intended to protect and preserve their traditional culture. For instance, in Thailand, rather than promoting products, billboards present pictures that honor their King and Queen. In 2007, the Thai government blocked citizens' access to YouTube, after a clip appeared on the site that insulted King Bhumibol Adulyadej. The clip showed graffiti-like elements superimposed over photographs of the King, including pictures of feet over the king's image—a major taboo.

Economic Structure. Proponents of media reform in the United States are concerned about the concentration of media ownership in the hands of a few mega-conglomerates (see Chapter 7, Structure). But within a global perspective, private ownership is but one of three types of media ownership systems, each of which exercises a distinctive influence on the construction of media messages: State Ownership, Public Ownership, and Private Ownership.

State-Owned System. In authoritarian countries such as China, Cuba, and North Korea, the media industry is controlled by the government. Under this system, television programs, radio shows, films, and newspapers, as well as books and magazines, are owned, produced, and distributed under the close supervision of the government.

Public Ownership. Under this system of ownership, the media are owned by the public but operated by the government. In countries such as Sweden, the Netherlands, and Kazakstan, the revenue required to cover the operating costs of newspapers, television stations, and radio stations are generated through public taxes.

Private Ownership. In countries such as the United States, newspapers, magazines, radio stations, film studios, and television stations are privately owned—either by individuals or, increasingly, by large, multinational corporations. Under this market-driven system, the primary purpose, or function, is to generate the maximum possible profit.

Currently, the private ownership model is encroaching on the established media model of many countries. Thus, many countries now operate on a *hybrid media system,* in which several ownership systems co-exist. For instance, in the United States the media are predominantly privately owned. However, NPR and PBS are publicly owned radio and television systems, respectively.

The economic framework of a country plays a major role in the content of its media. For instance, in state-owned media systems like China, independent sources of information are not available. Consequently, stories are difficult to substantiate, which undermines public confidence in the media. In England, the broadcast media are owned by the government and financed through public taxes. The staff of the British Broadcasting System (BBC) consists of civil employees who are not subject to market-driven pressures. In this system, the content of the programs is not determined by the audience; thus, although the quality of the programs may be, in their estimation, superior, they may not be as successful in attracting an audience as in the American system.

Although a country's policy with respect to freedom of the press is influenced by its political system, the economic structure of a country can also place restrictions on what is conveyed through the channels of mass communication. Zlobin explains,

> If you ask a British journalist who has more freedom, you or an American journalist working for a private company, he will say, "No question, me ... because I am defended by law. They can't kick me out, my salary is guaranteed. I am working for the British government—not the particular administration that might happen to be in power at the moment."[103]

In this case, the British government protects the media from the pressures of the market and foreign influence. In contrast, the U.S. media maintains a strict independence from government. However, the American media industry struggles with freedom from market-forces which shapes the coverage of issues.

Changes in a country's media system can bring about broader changes in the cultural, political, and economic life of the nation. For instance, as the former Soviet Union moved toward democracy, Soviet President Mikhail Gorbachev first introduced the policy of *glasnost*, or openness, which encouraged more freedom of expression in the press, including criticism of the authorities. And as part of the movement toward a market economy, in July 1990, Gorbachev ordered the privatization of the nation's radio and television industries.

Case Studies. Because a country's media system reflects its historical, political, cultural, and cultural orientation, an interesting approach to the study of a foreign country consists of an examination of its media system. To illustrate, consider the following *brief* descriptions:

- *The American media system.* The American media industry is shaped by the relationship between its democratic political system and its capitalistic economic structure. The First Amendment to the Constitution insures that a range of opinions and ideas are brought before the public. At the same time, the American media are privately owned by individuals and corporations, who make programming decisions in hopes of maximizing their profit. As mentioned earlier, this market imperative affects the selection of programming in the media.

- *The People's Republic of China.* The People's Republic of China operates within a socialistic economic system; consequently, the media are owned by the state. However, in the communist system, information is tightly controlled as a means of maintaining order and serving the interests of the government.

  To illustrate, in 2000, China finally broke its silence on the devastation surrounding an earthquake that had killed more than 15,000 people in southwestern China in 1970. At the time of the quake, the official Xinhua News Agency ran a brief dispatch for foreign readers, reporting a lower magnitude and omitting information on casualties and damage. After 30 years, the *Beijing Morning Post* newspaper finally reported the story, as relatives of the victims gathered for a memorial service commemorating the anniversary of the tragedy.
- *The Netherlands.* In this social democratic country, this media industry is based largely on the principles of "accessibility, variety, non-commercialism, and cooperation." Operating costs are taken from tax revenues. Programming time is distributed among many social and political groups, on the basis of the number of members in their group. Production facilities (complete with crews) are made available upon request.

Global Hegemony. The flow of global information has long been dominated by Western culture—particularly the United States. Four of the five major news agencies are Western; these agencies account for 90 percent of the global news flow. The Western dominance of international communications has long come under criticism by the international community. Developing countries in particular have accused the United States of promoting its ideology by monopolizing media programming on a global scale. In 1976, the United Nations Educational, Scientific and Cultural Organization (UNESCO) called for a New World Information and Communication Order to respond to the following inequities:

1. *The flow of information is unequal, with too much information originating in the West and not enough representing the developing nations.*
2. *There is too much bias against, and stereotyping of, the developing or "less developed" countries.*
3. *Alien values are foisted on the Third World by too much Western (mainly American) "communication imperialism."*
4. *Western communication places undue emphasis on "negative" news of the Third World—disasters, coups, government corruption, and the like.*
5. *Finances are unequally distributed around the world for technology and communication development.*
6. *The Western definition of "news" (meaning atypical and sensational items) is unrealistic and does not focus enough attention on development news (items helping in the progress and growth of the country).*
7. *Communication and journalism education in universities is too Western-oriented, and too many textbooks used in the Third World are authored by First-World writers, especially by Americans.*

8. Too much of the world's information is collected by the big five news agencies, all but one representing the First (advanced capitalist) World.[104]

However, American popular culture no longer has quite the influence of the past, for several reasons. As discussed previously, at long last, the domestic media systems in many countries are catching up to the United States. For instance, India's Bollywood's films reach up to 3.6 billion people around the world—a billion more than the audience for Hollywood.[105] Moreover, in an effort to preserve cultural integrity, countries such as Canada, Israel, and France have imposed quotas on the amount of foreign media presentations (i.e., music, films, and television programs) that can be imported into the country. In addition, digital media technology "levels the playing field," enabling individuals to produce, edit, and distribute media around the globe.

The international community has developed initiatives designed to contend with the inequality of global information systems. UNESCO has adopted a strategy of providing support for individual countries as they develop their own communication systems. In addition, numerous countries support domestic media production through government subsidies to artists and media communicators, including Norway, Denmark, Spain, Mexico, Canada, and South Africa.

And finally, private organizations are working to provide digital access to remote communities, so that individuals throughout the globe will be able to participate fully in the opportunities presented by unlimited access to information. For instance, the nonprofit organization One Laptop Per Child is developing a laptop computer at a cost of $100, which is designed to connect 1.2 billion children in the developing world to the resources of a global network.[106]

NOTES

1. "Is Torture on Hit Fox TV Show '24' Encouraging US Soldiers to Abuse Detainees?" Democracy Now! February 22, 2007 (www.democracynow.org).

2. Frank Baker, "Media Use Statistics," Media Literacy Clearinghouse (www.frankwbaker.com).

3. Henry J. Kaiser Family Foundation, "Fact Sheet: TV Violence" (Menlo Park, CA: 2003).

4. Ibid.

5. Lawrie Mifflin, "An Increase Is Seen in the Number of Violent Television Programs," *New York Times*, April 17, 1998, A16.

6. Richard Rosenfeld, associate professor of criminology, University of Missouri–St. Louis, interview by author, August 12, 1992.

7. Ibid.

8. Carey Goldberg, with Marjorie Connelly, "Polls Finds Decline in Teen-age Fear and Violence," *New York Times*, October 20, 1999, A1.

9. Mifflin, "An Increase Is Seen."
10. Baker, "Media Use Statistics."
11. Internet Movie Database (www.imdb.com).
12. A. Bandurfa, D. Ross, and S. D. Ross, "Transmission of Aggression Through Imitation of Aggressive Model," *Journal of Abnormal and Social Psychology,* 63 (1961), 575–582.
13. Robert M. Liebert and Joyce Sprafkin, *The Early Window: Effects of Television on Children and Youth,* 3rd ed. (New York: Pergamon Press, 1988), 140, 41.
14. Ibid., 157.
15. Ibid., 147.
16. Daniel Linz, Edward Donnerstein and Steven Penrod Steven, "The Effects of Multiple Exposures to Filmed Violence against Women," *Journal of Communication* 34(Summer 1984), 130–147.
17. Fred Emery and Merrelyn Emery, *A Choice of Futures* (Leiden, Netherlands: Martinus Nijhoff Social Sciences Division, 1976), 82.
18. N. M. Malmauth and J. V. P. Check, "The Effects of Mass Media Exposure on Acceptance of Violence Against Women: A Field Experiment," *Journal of Research in Personality* (1981), n. s. 15.
19. G. S. Lesser, *Children and Television: Lessons From Sesame Street* (New York: Vintage Books, 1974), 4.
20. Ibid., 3.
21. Charles W. Turner, Bradford W. Hesse and Sonja Peterson-Lewis, "Naturalistic Studies of the Long-Term Effects of Television Violence," *Journal of Social Issues* 42:3(1986).
22. Richard Frost and John Stauffer, "The Effects of Social Class, Gender, and Personality on Psychological Responses to Filmed Violence," *Journal of Communication* (Spring 1987).
23. Charles W. Turner and Leonard Berkowitz, "Identification with Film Aggressor (Covert Role Taking) and Reactions to Film Violence," *Journal of Personality and Social Psychology* 21:2 (1972), 256–264.
24. Joanne R. Cantor, Dolf Zillmann and Edna F. Einsiedel, "Female Response to Provocation after Exposure to Aggressive and Erotic Films," *Communication Research* 5 (October 1978), 395–412.
25. Frost and Stauffer, "Responses to Violence," 30.
26. Ibid., 4l.
27. Mark Crispin Miller, "Hollywood; the Ad," *The Atlantic Monthly (*April 1990), 53.
28. Don West, "V-Chips, Kids TV Have All American Appeal," *Broadcasting and Cable* 127:43(October 20, 1997), 6(1).
29. Kaiser Family Foundation, December 21, 1999 (http://kff.org/content/archive/1477/vchip.html).
30. Ibid.
31. David Rosenbaum, "Panel Documents How Violent Fare Is Aimed at Youth," *New York Times*, September 12, 2000.
32. Mabel Rice, Altha C. Huston and John C. Wright, "The Forms of Television: Effects on Children's Attention, Comprehension, and Social Behavior," in *Television and Behavior: Ten Years of Scientific Progress and Implications for the*

Eighties, vol. 2, *Technical Reviews* eds. David Pearl, Lorraine Bouthilet and Joyce Laza (Rockville, MD: National Institute for Mental Health, 1982), 26.

33. Frank Rich, "Washington's Post-Littleton Looney Tunes," *New York Times,* June 19, 1999, A27.

34. "Study Finds US Children Spend a Full Work Week Using TV, Computers, Games," Agence France Presse, November 17, 1999.

35. Baker, "Media Use Statistics."

36. Ibid.

37. Ibid.

38. *Washington Post*, February 6, 2006, quoting Pew Internet & American Life Project surveys conducted October–November 2004 (teens) and January–June 2005 (adults).

39. Pittsburgh Consortium of Independent Schools PCIS(www.pittsburghindependentschools.org/resources/quick_facts.php).

40. Media Mark Research (www.mediamark.com/mri/docs/press.html).

41. Fiscal Notes (www.cpa.state.tx.us/comptrol/fnotes/fn0508/teens.html).

42. Stephanie Rosenbloom, "Mommy and Daddy's Little Life Coach," *New York Times*, April 5, 2007, E1.

43. James U. McNeal, *Children as Consumers* (Lexington, MA: Lexington Books, 1987).

44. Media Mark Research.

45. "National Study Reveals Kids Favorite TV Ads," *Advertising Age* (March 1998) (www.adage.com).

46. Paul M. Fischer and others, "Brand Logo Recognition by Children Aged 3 to 6 Years," *Journal of the American Medical Association* (December 11, 1991), 3145.

47. *Buy Me That: A Kid's Survival Guide to TV Advertising*, VHS, produced by Public Media, Inc. (Chicago: Films Incorporated Video, 1990).

48. John Lyons, *Guts: Advertising from the Inside Out* (New York: Amacom, 1987), 292.

49. Kate Louise Roberts, ed., *Hoyt's New Cyclopedia of Practical Quotations* (New York: Funk and Wagnalls, 1922), 520.

50. *Parenting in a Television Age: A Media Literacy Workshop Kit on Children and Television* (Los Angeles: Center for Media and Values, 1991), handout no. 1.

51. John P. Murray and Barbara Lonnborg, *Children and Television: A Primer for Parents* (Boys Town, 1991), 2–3.

52. *Parenting in a Television Age*, handout no. 1.

53. Ibid.

54. Peterson, "Three Recent Cases."

55. Ibid.

56. Amiee Dorr, Sherryl Browne Graves and Erin Phelps, "Television Literacy for Young Children," *Journal of Communication* (Summer 1980), 73.

57. Ibid.

58. "National Study Reveals Kids Favorite TV Ads," *Advertising Age* (March 1998) (www.adage.com)

59. Ibid.

60. D. Sweet and R. Singh, "TV Viewing and Parental Guidance," *Education Consumer Guide*, April 2, 1997 (http://inet.ed.gov/pubs/OR/Consumer/tv.html).

61. George Gerbner, "The 1998 Screen Actors Guild Report: Casing the American Scene," November 16, 1999 (www.sag.com/special/americanscene.html).

62. Linda Holtzman, Med 315: Content Analysis-Cartoons (Summer 1992).

63. Megan Rosenfeld, "Girls Find Less to Like on the Tube, Survey Says," *Washington Post*, carried in the *St. Louis Post-Dispatch,* January 17, 1996, 1E.

64. Betty Debman, "Mini-Page: South American Countries," St. Louis Post-Dispatch, October 1999, C3-4.

65. W. Andrew Collins, "Cognitive Processing in Television Viewing," in *Television and Behavior: Ten Years of Scientific Progress and Implications for the Eighties,* vol. 2, *Technical Reviews,* ed. by David Pearl, Lorraine Bouthilet, and Joyce Lazar (Rockville, MD: National Institute for Mental Health, 1982), 11.

66. Ibid.

67. Ellen Edwards, "More Than Ever, Kids Are at Home with Media," *Washington Post*, November 18, 1999.

68. David Considine and Gail Haley, *Visual Messages: Integrating Imagery into Instruction* (Englewood, CO: Teacher Ideas Press, 1992), 80.

69. John Tebbel, *The Media in America* (New York: Thomas Y. Crowell Company, 1974).

70. Ibid., 39

71. Sylvester Brown Jr., "Some Video Games Make a Point with Their Violence," *St. Louis Post-Dispatch*, July 2, 2006.

72. Ibid.

73. Edward Herman and Noam Chomsky, *Manufacturing Consent* (New York: Pantheon Books, 1988), 2.

74. Ibid., 17.

75. Ibid., 26.

76. Francesca M. Cancian and Bonnie L. Ross, "Mass Media and the Women's Movement," *Journal of Applied Behavioral Science* 12:1(1981), 11.

77. Ibid., 18.

78. Ibid., 25.

79. Ibid., 18.

80. Ibid., 20.

81. Herbert Gans, *Deciding What's News* (New York: Pantheon Books, 1979), 31–37.

82. Philip Gault, *Choosing the News: The Profit Factor in News Selection* (New York: Greenwood Press, 1990), 127.

83. Johnson Russia List, http:www.cdi.org/russia/Johnson/defzault.cfm

84. W. James Potter, News from Three Worlds in Prestige U.S. Newspapers," in *Current Issues in International Communications* by L. John Martin and Ray Eldon Hiebert, New York: Longman, 1990, 280.

85. Harold D. Lasswell, Propaganda Technique in the World War (New York: Peter Smith, 1927), 195.

86. Simon Romero, "When Villages Go Global," *New York Times*, April 23, 2000.

87. Doreen Carvajal, "1,000 Journalists Killed ... and more than 140 were jailed—its highest level in a decade," Forbes.com (www.forbes.com/feeds/ap/2007/02/01/ap3386569.html).

88. Ibid.

89. Ibid.
90. Nikolai Zlobin, Interview by author, July 20, 1999, St. Louis, MO.
91. Ibid.
92. Ibid.
93. Peter Kenyon, "Provocative 'Yacoubian' Film Opens in Cairo," All Things Considered, National Public Radio, June 21, 2006.
94. Ibid.
95. Nikolai Zlobin, interview.
96. Ibid.
97. Asep Sutresna, "International Communication and Popular Culture in Indonesia," Paper presented to MED 531, Media and Culture, Webster University (May 1993), 6.
98. Ibid., 7.
99. Ibid., 13.
100. Anand Giridharadas, "Playboy Makes Move in India, but Without the Centerfold," *New York Times*, January 2, 2006.
101. Ibid.
102. Ibid.
103. Nikolai Zlobin, interview.
104. John C. Merrill, John Lee, and Edward J. Friedlander, *Modern Mass Media* (New York: Harper & Row, 1990), 428.
105. Pankaj Mishra, "Hurray for Bollywood," *New York Times*, February 28, 2004, A15.
106. John Markoff, "At Davos, the Squabble Resumes on How to Wire the Third World," *New York Times*, January 29, 2007.

CHAPTER 17

OUTCOMES

It is now appropriate to consider the "quintessential so-what"—that is, given what you know about the media, what steps can be taken to improve our communications environment? The Aspen Institute National Leadership Conference on Media Literacy has considered this critical issue of possible *outcomes*:

> Is media literacy important only to the extent that it enables one to be a better citizen in society? What is the role of ideology in the process? To what extent is an individual "media literate" if she just appreciates the aesthetics of a message without going further with it?[1]

The range of outcomes falls into the following categories:

Personal Responses. The most immediate outcome is that you are now in a position to make independent, critical choices about media consumption. Media technology such as DVDs, cable television, and CDs give you control over your personal media usage. Moreover, the Internet supplies you with immediate access to your choice of information.

In addition, alternative media presentations such as the *Progressive*, *Nation*, *American Prospect*, *Adbusters*, and *CovertAction* offer a range of perspectives on issues. Michael Parenti declares, "To create a more democratic climate of opinion in our country we must ... support and strengthen alternative media with subscriptions and contributions, recognizing them as a crucial and liberating source of information and analysis."[2]

The range of your personal responses includes:

- *Becoming well-informed in matters of media coverage.*
- *Maintaining a "balanced media diet"; that is, checking several media (e.g., both newspapers and television) to examine the coverage of issues.*
- *Being aware of your everyday contact with the media and its influence on your lifestyle, attitudes, and behaviors.*
- *Applying the media literacy analysis tools (Keys to Interpreting Media Messages) to media presentations to derive insight into media messages.*
- *Examining media programming to learn about cultural attitudes, values, behaviors, preoccupations, and myths.*
- *Developing an awareness of programming as "text" that furnishes trends as a way of learning about changes in the culture.*
- *Keeping abreast of patterns in ownership and government regulations that affect the media industry.*
- *Promoting discussions about the media industry, media programming, and issues with friends, colleagues, and children.*

Becoming Involved in the Media Literacy Community. Media literacy organizations promote the field of media literacy by collecting and disseminating media literacy information. They also sponsor programs and conferences throughout the country. Examples of media literacy organizations include:

- Center for Media Literacy
- Center for Media Education
- Gateway Media Literacy Partners (GMLP)
- National Telemedia Council

Many other organizations promote goals that are associated with media literacy. Some of these organizations include:

- Children Now
- Action for Children's Television
- Children's Advertising Review Unit
- National Alliance for Non-Violent Programming

Media Activism. Media activism involves taking steps to democratize the communications environment, both nationally and globally.

Individual Activism. Individuals may make the following personal choices in response to media programming:

- Cancel your subscription or turn off objectionable programming.
- If you have concerns about a newspaper article, write a letter to the editor.

- If you have concerns about a television or radio program, write to the general manager of the station.
- Register a complaint with the Federal Communications Commission (FCC).

  The FCC can respond to public complaints by investigating broadcast stations. On the basis of their findings, the FCC is authorized to levy fines on stations. In extreme cases, the FCC can suspend station operations, refuse to renew a station's broadcast license, or even withdraw a station's current license. However, the First Amendment (freedom of speech) provides considerable latitude for the expression of ideas—even those that are in "poor taste."

  Federal Communications Commission regulations require that stations keep all public correspondence on file. Consequently, station management must make a formal acknowledgement of your point of view.
- Meet in person with the staff of the newspaper, TV, or radio station.

Grassroots Organizing activities begin at the local level and focus on organizing community resources. The goal of the following activities is to develop awareness within communities and work for change in the media landscape.

- *Picketing.* This strategy draws public attention to an issue and a media organization. The trick is to attract the attention of the media through this action.
- *Letter writing Campaigns.* Carol Rubin-Schlansky of Richmond Heights, Missouri, orchestrated an effective letter-writing campaign in response to the placement of an objectionable ad during her young daughters' favorite television program. Rubin-Schlansky contacted the station manager but found him unresponsive. She then composed a complaint letter, leaving it unsigned, and distributed copies to friends and acquaintances. They were instructed that if they agreed with her position, they should sign their names and mail the letters on *the same day.* This strategy had a definite impact. The station manager admitted, "Anytime you get 50 letters about something, it gets your attention."[3]

  Social action groups have found success in incorporating the Internet into the process of letter writing by supplying the text and e-mail address of the recipient. The "author" of the letter simply has to fill out his or her name and click on the designated link.
- *Petition Drives.* Media organizations are always more impressed by complaints by numbers of people than the opinions of one individual. The Internet has greatly facilitated the process of circulating a petition and gathering a list of supporters. However, the list of names on a petition also may be easily dismissed, since it takes relatively little effort on the part of the people signing the petition.
- *Contacting Advertisers.* Media organizations are very sensitive to the concerns of their advertisers who, in turn, strive to maintain the goodwill of the public. Consequently, explaining your concerns and listing the program's advertisers can be an effective action. As an example, in 2007, radio "shock jock" Don Imus referred to the members of the Rutgers University women's basketball team as "nappy-headed hos," and outraged groups brought the names of the program's sponsors—Procter & Gamble, and Sprint—to public attention.[4] The sponsors

then withdrew their sponsorship, and shortly thereafter, NBC and CBS radio fired Imus. (For further discussion, see Chapter 3.)

Becoming a Stockholder. Becoming a stockholder in one of the media conglomerates can be an effective way to exercise some influence over the direction of these companies. By purchasing only one share of a company's stock, you become a shareholder who can bring issues of concern to the attention of other stockholders and vote on policy issues. The goal is to broaden stockholders' definitions of corporate success to include responsible, quality programming. To illustrate, these stockholders are often parents who are privately concerned about the impact of media programming. Consequently, the hope is that they will take a long-term look at their company beyond simply its quarterly profits. "Educating" stockholders can free producers to follow their best instincts to generate quality programming.

- *Monitoring Local Media.* Groups that do not feel served by the media in their community can monitor the programming and challenge the license renewal with the Federal Communications Commission (FCC). As an example, between 1953–1979, the members of the United Church of Christ in Jackson, Mississippi, fought when they felt that their local television station refused to cover civil rights stories. Citizens monitored the programming around the clock to show how it was excluding a vast part of the population, and they ultimately prevailed when the license of WLBT-TV was not renewed. Professor Eric Klinenberg explains,

> (United Church of Christ) challenged a station renewal license in Jackson, Mississippi, for a local station, local television station, that refused to air a lot of civil rights coverage, that would preempt national coverage when it was against the interest of the small number of station owners, who had quite discriminatory politics built into their programming. They served a community in Jackson that was overwhelmingly African American, and they misserved them, in fact, and failed to be accountable in ways that a broadcaster needs to be. The United Church of Christ fought a long legal battle to say, "We have standing as members of this community, that when a broadcast station discriminates against its own audience, when it doesn't serve their interest, because they use the public airwaves—they depend on the public airwaves—we can challenge the license." They won that case, and the result is, citizens now have a number of legal resources to fight back when the media misserves them....[5]

Organizational Activism. National organizations with large memberships can most assuredly influence the policies of media corporations. Thanks to the efforts of organizations such as Free Press (www.freepress.com) and Action Coalition for Media Education (ACME), media activists from around the country are working together, employing different strategies that share the common goal of broadening and diversifying corporate ownership of the media industry. Thus, in 2006, thanks largely to an enormous grassroots movement organized by Free Press, language about "net neutrality" was included as part of an agreement for a merger between AT&T and the Bell companies, and a two-year moratorium was established, preserving the principle of "net neutrality."

Three thousand activists from around the country gathered in Memphis, Tennessee, at the 2007 Media Reform conference, to share ideas and achievements with respect to the democratization of the U.S. media industry. Workshops included the following topics:

- Effective Grassroots Lobbying
- How to Challenge a Broadcast License
- Connecting Community-Based Media Organizations Across America
- Get Radio: What You Need to Know to Start Your Own Station

Media reform has also emerged as a national political issue. Congressional legislators Bernie Sanders, Dennis Kucinich, and Ed Markey announced plans to hold congressional hearings to discuss the need to democratize the media, taking a careful look at the criteria for awarding broadcast licenses through the auctioning of the public airwaves—particularly these conglomerates' record of public service.

Sectors

Media literacy is an area of study that prepares students for careers in a range of fields. In 2005, Elizabeth Van Ness wrote an opinion column in the *New York Times*, entitled, "Is a Cinema Studies Degree the New M.B.A.?" in which she argued that Cinema Studies imbues students with the critical skills that make them sought-after in the workplace:

> Rick Herbst, now attending Yale Law School, may yet turn out to be the current decade's archetypal film major. Twenty-three years old, he graduated last year from the University of Notre Dame, where he studied filmmaking with no intention of becoming a filmmaker. Rather, he saw his major as a way to learn about power structures and how individuals influence each other.
>
> "People endowed with social power and prestige are able to use film and media images to reinforce their power—we need to look to film to grant power to those who are marginalized or currently not represented," said Mr. Herbst, who envisions a future in the public policy arena. The communal nature of film, he said, has a distinct power to affect large groups, and he expects to use his cinematic skills to do exactly that.
>
> At a time when street gangs warn informers with DVD productions about the fate of "snitches" and both terrorists and their adversaries routinely communicate in elaborately staged videos, it is not altogether surprising that film school—promoted as a shot at an entertainment industry job—is beginning to attract those who believe that cinema isn't so much a profession as the professional language of the future.[6]

Substituting the term "Media Literacy" for "Cinema Studies" makes a compelling case for the value of a degree in Media Literacy, which expands this theoretical and diagnostic focus to include all forms of media. As

Elizabeth Daley, dean of the School of Cinema-Television at the University of Southern California observes, "The greatest digital divide is between those who can read and write with media, and those who can't. Our core knowledge needs to belong to everybody.... If I had my way, our multimedia literacy honors program would be required of every student in the university,"[7] Indeed, today's geopolitical world requires that professionals in the public realm understand the nuances of media messages. Van Ness explains,

> (In 2005), members of a Baltimore street gang circulated a DVD that warned against betrayal, packaged in a cover that appeared to show three dead bodies. That and the series of gruesome execution videos that have surfaced in the Middle East are perhaps only the most extreme face of a complex sort of post-literacy in which cinematic visuals and filmic narrative have become commonplace.[8]

Graduates of film studies and media literacy programs have pursued careers in museums, leisure businesses, and in the public policy arena.

Media literacy is a discipline with career applications in the following sectors: Education, Public Policy, Community Media, Media Arts, Professional Media, and Writing and Research.

Education Sector. Media literacy is an established field of study within the international academic community. England and Australia have emerged as leaders in the discipline of media education, with performance and content standards, norm-referenced tests, and pre-service university training for a specialty in media education. In 2002, the U.K. passed a Communications Bill, charging a new super-regulator, Ofcom, with the duty to encourage "a better public understanding of the nature and characteristics of material published by means of electronic media." It also allows for greater use of rating systems, filters, and other devices which block out objectionable content.[9]

Canada is also at an advanced stage in the development of media literacy, thanks in large measure to the Canadian Association for Media Education Organizations, a national network of media literacy organizations. Ontario has the most advanced media education standards. As of 2006, its language curriculum contains a discreet media strand with elaborate learning goals and supports for each grade K–12.[10]

Other countries have also made significant inroads into the field of media literacy, including New Zealand, Chile, India, Scotland, South Africa, Japan, France, Italy, Spain, and Jordan.

Significantly, the United States has lagged behind these other countries in the media literacy movement. According to a 2006 study by the National Center for Public Policy and Higher Education, more than 50 percent of college students lack the skills to perform tasks that fall under the broad umbrella of "literacy," which includes understanding the arguments of a newspaper editorial and summarizing the results of a survey, defined as "complex literacy tasks."[11]

Some form of media literacy education in primary and secondary schools is required in all 50 states[12]; however, many teachers ignore this mandate—in part because of the pressure to prepare for the standardized tests that accompany the No Student Left Behind education initiative. Schools' certifications and teachers' promotions are predicated on students' performance on this test. Consequently, Baker observes, "Teachers, who know what is on the test, teach only that material, and thus media literacy gets left out."[13]

But significantly, media literacy is a discipline that actually *enhances* critical thinking and literacy skills—major areas of focus in the No Child Left Behind program. A study conducted by Hobbs and Frost reveals that media literacy education improved students' reading, viewing and listening comprehension of print, audio and video texts, message analysis and interpretation, and writing.[14]

However, in recent years, the media literacy movement has gained momentum in the American academic community. A number of national associations promote media literacy in the United States, including: The Center for Media Literacy in Los Angeles, The National Telemedia Council in Madison, Wisconsin, and the New Mexico Media Literacy Project (NMMLP). Regional media literacy associations include the Gateway Media Literacy Partners (GMLP) in the St. Louis, MO, area.

Moreover, a 2007 survey found that 180 two-year and four-year institutions offered media literacy courses or programs.[15] These course offerings are offered through a number of academic disciplines, although they can most often be found in departments of Communication or Education.

Public Policy Sector. A number of organizations are working with educational institutions, community organizations, or media literacy associations to promote legislative and regulatory reforms in media policy. Some of the areas of media policy legislation that are being addressed include:

- *Media Ownership*
  Imposing limits on mergers that further concentrate media ownership.
  Restoring the FCC's fairness doctrine on the public airwaves, so that broadcast license renewals will be predicated on whether a station has met its public interest obligations.
  Using the proceeds from the auction of the public airwaves and awarding of broadcast licenses to support local and independent media.
  Expanding the ownership base of the media industry, particularly to members of minority groups.
  Enforcing anti-trust laws to break up the media oligopolies.
- *Political Campaign Reform*
  Increasing public financing of political campaigns.
  Providing free television air time for candidates during campaigns.
- *Digital Media Protections*
  Guarantying the principle of "net neutrality," so that all users of the Internet will have equal opportunities to access and disseminate information.

Addressing the Digital Divide by taking steps to insure that the Internet is accessible and affordable.

Taking steps to insure that Intellectual Property Rights of individuals are protected.

Supporting policies designed to protect the privacy of Internet users.

- *Education*
  Implementing the Education Standards of states, which mandates the instruction of media literacy in schools.
- *Community Media*
  Urging local officials to demand public interest obligations and safeguards for PEG (public, education, and government) television in return for the cable companies' use of public rights-of-way.
- *Media and Children*
  Requiring broadcasters to air a minimum amount of educational programming for children as part of their public service obligation.
- *Public Broadcasting*
  Expanding the public broadcasting system (especially news).

Community Media Sector. Community-based media organizations' outreach efforts reach audiences typically not in contact with academic institutions, including religious organizations, public access groups, and privately funded organizations. The media organizations are distinctly local in nature. The stations are staffed by members of the community. Often, a large percentage of the positions is made of up volunteers.

Community radio and television stations are almost entirely supported by individual donations. Because their operation is free of the economic imperatives that characterize commercial stations, their programming reflects the interests of its audience (some of whom volunteer at the station). Community media stations produce programming that promotes an awareness of issues, challenges, and opportunities facing their communities. In addition, community stations promote the local arts; indeed, until the Hurricane Katrina disaster, the most popular radio station in New Orleans was WWOZ, which played the music of local artists, as well as older examples of their rich musical heritage.

As an example, a number of community media organizations operate in St. Louis, Missouri. To illustrate, the mission of the Homeless Empowerment Project publishes *Whats Up Magazine* that mobilizes the public around poverty issues, and organizes, educates, and builds alliances to find community-based solutions to homelessness and poverty. The publication is sold by St. Louis's homeless citizens, and helps them earn the money they need to get ahead. The publication covers issues surrounding poverty and homelessness, and includes stories about labor, the environment, public health, and civil liberties. Another community media organization is Double Helix, the community television and radio station. The mission of these media stations is as follows:

- The Double Helix Corporation is an arts and educational organization dedicated to fostering community participation, knowledge, and training through mass media with the following values:

  Developing volunteer participation

  Supporing cultural diversity

  Promoting local talent

  Providing a forum for the public discourse

  Educating through programming and training[16]

Media Arts. Media arts programs promote media literacy through both production and critical analysis. These programs are primarily directed at young people. Media arts programs encourage self-discovery and growth through artistic expression. The topics of these films, videos, and web sites examine issues rarely addressed in mainstream media. In addition, the process of producing media presentations can provide insight into how messages are constructed in the media.

Writing and Research. A number of publications, both print and on the Internet, analyzes media coverage and trends in the media industry. Some of these publications include FAIR (Fairness and Accuracy in Media), Media Reality Check, American Journalism Review, and the Project for Excellence in Journalism.

In addition, media literacy analysis can be found throughout the popular press. Many newspapers and magazines throughout the country include media critics on their staff who discuss cultural trends found in programming. Also, features and entertainment journalism pieces often focus on trends in media programming that serve as a barometer of cultural attitudes.

As an example, journalist David Carr authored an article in the *New York Times* in 2006 entitled "Hollywood Gives the Press A Bad Name," that looks at how journalists are depicted in popular films. Carr observes,

> The movies in which the press is seen as holding business and government to account—how the press likes to think of itself—are far outnumbered by the films in which the news media come off as entirely unaccountable.
>
> When Hollywood has a role requiring greasy self-interest, it knows it can insert a fast-talking guy with a notebook and soup stains on his tie … *King Kong* offers a typical scenario. The poor gorilla is chained to a stage for the entertainment of others and photographers shower him with flashbulbs until he goes ballistic, flattens New York and then tumbles to his death. And, oh yeah, the journalists are there to climb atop the carcass for some more pictures. Not much has changed in public perception of the craft since the original *King Kong* was made back in 1933. In *Capote*, the journalist sells out his subject, while in *Munich* a frantic electronic press in pursuit of the story tips off the terrorists.[17]

According to Carr, this tarnished view of journalists is an indication of a lack of public confidence in journalists in the wake of examples of discreditable behavior by members of the press:

> The business in general seems to be playing to type. Myriad plagiarism scandals, most notably one involving *The New York Times* and Jayson Blair and CBS's failure to verify a memo related to President Bush's National Guard service, conjure their own images of journalistic malfeasance.

There were the travails of Judith Miller, the former reporter for *The New York Times*, and now even Bob Woodward of *The Washington Post*—whose work with Carl Bernstein provided grist for *All the President's Men*, a journalistic paean—is starring in a far less praiseworthy role.[18]

Professional Sector. The professional media sector can be a very powerful and effective voice for media literacy. The newspaper, film, and television industries have established programs designed to promote critical understanding of media and media content. In some cases, media professionals work in partnership with educational institutions, community groups, or media literacy organizations. Organizations of media professionals with interests in media literacy include: Creating Critical Viewers, Newspaper Association of America Foundation, Show Coalition, Taos Film Festival.

In addition, media professionals do produce responsible and informative programming that improves the industry by applying the principles of media literacy. Documentary programs such as "Frontline" and "On the Media" heighten awareness of the impact of the media on our culture. And news programming like "Democracy Now" (democracynow.com) call attention to issues and challenge its audience to think critically about the information that they receive through the mainstream media.

Independent video producers also promote media literacy by examining issues that are not covered by corporate media. One notable example is *An Inconvenient Truth* (2006), a film produced by former Vice President Al Gore, which brought the issue of global warming to public attention. Companies that produce independent media literacy programming include: The Association for Independent Video and Filmmakers, the Foundation for Independent Video and Film, Boston Film and Video Foundation, and The Northwest Film Center.

Presentations produced for theatrical release also can bring social issues to the consciousness of the public. Most famously, *All the President's Men* (1976) dramatized how American investigative journalists Woodward and Bernstein uncovered the Watergate scandal. More recently, *The Girl in the Café* (2005) is a charming romance set amid the G8 Summit in Reykjavik, Iceland. A summary of the film is as follows:

A May-December comedy becomes a political drama. Lawrence (Bill Nighy), a spindly, self-effacing civil servant, is a senior researcher for the Chancellor of the Exchequer, preparing for a G-8 summit that will determine the scope of the world's effort to reduce extreme poverty. In a crowded café, he chats awkwardly with Gina (Kelly McDonald), a young Scot with time on her hands. They share a couple of meals, and he invites her to accompany him to the summit in Reykjavík. Once there, as romance blooms, Gina's past, Lawrence's work and proclivity to compromise, and the presence of ministers and presidents spur her to act.[19]

The romance between the two characters serves as a metaphor for the process at the summit. Lawrence's emotional baggage that prevents him from realizing any relationship is also found in the bureaucratic roadblocks that prevent the G-8 from finding bold solutions to end child poverty in the world.

Popular music groups, from the Dixie Chicks to Eminem and the Dead Presidents also raise questions and call on their audiences to take action on social issues.

MEDIA & SOCIAL CHANGE

CUTLINE

Presentations produced for theatrical release such as *The Girl in the Café* (2005) can bring social issues to the consciousness of the public.

NOTES

1. Aspen Institute, "National Leadership Conference on Media Literacy," Queenstown, Maryland, December 7–9, 1992.
2. Michael Parenti, "Does the U.S. Have a Free Press?" *The Witness* (March 1985), 45–50.
3. Eric Mink, "Mother's Anger Turns Into Primer On Activism," *St. Louis Post-Dispatch*, April 11, 1993, 14C.
4. Noam Cohen, "Bloggers Take on Talk Radio Hosts," *New York Times,* January 15, 2007, C3.
5. Eric Klinenberg, interview on Democracy Now!, January 26, 2007 (www.democracynow.com).
6. Elizabeth Van Ness, "Is a Cinema Studies Degree the New M.B.A.?" *New York Times*, March 6, 2005.
7. Ibid.
8. Ibid.
9. Nick Higham, "UK Broadcasting Is Leaving Its 1950s Roots Far Behind," media-l@nmsu.edu, December 3, 2002.
10. Neil Anderson, English and Media Consultant, Toronto Board of Education, e-mail, June 11, 2006.

11. Michelle Oyola, "Students Not Life-Literate, Says Study," *Webster University Journal*, February 23, 2006.

12. Robert Kubey and Frank Baker, "Has Media Literacy Found a Curricular Foothold?" 2000 Editorial Projects in Education Vol. 19, number 9, pp. 56, 38.

13. Frank Baker, e-mail to author, June 11, 2006.

14. Renee Hobbs and Richard Frost, "Measuring the Acquisition of Media Literacy Skills," *Reading Research Quarterly* (Spring 2003).

15. Art Silverblatt, Frank Baker, Kathleen Tyner, and Laura Stuhlman, "Media Literacy in U.S. Institutions of Higher Education," July 25, 2002 (www.webster.edu/medialiteracy/survey/survey_Report.htm).

16. KDHX-TV Saint Louis Community Television (www.dhtv.org/about.htm).

17. David Carr, "Hollywood Gives the Press a Bad Name," *New York Times,* December 12, 2005, C1.

18. Ibid.

19. Film review, jhailey@hotmail.com, *The Girl in the Café,* Internet Movie Database (www.imdb.com/).

GLOSSARY

active-negative personality Political scientist James David Barber devised a formula for predicting presidential performance, based on distinct character types. Barber has identified four character patterns based on level of activity (activity-passivity) and enjoyment (positive-negative affect). The active-negative character combines intense effort with a relatively low emotional reward. The active-negative figure is compulsive, and his or her goal is to obtain and maintain power.

active-positive personality Political scientist James David Barber devised a formula for predicting presidential performance, based on distinct character types. Barber has identified four character patterns based on level of activity (activity-passivity) and enjoyment (positive-negative affect). The active-positive personality is distinguished by an industrious nature, combined with the enjoyment of this level of activity.

advertorials Ads that appear in newspapers in the form of editorial content.

affective response In contrast with print, visual and aural stimuli initially touch us on an emotional, or affective, level. Media communicators can influence the attitude and behavior of audiences by appealing to emotions and evoking an affective, or emotional, response.

affective strategies Media communicators can influence the attitudes and behavior of audiences by developing communications strategies designed to appeal to the emotions of the audience. For instance, ads frequently are directed at emotions such as guilt or the need for acceptance to sell their product.

agenda setting Even if newspapers don't tell us what to think, they do tell us what to think *about*. An issue can become a topic of national debate through the news media.

American mass communications model Because the American media is a market-driven system, the audience has emerged as the primary consideration in the communication process, calling for yet another configuration of the mass communications model:

Channel
Audience
Communicator
Message

angle Angle refers to the level at which the camera is shooting in relation to the subject. The choice of angle can affect the audience's attitude toward the subject. A person filmed from a high angle looks small, weak, frightened, or vulnerable. In contrast, a person filmed from a low angle appears larger, more important, and powerful.

arousal theory of media violence A theory of media violence effects that maintains that violent programming stimulates aggression in audience members and can lead to aggressive behavior. An illustration of the arousal theory is John Hinckley who, after watching the film *Taxi Driver* in 1981, attempted to assassinate President Ronald Reagan.

artistic expression Artists are often able to find a creative outlet through their work. Novelists, painters, or experimental videographers express themselves through their art and share their artistic vision with the audience.

audience attention span Attention span can be a factor in audience interference. Communication is an active process that demands concentration and energy. Occasionally, members of the audience will just tune out the speaker and take a brief rest.

audience behavior patterns Audience behavior patterns refer to the ways in which individuals use particular media, as well as the expectations that the individual brings to that medium.

audience identification Audience identification is perhaps the most pressing challenge facing a media communicator. Media communicators devote enormous resources to developing a clear sense of audience. Different sectors of audience have distinct, identifiable interests and look for specific objectives or gratifications in media programming, based on their stage of life. Audience identification can affect content, style, and communications strategies.

audience interference Audience interference refers to instances in which the audience obstructs the communication process. Several factors may influence the way in which individuals select and process information, including selective exposure, selective perception, selective retention, attention span, and the ego of the audience member.

biased interviewing techniques A reporter can slant a story through the type of questions posed to subjects while conducting research for the story. Types of biased interviewing strategies include compliance as assertion, leading or loaded questions, hypothetical questions, and presenting questions with "either/or" choices.

big promise The big promise refers to an ad strategy in which an advertisement makes claims that are far beyond the capacity of the product.

broadcasting Broadcasting is a concept tied to the early stages of American media. Because the overall audience was limited, the mass communicator had to produce general programming that would appeal to the mass culture.

camouflaged warnings Product warnings are designed to be as inconspicuous as possible. For example, the disclaimers on cigarette advertisements appear in very small print. The warning is generally separated from the main visual field. And sometimes the print is camouflaged by the color and graphics of the ad.

cathartic theory of media violence A theory of media effects that holds that violent programming may at times provide a healthy release for aggressions. After watching a violent program, the audience may feel drained and purified, purged of violent impulses. In this sense, media violence could be regarded as positive and constructive.

channel interference One of the sources of communications interference. Channel interference occurs when a glitch in the channel prevents the audience from understanding the message. In mass communications, channel interference occurs when the television picture suddenly goes blank or the sound becomes inaudible. Channel interference can also result from using an inappropriate channel to send a particular type of message.

character development By the end of a narrative, characters often have changed dramatically. Focusing on these changes can provide insight into media messages.

civic journalism An approach which represents a departure from the notion of journalism as a detached, objective record of events. Civic journalism calls for the press to assume an active role in strengthening citizenship, improving political debate, and reviving public life. Critics contend that this approach undermines the traditional watchdog function of the press.

code words Code words are terms that have clear and distinct messages for targeted audiences.

color A visual element that can have a powerful effect on the way that audiences respond to a media presentation.

commencement words Commencement words suggest immediacy, importance, and a sense of urgency (e.g., *introducing, announcing, now, suddenly*).

communication strategy An approach designed to reach and influence a particular target audience by capitalizing on their interests, concerns, and preoccupations.

communications model The basic communications model consists of the following elements: the *communicator*, who delivers the message; the *message*, which is the information being communicated; the *channel*, the passage through which the information is being conveyed; and the *audience*, which consists of the person or people who are receiving the message.

communicator interference One source of communications interference. Communicator interference occurs when the communicator makes it difficult for the audience to understand the message. For instance, the communicator may not know what he or she wants to say or may send mixed messages to the audience.

comparative media Comparative media refers to the characteristics that distinguish one medium from another. The effective media communicator takes advantage of the unique properties of each medium to convey media messages.

competing functions Competing functions refers to instances in which media productions attempt to fulfill several competing functions simultaneously, which undermines the effectiveness of the presentation.

compliance as assertion In this biased interviewing technique, reporters may come prepared with a point of view (and a quote) ready to include in an article and is interviewing only for the *consent* of the subject. In this case, reporters may phrase a question, "Would you agree that ..." or "Would you say that ..." or "So what you are saying is ...".

computer operating system Software that determines your interactions with your computer and how the computer operates.

connotation Connotation refers to the meaning associated with a word beyond its denotative, or dictionary, definition. The meaning of a connotative word is universally understood and agreed upon.

connotative images Images appearing in photographs, film, or video that possess universal associative properties.

consequences Events in a media presentation that are caused, directly or indirectly, by a character's actions. A media-literate viewer may ask if the consequences of a character's actions are accurately depicted.

content analysis Content analysis is a quantitative methodology that can be employed to look for patterns in messages, symbols, language, art forms, and potential bias in the media.

context Context refers to those surrounding elements that subtly shape meaning and convey message. Elements of context include historical context, cultural context, and structure.

convenience words Convenience words appeal to the consumers' interest in products that will make their lives easier (e.g., *easy*, *quick*).

convention A convention is a practice or object that appears so often in the media that it has become standard. Conventions furnish cues about people, events, and situations.

conventional setting Conventional settings refer to a standard background against which the action takes place. The conventional setting for a sitcom is the home or workplace.

conventional storyline A conventional storyline is a recurrent incident that is characteristic of a particular genre. Examples include the gun duel in a western, the wedding scene in a romance, or the car chase in the action genre.

conventional trappings Conventional trappings include props and costumes that are common to a genre. These trappings furnish the audience with clues about the action.

cookies A piece of software which plants small, traceable files on the computers of the people who visit a site. This interactive technology can track all of your activities on the Internet, raising serious issues about privacy.

critical responses A category of mass communication feedback, in which critics provide their assessment of the quality of a media presentation.

critical studies Critical theorists argue that the worldview presented through the media does not merely *reflect* or *reinforce* culture but in fact *shapes* thinking by promoting the dominant ideology of a culture. The media largely present the ideology of the dominant culture as a means of maintaining control. In that sense, the media can create (or *re-create*) representations of reality that reflect the dominant ideology.

cross-cutting Cross-cutting is an editing technique in which footage from different locations is juxtaposed to give the impression of events occurring at the same moment.

cultural context Anthropologists study ancient civilizations by unearthing artifacts in order to reconstruct a portrait of the society. In the same way, the study of media productions furnishes a means of understanding culture.

cultural myths Cultural myths are sets of beliefs that may not be true but nevertheless tell us about how we see ourselves and our culture.

cultural preoccupations The relative importance that a culture places on particular issues as reflected through media content; for example, the amount of attention given to sexually oriented content.

cultural studies A critical approach to communication analysis that regards the media as a reflection of multiple realities (e.g., cultural subgroups).

cumulative effects theory of media violence This theory of media violence effects maintains that cumulative media messages regarding violence may have long-term, *indirect* effects on individuals.

cumulative messages Messages often appear in the media with such frequency that they form new meanings, independent of any individual presentation. Examples would include messages regarding gender roles, definitions of success, and racial and cultural stereotypes.

customer advantage words Customer advantage words offer the consumer a sense of control, vision, wisdom, and superiority (e.g., *bargain, offer, free, sale*).

damage control Damage control refers to the management of information during a crisis. This strategy is designed to minimize potentially harmful stories.

deep background In journalism, information provided by a source that puts a story into a broader perspective and guides the report in a particular direction.

demographic research Demographic research refers to the study of human populations. Demographic considerations such as geographic location can play a large role in consumer buying patterns. Other demographic categories include age, gender, income, education, occupation, race, religion, and family size.

description This common communication function occurs when a communicator provides details, elaborates on general statements, or offers concrete examples as a way of enhancing the understanding of the audience.

desensitizing theory of media violence Some researchers have found that frequent exposure to media violence can have a numbing effect on the audience.

designated spokesperson Sometimes the press anoints a spokesperson to represent a particular cause. They may be leaders of an organization or an "expert" (e.g., university professor). But whether these people actually enjoy the support of a broad constituency is open to question.

dialogue Dialogue is written material that is intended to *sound* like conversation. A script may contain a great deal of information and complex layers of meaning. This material is presented very rapidly, like speech, so that the audience member easily can confuse the message being delivered.

directive response Media content such as advertising, political spots, and public service messages have very specific cognitive, attitudinal, and behavioral response objectives on the part of the media communicator.

directives Directives tell the consumer what to do (e.g., *hurry, compare*).

disengagement This function applies to situations in which the objective is to discourage extended conversation.

dissemination schedule The dissemination schedule refers to the amount of time that it takes for information to reach the audience, when conveyed through a particular medium, as well as the route that it takes to get to the public.

editing Editing refers to the selection and arrangement of information.

editorial content Editorial content refers to news content—everything in the newspaper that is not paid space.

ego A factor in audience interference, in which the audience member focuses on those aspects of a conversation or media presentation that relate to him or her, ignoring the rest of the message.

elite art Elite art is directed at a select, educated audience. The responsibility for comprehending and appreciating the content rests with the audience (as opposed to the artist, as is the case with popular art). Elite art is defined by the following characteristics: exclusivity, aesthetic complexity, historical context, and exploration.

embedded values Media content often reflects the value of the media communicator, as well as widely held cultural values and attitudes. Values may be embedded in the text through such production techniques as editing decision, point of view, and connotative words and images.

emotional benefits Advertisers recognize that products are purchased for psychological as well as product satisfaction. Consequently, ads may focus on the impact that the product has on the consumer.

emotional catharsis One of the possible functions of a communications exchange, this would include spontaneous expressions of love, passion, anger, pain, happiness, or the release of tension.

entertainment One of the possible functions of a communications exchange, this refers to communication that is devoted to amusement, often as a tool of persuasion.

environment Environment refers to the physical surroundings that can affect communication.

environmental interference One of the sources of communications interference. Environmental interference refers to distractions that occur in the setting in which the information is received.

euphemism Euphemisms are words that have an innocuous connotation; these neutral terms often are substituted for language that could offend the audience.

explicit content Explicit content consists of events and activities in the plot that are displayed through visible action. The viewer constructs meaning by selecting the essential pieces of explicit information in the story.

exploration One of the possible functions of a communications exchange, this refers to instances in which media communicators are actively composing their message during the course of the presentation. Mass communicators generally present polished information that has been prepared in advance. However, media communicators are sometimes subject to slipups when they work without a script.

expression One common function of communication is to inform the listener of the speaker's frame of mind. In these situations, speakers might talk about what they are thinking at that moment, how they are feeling or their attitudes toward people and issues.

extraneous inclusion A journalistic technique that can be used to present a particular point of view, in which information is added to a story that, on the surface, appears to be immaterial. However, these details add a context to the story that establishes a distinct point of view toward the subject.

extreme close-up (XCU) Film and television can *approximate* the first-person perspective through use of the extreme close-up camera shot. This shot studies a character's reaction to events and people.

extreme long shot (XLS) The extreme long shot, which is used in film and television, takes in a wide expanse of visual information and often establishes the setting at the beginning of a scene. This shot provides a broad context for the subsequent action.

false and misleading ads In some cases, ads make false claims that are intended to mislead the consumer.

false function Media programs may offer the appearance of serving one function while actually fulfilling other purposes. Examples include "infotainment" TV programs like "Entertainment Tonight" and "A Current Affair," which are entertainment programs presented in a news format. People may look to these programs for legitimate news, although their predominant functions are to amuse and titillate.

feedback Part of the communication process, feedback furnishes an opportunity for the audience to respond to the communicator. Listeners ask questions or comment to better understand what the communicator is trying to say. Feedback also provides vital reassurance for the communicator.

file photos File photos are pictures that are kept by newspapers and published when the need arises. Consequently, some photos that accompany newspaper articles may have been taken long before the event being covered.

first-person point of view The first-person point of view presents the action through the eyes of one character. The reader's understanding therefore is colored by the predispositions and values of the first-person narrator.

flak Flak refers to organized responses to media content, which can take the form of letters, phone calls, petitions, lawsuits, and legislative initiatives, with the expressed purpose of influencing media content. Part of E. S. Herman and N. Chomsky's propaganda model.

formula Formula refers to patterns in *function, premise, structure, plot,* and *character.* Individual programs generally conform to the formula of the genre.

formulaic function A genre shares a common manifest objective. For instance, the primary function of the sitcom is to entertain or amuse the audience. In addition, a genre may contain shared latent functions.

formulaic plot Only a finite number of general plots, or stories, appear within a given genre. While these general plots appear regularly, the embellishments, detail, and small nuances within these plots keep each episode fresh and interesting.

formulaic premise A formulaic premise refers to an identifiable situation that characterizes a genre.

formulaic structure A genre generally fits within an identifiable, unvarying structure, or organizational pattern. In many genres (including the sitcom) the standard formula is order/chaos/order.

frame In interactive media, a frame is a software feature that allows the home page to be divided into different sections, each of which is a window to another website.

framework Framework refers to various structural elements of a production, including introduction, plot, genre, and logical conclusion.

function A simple communication activity may be motivated by many purposes, or functions, which include expression, description, education, information exchange, persuasion, entertainment, creative expression, artistic expression, ritual, performance, emotional catharsis, disengagement, and profit.

genre A genre is a standardized format that is distinctive and easily identifiable. Examples include horror films, romances, sci-fi, situation comedies, westerns, and the evening news. A genre is not confined to one medium. For instance, at one time or another, westerns have appeared in print, on radio, television, and film.

gestalt A natural predisposition to order. For example, human beings tend to look for balance, that is, equal distribution around the center.

global hegemony The control of global information as a means of establishing a position of dominance among nations.

graphical user interface A navigational element in a website that furnishes information about the web page, such as links, and index of pages in the site.

hard news Hard news stories deal with topical events and issues that have an impact on the lives of the readers. The principal function of hard news is to inform. This information provides readers with a vital connection to the nation and the world.

hegemonic model A school of thought with regard to the role of the audience in the mass communication process, in which the audience assumes a passive role in the communications process, responding in a uniform way to messages constructed by the media communicator.

hegemony The imposition of an ideology within a culture is referred to as hegemony. Critical theorists like Stuart Hall argue that the worldviews presented through the media do not merely reflect or reinforce culture but in fact shape thinking by promoting the dominant ideology of a culture.

hermeneutics Hermeneutic refers to the study of the methodological principles of interpretation. The study of media has a hermeneutic, or interpretive, function, furnishing a means of understanding culture.

historical context Media content often derives its significance from the events of the day. As a result, understanding the historical context can provide insight into media messages. At the same time, media presentations can furnish information into the period in which they were produced, as well as providing perspective on cultural changes.

home page The page at a website that serves as the starting point for accessing other pages at the site. The home page serves as the introduction, providing information and attracting visitors to the site.

hybrid media As media technology has evolved, existing media systems have begun to overlap, creating hybrid channels of mass communications. One example is the VCR, which now presents film on television.

hyperbole An ad strategy that relies on exaggeration or absurd overstatement to make a point.

ideology The manner or the content of thinking characteristic of an individual group or culture.

illogical ads Advertisements that appear perfectly reasonable on the surface often do not hold up under logical scrutiny.

illogical conclusion The assumption behind the concept of logical conclusion holds that the conclusion of a presentation must be a logical extension of the initial premise, characters, and worldview, free of intrusion by the artist. In light of this, it is striking that the conclusions to popular media presentations so frequently violate this principle of logical progression. Conclusions are often false, confused, or simply illogical when considered within the flow of the program.

implicit content Implicit content refers to those elements of plot that remain under the surface, including motivation, the relationship between events, and the consequences of earlier actions.

inaccurate paraphrase A journalistic technique that can be used to present a particular point of view, in which reporters paraphrase what their subject said instead of quoting directly. In the process, the reporter's summary may not always be accurate.

incomplete/distorted message This type of ad strategy tells only a half-truth in order to present its product in the best possible light.

indirect feedback mechanisms Since immediate responses are not observable, most mass communications feedback is delayed and cumulative. Media organizations depend on a variety of indirect audience feedback mechanisms including ratings, generated revenue, delayed audience response, audience research, critical response, and intuition.

information appliance As cable television becomes a primary Internet carrier, an individual can receive e-mail, conduct research and business, and be entertained through the television set.

information exchange This function occurs in interpersonal communication when all parts benefit from an exchange of information.

information management This public relations approach to government/press relations, first used by the Reagan administration, emphasized the following principles: plan ahead, stay on the offensive, manage the flow of information, limit reporters' access to the president, speak in one voice, make it easy on the press, exploit the medium, and mislead when necessary.

infotainment Entertainment programming that has taken on the trappings of journalism.

initiator In digital media, we both *retrieve* and *impart* information. As is the case with interpersonal communications, our role changes as we move from media communicator (the person initiating the dialogue) to audience (the recipient of information—both solicited and unsolicited) and back again.

instruction This communication function refers to occasions in which the purpose is either (1) to inform someone about a subject with which he or she is unfamiliar or (2) to furnish *additional* information about a subject with which the audience is already acquainted.

interactive media Refers to communication between an initiator and receiver, using a combination of established media to emulate humans' communication patterns through a transparent machine. Interactive media combines existing media (print, photography, graphics, video, and audio). As such, this medium combines many of the distinctive characteristics of established media, including printed text, photographic images, sound, and motion.

interference Interference refers to those factors that can hinder the communications process (e.g., communicator interference, channel interference, and audience interference).

internal structure The internal structure of a media organization consists of the following elements: the resources of the production company, the organizational framework (i.e., different departments, lines of responsibility), and the process of decision making.

interpersonal communication Interpersonal communication refers to face-to-face interaction with another person.

intrapersonal communication Intrapersonal communication takes place within ourselves. It is the basis of all forms of communication.

introduction The introduction often acquaints the audience with the most important information, primary characters, and premise of the media presentation. The opening of a film, television, or radio program may serve as a preview of the entire presentation.

jump In journalism, a jump refers to the continuation of a story to another page.

labels Labels are connotative words or phrases that describe a person or group. Labels often appear with such frequency in the media that they no longer simply *describe* but in fact *define* the group.

language collectives Language collectives refers to a use of language in media communications which ascribes human qualities to a large, all-encompassing organization or entity (e.g., "the Supreme Court said today," or "the White House claimed ..."). In addition, language collectives make absolute, authoritative claims, overlooking individual dissent or disagreement among people within the organization.

latent function Latent function refers to purposes behind the communication of information that may not be immediately obvious to the audience.

latent message Latent messages are indirect and beneath the surface and consequently escape our immediate attention. Latent messages may reinforce manifest messages or may suggest entirely different meanings.

lifestyle indicators (LSIs) Lifestyle indicators refers to a type of advertising research that predicts consumer buying patterns on the basis of a consumer's previous purchases.

lighting The amount of light used in a visual medium can affect the mood. Brightly lit presentations evoke a feeling of security and happiness, while a dimly lit presentation creates an atmosphere of mystery and apprehension. The source of the light can also convey messages.

link In interactive media, links are virtual passageways that lead to another part of a website or to an entirely different site. A link normally appears as an underlined word, phrase, or image. Clicking on the link automatically transports the user to that particular destination.

manifest message Manifest messages are direct and clear to the audience. We generally have little trouble recognizing these messages when we are paying full attention to a media presentation.

mass communication In mass communication, messages are communicated through a mass medium (e.g., radio or television) to a large group of people who may not be in direct contact with the communicator.

media literacy The author's definition of media literacy emphasizes the following:

- — An awareness of the impact of the media on the individual and society.
- — An understanding of the process of mass communication.
- — The development of strategies with which to analyze and discuss media messages.
- — An awareness of media content as a "text" that provides insight into our contemporary culture and ourselves.
- — The cultivation of an enhanced enjoyment, understanding, and appreciation of media content.

media messages Media messages are the underlying themes or ideas contained in a media presentation.

media presentations Media presentations refers to the specific programming that is produced within each medium—for instance, particular films (e.g., *The Fugitive*), newspapers (e.g., the April 2000 edition of the *Washington Post*), or television programs (e.g., the January 12, 2000, episode of *Will and Grace*).

medium A channel of mass communications that enables people to communicate with large groups of people who are separated in time and space from the communicator. Examples of media include print, photography, radio, film, and television.

medium shot (MS) The medium shot, which is used in film and television, is analogous to the third-person perspective in print. This shot often includes several actors interacting in the shot.

meta information Information about the information acquired by a person on the Internet. Computer software records not only who has been in contact with a web site but also records the sequence of hits.

microcasting A concept tied to the evolution of American media. In interactive media, an initiator can now identify individuals—including their backgrounds, finances, lifestyles, and buying habits—and tailor the message to them.

motivation Those reasons that compel a character in a media presentation to behave in the ways that they do. If a character's motivation is poorly presented, the character's actions may not make sense to the viewer.

multiple function A communications exchange may serve more than one function at a time. While these functions are often compatible, at other times they may be in conflict.

multiple realities This term is used in cultural studies. It refers to a phenomenon in which media content is subject to different interpretations, depending on the experience and orientation of the audience member.

mythic reality Mythic reality refers to cultural myths that assume a degree of reality over time as people buy into it. The danger presented by mythic realities is that people sometimes make decisions on the basis of these myths.

narrowcasting Narrowcasting is a concept tied to the evolution of American media. Over time, the consumer media market has become so large that it is now profitable to direct messages at specialized interests, tastes, and groups.

natural sound The noises that normally occur within a given setting (e.g., crowd noise at a baseball game). Natural sound is frequently added to the audio tracks of media presentations to add a feeling of verisimilitude.

neologism Neologisms are words that advertisers invent for products—for example, Acura.

news director In broadcast journalism, the news director is directly responsible for the station's daily newscasts.

newspaper chain A series of newspapers in different locations throughout the country owned by one large company.

no-effects theory of media violence This theory holds that media violence has a minimal effect on audiences.

nonverbal performance skills Nonverbal skills refers to communications vehicles other than language. Nonverbal communication elements include gestures, facial expressions, posture, and dress.

not-available ploy A journalistic technique, in which an article includes a statement that the subject was unavailable for comment. The inclusion of this statement often implies that the subject was uncooperative, ducking the reporter, or had something to hide. This statement often neglects to clarify the circumstance: whether the person was in town, when the person was contacted, where the person was contacted, how often the reporter attempted to reach the person, and the time frame in which the reporter attempted to contact the subject.

omniscient camera The omniscient camera, which is used in film and television, is analogous to the omniscient narrator in print. This all-seeing or all-knowing camera enables the director to focus on characters in different settings (unbeknownst to the other characters).

omniscient point of view The omniscient or all-knowing point of view enables the author to enter the heads of any and all of the characters so that the reader has a comprehensive exposure to the people and events depicted in the work.

one-person cross-section A journalistic technique in which one person is positioned as representative of a larger group—which may not be the case. This technique can be used to present a particular point of view in the story.

opiate theory of media violence A theory of media violence that holds that after watching enough programming people may become passive and incapable of feeling anything.

pace Pace refers to the rhythm of rate at which information should be assimilated.

panoramic point of view In a panoramic point of view, the perspective is constantly shifting.

parallel action Filmmakers use the narrative strategy of parallel action to create the illusion that events on screen are occurring simultaneously. This can be accomplished by the editing technique of cross-cutting, in which footage from different locations is juxtaposed to give the impression of events occurring at the same moment.

parasocial relationship A dynamic in mass communication in which the media communicator creates the *appearance* of a personal relationship with the audience.

parity statement An ad strategy in which the wording suggests that a product is unique when in fact it is indistinguishable from its competition.

participatory response This phrase refers to a form of mass communication feedback. Individuals can respond directly to programs through laughter, anger, and even personal boycotts of programs and products. Some audience members also participate through call-ins, community productions, and the like.

passive catchphrase A journalistic technique, in which the subject of a sentence (the person/thing responsible for the action) is omitted. This technique can affect the point of view of the story by creating the impression that an opinion is common knowledge.

passive-negative personality Political scientist James David Barber devised a formula for predicting presidential performance, based on distinct character types. Barber has identified four character patterns based on levels of activity (activity-passivity) and enjoyment (positive-negative affect). The passive-positive figure "does little in politics and enjoys it less." Withdrawn by nature and possessing a low sense of self-esteem, this personality type regards politics as a civic duty, often serving his term of office with reluctance.

passive-positive personality This is part of political scientist James David Barber's formula for predicting presidential performance based on character type. A passive-positive president is a compliant figure who combines a low self-esteem with a "superficial optimism." As a result, this personality is looking for acceptance, which can interfere with an aggressive approach to the implementation of policy.

performance This function of communication refers to occasions in which the purpose of the conversation is to create a favorable impression.

persuasion In this communications function, the objective is to promote a particular idea or motivate the audience to action.

photo opportunity Events which are staged in order to give photographers the opportunity to snap pictures.

platform (political) ads A political ad that outlines a position on a specific issue.

plot A series of actions planned by the artist to build on one another, with an introduction, body, and conclusion. The foundation of plot is *conflict*. Characters are initially confronted with a dilemma, which is resolved by the end of the story.

plot convention A storyline that can appear within a number of genres. Examples include the wedding at the end of the story, and the "boy meets girl" scenario.

point of view Point of view refers to the source of information—who tells the story.

political action committees (PACs) The Federal Election Campaign Act (FECA) of 1971, amended in 1975 and 1976, permits corporations, labor unions, and religious organizations to support political candidates through the formation of political action committees (PACs).

popular culture Popular culture describes those productions, both artistic and commercial, designed for mass consumption, which appeal to and express the tastes and understanding of the majority of the public, free of control by minority standards. They reflect the values, convictions, and patterns of thought and feeling generally dispersed through and approved by American society.

portals Initial points of entry into the Internet. Examples include Yahoo, Excite, and Lycos.

post-modern mass communications model In this rapidly evolving media landscape, producers must take their audience into consideration at an earlier stage of the communication process:

Channel
Audience
Communicator
Message

In many instances, the audience now determines the choice of the *medium*, *media communicator*, and the *content* of a media presentation. In this post-modern communications model, the audience is able to bypass the traditional media gatekeepers and act as their own content providers.

preferred conclusion When examining the logical conclusion to a presentation, it can be beneficial for audience members to consider how they would have preferred for the story to end. This response can reveal a great deal about their personal belief system.

preferred reading A key concept in the *hegemonic* model of audience interpretation, in which the sympathies of the audience are aligned with the values and beliefs of the dominant culture (i.e., those people, groups, and interests which maintain economic and social control of the culture). The production positions the audience to assume the role, perspective, and orientation of the primary figure, who represents the dominant culture.

premise The initial circumstances, situation, or assumption which serves as the point of origin in the narrative. A description of premise usually answers the question, "What is this program about?"

preproduction editing process Preproduction editing process refers to the decisions regarding both what to include and what to omit from a media presentation. These decisions have been reached before the presentation reaches the public, so the audience is not in a position to make a critical judgment about the selection process.

presentation of opinion as fact A journalism technique, in which reporters present opinion disguised as fact in news stories.

process The dynamics of communications, including function, comparative media, media communicator, and audience.

production values The *style* and *quality* of a media presentation. Production values often create a mood that reinforces manifest messages or themes. Production values include editing, color, lighting, shape, scale, relative position, movement, point of view, angle, connotation, performance, and sound.

product placement A practice in which advertisers pay a hefty fee to film studios to ensure that their products are displayed in a commercial film.

profit An underlying function driving American media industry is profit. Of course, advertising and commercial television are geared to generate income.

However, journalists are also torn between serving the public's right to know and making a profit.

propaganda Propaganda refers to the systematic development and dissemination of information to propagate the views and interests of a particular group.

psychographic research Psychographic research identifies the attitudes, values, and experiences shared by groups.

pyramid style The pyramid style refers to a construct in American journalism, in which the most important information should be included in the first paragraph. Readers should therefore expect to find the answers to the following questions in the paragraph: *who, what, when, how,* and *why.*

qualifier words An ad strategy in which phrases such as "some restrictions apply" are added inconspicuously, signaling that this information is insignificant.

radio frequency ID devices (RFID) These are melded into personal clothing, products, animals, and people for purposes of identification, using radio waves.

reassurance appeals In political advertising, reassurance appeals promote a sense of confidence in the candidate.

receiver In digital media, we both *retrieve* and *impart* information. As is the case with interpersonal communications, our role changes as we move from media communicator (the person initiating the dialogue) to audience (the recipient of information—both solicited and unsolicited) and back again.

reception theory A school of thought in regard to the audience's interpretation of media content that recognizes the unique perspective of the individual. According to this construct, the audience assumes an active role in interpreting the information they receive through mass media. Different groups make sense of content in different ways.

relative position Relative position refers to where a character or subject appears on the screen (or page). Objects appearing toward the front attract immediate attention, whereas things in the background are generally considered of secondary importance.

rhythm The rate or pace at which movement occurs.

ritual As it pertains to communication, a ritual is a verbal or written exchange that has a social significance beyond the surface.

romantic ideal An ideal worldview that often appears in media presentations. This ideal presumes an ordered universe that operates according to absolute values: truth, justice, beauty, faith, and love.

scale The relative size between objects. The larger an object appears, the most important it seems.

search engine In interactive media, a search engine is a navigational device that enables an individual to conduct research by searching for words or phrases on a large number of World Wide Web pages.

second-person point of view The second-person point of view makes the reader the primary participant in the story. This perspective makes use of the pronoun *you.*

sectors The various career applications of media literacy: *Education, Public Policy, Community Media, Media Arts, Professional Media*, and *Writing and Research*.

selective exposure A category of audience interference. Selective exposure refers to the programming choices that individuals make, based on their personal interests and values. For instance, sports fans may watch ESPN, while people uninterested in sports will tune in something else.

selective perception A category of audience interference. The phenomenon by which people's interpretation of content is colored by their predispositions and preconceptions.

selective quotes A journalistic technique, in which reporters color a story by choosing when to use quotes, whose quotes to include, and which parts of the person's interview to extract into a quote.

selective retention A category of audience interference. Selective retention occurs when people mentally edit what they see or hear by remembering (or forgetting) selected information.

sidebar In journalism, a story appearing on the same page with a larger, related story. Often, a sidebar story presents specific information related to the topic of the main story (i.e., background information or personal anecdotes). A typical sidebar might be about how a labor strike has affected a particular town or family.

simile An ad strategy that makes a direct comparison between the product and something else; such comparisons are introduced by *like* or *as*.

slanted sample A journalistic technique, in which the sample of the public asked for their response to issues and events has been selected in an arbitrary fashion. Consequently, their views are not representative of the public at large.

slogan (political) ads A political advertisement in which a candidate expresses an emotional response toward an issue.

soft news Soft news is not necessarily timely, has minimal societal consequences, and is primarily designed to entertain.

sound bite An excerpt of a political figure's speech broadcast by the news media.

sound effects The sounds that are added to broadcast presentations for dramatic emphasis.

spam Unsolicited information from the Internet.

spin control This information strategy is employed by political communications teams to manage how information is presented, reported, and received by the public.

stereotypes A stereotype is an oversimplified conception of a person, group, or event. This term derives from the Greek word *steros* (hard or solid), which underscores the inflexible, absolute nature of stereotypes. Stereotype is an *associative* process; ideas about groups are based on a shared understanding about a group.

stock characters A stock character refers to a character who appears so frequently in the media that he or she has become a conventional and recognizable type.

structure Structure refers to the impact of ownership, internal organization, and government regulations on the content of media programming.

structured motion Structured motion refers to the ways in which a print ad is designed so it dictates the order in which the audience looks at the layout.

subjective camera technique Filmmakers can create a literal first-person point of view by employing a subjective camera technique. In this technique, the camera assumes the perspective of the protagonist, so the audience sees the world through the eyes of the main character.

subplot Some narratives contain secondary stories, called subplots. Subplots often may initially appear to be unrelated to the main theme. However, the subplots may tie together at the conclusion, underscoring the themes of the primary plot.

temporal and spatial inferences Through editing, media communications are able to manipulate time and space in order to establish relationships between people, locations, and events.

third-person point of view The third-person point of view describes the activities and internal processes of one character. The third-person point of view commonly employs the pronouns *he* or *she*. The author is privy to the thoughts and activities of this character but retains some critical distance and is therefore not accountable for the behavior of the character.

transformational words Transformational words are employed in advertising; they promise new levels of experience (e.g., *sensational, startling, amazing, remarkable*).

transparent machine In interactive communication, a goal is to produce a computer that no longer intrudes on the computer process (e.g., freezes, requires "booting up," or needs specific commands).

ubiquitous computers A stage in the evolution of interactive technology, in which the computer will be fully integrated into the environment.

undefined function This refers to instances in which the communicator does not have a clear intention of what he or she intends to say. Consequently, the presentation of information can be muddled, directionless, and ineffective.

unfinished statements Unfinished statements make implied claims by leaving it to the consumer to complete the statement (e.g., "Magnavox gives you more.").

uniform resource locater (URL) A unique identification code that enables an individual to locate a web page on the Internet.

vague authority In this journalistic bias technique, reporters use undocumented and generalized groups to impose a particular point of view.

value hierarchy Value hierarchy refers to the value system operating within the worldview of a media presentation.

vector In film or television, every moving object has a vector, or *implied* direction of movement.

verbal performance skills Verbal performance skills refers to the media communicator's voice quality and delivery. Verbal performance elements include volume, tone, clarity, and pacing.

verisimilitude Verisimilitude is defined as the appearance of truth. In its ability to instantaneously preserve a moment of space, photography creates an illusion of verisimilitude, or lifelike quality.

virtual presence systems The next generation of interactive devices, in which microprocessors are installed in the environment.

web page One component of a web site, identifiable by a distinctive URL address.

web site A virtual arena on the Internet which revolves around a particular subject. The site contains a collection of web pages, as well as links to other related sites.

worldview Popular artists construct complete worlds out of their imaginations. The premise, plot, and characters of fictional narratives are based on certain fundamental assumptions about how this world operates. Even when we watch nonfiction content like the news, we receive overall impressions about worldview. Media presentations establish *who* and *what* are important within the worldview of the program.

SUGGESTED READING

Alexander, Janet E., and Marsha Ann Tate. *Web Wisdom: How to Evaluate and Create Information Quality on the Web*. Mahwah, NJ: Lawrence Erlbaum Associates, 1999.

Altheide, David L., and Robert P. Snow. *Media Logic*. Beverly Hills, CA: Sage Publications, 1979.

Arnheim, Rudolf. *Art and Visual Perception*. Berkeley and Los Angeles: University of California Press, 1974.

Bagdikian, Ben. *The Media Monopoly*. 3rd ed. Boston: Beacon Press, 1990.

Braudy, Leo. *The Frenzy of Renown: Fame and Its History*. Oxford, New York, Toronto: Oxford University Press, 1986.

Buckingham, David. *Moving Images*. Manchester, UK: Manchester University Press, 1997.

Buckingham, David. *After the Death of Childhood: Growing Up in the Age of Electronic Media*. Cambridge: Polity Press, 2000.

Collins W. Andrew. "Children's Comprehension of Television Content," in *Children Communicating*, ed. Ellen Wartella. Beverly Hills, CA: Sage Publications, 1979.

Considine, David, and Gail Haley. *Visual Messages: Integrating Imagery into Instruction*. Englewood, CO: Teacher Idea Press, 1992.

Ewen, Stuart. *All Consuming Images*. New York: Basic Books, 1988.

Finnegan, Lisa. *No Questions Asked: News Coverage Since 9/11*. Westport, CT: Praeger, 2006.

Gans, Herbert. *Deciding What's News*. New York: Pantheon Books, 1979.

Gault, Philip. *Choosing the News: The Profit Factor in News Selection*. Westport, CT: Greenwood Press, 1990.

Goffman, Erving. *Gender Advertisements*. New York: Harper & Row, 1976.

Holtzman, Linda. *Media Messages: What Film, Television and Popular Music Teach Us about Race, Class, Gender and Sexual Orientation.* Armonk, NY: M.E. Sharpe, 2000.

Jamieson, Kathleen Hall. *Packaging the Presidency.* New York: Oxford University Press, 1992.

Jenkins, Henry. *Textual Poachers: Television Fans and Participatory Culture.* London and New York: Routledge, 1992.

Klein, Naomi. *No Logo: Taking Aim at the Brand Bullies.* New York: Picador, 2000.

Klinenberg, Eric. *Fighting for Air: The Battle to Control America's Media.* New York: Metropolitan Books, 2007.

Kress, Gunther, and Theo van Leeuwen. *Reading Images: The Grammar of Visual Design.* London and New York: Routledge, 1995.

Lee, Martin A., and Norman Soloman. *Unreliable Sources: A Guide to Detecting Bias in the News Media.* Secaucus, NJ: Carol Publishing Group, 1990.

Lessig, Lawrence. *Free Culture: The Nature and Future of Creativity.* New York: Penguin, 2005.

MacLean, Eleanor. *Between the Lines.* Montreal: Black Rose Books, 1981.

Masterman, Len. *Teaching the Media.* London and New York: Routledge, 1985.

McChesney, Robert. *Rich Media, Poor Democracy.* Champaign, IL: University of Illinois, 1999.

McLuhan, Marshall. *Understanding Media: The Extensions of Man.* New York: McGraw-Hill Book Company, 1964.

Mitroff, Ian I., and Warren Bennis. *The Unreality Industry.* New York: Oxford University Press, 1989.

Parenti, Michael. *Make Believe Media.* New York: St. Martin's Press, 1992.

Sabato, Larry J. *The Rise of Political Consultants.* New York: Basic Books, Inc., 1981.

Saven, Leslie. *The Sponsored Life.* Philadelphia: Temple University Press, 1993.

Schwartz, Tony. *The Responsive Chord.* Garden City, NY: Anchor Books, 1973.

Silverblatt, Art, Jane Ferry, and Barb Finan. *Approaches to Media Literacy*, Armonk, NY: M.E. Sharpe, 1999.

Twitchell, James B. *Adcult USA.* New York: Columbia University Press, 1997.

Tyner, Kathleen. *Literacy in a Digital World.* Mahwah, NJ: Lawrence Erlbaum Associates, 1998.

Wasko, Janet. *Understanding Disney: The Manufacture of Fantasy.* Cambridge: Polity Press, 2001.

Wolf, Naomi. *The Beauty Myth.* New York: William Morrow and Company, Inc., 1991.

INDEX

About the Author

ART SILVERBLATT is professor of communications and journalism at Webster University in St. Louis. He is the author of numerous books and articles, including *Media Literacy: Keys to Interpreting Media Messages* (Praeger, 1995, 2001), *The Dictionary of Media Literacy* (Greenwood, 1997), *Approaches to the Study of Media Literacy* (1999), and *International Communications: A Media Literacy Approach* (2004). Another book, *Approaches to Genre Study*, is scheduled to be published in spring 2008.